Rick Steves'

ITALY
2006

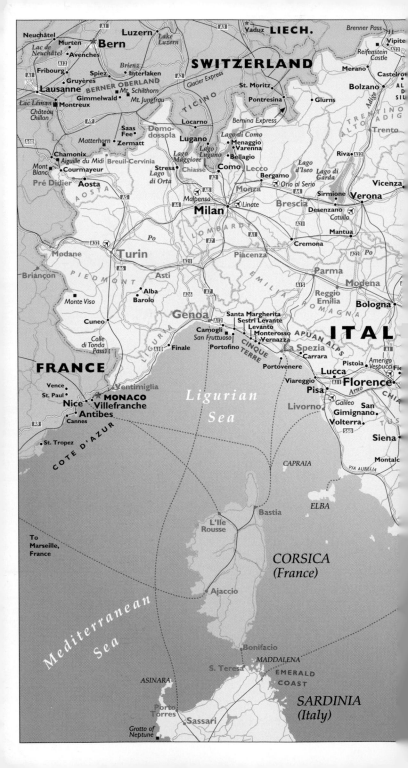

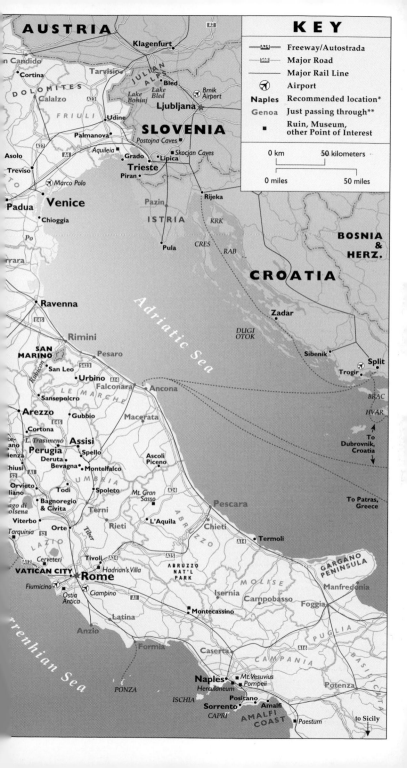

VENICE

1. Accademia Gallery
2. Bridge of Sighs
3. Ca' d'Oro
4. Ca' Rezzonico
5. Campanile (Bell Tower)
6. Clock Tower
7. Correr Museum
8. To Dalmation School
9. Diocesan Museum
10. Doge's Palace
11. Frari Church
12. Galleria San Marco Glass Blowers
13. Harry's American Bar
14. To Jewish Ghetto & Museum
15. La Fenice Opera House
16. La Salute Church
17. Palazzo Grassi
18. Peggy Guggenheim Collection
19. Rialto Bridge
20. San Giorgio Maggiore Church
21. San Polo Church
22. San Silvestro Church
23. San Zaccaria Church
24. Scala Contarini del Bovolo
25. Scuola Grande di San Rocco
26. Scuola San Teodoro
27. St. Mark's Basilica
28. St. Mark's Square
29. Teatro Goldoni

Transport:
30. Train Station
31. Boats to Murano, Burano & Torcello
32. To Tronchetto (Main Parking Lot)

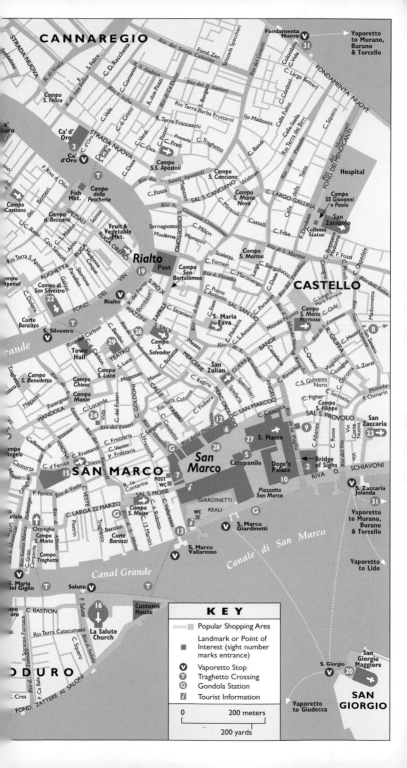

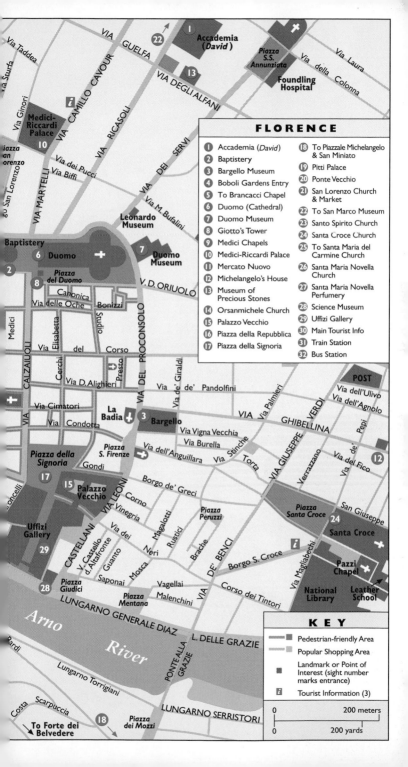

FLORENCE

1. Accademia (David)
2. Baptistery
3. Bargello Museum
4. Boboli Gardens Entry
5. To Brancacci Chapel
6. Duomo (Cathedral)
7. Duomo Museum
8. Giotto's Tower
9. Medici Chapels
10. Medici-Riccardi Palace
11. Mercato Nuovo
12. Michelangelo's House
13. Museum of Precious Stones
14. Orsanmichele Church
15. Palazzo Vecchio
16. Piazza della Repubblica
17. Piazza della Signoria
18. To Piazzale Michelangelo & San Miniato
19. Pitti Palace
20. Ponte Vecchio
21. San Lorenzo Church & Market
22. To San Marco Museum
23. Santo Spirito Church
24. Santa Croce Church
25. To Santa Maria del Carmine Church
26. Santa Maria Novella Church
27. Santa Maria Novella Perfumery
28. Science Museum
29. Uffizi Gallery
30. Main Tourist Info
31. Train Station
32. Bus Station

KEY

- Pedestrian-friendly Area
- Popular Shopping Area
- Landmark or Point of Interest (sight number marks entrance)
- *i* Tourist Information (3)

| 0 | 200 meters |
| 0 | 200 yards |

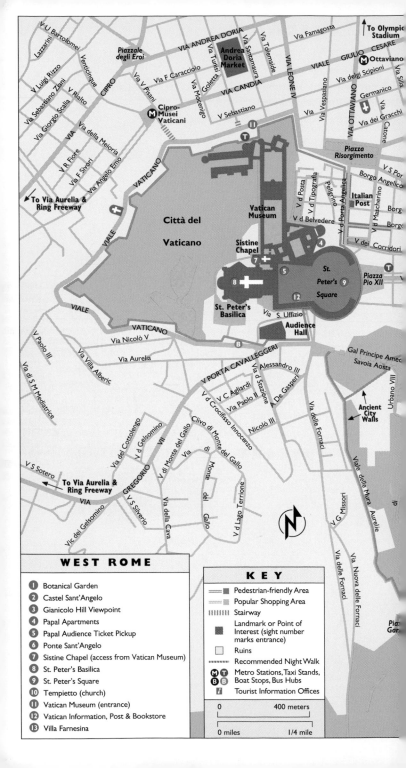

WEST ROME

1 Botanical Garden
2 Castel Sant'Angelo
3 Gianicolo Hill Viewpoint
4 Papal Apartments
5 Papal Audience Ticket Pickup
6 Ponte Sant'Angelo
7 Sistine Chapel (access from Vatican Museum)
8 St. Peter's Basilica
9 St. Peter's Square
10 Tempietto (church)
11 Vatican Museum (entrance)
12 Vatican Information, Post & Bookstore
13 Villa Farnesina

KEY

Pedestrian-friendly Area
Popular Shopping Area
Stairway
Landmark or Point of Interest (sight number marks entrance)
Ruins
Recommended Night Walk
M T Metro Stations, Taxi Stands,
B B Boat Stops, Bus Hubs
i Tourist Information Offices

0   400 meters

0 miles   1/4 mile

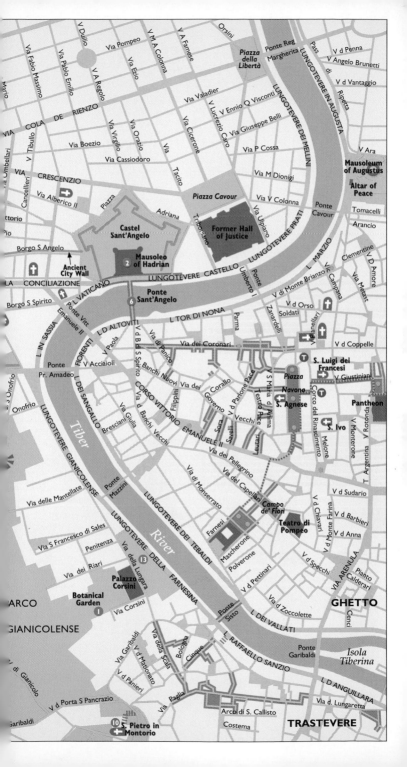

Rick Steves'

ITALY

2006

AVALON
TRAVEL

CONTENTS

INTRODUCTION

Bella Italia! It has Europe's richest, craziest culture. If you take it on its own terms, Italy is a cultural keelhauling that actually feels good.

Some people, often with considerable effort, manage to hate it. Italy bubbles with emotion, corruption, stray hairs, inflation, traffic jams, body odor, strikes, rallies, holidays, crowded squalor, and irate ranters shaking their fists at each other one minute and walking arm in arm the next. Have a talk with yourself before you cross the border. Promise yourself to relax and accept it as a package deal.

This book will help you make the most of your trip. It breaks Italy into its top big-city, small-town, and rural destinations. You'll get all the information and opinions necessary to wring the maximum value out of your limited time and money in each of these destinations.

If you plan a month or less in Italy and have a normal appetite for information, this lean and mean little book is all you need. If you're a travel-info fiend (like me), you'll find this book sorts through all the superlatives and provides a handy rack upon which to hang your supplemental information.

Italy is my favorite country. Experiencing its culture, people, and natural wonders economically and hassle-free has been my goal for three decades of traveling, researching, and tour guiding. With this book, I pass on to you the lessons I've learned, updated for 2006.

Rick Steves' Italy is a tour guide in your pocket, offering a comfortable mix of big cities and cozy towns, from brutal but *bella* Rome to *tranquillo,* traffic-free Riviera villages. It covers the predictable biggies and adds a healthy dose of "Back Door" intimacy.

Along with marveling at Michelangelo's masterpieces, you'll enjoy a bruschetta snack as a village boy rubs fresh garlic on your toast. I've been selective, including only the top sights. For example, after visiting many hill towns, I recommend just the best.

The best is, of course, only my opinion. But after spending half my adult life researching Europe, I've developed a sixth sense for what travelers enjoy.

This Information Is Accurate and Up-to-Date

This book is updated every year. Most publishers of guidebooks can afford an update only every two or three years (and even then, it's often by e-mail or fax). Since this book is selective, I can update it in person each summer. The telephone numbers and hours of sights listed in this book are accurate as of mid-2005—but once you pin Italy down, it wiggles. Still, if you're traveling with the current edition of this book, I guarantee you're using the most up-to-date information available in print. For any updates, see www.ricksteves .com/update. Also at our Web site, you'll find a valuable list of reports and experiences—good and bad—from fellow travelers who have used this book (www.ricksteves.com/feedback).

Use this year's edition. People who try to save a few bucks by traveling with an old book are not smart. They learn the seriousness of their mistake...in Italy. Your trip costs about $10 per waking hour. Your time is valuable. This guidebook saves lots of time.

About This Book

This book is organized by destinations. Each destination is a mini-vacation on its own, filled with exciting sights and comfortable, good-value places to stay. In the following chapters, you'll find:

Planning Your Time, a suggested schedule with thoughts on how best to use your limited time.

Orientation, including tourist information, city transportation, and an easy-to-read map designed to make the text clear and your arrival smooth.

Self-Guided Walks to take you through interesting neighborhoods, personal tour guide in hand.

Sights with ratings: ▲▲▲—Don't miss; ▲▲—Try hard to see; ▲—Worthwhile if you can make it; no rating—Worth knowing about.

Sleeping and **Eating,** with addresses and phone numbers of my favorite hotels and restaurants.

Transportation Connections to nearby destinations by train, and route tips for drivers.

The **appendix** is a traveler's tool kit, with telephone tips, a climate chart, events calendar, and survival phrases.

Browse through this book, choose your top destinations, and link them up. Then have a great trip! You'll travel like a temporary local, getting the absolute most out of every mile, minute, and euro. As you travel the route that I know and love, I'm happy you'll be meeting some of my favorite Italian people.

PLANNING

Trip Costs

Six components make up your trip cost: airfare, surface transportation, room and board, sightseeing/entertainment, shopping/miscellany, and gelato.

Airfare: Don't try to sort through the mess. Find and use a good travel agent. A basic round-trip United States-to-Milan (or Rome) flight should cost $700–1,000, depending on where you fly from and when (cheapest in winter). Always consider saving time and money in Europe by flying "open jaw" (into one city and out of another).

Surface Transportation: For a three-week whirlwind trip to all my recommended destinations, allow $300 per person for public transportation (train and buses) or $800 per person (based on 2 people sharing a car) for a three-week car rental, including insurance, tolls, gas, and parking. Car rental is cheapest if arranged from the United States. Some train passes are available only outside of Europe. You might save money by getting an Italian railpass or buying tickets as you go (see "Transportation," page 16).

Room and Board: You can easily manage in Italy on $100 a day for room and board. This allows $10 for lunch, $5 for snacks, $20 for dinner, and $65 for lodging (based on 2 people splitting the cost of a $130 double room that includes breakfast). If you've got more money, I've listed great ways to spend it. And students and tightwads can enjoy Italy for as little as $50 a day ($25 for a bed, $25 for meals and snacks).

Sightseeing and Entertainment: In big cities, figure about $6–15 per major sight (museums, Colosseum), $3 for minor ones (climbing church towers), and $30 for splurge experiences (such as tours and concerts). An overall average of $15 a day works for most. Don't skimp here. After all, this category is the driving force behind your trip—you came to sightsee, enjoy, and experience Italy.

Shopping and Miscellany: Figure $2 per postcard, coffee, soft drink, or gelato. Shopping can vary in cost from nearly nothing to a small fortune. Good budget travelers find that this category has little to do with assembling a trip full of lifelong and wonderful memories.

Italy's Best Three-Week Trip (By Car)

Day	Plan	Sleep in
1	Arrive in Milan	.Milan
2	Milan to Lake Como	.Varenna
3	Lake Como.	.Varenna
4	To Dolomites via Verona	.Castelrotto
	(pick up car in Milan or Verona)	
5	Dolomites	.Castelrotto
6	To Venice.	.Venice
7	Venice.	.Venice
8	To Florence	.Florence
9	Florence	.Florence
10	To Cinque Terre.	.Vernazza
11	Cinque Terre.	.Vernazza
12	To Siena.	.Siena
13	Siena	.Siena
14	To Assisi	.Assisi
15	To Civita	.Civita or Orvieto
16	To Sorrento via Pompeii	.Sorrento
17	Sorrento	.Sorrento
18	To Paestum via Amalfi Coast	.Sorrento
19	To Rome, drop car	.Rome
20	Rome	.Rome
21	Rome	.Rome
22	Rome, fly home	

Modifications for Train Travelers: This trip is designed to be done by car, but works fine by rail with a few modifications. A TrenItalia Pass (4 days in 2 months) can be convenient if you avoid trains that require reservations; pay out of pocket for short runs, such as Milan to Varenna, or the hops between villages in the Cinque Terre. Consider basing yourself in the Dolomites in

When to Go

Italy's best travel months are May, June, September, and October. November and April usually have pleasant weather, with generally none of the sweat and stress of the tourist season. Off-season, expect shorter hours, more lunchtime breaks, and fewer activities.

Peak season (May–Sept) offers the longest hours and the most exciting slate of activities—but terrible crowds and, at times, suffocating heat. During peak times, many resort-area hotels maximize business by requiring that guests take half-pension, which means buying a meal per day (usually dinner) in their restaurants. August, the local holiday month, isn't as bad as many make it out to be, but big cities tend to be quiet (with discounted hotel prices), and beach

Bolzano. From Venice, go directly to the Cinque Terre, then do Florence and Siena. A car is efficient in the hill towns of Tuscany and Umbria, but a headache elsewhere. Sorrento is a good home base for Naples and the Amalfi Coast. Skip Paestum unless you love Greek ruins. To save Venice for last, start in Milan, seeing everything but Venice on the way south, then sleeping through everything you've already seen by catching the night train from Naples or Rome to Venice. This saves you a day and gives you an early arrival in Venice.

and mountain resorts are jammed (with higher hotel prices). Note that Italians generally wear shorts only at beach resort towns. If you want to blend in, wear lightweight long pants in Italy, even in summer, except at the beach.

Summer temperatures range from the 70s and 80s in Milan to the high 80s and 90s in Rome. Air-conditioning, when available, usually doesn't kick in until June 1 and shuts off September 30. Most mid-range hotels come with air-conditioning—a worthwhile splurge in the summer. Spring and fall can be cold, and many hotels do not turn on their heat until November 1. In the winter, it often drops to the 40s in Milan and the 50s in Rome.

For weather specifics, see the climate chart in the appendix.

Sightseeing Priorities

Depending on the length of your trip, here are my recommended priorities:

4 days:	Florence, Venice
6 days, add:	Rome
8 days, add:	Cinque Terre
10 days, add:	Civita and Siena
14 days, add:	Sorrento, Naples, Pompeii, Amalfi Coast, Paestum
18 days, add:	Milan, Lake Como, Varenna, Assisi
21 days, add:	Dolomites, Verona, Ravenna

(This includes everything on the "Italy's Best Three-Week Trip" map on page 5.)

Travel Smart

Many people travel through Italy thinking it's a chaotic mess. They feel any attempt at efficient travel is futile. This is dead wrong—and expensive. Italy, which seems as orderly as spilled spaghetti, actually functions quite well. Only those who understand this and travel smart can enjoy Italy on a budget.

Your trip to Italy is like a complex play—easier to follow and really appreciate on a second viewing. While no one does the same trip twice to gain that advantage, reading this book in its entirety before your trip accomplishes much the same thing.

Design an itinerary that enables you to hit the festivals and museums on the right days. As you read this book, note that Monday is a problem day, when many museums are closed. Sundays have the same pros and cons as they do for travelers in the United States. Sightseeing attractions are generally open but have shorter hours, shops and banks are closed, and minor transportation connections are more frustrating (e.g., no bus service to or from Civita). City traffic is light. Rowdy evenings are rare on Sundays. Saturdays are virtually weekdays with earlier closing hours (though transportation connections can be less frequent than on Mon–Fri). Hotels in tourist areas are often booked up on Easter weekend, in August, and on Fridays and Saturdays year-round. Religious holidays and train strikes can catch you by surprise anywhere in Italy.

Be sure to mix intense and relaxed periods in your itinerary. Plan ahead for banking, laundry, post-office chores, and picnics. Every trip (and every traveler) needs at least a few slack days. Pace yourself. Assume you will return.

Reread this book as you travel and visit local tourist information offices. Upon arrival in a new town, lay the groundwork for a smooth departure; write down the schedule for the train or bus you'll take when you depart. Buy a phone card (or mobile phone) and use it for reservations, reconfirmations, and double-checking hours of sights. Use taxis in the big cities, bring along a water bottle, and linger in the shade.

Connect with the cultures. Set up your own quest for the best gelato, sculpture, cheesy souvenir, or whatever. Enjoy the friendliness of the local people. Ask questions. Most locals are eager to point you in their idea of the right direction. Keep a notepad in your pocket for organizing your thoughts. Those who expect to travel smart, do.

RESOURCES
Tourist Information Offices
In the United States

Before your trip, contact the nearest Italian tourist office in the United States and briefly describe your trip and request information. You'll get the general packet and, if you ask for specifics (city map, calendar of festivals, etc.), an impressive amount of help. If you have a specific problem, they're a good source of sympathy.

Contact the office nearest you:

In New York: 630 Fifth Ave. #1565, New York, NY 10111, brochure hotline tel. 212/245-4822, tel. 212/245-5618, fax 212/586-9249, enitny@italiantourism.com.

In Illinois: 500 N. Michigan Ave. #2240, Chicago, IL 60611, tel. 312/644-0996, fax 312/644-3019, enitch@italiantourism.com.

In California: 12400 Wilshire Blvd. #550, Los Angeles, CA 90025, brochure hotline tel. 310/820-0098, tel. 310/820-4498, fax 310/820-6357, enitla@italiantourism.com.

Web Sites: www.italiantourism.com (Italian Tourist Board in the U.S.), www.museionline.it (museums in Italy), and www.trenitalia.com (train info and schedules).

In Italy

During your trip, your first stop in each town should be the tourist information office (abbreviated **TI** in this book, and marked "i," "*turismo*," and "APT" in Italy). While Italian TIs are about half as helpful as those in other countries, their information is twice as important. Prepare. Have a list of questions and a proposed plan to double-check. If you're arriving late, telephone ahead (and try to get a map for your next destination from a TI in the town you're departing from). Since Italy is ever-changing, ask the local TI for a current list of the city's sights, hours, and prices.

Be wary of the travel agencies or special information services that masquerade as TIs but serve fancy hotels and tour companies. They are crooks and liars selling things you don't need.

While the TI is eager to book you a room, use its room-finding service only as a last resort. Across Europe, room-finding services are charging commissions from hotels, taking fees from travelers, and blacklisting establishments that buck their materialistic rules. They are unable to give hard opinions on the relative value of one place over another. The accommodations stakes are too high to go potluck through the TI. You'll do better going direct with the listings in this book.

Rick Steves' Guidebooks, Public Television Show, and Radio Show

Rick Steves' Europe Through the Back Door gives you budget-travel skills, such as minimizing jet lag, packing light, planning your itinerary, traveling by car or train, finding rooms, changing money, avoiding rip-offs, buying a mobile phone, hurdling the language barrier, staying healthy, taking great photographs, using a bidet, and much more. The book also includes chapters on 38 of my favorite "Back Doors," five of which are in Italy.

Country Guides: These annually updated books offer you the latest on the top sights and destinations, with tips on how to make your trip efficient and fun. Here are the titles:

Rick Steves' Best of Europe	*Rick Steves' Great Britain*
Rick Steves' Best of	*Rick Steves' Ireland*
Eastern Europe	*Rick Steves' Italy*
Rick Steves' England	*Rick Steves' Portugal*
(new in 2006)	*Rick Steves' Scandinavia*
Rick Steves' France	*Rick Steves' Spain*
Rick Steves' Germany	*Rick Steves' Switzerland*
& Austria	

City and Regional Guides: Updated every year, these focus on Europe's most compelling destinations. Along with specifics on sights, restaurants, hotels, and nightlife, you'll get self-guided, illustrated tours of the outstanding museums and most characteristic neighborhoods. For travel in Italy, my very portable Venice, Florence and Tuscany, and Rome guidebooks earn their keep after one major museum visit, where you won't need to buy an interpretive guide to understand what you're seeing.

Rick Steves' Amsterdam,	*Rick Steves' Prague*
Bruges & Brussels	*& the Czech Republic*
Rick Steves' Florence	*Rick Steves' Provence*
& Tuscany	*& the French Riviera*
Rick Steves' London	*Rick Steves' Rome*
Rick Steves' Paris	*Rick Steves' Venice*

Rick Steves' Phrase Books: In Italy, a phrase book is as fun as it is necessary. This practical and budget-oriented series covers

Italian, French, German, Portuguese, Spanish, and French/Italian/German. You'll be able to ask the gelato man for a free little taste, chat with your cabbie, and make hotel reservations over the phone.

And More Books: *Rick Steves' Europe 101: History and Art for the Traveler* (with Gene Openshaw) gives you the story of Europe's people, history, and art. It's heavy on Italy's ancient, Renaissance, and modern eras. Written for smart people who were sleeping in their history and art classes before they knew they were going to Europe, *101* helps Europe's sights come alive. This book is especially useful for travel in Italy, where art is everywhere.

Rick Steves' Easy Access Europe, geared for travelers with limited mobility, covers London, Paris, Bruges, Amsterdam, and the Rhine River.

Rick Steves' Postcards from Europe, my autobiographical book, packs 25 years of travel anecdotes and insights into the ultimate 2,000-mile European adventure. Nearly half this book is set in Italy.

My latest book, *Rick Steves' European Christmas*, covers the joys, history, and quirky traditions of the holiday season in seven European countries.

Public Television Show: My series, *Rick Steves' Europe,* keeps churning out shows. Several of the more than 60 episodes feature sights covered in this book.

Radio Show: My new weekly radio show, which combines call-in questions (à la *Car Talk*) and interviews with travel experts, airs on public radio stations. For a schedule of upcoming topics, an archive of past programs, and details on how to call in, see www.ricksteves.com/radio.

Other Guidebooks

Especially if you'll be traveling beyond my recommended destinations, you may want some supplemental information. When you consider the improvements they'll make in your $3,000 vacation, $30 for extra maps and books is money well spent. Particularly for several people traveling by car, the weight and expense are negligible. One budget tip can save the price of an extra guidebook.

Lonely Planet's *Italy* is thorough, well-researched, and packed with travel information, maps, and hotel recommendations for various budgets. The similar *Rough Guide to Italy* is also good and more insightful, updated by British researchers. Neither of these is updated annually—use them only with a one- or two-year-old copyright. The highly opinionated *Let's Go: Italy*, researched every year by Harvard students, is great for students and vagabonds. If you're a low-budget train traveler interested in hosteling and the youth and nightlife scene (which I have largely ignored), get *Let's Go: Italy*. The Italy section in the bigger *Let's Go: Europe* is sparse.

Cultural and Sightseeing Guides: The colorful Eyewitness

Begin your trip at www.ricksteves.com

At www.ricksteves.com you'll find a wealth of **free information** on destinations covered in this book, including fresh European travel and tour news every month and helpful "Graffiti Wall" tips from thousands of fellow travelers.

While you're there, the **online Travel Store** is a great place to save money on travel bags and accessories designed by Rick Steves to help you travel smarter and lighter, plus a wide selection of guidebooks, planning maps, and DVDs.

Traveling through Europe by rail is a breeze, but choosing the right railpass for your trip—amidst hundreds of options—can drive you nutty. At www.ricksteves.com, you'll find **Rick Steves' Annual Guide to European Railpasses**—your best way to convert chaos into pure travel energy. Buy your railpass from Rick, and you'll get a bunch of free extras to boot.

Travel agents will tell you about mainstream tours of Europe, but they won't tell you about **Rick Steves' tours.** Rick Steves' Europe Through the Back Door travel company offers more than two dozen itineraries and 300 departures reaching the best destinations in this book...and beyond. You'll enjoy the services of a great guide, a fun bunch of travel partners (with group sizes in the twenties), and plenty of room to spread out in a big, comfy bus. You'll find trips to fit every vacation size, from week-long city getaways to longer cross-country adventures. For details, visit www.ricksteves.com or call 425/771-8303 ext 217.

series is popular with travelers; editions include Italy, Florence/Tuscany, Venice/Veneto, Rome, Taste of Tuscany, Umbria, Milan/Lakes District, Naples/Amalfi Coast, and Sicily. They are fun for their great, easy-to-grasp graphics and photos, and just right for people who want only factoids. But the Eyewitness written content is relatively skimpy, and the books weigh a ton. I buy them in Italy (no more expensive than in the U.S.) or simply borrow them for a minute from other travelers at certain sights to make sure I'm aware of that place's highlights. The tall, green Michelin guides to Italy and Rome have minimal information on room and board, but include great maps for drivers and lots of solid, encyclopedic coverage of sights, customs, and culture (sold in English in Italy). The Cadogan guides to various parts of Italy offer a thoughtful look at the rich and confusing local culture.

Recommended Reading

To get the feel of Italy past and present, consider reading some of these books:

Non-fiction: *That Fine Italian Hand* (Paul Hofmann), *Italian Days* (Barbara Grizzuti Harrison), *Under the Tuscan Sun* (Frances Mayes), *Desiring Italy* (Susan Cahill), *The Italians* (Luigi Barzini), *Italian Neighbors* (Tim Parks), *The Decline and Fall of the Roman Empire* (Edward Gibbon), *The House of Medici* (Christopher Hibbert), *The Architecture of the Italian Renaissance* (Peter Murray), and *Travelers' Tales Italy* (Anne Calcagno). Gourmets like *The Marling Menu-Master for Italy.*

Fiction: *The Agony and the Ecstasy* (Irving Stone), *Room with a View* (E.M. Forster), *Angels and Demons* (Dan Brown), *The Light in the Piazza* (Elizabeth Spencer), *The Birth of Venus* (Sarah Dunant), *A Soldier of the Great War* (Mark Helprin), *Pompeii: A Novel* (Robert Harris), *The Divine Comedy* (Dante), *Decameron* (Giovanni Boccaccio), *The Leopard* (Giuseppe Tomasi di Lampedusa), *Romeo and Juliet* (William Shakespeare), and *I, Claudius* (Robert Graves).

Maps

The black-and-white maps in this book, drawn by Dave Hoerlein, are concise and simple. Dave, who is well-traveled in Italy, designed the maps to help you locate recommended places and the tourist offices, where you can pick up more in-depth maps of the city or region (cheap or free). Better maps are sold at newsstands—take a look before you buy to be sure the map has the level of detail you want.

Michelin maps are available—and cheaper than in the United States—throughout Italy in bookstores, newsstands, and gas stations. Train travelers can do fine with a simple rail map (such as the one that comes with a train pass) and city maps from the TIs. Drivers should invest in a good 1:200,000 map and learn the key to maximize the sightseeing value.

PRACTICALITIES

Red Tape: You need a passport but no visa and no shots to travel in Italy.

Time: In Italy—and in this book—you'll use the 24-hour clock. It's the same through 12:00 noon, then keep going—13:00, 14:00, and so on. For anything over 12, subtract 12 and add p.m. (14:00 is 2:00 p.m.).

Italy, like most of continental Europe, is six/nine hours ahead of the East/West Coast of the United States.

Business Hours: Traditionally, Italy uses the siesta plan. People usually work from about 8:00–13:00 and from 15:30–19:00, Monday through Saturday. Nowadays, however, many businesses have adopted the government's new recommended 8:00–14:00 workday. In tourist areas, shops are open longer.

Discounts: Don't expect discounts on sights in Italy if you're a youth or senior. Discounts are generally available only to people who are members of the European Union and "reciprocating countries," meaning countries that offer discounts to European youth and seniors. The U.S. isn't big on price breaks for Europeans.

Metric: Get used to metric. A liter is about a quart, four to a gallon; a kilometer is about six-tenths of a mile. Figure kilometers to miles by cutting them in half and adding back 10 percent of the original (120 km: 60 + 12 = 72 miles, 300 km: 150 + 30 = 180 miles).

Watt's up? If you're bringing electrical gear, you'll need a two-prong adapter plug (sold cheap at travel stores in the United States) and a converter. Travel appliances often have convenient, built-in converters; look for a voltage switch marked 120V (U.S.) and 240V (Europe).

News: Americans keep in touch with the *International Herald Tribune* (published almost daily via satellite). Every Tuesday, the European editions of *Time* and *Newsweek* hit the stands with articles of particular interest to European travelers. Sports addicts can get their fix from *USA Today*. Good Web sites include www.europeantimes.com and http://news.bbc.co.uk.

Language Barrier: Many Italians in larger towns and the tourist trade speak at least some English. Still, you'll get more smiles and results by using at least the Italian pleasantries. In smaller, nontouristy towns, Italian is the norm. See the "Survival Phrases" near the end of this book.

Note that Italian is pronounced much like English, with a few exceptions, such as: *c* followed by *e* or *i* is pronounced *ch* (to ask, *"Per centro?"*—"To the center?"—you say, pehr CHEHN-troh). In Italian, *ch* is pronounced like the hard *c* in Chianti (*chiesa*—church—is pronounced kee-AY-zah). Give it your best shot. Italians appreciate your efforts.

MONEY

Exchange Rate

I list prices in euros throughout this book.

> **1 euro (€) = about $1.20**

Just like the dollar, the euro is broken down into 100 cents. You'll find coins ranging from 1 cent to 2 euros, and bills from 5 euros to 500 euros. To roughly convert prices in euros to dollars, add 20 percent to Italian prices: €20 is about $24, €45 is about $55, and so on.

Look carefully at any €2 coin you get in change. Some unscrupulous merchants are giving out similar-looking, gold-rimmed,

Damage Control for Lost or Stolen Cards

If you lose your credit, debit, or ATM card, you can stop people from using your card by reporting the loss immediately to the respective global customer-assistance centers. Call these 24-hour U.S. numbers collect: Visa (tel. 410/581-9994), MasterCard (tel. 636/722-7111), and American Express (tel. 336/393-1111).

Have, at a minimum, the following information ready: the name of the financial institution that issued you the card, along with the type of card (classic, platinum, or whatever). Ideally, plan ahead and pack photocopies of your cards—front and back—to expedite their replacement. Providing the following information will allow for a quicker cancellation of your missing card: full card number, whether you are the primary or secondary cardholder, the cardholder's name exactly as printed on the card, billing address, home phone number, circumstances of the loss or theft, and identification verification (your birthdate, your mother's maiden name, or your Social Security number—memorize this, don't carry a copy). If you are the secondary cardholder, you'll also need to provide the primary cardholder's identification verification details. You can generally receive a temporary card within two or three business days in Europe.

If you promptly report your card lost or stolen, you typically won't be responsible for any unauthorized transactions on your account, although many banks charge a liability fee of $50.

old 500-lire coins (worth $0) as change instead of €2 coins (worth $2.40). You are now warned!

Banking

Bring plastic (ATM, credit, or debit cards) along with several hundred dollars in hard cash as an emergency backup. Traveler's checks are a waste of time and money.

To withdraw cash from a bank machine *(bancomat)*, you'll need a PIN code (numbers only, no letters on European keypads) and your bank card. Before you go, verify with your bank that your card will work and alert them that you'll be making withdrawals in Europe; otherwise, the bank may not approve transactions if it perceives unusual spending patterns. Ask about fees whether you're using a cash machine (can be $5 per transaction) or getting cash advances with your regular credit card.

It's smart to bring two cards in case one gets demagnetized or eaten by a temperamental machine. If your card doesn't work, try again, and request a smaller amount; some cash machines won't let

Tips on Sightseeing in Italy

- Churches offer some amazing art (usually free), a cool respite from heat, and a welcome seat. A modest dress code (no bare shoulders or shorts for anyone) is enforced at larger churches, such as Venice's St. Mark's and the Vatican's St. Peter's, but is often overlooked elsewhere. Some churches have coin-operated audioboxes that describe the art and history. Coin boxes near a piece of art illuminate the art (and present a better photo opportunity). Whenever possible, let there be light.

- Reservations are highly advisable for some of the more famous museums (Florence's Uffizi Gallery and Accademia with *David*—to book these through your hotel, see "Make Reservations to Avoid Lines," page 331) and mandatory at others (Florence: Brancacci Chapel, Milan: da Vinci's *The Last Supper*, Padua: Scrovegni Chapel, Rome: Borghese Gallery and Nero's Golden House). The process is simple for English-speakers and generally free or nearly free. Lately, reservations to see both the Uffizi in Florence and *The Last Supper* in Milan have been booked over a month in advance. Plan ahead.

- Hours listed anywhere can vary. On holidays, expect shorter hours or closures. In summer, some sights are open late, allowing easy viewing without crowds. Ask the local TI for a current listing of museum hours. You can confirm sightseeing plans each morning with a quick telephone call asking, "Are you open today?" (*"Aperto oggi?"*; ah-PER-toh OH-jee) and "What time do you close?" (*"A che ora chiuso?"*; ah kay OH-rah kee-OO-zoh). I've included telephone numbers for this purpose.

you take out more than about €150 (don't take it personally). Also be aware that some ATMs will tell you to take your cash within 30 seconds, and if you aren't fast enough, your cash may be sucked back into the machine...and you'll have a hassle trying to get it from the bank.

Visa and MasterCard are more commonly accepted than American Express. Just like at home, credit or debit cards work easily at larger hotels, restaurants, and shops, but smaller businesses prefer payment in local currency. If you have lots of large bills, break them at a bank, especially if you like shopping at mom-and-pop places; they rarely have huge amounts of change.

Regular banks have the best rates for changing cash and traveler's checks. For a large exchange, it pays to compare rates and fees. Banks—not exchange offices—have the best rates for cashing traveler's checks. Banking hours are generally 8:30–13:30 and

- Art historians and Italians refer to the great Florentine centuries by dropping a thousand years. The *Trecento* (300s), *Quattrocento* (400s), and *Cinquecento* (500s) were the 1300s, 1400s, and 1500s.
- In Italian museums, art is dated with *sec* for *secolo* (century, often indicated with Roman numerals), A.C (for Avanti Cristo, or B.C.), and A.D. (for Dopo Cristo, or A.D.). O.K.?
- The greedy practice of jacking up admission prices by charging a few euros extra for a special exhibition, which you have to pay whether you want to see it or not, has become quite typical.
- Audioguides are becoming increasingly common at museums. These small, portable devices give you information in English on what you're seeing. After you dial a number that appears next to a particular work of art, you listen to the spiel (cutting it short if you want). Though the information can be dry, it's usually worthwhile (about €4; extra for 2 sets of headphones or bring your own 2nd set of standard Y-jack or MP3 player headphones).
- About half the visitors at Italian museums are English (not Italian) speakers. If a museum lacks audioguides and the only English you encounter explains how to pay, politely ask if there are plans to include English descriptions of the art. Think of it as a service to those who follow.
- In museums, rooms can begin closing about 30–60 minutes before actual closing time. Don't save the best for last.
- WCs at museums are usually free and clean.

15:30–16:30 Monday–Friday, but they can vary wildly. Banks are slow; simple transactions can take 15 to 30 minutes. Post offices and train stations usually change money if you can't get to a bank.

You should use a money belt (a pouch with a strap that you buckle around your waist like a belt and wear under your clothes). Thieves target tourists. A money belt provides peace of mind, allowing you to carry lots of cash safely.

Don't be petty about withdrawing money. You don't need to waste time every few days tracking down a cash machine. Change a week's worth of money, get big bills, stuff them in your money belt, and travel!

VAT Refunds and Customs Regulations

Wrapped into the purchase price of your Italian souvenirs is a Value Added Tax (VAT) that's generally about 20 percent. If you purchase more than €155 worth of goods at a store that participates in the VAT refund scheme, you're entitled to get most of that tax back. Personally, I've never felt that VAT refunds are worth the hassle, but if you do, here's the scoop.

If you're lucky, the merchant will subtract the tax when you make your purchase (this is more likely to occur if the store ships the goods to your home). Otherwise, you'll need to do this:

Get the paperwork. Have the merchant completely fill out the necessary refund document, called a "cheque." You'll have to present your passport at the store.

Have your cheque(s) stamped at the border or airport at your last stop in the European Union by the customs agent who deals with VAT refunds. It's best to keep your purchases in your carry-on for viewing, but if they're too large or dangerous (such as knives) to carry on, then track down the proper customs agent to inspect them before you check your bag. You're not supposed to use your purchased goods before you leave. If you show up at customs wearing your stylish new leather shoes, officials might look the other way—or deny you a refund.

To collect your refund, you'll need to return your stamped documents to the retailer or its representative. Many merchants work with services such as Global Refund or Premier Tax Free, which have offices at major airports, ports, or border crossings. These services, which extract a 4 percent fee, can refund your money immediately in your currency of choice or credit your card (within two billing cycles). If you have to deal directly with the retailer, mail the store your stamped documents and then wait. It could take months.

Customs Regulations: You can take home $800 in souvenirs per person duty-free. The next $1,000 is taxed at a flat 3 percent. After that, you pay the individual item's duty rate. You can also bring in duty-free a liter of alcohol (slightly more than a standard-sized bottle of wine), a carton of cigarettes, and up to 100 cigars. As for food, anything in cans or sealed jars is acceptable. Don't bring back dried meats, cheeses, and fresh fruits and veggies. To check customs rules and duty rates, visit www.customs.gov.

TRANSPORTATION

By Car or Train?

Each mode of transportation has pros and cons. Public transportation is one of the few bargains in Italy. Trains and buses are inexpensive and good. City-to-city travel is faster, easier, and cheaper by train than by car. Trains give you the convenience and economy of doing long stretches overnight. By train, I arrive relaxed and well-rested—not so by car.

Italy's Public Transportation

NOT TO SCALE

KEY: —— RAIL ···· SHIP ⊥ PRIVATE RAIL --- BUS

Parking, gas (about $5/gallon), and freeway tolls (about $6/hr) are expensive in Italy. But drivers enjoy more control, especially in the countryside. Cars carry your luggage for you, generally from door to door—especially important for heavy packers (such as chronic shoppers and families traveling with children). And groups know that the more people you pack into a car or minibus, the cheaper it gets per person.

Considering how handy and affordable Italy's trains and buses are (and that you're likely to go both broke and crazy driving in Italian cities), I'd do most of Italy by public transportation. If you want to drive, consider doing the big, intense stuff (Rome, Naples area, Milan, Florence, and Venice) by train or bus and renting a car for the hill towns of Tuscany and Umbria and for the Dolomites. A car is a worthless headache on the Riviera and in the Lake Como area.

Trains

To travel by train cheaply in Italy, you can simply buy tickets as you go, though train station lines can be long and the fast-train supplement charges are confusing. You'll potentially save some hassle but not money by buying the Italian State Railway's **TrenItalia Pass** (see chart on page 22). Although the pass covers most supplements, it doesn't cover reservations (purchased separately, optional for most trains—€4, required for Eurostar Italia—€8–11, more for *cuccetta* berths and sleepers on overnight trains). Pay all ticket costs in the station before you board or pay a nasty penalty on the train.

Since the cost difference between the TrenItalia Pass and point-to-point tickets is usually negligible, the biggest advantage of the pass is not having to wait in line to buy tickets. However, if you'll be reserving seats anyway, you'll still have to spend time in line—essentially eliminating the point of buying this pass. For most travelers, point-to-point tickets make more sense.

Multi-Country Railpasses: For travel exclusively in Italy, a 17-country **Eurailpass** is a bad value. If you're branching out beyond Italy, the **Eurail Selectpass** allows you to tailor a pass to your trip, provided you're traveling in three, four, or five adjacent countries directly connected by rail or ferry. For instance, with a three-country pass allowing 10 days of train travel within a two-month period ($564 in 2005), you could choose France–Italy–Greece or Germany–Austria–Italy. A **France and Italy Pass** combines just those two countries and covers night trains to and from Paris via Switzerland (but if your route crosses Switzerland by day, you'll pay extra—so the Selectpass is a better choice if you want to see the Alps).

Timetables: Newsstands sell up-to-date regional and all-Italy **timetables** (€5, ask for the *orario ferroviaro*). On the Web, check Germany's excellent all-Europe Web site, http://bahn.hafas.de/bin/query.exe/en, or Italy's www.trenitalia.com. The train

Deciphering Italian Train Schedules

At the station, look for the big yellow posters labeled *Partenze*—Departures (ignore the white posters, which show arrivals).

Schedules are listed chronologically, hour by hour, showing the trains leaving the station throughout the day. Each schedule has columns:

- The first column *(Ora)* lists the time of departure.
- The next column *(Treno)* shows the type of train.
- The third column *(Classi Servizi)* lists the services available (1st- and 2nd-class cars, dining car, *cuccetta* berths, etc.) and, more important, whether you need reservations (usually denoted by an *R* in a box).
- The next column lists the destination of the train *(Principali Fermate Destinazioni)*, often showing intermediate stops, followed by the final destination, with arrival times listed throughout in parentheses. Note that *your* final destination may be listed in fine print as an intermediate destination. If you're going from Milan to Florence, scan the schedule and you'll notice that virtually all trains that terminate in Rome stop in Florence en route. Travelers who read the fine print end up with a greater choice of trains.
- The next column *(Servizi Diretti e Annotazioni)* has pertinent notes about the train, such as "also stops in..." *(ferma anche a...)*, "doesn't stop in..." *(non ferma a...)*, "stops in every station" *(ferma in tutte le stazioni)*, and so on.
- The last column lists the track *(Binario)* the train departs from. Confirm the *binario* with an additional source: a ticket seller, the electronic board listing immediate departures, TV monitors on the platform, or the railway officials who are usually standing by the train unless you really need them.

For any odd symbols on the poster, look at the key at the end. Some of the phrasing can be deciphered easily, such as *servizio periodico* (periodical service—doesn't always run). For the trickier ones, ask a local or railway official or simply take a different train.

information telephone number is 848-888-8088.

Types of Trains: Along with the various milk-run trains, there are the slow IR (Interregional) and *diretto* trains, the medium *espresso*, the fast IC (InterCity), and the Eurostar Italia bullet train (abbreviated "ES," a.k.a. the T.A.V., which stands for *Treno Alta Velocità*). Compared to fast InterCity trains, the speedier Eurostar Italia may not be worth the extra expense because it shaves only a little time off typical trips (15–45 min faster between Venice and

Anatomy of an Italian Train Ticket

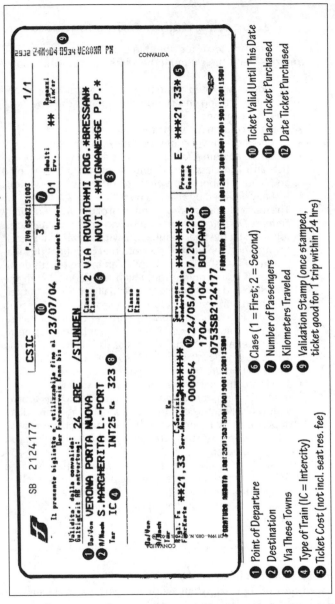

1. Point of Departure
2. Destination
3. Via These Towns
4. Type of Train (IC = Intercity)
5. Ticket Cost (not incl. seat res. fee)
6. Class (1 = First; 2 = Second)
7. Number of Passengers
8. Kilometers Traveled
9. Validation Stamp (once stamped, ticket good for 1 trip within 24 hrs)
10. Ticket Valid Until This Date
11. Place Ticket Purchased
12. Date Ticket Purchased

Italy by Train

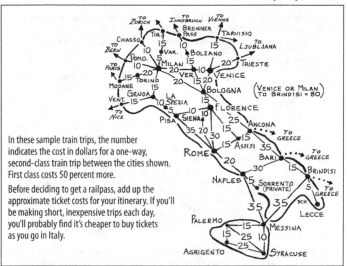

In these sample train trips, the number indicates the cost in dollars for a one-way, second-class train trip between the cities shown. First class costs 50 percent more.

Before deciding to get a railpass, add up the approximate ticket costs for your itinerary. If you'll be making short, inexpensive trips each day, you'll probably find it's cheaper to buy tickets as you go in Italy.

Florence, 30–60 min on Florence–Rome trip, and 10–20 min on Rome–Naples journey) and requires a reservation before boarding (€8-11 with railpass). If you're buying tickets as you go, fast trains are affordable (e.g., a 2nd-class Rome-to-Venice Eurostar ticket costs about $50 with a reservation at any ticket window or machine, only $7 more than the IC train).

Buying Tickets: Avoid big-city train station ticket lines whenever you can by buying tickets at:

1. Automated ticket machines, found in most major train stations in Italy. You can pay by cash (gives change) or by debit or credit card. Select English, then wade through a menu of destinations. If you don't see the city you're traveling to, keep keying in the spelling until it's listed. You can choose from first and second class seats, request tickets for more than one traveler, and (on the high-speed Eurostar trains) choose an aisle or window seat. When the machine prompts, "Fidelity Card?," choose no. Americans will need to select full-price tickets, since we're not eligible for any EU or resident discounts. You can even validate your ticket in the same machine if you're boarding your train right away.

2. Local travel agencies, such as CIT or American Express, where you can also make reservations and book a *cuccetta* (overnight berth) or sleeper. The cost is the same or minimally higher (about €2), the lines and language barrier are smaller than at the train station, and you'll save time.

First-class tickets cost 50 percent more than **second-class.** While second-class cars go as fast as their first-class neighbors,

Railpasses

Prices listed are for 2005. For up-to-date prices and details (and easy online ordering), see my comprehensive Guide to European Railpasses at www.ricksteves.com/rail. TrenItalia passes are also sold in Italy at travel agencies and major train stations.

TRENITALIA PASS

Type of Pass	1st Class Individual	1st Class Saver	2nd Class Individual	2nd Class Saver	2nd Class Youth
4 days in 2 months	$260	$221	$206	$175	$174
Extra rail days (max. 6)	27	23	22	19	18

Youthpasses: Under age 26 only. Kids 4–11 pay half adult fare. Under 4: free. Saverpass: Price is per person for two or more traveling together.

ITALY RAIL & DRIVE PASS

Any 4 days of rail travel + 2 days of Hertz car rental in 1 month.

Car Category	1st Class	2nd Class	Extra car day
Economy	$316	$260	$49
Compact	338	282	65
Intermediate	348	293	75
Small Automatic	348	293	75

Rail & Drive prices are approximate per person, two traveling together. Solo travelers pay about 20% more. No extra rail days. For more info, call your travel agent or Rail Europe at 800-438-7245.

FRANCE–ITALY PASS

Type of Pass	1st Class Individual	1st Class Saver	2nd Class Individual	2nd Class Saver	2nd Class Youth
4 days in 2 months	$309	$269	$269	$239	$199
Extra rail days (max. 6)	34	30	30	26	23

Youthpasses: Under age 26 only. Kids 4–11 pay half adult fare. Under 4: free. Saverpass: Price is per person for two or more traveling together. Be aware of your route. Many daytime connections from Paris to Italy pass through Switzerland (an additional $50 2nd class or $75 1st class if not covered by your pass). Night trains to/from Paris, and routes via Nice, Torino, or Modane are okay.

GREECE–ITALY FLEXIPASS

Type of Pass	1st Class Individual	1st Class Saver	2nd Class Individual	2nd Class Saver	2nd Class Youth
4 days in 2 months	$299	$255	$239	$204	$200
Extra rail days (max. 6)	30	25	24	20	20

Youthpasses: Under age 26 only. Kids 4–11 pay half adult fare. Under 4: free. Saverpass: Price is per person for two or more traveling together. Covers deck passage on overnight Superfast Ferries between Patras, Greece and Bari or Ancona, Italy (starts use of one travel day). Or 50% discount on Hellenic Med. Line ferry with basic cabin Patras-Corfu-Brindisi (does not use a travel day). Does not cover travel to or on Greek islands.

EURAIL SELECTPASSES

This pass covers travel in three adjacent countries. For details and four- or five-country options, see *Rick Steves' Guide to European Railpasses* at www.ricksteves.com/rail.

Type of Pass	1st Class Selectpass	1st Class Saverpass	2nd Class Youthpass
5 days in 2 months	$370	$316	$241
6 days in 2 months	410	348	267
8 days in 2 months	488	414	317
10 days in 2 months	564	480	367

Youthpasses: Under age 26 only. Kids 4–11 pay half adult fare. Under 4: free. Saverpass: Price is per person for two or more traveling together.

Italy is one country where I would consider the splurge of first class. The easiest way to "upgrade" a second-class ticket once on board a crowded train is to nurse a drink in the snack car.

Some travelers can get a discount on already-cheap point-to-point tickets purchased in Italy. **Youths** under 26 can buy a €40 Carta Verde discount card at any train station and save 10 percent on second- and first-class tickets for one year. If you're 60 or over, you can purchase a €30 Carta d'Argento discount card, which saves you 15 percent on second- and first-class tickets for a year. The **Tariffa Famiglia** discount allows one child (aged 4–11) to travel for free with two adults when they buy first- or second-class point-to-point tickets in Italy (no card needed). See www.trenitalia.com for details.

Before boarding the train, you must **validate** (stamp) your train documents in the machine near the platform. This includes whatever you need to take a particular trip, which can be as simple as a single ticket, but can also involve a supplement, seat reservation, or *cuccetta* reservation on an overnight train. You don't need to stamp Eurailpasses or TrenItalia Pass. If you forget to stamp your ticket, go right away to the train conductor—before he comes to you—or you'll pay a fine.

Reservations: Trains can fill up, even in first class; if a popular train route originates at your departure point (e.g., you're catching the Milan-to-Venice train in Milan), arrive a minimum of 15 minutes before the departure time to snare a seat. If you anticipate a crowd, you can get a firm seat reservation in advance for about €4. Some major stations have train composition posters on the platforms showing where first- and second-class cars are located when the trains arrive (letters on the poster are supposed to correspond to letters posted over the platform—but they don't always). Be aware that conductors are no longer marking reserved seats with a card—instead, they are simply posting a list of the reservable and non-reservable seat rows (sometimes in English) in each train car's vestibule. This means that if you board a crowded train and get one of the last seats, you may be ousted when the reservation holder comes along. To avoid this situation, reserve a seat when possible.

Theft: Italian trains are famous for their thieves. Never leave a bag unattended. I've noticed that police now ride the trains, and things seem more controlled. Still, for an overnight trip, I'd feel safe only in a *cuccetta* (a berth in a special sleeping car with an attendant who keeps track of who comes and goes while you sleep—approximately €15 in a 6-bed compartment, €20 in a less-cramped 4-bed compartment).

Baggage Storage: Many stations have *deposito bagagli* where you can safely leave your bag for €3 per 12-hour period (payable when you pick up the bag, double-check closing hours). Since the terrorist attacks of September 11, 2001, no stations have lockers.

Strikes: Strikes, which are common, generally last a day. Train employees will simply explain, "*Sciopero*" (strike). But in actuality, sporadic trains, following no particular schedule, lumber down the tracks during most strikes. When a strike is pending, travel agencies (and Web-savvy hoteliers) can check the Web for you to see when the strike goes into effect and which trains will continue to run.

Car Rental

Research car rentals before you go. It's cheaper to arrange car rentals from the U.S., either with your travel agent or directly with the companies. Rent by the week with unlimited mileage. I normally rent the smallest, least expensive model. For a three-week rental, allow $800 per person (based on 2 people sharing a car), including insurance, tolls, gas, and parking. If you'll be renting for three weeks or more, consider leasing; you'll save money on insurance and taxes. Explore your drop-off options and costs (south of Rome can be a problem).

For peace of mind, I spring for the Collision Damage Waiver insurance (CDW, about $15 per day), but it has a high deductible hovering around $1,000–1,500. Car-rental companies may try to sell you "super CDW" at an additional cost of $7–15 per day to lower the deductible to zero.

Some credit cards cover CDW insurance; quiz your credit card company on the worst-case scenario. If you use the coverage offered by your credit card, you'll have to decline the CDW offered by your car-rental company. In this situation, some car-rental companies put a hold on your credit card for the amount of the full deductible (which can equal the value of the car). This is bad news if your credit limit is low—particularly if you plan on using that card for other purchases during your trip.

In sum, buying CDW—and the supplemental insurance to buy down the deductible, if you choose—is the easiest but priciest option. Using the coverage that comes with your credit card is cheaper, but can involve

more hassle. For longer trips, leasing is the best way to go.

In Italy, theft insurance (separate from CDW insurance) is mandatory. The insurance usually costs about $10–15 a day, payable when you pick up the car.

A rail-and-drive pass (such as a EurailDrive, Selectpass Drive, or Italy Rail and Drive) can be put to thoughtful use. Certain areas are great by car, such as the Dolomites and the hill towns of Tuscany and Umbria, while most of Italy is best by train. If comparing rates between this kind of pass and a separate car rental, note that with an Italy Rail and Drive pass, you pay $160–180 per day for the first two car days, then $50–75 for each additional day (with 4 days of rail in 2 months, includes theft insurance and CDW).

Driving

Driving in Italy can be scary—a video game for keeps, and you only get one quarter. All you need is a car, internal fortitude, and an international driver's license (get it at your local AAA office for $10, plus the cost of 2 passport photos). Note that you need to carry along your American driver's license, too.

Autostrada: Italy's freeway system is as good as our interstate system, but you'll pay about a dollar for every 10 minutes of use. (I paid €20 for the four-hour drive from Bolzano to Pisa.) While I favor the freeways because I feel they're safer, cheaper (saving time and gas), and less nerve-racking than smaller roads, savvy local drivers know which toll-free "superstradas" are actually faster and more direct than the *autostrada* (e.g., Florence to Pisa). For more information, visit www.autostrade.it.

Gas: Most cars take unleaded gas (*senza piombo,* from green pumps, available everywhere). *Autostrada* rest stops are self-service stations open daily without a siesta break. Small-town stations are usually cheaper and offer full service but shorter hours. Many 24-hour-a-day stations are entirely automated, with machines that trade gas for paper money.

Parking: White lines generally mean parking is free. Blue lines mean you'll have to pay—usually €1 per hour (use machine, leave time-stamped receipt on dashboard). If there's no meter, there is probably a roving attendant who will take your money. Study the signs. Many free zones are cleared out (by car owners or tow trucks) one day a week for street cleaning. Often the free zones have a 30- or 60-minute time limit. *Zona disco* has nothing to do with dancing. Italian cars have a time disk (a cardboard clock), which you set at your arrival time and lay on the dashboard so the attendant knows how long you've been parked. This is a fine system that all drivers should take advantage of. (If your rental car doesn't come with a *zona disco,* pick one up at a tobacco shop or just write your arrival time on a piece of paper and place it on the dashboard.)

Driving in Italy: Distance and Time

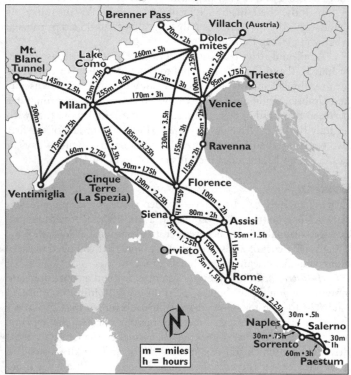

Garages are safe, save time, and help you avoid the stress of parking tickets. Take the parking voucher with you to pay the cashier before you leave.

Theft: Cars are routinely vandalized and stolen. Try to make your car look locally-owned by hiding the "tourist-owned" rental-company decals and putting a local newspaper in your back window.

COMMUNICATING

Telephones

Smart travelers learn the phone system and use it daily to reserve or reconfirm rooms, get tourist information, or phone home.

If you have to spell out your name on the phone when making a reservation, you might have trouble with *a* (pronounced "ah" in Italian), *e* (pronounced "ay"), and *i* (pronounced "ee"). Say "*a*, Ancona," "*e*, Empoli," and "*i*, Italia" to clear up that problem. If you plan to access your voice mail from Italy, be advised that you can't always dial extensions or secret codes once you connect (you're on vacation—relax).

Types of Phones

You'll encounter various kinds of phones in your European travels.

Telecom **pay phones** are everywhere, and take cards only (no coins). About a quarter of the phones are broken. The rest work reluctantly. Dial slowly and deliberately, as if the phone doesn't understand numbers very well. Often a recorded message in Italian will break in, brusquely informing you that the phone number does not exist *(non-esistente)*, even if you're dialing your own home phone number. Dial again with an increasing show of confidence, in an attempt to convince the phone of your number's existence. If you fail, double-check your prefixes (see "European Calling Chart" on page 708) or try a different phone. Repeat as needed.

Hotel room phones are fairly cheap for local calls, but pricey for international calls, unless you use an international phone card (see below).

American mobile phones work in Europe if they're GSM-enabled, tri-band (or quad-band), and on a calling plan that includes international calls. With a T-Mobile phone, you can roam using your home number, and pay $1–2 per minute for making or receiving calls.

Some travelers buy a **European mobile phone** in Europe. For about $125, you can get a phone that will work in most countries once you pick up the necessary chip (about $30) per country. Or you can buy a cheaper, "locked" phone that only works in the country where you purchased it (about $100, includes $20 worth of calls). If you're interested, stop by any European shop that sells mobile phones; you'll see prominent store window displays. You aren't required to (and shouldn't) buy a monthly contract—buy pre-paid calling time instead (as you use it up, buy additional minutes at newsstands or mobile-phone shops). If you're on a budget, skip mobile phones and use international phone cards instead.

Paying for Calls

You can spend a fortune making phone calls in Europe...but why would you? Here's the skinny on different ways to pay, including the best deals.

Italian Phone Cards come in two types: official phone cards that you insert into a pay phone, and international phone cards that can be used from virtually any phone.

Insertable phone cards are used to make calls from pay phones. You can buy these Telecom cards (in denominations of €5 or €10) at *tabacchi* shops, post offices, and machines near phone booths (many phone booths indicate where the nearest phone-card sales outlet is located). Rip off the perforated corner to "activate" the card, then physically insert it into a slot in the pay phone. It displays how much money you have remaining on the card. Then just dial away to anywhere in the world. The price of the call is automatically deducted while you talk. These cards give you your best deal for calls within Italy, and are reasonable for international calls.

International phone cards are an even better deal for overseas calls (as cheap as 2 cents per minute to the United States). Unlike the official phone cards, an international phone card is *not* inserted into the phone. Instead, you dial the toll-free number listed on the card, reaching an automated operator. When prompted, you dial in a scratch-to-reveal code number, also written on the card. Then dial your number. You can use the cards to make local and domestic long-distance calls as well. Since they're not insertable, you can use them from any phone—including the one in your hotel room (if your phone is set on pulse, switch it to tone). Generally you'll get more minutes out of a card if you use it from your hotel room, rather than from a pay phone. (For a €5 card, for example, you may get 180 minutes from your hotel room phone, compared to 40 minutes from a pay phone.) Buy cards at small newsstand kiosks, *tabacchi* shops, and hole-in-the-wall long-distance phone shops. Because there are so many brand names, simply ask for an international phone card (*carta telefonica prepagata internazionale*, KAR-tah teh-leh-FOHN-ee-kah pray-pah-GAH-tah in-ter-naht-zee-oh-NAH-lay). Tell the vendor where you'll be making most calls (*"per Stati Uniti"*—to America), and he'll select the brand with the best deal. Buy a lower denomination in case the card is a dud. I've had good luck with the Europa card, which offers 180 minutes from Italy to the United States for €5. If you have time left on your card when you leave the country (as you likely will), simply give it to another traveler—anyone can use it.

Dialing direct from your hotel room without using an international phone card is usually quite expensive for international calls, but it's convenient. I always ask first how much I'll be charged. Keep in mind that you have to pay for local and occasionally even toll-free calls.

Receiving calls in your hotel room is often the cheapest way to keep in touch with the folks back home—especially if your family has an inexpensive way to call you (either a good deal on their long-distance plan, or a prepaid calling card with good rates to Europe). Give them a list of your hotels' phone numbers before you go. As you travel, send your family an e-mail or make a quick payphone call to set up a time for them to call you, and then wait for the ring.

Metered phones are sometimes available in bigger post offices. You can talk all you want, then pay the bill when you leave—but be sure you know the rates before you have a lengthy conversation.

Coin-operated phones, while rare, still exist in some areas. If making a call, have a bunch of coins handy—they go fast.

U.S. Calling Cards (such as the ones offered by AT&T, MCI, or Sprint) are the worst option. You'll nearly always save a lot of money by paying for your call in any of the other ways described above.

How to Dial

Calling from the United States to Italy, or vice versa, is simple—once you break the code. The "European Calling Chart" on page 708 will walk you through it. Remember that European time is six/nine hours ahead of the East/West Coast of the United States.

Dialing within Italy: Italy has a direct-dial phone system (no area codes). To call anywhere within Italy, just dial the number. For example, the number of one of my recommended Florence hotels is 055-293-451. To call it from a Florence train station, dial 055-293-451. If you call it from Venice, it's the same: 055-293-451. Italian mobile phone numbers no longer start with zero (these are dialed direct like fixed phone numbers).

Italian phone numbers vary in length; a hotel can have, say, an eight-digit phone number and a nine-digit fax number.

Italy's toll-free numbers start with 800 (like U.S. 800 numbers, though in Italy you don't need to dial a "1" first). In Italy, these 800 numbers—called *freephone* or *numero verde* (green number)—can be dialed free from any phone without using a phone card or coins. Note that you can't call Italy's toll-free numbers from America, nor can you count on reaching America's toll-free numbers from Italy.

Dialing International Calls: When calling internationally, dial the international access code (00 if you're calling from Europe, 011 from the United States or Canada), the country code of the country you're calling (39 for Italy; see appendix for list of other countries), and the local number. Note that in most European countries, you have to drop the zero at the beginning of the local number—but in Italy, you dial it. So, to call the Venice hotel from the United States, dial 011 (the U.S. international access code), 39 (Italy's country code), then 041-528-5174. To call my office in Edmonds, Washington, from Italy, I dial 00 (Europe's international access code), 1 (the U.S. country code), 425 (Edmonds' area code), and 771-8303.

E-mail and Mail

E-mail: E-mail use among Italian hoteliers is common. Sometimes hotels have one or more computers in the lobby where you can check your e-mail; don't expect to plug in your own laptop. Wi-Fi access is rarely available in hotels. Drab little Internet cafés are popular, especially in big cities. Your hotelier can steer you to one near your hotel.

When you see a cluster of orange public phones in a room off a busy street, you might see several computers in the batch. With these, you can use your Italian phone card to access the Internet. You won't be comfortable (no seat), and you'll get cut off if your phone card runs out of time, but this can be a handy, quick way to check your e-mail.

Mail: Mail service in Italy has improved over the last few years, but even so, mail nothing precious from Italy. If you need to receive mail while traveling, consider a few pre-reserved hotels along your route. Allow 14 days for United States-to-Italy mail delivery, but don't count on it. Federal Express, UPS, and DHL all make pricey two-day deliveries. E-mailing and phoning is so easy that I've completely dispensed with mail stops.

SLEEPING

For hassle-free efficiency, I favor hotels and restaurants handy to sightseeing activities. Rather than list hotels scattered throughout a city, I describe two or three favorite neighborhoods and recommend the best accommodations values in each, from $20 bunks to plush $450 doubles with all the comforts.

Sleeping in Italy is expensive. Cheap big-city hotels can be depressing. Tourist information services cannot give opinions on quality. A major feature of this book is its extensive listing of good-value rooms. I like places that are clean, small, central, quiet at night, traditional, inexpensive, and friendly, with firm beds—and those not listed in other guidebooks. (In Italy, for me, 6 out of these 9 criteria means a keeper.)

Types of Accommodations

Hotels

Double rooms listed in this book will range from about $50 (very simple, toilet and shower down the hall) to $300 (maximum plumbing and more), with most clustering around $100 (with private bathrooms). Prices are higher in big cities and heavily touristed cities, and lower off the beaten path. Three or four people can economize by requesting larger rooms. Solo travelers find that the cost of a *camera singola* is often only 25 percent less than a *camera doppia*, and single travelers using double rooms enjoy hardly any savings at all. Most listed hotels have rooms for anywhere from one to five people. If there's room for an extra cot, they'll cram it in for you.

The Italian word for "hotel" is *hotel*, and in smaller, nontouristy towns, *albergo*. A few places have kept the old titles, *locanda* or *pensione*, indicating that they offer budget beds.

You normally get close to what you pay for. Prices are fairly standard. Shopping around earns you a better location and more character, but rarely a cheaper price.

Sleep Code

To help you easily sort through these listings, I've divided the rooms into three categories based on the price for a standard double room with bath:

$$$ **Higher Priced**
$$ **Moderately Priced**
$ **Lower Priced**

To pack maximum information into minimum space, I use this code to describe accommodations in this book. When there is a range of prices in one category, that means the price fluctuates with the season, size of room, or length of stay. Prices listed are per room, not per person.

S = Single room (or price for one person in a double).
D = Double or Twin room. "Double beds" are often two twins sheeted together and are usually big enough for nonromantic couples.
T = Triple (generally a double bed with a single).
Q = Quad (usually two double beds).
b = Private bathroom with toilet and shower or tub.
s = Private shower or tub only (the toilet is down the hall).

According to this code, a couple staying at a "Db-€85" hotel would pay a total of 85 euros (about $100) for a double room with a private bathroom. You can assume a hotel takes credit cards unless you see "cash only" in the listing. The hotel staff speaks basic English unless otherwise noted.

However, prices at nearly any hotel can get soft if you do any of the following: arrive direct (without using a pricey middleman like the TI or a Web booking service), offer to pay cash, mention this book, stay at least three nights, or visit off-season. Breakfasts are legally optional (though some hotels insist they're not). Initial prices quoted often include breakfast and a private bathroom. Offer to skip breakfast for a better price.

Few hotels still have rooms with no private shower, but if they do, requesting this will save you $20–40. Generally, rooms with a bath or shower also have a toilet and a bidet (which Italians use for quick sponge baths). If a shower has no curtain, the entire bathroom showers with you. The cord that dangles over the tub or shower is not a clothesline. You pull it when you've fallen and can't get up.

Double beds are called *matrimoniale*, even though hotels aren't interested in your marital status. Twins are *due letti singoli*.

When you check in, the receptionist will ask for your passport and keep it for a couple of hours. Hotels are required to register each guest with the police. Relax. Americans are notorious for making this chore more difficult than it needs to be.

Rooms are safe. Still, zip cameras and keep money out of sight. More pillows and blankets are usually in the closet or available on request. In Italy, towels and linen aren't always replaced every day. Hang your towel up to dry.

Many hotel rooms have a TV and phone. Rooms in fancier hotels usually come with a tiny safe, a small stocked fridge (called a *frigo* bar, FREE-goh bar; you pay for what you use; if it's noisy at night, unplug it), and air-conditioning. Sometimes you pay an extra per-day charge for air-conditioning, and it may only be turned on during the heat of the day (around 10:00–24:00). Conveniently, many business-class hotels drop their prices in July and August, just when the air-conditioned comfort they offer is most important.

Most hotel rooms with air conditioners come with a control stick (like a TV remote) that generally has the same symbols and features: fan icon (click to toggle through wind power, from light to gale); louver icon (choose steady airflow or waves); snowflake and sunshine icons (cold air or heat, depending on season); clock ("O" setting: run x hours before turning off; "I" setting: wait x hours to start); and the temperature control (20 or 21 degrees Celsius is comfortable).

Many American travelers are shocked to learn that hotels aren't allowed to fire up their air-conditioners except between (about) June 1 and Sept 30. To conserve energy, the Italian government tightly regulates when hotels can provide air-conditioning in summer and heat in winter. As Americans, the world's energy gluttons, we often have a tough time understanding the importance of these serious conservation measures enacted by far-sighted governments. Be prepared to sweat a little...like everyone else.

The hotel breakfast, while convenient, is often a bad value—$12 for a roll, jelly, and usually unlimited *caffè latte*. You can sometimes request cheese or salami (about $3 extra). I enjoy taking breakfast at the corner café. It's OK to supplement what you order with a few picnic goodies.

Many hotels in resort areas will charge you for half-pension, called *mezza pensione*, during peak season (which can run from May through mid-October for resorts). Half-pension means that you pay for one meal per day per person (lunch or dinner, though usually dinner), whether you want to or not. Wine is rarely included. If half-board is required, you can't opt out and pay less. Some places offer half-board as an option; it can be worth considering. If they charge you less per meal than you've been paying for an average restaurant meal on your trip, half-board is a fine value if the chef is good. Ask other guests about the quality or check out their restaurant yourself.

You can usually save time by paying your bill the evening before you leave instead of paying in the busy morning, when the reception desk is crowded with tourists wanting to pay up, ask questions, or check in.

Hotels near Airports: If you have an early-morning flight, I'd suggest staying in the center of town and getting to the airport via bus, train, or taxi. But if you really want a hotel near an airport for the first or last night of your trip, try www.worldairportguide.com.

Private Rooms and Apartments: In small towns, there are often few hotels to choose from, but an abundance of *affitta camere,* or rental rooms. This can be anything from a set of keys and a basic bed to a cozy B&B with your own Tuscan grandmother. The local TI can give you a list of possibilities. These rooms are generally a good budget option, but since they vary in quality, shop around to find the best value. Apartment rentals, a great value for families or couples traveling together, are also listed at the TI and are very common in small towns. Apartments generally offer a couple of bedrooms, a sitting area, and a teensy *cucinetta,* usually stocked with dishes and flatware. Once you have the keys, you will probably be on your own.

Agritourism: *Agriturismo* (or agricultural tourism) began in the 1980s as a way to encourage farmers to remain on their land, produce food, and offer accommodations to tourists. A peaceful home base for exploring the region, these rural Italian B&Bs are ideal for couples or families traveling by car.

As the name implies, *agriturismi* are in the countryside, although some are located within a mile of town. Most are family-run and can vary wildly in quality. Some properties are simple and rustic, while others are downright luxurious, offering amenities such as swimming pools and riding stables. The rooms are usually clean and comfortable. Breakfast is often included, and half-pension (which in this case means a home-cooked dinner) may be built into the price. Kitchenettes are often available to cook up your own feast. Make sure you know how to operate the appliances. To maximize your time, ask the owner for suggestions on local restaurants, sights, and activities.

It's wise to book several months in advance for high season (May–Sept). Weeklong stays are preferred in July and August, but shorter stays may be possible. To sleep cheaper, avoid peak season. A Tuscan farmhouse that rents for as much as $2,000 a week at peak times can go for as little as $700 in late September or October. In the winter, you might be charged extra for heat, so confirm the price ahead of time. Payment policies vary, but generally a 25 percent deposit is required (lost if you cancel), and the balance is due one month before arrival.

I've listed some *agriturismi* in this book, but there are thousands. Be aware that agricultural tourism is organized "*all'Italiana,*" which means, among other things, a lack of a single governing body. Local TIs can give you a list of farms in their area. Also visit www.agriturist.it or www.agriturismoitaly.it (among dozens of Web sites). For a booking agency, consider Farm Holidays in Tuscany. They book rooms and apartments at farms in Tuscany, Umbria, and elsewhere in Italy (closed Sat–Sun, tel. 0564-417-418, www.byfarmholidays.com, info@byfarmholidays.com).

Making Reservations

Given the increasing popularity of travel to Italy, the high prices, and the quality of the gems I've found for this book, I'd recommend reserving rooms. You can call long in advance from home or grab rooms a few days to a week in advance as you travel. Note that for Florence, it's smart to book at least a month in advance for the handy benefit of having your hotelier make museum reservations for you (see page 331).

If you prefer the flexibility of traveling without reservations, you'll have greater success of snaring rooms if you arrive early in the day. When you anticipate crowds, call hotels between 9:00 and 10:00 on the day you plan to arrive, when the hotel clerk knows who'll be checking out and just which rooms will be available.

I've taken great pains to list telephone numbers with long-distance instructions (see "Telephones," page 26; also see the appendix). Use the telephone and convenient telephone cards. Most hotels listed are accustomed to English-only speakers. (If you have difficulty, ask the fluent receptionist at your current hotel to call for you.) A hotel receptionist will usually trust you and hold a room until 16:00 without a deposit, though some will ask for a credit-card number.

If you know where you want to stay each day (and you don't need or want flexibility), reserve your rooms a month or two in advance. To reserve from home, e-mail, phone, or fax your request. Phone and fax costs are reasonable, e-mail is a steal (and preferred by most hotels), and simple English is usually fine. To fax, use the handy form in the appendix (online at www.ricksteves.com /reservation). If you don't get an answer to your fax request, consider that a "no." (Many little places get 20 faxes a day after they're full, and they can't afford to respond.)

A two-night stay in August would be "2 nights, 16/8/06 to 18/8/06." (Europeans write the date in this order—day/month/ year—and hotel jargon uses your day of departure.)

If you receive a response from the hotel stating its rates and room availability, it's not a confirmation. You must confirm that you indeed want a room at the given rate. One night's deposit is generally required. Your credit-card number will usually be accepted as the deposit. Be sure to fax your card number (rather than e-mail it) to keep it private, safer, and out of cyberspace. You can pay with your card or cash when you arrive; if you don't show up, your card will be billed for one night. To make things easier on yourself and the hotel, be sure you really intend to stay at the hotel on the dates you requested. These family-run businesses lose money if they turn away customers while holding a room for someone who doesn't show up. Understandably, some hotels bill no-shows for one night. *If you must cancel, do so well in advance.* Long distance is cheap and easy from public phone booths. Don't let these people down—I promised you'd call and cancel if for some reason you won't show up.

Reconfirm your reservations a few days in advance for safety, and let them know about what time you'll arrive. Don't needlessly confirm rooms through the tourist office or Web services; they'll take a commission of up to 20 percent. On the small chance that a hotel loses track of your reservation, bring along their faxed confirmation or a hard copy of their e-mailed confirmation.

EATING

The Italians are masters of the art of fine living. That means eating…long and well. Lengthy, multicourse lunches and dinners and endless hours sitting in outdoor cafés are the norm. Americans eat on their way to an evening event and complain if the check is slow in coming. For Italians, dining is an end in itself, and only rude waiters rush you. When you want the bill, mime-scribble on your raised palm or ask for it: *"Il conto?"* You may have to ask for it more than once. To save time, ask for the check when you receive the last item you order.

Even those of us who liked dorm food will find that the local cafés, cuisine, and wines become a highlight of our Italian adventure. Trust me, this is sightseeing for your palate, and even if the rest of you is sleeping in cheap hotels, your taste buds will relish an occasional first-class splurge. You can eat well without going broke. But be careful; you're just as likely to blow a small fortune on a disappointing meal as you are to dine wonderfully for €20.

Restaurants

When restaurant-hunting, choose places filled with locals, not the place with the big neon signs boasting, "We speak English and accept credit cards." Restaurants parked on famous squares generally serve bad food at high prices to tourists. Locals eat better in lower-rent locales. Family-run places operate without hired help and can offer cheaper meals. The word *osteria* (normally a simple, local-style restaurant) makes me salivate.

Tips on Tipping

Tipping in Italy isn't as automatic and generous as it is in the United States, but for special service, tips are appreciated, if not expected. As in the United States, the proper amount depends on your resources, tipping philosophy, and the circumstance, but some general guidelines apply.

Restaurants: Tipping is an issue only at restaurants that have waiters and waitresses. If you order your food at a counter, don't tip. Many Italians don't ever tip.

At restaurants with table service, menus list if there is a *pane e coperto* charge (bread and cover charge, usually €2 per person) and if service is included (*servizio incluso*, generally 15 percent). If the service is included, there's no need to tip beyond that, but if you like to tip and you're pleased with the service, throw in €1–2 per person.

If service is not included (*servizio non incluso*), you could tip 5 to 10 percent by rounding up or leaving the change from your bill. Leave the tip on the table or hand it to your server. It's best to tip in cash even if you pay with your credit card. Otherwise the tip may never reach your server.

Taxis: To tip the cabbie, round up. For a typical ride, round up to the next euro on the fare (to pay a €13 fare, give €14); for a long ride, to the nearest 10 (for a €75 fare, give €80). Note that if the cabbie hauls your bags, you'll be charged an automatic supplement, so no need to tip extra. In Venice, tip a water taxi like you would a land taxi, but don't bother tipping for quick *traghetto* rides or already-pricey gondola rides.

Special Services: It's thoughtful to tip a couple of euros to someone who shows you a special sight and who is paid in no other way (such as the man who shows you an Etruscan tomb in his backyard). Tour guides at public sites often hold out their hands for tips after they give their spiel; if I've already paid for the tour, I don't tip extra, though some tourists do give a euro or two, particularly for a job well done. I don't tip at hotels, but if you do, give the porter a euro for carrying bags and leave a couple of euros in your room at the end of your stay for the maid if the room was kept clean. In general, if someone in the service industry does a super job for you, a tip of a couple of euros is appropriate...but not required.

When in doubt, ask. If you're not sure whether (or how much) to tip for a service, ask your hotelier or the TI; they'll fill you in on how it's done on their turf.

Eating with the Seasons

Italian cooks love to serve you fresh produce and seafood at its tastiest. If you must have porcini mushrooms outside of October and November, they'll be frozen. To get the freshest veggies at a fine restaurant, request *"Il piatto di verdure della stagione, per favore"* (A plate of seasonal vegetables, please). Here are a few examples of what's fresh when:

April–May:	Squid, green beans, asparagus, artichokes, and zucchini flowers
April, May, Sept, Oct:	Black truffles
May–June:	Asparagus, zucchini, cantaloupe, and strawberries
May–Aug:	Eggplant
Oct–Nov:	Mushrooms and white truffles
Fresh year-round:	Clams, meats, and cheese

For unexciting but basic values, look for a *menu turistico* (also called *menu del giorno—menu* of the day), a three- or four-course, set-price meal (price includes service charge, no need to tip). Galloping gourmets order à la carte with the help of a menu translator. (The *Marling Italian Menu Master* is excellent. *Rick Steves' Italian Phrase Book* has enough phrases for intermediate eaters.) Some restaurants have self-serve antipasti buffets, offering a variety of cooked appetizers spread out like a salad bar (pay per plate, not weight; usually costs around €6–8); a plate of antipasti combined with a pasta dish makes a healthy, affordable, interesting meal.

A full meal consists of an appetizer (antipasto, €3–5), a first course (*primo piatto,* pasta or soup, €5–10), and a second course (*secondo piatto,* expensive meat and fish dishes, €7–15). Vegetables *(contorni, verdure)* may come with the *secondo* course or cost extra (€3–5) as a side dish.

Seafood and steak are sometimes sold by weight (if you see "100 g" or "*l'etto*" by the price on the menu, you'll pay that price *per* 100 grams—about a quarter pound; sometimes also abbreviated *s.q.,* or "according to quantity"). Tourists without good language skills are commonly shell-shocked by the bill when ordering dishes sold by the weight. Some special dishes come in large quantities meant for two people; the shorthand way of showing this on a menu is "X2" (meaning "for two people").

Restaurants normally pad the bill with a cover charge (*pane e coperto,* around €2) and a service charge (*servizio,* 15 percent); see "Tips on Tipping," page 36.

As you will see, the euros add up in a hurry. Light and budget eaters get by with a *primo piatto* each and a shared antipasto.

Italians admit that *secondi* are the least interesting aspect of the local cuisine. My standard ordering procedure is to mix *antipasti* and *primi piatti* family-style with my dinner partners (skipping *secondi*) to keep the prices down and the experience up. When done well (e.g., under-ordering, since courses are often bigger than necessary), we eat well in better places for less than the cost of a tourist *menu* in a cheap place.

Delis, Cafeterias, Pizza Shops, and *Tavola Calda* (Hot Table) Bars

Italy offers many cheap alternatives to restaurants. Stop by a *rosticcerìa* for great cooked deli food; a self-service cafeteria (called "free flow" in Italian) that feeds you without the add-ons; a *tavola calda* bar for an assortment of veggies or first courses; or a Pizza Rustica shop for stand-up or take-out pizza.

Pizza is cheap and everywhere. Key pizza vocabulary: *capricciosa* (generally ham, mushrooms, and artichokes), *funghi* (mushrooms), *margherita* (tomato sauce and mozzarella), *marinara* (tomato sauce, oregano, garlic, no cheese), *quattro formaggi* (four different cheeses), and *quattro stagioni* (different toppings on each of the four quarters— for those who can't choose just one menu item). If you ask for *peperoni* on your pizza, you'll get green or red peppers, not sausage. Kids like simple, plain *margherita* (tomato and cheese) or spicy *diavola* (closest thing in Italy to American "pepperoni"). At Pizza Rustica take-out shops, slices are sold by weight (100 grams, or *un etto*, is a hot, cheap snack; 200 grams, or *due etti*, makes a light meal).

For a fast, cheap, and healthy lunch, find a *tavola calda* bar with a buffet spread of meat and vegetables and ask for a mixed plate of vegetables with a hunk of mozzarella *(piatto misto di verdure con mozzarella)*. Don't be limited by what you can see. If you'd like a salad with a slice of cantaloupe and a hunk of cheese, they'll whip that up for you in a snap. Belly up to the bar and, with a pointed finger and key words from the chart in this chapter, you can get a fine mixed plate of vegetables. If something's a mystery, ask for "*un assaggio*" ("a little taste").

Italian Bars/Cafés

Italian "bars" are not taverns, but cafés. These local hangouts serve coffee, mini-pizzas, sandwiches, and cartons of milk from the cooler. Many dish up plates of fried cheese and vegetables from under the glass counter, ready to reheat. This is my budget choice, the Italian equivalent of English pub grub.

For quick meals, bars usually have trays of cheap, ready-made sandwiches (*panini* or *tramezzini*)—some kinds are delightful grilled *(riscaldato)*. To save time for sightseeing and room for dinner, my favorite lunch is a ham and cheese *panini* at a bar (called

Ordering Food at *Tavola Caldas*

"Heated, please."	*"Scaldare, per favore."*	skahl-DAH-ray, pehr fah-VOH-ray
"A taste, please."	*"Un assaggio, per favore."*	oon ah-SAH-joh, pehr fah-VOH-ray
plate of mixed veggies	*piatto misto di verdure*	pee-AH-toh MEES-toh dee vehr-DOO-ray
artichoke	*carciofi*	kar-CHOH-fee
asparagus	*asparagi*	ah-spah-rah-jee
beans	*fagioli*	fah-JOH-lee
green beans	*fagiolini*	fah-joh-LEE-nee
broccoli	*broccoli*	BROK-oh-lee
cantaloupe	*melone*	May-LOH-nay
carrots	*carote*	kah-ROT-ay
ham	*prosciutto*	proh-SHOO-toh
mushrooms	*funghi*	FOONG-ghee
potatoes	*patate*	pah-TAH-tay
rice	*riso*	REE-zoh
spinach	*spinaci*	speen-AH-chee
tomatoes	*pomodori*	poh-moh-DOH-ree
zucchini	*zucchine*	zoo-KEE-nay
breadsticks	*grissini*	gree-SEE-nee

(Excerpted from *Rick Steves' Italian Phrase Book*)

tost, grilled twice to get really hot). To get food "to go," say, *"Da portar via"* ("for the road"). All bars have a WC *(toilette, bagno)* in the back, and customers (and the discreet public) can use it.

Bars serve great drinks—hot, cold, sweet, or alcoholic. Chilled bottled water (*naturale* or *frizzante*) is sold cheap to go.

Coffee: If you ask for *"un caffè,"* you'll get espresso. Cappuccino is served to locals before noon and tourists any time of day. (To an Italian, cappuccino is a breakfast drink and a travesty after anything with tomatoes.) Italians like it only warm. To get it hot, request *"Molto caldo"* (very hot) or *"Più caldo, per favore"* ("hotter, please"; pew KAHL-doh, pehr fah-VOH-ray).

Experiment with a few of the options...

- *caffè macchiato* (mah-kee-AH-toh): espresso with only a splash of milk
- *caffè latte:* coffee with lots of hot milk, no foam
- *caffè Americano:* espresso diluted with hot water

- *caffè corretto:* espresso with a shot of liquor, usually *grappa* (but Sambuca is good, too)
- *caffè freddo:* sweet and iced espresso
- *cappuccino freddo:* iced cappuccino
- *caffè hag:* instant decaf (any coffee drink is available decaffeinated; ask for it *decaffeinato:* day-kah-fay-een-AH-toh)

Beer: Beer on tap is *alla spina.* Get it *piccola* (11 oz), *media* (17 oz), or *grande* (34 oz, or 1 liter).

Wine: To order a glass (*bicchiere*; bee-kee-AY-ray) of red *(rosso)* or white *(bianco)* wine, say, "*Un bicchiere di vino rosso/bianco.*" *Corposo* means full-bodied. House wine often comes in a quarter-liter carafe (8.5 oz, *un quarto*), half-liter pitcher (17 oz, *un mezzo*), or one-liter pitcher (34 oz, *un litro*). Trendy wines with small production (such as Brunello di Montalcino) are good but overpriced. There are better values on wines with greater production and less demand (such as Frescobaldi Montisodi).

Prices: You'll notice a two-tiered price system. Drinking a cup of coffee while standing at the bar is cheaper than drinking it at a table. If you're on a budget, don't sit without first checking out the financial consequences. Ask "Same price if I sit or stand?" by saying, "*Costa uguale al tavolo o al banco?*" (KOH-stah oo-GWAH-lay ahl TAH-voh-loh oh ahl BAHN-koh).

If the bar isn't busy, you'll often just order and pay when you leave. Otherwise: 1) decide what you want; 2) find out the price by checking the price list on the wall or the prices posted near the food, or by asking the barman; 3) pay the cashier; and 4) give the receipt to the barman (whose clean fingers handle no dirty euros) and tell him what you want.

Picnics

In Italy, picnicking saves lots of euros and is a great way to sample local specialties. In the process of assembling your meal, you get to deal with the Italians in the market scene. On days you choose to picnic, gather supplies early. You'll probably visit several small stores or market stalls to put together a complete meal, and many close around noon. While it's fun to visit the small specialty shops, a local *alimentari* is your one-stop corner grocery store (most will slice and stuff your sandwich for you if you buy the ingredients there). A *supermercato* gives you more efficiency with less color for less cost.

Juice-lovers can get a liter of O.J. for the price of a Coke or coffee. Look for "100% *succo*" (juice) on the label. Hang on to the half-liter mineral-water bottles (sold everywhere for about €0.50). Buy juice in cheap liter boxes, drink some, and store the extra in your water bottle. (I drink tap water—*acqua del rubinetto.*)

Picnics can be an adventure in high cuisine. Be daring. Try

Send Me a Postcard, Drop Me a Line

If you enjoy a successful trip with the help of this book and would like to share your discoveries, please fill out the survey at www.ricksteves.com/feedback. I personally read and value all feedback.

---

the fresh mozzarella, *presto* pesto, shriveled olives, and any UFOs the locals are excited about. Shopkeepers are generally happy to sell small quantities of produce. A typical picnic for two might be fresh rolls, 100 grams of cheese, 100 grams of meat, two tomatoes, three carrots, two apples, yogurt, and a liter box of juice. Total cost—about €10.

TRAVELING AS A TEMPORARY LOCAL

We travel all the way to Italy to enjoy differences—to become temporary locals. You'll experience frustrations. Certain truths that we find "God-given" or "self-evident," such as cold beer, ice in drinks, bottomless cups of coffee, hot showers, and bigger being better, are suddenly not so true. One of the benefits of travel is the eye-opening realization that there are logical, civil, and even better alternatives. A willingness to go local ensures that you'll enjoy a full dose of Italian hospitality.

If there is a negative aspect to the image Italians have of Americans, it is that we are big, aggressive, impolite, rich, loud, and a bit naive. Americans tend to be noisy in public places, such as restaurants and trains. Our raised voices can demolish Europe's reserved and elegant ambience. Talk softly.

While Italians, flabbergasted by our Yankee excesses, say in disbelief, *"Mi sono cadute le braccia!"* ("I throw my arms down!"), they nearly always afford us individual travelers all the warmth we deserve.

Judging from all the happy postcards I receive from travelers who have used this book, it's safe to assume you'll enjoy a great, affordable vacation—with the finesse of an independent, experienced traveler.

Thanks, and *buon viaggio!*

BACK DOOR TRAVEL PHILOSOPHY
From *Rick Steves' Europe Through the Back Door*

Travel is intensified living—maximum thrills per minute and one of the last great sources of legal adventure. Travel is freedom. It's recess, and we need it.

Experiencing the real Europe requires catching it by surprise, going casual..."Through the Back Door."

Affording travel is a matter of priorities. (Make do with the old car.) You can travel—simply, safely, and comfortably—anywhere in Europe for $100 a day plus transportation costs. In many ways, spending more money only builds a thicker wall between you and what you came to see. Europe is a cultural carnival, and, time after time, you'll find that its best acts are free and the best seats are the cheap ones.

A tight budget forces you to travel close to the ground, meeting and communicating with the people, not relying on service with a purchased smile. Never sacrifice sleep, nutrition, safety, or cleanliness in the name of budget. Simply enjoy the local-style alternatives to expensive hotels and restaurants.

Extroverts have more fun. If your trip is low on magic moments, kick yourself and make things happen. If you don't enjoy a place, maybe you don't know enough about it. Seek the truth. Recognize tourist traps. Give a culture the benefit of your open mind. See things as different but not better or worse. Any culture has much to share.

Of course, travel, like the world, is a series of hills and valleys. Be fanatically positive and militantly optimistic. If something's not to your liking, change your liking. Travel is addictive. It can make you a happier American as well as a citizen of the world. Our earth is home to six billion equally important people. It's humbling to travel and find that people don't envy Americans. They like us, but, with all due respect, they wouldn't trade passports.

Globe-trotting destroys ethnocentricity. It helps you understand and appreciate different cultures. Regrettably, there are forces in our society that want you dumbed down for their convenience. Don't let it happen. Thoughtful travel engages you with the world—more important than ever these days. Travel changes people. It broadens perspectives and teaches new ways to measure quality of life. Many travelers toss aside their hometown blinders. Their prized souvenirs are the strands of different cultures they decide to knit into their own character. The world is a cultural yarn shop. And Back Door travelers are weaving the ultimate tapestry. Come on, join in!

ITALY

(Italia)

There are two Italys: The North is industrial, aggressive, and "time is money" in its outlook. The South is crowded, poor, relaxed, farm-oriented, and traditional. (For more on this, see sidebar on page 215.) Families here are very strong and usually live in the same house for many generations. Loyalties are to family, city, region, soccer team, and country—in that order.

Economically, Italy has had its problems, but somehow things have always worked out. Today, Italy is the Western world's seventh-largest industrial power. Its people earn more per capita than the British. Italy is the world's leading wine producer. It is sixth in cheese and wool output. Tourism is big business. Cronyism, which complicates my work, is an integral part of the economy.

Italy, home of the Vatican, is 98 percent Catholic, but the dominant religion is life—motor scooters, soccer, fashion, girl-watching, boy-watching, good coffee, good wine, and *il dolce far niente* ("the sweetness of doing nothing"). The Italian character shows itself on the streets in the skilled maniac drivers and the classy dressers who star in the ritual evening stroll, or *passeggiata*.

The language is fun. Be melodramatic and talk with your hands. Hear the melody; get into the flow. Italians are outgoing. They want to communicate, and they try harder than any other Europeans. Play with them.

Italy, a land of extremes, is also the most thief-ridden country you'll visit. Tourists suffer virtually no violent crime—but there are plenty of petty purse-snatchings, pickpocketings, and shortchangings. Wear your money belt! The scruffy-looking women and children loitering around the major museums aren't there for the art.

Take advantage of the cheap, colorful, and dry-but-informative city guidebooks sold on the streets. Use the information telephones you'll find in most historic buildings. Just set the dial on English, pop in your coins, and listen. The narration is often accompanied by a brief slide show.

Some important Italian churches require modest dress: No shorts or bare shoulders on men, women, and sometimes even

Italy Almanac

Population: 58 million. The population is almost entirely indigenous Italians who speak Italian (with German and French spoken in some Alpine regions) and are nominally Roman Catholic (98 percent). One in five Italians is over 65, and one in three uses the Internet.

Area: 116,000 square miles, including the islands of Sicily, Sardinia, and others.

Latitude and Longitude: 43°N and 12° E (similar to Oregon or Maine).

Geography: Italy is shaped like a boot, 850 miles long and 150 miles wide, jutting into the central Mediterranean. (Florida is 500 miles long.) The terrain is generally mountainous or hilly, with the Alps in the north and a north-south "spine" of the Apennine Mountains.

Highs and Lows: The highest point is Mont Blanc, on the border with France. Besides the Alps, the highest point is Monte Cimone (7,100 feet). The lowest point is sea level. Italy has 5,000 miles of coastline.

Rivers: Po (the longest, 400 miles), Arno, Adige, and Tiber.

Active Volcanoes: Vesuvius, Etna, and Stromboli.

Major Cities: Rome (the capital, 2.6 million), Milan (1.3 million), and Naples (1 million).

Italian Inventions: Cologne, thermometer, barometer, pizza, wireless telegraph, espresso machine, typewriter, batteries,

children. With a little imagination (except at the ultrastrict Vatican's St. Peter's), those caught by surprise can improvise something—a jacket for your knees and maps for your shoulders. I wear a super-lightweight pair of long pants for my hot and muggy big-city Italian sightseeing.

While no longer a cheap country, Italy is still a hit with shoppers. Glassware (Venice), gold, silver, leather, prints (Florence), and high fashion (Rome and Milan) are good souvenirs, but do some price research at home so you'll recognize the good values.

Il dolce far niente is a big part of Italy. Zero in on the fine points. Don't dwell on the problems. Accept Italy as Italy. Savor your cappuccino, dangle your feet over a canal (if it smells, breathe through your mouth), and imagine what it was like centuries ago. Ramble through the rabble and rubble of Rome and mentally resurrect those ancient stones. Look into the famous sculpted eyes of Michelangelo's *David* and understand

nitroglycerin, and the ice cream cone.

Gross Domestic Product: $1.5 trillion.

Economy: Sixty-five percent of the economy consists of service jobs (especially tourism), 30 percent is industry (textiles, chemicals), and five percent is agriculture (fruit, vegetables, olives, wine, plus fishing). Pollution remains a greater problem in Italy than elsewhere in Europe. There are 10,000 miles of train lines (mostly government-run) and 4,300 miles of freeway (*autostrada*).

Museums: 3,000.

Government: Italy is a republic, with three branches of government. The chief executive is the prime minister (currently Silvio Berlusconi, a media-owning billionaire—see sidebar on page 702), who assumes office as the head of the leading vote-getting party in legislative elections. The bicameral legislature is elected by (mostly) direct voting. Since World War II, the fragmented country has had 60 national governments.

Regions: Italy is divided into 20 regions (including Tuscany, Umbria, Veneto, and Lazio). Locally, there are some 8,000 "communes," with a community council and mayor.

Flag: Three vertical bands of green, white, and red.

Average "Gio": The average Italian is 41 years old, makes $27,000 a year, and has 1.27 kids. Every day, he or she consumes two servings of pasta, a half pound of bread, and two glasses of wine, and will live to the average age of 79 years, 6 months, and two days.

Renaissance man's assertion of himself. Sit silently on a hilltop rooftop. Get chummy with the winds of the past. Write a poem over a glass of local wine in a sun-splashed, wave-dashed Riviera village. If you fall off your moral horse, call it a cultural experience. Italy is for romantics.

VENICE

(Venezia)

Soak all day in this puddle of elegant decay. Venice is Europe's best-preserved big city. This car-free urban wonderland of a hundred islands—laced together by 400 bridges and 2,000 alleys—survives on the artificial respirator of tourism.

Born in a lagoon 1,500 years ago as a refuge from barbarians, Venice is overloaded with tourists and is slowly sinking (unrelated facts). In the Middle Ages, the Venetians, becoming Europe's clever middlemen for East-West trade, created a great trading empire. By smuggling in the bones of St. Mark (San Marco) in A.D. 828, Venice gained religious importance as well. With the discovery of America and new trading routes to the Orient, Venetian power ebbed. But as Venice fell, her appetite for decadence grew. Through the 17th and 18th centuries, Venice partied on the wealth accumulated through earlier centuries as a trading power.

Today, Venice is home to about 65,000 people in its old city, down from a peak population of nearly 200,000. While there are about 500,000 in greater Venice (counting the mainland, not counting tourists), the old town has a small-town feel. Locals seem to know everyone. To see small-town Venice away from the touristic flak, escape the Rialto-San Marco tourist zone and savor the town early and late without the hordes of vacationers day-tripping in from cruise ships and nearby beach resorts. A 10-minute walk from the madness puts you in an idyllic Venice few tourists see.

Planning Your Time

Venice is worth at least a day on even the speediest tour. Hyperefficient train travelers take the night train in and/or out.

Venice Overview

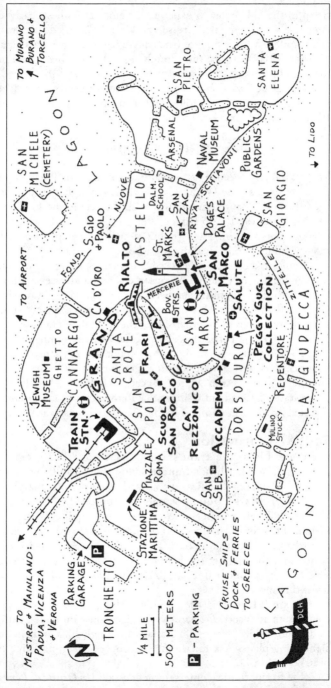

Sleep in the old center to experience Venice at its best: early and late. For a one-day visit, cruise the Grand Canal, do the major sights on St. Mark's Square (the square itself, Doge's Palace, and St. Mark's Basilica), see the Church of the Frari (Chiesa dei Frari) for art, and wander the backstreets on a pub crawl (described in "Eating," page 102). Venice's greatest sight is the city itself. Make time to simply wander. While doable in a day, Venice is worth two. It's a medieval cookie jar, and nobody's looking.

ORIENTATION

The island city of Venice is shaped like a fish. Its major thorough-fares are canals. The Grand Canal winds through the middle of the fish, starting at the mouth where all the people and food enter, passing under the Rialto Bridge, and ending at St. Mark's Square (Piazza San Marco). Park your 21st-century perspective at the mouth and let Venice swallow you whole.

Venice is a car-less kaleidoscope of people, bridges, and odor-less canals. The city has no major streets, and addresses are hope-lessly confusing. There are six districts: San Marco (most touristy), Castello (behind San Marco), Cannaregio (from the train station to the Rialto), San Polo (other side of the Rialto), Santa Croce, and Dorsoduro. Each district has about 6,000 address numbers.

To find your way, navigate by landmarks, not streets. Many street corners have a sign pointing you to *(per)* the nearest major landmark, such as San Marco, Accademia, Rialto, and Ferrovia (train station). Obedient visitors stick to the main thoroughfares as directed by these signs and miss the charm of backstreet Venice.

Tourist Information

There are TIs at the **train station** (daily 8:00–18:30, crowded and surly); at **St. Mark's Square** (daily 9:00–20:00; with your back to St. Mark's Basilica, it's in far left corner of square); and near the **St. Mark's Square vaporetto stop** on the lagoon (daily 10:00–18:00, sells vaporetto tickets, rents audioguides with a GPS system at €15 for self-guided walking tours—they work erratically, and when they do, they're boring). Smaller offices are at **Piazzale Roma** and the **airport** (daily 9:30–19:30). For a quick question, save time by phoning 041-529-8711. The TI's official Web site is www.turismovenezia.it.

At any TI, pick up the free bimonthly magazine *Leo,* which comes with an insert, *Leo Bussola,* that lists museum hours, exhibi-tions, and musical events (in Italian and English). Confirm your sightseeing plans. Ask for the fine brochures outlining three off-beat Venice walks.

The free periodical entertainment guide *Un Ospite di Venezia*

Arrival in Venice

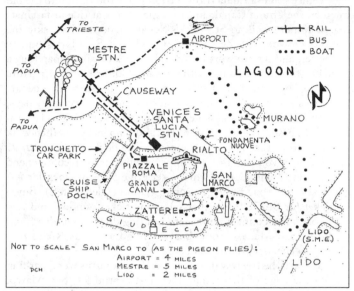

Map labels:
- TO TRIESTE
- AIRPORT
- MESTRE STN.
- TO PADUA
- LAGOON
- CAUSEWAY
- VENICE'S SANTA LUCIA STN.
- MURANO
- TO PADUA
- FONDAMENTA NUOVE
- TRONCHETTO CAR PARK
- RIALTO
- PIAZZALE ROMA
- SAN MARCO
- CRUISE SHIP DOCK
- GRAND CANAL
- ZATTERE
- GIUDECCA
- LIDO (S.M.E.)
- LIDO
- RAIL
- BUS
- BOAT
- NOT TO SCALE - SAN MARCO TO (AS THE PIGEON FLIES):
  - AIRPORT = 4 MILES
  - MESTRE = 5 MILES
  - LIDO = 2 MILES
- DCH

(a monthly listing of events, nightlife, museum hours, train and vaporetto schedules, emergency telephone numbers, and so on) is available at the TI or fancy hotel reception desks (www .aguestinvenice.com).

More Web Sites on Venice: www.veniceforvisitors.com, www.museiciviciveneziani.it (civic museums in Venice), www .venicexplorer.net (interactive maps), and www.meetingvenice.it.

Maps: Of all places, Venice requires a good map. Hotels give away lousy freebies. The TI sells a simple one that isn't much better. Bookshops, newsstands, and postcard stands sell a wider range of maps; the €3 maps that are pretty bad, but if you spend €5, you'll get a map that shows you everything. Invest in a good map and use it—this can be the best €5 you spend in Venice.

Arrival in Venice

A two-mile-long causeway (with both highway and train lines) connects Venice to the mainland. Mestre, the sprawling mainland industrial base, has fewer crowds, cheaper hotels, and plenty of cheap parking lots, but no charm. Don't stop here, unless you're parking your car in a lot.

By Train: Trains to Venice stop at either Venezia Mestre (on the mainland) or at the Santa Lucia station on the island of Venice itself. If your train only stops at Mestre, worry not. Shuttle trains regularly connect Mestre's station with Venice's Santa Lucia station—your train ticket to Mestre will let you ride free (6/hr, 10 min).

Venice's **Santa Lucia train station** plops you right into the old town on the Grand Canal, an easy vaporetto boat ride or fascinating 40-minute walk to St. Mark's Square. Upon arrival, skip the station's crowded TI, because the two TIs at St. Mark's Square are better, and it's not worth a long wait for a minimal map (buy a good one from a newsstand with no wait). Confirm your departure plan (stop by train info desk or just study the *partenze*—departure—posters on walls). Consider storing unnecessary heavy bags, even though lines for **baggage check** may be very long (platform #14, €3/12 hrs, €5/24 hrs, daily 6:00–24:00, no lockers). Then walk straight out of the station to the canal. The dock for *vaporetti* #1 and #82 is on your left (for downtown Venice, most recommended hotels, and Grand Canal Cruise—see page 59); the dock for #51 and #52 is on your right (for some recommended hotels). Buy a €5 ticket (or €10.50 24-hour pass) at the ticket window and hop on a boat, after confirming that it's heading downtown (direction: Rialto or San Marco). Some boats only go as far as Rialto *(solo Rialto)*, so check with the conductor.

By Car: The freeway dead-ends at Venice, near several parking lots on the edge of the island. The most central lot, San Marco, is very busy and too expensive. Follow the green lights directing you to an alternative parking lot with space, probably Tronchetto (across the causeway and on the right), which has a huge, multistoried garage (€18/day, tel. 041-520-7555). From there, avoid the travel agencies masquerading as TIs and head directly for the vaporetto docks for the boat connection (#82) to the town center. Don't let taxi boatmen con you out of the relatively cheap €5 vaporetto ride. Parking in Mestre is easy and cheap (open-air lots €4/day, €5/day garage across from Mestre train station, easy shuttle-train connections to Venice's Santa Lucia Station—6/hr, 10 min). There are also huge and economical lots in Verona, Padua, and Vicenza.

By Plane: For information on Venice's airport and connections into the city, see page 111.

Passes for Venice

To help control (and confuse?) its flood of visitors, Venice offers cards and passes that cover some museums and/or transportation. For most visitors, the simple Museum Card (the Doge's Palace/Correr Museum combo-ticket) or Museum Pass will do.

The **Museum Card** covers the museums of St. Mark's Square: Doge's Palace, clock tower *(torre dell'orologio)*, Correr Museum, and the two museums accessed from within the Correr—the National Archaeological Museum and the Monumental Rooms of Marciana National Library (€11, called *"Museum Card per i Musei di Piazza San Marco,"* valid for 3 months, 1 entry per museum; to bypass long line at Doge's Palace, purchase card at the Correr Museum, then enter Doge's Palace).

The pricier **Museum Pass** includes the St. Mark's Square museums listed above, plus Ca' Rezzonico (Museum of 18th-Century Venice), Mocenigo Palace museum (textiles and costumes), Casa Goldoni (home of the Italian playwright), and museums on the islands—Murano's Glass Museum and Burano's Lace Museum (€15.50, valid for 3 months, 1 entry per museum).

The **Chorus Pass** gives access to 15 of Venice's churches (including San Polo and the Frari, covered in this book) and their works of art (€8, or pay €2.50 per church). You'd need to visit four churches to save money.

Venice also (pointlessly) offers two other Museum Cards: €8 for the **museums of the 18th century** (called *"Museum Card per area del Settecento";* the museums are Ca' Rezzonico, Casa Goldoni, and Palazzo Mocenigo) and €6 for the **island museums** (called *"Museum Card per i musei delle isole,"* covering Murano's Glass Museum and Burano's Lace Museum).

No cards or passes cover these top attractions: Accademia, Peggy Guggenheim Collection, Scuola Grande di San Rocco, Campanile, and the three sights within St. Mark's Basilica that charge admission.

Venice Cards: These cards include Venice's public transportation, public toilets, and, if you get the "orange" version, some sights. Personally, I don't think these are worth the bother, but here's the information: The **Blue Venice Card** covers all your vaporetto rides, plus entry to public toilets (€11/1 day, €23/3 days, €41/7 days, cheaper for "Juniors" under 30). The **Orange Venice Card** includes transportation and toilets, as well as the museums covered by the Museum Pass—so it's like getting a Blue Venice Card and a Museum Pass (€26/1 day, €43/3 days, €58/7 days, cheaper for "Juniors" under 30). To order either card, book online at www.venicecard.com (tel. 041-2424). Better yet, if all you want is a vaporetto pass, you can get a 24-hour pass for €10.50 at any vaporetto dock; described under "Getting Around Venice," below.

"Rolling Venice" Youth Discount Pass: To those under age 30, this worthwhile €3 pass gives discounts on sights and transportation, plus information on cheap eating and sleeping. It is sold at kiosks at major vaporetto stops, including Ferrovia (train station), Rialto, Accademia, and San Marco/Vallaresso (St. Mark's Square).

Helpful Hints

Rip-offs, Theft, and Help: The dark, late-night streets of Venice are safe. Even so, pickpockets (often elegantly dressed) work the crowded main streets, docks, and *vaporetti* (wear your money belt and carry your daybag in front). Your biggest risk

Daily Reminder

Need a calendar? See the appendix.

Sunday: The Church of San Giorgio Maggiore (on an island near St. Mark's Square) hosts a Gregorian Mass at 11:00. The Rialto open-air market consists mainly of souvenir stalls today (fish and produce sections closed). These sights are open only in the afternoon: Frari Church (13:00–17:00, closed Sun in Aug) and St. Mark's Basilica (14:00–16:00). It's a bad day for a pub crawl, as most pubs are closed.

Monday: All sights are open except for the Rialto fish market, Dalmatian School, the skippable Palazzo Mocenigo (textiles), and Torcello Museum (on Torcello Island). The Accademia and Ca' d'Oro (House of Gold) close at 14:00. Don't side-trip to Verona or Vicenza today, as most sights in these towns are closed.

Tuesday: All sights are open except the Peggy Guggenheim Collection, Ca' Rezzonico (Museum of 18th-Century Venice), and the Lace Museum (on Burano island).

Wednesday: All sights are open except the Glass Museum (on Murano Island).

Thursday/Friday: All sights are open.

Saturday: All sights are open (Peggy Guggenheim Collection until 22:00 June–July) except the Jewish Museum.

Notes: The Accademia is open earlier (daily at 8:15) and closes later (19:15 Tue–Sun) than most sights in Venice. Some sights close earlier off-season (e.g., Doge's Palace, Correr Museum, Campanile, and St. Mark's Basilica).

Churches: Modest dress is recommended at churches and required at St. Mark's Basilica—no bare shoulders, shorts, or short skirts. Some churches are closed to sightseers on Sunday morning (e.g., St. Mark's Basilica and Frari Church) and many are closed from roughly 12:00 to 14:30 or 15:00 Monday through Saturday (e.g., La Salute and San Giorgio Maggiore).

Crowd Control: Crowds can be a serious problem at the Accademia (to minimize crowds, go early or late, or call 041-520-0345 to reserve tickets in advance); St. Mark's Basilica (try going early or late, or you can skip the line if you have a bag to check—see "St. Mark's Basilica," page 70); Campanile (go early or late—it's open until 21:00 July–Sept); and the Doge's Palace. For the Doge's Palace, you have three options for avoiding the ticket-sales line: Buy your Museum Card or Museum Pass at the Correr Museum (then step right up to the Doge's Palace turnstile, thus skipping the long line); visit the Doge's Palace at 17:00 (if it's April–Oct), when lines disappear; or book a "Secret Itineraries" tour (see page 75). All of the sights that have crowd problems (St. Mark's Basilica, Doge's Palace, and Accademia) get more crowded when it rains.

of pickpockets is actually inside St. Mark's Basilica. A service called Counter of Tourist Mediation handles complaints about local crooks, but does not give out information (tel. 041-529-8710, complaint@turismovenezia.it).

Get Lost: Accept the fact that Venice was a tourist town 400 years ago. It was, is, and always will be crowded. While 80 percent of Venice is, in fact, not touristy, 80 percent of the tourists never notice. Hit the back streets. Venice is the ideal town to explore on foot. Walk and walk to the far reaches of the town. Don't worry about getting lost. Get as lost as possible. Keep reminding yourself, "I'm on an island, and I can't get off." When it comes time to find your way, just follow the directional arrows on building corners or simply ask a local, *"Dov'è San Marco?"* ("Where is St. Mark's?") People in the tourist business (that's most Venetians) speak some English. If they don't, listen politely, watching where their hands point, say *"Grazie,"* and head off in that direction. If you're lost, pop into a hotel and ask for their business card—it comes with a map and a prominent "you are here."

Don't Cheap Out: Venice is expensive for locals as well as tourists. The demand is huge, supply is limited, and running a business is costly. Things just cost more here; everything must be shipped in and hand-trucked to its destination. Perhaps the best way to enjoy Venice is just to succumb to its charms and blow a lot of money.

Take Breaks: Venice's endless pavement, crowds, and tight spaces are hard on the tourist. Schedule breaks in your sightseeing. Grab a cool place to sit down, relax, and recoup—meditate on a pew in an uncrowded church, or buy a cappuccino and a fruit cup in a café.

Etiquette: Walk on the right and don't loiter on bridges. Picnicking is technically forbidden (keep a low profile). Dress modestly. Men should keep their shirts on. (Women, too.) When visiting St. Mark's Basilica or other major churches, men, women, and even children should cover their knees and shoulders (or risk being turned away). Remove hats when entering a church.

Pigeon Poop: If bombed by a pigeon, resist the initial response to wipe it off immediately—it'll just smear into your hair. Wait until it dries and flake it off cleanly.

Public Toilets: There are handy public WCs near St. Mark's Square, the Rialto, and the Accademia Bridge. You'll find public pay toilets near most major landmarks. Use free toilets—in a museum you're visiting or a café you're eating in—when you can.

Water: Venetians pride themselves on having pure, safe, and tasty tap water piped in from the foothills of the Alps. You can actually see the mountains from Venice's bell towers on crisp, clear winter days.

Lingo: *Campo* means square, *campiello* is a small square, *calle* is street, *fondamenta* is the road running along a canal, *rio* is a small canal, *rio terra* is a street that was once a canal and has been filled in, and *ponte* is a bridge.

Services

Money: The plentiful ATMs are the easiest way to go. If you must exchange currency, be aware that bank rates vary. The American Express change desk is just off St. Mark's Square (see "Travel Agencies," below). Non-bank exchange bureaus, such as Exacto, will charge you $10 more than a bank for a $200 exchange.

Internet Access: You'll find handy little Internet places all over town. They're all equally good.

Post Office: A large post office is just outside the far end of St. Mark's Square (the end farthest from the basilica; Mon–Fri 8:30–14:00, Sat 8:30–13:00, closed Sun, shorter hours off-season). The main P.O. is near the Rialto Bridge (on St. Mark's side, Mon–Fri 8:10–13:30, Sat 8:10–12:30, closed Sun). Use post offices only as a last resort, as simple transactions can take 45 minutes if you get in the wrong line. You can buy stamps from tobacco shops and mail postcards from any of the red postboxes around town.

Bookstores: Libreria Studium stocks all the English-language guidebooks (including mine for Venice, Florence, and Rome) just a block behind St. Mark's Basilica (daily 9:00–19:30, Calle de la Canonica, tel. 041-522-2382).

Laundry: I list several laundry options below, but your hotelier can direct you to one nearest your hotel. A modern **self-service** *lavanderia* is near St. Mark's Square on Ruga Giuffa at #4826 (daily 8:30–23:00, next to recommended Hotel al Piave—see page 93, tel. 393-760-7499, run by Massimo). **Lavanderia Gabriella** is also near St. Mark's Square (€14/load wash and dry, Mon–Fri 8:00–12:30, closed Sat–Sun; Rio Terra Colonne 985, from San Zulian Church go over Ponte dei Ferali, then take first right down Calle dei Armeni; tel. 041-522-1758). A **self-service launderette** near the train station is a few steps from the recommended hotel Albergo Marin—see page 99 for directions (daily 7:30–22:30, Campiello delle Muneghe 665a/b, San Polo, tel. 348-301-7457).

Travel Agencies: If you need to get train tickets, pay supplements, make reservations, or arrange a *cucetta* (koo-CHET-tah—bunk on a night train), avoid the time-consuming trip to the crowded train station by using a downtown travel agency.

While American Express charges railpass holders a €3 service fee for reservations, the other agencies do basically everything the train station does for the same price with no fee. All can give advice on cheap flights. Note that you'll get a far better price if you're able to book at least a week in advance. Consider booking flights for later in your trip while you're here (and remember that in Europe, you don't have to buy a round-trip ticket to get the best price).

Kele & Teo Viaggi e Turismo is reliable and handy, selling train tickets with no fees (Mon–Fri 8:30–18:00, Sat 9:00–12:00, closed Sun, at Ponte dei Bareteri on the Mercerie midway between Rialto and St. Mark's Square, tel. 041-520-8722, www.keleteo.com, incoming@keleteo.com).

Oltrex, just one bridge past the Bridge of Sighs, is a great little agency. They sell train and plane tickets and happily book train reservations for no extra fee (daily 9:00–19:00, Riva Degli Schiavoni, tel. 041-524-2828).

American Express books flights, sells train tickets, and makes train reservations for a €3 fee (Mon–Fri 9:00–17:30, closed Sat–Sun, about 2 blocks off St. Mark's Square en route to Accademia at 1471 San Marco, tel. 041-520-0844).

Church Services: The **San Zulian Church** (the only church in Venice that you can actually walk around) offers a Mass in English at 9:30 on Sunday (May–Sept, 2 blocks toward Rialto off St. Mark's Square). Gregorians enjoy the sung Gregorian Mass on Sundays at 11:00 (plus Mon–Sat at 8:00) at the **Church of San Giorgio Maggiore** (on island of San Giorgio Maggiore, visible from Doge's Palace, see page 76). Call 041-522-7827 to confirm times.

Haircuts: I've been getting my hair cut at **Coiffeur Benito** for 15 years. Benito has been keeping local men and women trim for 25 years. He's an artist—actually a "hair sculptor"—and a cut here is a fun diversion from the tourist grind (€19.50 for women, €16.50 for men, Tue–Sat 8:30–13:00 & 15:30–19:30, closed Sun–Mon, behind San Zulian Church near St. Mark's Square, Calle S. Zulian Gia del Strazzariol 592a, tel. 041-528-6221).

Getting Around Venice

By Vaporetto: The public transit system is a fleet of motorized bus-boats called *vaporetti*. They work like city buses except that they never get a flat, the stops are docks, and if you get off between stops, you may drown.

For most travelers, only two lines matter: #1 is the slow boat, which takes 45 minutes to make every stop along the entire length of the Grand Canal (leave every 10 min); #82 is the fast boat that zips down the Grand Canal in 25 minutes (leaves every 20 min), stopping mainly at Tronchetto (parking lot), Piazzale Roma (bus station), Ferrovia (train station), Rialto Bridge, San Tomà (Frari Church), the Accademia Bridge, and St. Mark's Square (specifically, the San Marco/Vallaresso dock). Some #82 boats go only as far as Rialto *(solo Rialto)*—check with the conductor before boarding.

It's a simple system, but there are a few quirks. Some stops have just one dock for boats going in both directions, while others have docks across the canal from each other—one side of the canal if you're going upstream, the other side for downstream. Electric reader boards on busy docks indicate which boats are coming next and when. Signs on board indicate upcoming stops.

Some lines don't run early or late. For example, the #82 fast vaporetto often doesn't leave the San Marco/Vallaresso stop (at St. Mark's Square) until 9:30; if you're trying to get from St. Mark's Square to the train station to catch an early train, you'd need to take slow #1 instead. If there's any doubt, ask a ticket-seller or conductor. If you plan to ride a lot of *vaporetti*, consider picking up the most current ACTV timetable (€0.60, in English and Italian, www.actv.it).

Tickets are €5 to travel up or down the Grand Canal, and €3.50 for other routes. They're good for 90 minutes in one direction (you can hop on and off during that time). Technically, you're not allowed a round-trip, even if you can do it within the 90-minute span. Buy tickets at the dock from ticket booths or from a conductor on board (do it before you sit down, or you risk being fined).

A 24-hour pass (€10.50) saves money after two trips. Also consider the 72-hour pass (€22). It's fun to be able to hop on and off spontaneously. There are also two round-trip tickets available: one for €6 (good for any route that doesn't go on the Grand Canal) and another for €7 (includes 1 trip on the Grand Canal). Technically, luggage costs the same as dogs—€3.50—but I've never been charged for either.

To avoid a fine, make sure your ticket is stamped with a time before boarding. Tickets come already stamped unless you specify otherwise; if, for whatever reason, your ticket lacks a stamp, stick it into the time-stamping yellow machine before boarding. A 24- or 72-hour pass must be stamped before the first use. Riding free? There's a one-in-10 chance a conductor will fine you €23.

For vaporetto fun, take my self-guided cruise of the Grand Canal (see page 59). During rush hour (about 9:00 from the Tronchetto parking lot and train station towards St. Mark's, about 17:00 in the other direction), boats are jam-packed. If you like joyriding on *vaporetti*, ride a boat around the city and out into the lagoon, then over to the Lido, and back. Ask for the circular route—*circulare* (cheer-koo-LAH-ray). It's usually the #51 or #52,

Venice

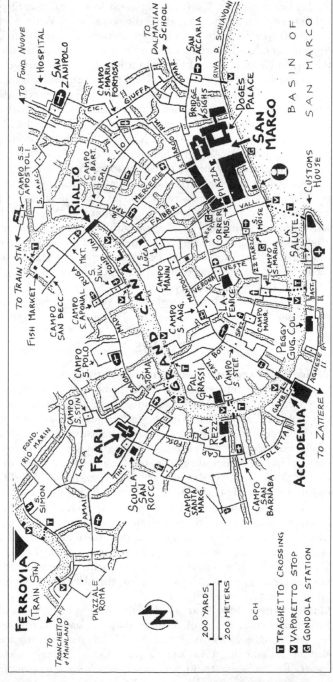

leaving from the San Zaccaria vaporetto stop (near the Doge's Palace) and from all the stops along the perimeter of Venice.

By *Traghetto*: Only three bridges cross the Grand Canal, but *traghetti* (gondolas) shuttle locals and in-the-know tourists across the Grand Canal at several handy locations (see map on page 60; routes also marked on pricier maps sold in Venice). Take advantage of these time-savers—they can also save money. For instance, while most tourists take the €5 vaporetto to connect St. Mark's with La Salute Church, a €0.50 *traghetto* does the job just as well. Most people stand while riding (generally run 6:00–20:00, sometimes until 23:00, tel. 041-2424 for schedule).

By Water Taxi: Venetian taxis, like speedboat limos, hang out at most busy points along the Grand Canal. Prices, which average €50 (about €90 to the airport, €50 to the train station, with extra fees for very early or late runs), are a bit soft. Negotiate and settle before stepping in. For travelers with lots of luggage or small groups who can split the cost, taxi rides can be a worthwhile and time-saving convenience—and skipping across the lagoon in a classic wooden motorboat is a cool indulgence. For €80 an hour, you can have a private taxi-boat tour.

By Gondola: To hire a gondolier for your own private cruise, see "Gondola Rides," page 83.

TOURS

Venice Walks and Tours—This company offers a selection of historic and entertaining walks, including the basic St. Mark's Square introduction (daily at 11:00), Cannaregio and the Jewish Ghetto, San Polo and Dorsoduro, Ghosts and Legends, Casanova, and Secret Gardens (€20 per person, cheaper for returnees and students, €5 discount with this book through 2006, group size 8–20, English language only—guides are native-speaking expats, 2 hours each, rain or shine, also day trips into the mainland; tel. 041-520-8616, mobile 340-050-2444, www.tours-italy.com, Monica or Jonathan).

Their 75-minute Grand Canal boat tour, offered daily at 16:30 and 17:30 (€40), is good. Tours are limited to about eight passengers (sitting awkwardly in a taxi not designed for sightseeing). You'll enjoy a fascinating, relaxing look at the wonders of the Grand Canal as well as the intimate back canals with a motor-mouthed (and interesting) guide. Departures are timed to give photographers the best possible light.

Classic Venice Bars Tour—Debonair local guide Alessandro Schezzini is a connoisseur of Venetian *bacari*—classic old bars serving traditional *cicchetti* (local munchies). He offers evening tours that involve sampling a snack and a glass of wine at three different *bacari*. The fee—about €30 per person—includes wine, *cicchetti*, and a chat with Alessandro, who will answer all of your questions about Venice (April–Oct Wed and Sat at 18:00, other evenings and off-season by request and with demand, 6–8 per group, tours must have at least 6, call or e-mail a day or two in advance to confirm, meet at top of Rialto Bridge, tel. & fax 041-534-5367, mobile 335-530-9024, venische@tiscalinet.it).

Venicescapes—Michael Broderick's private theme tours of Venice are intellectually demanding and beyond the attention span of most mortal tourists. Rather than a "sightseeing tour," consider your time with Michael a rolling, graduate-level lecture. Michael's challenge: To help visitors gain a more solid understanding of Venice. For a description of his various itineraries, see www.venicescapes.org (book well in advance, 4–6-hr tour: €275 for 2, €50 per person after that, plus admissions and transportation, tel. 041-520-6361, info@venicescapes.org).

Local Guides—Licensed guides are carefully trained and love explaining Venice to visitors. The following companies and guides give excellent tours to individuals, families, and small groups. If you organize a small group from your hotel at breakfast to split the cost (€65/hour with 2-hour minimum), the fee becomes quite reasonable.

Elisabetta Morelli is reliable, personable, and informative, giving good insight into daily life in Venice (€60/hr for Rick Steves' readers, usually 2–3-hour tours, tel. 041-526-7816, mobile 328-753-5220, bettamorelli@inwind.it). **Venice With a Guide** is a co-op of 10 equally good guides (www.venicewithaguide.com). **Walks Inside Venice** is a group of three women enthusiastic about their teaching (Roberta Curiel, tel. 041-524-1706, mobile 347-253-0560, www.walksinsidevenice.com, info@walksinsidevenice.com).

Alessandro Schezzini isn't a licensed Italian guide (and is therefore unable to take you into actual sights), but he does a great job getting you beyond the clichés and into offbeat Venice (€90, 2.5 hrs, listed above in "Classic Venice Bars Tour"). He also does Ghost Tours for spooky evening fun.

SELF-GUIDED CRUISE

"Welcome to Venice" Grand Canal Cruise

For a ▲▲▲ joyride, introduce yourself to Venice by boat. Cruise the Canal Grande from Tronchetto (parking lot) or Ferrovia (Santa Lucia train station) all the way to San Marco. You can ride boat #1 (slow and ideal, 45 min) or #82 (too fast to comfortably follow this tour, 25 min). When catching either boat, confirm that you're on a "San Marco via Rialto" boat (some boats finish at the Rialto Bridge and others take a non-scenic outside route). The conductor announces *"Solo Rialto!"* for boats going only as far as Rialto. You

Venice's Grand Canal

do not want boats heading for Piazzale Roma. Note that the San Marco vaporetto stop is actually called San Marco/Vallaresso.

If you can't snag a front seat, lurk nearby and take one when it becomes available or find an outside seat in the stern. This ride has the best light and fewest crowds early or late. Twilight is magic. After dark, chandeliers light up the building interiors. While Venice is a barrage on the senses that hardly needs a narration, these notes give the cruise a little meaning and help orient you to this great city. Some city maps (on sale at postcard racks) have a handy Grand Canal map on the back.

Overview

The Grand Canal is Venice's "Main Street." At more than two miles long, nearly 150 feet wide, and nearly 15 feet deep, it's the biggest canal with the most impressive palaces. The canal is the remnant of a river that once spilled from the mainland into the Adriatic. The sediment it carried formed barrier islands that cut off the sea, forming a lagoon.

Venice is a city of palaces, dating from the days when Venice was the world's richest city. The most lavish palaces formed a grand chorus line along the Grand Canal. Once frescoed in reds and blues, with black-and-white borders and gold-leaf trim, they made Venice a city of dazzling color. This cruise is the only way to really appreciate the palaces, approaching them at water level, where their main entrances were located. Today, strict laws prohibit any changes in these buildings, so while landowners gnash their teeth, we can enjoy Europe's best-preserved medieval city—slowly rotting. Many of the grand buildings are now vacant. Others harbor chandeliered elegance above mossy, empty ground floors.

The Tour Begins

Start at the **train station** or **Tronchetto** parking lot. We'll orient by the vaporetto stops.

Venice's main thoroughfare is busy with all kinds of **boats:** taxis, police boats, garbage boats, ambulances, construction cranes, and even brown-and-white UPS boats. Venice's sleek, black, graceful **gondolas** are a symbol of the city. While used gondolas cost about €10,000, new ones run up to €35,000 apiece. Today, with more than 400 gondoliers joyriding amid the churning *vaporetti*, there's a lot of congestion on the Grand Canal. Watch your vaporetto driver curse the better-paid gondoliers.

Ferrovia: The **Santa Lucia train station** (on the left bank of the canal), one of the few modern buildings in town, was built in 1954. It's been the gateway into Venice since 1860, when the first station was built. "F.S." stands for "Ferrovie dello Stato," the Italian state railway system.

The **bridge** at the station is the first of only three (so far) that cross the Grand Canal. Over 20,000 a day commute in from mainland, making this the busiest part of Venice during each rush hour. To alleviate some of the congestion and make the commute easier, a new fourth bridge over the Grand Canal (made of glass) is being built between the train station and Piazzale Roma (bus station).

Opposite the train station, atop the green dome of **San Simeone Piccolo** church, Saint Simon waves *ciao* to whoever enters or leaves the "old" city.

Riva di Biasio: Just past the Riva di Biasio stop, look left down the broad **Cannaregio Canal**. The twin pale-pink six-story "skyscrapers" are a reminder of how densely populated the world's original **ghetto** was. Set aside as the local Jewish quarter in 1516, the area (located behind the San Marcuola stop) became extremely crowded. This urban island developed into one of the most closely knit business and cultural quarters of all the Jewish communities in Italy, and gave us our word ghetto (from *geto,* the copper foundry located here). For more information, visit the Jewish Museum in this neighborhood (see page 80).

San Marcuola: The gray **Turkish "Fondaco" Exchange** (right side, opposite San Marcuola vaporetto stop) is considered the oldest house in Venice. Its horseshoe arches and roofline of triangles-and-dingleballs are a reminder of its Byzantine heritage. Turkish traders in turbans docked here, unloaded their goods into the warehouse on the bottom story, then went upstairs for a home-style meal and a place to sleep. Venice in the 1500s was very cosmopolitan, welcoming every religion and ethnicity...so long as they carried cash.

Venice's **Casino** (left-hand side) is housed in the palace where German composer Richard *(The Ring)* Wagner died in 1883. See his distinct, strong-jawed profile in the white plaque on the brick wall. In the 1700s, Venice was Europe's Vegas, with casinos and prostitutes everywhere. Today, this elegant Casino welcomes men in ties and ladies in dresses. "Casinos" (literally "little houses") have long provided Italians with a handy escape from daily life.

San Stae: Opposite the San Stae stop, look for the **faded frescoes** (left bank, on lower story). Imagine the facades of the Grand Canal at their finest. As colorful as the city is today, it's still only a sepia-toned snapshot of a long-gone era of lavishly decorated and brilliantly colored palaces.

Ca' d'Oro: The lacy **Ca' d'Oro,** or "House of Gold," (left bank, just before the vaporetto stop) is the best example of "Venetian Gothic" on the canal. Its three stories offer different variations on balcony design, topped with a spiny white roofline. Venetian Gothic mixes traditional Gothic (pointed arches and round medallions stamped with a four-leaf clover) with Byzantine styles (tall, narrow arches atop thin columns), filled in with Islamic frills. Like all the palaces, this was originally painted and gilded to make it even more glorious than it is now. *"Ca'"* means "house." Because only the house of the doge (Venetian ruler) could be called a palace *(palazzo),* all other palaces are technically *"Ca'."* Today the Ca' d'Oro is a museum, but, other than temporary exhibits, there's little to see inside (see page 81).

Farther along, on the right, the outdoor arcade of the **fish and produce market** bustles with people in the morning but is quiet the rest of the day. This is a great scene to wander through—even though European hygiene standards recently required a less-colorful remodeling job. Find the *traghetto* gondola ferrying shoppers back and forth, standing like Washington crossing the Delaware.

The huge **post office** (left side, just before the Rialto Bridge), with *servizio postale* boats moored at its blue posts, was the German

Exchange in the early 1500s, the trading center for German metal merchants. The building's top story has a rare sight in frilly Venice—square windows. Rising above the post office, you can see in the distance the golden angel of the Campanile (bell tower) at St. Mark's Square, where this tour will end.

As the canal bends, we pass beneath the impressive Rialto Bridge. Singing gondoliers love the acoustics here: *"O sole mio..."*

Rialto: A major landmark of Venice, the **Rialto Bridge** is lined with shops and tourists. Constructed in 1588, it's the third bridge built on this spot. With a span of 160 feet and foundations stretching 650 feet on either side, the Rialto was an impressive engineering feat in its day. Earlier Rialto Bridges could open to let in big ships, but not this one. When this new bridge was completed, much of the Grand Canal was closed to shipping and became a canal of palaces.

Rialto, a separate town in the early days of Venice, has always been the commercial district, while San Marco was the religious and governmental center. Today, a winding street called the Mercerie connects the two, providing travelers with human traffic jams and a mesmerizing gauntlet of shopping temptations. The restaurants that line the canal feature great views, midrange prices, and low-quality food.

San Silvestro: On the left side, opposite the vaporetto stop, **two palaces stand side by side,** with stories the same height, creating the effect of one long balcony.

We now enter a long stretch of important **merchants' palaces,** each with proud and different facades. Since ships couldn't navigate beyond the Rialto Bridge to reach the section of the Grand Canal you just came from, the biggest palaces—with the major shipping needs—lie ahead.

Palaces like these were multifunctional: ground floor for the warehouse, offices and showrooms upstairs on the "noble floor" (with big windows designed to allow in maximum light), and living quarters on the top.

Sant'Angelo: Just past the Sant'Angelo stop (ahead on the right, with twin obelisks on the rooftop) stands the **palace of a 15th-century captain general** of the sea. These Venetian equivalents of five-star admirals were honored with twin obelisks decorating their palaces. This palace flies three flags: those of Italy (green-white-red), the European Union (blue with ring of stars), and Venice (the lion).

Notice how many buildings have a foundation of waterproof white stone *(pietra d'Istria)* upon which the bricks sit high and dry. Many canal-level floors are abandoned; the rising water level takes its toll. The **posts**—historically painted gaily with the equivalent of family coats of arms—don't rot under water. But the wood at the waterline does.

Venice at a Glance

▲▲▲St. Mark's Square Venice's grand main square. **Hours:** Always open.

▲▲▲St. Mark's Basilica Cathedral with mosaics, saint's bones, treasury, museum, and viewpoint of square. **Hours:** Basilica open to tourists Mon–Sat 9:30–17:30, until 16:30 off-season, Sun 14:00–16:00; San Marco Museum open Mon–Sat 9:45–16:30, Sun 9:45–16:00.

▲▲▲Doge's Palace Art-splashed palace of former rulers, with prison accessible through Bridge of Sighs. **Hours:** Daily April–Oct 9:00–19:00, Nov–March 9:00–17:00.

▲▲▲Rialto Bridge Distinctive bridge spanning the Grand Canal, with a market nearby for locals and tourists. **Hours:** Bridge—always open; market—souvenir stalls open daily, produce market closed Sun, fish market closed Sun–Mon.

▲▲Correr Museum Venetian history and art. **Hours:** Daily April–Oct 9:00–19:00, Nov–March 9:00–17:00.

▲▲Accademia Venice's top art museum. **Hours:** Mon 8:15–14:00, Tue–Sun 8:15–19:15, shorter hours off-season.

▲▲Peggy Guggenheim Collection Popular display of 20th-century art. **Hours:** Wed–Mon 10:00–18:00, June–July open until 22:00 on Sat, always closed Tue.

▲▲Frari Church Franciscan church featuring Renaissance masters. **Hours:** Mon–Sat 10:00–18:00, Sun 13:00–17:00 (closed Sun in Aug).

▲▲Scuola Grande di San Rocco "Tintoretto's Sistine Chapel." **Hours:** Daily April–Oct 9:00–17:30, Nov–March 10:00–16:00.

▲Campanile Dramatic bell tower on St. Mark's Square with elevator to top. **Hours:** Daily July–Sept 9:00–21:00, Oct–June 9:00–19:00.

▲Bridge of Sighs Famous enclosed bridge, part of Doge's Palace, near St. Mark's Square. **Hours:** Always viewable.

▲San Giorgio Maggiore Island across the lagoon featuring church with Palladio architecture, Tintoretto paintings, and fine views back on Venice. **Hours:** Daily May–Sept 9:30–12:30 & 14:30–18:30, Oct–April 9:30–12:30 & 14:30–16:30, closed Sun to sightseers during Mass.

▲**Ca' Rezzonico** Posh Grand Canal palazzo with 18th-century Venetian art. **Hours:** April–Oct Wed–Mon 10:00–18:00, Nov–March Wed–Mon 10:00–17:00, closed Tue.

Church of San Zaccaria Final resting place of St. Zechariah (San Zaccaria), plus a Bellini altarpiece. **Hours:** Mon–Sat 10:00–12:00 & 16:00–18:00, Sun 16:00–18:00 only.

La Salute Church Striking church dedicated to the Virgin Mary. **Hours:** Daily 9:00–12:00 & 15:00–18:00.

Church of San Polo Ninth-century church with works by Tintoretto, Veronese, and Tiepolo. **Hours:** Mon–Sat 10:00–17:00, Sun 10:00–13:00.

Jewish Ghetto Neighborhood and Jewish Museum. **Hours:** June–Sept Sun–Fri 10:00–19:00, Oct–May Sun–Fri 10:00–17:30, closed Sat and Jewish Holidays.

Ca' d'Oro Venetian Gothic palace with temporary exhibits, fronting the Grand Canal. **Hours:** Mon 8:15–14:00, Tue–Sun 8:15–19:15.

Dalmatian School Exquisite Renaissance meeting house. **Hours:** Tue–Sat 9:30–12:30 & 15:30–18:30, Sun 9:30–12:30, closed Mon.

Santa Elena 100-year-old neighborhood with few tourists. **Hours:** Always open.

Murano Island famous for glass factories and glassmaking museum. **Hours:** Museum—April–Oct Thu–Tue 10:00–17:00, Nov–March Thu–Tue 10:00–16:00, closed Wed.

Burano Sleepy lacemaking island with lace museum. **Hours:** Museum—April–Oct Wed–Mon 10:00–17:00, Nov–March Wed–Mon 10:00–16:00, closed Tue.

Torcello Near-deserted island with old church and museum. **Hours:** Church—daily 10:30–17:30; museum—Tue–Sun 10:30–17:30, closed Mon.

Take a deep whiff of Venice. What's all this nonsense about stinky canals? All I smell is my shirt. By the way, how's your captain? Smooth dockings? To get to know him, stand up in the bow and block his view.

San Tomà: After the San Tomà stop, look down the side canal (on the right, before the bridge) to see the traffic light, the **fire station,** and the fireboats ready to go.

We now prepare to round the corner and double back toward St. Mark's. The impressive **Ca' Foscari** (right side) dominates the bend in the canal. Its four stories get increasingly ornate as they rise from the water—from simple Gothic arches at water level, to Gothic with a point, to Venetian Gothic arches topped with four-leaf clovers, to still more medallions and laciness that look almost Moorish. Wow.

These days, when buildings are being renovated, huge murals with images of the building mask the ugly scaffolding. Corporations sponsor these multistory covers, hiding the scaffolding for the goodwill—and the publicity.

Ca' Rezzonico: The grand, heavy, white **Ca' Rezzonico,** directly at the stop of the same name, houses the Museum of 18th-Century Venice (see page 78). Across the canal is the cleaner and leaner **Palazzo Grassi,** which often showcases special exhibitions. This was the last major palace built on the canal, erected in the late 1700s.

Accademia: The wooden **Accademia Bridge** crosses the Grand Canal and leads to the **Accademia** art museum (right side), filled with the best Venetian paintings (see page 76). The bridge was put up in 1932 as a temporary one. Locals liked it, so it stayed. Cruising under the bridge, you'll get a classic view of the domed La Salute Church ahead.

The low, white building among greenery (on the right, between the bridge and the church) is the **Peggy Guggenheim Collection.** The American heiress "retired" here, sprucing up the palace that had been abandoned in mid-construction; the locals call it the *"palazzo non finito."* Peggy willed the city her fine collection of modern art (see page 77).

Salute: A crown-shaped dome supported by scrolls stands atop **La Salute Church** (see page 78). This Church of Saint Mary of Good Health was built to thank God for delivering Venetians from the devastating plague of 1630 (which had killed about a third of the city's population).

Across the canal (left side), several **fancy hotels** have painted facades that hint at the canal's former glory.

As the Grand Canal opens up into the lagoon, the last building on the right with the golden ball is the 16th-century **Customs House** (Dogana da Mar, not open to the public). Its two bronze

Atlases hold a statue of Fortune riding the ball. Arriving ships stopped here to pay their tolls.

As you prepare to disembark at the San Marco/Vallaresso stop, look from left to right out over the lagoon. On the left, a wide harborfront walk leads past the town's most elegant hotels to the green area in the distance. This is the public garden, the largest of Venice's few parks, which hosts the Biennale art show. Farther in the distance is the **Lido,** the island with Venice's beach. It's tempting, with sand and casinos, but its car traffic breaks into the medieval charm of Venice.

The ghostly white church that seems to float is the architect Andrea Palladio's **San Giorgio Maggiore.** It's just a vaporetto ride away (#82 from the San Zaccaria Jolanda stop, just past the Bridge of Sighs; see page 76). Across the lagoon (to your right) is a residential island called **Giudecca.**

San Marco/Vallaresso: Get off at the San Marco/Vallaresso stop. Directly ahead is **Harry's Bar.** Hemingway drank here when it was a characteristic no-name *osteria* and the gondoliers' hangout. Today, of course, it's the overpriced hangout of well-dressed Americans who don't mind paying triple for their Bellinis (peach juice with Prosecco—a sparkling white wine) to make the scene. St. Mark's Square is just around the corner.

SIGHTS

St. Mark's Square

For information on Venice's Museum Card and pricier Museum Pass, which cover most of the sights on the square, see page 50.

▲▲▲**St. Mark's Square (Piazza San Marco)**—This grand square is surrounded by splashy, historic buildings and sights (each one described in more detail below): St. Mark's Basilica, the Doge's Palace, the Campanile (bell tower), and the Correr Museum. The square is filled with music, lovers, pigeons, and tourists by day, and is your private rendezvous with the Venetian past late at night, when Europe's most magnificent dance floor is *the* romantic place to be.

With your back to the church, survey one of Europe's great urban spaces, and the only square in Venice to merit the title "Piazza." Nearly two football fields long, it's surrounded by the offices of the republic. On the right are the "old offices" (16th-century Renaissance). At left are the "new offices" (17th-century Baroque). Napoleon, after enclosing the square with the more simple and austere neoclassical wing across the far end, called this "the most beautiful drawing room in Europe."

For a slow, pricey evening thrill, invest about €15 (including the cover charge for the music) in a glass of wine or coffee at one of the elegant cafés with the dueling orchestras (see "Cafés on St. Mark's

St. Mark's Square

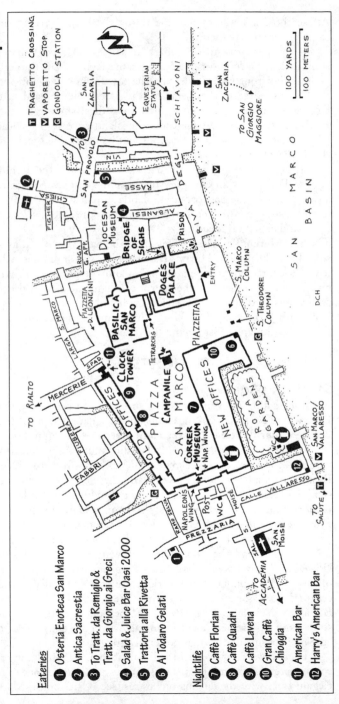

Eateries
1. Osteria Enoteca San Marco
2. Antica Sacrestia
3. To Tratt. da Remigio & Tratt. da Giorgio ai Greci
4. Salad & Juice Bar Oasi 2000
5. Trattoria alla Rivetta
6. Al Todaro Gelati

Nightlife
7. Caffè Florian
8. Caffè Quadri
9. Caffè Lavena
10. Gran Caffè Chioggia
11. American Bar
12. Harry's American Bar

🛶 Traghetto Crossing
Ⓥ Vaporetto Stop
Ⓖ Gondola Station

100 Yards
100 Meters

Cafés on St. Mark's Square

Cafés line the square. All of the café orchestras feature similar food, prices, and a three- or four-piece combo playing a selection of classical and pop hits, from Brahms to "Bésame Mucho." If you get just a drink, expect to pay about €15, including the cover charge. It's perfectly acceptable to nurse a cappuccino for an hour, since you're paying for the music with the cover charge.

Caffè Florian (on the right as you face the church) is the most famous Venetian café and one of the first places in Europe to serve coffee. It's been a popular spot for a discreet rendezvous in Venice since 1720. The orchestra plays a more classical repertoire than the other cafés. The outside tables are the main action, but do walk inside through the richly decorated, 18th-century rooms where Casanova, Lord Byron, Charles Dickens, and Woody Allen have all paid too much for a drink (reasonable prices at bar in back).

Caffè Quadri, exactly opposite the Florian, has an equally illustrious history of famous clientele, including the writers Stendhal and Dumas, and composer Richard Wagner. **Caffè Lavena,** near the clock tower, is newer and less prestigious.

Gran Caffè Chioggia, on the Piazzetta facing the Doge's Palace, charges slightly less, with one or two musicians playing cocktail jazz.

Square," above). For an unmatched experience that offers the best people-watching, it's worth the small splurge. But if all you have is €1, buy a bag of pigeon feed and become popular in a flurry. (To control the poopulation, the city adds bird birth control to the feed.) To get the flock airborne, toss your sweater in the air.

The **clock tower** *(torre dell'orologio)*, built during the Renaissance in 1496, marks the entry to the main shopping drag, called the Mercerie, which connects St. Mark's Square with the Rialto. From the piazza, you can see the bronze men (Moors) swing their huge clappers at the top of each hour. In the 17th century, one of them knocked an unsuspecting worker off the top and to his death—probably the first-ever killing by a robot. Notice one of the world's first "digital" clocks on the tower facing the square (with dramatic flips every 5 min). The clock tower, which opens for visitors in 2006, is included in the Museum Card and the pricier Museum Pass (both cover the museums of St. Mark's Square—see "Passes for Venice," page 50).

Venice's best TI is in the far left corner of the square (daily 9:00–20:00), and a €0.50 WC is 30 yards beyond St. Mark's Square (see *Albergo Diorno* sign marked on pavement, WC open daily 9:00–17:30). The other TI is on the lagoon (daily 10:00–18:00, walk toward the water by the Doge's Palace and go right, pay WCs nearby).

▲▲▲**St. Mark's Basilica**—Built in the 11th century to replace an earlier church, this basilica's distinctly Eastern-style architecture underlines Venice's connection with Byzantium (which protected it from the ambition of Charlemagne and his Holy Roman Empire). It's decorated with booty from returning sea captains—a kind of architectural Venetian trophy chest. The interior glows mysteriously with gold mosaics and colored marble. Since A.D. 828, the saint's bones have been housed on this site.

Cost and Hours: The church is free (except for the "Additional Sights" described below) and open Mon–Sat 9:30–17:30 (until 16:30 off-season), Sun 14:00–16:00 (tel. 041-522-5205). The line can be very long during peak season. No photos are allowed inside the church.

Bag Check: While small purses are allowed inside the church, larger bags and backpacks are not. Check them for free at the nearby Ateneo S. Basso, a former church (open roughly Mon–Sat 9:30–17:30, Sun 14:00–16:30; from Piazzetta dei Leoncini to the left of basilica, head down Calle S. Basso, 2nd door on your right). Those with a bag to check actually get to skip the line. Here's how it works: Drop by Ateneo S. Basso. (Consider watching the free 12-min intro video about St. Mark's Basilica.) Leave your bag and pick up the tag. Two people per tag are allowed to go to the basilica's gatekeeper and scoot directly in (ahead of the line). After touring the church, come back and pick up your bag.

Dress Code: To enter the church, modest dress is required even of kids (no shorts or bare shoulders). People who ignore the dress code hold up the line while they plead fruitlessly with the dress-code police.

Theft Alert: St. Mark's Basilica is the most dangerous place in Venice for pickpocketing—inside, it's always a crowded jostle.

Tours: In the atrium, see the schedule board that lists free English-language guided tours (schedules vary, but generally May–Oct Tue, Wed, and Thu at 11:00, 1 hr, meet guide just to the right of main doors, tel. 041-270-2421).

Inside the Church: St. Mark's Basilica has 43,000 square feet of Byzantine mosaics, the best and oldest of which are in the atrium (turn right as you enter and stop under the last dome—this may be roped off, but dome is still visible). Facing the church, gape up (it's OK, no pigeons) and read the story of Adam and Eve that rings the bottom of the dome. Now, facing the piazza, look domeward for the story of Noah, the ark, and the flood (two by two, the wicked being drowned, Noah sending out the dove, a happy rainbow, and a sacrifice of thanks).

St. Mark's Basilica

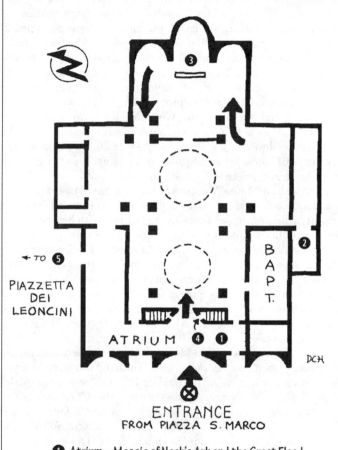

TO ⑤
PIAZZETTA
DEI
LEONCINI

B A P T.

A T R I U M

DCH

ENTRANCE
FROM PIAZZA S. MARCO

① Atrium — Mosaic of Noah's Ark and the Great Flood
② Treasury
③ Golden Altarpiece
④ Stairs up to Loggia: San Marco Museum & Bronze Horses
⑤ To Ateneo S. Basso Bag Check across Square

Step inside the church (the stairs on the right lead to the bronze horses in the San Marco Museum, described below—save these for later). The interior glows mysteriously with gold mosaics and colored marble. Notice the marble floor richly decorated in mosaics. As in many Venetian buildings, because the best foundation pilings were made around the perimeter, the floor rolls. As you shuffle under the central dome, look up for the Ascension. As you follow the one-way tourist route, consider stopping off at the Treasury and the Golden Altarpiece, described below.

Additional Sights in the Church: There are three sights within St. Mark's that each charge a small admission fee: the San Marco Museum (€3, Mon–Sat 9:45–16:30, Sun 9:45–16:00), Treasury (€2, includes audioguide, open same hours as church), and Golden Altarpiece (€2, same hours as church).

In the **San Marco Museum** (Museo di San Marco) upstairs, you can see an up-close mosaic exhibition, a fine view of the church interior, a view of the square from the balcony with bronze horses, and (inside, in their own room) the original horses. These well-traveled horses, made during the days of Alexander the Great (4th century b.c.), were taken to Rome by Nero, to Constantinople/Istanbul by Constantine, to Venice by crusaders, to Paris by Napoleon, back "home" to Venice when Napoleon fell, and finally indoors and out of the acidic air. The staircase up to the museum is in the atrium, near the basilica's entrance, marked by a sign that says "Loggia dei Cavalli, Museo."

San Marco's **Treasury** (ask for the included and informative audioguide when you buy ticket) and **Golden Altarpiece** give you the best chance outside of Istanbul or Ravenna to see the glories of Byzantium. Venetian crusaders looted the Christian city of Constantinople and brought home piles of lavish loot (perhaps the lowest point in Christian history until the advent of TV evangelism). Much of this plunder is stored in the Treasury (Tesoro) of San Marco. As you view these treasures, remember that most were made around a.d. 500, while Western Europe was stuck in the Dark Ages. Beneath the high altar lies the body of St. Mark ("Marce") and the Golden Altarpiece (Pala d'Oro), made of 250 blue-backed enamels with religious scenes, all set in a gold frame and studded with 15 hefty rubies, 300 emeralds, 1,500 pearls, and assorted sapphires, amethysts, and topaz (c. 1100). Both of these sights are interesting and historic, but neither is as much fun as two bags of pigeon feed.

▲▲▲**Doge's Palace (Palazzo Ducale)**—The seat of the Venetian government and home of its ruling duke, or doge, this was the most powerful half-acre in Europe for 400 years.

The Doge's Palace was built to show off the power and wealth of the republic and remind all visitors that Venice was number one.

Floods and a Dying City

Venice floods about 100 times a year—normally in March and November, when the wind blowing from the south (Egypt) and high barometric pressure on the lower Adriatic Sea are most likely to combine to push water up to this top end of the sea. (The lunar tide in the Mediterranean is miniscule.)

Floods start in St. Mark's Square. The entry of the church is nearly the lowest spot in town. You might see stacked wooden benches; when the square floods, these are placed end to end to make elevated sidewalks. If you think the square is crowded now, in times of floods it turns into total gridlock, as everyone jostles for space on the wooden walkways.

The measuring devices at the outside base of the Campanile (near the exit, facing St. Mark's Square) show the current sea level *(livello marea)*. When the water level rises one meter, a warning siren sounds. It repeats if a serious flood is imminent. Find the mark that shows the high-water level from the terrible floods of 1966 (waist-level, on right). Imagine being a Venetian and hearing the alarm. You rush home to remove your carpets and raise your furniture above the (salt) water level. Many doorways have three-foot-tall wooden or metal barriers to fight the *acqua alta,* but the seawater still seeps through floors and drains, rendering the barriers nearly useless. After the water recedes, you have to carefully clean everything it touched to minimize the damage caused by the corrosive salt water.

In 1965, Venice's population was more than 150,000. Since the flood of 1966, the population has been shrinking. Today the population is about 65,000...and geriatric. Sad, yes, but imagine raising a family here: The fragile nature of the city means piles of regulations (for example, no biking), and costs are high—even though the government is now subsidizing rents to keep people from moving out. You can easily get glass and tourist trinkets, but it's hard to find groceries. And floods and the humidity make house maintenance an expensive pain.

You may notice construction work going on along the waterfront near St. Mark's Square. They're raising the entire level of the square by bringing up the pavement stones, adding a layer of sand, and replacing the stones. If the columns along the ground floor of the Doge's Palace look stubby, it's because this process has been carried out many times over the centuries.

In typical Venetian Gothic style, the bottom has pointy arches and the top has an Eastern or Islamic flavor. Its columns sat on pedestals, but in the thousand years since they were erected, the palace has settled into the mud and the bases have vanished.

Enjoy the newly restored facades from the **courtyard.** Notice a grand staircase (with nearly naked Moses and Paul Newman at the top). Even the most powerful visitors climbed this to meet the doge. This was the beginning of an architectural power trip. The doge, the elected-for-life duke or leader of this "dictatorship of the aristocracy," lived with his family on the first floor near the halls of power. From his living quarters (once lavish, now sparsely furnished), you'll follow the one-way route through the public rooms of the top floor, finishing with the Bridge of Sighs and the prison. The place is wallpapered with masterpieces by Veronese and Tintoretto. Don't worry much about the great art. Enjoy the building.

In Room 12, the **Senate Room,** the 120 senators met, debated, and passed laws. From the center of the ceiling, Tintoretto's *Triumph of Venice* shows the city in all her glory. Lady Venice, in heaven with the Greek gods, stands high above the lesser nations, who swirl respectfully at her feet with gifts.

The **Armory**—a dazzling display originally assembled to intimidate potential adversaries—shows remnants of the military might that the empire employed to keep the East-West trade lines open (and the local economy booming). Squint out the window to see Palladio's San Giorgio Maggiore and, to the left in the distance, the tiny green dome at Venice's Lido (beach).

The giant **Hall of the Grand Council** (175 feet long, capacity 2,600) is where the entire nobility met to elect the senate and doge. Ringing the room are portraits of 76 doges (in chronological order). One, a doge who opposed the will of the Grand Council, is blacked out. Behind the doge's throne, you can't miss Tintoretto's monsterpiece, *Paradise,* the largest oil painting in the world. Christ and Mary are surrounded by a heavenly host of 500 saints. Its message to electors who met here: Make wise decisions and you'll ultimately join that holy crowd.

Cross the covered **Bridge of Sighs** over the canal to the **prisons** (at the fork in the route, descend the stairs rather than continuing right into a cell or you'll miss the basement altogether and end up at the bookshop at the end of the palace visit). In the privacy of his own home, a doge could sentence, torture, and jail his opponents secretly. Circle the cells. Notice the carvings made by prisoners—from olden days up until 1930—on some of the stone windowsills of the cells, especially in the far corner of the building.

As you walk back over the bridge, squeeze your arm through the marble lattice window and wave to the gang of tourists gawking at you.

Cost: €11 Museum Card (also includes admission to the Correr Museum). If the line is very long at the Doge's Palace, buy your ticket at the Correr Museum across the square. With that, you can go directly through the Doge's Palace turnstile without waiting in the long line.

Hours: Daily April–Oct 9:00–19:00, Nov–March 9:00–17:00, last entry 1 hr before closing.

Tours: Consider the €5.50 audioguide or "Secret Itineraries Tour," which follows the doge's footsteps through rooms not included in the general admission price. Tours must be booked in advance (€12.50; in English at 9:55, 10:45 and 11:35; 75 min, arrive 20 min early to check in, no need to wait in line, just *"scusi"* your way to the information desk in the room before the ticket counter). To make the reservation for the tour, call 041-291-5911 if you're reserving for visits on the same day or the day before, or call 041-520-9070 for visits more than two days in advance. While the tour skips the main halls inside, it finishes inside the palace and you're welcome to visit the halls on your own.

▲▲**Correr Museum (Museo Civico Correr)**—This uncrowded museum gives you a good overview of Venetian history and art. In the Napoleon Wing, you'll see fine neoclassical sculpture by Canova. Then peruse armor, banners, and paintings re-creating festive days of the Venetian republic. The upper floor lays out a good overview of Venetian art, including several paintings by the Bellini family. And just before the cafeteria is a room filled with traditional games. There are English descriptions and breathtaking views of St. Mark's Square throughout (€11 Museum Card also includes the Doge's Palace, daily April–Oct 9:00–19:00, Nov–March 9:00–17:00, last entry 70 min before closing, enter at far end of square directly opposite church, tel. 041-240-5211).

▲**Campanile (Campanile di San Marco)**—This dramatic bell tower replaced a shorter lighthouse, once part of the original fortress/palace that guarded the entry of the Grand Canal. The lighthouse crumbled into a pile of bricks in 1902, a thousand years after it was built. Ride the elevator 300 feet to the top of the reconstructed bell tower for the best view in Venice. For an ear-shattering experience, be on top when the bells ring (€6, daily July–Sept 9:00–21:00, Oct–June 9:00–19:00). The golden angel at the top always faces into the wind. Lines are longest at midday; beat the crowds and enjoy crisp morning air at 9:00, or try in the early evening (around 18:00).

Behind St. Mark's Basilica

Diocesan Museum (Museo Diocesano)—This little-known museum circles a peaceful Romanesque courtyard immediately behind the basilica (just before the Bridge of Sighs). It's filled with plunder from the Venetian Empire that never found a place in St. Mark's. While free and in a state of disarray in 2005, it expects to be presentable and worth an admission charge in 2006 (Mon–Sat 10:00–12:30, closed Sun).

▲**Bridge of Sighs**—Connecting two wings of the Doge's Palace high over a canal, this enclosed bridge was popularized by travelers in the Romantic 19th century. Supposedly, a condemned man would be led over this bridge on the way to the prison, take one last look at the glory of Venice, and sigh. While overhyped, the bridge is undeniably tingle-worthy—especially after dark, when the crowds have dispersed and it's just you and floodlit Venice. It's around the corner from the Doge's Palace: Walk towards the waterfront, turn left along the water, and look up the first canal on your left.

Church of San Zaccaria—This historic church is home to a sometimes-waterlogged crypt, a Bellini altarpiece, a Tintoretto painting, and the final resting place of St. Zechariah—the father of John the Baptist (free, €1 to enter crypt, €0.50 coin to light up Bellini's altarpiece, Mon–Sat 10:00–12:00 & 16:00–18:00, Sun 16:00–18:00 only, 2 canals behind St. Mark's Basilica).

Across the Lagoon from St. Mark's Square

▲**San Giorgio Maggiore**—This is the dreamy island you can see from the waterfront by St. Mark's Square. The striking church, designed by Palladio, features art by Tintoretto and good views of Venice (free entry to church, daily May–Sept 9:30–12:30 & 14:30–18:30, Oct–April 9:30–12:30 & 14:30–16:30, closed Sun to sightseers during Mass, Gregorian Mass sung Mon–Sat at 8:00, Sun at 11:00). The church's bell tower, which usually provides oh-wow views over Venice, will be closed for restoration through 2006 (when it's open, it costs €3 and is accessible by elevator until 30 min before church's closing time). To reach the island from St. Mark's Square, take the five-minute vaporetto ride on #82 from the San Zaccaria Jolanda stop, just past the Bridge of Sighs, closest to the big statue.

Dorsoduro District

▲▲**Accademia (Galleria dell'Accademia)**—Venice's top art museum, packed with highlights of the Venetian Renaissance, features paintings by the Bellini family, Titian, Tintoretto, Veronese, Tiepolo, Giorgione, Canaletto, and Testosterone. It's just over the wooden Accademia Bridge. Expect long lines in the late morning because they allow only 300 visitors in at a time; visit early or late to miss crowds, or call 041-520-0345 to book tickets at least a day in advance (€7.50, Mon 8:15–14:00, Tue–Sun 8:15–19:15, shorter hours off-season, last entry 45 min before closing, no photos allowed,

Accademia Overview

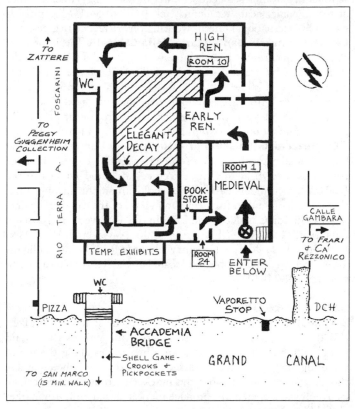

tel. 041-522-2247). The dull audioguide doesn't let you fast-forward to works you want to hear about; you have to listen to the whole spiel for each room (€4/person, €6/double set, or €6/PalmPilot).

At the Accademia Bridge, there's a decent canalside pizzeria (Pizzeria Accademia Foscarini—see page 106) and a public WC at the base of the bridge.

▲▲**Peggy Guggenheim Collection**—The popular museum of far-out art, housed in the American heiress' former retirement palazzo, offers one of Europe's best reviews of the art of the first half of the 20th century. Stroll through styles represented by artists whom Peggy knew personally—Cubism (Picasso, Braque), Surrealism (Dalí, Ernst), Futurism (Boccioni), American Abstract Expressionism (Pollock), and a sprinkling of Klee, Calder, and Chagall (€10, Wed–Mon 10:00–18:00, closed Tue, June–July open until 22:00 on Sat, audioguide-€5, guidebook-€18, free and mandatory baggage check, pricey café, photos allowed only in garden and terrace—a fine and relaxing perch overlooking Grand Canal, free concerts in

summer in garden—see ticket counter or www.guggenheim-venice
.it for schedule, near Accademia, tel. 041-240-5411). The place is
staffed by international interns working on art-related degrees.

La Salute Church (Santa Maria della Salute)—The impressive
church with a crown-shaped dome was built and dedicated to the
Virgin Mary by grateful survivors of the 1630 plague (free, daily
9:00–12:00 & 15:00–18:00, tel. 041-522-5558 to confirm). It's a
10-minute walk from Accademia Bridge, or a vaporetto ride (stop:
Salute), or an inexpensive *traghetto* crossing from near St. Mark's
Square—catch it on the lagoon next to the TI and Harry's Bar.

▲**Ca' Rezzonico (Museum of 18th-Century Venice)**—A grand
Grand Canal palazzo, Ca' Rezzonico (ret-ZON-ee-koh) offers the
best look in town at the life of Venice's rich and famous in the
1700s. Wander under ceilings by Tiepolo, among furnishings from
that most decadent century, enjoying views of the canal and paintings by Guardi, Canaletto, and Longhi (€6.50, covered by Museum
Pass, April–Oct Wed–Mon 10:00–18:00, Nov–March Wed–Mon
10:00–17:00, closed Tue, last entry 1 hour before closing, audiogu-
ide-€4/person or €6/double set, located at Ca' Rezzonico vaporetto
stop, tel. 041-241-0100).

Santa Croce District

▲▲▲**Rialto Bridge**—One of the world's most famous bridges,
this distinctive and dramatic stone structure crosses the Grand
Canal with a single confident span. The arcades along the top of
the bridge help reinforce the structure...and offer some enjoyable
shopping diversions, as does the **market** surrounding the bridge
(souvenir stalls open daily, produce market closed Sun, fish market
closed Sun–Mon).

San Polo District

▲▲**Frari Church (Chiesa dei Frari)**—My favorite art experience in Venice is seeing art *in situ*—the setting for which it was
designed—and my favorite example is the Chiesa dei Frari. The
Franciscan "Church of the Brothers" and the art that decorates it
are warmed by the spirit of St. Francis. It features the work of three
great Renaissance masters: Donatello, Bellini, and Titian—each
showing worshipers the glory of God in human terms.

In **Donatello's wood carving of St. John the Baptist** (just to
the right of the high altar), the prophet of the desert—dressed in
animal skins and nearly starving from his diet of bugs 'n' honey—
announces the coming of the Messiah. Donatello was a Florentine
working at the dawn of the Renaissance.

Bellini's *Madonna and Child with Saints and Angels* painting
(in the chapel farther to the right) came later, done by a Venetian
in a more Venetian style—soft focus without Donatello's harsh

Frari Church

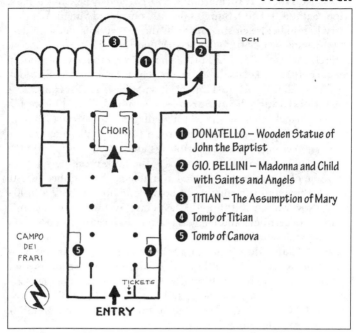

1 DONATELLO – Wooden Statue of John the Baptist

2 GIO. BELLINI – Madonna and Child with Saints and Angels

3 TITIAN – The Assumption of Mary

4 Tomb of Titian

5 Tomb of Canova

realism. While Renaissance humanism demanded Madonnas and saints that were accessible and human, Bellini places them in a physical setting so beautiful it creates its own mood of serene holiness. The genius of Bellini, perhaps the greatest Venetian painter, is obvious in the pristine clarity, rich colors (notice Mary's clothing), believable depth, and reassuring calm of this three-paneled altarpiece. It's so good to see a painting in its natural setting.

Finally, glowing red and gold like a stained-glass window over the high altar, **Titian's** *The Assumption of Mary* sets the tone of exuberant beauty found in the otherwise sparse church. Titian the Venetian—a student of Bellini—painted steadily for 60 years... you'll see a lot of his art. As stunned apostles look up past the swirl of arms and legs, the complex composition of this painting draws you right to the radiant face of the once-dying, now-triumphant Mary as she joins God in heaven.

Be comfortable discreetly freeloading off passing tours. For many, these three pieces of art make a visit to the Accademia Gallery unnecessary (or they may whet your appetite for more). Before leaving, check out the neoclassical, pyramid-shaped tomb of Canova and (opposite that) the grandiose tomb of Titian. Compare the carved marble Assumption behind Titian's tombstone portrait with the painted original above the high altar.

Cost, Hours, Information: €2.50, covered by €8 Chorus Pass, Mon–Sat 10:00–17:00, Sun 13:00–17:00 but closed Sun in Aug (last entry 15 min before closing, no visits during services, audioguides- €1.60/person or €2.60/double set). Modest dress is recommended. Church info: tel. 041-272-86118. The church often hosts evening **concerts** (€15, tickets sold at the church; for concert details, look for fliers, call 041-272-8611, or check www.basilicadeifrari.it).

▲▲**Scuola Grande di San Rocco**—Sometimes called "Tintoretto's Sistine Chapel," this lavish meeting hall (next to the Frari Church) has some 50 large, colorful Tintoretto paintings plastered to the walls and ceilings. The best paintings are upstairs, especially the *Crucifixion* in the smaller room. View the neck-breaking splendor with one of the mirrors *(specchio)* available at the entrance (€5.50, includes free and informative audioguide, daily April–Oct 9:00– 17:30, Nov–March 10:00–16:00, last entry 30 min before closing, or see a concert here and enjoy the art as an evening bonus, www .scuolagrandesanrocco.it).

Church of San Polo—This nearby church, which pales in compari- son to the two sights listed above, is worth a visit for art-lovers. One of Venice's oldest church (from the 9th century), San Polo features works by Tintoretto, Veronese, and Tiepolo and son (€2.50, cov- ered by €8 Chorus Pass, Mon–Sat 10:00–17:00, Sun 10:00–13:00, last entry 15 min before closing).

Cannaregio District

Jewish Ghetto—The word "ghetto" comes from *geto*, which means "foundry" in the Venetian dialect. In 1516, Venice forced its Jews to live on an undesirable and easy-to-isolate island that was once home to the city's foundry. Restricted within their tiny neigh- borhood (the Ghetto Nuovo, or "New Ghetto"), they expanded upward, building six-story "skyscrapers" that stand today. The main square, Campo di Ghetto Nuovo, must have been quite a scene, with 70 shops ringing it and all of Venice's Jewish com- merce compressed onto this one spot. The island's two bridges were locked up at night, when only Jewish doctors—coming to the aid of Venetians—were allowed to come and go. Eventually the ghetto community outgrew its original island, and the ghetto spread to adjacent blocks. As late as the 1930s, 12,000 Jews called Venice home, but today there are only 200—and only a handful live in the actual Ghetto. Of the original five synagogues, only two are still active. You can spot them (with their 5 windows) from the square, but you can visit them only with a tour booked through the Jewish Museum (listed below).

This original ghetto becomes most interesting after touring the **Jewish Museum** (Museo Ebraico), with a humble two-room collection of silver and cloth worship aids and artifacts of the old community (€3, June–Sept Sun–Fri 10:00–19:00, Oct–May Sun–Fri 10:00–17:30, closed Sat and Jewish holidays, Campo di Ghetto Nuovo, tel. 041-715-359). Synagogue tours in English are offered hourly (€8, 30 min, Sun–Fri 10:30–17:30, until 16:30 in winter, contact museum for details).

Ca' d'Oro—This "House of Gold" palace, fronting the Grand Canal, is quintessential Venetian Gothic (Gothic seasoned with Byzantine and Islamic accents). Inside, there's little to see aside from special exhibitions (€5, Mon 8:15–14:00, Tue–Sun 8:15–19:15, free peek through hole in door of courtyard, Cannaregio 3932).

Castello District
Dalmatian School (Scuola Dalmata di San Giorgio)—This "school" (which means "meeting place") is a reminder that Venice was Europe's most cosmopolitan place in its heyday. It was here that the Dalmatians (from the present-day country of Croatia) worshipped in their own way, held neighborhood meetings, and worked to preserve their culture. The chapel on the ground floor happens to have the most exquisite Renaissance interior in Venice, with a cycle of paintings by Carpaccio ringing the room (€3, Tue–Sat 9:30–12:30 & 15:30–18:30, Sun 9:30–12:30, closed Mon, between St. Mark's Square and Arsenale, on Calle dei Furlani, 3 blocks southeast of Campo San Lorenzo, tel. 041-522-8828).

Santa Elena—For a pleasant peek into a completely non-touristy, residential side of Venice, walk or catch vaporetto #1 from St. Mark's Square to the neighborhood of Santa Elena (at the fish's tail). This 100-year-old suburb lives as if there were no tourism. You'll find a kid-friendly park, a few lazy restaurants, and beautiful sunsets over San Marco.

The Biennale—Every odd year (next in 2007), Venice hosts a world's fair of contemporary art in the Giardini park and Arsenale (June–Oct 2007, take vaporetto #1 or #82 to Giardini/Biennale; for the latest, visit www.labiennale.org). For more information, see page 84.

Venice Lagoon
The island of Venice sits in a lagoon—a calm section of the Adriatic protected from wind and waves by the neutral breakwater of the Lido. Beyond the church-topped island of San Giorgio Maggiore (directly in front of St. Mark's Square—see page 76—three interesting islands hide out in the lagoon: Murano, Burano, and Torcello. Pick up a free map of the islands from any TI.

Getting There: Murano, Burano, and Torcello are reached easily, cheaply, and slowly by **vaporetto**. Depart from the San Zaccaria Jolanda dock, past the Bridge of Sighs and near the big statue. Line #12 connects all three islands, or take #41 to Murano (get off at

Venice's Lagoon

Murano Colonna), and then #12 to the other islands. If you plan to visit even two of these islands, get a 24-hour €10.50 vaporetto pass or a 12-hour €8.50 "Laguna Tour" pass for convenience. **Speedboat tours** of these three lagoon destinations take three to five hours, and leave twice a day from the dock past the Doge's Palace near the shuttle dock (look for the signs and booth); the tours are speedy indeed, stopping for roughly 40 minutes at each island (for glass-blowing and lacemaking demonstrations followed by sales pitches; €20, April–Oct usually at 9:30 and 14:30, Nov–March 14:30 only, tel. 041-523-8835). Many tourists are almost kidnapped from St. Mark's Square by sales reps who bundle you onto a **free speedboat shuttle to Murano**, with no obligation other than to check out their factory/salesroom. It's a free and handy way to get to Murano. You must watch the 20-minute glassmaking show (and sales pitch), but then you're free to escape and see the rest of the island.

Murano is famous for its glass factories. Upon arrival, wander up Via Fondamenta Vetrai (along the canal of the glassmakers), and check out the various factories (*fabricca* or *fornace*), each offering a free 20-minute glassblowing demonstration of an artisan in action firing up something in a furnace, followed by an almost comically high-pressure sales pitch. (The spiel is brief, and there's absolutely no obligation to buy anything.) The Glass Museum displays the very best of 700 years of Venetian glassmaking, as well as exhibits on ancient and modern glass art. While the display is pretty old-school musty, it's well-described in English (€4, covered by €15.50 Museum Pass, April–Oct Thu–Tue 10:00–17:00, Nov–March Thu–Tue 10:00–16:00, closed Wed, last entry 30 min before closing, tel. 041-739-586). When you're ready to go, head to the Faro vaporetto stop and take the #12 to Burano or the #41 back to San Zaccaria.

Burano, known for its lace, is a sleepy island with a sleepy community—village Venice without the glitz. Lace fans enjoy the Lace Museum (Museo del Merletto di Burano, €4, covered by €15.50 Museum Pass, April–Oct Wed–Mon 10:00–17:00, Nov–March Wed–Mon 10:00–16:00, closed Tue, tel. 041-730-034). The main drag from the vaporetto stop into town is packed with tourists and lined with shops, some of which sell Burano's locally produced white wine. Simply wander to the far side of the island, and the mood shifts. Explore to the right of the leaning tower for a peaceful yet intensely pastel, small-town lagoon world. Benches lining a little promenade at the water's edge make another pretty picnic spot.

Torcello is the birthplace of Venice, where the first mainland refugees settled, escaping the barbarian hordes. Yet today, it's the least-developed island (pop. 20), showing off the marshy, shrub-covered ecosystem of the lagoon. There's little for the tourist to see except the church (a 10-min walk from the dock), which claims to be the oldest in Venice and has impressive mosaics (still, it's not worth seeing on a short visit unless you really love mosaics and can't make it to Ravenna). The complex consists of the church itself, the bell tower (behind the church, climb a ramped stairway for great lagoon views), a sacristy, and a small museum (facing the church, in two separate buildings) that displays Roman sculpture and medieval sculpture and manuscripts. A €6 combo-ticket gets you into all the sights, or pay €2 for each (most open daily 10:30–17:30, museum closed Mon, tel. 041-730-761). There's a pay WC between the museum's two buildings.

EXPERIENCES

Gondola Rides

A rip-off for some, this is a traditional must for romantics. Gondoliers charge about €65–80 for a 50-minute ride during the day; from 20:00 on, figure on €80–105 (for *musica*—singer and accordionist—it's an additional €90 during day, €100 after 20:00). You can divide the cost—and the romance—among up to six people per boat. Note that only two seats (the ones in back) are next to each other. If you want to haggle, you'll find softer prices on back lanes where single gondoliers hang out, rather than at the bigger departure points. Establish the price and duration before boarding, enjoy your ride, and pay only when you're finished.

Though they cost nearly double after dark, gondolas are triply romantic and relaxing under the moon. Glide through nighttime Venice with your head on someone's shoulder. Follow the moon as it sails past otherwise unseen buildings. Silhouettes gaze down from bridges while window glitter spills onto the black water. You're anonymous in the city of masks, as the rhythmic thrust of your striped-shirted gondolier turns old crows into songbirds. This is extremely relaxing (and, I think, worth the extra cost to experience at night). Since you might get a narration plus conversation with your gondolier, talk with several and choose one you like who speaks English well. Women, beware...while gondoliers can be extremely charming, local women say anyone who falls for one of these Romeos "has slices of ham over her eyes."

For cheap gondola thrills during the day, stick to the €0.50 one-minute ferry ride on a Grand Canal *traghetto.*

Festivals

Venice's most famous festival is **Carnevale,** the celebration Americans call Mardi Gras (Feb 17–28 in 2006, www.carnevale .venezia.it). Carnevale, which means "farewell to meat," originated centuries ago as a wild two-month-long party leading up to the austerity of Lent. In Carnevale's heyday—the 1600s and 1700s—you could do pretty much anything with anybody from any social class if you were wearing a mask. These days it's a tamer 10-day celebration, culminating in a huge dance lit with fireworks on St. Mark's Square. Sporting masks and costumes, Venetians from kids to businessmen join in the fun. Drawing the biggest crowds of the year, Carnevale has nearly been a victim of its own success, driving away many Venetians (who skip out on the craziness to go ski in the Dolomites).

Every odd year (next in 2007), the city hosts the **Venice Biennale International Art Exhibition,** a world-class contemporary fair. Artists representing 65 nations from around the world send their best and most outrageous art—video, computer art, performance art, digital photography, painting, and sculpture—to be displayed in buildings and pavilions in the Arsenale and sprawling Castello Gardens (located in Venice's "fish tail"). Some artists convert entire buildings into a single installation, creating a weird wonderland of colors, video images, stage fog, laser lights, and piped-in sound. The festival is an excuse for temporary art exhibitions, concerts, and other cultural events around the city (June–Oct 2007, take vaporetto #1 or #82 to Giardini/Biennale, www.labiennale.org).

Other typically Venetian festival days filling the city's hotels with visitors and its canals with decked-out boats are: **Feast of the Ascension Day** (May 25), **Feast and Regatta of the Redeemer** (July 16), and the **Historical Regatta** (Sept 3). Smaller regattas include the **Murano Regatta** (July 3) and the **Burano Regatta** (Sept 17).

Venice's patron saint, **St. Mark,** is commemorated every April 25. Venetian men celebrate the day by presenting roses to the women in their lives (mothers, wives, and lovers).

Every November 21 is the **Feast of Our Lady of Good Health.** On this local "Thanksgiving," a bridge is built over the Grand Canal so that the city can pile into La Salute Church and remember how Venice survived the gruesome plague of 1630. On this day, Venetians eat smoked lamb from Dalmatia (which was the cargo of the first ship admitted when the plague lifted).

Venice is always busy with special musical and artistic events. The free monthly *Un Ospite di Venezia* lists all the latest in English (free at TI or from fancy hotels). For a comprehensive list of festivals, contact the Italian tourist information office in the United States (see page 7) and visit www.turismovenezia.it.

SHOPPING

Shoppers like Murano glass (described below), Burano lace (fun lace umbrellas for little girls), Carnevale masks (fine shops and local artisans all over town), art reproductions (posters, postcards, and books), calendars or prints of Venetian scenes, traditional stationery (pens and marbled paper products of all kinds), silk ties, scarves, and plenty of goofy knickknacks (Titian mousepads, gondolier T-shirts, and little plastic gondolas).

If you're buying a substantial amount from nearly any shop, bargain. It's accepted and almost expected. Offer less and offer to pay cash; merchants are very conscious of the bite taken by credit-card companies.

Popular **Venetian glass** is available in many forms: vases, tea sets, decanters, glasses, jewelry, lamps, mod sculptures (such as solid-glass aquariums), and on and on. Shops will ship it home for you (snap a photo of it before it's packed up). For a cheap, packable souvenir, consider the glass-bead necklaces sold at vendors' stalls throughout Venice.

If you're serious about glass, visit the small shops on **Murano Island.** Murano's glassblowing demonstrations are fun; you'll usually see a vase and a "leetle 'orse" made from molten glass.

Around St. Mark's Square, various companies offer glassblowing demos for tour groups. **Galleria San Marco,** a tour-group staple, offers great demos just off St. Mark's Square every few minutes.

They have agreed to let individual travelers flashing this book sneak in with tour groups to see the show (and sales pitch). And, if you buy anything, show this book and they'll take 20 percent off the listed price. The gallery faces the square behind the orchestra nearest the church; at #139, go through the shop and climb the stairs (daily 9:00–18:00, tel. 041-271-8650, manager Adriano).

Along Venice's many shopping streets, you'll notice fly-by-night vendors selling knockoffs of famous-maker handbags (Louis Vuitton, Gucci, etc.). These vendors are willing to bargain. Buyer beware. Legitimate manufacturers are raising a stink about these street merchants, and the government is trying to rid the city of them. As authorities are frustrated in attempts to actually arrest the merchants, they are considering making it illegal to buy items from them. Their hope: The threat of a huge fine will scare potential customers away from them—so unlicensed merchants will be driven out of business and off the streets.

NIGHTLIFE

Venice is quiet at night, as tour groups are back in the cheaper hotels of Mestre on the mainland, and the masses of day-trippers return to their beach resorts. **Gondolas** cost more, but are worth the extra expense (see page 83). *Vaporetti* are uncrowded, and it's a great time to cruise the Grand Canal on slow boat #1.

Venice has a busy schedule of events, festivals, and entertainment. Check at the TI for listings in publications such as the free *Leo* magazine (bimonthly, in Italian and English) and in the free *Un Ospite di Venezia* magazine (monthly, bilingual, also available at top-end hotels, www.aguestinvenice.com).

Concerts—Take your pick of traditional Vivaldi concerts in churches throughout town. Homegrown Vivaldi is as trendy here as Strauss is in Vienna and Mozart is in Salzburg. In fact, you'll find frilly young Vivaldis all over town hawking concert tickets. The TI has a list of this week's Baroque concerts (tickets from €18, shows start at 21:00 and generally last 90 min). You'll find posters in hotels all over town. There's music most nights at Scuola San Teodoro (east side of Rialto Bridge) and San Vitale Church (north end of Accademia Bridge), among others. Consider the venue carefully. The general rule of thumb: Musicians in wigs and tights offer better spectacle, musicians in black-and-white suits are better performers. For the latest on church concerts, check at any TI or call 041-962-9999. On summer Saturdays, the Guggenheim hosts evening concerts of contemporary music in the museum's garden (June–July, starts about 20:30, included with €10 museum entry, www.guggenheim-venice.it).

St. Mark's Square—For tourists, St. Mark's Square is the high-light, with lantern light and live music echoing from the cafés. Just being here after dark is a thrill, as dueling café orchestras entertain (see sidebar on page 69). Every night, enthusiastic musicians play the same songs, creating the same irresistible magic. Hang out for free behind the tables (which allows you to easily move on to the next orchestra when the musicians take a break), or spring for a seat and enjoy a fun and gorgeously set concert. If you sit a while, it can be €15 well spent (for a drink and the cover charge for music). Dancing on the square is free (and encouraged).

Streetlamp halos, live music, floodlit history, and a ceiling of stars make St. Mark's magic at midnight. You're not a tour-ist—you're a living part of a soft Venetian night...an alley cat with money. In the misty light, the moon has a golden hue. Shine with the old lanterns on the gondola piers, where the sloppy lagoon splashes at the Doge's Palace...reminiscing.

SLEEPING

Virtually all of my recommended hotels are central. See the maps (on pages 89, 92, and 95) for hotel locations. I've listed rooms in three neighborhoods: the Rialto action, St. Mark's bustle, and the quiet Dorsoduro area behind the Accademia art museum. Hotel Web sites are particularly valuable in Venice, because they often come with a map.

Reserve a room as soon as you know when you'll be in town. Hotels in Venice are usually booked up on Carnevale (Feb 17–28 in 2006), Easter (April 16 in 2006), April 25, May 1, Nov 1, and on Fridays and Saturdays year-round. If everything's full, don't despair. Call a day or two in advance and fill in a cancellation. If you arrive on an overnight train, your room may not be ready. Drop your bag at the hotel and dive right into Venice.

Venetian hoteliers are hard to pin down. They're experts at perfect price discrimination: They list a huge range of rates for the same room (e.g., €90–160) and refuse to give a firm price, enabling them to judge the demand and charge accordingly. Once they know what the market will bear, they max it out. Also, hotels are being squeezed by the very popular online booking services (which take about a 20 percent commission). Between wanting to keep their gouging options open for high-season weekends and trying to recover these online commissions, hoteliers set their rack rates (the highest rates a hotel charges) sky-high.

My listings are more likely to give a straight price. I've assured hoteliers that my readers will book direct, so they'll get 100 percent of what you pay; therefore, you'll get the fair net rate. I've listed only prices for peak season: April, May, June, September, and October.

Sleep Code

(€1 = about $1.20, country code: 39)
S = Single, **D** = Double/Twin, **T** = Triple, **Q** = Quad, **b** = bath-room, **s** = shower only. Breakfast is included, credit cards are accepted, and English is spoken unless otherwise noted. Air-conditioning, when available, is usually only turned on in summer.

To help you sort easily through these listings, I've divided the rooms into three categories based on the price for a stan-dard double room with bath:

$$$ **Higher Priced**—Most rooms €180 or more.
$$ **Moderately Priced**—Most rooms between
                            €130–180.
$ **Lower Priced**—Most rooms €130 or less.

Prices will be higher during festivals, and virtually all places drop prices from November through March (except during Carnevale) and in July and August.

If you book via a Web service, I wash my hands of your prob-lems. If you book direct, help me enforce honest business practices by reporting any hotel charging more than the listed rates in 2006. E-mail me at rick@ricksteves.com. Thanks.

Near St. Mark's Square

East of St. Mark's Square

Located near the Bridge of Sighs, just off the Riva degli Schiavoni waterfront promenade, these places rub drainpipes with Venice's most palatial five-star hotels. The first, while a bit pricey because of its location, is professional and comfortable. Ride the vaporetto to San Zaccaria (#51 from train station, #82 from Tronchetto parking lot).

$$$ Hotel Campiello, lacy and bright, was once part of a 19th-century convent. Ideally located 50 yards off the waterfront, its 16 rooms offer a tranquil, friendly refuge for travelers who appre-ciate affordable elegance (Sb-€120, Db-€190, 10 percent discount with cash, strict cancellation penalties enforced, air-con, elevator; from the waterfront street—Riva degli Schiavoni—take Calle del Vin, between Hotel Danieli and Hotel Savoia e Jolanda, to #4647, Castello; tel. 041-520-5764, fax 041-520-5798, www.hcampiello .it, campiello@hcampiello.it; family-run for 4 generations: sisters Monica and Nicoletta, and Thomas).

$$ Locanda al Leon has 14 renovated, 18th-century Venice-style rooms just off Campo S.S. Filippo e Giacomo (Db-€140,

St. Mark's Square Area Hotels

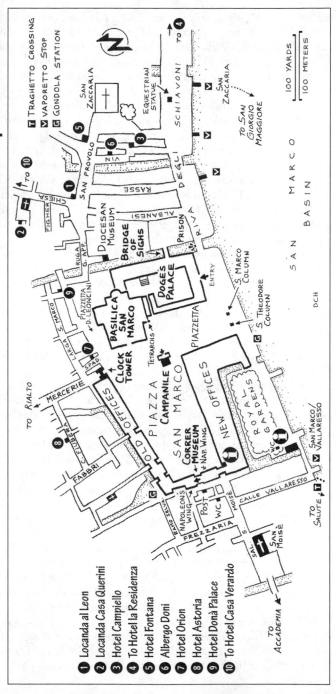

T TRAGHETTO CROSSING
V VAPORETTO STOP
G GONDOLA STATION

1 Locanda al Leon
2 Locanda Casa Querini
3 Hotel Campiello
4 To Hotel la Residenza
5 Hotel Fontana
6 Albergo Doni
7 Hotel Orion
8 Hotel Astoria
9 Hotel Donà Palace
10 To Hotel Casa Verardo

bigger Db-€165, these prices with cash and this book in 2006, Campo S.S. Filippo e Giacomo 4270, Castello, tel. 041-277-0393, fax 041-521-0348, www.hotelalleon.com, leon@hotelalleon.com, Juliano and Marcella). From the San Zaccaria vaporetto stop, take Calle delle Rasse (left of pink Hotel Danieli) to Salizada S. Provolo; turn left, then right to get to Campo S.S. Filippo e Giacomo. The hotel is on Calle dei Albanesi.

$$ Hotel Fontana is a two-star, family-run place with 14 rooms and lots of stairs on a touristy square two bridges behind St. Mark's Square (Sb-€110, Db-€155, family rooms, air-con, 10 percent discount with cash, quieter rooms on garden side, 2 rooms have terraces, Campo San Provolo 4701, Castello; tel. 041-522-0579, fax 041-523-1040, www.hotelfontana.it, info@hotelfontana .it, Diego and Gabriele). Take vaporetto #1 or #51 to San Zaccaria, find Calle delle Rasse—to the left of Hotel Danieli—take it, turn right at the end, and continue to the first square.

$$ Hotel la Residenza is a grand old palace facing a peaceful square. Its 15 great rooms ring a huge, luxurious lounge. Relaxing in the lounge, you'll really feel like you're in the Doge's Palace after hours. This is a great value for romantics (Sb-€95, Db-€150, air-con, Castello 3608, tel. 041-528-5315, fax 041-523-8859, www.venicelaresidenza.com, info@venicelaresidenza.com). From the Bridge of Sighs, walk east along Riva degli Schiavoni, cross three bridges, and take the first left up Calle del Dose to Campo Bandiera e Moro.

$ Locanda Casa Querini rents 11 plush rooms on a quiet square tucked away behind St. Mark's. You can enjoy your breakfast sitting right on a little square (Db-€130 with cash and this book through 2006, €5 more for view rooms, air-con, halfway between San Zaccaria vaporetto stop and Campo Santa Maria Formosa at Campo San Giovanni in Oleo 4388, Castello, tel. 041-241-1294, fax 041-241-4231, www.locandaquerini.com, casaquerini@hotmail .com, Patricia and Silvia). Take the street to the right of the Bridge of Sighs to Campo S.S. Fillipo e Giacomo, continue on Calle Rimpeto la Sacrestia, take the second left, and curl around to the left into the little square.

$ Albergo Doni is dark, hardwood, clean, and quiet—a bit of a time-warp—with 13 dim but classy rooms run by a likable smart aleck named Gina (S-€60, D-€90, Db-€115, T-€120, Tb-€155, Qb-€190, mention this book to get these special prices, reserve with credit card but pay in cash, ceiling fans, Castello 4656, tel. & fax 041-522-4267, www.albergodoni.it, albergodoni@libero.it; Gina, Nicolò, and Tessa). From the San Zaccaria vaporetto stop, cross one bridge to the right, take the first left past the Hotel Danieli, then turn left at the little square named Fondamenta del Vin.

North of St. Mark's Square

$$ Hotel Orion has 18 neat-as-a-pin, relaxing, and spacious rooms. Just off St. Mark's Square, it's a tranquil haven from the bustling streets (Db-€165 with this book in 2006, 5 percent discount with cash, air-con; from St. Mark's Square walk to the left of the facade and then turn left on Spadari, hotel is just before timbered overpass, Spadaria 700a, San Marco 30100; tel. 041-522-3053, fax 041-523-8866, www.hotelorion.it, info@hotelorion.it, Stefano).

$ Hotel Astoria has 24 simple, tidy rooms tucked away a few blocks off St. Mark's Square (Db-€120 promised with this book in 2006, 2 blocks from San Zulian Church at Calle Fiubera 951, San Marco; from Rialto vaporetto #1 dock, go straight inland on Calle Bembo—which becomes Calle dei Fabbri—and turn left on Calle Fiubera; tel. 041-522-5381, fax 041-528-8981, www .hotelastoriavenezia.it, info@hotelastoriavenezia.it, Giorgia).

Near the Rialto Bridge

Vaporetto #82 quickly connects the Rialto with both the train station and the Tronchetto parking lot.

West of the Rialto Bridge

$$$ Locanda Sturion, with 11 rooms, air-conditioning, and all the modern comforts, is pricey because it overlooks the Grand Canal (Db-€240, canal-view rooms cost €50 extra, 10 percent discount with cash, family deals, piles of stairs, 100 yards from Rialto Bridge, opposite vaporetto dock, Calle del Sturion 679, San Polo, tel. 041-523-6243, fax 041-522-8378, www.locandasturion.com, info@locandasturion.com).

$ Albergo Guerrato, above a handy and colorful produce market two minutes from the Rialto action, is run by friendly, creative, and hardworking Roberto and Piero. Giorgio takes the night shift. Their 800-year-old building—with 24 spacious, air-conditioned rooms—is simple, airy, and wonderfully characteristic (D-€90, Db-€115, top-floor "Guerratino" rooms go for Db-€135, Tb-€145, Qb-€170, prices promised through 2006 with this book and cash, a further 15 percent discount Nov–Feb and Aug, Calle drio la Scimia 240a, San Polo, tel. 041-522-7131 or 041-528-5927, fax 041-241-1408, www.pensioneguerrato.it, hguerrat@tin.it). Walk over the Rialto Brige away from St. Mark's Square, go straight about three blocks, turn right on Calle drio la Scimia (not simply Scimia, the block before), and you'll see the hotel sign. My tour groups book this place for 40 nights each year. Sorry. The Guerrato also rents family apartments in the old center (great for groups of 4–8) for around €55 per person.

Rialto Bridge Area Hotels

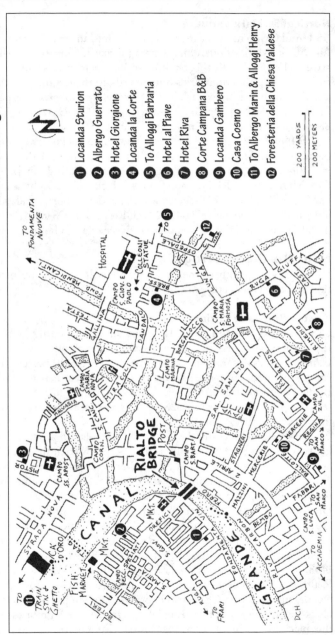

1. Locanda Sturion
2. Albergo Guerrato
3. Hotel Giorgione
4. Locanda la Corte
5. To Alloggi Barbaria
6. Hotel al Piave
7. Hotel Riva
8. Corte Campana B&B
9. Locanda Gambero
10. Casa Cosmo
11. To Albergo Marin & Alloggi Henry
12. Foresteria della Chiesa Valdese

200 YARDS
200 METERS

East of the Rialto Bridge
$$ **Locanda la Corte,** a three-star hotel, is perfumed with elegance. Its 18 attractive, high-ceilinged, wood-beamed rooms—done in pastels—circle a small, quiet courtyard (Sb-€120, standard Db-€150, superior Db-€170, 10 percent discount with cash, suites available, air-con, Castello 6317, tel. 041-241-1300, fax 041-241-5982, www .locandalacorte.it, info@locandalacorte.it, Marco and Raffaela). Take vaporetto #52 from the train station to Fondamente Nove, exit the boat to your left, follow the waterfront, and turn right after the second bridge to get to S.S. Giovanni e Paolo square. Facing the Rosa Salva bar, take the street to the left (Calle Bressana); the hotel is a short block away at #6317 before the bridge.

$ **Alloggi Barbaria** rents six quiet, spacious, Ikea-style rooms with the basic comforts. Beyond Campo S.S. Giovanni e Paolo, it's a long walk from the action but a good value (Db-€100 with this book in 2006, extra bed-€30, family deals, air-con, tel. 041-522-2750, fax 041-277-5540, www.alloggibarbaria.it, info@alloggibarbaria.it, Giorgio and Fausto). Take vaporetto #52 to Ospedale stop, turn left as you get off the boat, then right down Calle de le Capucine to #6573 (Castello).

Southeast of the Rialto Bridge
$$$ **Locanda Gambero,** with 31 pricey rooms, is a comfortable and very central three-star hotel (Sb-€130, Db-€230, Tb-€260, 10 percent discount with cash, air-con, Internet in lobby; from Rialto vaporetto dock walk away from the Rialto Bridge, cross one bridge, and take first left down skinny Calle Bembo/Calle dei Fabbri; or from St. Mark's Square go through Sotoportego dei Dai, then down Calle dei Fabbri; Calle dei Fabbri 4687, San Marco, tel. 041-522-4384, fax 041-520-0431, www.locandaalgambero.com, hotelgambero@tin.it, Sandro). Gambero runs the pleasant, Art Deco–style La Bistrot on the corner, which serves old-time Venetian cuisine.

$$ **Hotel al Piave,** with 27 fine air-conditioned rooms above a bright and classy lobby, is fresh, modern, and comfortable. You'll enjoy the neighborhood and always get a cheery welcome (Db-€150, Tb-€190, family suites-€250 for 4 or €280 for 5, prices good through 2006 with this book, discount for cash; vaporetto #82 to San Zaccaria, find your way to Ruga Giuffa, it's at #4838/40, Castello; tel. 041-528-5174, fax 041-523-8512, www.hotelalpiave .com, info@hotelpiave.com; Mirella, Paolo, and Ilaria speak English, faithful Molly doesn't).

$ **Hotel Riva,** with gleaming marble hallways and bright modern rooms, is romantically situated on a canal along the gondola serenade route. You could actually dunk your breakfast rolls in the canal (but don't). Sandro may hold a corner (*angolo*) room if you ask, and there are also a few rooms overlooking the canal.

Ten of the 32 rooms come with air-conditioning for the same price—request one when you reserve (Sb-€90, two D with adjacent showers-€100, Db-€120, Tb-€170, €10 extra for view, reserve with credit card but pay with cash only, Ponte dell'Angelo, tel. 041-522-7034, fax 041-528-5551). Facing St. Mark's Basilica, walk behind it on the left along Calle de la Canonica, take the first left (at blue *Pauly & C* mosaic in street), continue straight, go over the bridge (may be marked *Angelo* or *Anzolo*), and angle right to the hotel at Ponte dell'Angelo.

$ Corte Campana B&B, run by enthusiastic and helpful Riccardo, rents three quiet rooms just behind St. Mark's Square (Db-€129, Tb-€165, Qb-€200, cash only, air-con, Calle del Remedio 4410, Castello, tel. 041-523-3603, mobile 389-272-6500, www.cortecampana.com, info@cortecampana.com). Facing St. Mark's Basilica, take Calle de la Canonica (left of church); turn left before the canal on Calle dell'Anzolo. Take the second right (onto Calle del Remedio), cross the bridge, and follow signs. Ring the bell at the black gate; the door is across the courtyard on the left wall, and the B&B is up three flights of stairs.

$ Casa Cosmo is a humble little five-room place run by Davide and his parents. While it comes with minimal services and no public spaces, it's air-conditioned, extremely central, inexpensive, and quiet, with a tiny terrace (Db-€100 with this book and cash in 2006, on tiny Calle di Mezzo just off Calle delle Ballotte a block from the Merceria, San Marco 4976, tel. 041-296-0710, www.casacosmo.com, info@casacosmo.com).

Near the Accademia Bridge

When you step over the Accademia Bridge, the commotion of touristy Venice is replaced by a sleepy village laced with canals. This quiet area, next to the best painting gallery in town, is a 15-minute walk from St. Mark's Square and the Rialto, or you can take the Santa Maria del Giglio or Salute *traghetto* for a shortcut to St. Mark's. The fast vaporetto #82 connects the Accademia Bridge with both the train station (15 min) and St. Mark's Square (5 min).

South of the Accademia Bridge

To reach these hotels from the train station, you can take a vaporetto to the Accademia stop (more scenic, down Grand Canal) or the Zattere stop (less scenic, around outskirts of Venice, but cheaper and faster).

$$$ Hotel Belle Arti is a good bet if you want modern freshness in the old center. With a grand entry and all the American hotel comforts, it's a big, 67-room, three-star place sitting on a former schoolyard (Sb-€120, Db-€180-215, Tb-€265, plush public

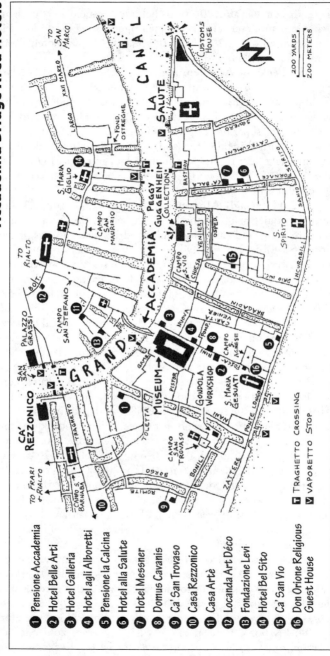

Accademia Bridge Area Hotels

1. Pensione Accademia
2. Hotel Belle Arti
3. Hotel Galleria
4. Hotel agli Alboretti
5. Pensione la Calcina
6. Hotel alla Salute
7. Hotel Messner
8. Domus Cavanis
9. Ca' San Trovaso
10. Casa Rezzonico
11. Casa Artè
12. Locanda Art Déco
13. Fondazione Levi
14. Hotel Bel Sito
15. Ca' San Vio
16. Don Orione Religious Guest House

T Traghetto Crossing
V Vaporetto Stop

areas, air-con, elevator; 100 yards behind Accademia art museum: facing museum, take left, then forced right, to Via Dorsoduro 912, Dorsoduro; tel. 041-522-6230, fax 041-528-0043, www.hotelbellearti .com, info@hotelbellearti.com).

$$$ Pensione Accademia fills the 17th-century Villa Maravege. Its 27 rooms are comfortable, elegant, and air-conditioned. You'll feel aristocratic gliding through its grand public spaces and lounging in its wistful, breezy gardens (Sb-€130, standard Db-€190, bigger "superior" Db-€240, Qb-€310, 10 percent discount promised with this book in hand in 2006; facing Accademia art museum, take first right, cross first bridge, go right to Dorsoduro 1058; tel. 041-523-7846, fax 041-523-9152, www.pensioneaccademia .it, info@pensioneaccademia.it).

$$$ Hotel agli Alboretti is a cozy, family-run, 23-room place in a quiet neighborhood a block behind the Accademia art museum. With red carpeting and wood-beamed ceilings, it feels plush (Sb-€105, Db-€180, Tb-€205, Qb-€230, air-con, elevator; 100 yards from the Accademia vaporetto stop on Rio Terra a Foscarini at Accademia 884, Dorsoduro; facing Accademia art museum, go left, then forced right; tel. 041-523-0058, fax 041-521-0158, www.aglialboretti.com, info@aglialboretti.com). They run a near-gourmet restaurant that is quickly becoming a local favorite.

$$ Pensione la Calcina, the home of English writer John Ruskin in 1876, maintains a 19th-century formality. It comes with all the three-star comforts in a professional yet intimate package. Its 33 rooms are squeaky clean, with good wood furniture, hardwood floors, and a peaceful canalside setting facing Giudecca island (Sb-€96, Sb with view-€106, Db-€148–186 depending on size of room and view, air-con, rooftop terrace, killer sundeck on canal and canalside buffet-breakfast terrace, Dorsoduro 780, at south end of Rio di San Vio, tel. 041-520-6466, fax 041-522-7045, www .lacalcina.com, la.calcina@libero.it). From the Tronchetto parking lot take vaporetto #82, or from the train station take #51 or #61, to Zattere (at vaporetto stop, exit right and walk along canal to hotel). Guests get a fine dinner at their La Piscina restaurant discounted to €22. Guests are welcome to use the terrace outside of meal times without buying anything.

$$ Casa Rezzonico is a silent getaway far from the madding crowds. Its private garden terrace has perhaps the lushest grass in Italy, and its seven spacious rooms have views of this garden and of the adjacent canal (Sb-€120, Db-€150, Tb-€180, Qb-€220, some rooms with air-con, Fondamenta Gherardini 2813, Dorsoduro, tel. 041-277-0653, fax 041-277-5435, www.casarezzonico.it, info @casarezzonico.it). Take vaporetto #1 to the Ca' Rezzonico stop, head up Calle del Traghetto, cross Campo San Barnaba to the canal, and continue forward on Fondamenta Gherardini to #2813.

$$ Hotel alla Salute, a basic retreat buried deep in Dorsoduro with 50 rooms and indifferent owners, works for those wanting a quiet Venice residence (Db-€140, cheaper if you pay in cash, facing the canal Rio delle Fornace near La Salute church, Salute 222, Dorsoduro, tel. 041-523-5404, fax 041-522-2271, www.hotelsalute .com, info@hotelsalute.com).

$$ Hotel Messner, a sprawling place popular with groups, rents 40 nondescript rooms in a peaceful canalside neighborhood near La Salute Church. While remote, it has cheap and handy *traghetto* access to St. Mark's Square (Sb-€110, Db with air-con-€140, Db without air-con in simpler annex-€115, Tb-€145, Qb-€160, peaceful garden, midway between lagoon and Grand Canal on Rio delle Fornace canal, Dorsoduro 216, tel. 041-522-7443, fax 041-522-7266, www.hotelmessner.it, messnerinfo@tin.it).

$ Hotel Galleria has nine tight, velvety rooms, most with views of the Grand Canal. Some rooms are quite narrow (S-€80, D-€110, Db-€120, big canal-view Db #8 and #10-€155, includes scant breakfast in room, fans, near Accademia art museum, and next to recommended Foscarini pizzeria, Dorsoduro 878a, tel. 041-523-2489, tel. & fax 041-520-4172, www.hotelgalleria.it, galleria@tin.it).

$ Ca' San Trovaso rents 14 classy, spacious rooms split between the main hotel and a nearby annex. The location is peaceful, on a small canal (Sb-€90, Db-€110, bigger canal-view Db-€130, Tb-€145, these prices promised with this book in 2006, breakfast in your room, fans, small roof terrace, Dorsoduro 1350/51, tel. 041-277-1146, fax 041-277-7190, www.casantrovaso.com, s.trovaso@tin .it, Mark and his son Alessandro). Take vaporetto #82 from the Tronchetto parking lot (or #51 from Piazzale Roma or the train station), get off at Zattere, exit left, turn right at tiny Calle Trevisan, cross the bridge, cross the adjacent bridge, take an immediate right, and then the first left.

$ Ca' San Vio is a tiny, new place run by the Ca' San Trovaso folks on a quiet canal with five fine air-conditioned rooms (small French bed Db-€100, bigger Db-€110, Tb-€140, breakfast in room, no public spaces, Calle delle Mende 531, Dorsoduro, tel. 041-277-1146, www.casanvio.com, Roberto and Marco).

$ Domus Cavanis, across the street from—and run by—Hotel Belle Arti (described above), is a big, practical, stark place, renting 30 quiet, simple rooms (Sb-€55, Db-€100, Tb-€135, family rooms, includes breakfast at Hotel Belle Arti, air-con, elevator, Dorsoduro 895, tel. 041-528-7374, fax 041-528-0043, info@hotelbellearti.com).

$ Don Orione Religious Guest House is a big cultural center dedicated to the work of a local man who became a saint in modern times. Filling an old monastery, it feels like a modern retreat center—clean, peaceful, and strictly run, with 50 rooms. It's beautifully located, comfortable, and a fine value (Sb-€70, Db-€115, Tb-€147, air-con, money raised funds their mission work in the developing world, groups welcome, on the Giudecca Canal directly across from the Accademia Bridge facing Campo Sant'Agnese, Zattere 909a, Dorsoduro, tel. 041-522-4077, fax 041-528-6214, www.donorione -venezia.it, info@donorione-venezia.it).

North of the Accademia Bridge

$$ Hotel Bel Sito, friendly for a three-star hotel, offers comfortable yet well-worn Old World character, 38 rooms, a peaceful courtyard, and a picturesque location—facing a church on a small square between St. Mark's Square and the Accademia (Sb-€98, Db-€160 promised with this book in 2006, air-con, elevator, some rooms with canal or church views; vaporetto #1 to Santa Maria del Giglio stop, take narrow alley to square, hotel at far end to your right; Santa Maria del Giglio 2517, San Marco, tel. 041-522-3365, fax 041-520-4083, www.hotelbelsito.info, info@hotelbelsito.info).

$$ Locanda Art Déco is a charming little place. While the Art Deco theme is scant, a wrought-iron staircase leads from the inviting lobby to seven thoughtfully decorated rooms (Db-€170, 3-night minimum on weekends, 5 percent discount with cash, 2 family rooms, air-con, just north of the Accademia Bridge off Campo Santo Stefano at 2966 Calle delle Botteghe, San Marco, tel. 041-277-0558, fax 041-270-2891, www.locandaartdeco.com, info@locandaartdeco.com, Giuseppe).

$ Casa Artè has eight homey rooms with high ceilings, old-style Venetian furnishings, air-conditioning, and thoughtful touches in a red-velvet ambience (Sb-€90, Db-€130, 10 percent discount with cash, family room sleeps up to 6, just north of Accademia Bridge, 100 yards west of Campo San Stefano on Calle de Frutariol, San Marco 2900/01, tel. 041-520-0882, fax 041-277-8395, www.casaarte.info, info@casaarte.info, Gian Carlo).

$ Fondazione Levi, run by a foundation that promotes research on Venetian music, offers 18 quiet, institutional, yet comfortable and spacious rooms (Sb-€65, Db-€105, Tb-€124, Qb-€145, twin beds only, elevator, San Vidal 2893, San Marco, tel. 041-786-711, fax 041-786-766, foresterialevi@libero.it). It's 80 yards from the base of the Accademia Bridge on the St. Mark's side. From the Accademia vaporetto stop, cross the Accademia Bridge, take an immediate left, crossing the bridge Ponte Giustinian and going down Calle Giustinian directly to the Fondazione. Buzz the *Foresteria* door to the right.

Near the Train Station

I don't recommend the train station area. It's crawling with noisy, disoriented tourists with too much baggage and people whose life's calling is to scam them out of their money. It's so easy to just hop a vaporetto upon arrival and get into the Venice of your dreams. Still, some like to park their bags near the station, and these two places work well.

$ Albergo Marin and its friendly, helpful staff offer 17 good-value, immaculate, quiet rooms handy to the train station (Sb-€80, Db-€95, these are the maximum prices with this book in 2006, 5 percent discount with cash, fans on request, Campiello delle Muneghe 670b, Santa Croce, tel. 041-718-022, fax 041-721-485, www .albergomarin.it, info@albergomarin.it). From the station, cross the Grand Canal and turn immediately right. Walk along the water, take the first left (after passing the church) down Calle del Traghetto di S. Lucia, and then jog left again to Campiello delle Muneghe.

$ Alloggi Henry, a homey little family-owned hotel, has eight ramshackle rooms in a quiet neighborhood a five-minute walk from the train station (Db-€90 with this book in 2006, no breakfast, Calle Ormesini 1506e, Cannaregio, tel. 041-523-6675, fax 041-715-680, www.alloggihenry.com, info@alloggihenry.com). From the station, follow Lista di Spagna, Rio Terra San Leonardo, and Rio Terra Farsetti, then take the second left on Calle Ormesini; the hotel's at #1506.

Big, Fancy Hotels

Here are three big, plush, four-star places with greedy, sky-high rack rates (around Db-€300) that often have great discounts (as low as Db-€160) for drop-ins, off-season travelers, or online booking through their Web site. If you want a sliding-glass-door, uniformed-receptionist kind of comfort and formality in the old center, these are worth considering: **$$$ Hotel Giorgione** (big, garish, shiny, near Rialto Bridge, www.hotelgiorgione.com); **$$$ Hotel Casa Verardo** (elegant and quietly parked on a canal behind St. Mark's, more stately, www.casaverardo.it); and **$$$ Hotel Donà Palace** (sitting like Las Vegas in the touristy zone just northeast of St. Mark's, www.donapalace.it).

Cheap Dormitory Accommodations

$ Foresteria della Chiesa Valdese, warmly run by the Methodist Church, offers 33 beds in doubles and three- to 10-bed dorms, halfway between St. Mark's Square and the Rialto Bridge. This run-down but charming old place has elegant ceiling paintings (dorm bed-€22, D-€58, Db-€75, includes breakfast, sheets, and lockers; must check in and out when office is open—9:00–13:00 & 18:00–20:00, Castello 5170, tel. 041-528-6797, fax 041-241-6238, foresteriavenezia@diaconiavaldese.org). From Campo Santa Maria Formosa, walk past Bar all'Orologio to the end of Calle Lunga and cross the bridge.

$ Venice's **youth hostel,** on Giudecca Island, is crowded and inexpensive (€21 beds with sheets and breakfast in 10- to 16-bed dorms, cheaper for hostel members, office open daily 7:00–9:30 & 13:30–23:30, catch vaporetto #82 from station to Zittele, tel. 041-523-8211, can reserve online at www.hostelbooking.com). The budget cafeteria welcomes non-hostelers (nightly 16:30–21:30).

EATING

While touristy restaurants are the scourge of Venice, and most restaurateurs believe you can't survive in Venice without catering to tourists, there are plenty of places that are still popular with locals and respect the tourists who happen in. First trick: Walk away from triple-language menus. Second trick: Order the daily special. Third trick: For freshness, eat fish. Most seafood dishes are the local catch-of-the-day.

For romantic—and usually pricey—meals along the water, see "Romantic Canalside Settings," page 108. For dessert, it's gelato (see end of this chapter).

Near the Rialto Bridge

North of the Rialto Bridge

These restaurants are located between Campo S.S. Apostoli and Campo S.S. Giovanni e Paolo.

Trattoria da Bepi is a classy, family-run place where Mamma scours the market for just the best ingredients and son, Loris, takes good care of the hungry clientele (€30 meals, Fri–Wed 12:00–14:30 & 19:00–22:00, closed Thu, half a block north of Campo S.S. Apostoli on Salizada Pistor, tel. 041-528-5031).

Osteria da Alberto has excellent €20 seafood dinners and €8 pastas (Mon–Sat 12:00–15:00 & 19:00–23:00, closed Sun, midway between Campo S.S. Apostoli and Campo S.S. Giovanni e Paolo, next to Ponte de la Panada on Calle Larga Giacinto Gallina, tel. 041-523-8153, run by Graziano and Giovanni).

Cicchetti: **Osteria al Bomba** is a *cicchetti* bar (see page 102) with a female touch. It's unusual (clean, no toothpicks, no cursing) but actually quite good, with lots of veggies. You can stand and eat at the bar, or oversee the construction of the house "*antipasto misto di cicchetti*" plate (€15, enough for 2), and then grab a seat at the long table (daily 18:00–23:00, near Campo S.S. Apostoli, a block off Strada Nuova on Calle dell'Oca, tel. 041-520-5175). You'll find more pubs nearby, in the side streets opposite Campo Santa Sofia, across Strada Nuova.

East of the Rialto Bridge, near Campo San Bartolomeo

Osteria di Santa Marina, on the wonderful Campo Marina square,

Rialto Area Restaurants

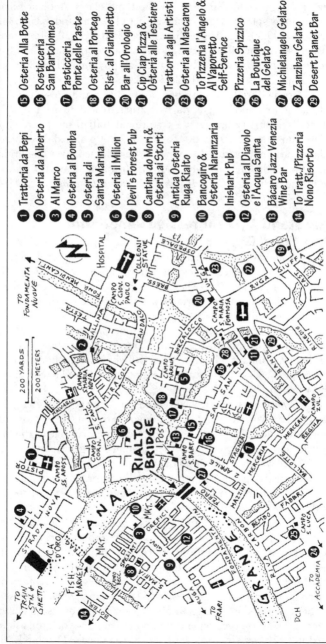

1. Trattoria da Bepi
2. Osteria da Alberto
3. Al Marco
4. Osteria al Bomba
5. Osteria di Santa Marina
6. Osteria il Milion
7. Devil's Forest Pub
8. Cantina do Mori & Osteria ai Storti
9. Antica Osteria Ruga Rialto
10. Bancogiro & Osteria Naranzaria
11. Inishark Pub
12. Osteria al Diavolo e l'Acqua Santa
13. Bácaro Jazz Venezia Wine Bar
14. To Tratt./Pizzeria Nono Risorto
15. Osteria Alla Botte
16. Rosticceria San Bartolomeo
17. Pasticceria Ponte delle Paste
18. Osteria al Portego
19. Rist. al Giardinetto
20. Bar all'Orologio
21. Cip Ciap Pizza & Osteria alle Testiere
22. Trattoria agli Artisti
23. Osteria al Mascaron
24. To Pizzeria l'Angelo & Al Vaporetto Self-Service
25. Pizzeria Spizzico
26. La Boutique del Gelato
27. Michielangelo Gelato
28. Zanzibar Gelato
29. Desert Planet Bar

serves pricey, near-gourmet food that's made with only the best seasonal ingredients. The quality food and classy ambience make this a good splurge (fun menu with €14 pastas and €25 *secondi*, Sun–Mon 19:30–21:30, Tue–Sat 12:30–14:30 & 19:30–21:30, reservations smart for dinner, eat indoors or outdoors on pleasant little square, midway between Rialto and Campo Santa Maria Formosa on Campo Marina, tel. 041-528-5239).

Osteria il Milion, with bow-tied waiters and dressy candlelit tables indoors and out, is quietly situated next to Marco Polo's home. It's touristy but tasty—traditional Italian meals are about €25 (Thu–Tue 12:00–15:00 & 18:30–23:00, closed Wed; near Rialto, head north from Campo San Bartolomeo, over one bridge, take first right off San Giovanni Grisostomo before the church, walk under the sign *Corte Prima del Milion o del forno*, it's at #5841; tel. 041-522-9302).

The Stand-Up Progressive Venetian Pub-Crawl Dinner

My favorite Venetian dinner is a pub crawl *(giro d'ombra)*—a tradition unique to Venice, where no cars means easy crawling. (*Giro* means stroll, and *ombra*—slang for a glass of wine—means shade, from the old days when a portable wine bar scooted with the shadow of the Campanile across St. Mark's Square.)

Venice's residential back streets hide plenty of characteristic bars *(baccari)* with countless trays of interesting toothpick munchies *(cicchetti)* and blackboards listing which wines are uncorked and served by the glass. This is a great way to mingle and have fun with the Venetians.

Cicchetti **bars** have a social stand-up zone and a cozy gaggle of tables where you can generally sit down with your *cicchetti* or order from a simple menu. In some of the more popular places, the local crowds spill happily out into the street. Food generally costs the same price whether you stand or sit.

I've listed plenty of pubs in walking order for a quick or extended crawl below. If you've crawled enough, most of these bars make a fine one-stop, sit-down dinner.

Try deep-fried mozzarella cheese, gorgonzola, calamari, artichoke hearts, and anything ugly on a toothpick. *Crostini* (small toasted bread with something on it) are popular, as are marinated seafood, olives, and prosciutto with melon. Meat and fish (*pesce;* PESH-shay) munchies can be expensive; veggies *(verdure)* are cheap, at about €3 for a meal-sized plate. In many places, there's a set price per food item (e.g., €1.50). To get a plate of assorted appetizers for €8 (or more, depending on how hungry you are), ask for: "*Un piatto classico di cicchetti misti da* €8" (oon pee-AH-toh KLAH-see-koh dee cheh-KET-tee MEE-stee da OH-toh ay-OO-roh).

Bread sticks *(grissini)* are free for the asking.

Drink the house wines. A small glass of house red or white wine *(ombra rosso* or *ombra bianco)* or a small beer *(birrino)* costs about €1. The house keg wine is cheap—€1 per glass, about €4 per liter. *Vin bon,* Venetian for fine wine, may run you from €1.50 to €6 per little glass. There are usually several fine wines uncorked and available by the glass. *Corposo* means full-bodied. A good last drink is *fragolino,* the local sweet wine—*bianco* or *rosso.* It often comes with a little cookie *(biscotti)* for dipping.

Bars don't stay open very late, and the *cicchetti* selection is best early, so start your evening by 18:00. Most bars are closed on Sunday.

Cicchetterie and Light Meals West of the Rialto Bridge

All of these places are within 200 yards of each other, in the neighborhood around the Rialto market. This area is very crowded by day but nearly empty after dark.

Cantina do Mori is famous with locals (since 1462) and savvy travelers (since 1982) as a classy place for fine wine and *francobolli* (a spicy selection of 20 tiny mayo-soaked sandwiches nicknamed "stamps"). Choose from the featured wines. Confirm the price, or they'll rip you off (Mon–Sat 12:00–20:30, closed Sun, stand-up only, arrive early before the *cicchetti* are gone, San Polo 429, tel. 041-522-5401). From Rialto Bridge, walk 200 yards down Ruga degli Orefici, away from St. Mark's Square—then left on Ruga Vecchia S. Giovanni, then right at Sotoportego do' Mori.

Osteria ai Storti, just opened in 2005, offers lots of veggies, great prices, a homey feel, and a wonderful, fun place to congregate outdoors. Check out the photo of the market in 1909, below the bar (Mon–Sat 12:00–22:30, closed Sun, 20 yards from Cantina do Mori on Calle do Spade).

Antica Osteria Ruga Rialto, "the Ruga," is a local fixture where Marco serves great bar snacks and wine to his devoted clientele (daily 11:00–14:30 & 19:00–24:00, easy to find, just past the Chinese restaurant on Ruga Vecchia S. Giovanni 692, tel. 041-521-1243).

Osteria al Diavolo el'Acqua Santa, three blocks west of the Rialto Bridge, serves good—if pricey—pasta and makes a handy lunch stop for sightseers and gondola-riders. While they list *cicchetti* and wine by the glass on the wall, I'd come here for a light meal rather than appetizers (Mon 12:00–15:00, Wed–Sun 12:00–15:00 & 19:00–23:00, closed Tue, hiding on a quiet street just off Rua Vecchia S. Giovanni, on Calle della Madonna, tel. 041-277-0307).

Al Marco, on Campo Cesare Battisti square, is a literal hole-in-the-wall where young locals gather to grab drinks and little snacks. The father-and-son team clearly lists the prices for wine and sandwiches (Mon–Sat 18:00–21:00, closed Sun, located on empty part of square just below courthouse).

Bancogiro (Osteria da Andrea), a simple bar behind the Rialto market, has stark yet powerfully-atmospheric outdoor seating overlooking the Grand Canal. Peruse their wine list and basic menu at the bar (strong local cheeses are *a forte*), order, and grab a table—worth the reasonable cover charge (Tue–Sat 10:30–24:00, closed Mon, less than 200 yards from Rialto Bridge on Campo San Giacometto, San Polo 122, tel. 041-523-2061). Consider their €15 fish and vegetable plate.

Osteria Naranzaria, which shares a prime piece of Grand Canal real estate with Bancogiro next door, is described below, under "Romantic Canalside Settings."

Cicchetterie and Light Meals East of the Rialto Bridge, near Campo San Bartolomeo

Osteria "Alla Botte" Cicchetteria is packed with a young, local, bohemian-jazz clientele. It's good for a *cicchetti* snack with wine at the bar or for a light meal in the small back room—find the posted menus (Fri–Tue 10:00–15:00 & 17:00–23:00, closed Thu and Sun eve, 2 short blocks off Campo San Bartolomeo in the corner behind the statue—down Calle de la Bissa, notice the "day after" photo showing a debris-covered Venice after the notorious 1989 Pink Floyd open-air concert, tel. 041-520-9775).

Rosticceria San Bartolomeo is a cheap—if confusing—self-service restaurant with a likeably surly staff. Take out, grab a table, or munch at the bar (good €6–7 pasta, great fried *mozzarella al prosciutto* for €1.30, delightful fruit salad, and €1 glasses of wine, prices listed on wall behind counter, no cover or service charge, Tue–Sun 9:00–21:30, closed Mon, tel. 041-522-3569). To find this venerable budget eatery, imagine the statue on the Campo San Bartolomeo walking backwards 20 yards, turning left, and going under a passageway—now, follow him.

From Rosticceria San Bartolomeo, continue over a bridge to Campo San Lio. Here, turn left, passing Hotel Canada on your right and following Calle Carminati straight about 50 yards over another bridge. On the left is the pastry shop *(pasticceria)* and straight ahead is Osteria Al Portego (at #6015). Both are listed below:

Pasticceria Ponte delle Paste is a feminine and pastel *salon de tè*, popular for its pastries and pre-dinner drinks. Italians love taking 15-minute breaks to sip a *spritz* aperitif with friends after a long day's work, before heading home. Ask sprightly Monica for a *spritz al bitter* (white wine, *amaro,* and soda water, €1.55; or choose from the menu on the wall) and munch some of the free goodies at the bar around 18:00 (daily 7:00–20:30, Ponte delle Paste).

Osteria al Portego is a friendly, local-style bar—one of the best in town—serving great *cicchetti* and good meals (Mon–Sat 10:30–15:00 & 18:00–22:00, closed Sun, Calle Malvasia 6015, Castello, tel. 041-522-9038). The *cicchetti* here can make a great meal, but you should also consider sitting down for an actual dinner. They have a fine menu.

On or near Campo Santa Maria di Formosa

These eateries can be found on the "Rialto Area Restaurants" map on page 101.

Campo Santa Maria Formosa is a classic Venetian square. For a balmy outdoor meal, have a pizza with wine on the square. **Bar all'Orologio** has a good setting and friendly service but mediocre "freezer" pizza (they're happy to let you split a pizza, Mon–Sat 6:00–23:00, closed Sun). To have a great pizza picnic on the square, cross the bridge behind the canalside *gelateria,* and grab a slice to go from **Cip Ciap Pizza** (Wed–Mon 9:00–21:00, closed Tue; facing *gelateria,* take bridge to the right; Calle del Mondo Novo). For a healthy snack, try the **fruit-and-vegetable stand** next to Campo Santa Maria Formosa's water fountain (Mon–Sat closes at about 19:30, closed Sun). Also on the square, the *gelateria* **Zanzibar** is perhaps too popular with tourists, but it's well-situated and the locals love it (daily 8:00–24:00, in winter 8:00–20:30).

Trattoria agli Artisti is efficient and friendly, with good food, especially the *frutti di mare*—spaghetti with seafood (Thu–Tue dinner from 18:00, closed Wed, half block off square down Ruga Giuffa, tel. 041-277-0029).

Ristorante al Giardinetto has white tablecloths, a formal but fun waitstaff, and a spacious, shady garden under a grape-vine canopy. While it used to be set up for big tour groups—and still feels it—groups no longer come here, and now the dining experience has improved (€9 pastas, €13 main courses, €2 *coperto*, closed Thu, at intersection of Ruga Giuffa and Calle Corona, tel. 041-528-5332).

Osteria alle Testiere is my most gourmet recommendation in Venice. Hugely respected, they are passionate about quality, serving up creative, artfully-presented market-fresh seafood (there's no meat on the menu) and fine wine in what the chef calls a "Venetian Nouvel" style. Reservations are required for their three daily sittings: 12:30, 19:00 and 21:15. With only 22 seats, it's tight and homey yet elegant (€15 pastas, €24 *secondi*, plan on spending €50 for dinner, closed Sun–Mon, Calle del Mondo Novo, tel. 041-522-7220).

Osteria al Mascaron is where I've come for 20 years to watch Gigi and his food-loving band of ruffians dish up rustic-yet-sumptuous pastas with steamy seafood (€13) to salivating local foodies. The €15 *antipasto misto* plate and two glasses of wine make a wonderful light meal (a block past Campo Santa Maria Formosa at Calle Longa Santa Maria Formosa 5225, tel. 041-522-5995).

In Dorsoduro

Near the Accademia

For locations, see the map on page 107.

Ristorante/Pizzeria Accademia Foscarini, next to the Accademia Bridge and Galleria, offers decent €7–8 pizzas in a great canalside setting. This place is both scenic and practical—I grab a quick lunch here on each visit to Venice (Wed–Mon 9:00–21:00 in summer, until 20:00 in winter, closed Tue, Dorsoduro 878C, tel. 041-522-7281).

Enoteca Cantine del Vino Gia Schiavi is much loved for its €1 *cicchetti*. It's also a good place for a €2 glass of wine and appetizers (Mon–Sat 8:00–20:30, closed Sun, 100 yards from Accademia Gallery on San Trovaso canal; facing Accademia, take a right and then a forced left at canal to the 2nd bridge—S. Trovaso 992, tel. 041-523-0034). You're welcome to enjoy your wine and finger food while sitting on the bridge.

Ai Gondolieri is considered one of the best restaurants for meat—not fish—in Venice. Its sauces are heavy and prices are high, but gourmet carnivores love it (€17 pastas, €25 *secondi*, €5 cover, Wed–Mon 12:00–15:00 & 19:00–22:00, closed Tue, closed for lunch July–Aug, reservations smart, Dorsoduro 366 San Vio, behind Peggy Guggenheim Collection on west end of Rio delle Torreselle, tel. 041-528-6396).

Near Campo San Barnaba

A number of less-touristed restaurants cluster around this small square. From the Accademia, head northwest, following the curve of the Grand Canal. In five minutes, you'll spill out onto Campo San Barnaba (and the nearby Campo Santa Margherita). Follow the straight and narrow path (Calle Lunga San Barnaba) west of the square for more restaurants.

Casin dei Nobili (Pleasure Palace of Nobles) has a diverse, reasonably-priced menu in a high-energy, informal, modern setting. The patio is filled with simple tables, happy tourists, and their inviting €10 daily specials (closed Mon, a half-block south of Campo San Barnaba, tel. 041-241-1841).

Ai Quattro Feri is a noisy, bustling, trattoria-style eatery, best for its catch-of-the-day seafood, especially the excellent grilled fish (€8 pastas, €12 *secondi*, closed Sun, just off the square on Calle Lunga San Barnaba 2757, tel. 041-520-6978).

Enoteca e Trattoria la Bitta, dark and woody, with a forgettable back patio, serves nicely-presented, traditional Venetian food with—proudly—no fish. Their small menu is clearly focused

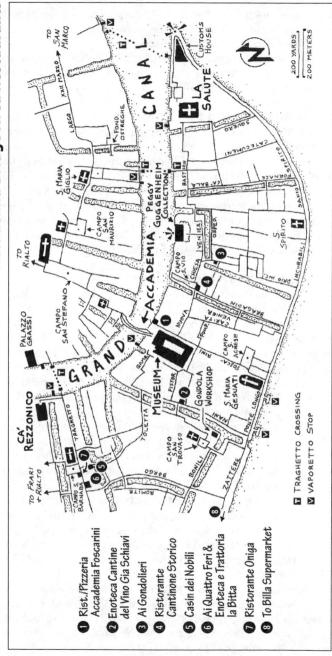

Accademia Bridge Area Restaurants

1. Rist./Pizzeria Accademia Foscarini
2. Enoteca Cantine del Vino Gia Schiavi
3. Ai Gondolieri
4. Ristorante Cantinone Storico
5. Casin dei Nobili
6. Ai Quattro Feri & Enoteca e Trattoria la Bitta
7. Ristorante Oniga
8. To Billa Supermarket

🔲 TRAGHETTO CROSSING
🔽 VAPORETTO STOP

on quality cooking (€9 pastas, €14 *secondi*, dinner only, Mon–Sat 18:30–23:00, closed Sun, cash only, next to Quattro Feri on Calle Lunga San Barnaba, tel. 041-523-0531).

Ristorante Oniga, right on Campo San Barnaba, is a wine bar/restaurant serving up Italian cuisine with a modern twist (closed Tue, tel. 041-522-4410).

On or near Campo San Polo

Antica Birraria la Corte is an everyday eatery on the very special Campo San Polo. Enjoy a pizza or simple meal on the far side of one of this great, homey, children-filled square (daily 12:00–14:30 & 19:00–22:30, on the way to Frari Church, Calle di Mezo 2168, San Polo, tel. 041-275-0570).

La Rivetta Ristorante offers a canalside setting and well-priced Venetian cuisine. Consider *spaghetti al nero di seppie* (spaghetti in squid ink) or *fegato alla Veneziana* (calf liver and onions; open daily, Calle di Mezo 1479, San Polo).

Romantic Canalside Settings

Of course, if you want a canal view, it comes with lower quality or a higher price. But the memory is sometimes most important.

At **Trattoria da Giorgio ai Greci,** a few blocks behind St. Mark's, Giorgio and sons Robert and Davide serve homemade pastas and fresh seafood. While they have inside seating, you come here for the canalside dining—it's the best I've found anywhere in town. Call to reserve a canalside table (€20 tourist menu, daily 12:00–24:00, closed Mon in winter, 2 canals east of St. Mark's on Ponte dei Greci 4988, tel. 041-528-9780).

Osteria Naranzaria is one of two wonderful eateries (Bancogiro, next door, is listed on page 104) on the Grand Canal between the market and the Rialto Bridge. Somehow they've taken a stretch of unbeatable but overlooked canalfront property and filled it with trendy candlelit tables. Stefano Monti loves sushi, and since Venice was the gateway to the Orient (remember Marco Polo), he includes it on his simple menu, along with coldcuts and fine wine. Peasants can take their glasses to the steps along the canal for bar prices, but the romantic table service doesn't cost that much extra. This is the best-value Grand Canal eatery I've found (closed Mon, tel. 041-724-1035).

Ristorante Cantinone Storico sits on a peaceful canal in Dorsoduro between the Accademia Bridge and the Peggy Guggenheim Collection. It's dressy, specializes in fish and traditional Venetian dishes, has six or eight tables on the canal, and is worth the splurge (€15 pasta, €20 *secondi*, €3 cover, Mon–Sat 12:30–14:30 & 19:30–21:30, closed Sun, be wise and make reservations, on the canal Rio de S. Vio, tel. 041-523-9577).

Rialto Bridge Tourist Traps: Locals are embarrassed by the lousy food and aggressive "service" of the string of joints dominating the best romantic Grand Canal real estate in town. Still, if you want to linger over dinner with a view of the most famous bridge and the romantic song of gondoliers oaring by (and don't mind eating with other tourists), this can be enjoyable. Don't trust the waiter's recommendations for special meals. Just get a simple pizza or pasta and a drink for €12, and you'll savor the ambience without getting ripped off.

Near St. Mark's Square

For the locations of these restaurants, see the "St. Mark's Square" map on page 68.

Osteria Enoteca San Marco offers beautifully-presented "creative new Italian" cuisine with a mod ambience in a classic medieval shell. They proudly offer fine wine by the glass. This place is pricey but the food is always top quality (€20 meals, Mon–Sat 12:30–23:00, closed Sun, a long block west of St. Mark's Square at Frezzeria 1610, tel. 041-528-5242, Carlo and his white-aproned army speak English).

At **Salad and Juice Bar Oasi 2000,** hardworking, English-speaking Paco serves big salads, sandwiches, and fresh-squeezed juice in a student cantina atmosphere just behind St. Mark's Basilica (Mon–Sat 8:00–19:00, closed Sun, off Calle San Provolo at Calle di Albanesi 4263, tel. 041-528-9937).

Trattoria alla Rivetta is a high-spirited hole-in-the-wall popular with gondoliers at lunch and mobbed with tourists at dinner. Even if they treat tourists as second-class eaters, pasta here for lunch is both a great meal and a great memory (just behind St. Mark's Basilica at the Ponte San Provolo bridge between Campo S.S. Filippo e Giacomo and Campo S. Provolo, tel. 041-528-7302). They also have bar munchies—see the *Prezzi al banco* price list on the wall by the bar.

Antica Sacrestia, a local institution, has à la carte choices and several different fixed-price menus: vegetarian, Venetian, tourist, seafood, fine pizza, and house specialties. I like the antipasto buffet. You can help the waiter construct your €14.50 plate with all the local goodies, including great seafood, and call it a meal (Tue–Sun 12:00–15:00 & 18:30–22:30, closed Mon, on Calle della Sacrestia 4442, 2 blocks behind St. Mark's, tel. 041-523-0749, www.anticasacrestia.com).

Trattoria da Remigio is well-known for high-quality, serious Venetian cuisine. Its indoors-only setting is a bit dressy, with a mix of tourists and locals and lots of commotion (Wed–Sun lunch from 12:30, dinner from 19:30, closed Mon–Tue, just past Rio dei Greci on a tiny square at the end of Calle Madonna, tel. 041-523-0089).

The **cafés on St. Mark's Square** offer music, inflated prices, and an unbeatable setting for a drink or light meal (for a description, see page 87).

Near the Train Station, in Cannaregio

For fast, cheap food near the station, consider **Brek,** a popular self-service cafeteria (after serving breakfast, it's open daily 11:30–22:00; with back to station, facing canal, go left on Rio Terra—it becomes Lista di Spagna in 2 short blocks, Lista di Spagna 124, tel. 041-244-0158).

Eating Elsewhere

Trattoria Pizzeria Nono Risorto is unpretentious, inexpensive, youthful, and famous for some of the best pizza in town. You'll sit in a gravelly garden, under a leafy canopy, surrounded by a young, enthusiastic waitstaff and Italian speakers enjoying huge salads, €9 pastas, and delicious €8 pizzas (€14 *secondi*, Wed–Mon 12:00–14:30 & 19:00–23:00, closed Tue; a 3-min walk from the Rialto fish market, find Campo San Cassiano and it's just over the bridge on Sotoportego de Siora Bettina; tel. 041-524-1169).

Osteria al Bacco, far beyond the crowds in a rustic Venetian setting, is worth the hike for its local cuisine (€35 for 3 courses and wine, Tue–Sun 12:00–14:00 & 19:00–22:00, closed Mon, reservations recommended, halfway between train station and northernmost tip of Venice, Fondamenta Cappuccine, Cannaregio 3054, tel. 041-717-493).

Osteria la Zucca, on the Rio del Megio canal, is hardworking, homey, and away from the crowds. You'll get good, typical Venetian cuisine at a moderate price (€20 meals, Mon–Sat 12:30–14:30 for lunch, dinner guests usually have 2 seating choices—19:00 or 21:00, closed Sun, mostly indoors, reserve for canal windows, a few outdoor tables with one on the canal, midway between train station and Rialto Bridge at San Giacomo dell'Orio 1762, Calle Larga, Santa Croce, tel. 041-524-1570). A short block away is the square called San Giacomo dell'Orio—a breezy scene with trees, families at play, and a couple of simple trattorias offering basic food and classic non-touristy outdoor seating.

Cheap Meals

A key to cheap eating in Venice is **bar snacks** (see page 102), especially stand-up mini-meals in out-of-the-way bars. Order by pointing. *Panini* (sandwiches) are sold fast and cheap at bars everywhere. Basic reliable ham-and-cheese sandwiches (white bread, crusts trimmed) come toasted—simply ask for "toast"; these make a great supplement to Venice's skimpy hotel breakfasts.

For budget eating, I like small *cicchetti* **bars** (see page 102). For speed, value, and ambience, you can get a filling plate of local appetizers at nearly any of the bars.

Pizzerias are cheap and easy—try for a sidewalk table at a scenic location.

Pizzeria l'Angelo serves up piping-hot pizza by the slice for under €2 or whole pizzas to go. Grab a beer or a soda and find a bench in nearby Campo Manin or Campo Sant'Angelo (Tue–Sun 11:30–22:00, Mon 11:30–16:00, Calle della Mandola 3711, tel. 041-277-1126). **Al Vaporetto Self-Service,** just across the street, is bright, efficient, and forgettable (€5 pastas, €6 *secondi*, Calle della Mandola). **Spizzico** is a cheap fast-food pizza shop on Campo San Luca. Here's a chance to compare American and Italian fast food—there's a Burger King nearby (between St. Mark's Square and the Rialto Bridge).

The **produce market** that sprawls for a few blocks just past the Rialto Bridge is a great place to assemble a picnic (best Mon–Sat 8:00–13:00, closed Sun). The adjacent fish market is wonderfully slimy. Side lanes in this area are speckled with fine little hole-in-the-wall munchie bars, bakeries, and cheese shops.

Gelato

For locations of first two places, see the "Rialto Area Restaurants" map on page 101. For the last place, see the "St. Mark's Square" map on page 68.

La Boutique del Gelato is considered the best *gelateria* in Venice (daily 10:00–20:30, closed Dec–Jan, 2 blocks off Campo Santa Maria Formosa on corner of Salizada San Lio and Calle Paradiso, next to Hotel Bruno, at #5727—just look for the crowd).

Late-Night Gelato: At the Rialto, try **Michielangelo,** just off Campo San Bartolomeo, on the St. Mark's side of the Rialto Bridge on Salizada Pio X (daily 10:00–23:00). At St. Mark's Square, the **Al Todaro** *gelateria* opposite the Doge's Palace is open late (daily 8:00–22:00, closes at 20:00 and on Mon in winter).

TRANSPORTATION CONNECTIONS

The train station can be crowded with long lines to buy train tickets, supplements, and *cuccetta* reservations. Consider taking care of these tasks at downtown travel agencies—such as Kele & Teo Viaggi e Turismo (see page 55). The cost is the same, the lines and language barrier are smaller, and you'll save time.

From Venice by Train to: Padua (3–5/hr, 30 min), **Vicenza** (2/hr, 1 hr), **Verona** (1/hr, 90 min), **Ravenna** (1/hr, 3–4 hrs, transfer in Ferrara or Bologna), **Florence** (9/day, 3 hrs), **Dolomites** (8/day to

Bolzano, about hrly, 4 hrs with 1 transfer; catch bus from Bolzano into mountains), **Milan** (1/hr, 3–4 hrs), **Monterosso/La Spezia/Cinque Terre** (2/day, 6 hrs, departs Venice at 10:00 and 15:00), **Rome** (8/day, 5 hrs, slower overnight), **Naples** (3/day, more with change in Rome, about 8–9 hrs), **Brindisi** (3/day, 11 hrs, change in Bologna), **Bern** (3/day, change in Milan, 8 hrs), **Munich** (2/day, 8 hrs), **Paris** (4/day, 11 hrs), and **Vienna** (3/day, 9 hrs).

Venice Airport

Venice's sleek, modern airport on the mainland, six miles north of the city, has a new wood-beam-and-glass terminal, with a TI, cash machines, car-rental agencies, and a few shops and eateries (airport info: tel. 041-260-9240). Check with your hotel or in *Un Ospite di Venezia* (the free tourist information guide from the TI and many hotels) for phone numbers and Web sites for all airlines serving Marco Polo and nearby airports.

There are three ways for you to get from the airport to downtown Venice (all covered below): speedboat, water taxi, and bus (to Venice with vaporetto connection).

If you're taking a boat from Venice to the airport, note that the dock and terminal—a 15-minute walk apart—are connected by a **free shuttle bus**. Airport-bound travelers unnecessarily stress and worry over this bus. Here's why: When your boat arrives, there may be no shuttle bus in sight, only taxi con-men, scaring travelers—nervous about catching their flights—into hiring their cabs (for a fortune). Don't believe them. There is always a free airport bus shuttling back and forth between the dock and the nearby check-in counters. While many travelers are advised to get to the airport two or more hours before departure (even for flights within Europe), I usually arrive about an hour before take-off and manage fine.

The **Alilaguna speedboat,** while not terribly speedy (making 3–4 stops in the lagoon as it sputters along), is the simplest transportation to and from downtown Venice (€10, 2/hr, 70 min, runs 6:15–24:00 from airport, generally departs airport at about :10 and :40 after the hour; runs 4:20–22:50 from Venice starting in Zattere, the Dorsoduro hotels; continues to San Marco/Giardinetti; tel. 041-523-5775, www.alilaguna.com). Another Alilaguna line goes between the airport and Fondamenta Nuove (€5, 40 min). Pick up a free schedule (or buy tickets) at the Alilaguna kiosk at the airport (far left of the arrivals hall as you exit baggage claim) or at any vaporetto stop which has Alilaguna service. You can also purchase tickets on board.

A **water taxi** zips directly between the airport and your hotel in 30 minutes for €80. While pricey, a small group may find it a smart investment—especially for an early departure.

The blue ATVO **shuttle buses** connect the airport and the Piazzale Roma vaporetto stop (€3, 2/hr, 20 min, 8:20–24:00 from airport, 5:30–20:40 to airport, schedule listed in *Un Ospite di Venezia*, www.atvo.it). The cheaper orange ACTV **bus** #5 also links the airport with Piazzale Roma (€2, 2/hr, 30–40 min; from airport to Piazzale Roma departs Mon–Sat at 5:25 and 6:07, then every 30 minutes at :05 and :35 past the hour until 20:05; Sun 1/hr from 7:05–20:05 at :05 past the hour; from Piazzale Roma to airport departing generally at :10 and :40 past the hour; confirm times at TI or airport).

NEAR VENICE

Padua, Vicenza, Verona, and Ravenna

While Venice is just one of many towns in the Italian region of Veneto (VEN-eh-toh), few venture off the lagoon. Four important towns and possible side trips, in addition to the lakes and the Dolomites, make zipping directly from Venice to Milan (or Florence) a route strewn with temptation.

Planning Your Time

The towns of Padua, Vicenza, Verona, and Ravenna are all, for various reasons, good stops. Each town gives the visitor a low-key slice of Italy that complements the urbanity of Venice, Florence, and Rome.

Visiting Verona, Padua, and Vicenza couldn't be easier: All are 30 minutes apart on the Venice–Milan line (hrly, 3 hrs). Spending a day town-hopping between Venice and Milan—with three-hour stops at Padua, Vicenza, and Verona—is exciting and efficient. Trains run frequently enough to allow flexibility and little wasted time. Of the towns included in this chapter, only Ravenna (2.5 hours from Padua or Florence) is not on the main Venice–Milan train line.

If you're Padua-bound, note that you need to reserve ahead to see the Scrovegni Chapel (see page 122). Most sights in Verona and Vicenza are closed on Monday.

Padua

Living under Venetian rule for four centuries seemed only to sharpen Padua's independent spirit. Nicknamed "the brain of Veneto," Padua (Padova) has a prestigious university (founded

Towns near Venice

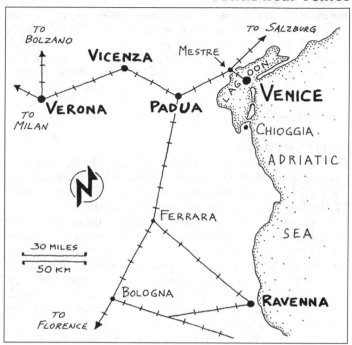

1222) that hosted Galileo, Copernicus, Dante, and Petrarch. The old town, even when packed with modern-day students, is a colonnaded time-tunnel experience. And Padua's museums and churches hold their own in Italy's artistic big league.

Even with all this, locals will tell you that Padua is a city with three "withouts": a saint without a name (since St. Anthony is merely referred to as the Saint), a field without grass (because the large square, Prato della Valle, is not a field as the word *prato* implies), and a café without doors (for in days past, Caffè Pedrocchi kept its doors open all day and all night).

ORIENTATION

Padua's main tourist sights lie on a north-south axis through the heart of the city: from the train station to Scrovegni Chapel to the market squares (the center of town) to the Basilica of St. Anthony. It's roughly a 10-minute walk between each of these sights, or about 30 minutes from end to end.

Tourist Information

The main TI, in the train station, is a good place to pick up a list of sights and a map upon arrival in Padua (Mon–Sat 9:30–18:30, Sun 9:30–12:30, shorter hours in winter, tel. 049-875-2077, infostazione@turismopadova.it). Another TI is located in an alley west of Caffè Pedrocchi (daily 9:00–13:30 & 15:00–19:00, tel. 049-875-2077). A third, seasonal TI shares a square with the Basilica of St. Anthony (April–Oct Mon–Sat 9:30–13:30 & 15:00–19:00, Sun 9:30–12:00 & 15:00–18:00, closed Nov–March).

Arrival in Padua

The baggage deposit office (€3.90, daily 6:00–21:30, bring your passport) is outside the train station lobby, under the colonnade—exit the lobby on the far right, just past an ATM and the main TI. Inside the station lobby, near the same far right exit, is a small office marked Bus Tickets, which sells city bus tickets (€0.85, also available at the *tabacchi* shop at the far right and at newsstands). Beyond the baggage deposit is a post office (Mon–Fri 8:30–14:00, Sat 8:30–13:00, closed Sun). If you have any train business, such as reservations, note that a travel agency, Leonardi Viaggi-Turismo, is half a block up the main drag in front of the station, on the left side of the street (Mon–Fri 9:00–19:00, Sat 9:00–13:00, closed Sun, Corso del Popolo 14, tel. 049-650-455).

Buses leave from in front of the station. Buses #3, #8, #12, and #18 go through town to the Basilica of St. Anthony (called "Santo" locally), departing from platform *(corsia)* #3. Get off at the end of Via Umberto I, just before Prato della Valle. If you're not sure where to get off, ask the driver, "Santo?" Due to pedestrian and car traffic, this relatively short distance can take 20 minutes. A taxi from the station into town costs about €5.

Helpful Hints

Festival Day: The Feast Day of St. Anthony, the town's patron saint, is celebrated on June 13, when many stores, restaurants, and sights (including the university) are closed.

Internet Access: Oddly for a college town, Padua has few Internet cafés. Internet Point is on Via Altinate (Mon–Sat 10:00–1:00, Sun 16:00–24:00, about 300 yards east of Piazza Garibaldi and Porta Altinate at #145, tel. 049-659-292).

Padua in Four Hours

Day-trippers can do a quick but enjoyable blitz of Padua—including a visit to the Scrovegni Chapel—in four hours. Your Scrovegni Chapel reservation will dictate the order of your sightseeing; see the booking procedure below.

Here's one possible plan: Take the bus from the train station to

Padua

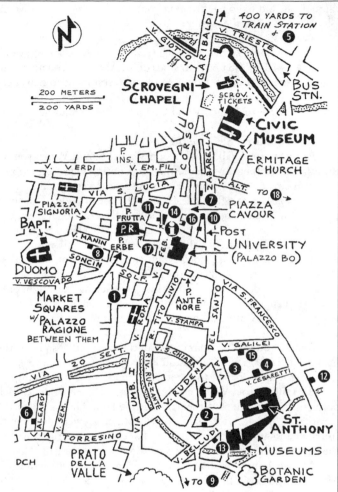

1 Majestic Hotel Toscanelli

2 Hotel al Fagiano

3 Hotel al Santo

4 Casa del Pellegrino Hotel & Rist.

5 To Hotel Grand'Italia, Hotel Monaco & Hotel al Cason

6 Ostello Città di Padova

7 La Cova Rist./Pizzeria

8 Marechiaro Pizzeria/Tratt.

9 To Zairo Ristorante/Pizzeria

10 Brek Cafeteria

11 Isola di Caprera Rist.

12 Gastro. San Francesco

13 Pollodoro la Gastro.

14 Caffè Pedrocchi

15 Pago Pago Pizzeria

16 PAM Supermarket

17 Bridge Entrance to Palazzo della Ragione

18 To Internet Point

the Basilica of St. Anthony at the south end of town, then walk back through the old town, sightseeing your way back to the Scrovegni Chapel, then on to the station.

Ready, set, go...

At zero hour: Arrive at Padua train station, check bags, catch bus #3, #8, #12, or #18 to the Basilica of St. Anthony. You may want to grab a take-out lunch from one of the recommended delis near the basilica and picnic in the peaceful cloisters. Note that parts of the basilica—the Sacristy and Chapel of the Reliquaries—close during lunch.

At 30 minutes: Sightsee the basilica.

At one hour: Walk north along Via del Santo. When you hit the wall, turn left onto Via San Francesco, noting Piazza Antenore's medieval sarcophagus on your left. Across the street from the piazza is a replica of Venice's gothic Ca' d'Oro (House of Gold). Continue on Via San Francesco, passing Feltrinelli International's English bookstore (Mon–Sat 9:00–13:00 & 15:30–19:30, closed Sun, under the porticos on your left) and arriving at Via VIII Febbraio.

Time to make a decision. To hit the markets first before they start to close (around 13:30), continue forward on Via San Francesco to reach Piazza delle Erbe. To continue sightseeing, turn right onto Via VIII Febbraio—the next square you'll reach has Palazzo del Bo (University), Caffè Pedrocchi, and the entrance to Palazzo della Ragione.

At 1:15 hours: Visit your choice of the two market squares, the Palazzo della Ragione, Caffè, and University. (Or go immediately to the Scrovegni Chapel, then return here for more sightseeing.)

At 1:50 hours: Walk north on Via VIII Febbraio (which becomes Via Cavour and then traffic-filled Via Garibaldi) to the Scrovegni Chapel. After Piazza Garibaldi, cross over one street to the right and head north again. The chapel is on your right, within the gardens of the old Roman Arena (don't overshoot it).

At two hours: Sightsee the Multimedia Room and Civic Museum, and get in line five minutes early for the Chapel.

At three hours: Visit the Scrovegni Chapel.

At 3:30 hours: Walk north to the train station (10–15 min) and reclaim your baggage.

At four hours: Catch your train. Ahhhh.

SIGHTS

▲▲**Basilica of St. Anthony**—Friar Anthony of Padua (1195–1231), "Christ's perfect follower and a tireless preacher of the Gospel," is buried here. For nearly 800 years, his remains and this impressive Romanesque Gothic church (building started immediately after the death of the saint in 1231) have attracted pilgrims to Padua

St. Anthony of Padua
(1195–1231)

Perhaps Christendom's most popular saint, Anthony is known as a powerful speaker, a miracle worker, and the finder of lost articles.

Born in Lisbon to a rich, well-educated family, his life changed at age 25, when he saw the mutilated bodies of some Franciscan martyrs. Their sacrifice inspired him to join the poor Franciscans and dedicate his life to Christ. He moved to Italy and lived in a cave, studying, meditating, and barely speaking to anyone.

One day, he joined his fellow monks for a service. The appointed speaker failed to show up, so Anthony was asked to say a few off-the-cuff words to the crowd. He started slowly but, filled with the Spirit, he became more confident and amazed the audience with his eloquence. Up in Assisi, St. Francis heard about Anthony and sent him on a whirlwind speaking tour.

Anthony had a strong voice, knew several languages, had encyclopedic knowledge of theology, and could speak spontaneously as the Spirit moved him. It's said he even stood on the shores of the Adriatic Sea in Rimini and enticed a school of fish to listen. Anthony also was known as a miracle worker—healing a sick horse, protecting a crowd from the rain, and making poisoned food harmless.

In 1230, Anthony retired to Padua, where he founded a monastery and initiated reforms for the poor. An illness cut off his life at age 36. Anthony once said: "Happy is the man whose words issue from the Spirit and not from himself!"

(daily in summer 6:30–19:45, in winter 6:30–19:00, modest dress code enforced). There is a helpful information desk with Anthony-related pamphlets in the cloisters (along with public WCs), located on the right side of the church (info desk open daily 8:30–13:00 & 14:00–18:30). To find English versions of the pamphlets—one on the saint's life and another about the basilica—head to the Chapel of the Reliquaries and offer a donation.

On the square in front of the church you'll find a handy **TI** (April–Oct Mon–Sat 9:30–13:30 & 15:00–19:00, Sun 9:30–12:00 & 15:00–18:00, closed Nov–March) and a couple of friendly cafés. (A 10-min stroll north up Via del Santo will take you back into the center of town.)

Exterior of Basilica: Nod to St. Anthony, who looks down from the red-brick facade and blesses us. He holds a book, a symbol of all the knowledge he accumulated as a quiet monk before his famous preaching career.

Guarding the church is Donatello's life-size equestrian statue of the Venetian mercenary general, Gattamelata. Though it looks like a thousand other man-on-a-horse statues, it was a landmark in Italy's budding Renaissance—the first life-size, secular, equestrian statue cast out of bronze in a thousand years.

Interior: Entering the basilica, gaze down the nave, past the crowds and through the incense haze, to Donatello's glorious crucifix arising from the altar, and realize this is one of the most important pilgrimage sites in Christendom.

Along with the crucifix, Donatello's bronze statues—Mary with Padua's six favorite saints—grace the high altar. Late in his career, the great Florentine sculptor spent a decade in Padua (c. 1444–1455), creating the altar and Gattamelata.

St. Anthony's Tomb (left side of nave): Pilgrims file slowly by the chapel containing St. Anthony's tomb. Nine marble reliefs, showing scenes and miracles from the life of the saint, circle this Renaissance masterwork from 1500.

As you enter the chapel, the first relief on the left depicts St. Anthony receiving the Franciscan habit. In the next, Anthony's compassion miraculously revives a woman stabbed to death by her jealous husband. Notice the etchings of familiar Paduan architecture at the top of the sculptures; in the third panel, the building with the keel-shaped roof is Palazzo della Ragione. On the back wall of the chapel, look for the miracle of the miser's heart. Anthony dips his hand into a moneylender's side to demonstrate the absence of his heart ("for where your treasure is, there your heart will be also"), which miraculously appeared in the dead man's treasure chest.

The next relief shows Anthony holding the foot of a young man who confessed to kicking his mother. Upon hearing of this act, Anthony declared that anyone so disrespectful to his mother ought to have his foot cut off. The boy took Anthony's word literally. His hysterical mother implored Anthony's help, and Anthony's prayers to God enabled him to reattach the foot.

The pilgrims believe Anthony is their protector—a confidant and intercessor of the poor. And they believe he works miracles. The faithful place offerings, votives, and prayers to ask for help or to give thanks for miracles they believe he's performed. By putting their hand on his tomb while saying a silent prayer, pilgrims show devotion to Anthony and feel the saint's presence.

Popular Anthony is the patron saint of dozens of things: of travelers, amputees, donkeys, pregnant women, sterile women, stewardesses, and pig farmers. Most pilgrims ask for his help in his role as the "finder of things"—from lost car keys to a life companion.

Chapel of the Reliquaries: This chapel sits toward the back of the basilica, in the apse. The most prized relic is in the glass case at center stage—Anthony's tongue. When Anthony's remains were exhumed thirty years after his death (1263), his body had decayed to dust, but his tongue was found miraculously unspoiled and red in color. How appropriate for the multilinguist who, full of the Spirit, couldn't stop talking about God (daily 7:00–12:45 & 14:30–19:30, shorter hours in winter, at far end of the church on the left side of the apse behind the altar).

Working clockwise around the curved chapel, start in front of the staircase at St. Anthony's holy, and holey, tunic *(tonaca)*. Using an imaginary clock, his coffin is at nine o'clock. His pillow—a comfy rock—is up the stairs. The center display case contains (top to bottom) the Saint's lower jaw *(il mento)*, his uncorrupted tongue *(lingua)*, and finally, his vocal chords (*apparato vocale*, discovered intact when his remains were examined in 1981). In the last display case, fragments of the True Cross *(la croce)* are held in a precious crucifix reliquary.

Cloisters: From the right side of the nave as you face the altar, follow signs to *chiostro;* from outside, find signs on the right side of the church.

Wander around the various cloisters. Picnic tables invite pilgrims and tourists to enjoy meals within the solitude of one of the cloisters (it's covered and suitable even when rainy, WCs in same cloister). In the far end, a fascinating little museum is filled with votives and folk art recounting miracles attributed to Anthony.

Prato della Valle—The so-called "field without grass" is 150 yards southwest of the basilica (down Via Luca Belludi). Once a Roman theater and later Anthony's preaching grounds, this square claims to be the largest in Italy. It's a pleasant 400-yard-long, oval-shaped piazza with fountains, walkways, dozens of statues of Padua's eminent citizens, and (yes) grass.

Orto Botanico—Green thumbs appreciate this botanical garden, which contains the university's vast collection of rare plants. It was founded in 1545 by the Faculty of Medicine to cultivate medicinal plants (€4, daily April–Oct 9:00–13:00 & 15:00–18:00, March–Nov Mon–Sat 9:00–13:00, closed Sun, entrance 150 yards south of Basilica of St. Anthony; with your back to the facade, take a hard left). A visitors center—in a little cottage, past the garden's entrance then to the right—houses models of the garden's layout and computer programs that describe the history and composition of the garden in English (same hours as the garden). WCs are just outside the visitors center, in the neighboring building.

▲▲▲**Scrovegni Chapel (Cappella degli Scrovegni)**—Reserve in advance to see this glorious, recently renovated chapel, wallpapered with Giotto's beautifully preserved cycle of nearly 40 frescoes, depicting scenes from the lives of Jesus and Mary.

Painted by Giotto and his assistants from 1303 to 1305, and

considered by many to be the first piece of modern art, this work makes it clear: Europe was breaking out of the Middle Ages. A sign of the Renaissance to come, Giotto placed real people in real scenes, expressing real human emotions. These frescoes were radical for their 3-D nature, lively colors, light sources, emotion, and humanism.

The chapel was built out of guilt for white-collar crimes. Reginaldo degli Scrovegni charged sky-high interest rates at a time when that practice was forbidden by the church. He even caught the attention of Dante, who placed him in one of the levels of hell in his *Inferno*. When Reginaldo died, the Church denied him a Christian burial. His son Enrico tried to buy forgiveness for his father's sins by building this superb chapel. After seeing Giotto's frescoes for the Franciscan monks of St. Anthony, Enrico knew he'd found the right artist to decorate the interior.

Cost and Hours: €12 entry fee for 15-minute visits includes Civic Museum and Multimedia Room (both described below); in summer after 19:00, 15-minute visits are €8 and 30-minute visits are €12 (visits don't include Civic Museum, which is closed then). The chapel is open daily 9:00–22:00 in summer, until 19:00 in off-season (people are allowed in every 15 min at :00, :15, :30, and :45 past the hour during the day, every half hour in eve, last entry 15 min before closing). The Multimedia Room has the same hours as the chapel.

Booking Your Reservation: To protect the paintings from excess humidity, only 25 people are allowed in the chapel at a time for a 15-minute visit. Reservations are obligatory (booking office open Mon–Fri 9:00–19:00, Sat 9:00–18:00, closed Sun, provide telephone number where you can be reached the day before, call 049-201-0020 or reserve online at www.cappelladegliscrovegni.it).

Book your visit at least 24 hours in advance; earlier is better to guarantee a spot. It's sometimes possible to buy a ticket for the same day at the ticket office, but don't count on it. If you book in person at the ticket office, you can pay cash rather than use a credit card. Visits scheduled after 19:00 are only €8 for a standard 15-minute visit, or you can stay in the chapel for a full 30 minutes for €12. The last booking for a 30-minute visit is at 21:45.

Pick up your tickets at the ticket office at least an hour before your visit (30 minutes early or up to the day before for 9:00 visits; present your booking receipt with online reservations) and be at the chapel doors (well-signed, 100 yards to the right of the ticket office as you exit) at least five minutes before your scheduled visit. The doors to the chapel are automatic and if you are even a minute late, you'll forfeit your visit and have to rebook and repay to enter.

At your appointed time, you first enter an anteroom to watch a 15-minute video (with English subtitles) and to establish humidity levels before continuing into the chapel (no photos are allowed).

Giotto di Bondone
(c. 1267–1337)

Though details of his life are extremely sketchy, we know that as a 12-year-old shepherd boy, Giotto was discovered painting pictures of his father's sheep on rock slabs. He became the wealthiest and most famous painter of his day. His achievement is especially remarkable, since painters at that time weren't considered anything more than craftsmen and weren't expected to be innovators.

After making a name for himself painting the life of St. Francis frescoes in Assisi, the Florentine tackled the Scrovegni Chapel (c. 1303–1305). At age 35, he was at the height of his powers. His scenes were more realistic and human than anything done for a thousand years. Giotto didn't learn technique by dissecting corpses or studying the mathematics of 3-D perspective. But he had innate talent, and his personality shines through in the humanity of his art.

The Scrovegni frescoes break ground by introducing nature—rocks, trees, animals—as a backdrop for religious scenes. Giotto's people, with their voluminous, deeply creased robes, are as sturdy and massive as Greek statues, a throwback to the Byzantine icon art of the Middle Ages. But these figures exude stage presence. Their gestures are simple but expressive: A head tilted down says dejection, an arm flung out is grief, clasped hands are hope. Giotto created his figures not just by drawing an outline and filling it in with a single color, but as a patchwork of lighter and darker shades, pioneering modern modeling techniques. Giotto's storytelling style is straightforward, and anyone with knowledge of the episodes of Jesus' life can read the chapel like a comic book.

The Scrovegni represents a turning point in European art and culture—away from scenes of heaven and toward a more down-to-earth, human-centered view.

Although you have only a short visit inside the chapel, it's divine. You're inside a Giotto time capsule, looking back at an artist ahead of his time.

Giotto's Frescoes in the Scrovegni Chapel: As you enter the long, narrow chapel, look down to the far end—the wall covered with Giotto's big *Last Judgment*. Christ in a bubble is flanked by crowds of saints and by scenes of heaven and hell. This is the final, climactic scene of the story told in the chapel's 38 panels—the story of Jesus and his mother Mary.

The story begins on the long north wall (with the windows) in the upper left corner. A priest scolds the man who will be Mary's father (Joachim, with the halo) and kicks him out of the Temple for the sin of being childless. In the next panel to the right, Joachim returns dejectedly to his sheep farm. Meanwhile (next panel), his wife is in the bedroom, hearing the miraculous news that their prayers have been answered—she'll give birth to Mary, the mother of Jesus.

From this humble start, the story of Mary and Jesus spirals clockwise around the chapel, from top to bottom. The top row (both north and south walls) covers Mary's life.

Jesus enters the picture in the center of the north (windowed) wall with his birth in a manger, the visit by the Magi, Presentation in the Temple, the Flight into Egypt, and so on. Spinning clockwise, you see Jesus being baptized, performing miracles, etc. Finally, Jesus is betrayed with a kiss (middle of north wall, bottom row), and is tried, humiliated, whipped, crucified, and buried. He ascends to heaven, where (on the big west wall) he reigns at the Last Judgment. The whole story unfolds beneath the blue, starry sky on the ceiling.

Some panels deserve a closer look:

Joachim Returns to the Sheepfold (north wall, upper left, second panel): Though difficult to appreciate from ground level, this oft-reproduced scene is groundbreaking. Giotto—a former shepherd himself—uses nature as a stage set, setting the scene in front of a backdrop of real-life mountains, and adding down-home details like Joachim's jumping dog, frozen in mid-air.

Betrayal of Christ, a.k.a. *Il Bacio,* "The Kiss" (north wall, bottom row, middle panel): Amid the crowded chaos of Jesus' arrest, Giotto focuses our eye on the central action, where Judas ensnares Jesus in his yellow robe (the color symbolizing envy), establishes meaningful eye contact, and kisses him.

Lamentation (south wall, bottom row, middle): Jesus has been crucified, and his followers weep and wail over the lifeless body. John spreads his arms wide and shrieks, his cries echoed by anguished angels above. Each face is a study in grief. Giotto de-emphasizes these saints' stoic response and highlights their human vulnerability.

Last Judgment (big west wall): Christ in the center is a glorious vision, but the fun stuff is in hell (lower right). Satan is a Minotaur-headed ogre munching on sinners. Around him, demons give sinners their just desserts in a scene right out of Dante...who was Giotto's friend and fellow Florentine. Front and center is Enrico Scrovegni in a violet robe (the color symbolizing penitence), donating the chapel to the Church in exchange for forgiveness for his father's sins.

Civic Museum (Musei Civici Eremitani)—This museum, next to the Scrovegni Chapel, was an Augustinian hermit's monastery. It displays Roman and Etruscan archaeological finds, including buckets of rare coins. The ruins of a Roman amphitheater ("arena") surround the Scrovegni Chapel (also called the "Arena" Chapel), a reminder that Padua was an important Roman town.

The museum also has 13th- to 18th-century paintings by Titian, Tintoretto, Giorgione, Tiepolo, Veronese, and other Veneto artists. The highlight is a Giotto crucifix. Near the crucifix is a statue of Enrico degli Scrovegni, looking as though he's wondering how to save his father's soul (€10 includes Multimedia Room, or covered by €12 Scrovegni ticket, Tue–Sun 9:00–19:00, closed Mon, mandatory and free bag check).

Multimedia Room (Sala Multimedia)—Rows of computer screens with English info offer a virtual chapel visit. There are explanations of the individual panels, Giotto's fresco technique, close-ups of the art, and a description of the restoration. They show a 12-minute video (English headphones available) that is similar—but not identical—to the one that precedes your visit (€10 with Civic Museum, or covered by €12 Scrovegni ticket, reduced to €8 after 19:00 with 15-min visits to the Scrovegni, or €12 after 19:00 with 30-min Scrovegni visits, daily April–Oct 9:00–22:00, Nov–March 9:00–19:00, mandatory and free bag check, no photos, Piazza Eremitani, tel. 049-820-4551).

Palazzo della Ragione—This grand 13th-century palazzo commonly called *il Salone* (great hall) once held the medieval law courts. The first floor consists of a huge hall—265 feet by 90 feet—that was once adorned with frescoes by Giotto. A fire in 1312 destroyed those paintings, and the palazzo was redecorated with the 15th-century art you see today: a series of 123 frescoes depicting the signs of the zodiac, labors of the month, symbols representing characteristics of people born under each sign, and finally, figures of saints to legitimize the power of the courts in the eyes of the church.

The hall is topped with a keel-shaped roof, which helps to support the structure without the use of columns—quite an architectural feat in its time, considering the building's dimensions. The curious stone in the right-hand corner near the entry is the "Stone of Shame," which was the seat of debtors being punished during the Middle Ages. Instead of being sentenced to death or prison (same thing back then), debtors sat upon this stone, renounced their possessions, and denounced themselves publicly before being exiled from the city (€4, more if there's an exhibition, Feb–Oct Tue–Sat 9:00–19:00, closed Sun–Mon, Nov–Jan closes 18:00, enter through City Hall across from University, up long staircase, tel. 049-820-5006).

▲▲Market Squares: Piazza delle Erbe and Piazza della Frutta—The stately Palazzo della Ragione (described above) provides a quintessentially Italian backdrop for Padua's almost exotic-feeling market, filling the surrounding squares—Piazza delle Erbe and Piazza della Frutta—each morning. Second only to the produce market in Italy's gastronomic capital of Bologna, this market has been renowned for centuries as having the freshest and greatest selection of herbs, fruits, and vegetables. Beneath the Palazzo della Ragione are various butchers, *salumerie* (delicatessens), cheese shops, bakeries, and fishmongers.

Explore this scene. Students gather here each evening, after the markets have closed, spilling out of colorful bars and cafés—drinks in hand—into the square. Their drink of choice is a *spritz,* an aperitif with Campari, Cynar (two bitter, alcoholic liquors), white wine, and sparkling water, garnished with an olive and a blood-orange wedge. **Bar Nazionale** offers outdoor seating for a ringside view of the action (at #41 under staircase of Palazzo della Ragione in Piazza delle Erbe). **Bar degli Spritz** is the students' hangout (at #36 near the middle of the palazzo at the passageway).

Get your *spritz* to take away *(da portar via)* and join the young people out on the piazza. This is a classic opportunity to enjoy a real discussion with smart, English-speaking students who see tourists not as pests but as interesting people from far away. For an instant conversation starter, ask about the current political situation in Italy or the cultural differences between the North and the South.

A typical snack stand selling all kinds of fresh, hot, and ready-to-eat seafood appetizers sets up in Piazza della Frutta between 17:00–20:30 (except Sun). Belly up to the bar with your drink and nosh on whatever's served.

Caffè Pedrocchi—This white-columned, neoclassical café is not just a café. A complex of meeting rooms and entertainment venues, it symbolizes progress. Built in 1831 during the period of Austrian rule, the Caffè Pedrocchi was inaugurated for the fourth Italian Congress of Scientists, convened during the mid–19th century to stir up nationalistic fervor as Italy struggled to become a united nation. As a symbol of patriotic hope, it's no surprise that students plotted an uprising here in 1848. You can still see a bullet hole in the wall of the Sala Bianca, where one of the insurgents was killed. Nowadays, you get more foam than fervor, but the café is still a marvel of interior design.

Each room is decorated and furnished in a different style. The simple color scheme of the café—red, white, and green—represents the colors of the Italian flag. The Sala Verde (Green Room) is the only room where people can sit and enjoy the beautiful interior without ordering anything or having to pay—in fact, you can even bring your own food and eat it free. Otherwise, take a seat in the Red or White rooms and order from the menu of teahouse fare, including salads, sandwiches and the writer Stendhal's beloved *zabayon*, a creamy custard (June–Sept Sun, Tue, and Wed 9:00–21:00, Thu–Sat 9:00–24:00, Oct–May also Mon 9:00–21:00, entrance is at intersection of Oberdan and VIII

Febbraio, between Piazza delle Erbe and Piazza Cavour, tel. 049-878-1231). On most Thursday evenings from March through November, the café hosts jazz concerts (€2 cover added to first round of drinks, reserve by phone).

Piano Nobile: This upper, noble floor, is much more elaborate. The rooms are all in different styles, such as Greek Etruscan or Egyptian, with English descriptions throughout. These rooms were intended to evoke memories of the glory of past epochs, which a united Italy had hopes of reliving.

The Piano Nobile also hosts a new, smaller **museum** that traces Padua's role in Italian history, from the downfall of the Venetian Republic (1797) to the founding of the Republic of Italy (1948). Exhibits, a few with English descriptions, include uniforms, medals, weaponry, old artillery, Fascist propaganda posters, and a video (in Italian) showing WWII bombardments on Padua. Pick up an English brochure as you enter (€4, Tue–Sun 9:30–12:30 & 15:30–18:00, closed Mon, access Piano Nobile from north entrance of building to right of Caffè entrance, tel. 049-820-5007).

University of Padua—The seat of this prestigious university, located in Palazzo del Bo, is adjacent to Caffè Pedrocchi. Founded in 1222 on the site of an old inn with an ox (*bue* in Italian, *bo* in dialect) painted on its sign, it's one of the first, greatest, and most progressive universities in Europe. Back when the Church controlled university curricula, a group of professors and students broke free from the University of Bologna, creating this liberal school, independent of Catholic constraints and accessible to people of alternative faiths.

A haven for free thought, it attracted intellectuals from all over Europe, including the great astronomer Copernicus, who realized here that the world didn't revolve around him. And Galileo—notorious for disagreeing with the Church's views on science—called his 18 years on the faculty here the best of his life. Students gather in ancient courtyards, surrounded by memories of illustrious alumni, including the first woman ever to receive a university degree (in 1678).

And just upstairs, Europe's first great **anatomy theater** (from the 1500s) is worth a look if you have time for a tour. Despite the Church' strict ban on autopsies, students would pack this theater to watch professors dissect human cadavers. If the Church came a-knockin', the table could be flipped, allowing the corpse to fall into a river below and be replaced with an animal instead (€3, guided tours 3/day except Sun; Mon, Wed, and Fri at 15:15, 16:15, and 17:15; Tue, Thu, and Sat at 9:15, 10:15, and 11:15). Only 30 may enter at a time, and school groups often book the entire visit. To confirm tour times and availability, call 049-827-3047 or stop by the university bookstore, located inside Palazzo del Bo on the right side of courtyard.

If the tour isn't booked, buy tickets from the bookstore 15 minutes before the visit. The tours take 45 minutes and include stops at the anatomy theater, Aula Magna (grand meeting hall plastered with the crests of important faculty), and Galileo's *cattedra* (lectern).

▲**Baptistery**—If you're an art lover but can't get in to see the Scrovegni Chapel, Padua's Baptistery is a good alternative. Located next to the Duomo, the Baptistery is decorated with Giusto de' Menabuoi's brilliant frescoes—the life of Jesus is depicted on the walls, and Christ in majesty with all the saints (yes, all of them) is on the octagonal ceiling (€2.50, audioguide-€1, daily 10:00–18:00, on Piazza del Duomo—it's the smaller building to the right of the Duomo as you're facing it).

SLEEPING

In the Center

$$$ **Majestic Hotel Toscanelli** is a fancy hotel with 32 pleasant, air-conditioned rooms, a touch of charm, and a relatively quiet location on a side street (Sb-€95–115, Db-€153–172, 10 percent discount with this book in 2006, superior rooms and suites available at extra cost, includes a wonderful breakfast, Via dell'Arco 2, about 2 blocks south of Piazza delle Erbe, tel. 049-663-244, fax 049-876-0025, www.toscanelli.com, majestic@toscanelli.com). From Piazza Erbe, head up Via dei Fabbri and take the first left, then turn right onto Via dell'Arco.

Near the Basilica of St. Anthony

$ **Hotel al Fagiano,** located on a side street west of Piazza del Santo, has 30 bright and cheery air-conditioned rooms decorated with Rosella Fagiano's modern art canvases (Sb-€55, Db-€78, Tb-€88, breakfast €3–6 extra; with your back to the church facade, take Via Belludi, then veer right onto Via Locatelli, #45 is under portico on the right; tel. & fax 049-875-0073, www.alfagiano.it, info@albergoalfagiano.191.it).

$ **Hotel al Santo,** run by the Tenan family, offers 16 rooms with all the comforts a few steps from the basilica (Sb-€55–60, Db-€90, Tb-€130, Qb-€145, double-paned windows, air-con, quieter rooms off street, some rooms have views of basilica, tel. 049-875-2131, fax 049-878-8076, www.alsanto.it, alsanto@alsanto.it).

$ **Casa del Pellegrino,** with 160 spotless, cheap, institutional rooms, is home to the pilgrims who come to pay homage to St. Anthony in the basilica, which is right next door (S-€44, Sb-€58, D-€55, Db-€69, Tb-€78, Qb-€90, most rooms have air-con, ask for a room off the street, breakfast-€6, elevator, Via Cesarotti 21, tel. 049-823-9711, fax 049-823-9780, www.casadelpellegrino.com, info@casadelpellegrino.it).

Sleep Code

(€1 = about $1.20, country code: 39)
S = Single, **D** = Double/Twin, **T** = Triple, **Q** = Quad, **b** = bathroom, **s** = shower only. Unless otherwise noted, credit cards are accepted, English is spoken, and breakfast is included in these rates.

To help you easily sort through these listings, I've divided the rooms into three categories, based on the price for a standard double room with bath:

$$$ **Higher Priced**—Most rooms €140 or more.
$$ **Moderately Priced**—Most rooms between €100–140.
$ **Lower Priced**—Most rooms €100 or less.

Down by the Station

$$$ **Hotel Grand'Italia** is the place for four-star elegance, convenience, and prices. Housed in a palace, its 61 rooms are comfortable, and the breakfast room is bright and inviting (Db-€165 but can be more during holidays and trade fairs, air-con, elevator, Corso del Popolo 81, right outside train station on the right side of main drag, tel. 049-876-1111, fax 049-875-0850, www.hotelgranditalia .it, booking@hotelgranditalia.it).

$$ **Hotel Monaco,** a three-star hotel with 57 darkly-decorated rooms, is a few doors away from the Grand'Italia and plain in comparison, but a heck of lot cheaper (Sb-€75, Db-€98–112, air-con, elevator, traffic noise, Piazzale Stazione 3; as you exit the station, it's to your right and across the street; tel. 049-664-344, fax 049-664-669, www.hotelmonacopadova.it, info@hotelmonacopadova.it).

$$ **Hotel al Cason,** just a seven-minute walk from the station, offers a good value for its 48 spacious, clean, and comfortable rooms (Db-€98, air-con, elevator, Internet access, free parking, handy restaurant, tel. 049-662-636, fax 049-875-4217, www.hotelalcason .com, info@hotelalcason.com). As you exit the station, cross the road and turn right, following the street as it curves around to the left. Cross the busy boulevard on your right—just after the overpass bridge but before the medieval tower—to get to Via Frà P. Sarpi. Follow Via F. P. Sarpi 100 yards and find the hotel ahead, on your right, at #40.

Hostel: $ **Ostello Città di Padova** is a well-run hostel with 120 beds in four-, six-, and eight-bed rooms (€15.50 beds with sheets and breakfast; 4-person family rooms-€60, with bath-€68; membership required or pay €3 supplement/night, Internet and laundry available, reception open 7:00–9:30 & 16:00–23:00, rooms locked during afternoon but reception staffed if you need to leave bags, 23:00 curfew, bus #3, #8 or #18 from station, get off at Prato della Valle, Via Aleardi 30, tel. 049-875-2219, www.ctgveneto.it/ostello, ostellopadova@ctgveneto.it).

EATING

The university population means cheap, good food in central *osterie, trattorie,* and take-out joints. These are all centrally located in the historic core.

La Cova Ristorante/Pizzeria, near Piazza Cavour, offers a pleasing range of pizza and pasta. But if you sit in the *ristorante* rather than the pizzeria, you're expected to have multiple courses (Wed–Mon 12:00–15:30 & 18:00–23:30, closed Tue, just off Piazza Cavour, Via P.F. Calvi 20, tel. 049-654-312).

Marechiaro Pizzeria/Trattoria is a popular, economical eatery just west of Piazza delle Erbe (Tue–Sun 12:00–14:30 & 18:30–22:30, closed Mon, Via D. Manin 37, tel. 049-875-8489).

Family-owned **Zairo** is a huge *ristorante*/pizzeria with reasonable prices, delicious and homemade pastas, Veneto specialties, snappy service, and local clientele (Tue–Sun 12:00–15:30 & 18:30–late, closed Mon, east side of Prato della Valle at #51, tel. 049-663-803).

Pago Pago dishes up €4–8 wood-fired Neapolitan pizzas (a local favorite), a variety of big €7 salads, and daily specials (Wed-Mon 12:00–14:30 & 19:00–22:30, pizza until 24:00, closed Tue, just 2 blocks from St. Anthony, heading north on Via del Santo take the first right onto Via G. Galilei to #59, a few steps ahead on the right, tel. 049-665-558).

Brek, tucked into a corner of Piazza Cavour 20, is an easy self-service *ristorante* with healthy and affordable choices (daily 11:30–14:30 & 18:30–22:00, tel. 049-875-3788).

Casa del Pellegrino Ristorante caters to St. Anthony pilgrims with simple, basic, and hearty meals, served in a cheery dining room, just north of the basilica (*primi*-€3–4, *secondi*-€6–12, pizza served only in evening, daily 12:00–14:00 & 19:30–21:00, Via Cesarotti 21, tel. 049-823-9711, Sun lunch by reservation only).

To dine rather than eat, consider **Isola di Caprera** for traditional Veneto cuisine (€22 menu or €37 seafood menu, cheaper à la carte options, Mon–Sat 12:00–15:00 & 19:30–22:30, closed Sun, air-con, Via Marsilio da Padova 11–15, a half block north of the eastern edge of Piazza della Frutta; to reserve, call 049-664-282 or 049-876-0244).

Take-Out Only: **Gastronomica San Francesco** serves up all kinds of homemade finger food, lasagna, roast meats, and vegetables by the *etto,* or 100 grams. A half kilo (about a pound) of lasagna and some vegetables make a light, portable lunch for two people; you can picnic at the nearby cloisters of the basilica. They'll set you up with to-go containers, plastic silverware, and napkins (Fri–Wed 10:00–13:30 & 17:00–20:00, closed Thu, Via San Francesco 214, tel. 049-876-2253). Facing the facade of the basilica, head down the left side 200 yards; the deli is on the corner at the end of the street.

Pollodoro la Gastronomica, another take-out deli near the basilica, sells roasted chicken and will make sandwiches (Wed–Sat and Mon 8:30–14:00 & 17:00–20:00, Sun 8:30–14:00, closed Tue; 100 yards from basilica, Via Belludi 34; with your back to the church entrance, it's under the arches on the left; tel. 049-663-718).

If the markets are closed, stock up on picnic items at **PAM supermarket,** tucked into the corner of a tiny piazzetta east of Caffè Pedrocchi (Mon–Sat 8:00–20:00, closed Wed evenings and Sun, Piazzetta Garzeria 3, tel. 049-657-006).

TRANSPORTATION CONNECTIONS

From Padua by Train to: Venice (4/hr, 30–40 min), **Vicenza** (2/hr, 25 min), **Milan** (hrly, generally leaving at :24 past the hour, 2.5 hrs), **Verona** (2/hr, 1 hr).

Vicenza

To many architects, Vicenza (vih-CHEHN-zah) is a pilgrimage site. Entire streets look like the back of a nickel. This is the city of Andrea Palladio (1508–1580), the 16th-century Renaissance architect who gave us the Palladian style that is so influential in countless British country homes.

Palladio's real name was Andrea di Pietro della Gondola, but his genius was such that one of his patrons—responsible for the architect's liberal arts education—gave him the nickname of Palladio, an allusion to Pallas Athena, Greek goddess of wisdom and the arts.

For the casual visitor, a quick stop offers plenty of Palladio—the last great artist of the Renaissance. Note that Vicenza's major sights are closed on Monday.

ORIENTATION

Tourist Information
The main TI is at Piazza Matteotti 12 (daily 9:00–13:00 & 14:00–18:00, tel. 0444-320-854, www.vicenzae.org); a second office is at Piazza dei Signori 8 (daily 10:00–14:00 & 14:30–18:30). Pick up a map and, if staying the night, an entertainment guide (in

Vicenza

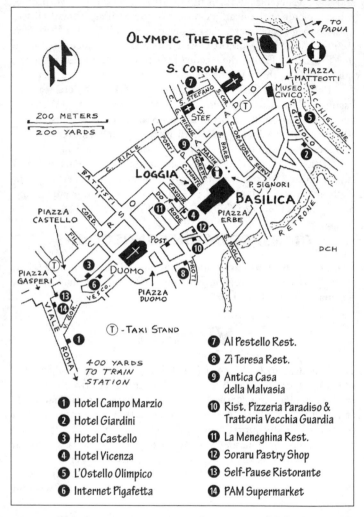

① - TAXI STAND

① Hotel Campo Marzio
② Hotel Giardini
③ Hotel Castello
④ Hotel Vicenza
⑤ L'Ostello Olimpico
⑥ Internet Pigafetta

⑦ Al Pestello Rest.
⑧ Zì Teresa Rest.
⑨ Antica Casa della Malvasia
⑩ Rist. Pizzeria Paradiso & Trattoria Vecchia Guardia
⑪ La Meneghina Rest.
⑫ Soraru Pastry Shop
⑬ Self-Pause Ristorante
⑭ PAM Supermarket

Italian, but *teatro* and *concerto* are easy enough to understand).
Architecture fans will appreciate the free, English *Vicenza Città del Palladio* brochure.

Arrival in Vicenza

From the train station, it's a five-minute **walk** up wide Viale Roma to the bottom of Corso Palladio. Or it's a short **bus** ride to Piazza Matteotti and the top of Corso Palladio. For a day trip, consider catching the bus to Piazza Matteotti and doing your sightseeing on the way back to the station: From the station, catch bus #1, #2, #4,

#5, or #7 (€1, tickets sold at *tabacchi* shop in station, stop is immediately to your left as you exit the station). Validate your ticket in the machine near the back of the bus. Get off at Piazza Matteotti, a skinny, park-like square in front of a white neoclassical building. A **taxi** to Piazza Matteotti costs about €6.

You can usually **check luggage** at the train station (€3.90, daily 9:00–13:00 & 15:00–19:00; with your back to the tracks, it's at the far left end of the station, past the WCs).

Helpful Hints

Combo-Tickets: Most of Vicenza's sights are covered by a combo-ticket called the Biglietto Unico (€8, good for 3 days, sold only at the Olympic Theater). In addition to the theater, the Biglietto Unico includes the Pinacoteca (paintings in Palazzo Chiericati on Piazza Matteotti), the Santa Corona Archaeological and Natural History Museum (next to the Church of Santa Corona), and the Museum of the Risorgimento and Resistance (2 miles outside of town). The pricier €11 combo-ticket (Biglietto Cumulativo) gets you into every sight in Vicenza except for exhibits in Basilica Palladiana.

Market Days: Vicenza hosts a Tuesday market (7:00–13:00) on Piazza dei Signori, and a larger Thursday market that also spills into Piazza Duomo, Piazza del Castello, and Viale Roma (7:00–13:00).

Internet Access: Internet Pigafetta has several terminals a few steps from Piazza Castello (Mon–Sat 7:00–20:00, closed Sun, Contrà Piazza Castello 15, tel. 0444-321-903).

Laundry: The self-service Euro Lavanderia Fai da Te is near the TI and a couple of blocks from Piazza Matteotti (daily 7:30–22:30; with your back to TI, turn left around corner, cross bridge, take the right-middle fork—of 5 streets—to Contrà XX Settembre 27, and go under the arches on left).

Tours: Guided tours of Vicenza may be offered in English in 2006; ask at the TI.

SIGHTS

Central Vicenza

▲▲**Olympic Theater (Teatro Olimpico)**—Palladio's last work is one of his greatest. It was commissioned by the Olympic Academy, a society of Vicenzan scholars and intellectuals (including Palladio), for the purpose of staging performances and intellectual debates. Begun in 1580, shortly before Palladio died, the theater was actually completed by a fellow architect, Scamozzi.

Modeled after the theaters of antiquity, this is a wood-and-stucco festival of classical columns, statues, and an oh-wow stage bursting with perspective tricks. Behind the stage, framed by a triumphal arch, five streets recede at different angles. The streets, depicting the idealized form of the city of Thebes, were created for the gala opening of the ancient Greek tragedy, *Oedipus Rex*, the first play ever performed in the theater and now a tradition for every season.

Many of the statues in niches on the stage are modeled after the people who funded the work—junior members are portrayed as Roman soldiers of antiquity, senior members as senators. The panels at the top show the labors of Hercules, in keeping with the classical antiquity theme that was all the rage in the 16th century. In contrast to the stunning stage, the audience's wooden benches are simple and crude (covered by €8 Biglietto Unico; dense 45-min audioguide-€3, or €5 for two; Tue–Sun 9:00–17:00, closed Mon, July–Aug until 19:00, last entry 15 min before closing, entrance to the left of TI, WC just past the ticket booth on the right, tel. 0444-222-800).

Performances: One of the oldest indoor theaters in Europe and considered one of the world's best, it's still used for performances from April through June (jazz and classical music) and from September through October (Greek tragedies and dramas, shows start at 21:00; for details, see www.vicenzae.org, info@vicenzae.org).

▲**Church of Santa Corona**—A block away from the Olympic Theater, this "Church of the Holy Crown" was built in the 13th century to house a thorn from the crown of thorns given to the Bishop of Vicenza by the French King Louis IX (free, Mon 15:00–18:00, Tue–Sun 8:30–12:00 & 15:00–18:00). It has Giovanni Bellini's fine *Baptism of Christ* (c. 1500, insert a coin for light, to the left of the altar). Study the incredible inlaid marble and mother-of-pearl work on the high altar (1670) and the inlaid wood complementing that in the stalls of the choir (1485).

Archaeological and Natural History Museum—Next door to the Church of Santa Corona, the ground floor of this humble museum features Roman antiquities (mosaics, statues, and artifacts excavated from Rome's Baths of Caracalla, plus swords) and a barbarian warrior skeleton complete with sword and helmet. Prehistoric scraps are upstairs, and there are a few English description sheets near exhibit entryways throughout (covered by €8 Biglietto Unico, Tue–Sun 9:00–17:00, closed Mon, last entry 15 min before closing, WC on 2nd floor at end of prehistoric hall, tel. 0444-320-440).

Corso Andrea Palladio—From the Olympic Theater or Church of Santa Corona, stroll down Vicenza's main drag, Corso Andrea Palladio, and see why they call Vicenza "Venice on terra firma." A steady string of Renaissance palaces and Palladian architecture is peopled by Vicenzans (considered by their neighbors to be as uppity as most of their colonnades) and punctuated by upper-class *gelaterie*.

After a few blocks, you'll see the commanding **Basilica Palladiana** (this was not a church but a meeting place for local big shots). With its 270-foot-tall, 13th-century tower, the basilica dominates the Piazza dei Signori, the town center since Roman times. It was young Palladio's proposal to redo Vicenza's dilapidated Gothic palace of justice in the neo-Greek style that established him as Vicenza's favorite architect. The rest of Palladio's career was a one-man construction boom. Opposite the basilica, the brick-columned **Loggia del Capitaniato**—home of the Venetian governor and one of Palladio's last works—gives you an easy chance to compare early Palladio (the basilica) with late Palladio (the loggia).

The basilica is open to tourists (€1, more during frequent special exhibitions—see www.vicenzae.org for specifics, Tue–Sun 9:00–13:00 & 15:00–19:00, closed Mon, tel. 0444-322-196). Even without a ticket, climb the 15th-century stairs. Halfway up the steps, you'll see the gargoyle-like lion's mouth (representing the long arm of the Venetian Republic). Centuries ago, people used to sneak notes into this mouth, anonymously reporting neighbors suspected of carrying communicable diseases that could bring on the plague. You can walk around the arcaded upper floor, which contains the entrance to the huge basilica. The basilica's roof, shaped like an upside-down keel, has a nautical feel, augmented by the porthole windows. Set in the wall in front, the winged lion (symbol of St. Mark and Venice) laid the course for this little town in the 15th century.

Outside, on the Piazza dei Signori, note the two tall **15th-century columns** topped with Jesus and the winged lion. When Venice took over Vicenza in the early 1400s, these columns were added—à la St. Mark's Square—to give the city a Venetian feel.

Finish your stroll along the Corso Palladio at Piazzale Gasperi (where the Pam supermarket is a handy place to grab a picnic for the train ride), dip into the park called Giardino Salvi (for one last Palladio loggia, closed to visitors but viewable from outside), and then walk five minutes down Viale Roma back to the station. Trains leave about every hour for Milan/Verona and Venice (less than an hour away).

Villas on the Outskirts of Vicenza

These two villas are worth a visit for architecture buffs with more time. Both houses are furnished with period pieces and have good English descriptions. Pick up the free English brochure on Palladio's villas from the TI if you plan to visit.

Villa la Rotonda—Thomas Jefferson's Monticello was inspired by Palladio's Rotonda (a.k.a. Villa Almerico Capra). Started by Palladio in 1566, it was finished by his pupil, Scamozzi. The white, gently domed building, with grand colonnaded entries, seems to have popped out of the grassy slope. Palladio, who designed a number of country villas, had a knack for using setting for dramatic effect. This private—but sometimes tourable—residence is on the edge of Vicenza (€5 to enter grounds, mid-March–mid-Nov Tue–Sun 10:00–12:00 & 15:00–18:00, closed Mon, shorter hours off season, confirm hours before heading out there; €10 for interior—open only Wed 10:00–12:00 & 15:00–18:00; Via Rotonda 29, tel. 0444-321-793). To get to the villa from Vicenza's train station, hop a bus (#8, 2/hr, stop is to the left of the station as you're facing it on Viale Venezia) or take a taxi. For a quick round-trip any time of day, you can zip out by cab (about €8, 5-min ride from train station) to see the building sitting regally atop its hill, and then ride the same cab back.

Villa Valmarana ai Nani—The 17th-century "Villa of the Dwarfs" is just up the street from Villa Rotonda. This is convenient if you want to see a villa interior and you're not in Vicenza on a Wednesday, when Villa la Rotunda is open. This elegant neoclassical estate features panoramic views and 18th-century murals by Tiepolo.

The villa's name comes from the local legend of an ancient manor house owned by a nobleman whose daughter was born a dwarf. Her father surrounded her with dwarf servants so she wouldn't realize she was small. One day as she was looking out the window, she saw a handsome prince ride by on his horse. Realizing she was a dwarf, she killed herself in anguish. Her servants—so saddened by her death that they turned to stone—now line the wall of the villa like petrified sentries.

The rooms in the main house include frescoes with scenes from the Trojan War, classical myths, and Italian lyrical poems. The frescoes in the guest house *(foresteria)* are nearly all by Tiepolo's son, Giandomenico, whose themes highlight 18th-century gentrified culture—the idealized tranquility of peasants, the exotic fashion and styles of the Chinese from a Western perspective, and scenes from Carnevale (€5, 10:00–12:00 & 15:00–18:00, closed Mon, and Tue and Fri mornings; from Villa Rotonda, head a few steps downhill, then up the slope on Stradella Valmarana about 200 yards; tel. 0444-321-803).

SLEEPING

(€1 = about $1.20, country code: 39)

$$$Hotel Campo Marzio, a four-star, American-style, pricey place with all the comforts, faces a park on the main drag, a few minutes' walk directly in front of the station (Db-€165–182; prices depend on season and size of room—"superior" means bigger, with a few more amenities; all rooms have air-con, elevator, free bikes, free and easy parking, Viale Roma 21, tel. 0444-545-700, fax 0444-320-495, www.hotelcampomarzio.com, info@hotelcampomarzio.com).

$$ Hotel Giardini, with three stars and 17 sleek rooms, has splashy pastel colors and a refreshing feel (Sb-€83, Db-€114, these prices promised with this book through 2006, air-con, elevator, on busy street but has double-paned windows, within a block of Piazza Matteotti/Olympic Theater on Via Giuriolo 10, tel. & fax 0444-326-458, www.hotelgiardini.com, info@hotelgiardini.com).

$ Hotel Castello, on Piazza Castello, has 18 homey, quiet rooms and lots of stairs (Sb-€77, Db-€98, air-con, Internet in lobby, new rooftop terrace; Contrà Piazza del Castello 24, down alley to the right of Ristorante agli Schioppi, 5-min walk from station, turn right after passing Hotel Campo Marzio and head up hill to square, take the street slightly to the left as you enter the square; tel. 0444-323-585, fax 0444-323-583, www.hotelcastelloitaly.com, info@hotelcastelloitaly.it).

$ Hotel Vicenza, in an 18th-century theater, is family owned and ideally located on a quiet street just off Piazza dei Signori. Its 34 peaceful rooms, some with small balconies, have a worn, Old World feel (D-€50, Db-€65, no breakfast, elevator, Stradella dei Nodari 5/7, tel. & fax 0444-321-512). They may be closing in 2006 for restoration, so call ahead.

Hostel: **$ L'Ostello Olimpico,** just a few years old, is wonderfully central on Piazza Matteotti, a few steps from the Olympic Theater (80 beds, 4– to 6-bed rooms-€16 per person, family rooms-€17.50 per person, Db-€19.50 per person, closed 9:30–15:15, curfew-23:30, breakfast-€1.85, lunch or dinner-€11, all eaten at nearby restaurant using vouchers from hostel, Internet access; bike rental-€1/hr, €8/day; laundry nearby on Contrà XX Settembre 27, best to reserve several weeks in advance by fax or e-mail, tel. 0444-540-222, fax 0444-547-762, ostello.vicenza@tin.it).

EATING

The local specialty is marinated cod, called *baccalà alla Vicentina*.

In **Al Pestello**'s casually elegant dining room, owner Fabio patiently and lovingly describes his menu of historic *cucina Vicentina* (including *baccalà*) from a menu written in dialect. The day's offerings are created from the freshest seasonal ingredients to complement an extensive list of local and national wines (expect to spend about €30 per person without wine, Mon 19:30–22:30, Tue–Sat 12:30–14:30 & 19:30–22:30, closed Sun, a block from the Church of Santa Corona at Contrà Santo Stefano 3, tel. 0444-323-721).

Zi Teresa is popular among locals for its romantic ambience and moderately priced traditional cuisine and pizzas (Thu–Tue 11:45–14:30 & 18:30–23:00, closed Wed, a couple blocks southwest of Piazza dei Signori, Contrà S. Antonio 1, at intersection with Contrà Proti, tel. 0444-321-411).

Antica Casa della Malvasia is a popular, atmospheric, cavernous trattoria serving up affordable regional favorites and homemade pastas (daily 12:00–14:30 & 19:00–24:00, Contrà delle Morette 5, just off Piazza dei Signori on a little alley directly across from the bell tower, tel. 0444-543-704). Their new attached *enoteca* offers wines (€0.80-€3.50/glass) and snacks.

Ristorante Pizzeria Paradiso offers dozens of inexpensive pasta and wood-fired pizza options and indoor/outdoor seating on a narrow square south of Piazza dei Signori and Piazza Erbe (Tue–Sun 12:00–14:30 & 18:30–22:30, closed Mon, Via Pescherie Vecchie 5, tel. 0444-322-320). When they're closed, try their sister restaurant next door, **Trattoria Vecchia Guardia** (different daily specials, Fri–Wed 12:00–14:30 & 18:30–22:30, closed Thu, Via Pescherie Vecchie 15, tel. 0444-321-231).

Cheap Eats: A cheap, self-service **Self-Pause Ristorante** is just off Piazza del Castello, in the shadow of the arch where Corso Andrea Palladio meets Viale Roma (Mon–Sat 12:00–14:30 & 19:00–22:00, Sun 19:00–22:00, Corso Andrea Palladio 10, tel. 0444-327-829). A few steps from that same arch is the **Pam supermarket,** perfect for picnics (Mon–Sat 8:00–20:00, Wed only until 13:00, closed Sun, follow the curve of the road just outside the city wall).

Pastry: La Meneghina is an atmospheric pastry shop (Tue–Sun 8:00–23:00, closed Mon; full meals 12:00–14:30 & 19:30–22:00 in summer, until 21:00 in winter; on Contrà Cavour 18, a short street between Piazza dei Signori and Corso Andrea Palladio, tel. 0444-323-305). Nearby, on Piazza dei Signori, the tiny **Soraru** pastry shop has lots of sidewalk tables within tickling distance of the Palladio statue (Thu–Tue 8:30–13:00 & 15:30–20:00, closed Wed, next to basilica, at far end of square from the two tall columns, tel. 0444-320-915).

TRANSPORTATION CONNECTIONS

From Vicenza by Train to: Venice (2/hr, 1 hr), **Padua** (2/hr, 20 min), **Ravenna** (about hrly, 3–4 hrs, depending on train, with changes in Padua and Ferrara or Bologna), **Verona** (2/hr, 40 min).

Verona

Romeo and Juliet made Verona a household word. Alas, a visit here has nothing to do with those two star-crossed lovers. You can pay to visit the house that falsely claims to be Juliet's (with an almost-believable balcony and a courtyard swarming with tour groups), take part in the tradition of rubbing the breast of Juliet's statue to ensure finding a lover (or picking up the sweat of someone who can't), and even make a pilgrimage to what isn't "La Tomba di Giulietta."

Despite the fiction, the town has been an important crossroads for 2,000 years and is therefore packed with genuine history. R and J fans will take some solace in the fact that two real feuding families, the Montecchi and the Capellis, were the models for Shakespeare's Montagues and Capulets. And, if R and J had existed and were alive today, they would recognize much of their "hometown."

Verona's main attractions are its wealth of Roman ruins; the remnants of its 13th- and 14th-century political and cultural boom; its 21st-century, quiet, pedestrians-only ambience; and a world-class opera festival each July and August (schedule at www.arena.it). After Venice's festival of tourism, the Veneto's second city (in population and in artistic importance) is a cool and welcome sip of pure Italy, where dumpsters are painted by schoolchildren as class projects. If you like Italy but don't need great sights, this town is a joy.

ORIENTATION

The most enjoyable core of Verona is along Via Mazzini between Piazza Brà and Piazza Erbe, Verona's market square since Roman times. Head straight for Piazza Brà—and stroll. All sights of importance are located within an easy walk through the old town, which is defined by a bend in the river. For a good day trip to Verona, see the Arena and take my self-guided walk (see page 141).

Tourist Information

Verona has two TIs (both open Mon–Sat 9:00–19:00, Sun 9:00–15:00, www.tourism.verona.it): at the train station (tel. 045-800-0861) and at Piazza Brà (as you face the large yellow-white building, TI is across street to your right, tel. 045-806-8680, public WC on Piazza Brà). At either TI, pick up the free city map that includes a list of sights, opening hours, and walking tours. If you're staying the night, ask the TI about concerts or pick up a monthly entertainment guide (either *Carnet Verona* or *Verona Live*) for about €1 at any newsstand. Both are in Italian, but *concerto di musica classica* is darn close to English.

The **Verona Card** covers bus transportation and entrance to most of Verona's sights (€8/day or €12/3 days, sold at participating sights and at the exchange office in the train station).

Arrival in Verona

By Train: Get off at Verona's Porta Nuova station. The station is modern, but so cluttered with shops that it can be hard to get oriented. From the tracks, an underground passage leads to the main hall. As you emerge from the passage, pay toilets and phones are to your left, and an ATM is to your right. Beyond the ATM to the right is a long hall; at the end of the hall, a smaller hall branches off to the right, where you'll find the baggage check (€4 for up to 5 hrs, passport required), TI (across from baggage check, in office labeled *Centro Accoglienza e Informazioni*), train information desk (same office as TI), and another ATM (to the right of the TI).

The boring 15-minute walk from the station to Piazza Brà is on busy streets; take the **bus** instead. Buses leave from directly in front of the station. You need to buy a ticket before boarding from a *tabacchi* shop inside the station (€1, good for 1 hr; or €3.10 for an all-day ticket valid until midnight). Confirm the route at the TI, or ask someone, *"Che numero per centro?"* (kay NOO-may-roh pehr CHEN-troh). You'll probably have a choice of orange bus #11, #12, #13, or #14, leaving from Platform A. Validate your ticket by stamping it in the machine in the middle of the bus. Buses stop on Piazza Brà, the square with the can't-miss-it Roman Arena. The TI is just a few steps beyond the bus stop (located along the medieval walls). Buses return to the station from the bus stop just outside the city wall (on the right), where Corso Porta Nuova hits Piazza Brà.

Taxis pick up only at taxi stands (at Piazza Brà and train station) and cost about €6 for a ride between the train station and Piazza Brà.

By Plane: From Verona's airport, catch a shuttle bus to the train station (€4.50, buy tickets on board, daily 6:00–23:30, departs every 20 min, trip takes 15 min). If going *to* the airport, catch the shuttle just to the left of the train station entrance (€4.50, departs every 20 min daily 5:40–23:10).

Helpful Hints

Sightseeing Schedules: Many sights are closed on Monday and are free on the first Sunday of every month.

Opera: In July and August, Verona's opera festival brings crowds and higher hotel prices (tickets €17–157, upper-level seats about €25, book tickets either online at www.arena.it or by calling tel. 045-800-5151, box office open Mon–Fri 9:00–12:00 & 15:15–17:15, Sat–Sun 9:00–12:00; in opera season, it's open daily 10:00–17:45, or until 21:00 on days when there's a show).

Internet Access: Try Internet Train (Mon–Fri 11:00–22:00, Sat–Sun 14:00–20:00, Via Roma 17A, a couple of blocks off Piazza Brà toward Castelvecchio, tel. 045-801-3394), Internetfast.it (Mon–Sat 10:00–20:00, closed Sun, Via Oberdan 16B, just off Porta Borsari toward Piazza Brà, tel. 045-803-3212), or Internet Etc. (Tue–Sat 10:30–20:00, Sun–Mon 15:30–20:00, off Via Mazzini on Via Quattro Spade 3B, tel. 045-800-0222).

Post Office: The post office is at Via Cattaneo 23E (Mon–Sat

8:30–18:30, closed Sun, from Piazza Brà take Via Roma and turn right on Via Cattaneo, 100 yards down on right).

Laundry: Mr. Lava Lava self-service laundry is near Ponte Nuovo (daily 9:00–23:00, last wash at 22:00, €5/load for wash and dry, soap vendor and change machine available, follow Via Carducci and turn right onto Via Interrato to #36).

Bikes: The TI at the train station has eight free loaner bikes (passport required for deposit, Mon–Sat 9:00–17:30, Sun 9:00–14:00, maybe summer only).

Gnocchi Festival: Ask a Veronese to tell you about Papa del Gnoccho (NYO-koh). About 500 years ago, at a time when the Veronese were nearly starving, the prince handed out gnocchi (potato dumplings) to everyone. To this day, it's customary for the Veronese to eat gnocchi on Friday during Lent. Every year someone from the San Zeno neighborhood is elected Papa del Gnoccho. On the Friday before Mardi Gras, he's dressed like a king—but instead of a scepter, he holds a huge fork piercing a *gnoccho*. Lots of people wear costumes, including little kids (who dress as gnocchi). The focal point of this celebration is the Church of San Zeno.

TOURS

Walking Tours—Juliet & Co. offers 75-minute tours in English (€10/person, doesn't include entry to any sights or monuments, April–Sept daily at 17:30, meet in front of equestrian statue on Piazza Brà, tel. 045-810-3173, www.julietandco.com).

Private Guides—To hire your own Verona guide, consider knowledgeable, enthusiastic, and friendly Marina Menegoi (€100/2–3 hour tour, itinerary varies according to your interests, she also does tours of the region—including wine-tasting tours, tel. 045-801-2174, mobile 328-958-1108, milanit@libero.it); or try the Verona guide association (tel. 049-869-8601). Even if you don't want to hire a guide, Marina is happy to help out my readers with information they might need—free of charge.

SELF-GUIDED WALK

Welcome to Verona

This walk will take you from Piazza Erbe to the major sights, ending at Piazza Brà. Allow an hour (including the tower climb and dawdling, but not the optional detours).

Piazza Erbe is a photographer's delight. Its pastel buildings corral the fountains, pigeons, and people that have congregated here since Roman times, when this was a forum. Notice the Venetian lion hovering above the square, reminding locals of their conquerors

Verona

1. Bus to Station
2. Bus from Station
3. Hotel Aurora
4. To L'Ospite Apartments
5. Hotel Europa
6. Hotel Bologna
7. Hotel Giulietta e Romeo
8. Hotel Torcolo
9. Locanda Catullo
10. To Villa Francescatti Hostel
11. Osteria al Duca
12. Osteria Giulietta e Romeo
13. Ristorante Greppia
14. Bottega del Vino
15. De Gusto Ristorante
16. Ristorante Sant'Eufemia
17. San Matteo Church Rest.
18. Osteria le Vecete
19. Oreste dal Zovo
20. Enoteca Can Grande
21. Brek Cafeteria
22. PAM Supermarket

since 1405. During medieval times, the stone canopy in the center held the scales where merchants measured the weight of things they bought and sold, such as silk, wool, and wood. The fountain has bubbled here for 2,000 years. Its statue, originally Roman, had lost its head and arms. After a sculptor added a new head and arms, the statue became Verona's Madonna. She holds a small banner that reads: "I want justice and I bring peace." In recent years, there has been an ongoing battle between market-stall owners, who earn their living from the tourists, and the community, which wants the square left free to be enjoyed as the open "living space" it was meant to be. The debate continues—notice whether the recently banned stall owners have bought their way back onto the square.

From the center of Piazza Erbe, head toward the river on Via della Costa. The street is marked by an **arch** with a whale's rib suspended from it. According to legend, the rib has hung there a thousand years, and will fall only when someone who's never lied walks under it. Give it a try.

The street soon opens up to a square, **Piazza dei Signori.** Center-stage is a white statue of the Italian poet Dante Alighieri. The pensive Dante seems to wonder why the tourists choose Juliet over him. Dante—expelled from Florence for political reasons—was granted asylum in Verona by the della Scala (a.k.a. Scaligeri) family. With the whale's rib behind you, you're facing the brick, crenellated, 13th-century della Scala residence. Behind Dante is the yellowish 15th-century Venetian Renaissance–style Portico of the Counsel. In front of Dante—and to his right (follow the white *WC* signs) is the 12th-century Romanesque **Palazzo della Ragione.**

Enter the courtyard. The impressive staircase—which goes nowhere—is the only surviving Renaissance staircase in Verona. For a grand city view, you can climb to the top of the 13th-century **Torre dei Lamberti** (€2 for stairs, €3 for elevator, Tue–Sun 8:30–19:30, Mon 13:30–19:30, last entry 45 min before closing). The elevator saves you 245 steps—but you'll still need to climb about 45 more to get to the first viewing platform. It's not worth continuing up the endless spiral stairs to the second viewing platform.

Exit the courtyard the way you entered and turn right, continuing down the whale-rib street. Within a block, you'll find the strange and very Gothic **tombs of the della Scala family,** who were to Verona what the Medici family were to Florence. Notice the dogs' heads near the top of the tombs. On the first tomb, the dogs peer over a shield displaying a ladder. The della Scala family got rich making ladders...but money can't buy culture. When Marco Polo returned from Asia boasting of the wealthy Kublai Khan, the della Scalas wanted to be associated with this powerful Khan by name. But misunderstanding Khan as *cane* (dog), one Scaligero changed his name to Can

Grande (big dog) and another to Can Signore (lord dog).

Continue straight for one long block and turn left on San Pietro Martire (you'll need to step into the street to check the road sign). After one block, you'll reach Verona's largest church, the brick **Church of Sant'Anastasia.** Consider visiting this church's interior—featuring surly stone hunchbacks and a Pisanello fresco (see church description on page 147)—before continuing the walk... or just peek in over the screen to get a sense of its size.

Facing the church, go right and walk along the length of it. Take a left on Via Sottoriva. In a block, you'll reach a small river-front park that usually has a few modern-day Romeos and Juliets gazing at each other rather than the view. Get up on the sidewalk right next to the river. You'll see the red-and-white bridge, **Ponte Pietra.** The white stones are from the original Roman bridge that stood here. After the bridge was bombed in World War II, the Veronese fished the marble chunks out of the river to rebuild it.

Head toward the Ponte Pietra. You'll also see, across the river and built into the hillside, the **Roman Theater**. Way above the theater is the fortress, **Castello San Pietro**. This is your chance to break away, cross the bridge, and visit the Roman Theater (see page 145 for details); or head up to the Castello for an expansive city view (go up the little road called Scalone Castello San Pietro at the end of the bridge, or climb the stairs to the left of the theater).

Me? I'm simply passing the bridge on the way to the next church. Leave the riverfront park and take the street to the right, Via Ponte Pietra, toward the bridge. One block before you reach the bridge (bridge entry clearly marked by an arch in a tower), turn left on Via Cappelletta. After two long blocks, you'll come to Via Duomo (the corner is marked by a little church). To tour another of Verona's historic churches—the **Duomo**—turn right and head up Via Duomo. (For more information about the Duomo—with Titian's *Assumption* and the foundations of a 10th-century church—see page 147.) To shortcut to the next stop, go left at the intersection, towards the Church of Sant'Anastasia.

With your back to the Church of Sant'Anastasia, walk down Corso S. Anastasia. In five minutes (at a brisk pace), you'll reach the ghostly white **Porta Borsari,** stretching across the road. This sturdy first-century Roman gate was one of the original entrances to this ancient town.

Continue straight (the name of the street changes to Corso Cavour). In a little park next to the castle is a first-century Roman triumphal arch, **Arco dei Gavi.** After being destroyed by French Revolutionary troops in 1796, it was rebuilt at this location in the 1900s.

Next to the arch is **Castelvecchio**—once the della Scala family's medieval castle, and now a sprawling art museum displaying

Christian statuary, some weaponry, and fine 13th- to 17th-century paintings. For more on this building and its exhibits, see page 146.

From the castle, you have several options. For a city view, you can walk out upon the grand bridge that leads from the castle over the river. For another church visit, walk a few blocks from the castle (following the river away from town) to the 12th-century **Basilica of San Zeno Maggiore** (with a triptych by Mantegna, bronze doors displaying Bible stories for illiterate medieval parishioners, and some prayerful 14th-century graffiti; described on page 147).

But to finish the walk, the castle's drawbridge points the way to Via Roma, taking you to Piazza Brà. Here you'll have a chance to rest at a sidewalk café (Brek is cheap—see page 151) and visit the remarkable **Roman Arena** (described below).

SIGHTS AND ACTIVITIES

▲▲**Evening *Passeggiata*** —For me, the highlight of Verona is the *passeggiata* (stroll)—especially in the evening—from the elegant cafés of Piazza Brà through the old town on Via Mazzini (one of Europe's many "first pedestrians-only streets") to the colorful Piazza Erbe.

Roman Arena—This elliptical 466-by-400-foot amphitheater is the third-largest in the Roman world. Dating from the first century B.C., it looks great in its pink marble. Over the centuries, crowds of up to 25,000 spectators have cheered Roman gladiator battles, medieval executions, and modern plays (including the popular opera festival that takes advantage of the famous acoustics every July and Aug). Climb to the top for a fine city view (€4, Tue–Sun 8:30–19:30, Mon 13:30–19:30, closes at 15:00 during opera season, hours can vary so check TI, last entry 1 hr before closing, WC near entry, located on Piazza Brà, tel. 045-800-3204).

House of Juliet—This bogus house is a block off Piazza Erbe (detour right to Via Cappello 23). The tiny, admittedly romantic courtyard is a spectacle in itself, with Japanese posing on the balcony, Nebraskans polishing Juliet's bronze breast, and amorous graffiti everywhere. The information boxes offer a good history (€1 for 2 people). ("While no documentation has been discovered to prove the truth of the legend, no documentation has disproved it either.") The "museum" exhibits art inspired by the love story, plus costumes and the bed from Franco Zeffirelli's film *Romeo and Juliet*—certainly not worth the €4 entry fee (Tue–Sun 8:30–19:30, Mon 13:30–19:30, tel. 045-803-4303).

Roman Theater (Teatro Romano)—Dating from the first century A.D., this ancient theater was discovered in the 19th century and restored. To reach the worthwhile museum, high up in the building above the theater, you can take the stairs or the elevator (to find the elevator, start at the stage and walk up the middle set of stairs, then continue straight on the path through the bushes).

The museum displays a model of the theater, a small Jesuit chapel, and lots of Roman artifacts (mosaic floors, busts and other statuary, clay and bronze votive figures, and other architectural fragments). You'll find helpful English information sheets in virtually every room (€3, free first Sun of month, WC to the right of theater entrance after ticket booth, Tue–Sun 8:30–19:30, Mon 13:30–19:30, last entry 45 min before closing, across the river near Ponte Pietra, tel. 045-800-0360). Every summer, the theater stages Shakespeare plays—only a little more difficult to understand in Italian than in Elizabethan English.

Giardino Giusti—If you'd enjoy a Renaissance garden with manicured box hedges and towering cypress trees, you could find this worth the walk and fee. Both the garden and its palazzo are up for sale, if you've got the cash (€5, daily 9:00–19:30, 8:00 until sunset off-season; cross river at Ponte Nuovo, continue 5 blocks up Via Carducci, then turn left to Via Giardino Giusti 2).

Castelvecchio—Verona's powerful della Scala family built this castle (1343–1356) as both a residence and a fortress to defend against their enemies. Today it's a museum showing off Verona in its glory days (€4, extra for exhibitions, Mon 13:30–19:30, Tue–Sun 8:30–19:30, last entry 45 min before closing, good English descriptions on sheets throughout, ask about audioguides, WC in third room past ticket booth).

The **ground floor** houses early Christian statues that were once vibrantly colored (notice the faint traces of paint). The homier first floor was the residential rooms of the castle (original wooden ceilings, traces of frescoes, religious paintings).

The **second floor** takes you out of the Middle Ages and into the Renaissance (paintings now have secular themes). Displayed on this floor are fine ancient bronze and gold artifacts and a collection of hair-raising medieval weaponry—pikes, halberds, helmets, breastplates, and enormous broadswords.

On the far side of the armaments exhibit, climb the skinny stairway for a grand view.

Churches

Verona has several historic churches. Three in particular—Sant'Anastasia, the Duomo, and San Zeno—are worth visiting, described below, and covered by the same €5 combo-ticket (combo-ticket sold at all the churches, or pay €2.50 apiece to enter, churches also covered by Verona Card—see page 139; tel. 045-592-813, no photos allowed, no tourists during Mass, modest dress expected). The San Lorenzo and San Fermo churches, also covered by the €5 combo-ticket, are not particularly worth a visit.

Church of Sant'Anastasia—This church was built from the late 13th century through the 15th century, but the builders ran out of steam, and the facade was never finished. The highlights of the interior are the grimacing hunchbacks holding basins of holy water on their backs (near entrance at base of columns) and Pisanello's fragmented fresco of *St. George and the Princess* (above chapel to right of altar; ask for English brochure, which describes the story of the church; April–Sept Mon–Sat 9:00–18:00, Sun 13:00–18:00, shorter hours March and Oct, open Sun afternoons only Nov–Feb).

Duomo—Started in the 12th century, this church was built over a period of centuries. Its bright interior demonstrates the tremendous leaps made in architecture over the course of its construction. (OK, so the white paint helps.) The highlights are Titian's *Assumption* and the ruins of an older church. To find the Titian, stand at the very back of the church and face the altar; the painting is to your left. Mary calmly rides a cloud—direction up—to the shock and bewilderment of the crowd below. To find the ruins of the older church, walk up toward the altar to the last wooden door on the left. (If the door's not open, ask someone for help.) Inside are the 10th-century foundations of the Church of St. Elena, turned intriguingly into a modern-day chapel (get the English descriptions at the entrance, April–Sept Mon–Sat 10:00–17:30, Sun 13:30–17:30, shorter hours March and Oct, open Sun afternoons only Nov–Feb).

Basilica of San Zeno Maggiore—This church is dedicated to the patron saint of Verona, whose remains are buried in the crypt under the main altar. In addition to being a fine example of Italian Romanesque, the basilica features Mantegna's *San Zeno Triptych* (sit on the right-side pews for the best view of Mantegna's perspective), peaceful double-columned cloisters, and a set of 48 paneled 11th-century bronze doors nicknamed "the poor man's Bible." Pretend you're an illiterate medieval peasant and do some reading. Facing the altar, on the far right of the nave you can see frescoes painted on top of other frescoes and graffiti dating from the 1300s. These were done by people who fled into the church in times of war or flooding to scratch prayers into the walls. Druidic-looking runes are actually decorated letters typical of the Gothic period, like those in illuminated manuscripts (April–Sept Mon–Sat 8:30–18:00, Sun 9:00–12:30 & 13:00–18:00, shorter hours March and Oct, open Sun afternoons only Nov–Feb).

SLEEPING

(€1 = about $1.20, country code: 39)
I've listed rates you'll pay in regular season. Prices soar above these in July and August (during opera season), the first week of April (during the Vinitaly wine festival), and any time of year for a trade

fair or holiday. Hotel Aurora and Hotel Torcolo are my favorites for their family-run feeling.

Near Piazza Erbe

$$ Hotel Aurora, just off Piazza Erbe, has friendly family management, a terrace overlooking the piazza, and 19 fresh, air-conditioned rooms (S-€68, Sb-€120, Db-€135, Tb-€158, cheaper off-season, reserve with traveler's check or personal check for deposit, good buffet breakfast, elevator, nearby church bells ring the hour early, Piazza Erbe, tel. 045-594-717, fax 045-801-0860, www.hotelaurora .biz, info@hotelaurora.biz). Their two quads (each with 2 rooms—1 double bed, 2 twin beds—and bathroom; €220/night) are better for families than couples because the bedrooms aren't private.

$ L'Ospite, a 10-minute walk from Piazza Erbe, has six cozy, immaculate, fully equipped apartments and lots of stairs. The rooms sleep up to four and include air-conditioning, breakfast, use of the washing machine, and weekly housekeeping (or as needed). Kind manager Federica Rossi can also organize excursions around the area or help you get opera tickets (about €35/person, depending on length of stay, monthly rates negotiable, on west side of Ponte Navi bridge, a few steps past San Paolo church on the left at Via XX Settembre #3, tel. 045-803-6994, mobile 329-426-2524, www .lospite.com, info@lospite.com).

Near Piazza Brà

Several fine places are in the quiet streets just off Piazza Brà, within 200 yards of the bus stop. From the square, yellow signs point you to the hotels.

$$$ Hotel Bologna, within a half block of the Arena, has 30 bright, classy, and well-maintained rooms; attractive public areas; and an attached restaurant (Sb-€101, Db-€140, Tb-€175, air-con, Piazzetta Scalette Rubiani 3, tel. 045-800-6830, fax 045-801-0602, www.hotelbologna.vr.it, hotelbologna@tin.it).

$$$ Hotel Giulietta e Romeo, just behind the Arena, is on a quiet side street. Its 30 decent rooms (9 have balconies) are decorated in dark colors, but on the plus side, they have non-smoking rooms and don't take tour groups (Sb-€110, Db-€190, air-con, elevator, Internet in lobby, bike rental-€5/half-day, laundry-€7.50/load, garage-€16/day, Vicolo Tre Marchetti 3, tel. 045-800-3554, fax 045-801-0862, www.giuliettaeromeo.com, info@giuliettaeromeo.com).

$$ Hotel Europa offers sleek, modern comfort. Nearly half of its 46 rooms are non-smoking—a rarity in Italy—and a few rooms have little balconies overlooking the *piazzetta* below (Db-€130, off-season mention this book when you reserve for a discount, air-con, elevator, Via Roma 8, tel. 045-594-744, fax 045-800-1852, www .veronahoteleuropa.com, hoteleuropavr@tiscali.it).

$ Hotel Torcolo offers 19 comfortable, lovingly maintained, non-smoking rooms in a good location near Piazza Brà (Sb-€70, Db-€100, breakfast-€7–12, breakfast is optional except during opera season, air-con, fridge in room, elevator, garage-€8–14/day; standing on Piazza Brà with your back to the gardens and the Arena over your right shoulder, head down the alley to the right of #16 and walk to Vicolo Listone 3; tel. 045-800-7512, fax 045-800-4058, www.hoteltorcolo.it, hoteltorcolo@virgilio.it, well-run by Silvia and Diana).

Between Piazza Brà and Piazza Erbe

$ Locanda Catullo is an inexpensive, quiet, and quirky place deeper in the old town, with 21 good, basic rooms up three flights of stairs. You can only reserve ahead if you're staying for three days or more, and you have to prepay the entire amount by personal check or bank transfer (they'll explain the procedure). This is a hassle, but it's the only cheap hotel in the center (S-€40, D-€55, Db-€65, Qb-€125, no breakfast; left off Via Mazzini onto Via Catullo, down an alley between 1D and 3A at Via Valerio Catullo 1; tel. 045-800-2786, fax 045-596-987, locandacatullo@tiscali.it, a leettle English spoken).

Hostel

$ Villa Francescatti is a good hostel (€13.50–15 beds with breakfast, 6-, 8-, and 10-bed rooms, some family rooms with private bathrooms, €3 extra for non-members, €8 dinners, launderette, Internet in lobby, rooms closed from 9:00–17:00 but reception open all day, 23:30 curfew; bus #73 from train station during the day or #90 at night and Sun to Piazza Isolo stop, walk over the river beyond Ponte Nuovo at Salita Fontana del Ferro 15; tel. 045-590-360, fax 045-800-9127).

EATING

Osteria al Duca has an affordable two-course *menu* (€15) and lots more options. For dessert, try the chocolate salami. Family-run with a lively atmosphere, it's popular—go early (Mon and Wed–Sat 12:00–14:30 & 18:30–22:30, Tue 18:30–22:30 only, closed Sun, Via Arche Scaligere 2, a half block from della Scala family tombs, tel. 045-594-474). Its sister restaurant, **Osteria Giulietta e Romeo,** serves up the same menu a block away with fewer crowds (Tue–Sat 12:15–14:30 & 19:00–22:30, Mon 19:00–22:30 only, closed Sun, Corso Sant'Anastasia 27, tel. 045-800-9177).

Ristorante Sant'Eufemia feels like a splurge, with tuxedoed waiters and an elegant Old World dining room. Let owners Luca and Mamma pamper you as you dine on the freshest grilled seafood or meats prepared *alla Veronese*. Several reasonably priced *menus*

The Wines of Verona

Wine connoisseurs appreciate the high-quality wines of this area. One of the most common, Valpolicella, has two forms: the red wine Amarone and dessert wine Recioto. To produce Amarone, grapes are partially dried *(passito)* before fermentation, then aged for a minimum of four years in oak casks, resulting in a rich, velvety, full-bodied red. Recioto, which in local dialect means "ears," uses only the grapes from the top of the cluster (they stick out like ears). Since these grapes get the most sun, they mature the fastest and have the highest concentration of sugar. The grapes are dried for months until all moisture has gone out before pressing, then aged for one to three years.

Sample these at Verona's many *enotecas* (wine-tasting bars) or restaurants. The first week of every April, Verona hosts Vinitaly, an important international convention of domestic and international wines. Vintners vie for prestigious awards and hotels are booked long in advance.

(including *coperto* and *servizio*) range from €13 for a *piatto completo* (a full meal in one course) to €32 for a four-course seafood feast. Light eaters could make a whole meal from their great antipasto buffet, which has lots of vegetarian choices (Mon–Sat 12:00–14:30 & 19:00–22:00, closed Sun except July–Aug; find alley directly across from Corso Porta Borsari 27 called Corte S. Gio in Foro, then go through gate at end of the alley; tel. 045-800-6865).

Other good choices include **Ristorante Greppia** for typical *cucina Veronese* (Tue–Sun 12:00–14:30 & 19:00–22:30, closed Mon, Vicolo Samaritana 3, first left off Via Mazzini if you're coming from Piazza Erbe, tel. 045-800-4577) and the pricier, venerable **Bottega del Vino,** renowned for its extensive wine list (Wed–Mon 12:00–15:00 & 19:00–24:00, closed Tue, Via Scudo di Francia 3, second left off Via Mazzini as you're coming from Piazza Erbe, tel. 045-800-4535).

San Matteo Church, a cheaper option, offers self-service and wood-fired pizza by day and full-service meals by night in a renovated church. Look for big, creative salads and regional dishes with market-fresh produce at reasonable prices (Mon–Fri 12:00–14:30 & 19:00–23:00, pizzas until 24:00, open for dinner Sat–Sun July–Aug only, tel. 045-800-4538). Located at Vicolo del Guasto 4, down a little alleyway between Via Catullo and Porta Borsari.

Osteria le Vecete offers an enjoyable, intimate pub setting. Choose from a dozen or so daily specials of homemade pastas and Veronese specialties, as well as simpler *bruschette* and salads—or select a few of the elaborately dressed *crostini* available in the case at the bar to go with your *vino* (kitchen open daily 12:00–15:00 & 18:30–22:30, but drinks are served between mealtimes and until late; it's buried in an alley between Via Mazzini and Corso Sant'Anastasia: from Piazza Brà, go down Via Mazzini and turn left onto Via Quattro Spade, then right onto Via Pelliciai, restaurant is about a half block down on your left at #3; tel. 045-594-748).

De Gusto offers an all-you-can-eat €7.50 lunch buffet featuring dozens of fresh salad ingredients, plus soups, pasta salads, roasted veggies, and drinks (water, wine, beer, soda). Supplemental plates of cheese and *salumi* are €4–5, and wine upgrades cost about €2. The à la carte dinners are just as good (Mon–Sat 12:00–14:30 & 19:30–22:30, closed Sun, around the corner from Juliet's balcony at Via Stella 13A, tel. 045-803-0066).

Oreste dal Zovo, run by enthusiastic Oreste and his Chicagoan wife Beverly, is a fun, local wine-and-grappa bar. There's no formal food, but an abundance of fun and hearty bar snacks. This historic *enoteca* was once the private chapel of the archbishop of Verona, and hiding between the bottles are traces of its past—ask Beverly to tell you the story. In addition to the wines, you can pick up high-quality aged balsamic vinegars from Modena and extra-virgin olive oils (March–Dec daily 8:00–20:00, closed Mon Jan–Feb, cash only, no chairs—just a couple of benches; it's on the alley—Vicolo San Marco in Foro 7—off Porta Borsari, just a block from Piazza Erbe; tel. 045-803-4369).

On Piazza Brà: For fast food with a great view of Verona's main square, consider the self-service **Brek** (daily, breakfast and sandwiches from 9:30, full menu 11:30–15:00 & 18:30–22:00, indoor/outdoor seating, cheap salad plates, Piazza Brà 20, right on the square between the historic city gate and the equestrian statue, tel. 045-800-4561). **Enoteca Can Grande** serves great wine (such as the local *Passito Bianco*) and delicious seasonal specialties thoughtfully paired with wines suggested by Giuliano and Corrina (Tue–Sun 10:00–24:00, always closed Mon, also closed Tue in winter; a block off Piazza Brà at Via dietro Liston 19D—if the equestrian statue jogged slightly right, he'd head straight here; tel. 045-595-022).

Picnic: **PAM supermarket** is just outside the historic gate on Piazza Brà (Mon–Sat 8:00–20:00, Sun 9:00–20:00, exit Piazza Brà through the gate and take the first right).

TRANSPORTATION CONNECTIONS

From Verona by Train to: Florence (4/day, 3 hrs, more with transfer in Bologna; note that all Rome-bound trains stop in Florence—listed as *Firenze* on train schedules), **Bologna** (nearly hrly, 2 hrs), **Milan** (hrly, 1.5–2 hrs), **Rome** (4/day, 5–6 hrs, more with transfer in Bologna), **Bolzano** (hrly, 1.5–2 hrs; note that Brennero-bound trains stop in Bolzano).

Parking in Verona: Drivers will find lots of cheap parking at the stadium, as well as cheap long-term parking near the train station and city walls and across the river from San Zeno. There are a few free spaces across the river from Castelvecchio. The most central lot is behind the Arena on Piazza Cittadella (guarded, €1/hr). Street parking costs €1.50 per hour (buy ticket at *tabacchi* shop to put on dashboard, spaces marked with blue lines). The town center is closed to regular traffic, but if you're staying here, you can drive to your hotel, and they'll get you permission—ask for details when you book.

Ravenna

Ravenna is on the tourist map for one reason: Its 1,500-year-old churches, decorated with best-in-the-West Byzantine mosaics. Known in Roman times as Classe, the city was an imperial port for the large naval fleet. Briefly a capital of eastern Rome during its fall, Ravenna was taken by the barbarians. Then, in A.D. 540, the Byzantine emperor Justinian turned Ravenna into the westernmost pillar of the Byzantine empire. A pinnacle of civilization in that age, Ravenna was a light in Europe's Dark Ages. Two hundred years later, the Lombards booted out the Byzantines, and Ravenna melted into the backwaters of medieval Italy, staying out of historical sight for a thousand years.

Today the local economy booms with a big chemical industry, the discovery of offshore gas deposits, and the construction of a new ship canal. The bustling town center is Italy's best for bicyclists. Locals go about their business, while busloads of tourists slip quietly in and out of town for the best look at the glories of Byzantium this side of Istanbul.

Ravenna is only a two-hour round-trip detour from the main Venice–Florence train line and worth the effort for those interested in old mosaics. While its sights don't merit an overnight stop, many find that the peaceful charm of this untouristy and classy town makes it a pleasant surprise in their Italian wandering.

ORIENTATION

Central Ravenna is quiet, with a pedestrian-friendly core and more bikes than cars. Keep to the sides of the streets; bikes take the center lane (subtly indicated by white brick paving) down the brick "pedestrian" streets. Listen for the outta-my-way bells.

On a quick visit to Ravenna, I'd see Basilica di San Vitale and its adjacent Mausoleum of Galla Placidia, Basilica di Sant'Apollinare

Nuovo, the covered market, and Piazza del Popolo.

Tourist Information

The TI is a 15-minute walk (or a 5-minute pedal) from the train station (April–Sept Mon–Sat 8:30–19:00, Sun 10:00–16:00; Oct–March Mon–Sat 8:30–18:00, Sun 10:00–16:00; Via Salara 8, tel. 0544-35404, www.turismo.ravenna.it). For directions to the TI, see "Orientation Walk," below. Most sights close early in the winter months; pick up a schedule from the TI when you arrive.

Helpful Hints

Combo-Tickets: There are two combo-tickets for Ravenna; you'll probably want the Visit Card. Many top sights can only be seen by purchasing the €7.50 Visit Card (sold at the sights), since there are no individual admissions to these attractions. This combo-ticket includes admission to the Basilica di San Vitale, the Basilica di Sant'Apollinare Nuovo, Spirito Santo (may be under restoration in 2006), Battistero Neoniano, and Cappella Arcivescovile. From March to mid-June—when school-group tours take over and space is limited—there's a €9.50 version of this combo-ticket that includes the Mausoleum of Galla Placidia; otherwise, the mausoleum is automatically included for free.

A different €5 combo-ticket covers admissions to the National Museum and the Mausoleum of Teodorico. A €6.50 version of this combo-ticket also includes the Church of Sant'Apollinare in Classe. This ticket is only worth buying if you'll be visiting two or more of the following sights, since—unlike with the other combo-ticket mentioned above—you can buy individual admissions to these: National Museum-€4 (Tue–Sun 8:30–19:30, closed Mon, last entry 30 min before closing), Mausoleum of Teodorico-€2 (daily 8:30–19:00, last entry 30 min before closing), and Church of Sant'Apollinare in Classe-€2 (Mon–Sat 8:30–19:30, Sun 13:00–19:30, last entry 30 min before closing).

Bike Rental: Yellow bikes are available free from the TI (passport required); the bikes are parked at the TI and other locations around town. Or rent bikes from the Coop San Vitale on Piazza Farini (€1/hour, €7.75/day, Mon–Sat 7:00–20:00, closed Sun, ID required, on the left just as you exit train station, tel. 0544-37031).

Local Guide: For a private guide, consider Claudia Frassineti (€85/half day, mobile 335-613-2996, www.abacoguide.it, abacoguide@tiscalinet.it).

Parking: You can park for free in the lot on north end of town just west of Via di Roma, or for €3 during the day and free overnight from 20:00–8:00 at Largo Giustiniano just north of San Vitale.

SIGHTS

Orientation Walk—A visit to Ravenna can be as short as a three-hour loop from the train station. From the station, walk straight down Viale Farini to Piazza del Popolo. This square was built around 1500, during a 60-year period when the city was ruled by Venice. Under the Venetian architecture, the people of Ravenna gather here as they have for centuries.

Most sights are within a few minutes' walk of Piazza del Popolo. A right on Via IV Novembre takes you a block to the colorful covered market, Mercato Coperto (Mon–Sat 7:00–13:00, closed Sun, good for picnic fixings). The TI is a block away (head up Via Cavour and take the first right onto Via Salara 8). Ravenna's two most important sights, Basilica di San Vitale and the Mausoleum of Galla Placidia, are two blocks from Piazza del Popolo (head down San Vitale). A few blocks from Piazza del Popolo in the opposite direction is the Basilica di Sant'Apollinare Nuovo, also worth a look. From there, it's about a 10-minute walk back to the station.

▲▲**Basilica di San Vitale**—Imagine: It's A.D. 540. The city of Rome has been looted, the land is crawling with barbarians, and the infrastructure of Rome's thousand-year empire is crumbling fast. Into this chaotic world comes the emperor of the East (Justinian), bringing order and stability, briefly reassembling the empire, and making Ravenna a beacon of civilization. His church of San Vitale—standing as a sanctuary of order in the midst of that madness—is covered with lavish mosaics: gold and glass chips the size of your fingernail. It's impressive enough to see a 1,400-year-old church. But rarer is to see one decorated in brilliant mosaics, still managing to convey the intended feeling that "this peace and stability was brought to you by your emperor and God."

In a medieval frame of mind, study the scene: High above the altar, God is in Heaven, portrayed as Christ sitting on a celestial orb. He oversees his glorious creation, symbolized by the four rivers. And running the show on earth is Justinian (left side), sporting both a halo and a crown to indicate that he's leader of the Church and the state. Here, Justinian brings together the military leaders and the church leaders, all united by the straight line of eyes. The bald bishop of Ravenna—the only person who was actually here—is portrayed most realistically.

Facing the emperor (from the right side) is his wife, Theodora, and her entourage. Decked out in jewels and pearls, the former dancer, who became Justinian's mistress and then empress, carries a chalice to consecrate the new church.

Ravenna

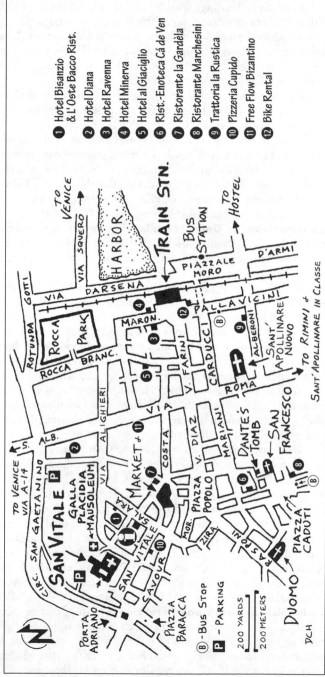

1 Hotel Bisanzio & L'Oste Bacco Rist.
2 Hotel Diana
3 Hotel Ravenna
4 Hotel Minerva
5 Hotel al Giaciglio
6 Rist.-Enoteca Cà de Ven
7 Ristorante la Gardèla
8 Ristorante Marchesini
9 Trattoria la Rustica
10 Pizzeria Cupido
11 Free Flow Bizantino
12 Bike Rental

The walls and ceilings sparkle with colorful biblical scenes told with a sixth-century exuberance. This was a time of transition, and many consider the mosaics of Ravenna both the last ancient Roman and the first medieval European works of art. For instance, you'll see a beardless Christ (as he was depicted by ancient Romans) next to a bearded Christ, his standard medieval portrayal.

The church's octagonal design—clearly Eastern—is similar to the construction of the Hagia Sofia, the mosque-turned-museum built 10 years earlier in Constantinople. Charlemagne visited Ravenna here in about A.D. 800. He was so impressed that when he returned to his capital, Aix-la-Chapelle (present-day Aachen in Germany), he built a church that many consider the first great stone building in northern Europe, modeled after this one (included in €7.50 Visit Card—see page 153, daily 9:00–19:00, off-season until 16:30, last entry 15 min before closing, tel. 0544-215-193).

▲▲**Mausoleum of Galla Placidia**—Just across the courtyard (and included in Basilica di San Vitale admission) is this tiny, humble-looking mausoleum, with the oldest—and to many, the best—mosaics in Ravenna.

The Mausoleum of Galla Placidia (plah-CHEE-dee-ah) is reputed to be the burial place of this daughter, sister, and mother of emperors, who died in A.D. 450. The little light that sneaks through the thin alabaster panels brings a glow and a twinkle to the early Christian symbolism that fills the little room. Opposite the door is St. Lawrence martyred on a fiery grill. He's legendary for mocking his executors, reportedly saying something like "I'm done on this side, you can turn me over now." He was famous as an example of the strength of the feisty early Christians. The four Gospels clearly labeled on the bookshelf were the source of this strength as they were persecuted by the Romans.

The dome is filled with stars. Along with Mark's lion, Luke's ox, and John's eagle, the golden cross rises from the east bringing life to all. Doves drink from fountains, symbolic of souls finding nourishment in the word of God. Cover the light of the door with your hand to see the standard Roman portrayal of Christ—beardless and as the Good Shepherd. Jesus, dressed in gold and purple like a Roman emperor, is King of Paradise—receiving the faithful (represented by lambs). The Eastern influence is apparent in the carpet-like decorative patterns (€9.50 for Visit Card March–mid-June, otherwise included in €7.50 Visit Card, daily 9:00–19:00, off-season until 16:30, last entry 45 before closing, tel. 0544-215-193).

▲▲**Basilica di Sant'Apollinare Nuovo**—This austere sixth-century church, with a typical early-Christian-basilica floor plan, has two huge and wonderfully preserved side panels. One is a procession of haloed virgins, each bringing gifts to the Madonna and the Christ Child. Opposite, Christ is on his throne with four angels, awaiting a solemn procession of 26 martyrs. Ignoring the Baroque altar from a thousand years later, we can clearly see the rectangular Roman hall of justice or basilica plan—which was adopted by churches and used throughout the Middle Ages (included in €7.50 Visit Card, daily April–Sept 9:00–19:00, March and Oct 9:30–17:30, Nov–Feb 10:00–17:00, on Via di Roma, tel. 0544-219-518).

▲**Church of Sant'Apollinare in Classe**—Featuring great Byzantine art, this church is a favorite among mosaic pilgrims (€2, included in upgraded €6.50 combo-ticket—described in "Combo-Tickets" on page 153—with National Museum and Mausoleum of Teodorico, Mon–Sat 8:30–19:30, Sun 13:00–19:30, confirm hours Oct–March, last entry 30 min before closing, tel. 0544-473-661).

The church is two miles out of town. Catch bus #4 or #44 across the street from the train station (on the corner by the park) or from Piazza Caduti (€1, 3/hr, 15 min, reduced service Sun; with your back to the *tabacchi* shop, stop is on the corner; buy bus tickets from any *tabacchi* shop). To head back to town, walk down the same road; the stop is about 100 yards ahead on the right. The **Self-Service Sant'Apollinare in Classe** is a cheap, air-conditioned, and efficient place for lunch right on the church grounds (daily 12:00–15:00, tel. 0544-35679).

Other Sights—The **Basilica di San Francesco** is worth a look for its simple interior and flooded, mosaic-covered crypt below the main altar (daily 7:00–12:00 & 15:00–18:30). Nearby in Via Dante Alighieri, the **Tomb of Dante** is the true site of his remains. After being exiled from Florence for his political beliefs, Dante lived out the rest of his life in Ravenna. The Florentines forgave Dante posthumously and wanted to bring their famous poet's bones home to rest. To protect his relics from theft by the Florentines, Ravenna hid his bones in the neighboring Basilica di San Francesco in 1519. They lay forgotten in the church for three centuries, until they were rediscovered and replaced in his tomb in 1865. The Dante memorial—often mistaken for a tomb—in Florence's Santa Croce Church is empty (daily April–Sept 9:00–19:00, Oct–March 9:00–12:00 & 14:00–17:00).

Overrated Sight—The nearby beach town of Rimini is a crowded mess.

SLEEPING

(€1 = about $1.20, country code: 39)

$$$ **Hotel Bisanzio** is a business-class splurge in the city center (Sb-€100, Db-€124, larger Db-€170, air-con; from Piazza del Popolo take Via IV Novembre to the Mercato, turn left onto Via Cavour and take the first right, Via Salara 30; tel. 0544-217-111, fax

0544-32539, www.bisanziohotel.com, info@bizanziohotel.com).

$$ Hotel Diana, with 33 bright and tasteful rooms, is a classy, peaceful haven with a restful terrace. Though a bit outside the town center, it's still an easy walk from the Basilica di San Vitale (Sb-€57, Db-€83, fancier rooms available, free Internet access in lobby, free parking nearby, Via G. Rossi 47, tel. 0544-39164, fax 0544-30001, www.hoteldiana.ra.it, info@hoteldiana.ra.it).

$$ Hotel Ravenna, with 24 spanking-clean rooms and double-paned windows, is located across from the train station (S-€40, Sb-€48, D-€55, Db-€90, no breakfast, Viale Maroncelli 12, tel. 0544-212-204, fax 0544-212-077, www.hotelravenna.ra.it, hotelravenna@ravennablu.it).

$$ Hotel Minerva, just to the right of the train station as you exit, has 18 renovated rooms (Sb-€55, Db-€90, breakfast-€6, elevator, air-con, nearby laundry service and Internet access, Viale Maroncelli 1, tel. 0544-213-711, fax 0544-211-420, www.minerva-hotel.com, hotel.minerva@libero.it).

$ Hotel al Giaciglio, also near the station, is recently renovated and a handy choice (S-€40, D-€50, Db-€65, Via R. Brancaleone 42, tel. & fax 0544-39403, www.albergoalgiaciglio .com, info@albergoalgiaciglio.com).

Hostel: **$ Ostello Dante Hostel,** a 15-minute walk from the station, has Internet access (with phone card), laundry service, free loaner bikes and bike rentals (€2.50/day), and a game room. There's a long lockout (10:00–17:00), but you can leave your bags if you arrive by noon (110 beds, €13.50/bed, €1 more in winter, 4–5 bed rooms, family rooms-€15/person with baths, €3/night extra for non-Italian members, includes breakfast and sheets, towels-€1, 23:30 curfew, Via Nicolodi 12, tel. & fax 0544-421-164, www.hostelravenna.com, hostelravenna@hotmail.com). From the station, follow signs for *Ostello Dante* or catch bus #1, #10, #11, or #70 from the station and get off at Via Gulli.

EATING

The atmospheric **Ristorante-Enoteca Ca' de Ven** (House of Wine) fills a 16th-century warehouse with locals enjoying quality wine and traditional cuisine. *Piadina* (peeah-DEE-nah) dominates the menu. An unleavened bread that kids are raised on here, it's served with cheese and prosciutto. Try their dessert specialty—*torta di marzipan*—made exclusively for them by a local bakery. This decadent almond-and-cocoa brownie is best with sweet red wine (Tue–Sat 12:00–14:00 & 19:00–22:00, Sun 17:30–22:15, closed Mon, 2-min walk from Piazza del Popolo on Via Cairoli which turns into Via C. Ricci, Via C. Ricci 24, tel. 0544-30163).

Locals like **Ristorante la Gardèla,** which offers reasonable prices and cuisine specialties from Italy's mountainous Emilia-Romagna region. These include *cappelletti in brodo,* a light, meat-stuffed pasta served in broth (Fri–Wed 12:00–14:30 & 19:00–22:00, closed Thu, from Piazza del Popolo follow Via IV Novembre past Piazza della Costa to corner of Via Ponte Marino 3, tel. 0544-217-147). **L'Oste Bacco** is run by the same owners with the same menu (homemade pastas from €5.50–7.50, Wed–Mon 12:15–14:30 & 19:15–22:30, closed Tue, just north of TI at Via Salara 20, tel. 0544-35363).

Ristorante Marchesini has a classy self-serve menu that includes some delicious salads and homemade pastas (Mon–Sat 12:00–14:30, Sat–Sun also 19:30–22:30 only by reservation for a fixed price *menu,* 5-min walk from Piazza del Popolo, on corner of Piazza Caduti at Via Mazzini 6—ride elevator to 1st floor, tel. 0544-212-309).

Trattoria la Rustica is also worthwhile, featuring grilled meats and homemade pasta like *cappelletti, garganelli,* and *tortelli* (about €20 for a 3-course dinner not including wine, Sat–Thu 12:00–14:30 & 19:00–22:30, closed Fri, located at Via Alberoni 55, tel. 0544-218-128).

Free Flow Bizantino, inside the covered market, is another self-serve place (Mon–Fri 11:45–14:30, for lunch only). Or assemble a picnic at the market and enjoy your feast in the shady gardens of the **Rocca Brancaleone** fortress (daily 8:00–20:00, closes at sunset off-season; 5-min walk from station, following Via Maroncelli until you see the walls).

For a cheap and traditional lunch or snack, try a *piadina* or *cresciolo* (calzone-like) sandwich from **Pizzeria Cupido** just up Via Cavour, past the covered market. These tasty sandwiches (€3–4.50) come stuffed with a variety of meats, cheeses, and vegetables. Try one filled with *squacquerone,* a soft regional cream cheese (daily 8:00–15:00; Mon, Thu, and Sun also open until 20:00; Via Cavour 43—through the archway, tel. 0544-37529).

TRANSPORTATION CONNECTIONS

From Ravenna by Train to: Venice (10/day, change in Ferrara or Bologna, sometimes Venice's Mestre station as well, 3–4 hrs), **Florence** (about hrly, requires transfer in Bologna, 2.5 hrs).

THE DOLOMITES

(Dolomiti)

Italy's dramatic limestone rooftop, the Dolomites, offers some of the best mountain thrills in Europe. Bolzano is the gateway to the Dolomites, and Castelrotto is a good home base for your exploration of Alpe di Siusi, Europe's largest alpine meadow.

The sunny Dolomites are well-developed, and the region's famous valleys and towns suffer from après-ski fever. The cost for the comfort of reliably good weather is a drained-reservoir feeling. Lovers of the Alps may miss the lushness that comes with the unpredictable weather farther north. But the bold limestone pillars, flecked with snow over green meadows under a blue sky, offer a worthwhile mountain experience.

A hard-fought history has left the region bicultural, with an emphasis on the German. Locals speak German first, and some wish they were still part of Austria. In the Middle Ages, as part of the Holy Roman Empire, the region faced north. Later, it was firmly in the Austrian Hapsburg realm. By losing World War I, Austria's South Tirol became Italy's Alto Adige. Mussolini did what he could to Italianize the region, including giving each town an Italian name. But even in the last decade, local secessionist groups have agitated violently for more autonomy with some success (see sidebar on page 162).

The government has wooed locals with economic breaks that make it one of Italy's richest areas (as local prices attest), and today all signs and literature in the province of Alto Adige/Süd Tirol are in both languages. Many include a third language, Ladin—an ancient, Latin-type language still spoken in a few traditional areas. (I have listed both the Italian and German, so the confusion caused by this guidebook will match that experienced in your travels.)

The Dolomites

In spite of all the glamorous ski resorts and busy construction cranes, the local color survives in a warm, blue-aproned, ruddy-faced, felt-hat-with-feathers way. There's yogurt and yodeling for breakfast. Culturally as much as geographically, the area is reminiscent of Austria. The Austrian Tirol is named for a village that is now part of Italy.

Planning Your Time

Train travelers should side-trip in from Bolzano (90 min north of Verona). To get a feel for the alpine culture, spend a night in Castelrotto. With two nights in Castelrotto, you can actually get

Ich bin ein Italiener

Four in 10 Italians living in the Dolomites region speak German. Many are fair-skinned and blue-eyed, eating strudel after their pasta, and feeling a closer bond with their ancestors in Austria than to their swarthy countrymen to the south. In the province of Alto Adige/Süd Tirol, along the Austrian border, German-speakers are the majority. Most have a passing knowledge of Italian, but they watch German-language TV, read newspapers in *Deutsch,* and live in Tirolean-looking villages.

At the end of World War I, the region was ceded by (loser) Austria to (winner) Italy. Mussolini suppressed the Germanic elements as part of his propaganda campaign praising all things Italian. Many German speakers hoped that Hitler would "liberate" them from Italy. But Hitler's close alliance with Mussolini prevented that from happening. Instead, in June 1939, residents were given six months to make a hard choice—move north to the Fatherland and become German citizens, or stay in their homeland *(Heimat)* under Italian rule. The vast majority (212,000, or 85 percent) made the decision to leave, but because of the outbreak of World War II, only 75,000 actually moved.

At the war's end, German-speakers were again disappointed when the Allied powers refused to grant them autonomy or repatriation (citizenship) with Austria, instead sticking with the pre-war arrangement.

The region rebuilt, and the two linguistic groups got along, but for the remainder of the 20th century there was always an underlying problem: German-speakers were continually outvoted by the Italian-speaking majority in the regional government (comprising both Italian-speaking Trentino and German-speaking Alto Adige/Süd Tirol). German-speakers lobbied the national government for more control on the provincial (not regional) level, even turning to demonstrations and violence. Over the years, Rome slowly and grudgingly granted increased local control.

Today, Alto Adige/Süd Tirol has a large measure of autonomy written into the country's 2001 constitution, though it's still officially tied to Trentino. Roads, water, electricity, communications, and schools are all under local control, including the new Free University of Bolzano/Bozen, founded in 1998.

out and hike. Tenderfeet ride the bus, catch a cable car, and stroll. For serious mountain thrills, do a six-hour hike. And for a thrill that won't soon fade away, spend a night in a mountain hut. This means two nights in Castelrotto straddling a night in a hut.

Car hikers with a day can drive the three-hour loop from Bolzano or Castelrotto (Val Gardena–Sella Pass–Val di Fassa) and ride one of the lifts to the top for a ridge walk. Connecting Bolzano and Venice by the Great Dolomite Road takes two hours longer than by the autostrada, but it is far more scenic (see "More Sights in the Dolomites," page 181). Note that in 2006, local authorities may impose a €5 toll, payable at toll booths, for cars driven by non-locals passing through the Alto Adige region (the money would be used to helped preserve the unique ecosystem).

Hiking season is mid-June through mid-October. The region is crowded, booming, and blooming from mid-July through mid-September. It's packed with Italian vacationers in August. Spring is usually pretty dead, with lifts shut down, huts closed, and the most exciting trails still under snow. Many hotels and restaurants close in April and November. Ski season (Dec–Easter) is busiest of all. For more information, visit www.suedtirol.com.

Bolzano
(Bozen)

Willkommen to the Italian Tirol! If it weren't so sunny, you could be in Innsbruck. This enjoyable old town of 100,000 is the most convenient gateway to the Dolomites, especially if you're relying on public transportation. It's just the place to take a Tirolean stroll. Everything mentioned in Bolzano is a 10-minute walk from the train station and the main square, Piazza Walther.

ORIENTATION

Tourist Information

Bolzano's TI is helpful (Mon–Fri 9:00–18:30, Sat 9:00–12:30, closed Sun, tel. 0471-307-000, www.bolzano-bozen.it). Pick up the city map (includes a walking tour). Don't bother with the €2.50 Museum Card (offering discounts at 5 Bolzano museums and the skippable Runkelstein Castle), because the only sight that merits your time is the archaeological museum with its famous Ice Man.

The excellent Dolomites Information Center is buried deep in the old town, on an alley between Portici/Lauben and Via Vintler Strasse at Galleria Vintler-Durchgàng 16 (Mon–Fri 10:00–12:00 & 15:00–17:00, closed Sat–Sun, tel. 0471-999-955).

Arrival in Bolzano

To get to the TI and downtown from the train station, veer left up the tree-lined Viale della Stazione/Bahnhofallee, and walk past the bus station (on your left) two blocks to **Piazza Walther.** You'll see the TI on your right.

From Piazza Walther, the medieval heart of town is a couple of blocks northwest. The arcaded Via dei Portici leads to **Piazza Erbe/Obstplatz,** with the Ice Man and an open-air produce market (see "Markets," page 166).

Helpful Hints

Internet Access: Try AthesiaBuch bookstore at Portici/Lauben 41 (free but €5 deposit required, Mon–Fri 9:00–12:25 & 14:30–19:00, Sat 9:00–12:50, closed Sun, 2 computers, 30 min max, terminals 2 floors down from street level, second entrance on Via Argentieri/Silbergasse, tel. 0471-927-211).

Baggage Storage: To find the baggage-check desk at the train station, exit the station to the right, then re-enter the station hall near the taxi stand (€4/day, daily 8:00–18:30). The nearby bus terminal (located a block northwest of the train station) also has lockers.

Laundry: Lava e Asciuga launderette is at Via Rosmini Strasse 81, about two blocks from the archaeological museum (daily 7:30–22:30, last wash 21:30, €3 wash, €3 dry, mobile 340-220-2323).

Bike Rental: There are plenty of bikes for rent just off Piazza Walther on Viale della Stazione/Bahnhofallee (€1/6 hrs, €2/day, €10 refundable deposit, ID required, May–Oct Mon–Sat 9:00–18:30, closed Sun and Nov–April). The TI also has 10 bikes to rent for €5 per day (€10 refundable deposit, ID required, year-round).

SIGHTS

▲▲South Tirol Museum of Archaeology (Museo Archeologico dell'Alto Adige/Südtiroler Archäologiemuseum)—This excellent museum features the original "Ötzi the Ice Man." The frozen body was discovered high in the mountains on the Italian/Austrian border by some German hikers in 1991. Initially thinking it was the corpse of a lost hiker, officials chopped him out of the glacier, damaging his left side. But upon discovering his older-than-Bronze Age hatchet, they realized what they had found—a 5,300-year-old, nearly perfectly preserved man with clothing and gear in excellent condition for his age. With Ötzi as the centerpiece, the museum takes you on an intriguing journey through time, recounting the evolution of man—from the Paleolithic era to the Roman period and finally to the Middle Ages—in vivid detail. The exhibit offers

Bolzano

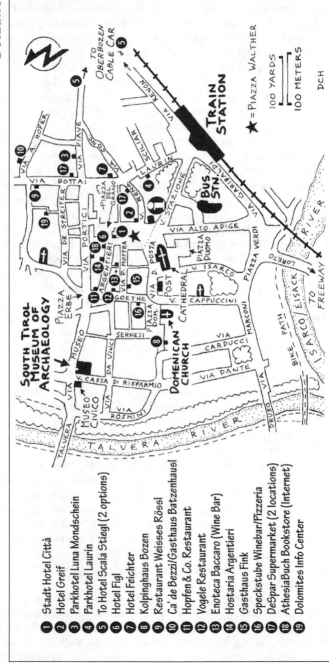

SOUTH TIROL OF MUSEUM OF ARCHAEOLOGY

TO OBERBOZEN CABLE CAR & ⑤

TRAIN STATION

BUS STN.

PIAZZA WALTHER

★ = PIAZZA WALTHER

100 YARDS
100 METERS

DCH

TALVERA RIVER

ISARCO/EISACK RIVER

① Stadt Hotel Città
② Hotel Greif
③ Parkhotel Luna Mondschein
④ Parkhotel Laurin
⑤ To Hotel Scala Stiegl (2 options)
⑥ Hotel Figl
⑦ Hotel Feichter
⑧ Kolpinghaus Bozen
⑨ Restaurant Weisses Rössl
⑩ Ca' de Bezzi/Gasthaus Batzenhausl
⑪ Hopfen & Co. Restaurant
⑫ Vögele Restaurant
⑬ Enoteca Baccaro (Wine Bar)
⑭ Hostaria Argentieri
⑮ Gasthaus Fink
⑯ Speckstube Winebar/Pizzeria
⑰ DeSpar Supermarket (2 locations)
⑱ AthesiaBuch Bookstore (Internet)
⑲ Dolomites Info Center

informative displays and models, video demonstrations of the extraction of Ötzi and his personal effects, a great audioguide, and interactive computers. You'll see Ötzi himself—still frozen—and glass cases displaying his incredibly well-preserved and fascinating clothing and gear, including a two-color, finely-stitched coat, his loincloth, a fancy hat, shoes, a finely crafted hatchet, and fire-making gadgets (€8, Tue–Sun 10:00–18:00, Thu until 20:00, last entry 1 hour before closing, closed Mon, essential audioguide–€2, near the river at Via Museo/Museumstrasse 43, tel. 0471-320-121, www.iceman .it). The museum may be splitting into two in 2006, with the Ice Man exhibits in one museum and everything else in the other.

Markets—Piazza Erbe/Obstplatz hosts an ancient and still-thriving open-air produce market (daily except Sat afternoon and all day Sun). Wash your produce in the handy drinking fountain in the middle of the market. Another market (offering more variety, not just food) is held Saturday mornings on Piazza della Vittoria.

Dominican Church (Chiesa dei Domenicani)—If you're an art-lover who won't make it to Padua to see Giotto's Scrovegni Chapel (see page 121), drop by this 13th-century church to see its Chapel of St. John (San Giovanni; chapel near altar to the right), frescoed by the Giotto School. It lacks the high quality and that divine "Smurf" blue of the Scrovegni Chapel, but it gives you a sense of Giotto's vision (free, Mon–Sat 9:30–17:00, Sun 12:00–17:00, also see peaceful cloisters farther to right of Piazza Domenicani, entrance at #19).

Cable Car to Oberbozen—Of the three different cable cars that can whisk you out of Bolzano, the most popular is the Ritten lift to the touristy town of Oberbozen (€3.50 round-trip, runs daily about 7:00–19:00, 3/hr in summer, 1/hr and shorter opening times off-season, 12 min, toll-free tel. 800-846-047 or tel. 0471-345-245 for cable-car info and trail conditions, operates year-round; from Bolzano train station, walk about 5 blocks down Via Renon to Renon/Rittner Sielbahn cable car). More interesting than Oberbozen are the nearby "earth pyramids," which are a 20-minute walk from the cable-car station. The pyramids are Bryce Canyon-like pinnacles rising out of the ridge. A little train runs along the ridge, connecting Oberbozen with other villages nearly hourly, including Collalbo (€3.50 round-trip). From Collalbo, you can hike another 45 minutes to more pyramids. (Oberbozen TI tel. 0471-356-100.)

Many are tempted to wimp out on the Dolomites and see them from a distance by hiking from Oberbozen to the Pemmern chairlift (€7.20 one-way including Renon/Rittner gondola, €8.90 round-trip), riding to Schwarzseespitze, and walking 45 more minutes to the Rittner Horn. You'll be atop a 7,000-foot peak with distant but often-hazy Dolomite views. It's not worth the trouble.

SLEEPING

All of the listed hotels are in the city center.

$$$ Stadt Hotel Città is ideally situated on Piazza Walther. The hotel's café spills out onto the piazza, offering a prime spot for people-watching. While the hotel is expensive for singles, it's a fine value for couples, especially if you plan to spend an afternoon in their free-for-guests Wellness Center (daily 16:30–22:00, Turkish bath, massage by appointment, whirlpool, Finnish sauna), which is the perfect way to unwind after a day of hiking or skiing in the Dolomites (Sb-€70–98, Db-€98–155, Tb-€120–190, air-con, elevator, Piazza Walther 1, tel. 0471-975-221, fax 0471-976-688, www .hotelcitta.info, info@hotelcitta.info).

$$$ Hotel Greif is also right on Piazza Walther. When you walk into any of their 33 rooms, which were designed by artists, you'll feel like you're in a modern-art installation. It's not cozy, but it is striking, and a stay here comes with perhaps the best breakfast in Italy (Sb-€115, "comfort" Db-€173, "superior" Db-€220, most rooms non-smoking, air-con, in-room Internet access, expensive laundry, Piazza Walther, entrance on Via della Rena/Raing, tel. 0471-318-000, fax 0471-318-148, www.greif.it, info@greif.it). Drivers follow signs to Parking Walther and enter hotel from the garage.

$$$ Parkhotel Luna Mondschein is an elegant, well-maintained hotel in a lush park setting, offering 76 posh rooms a five-minute walk from Piazza Walther (Sb-€87, Db-€132, buffet breakfast-€12, parking-€14/day, Internet in lobby, tel. 0471-975-642, fax 0471-975-577, www.hotel-luna.it, info@hotel-luna.it).

$$$ Parkhotel Laurin is an Old World luxury hotel, with 96 tastefully decorated rooms, marble bathrooms, a classy dining room and terrace, a swimming pool, extensive garden, attentive

---

Sleep Code

(€1 = about $1.20, country code: 39)
S = Single, **D** = Double/Twin, **T** = Triple, **Q** = Quad, **b** = bathroom, **s** = shower only. Unless otherwise noted, credit cards are accepted, English is spoken, and breakfast is included.

To help you sort easily through these listings, I've divided the rooms into three categories based on the price for a standard double room with bath:

   $$$ **Higher Priced**—Most rooms €100 or more.
    $$ **Moderately Priced**—Most rooms between €60–100.
     $ **Lower Priced**—Most rooms €60 or less.

staff, and frescoes throughout the grand lobby depicting the legend of King Laurin (Db-€170, parking-€13/day, Via Laurin 4, tel. 0471-311-000, fax 0471-311-148, www.laurin.it, info@laurin.it).

$$$ Scala Stiegl, with a traditional feel with modern touches, is convenient to the station, Rittner lift, and Piazza Walther. It also has a garden with a swimming pool (May–Sept only) and free loaner bikes (Sb-€88, Db-€140, some with garden views, parking-€8/day, Internet in lobby, Via Brennero/Brenner Strasse 11, tel. 0471-976-222, fax 0471-981-141, www.scalahot.com, info@scalahot.com).

$$ Hotel Figl, warmly run by Anton and Helga Mayr, has 23 comfy, Ikea-style rooms and an attached café on a pedestrian square located a block from Piazza Walther (Sb-€80, Db-€100, junior suite-€110, €5 discount with this book through 2006 if you ask, breakfast extra, air-con, elevator, Kornplatz 9, tel. 0471-978-412, fax 0471-978-413, www.figl.net, info@figl.net).

$$ Hotel Feichter is a bright, cheery lodging with a characteristic alpine feel and 30 rooms overlooking the rooftops of Bolzano (Sb-€55, Db-€83, Tb-€100; leave Piazza Walther on Via Rena/Raing, then take left fork to Via Grappoli/Weintraubengasse, hotel is a few steps ahead on the right at #15; tel. 0471-978-768, fax 0471-974-803, www.paginegialle.it/feichter, hotel.feichter@dnet.it, Hannes Feichter and family).

$$ Kolpinghaus Bozen, modern, clean, and church-run, has 40 rooms with twin beds (placed head to toe) and all the comforts. It makes one feel thankful (Sb-€55, Db-€84, Tb-€126, elevator, 4 blocks from Piazza Walther near Piazza Domenicani at Spitalgasse 3, tel. 0471-308-400, fax 0471-973-917, www.kolping.it/bz, kolping @tin.it). The lineup in front of the building at lunchtime consists mainly of workers waiting for the institutional cafeteria to open up (€9.50 meals, open to public, Mon–Fri 11:45–14:00 & 18:30–19:30, Sat 11:45–14:00, closed Sun).

EATING

All listings are in the downtown core. Prices are pretty consistent (you can generally get a good plate of meat and veggies for €10) and nearly every local-style place serves a mix of Germanic Tiroler and Italian fare.

Weisses Rössl offers affordable—mostly Tirolean—food with fine vegetarian options. Located in a traditional woody setting, it's good for dining indoors with lots of locals (€10 plates, Mon–Fri 11:00–23:00, Sat afternoon only, closed Sat eve and all Sun, Via Bottai/Bindergasse 6, 2 blocks north of Piazza Municipio, tel. 0471-973-267).

Ca' de Bezzi/Gasthaus Batzenhausl is historic, with a Teutonic-feeling upper floor; in contrast, the patio and back room

Tirolean Cuisine

During your visit to the Dolomites, take a break from Italian-style pizzas and pastas to sample some of the region's traditional cuisine...with a distinctly Austrian flavor. To reduce confusion, I've generally listed Italian names here, though local menus are in both Italian and German (and, usually, English).

Wurst and sauerkraut are the Tirolean clichés. More adventurous eaters seek out *speck,* a raw ham smoked for five months, then thinly sliced and served as an antipasto or in sandwiches. *Canederli*—large dumplings with bits of *speck,* liver, spinach, or cheese—are often served in broth, or with butter and cheese.

The stars of Tirolean cuisine are the hearty meat dishes—which, unlike traditional Italian main courses, are nearly always served with side dishes of doughy dumplings or vegetables and potatoes. Try *stinco di maiale* (roasted pork shank, usually garnished with potatoes) and *crauti rossi* (a sweetish sauerkraut made from red cabbage). *Carrè affumicato* is pork shank that is first smoked, then boiled. *Selvaggine,* or wild game, comes in the form of *capriolo* (fawn), *cervo* (venison), or *camoscio* (chamois/antelope). Game is eaten smoked and thinly sliced in *antipasti*; in meat sauce *(ragù)* with fresh pasta or as ravioli stuffing; or in entrees, as tender chunks grilled or roasted in a rich sauce *(spezzatino)*.

For dessert, strudel is everywhere, filled with the harvest from this region's renowned apple orchards. Cakes and pies are loaded with other locally grown fruits, raisins, and nuts. *Kaiserschmarrn* is an interesting alternative: a tall, eggy crêpe prepared with raisins and topped with powdered sugar and red currant jam.

Bier (birra) is king in the Alto Adige (the best-known brand, Forst, is brewed in nearby Merano), but wines of the area are well matched to the local fare. *Magdalaner* is a light, dry red made from schiava grapes. *Lagrein scuro* is a full-bodied red, dry and fruity, similar to a Cabernet or Merlot. *Gewürztraminer* is a dry white wine with spicy, fruit flavor. For something stronger, try *grappa* made from Williams pears (and served with a wedge of fresh pear), or *grappa Nocino*—a darker, sweeter brew similar to Jägermeister. *Guten Appetit und Prost!*

are refreshingly modern and untouristy. They make their own breads and pastas and serve traditional Tirolean fare, with a focus on fine wine—about 30 bottles are open to serve by the glass (daily 11:30–14:30 & 19:00–24:00, limited menu between mealtimes, a rare place open on Sun, Via Andreas Hofer Strasse 30, tel. 0471-050-950).

Hopfen and Co. fills an 800-year-old house. While it's been a tavern since the 1600s, it feels stylish and fresh. It's a high-energy place packed with locals who come for its homemade beer, delicious Tiroler/Italian food, and reasonable prices (first course-€5–7, main course-€10–15, Mon–Sat 9:30–24:00, Piazza Erbe/Obstplatz 17, tel. 0471-300-788).

Vogele, a half-block south, serves Tirolean/Italian cuisine with modern flair and has fine outdoor seating under the arcade (main course-€10–15, Mon–Sat 12:00–16:00 & 18:00–23:00, closed Sun, Via Goethe Strasse 3, tel. 0471-973-938).

Enoteca Baccaro, a wine bar a half-block east of Vogele, is an intriguing spot for a glass of wine (from €0.90–3) and bar snacks amid locals (Mon–Fri 9:00–21:00, Sat 9:00–15:00, plus Sat until 21:00 in winter, closed Sun, located on a hidden alley off Via Argentieri/Silbergasse 17, look for *vino* sign next to fountain on south side of street, tel. 0471-971-421).

Hostaria Argentieri, pricier than the rest, serves Italian and German cuisine, plus seafood, in a classy setting a block away from Kornplatz (Mon–Sat 12:00–14:30 & 19:00–22:30, closed Sun, Via Argentieri/Silbergasse 14, tel. 0471-981-718).

Gasthaus Fink has typical Tirolean and Italian dishes priced just right, on a quiet pedestrian street just off Piazza Walther (Fri–Wed 9:30–21:30, limited menu between mealtimes, closed Thu, Via della Mostra 9, tel. 0471-975-047).

The economical **Speckstube Winebar/Pizzeria** specializes in wood-fired pizzas and offers a salad bar and local fare (daily 12:00–15:30 & 18:00–22:00, Via Goethe Strasse 32, tel. 0471-970-070).

Picnic: Assemble the ingredients at the **Piazza Erbe/Obstplatz** market; dine in a superb setting in Piazza Walther or in the park along the Talvera River. A **DeSpar supermarket** is on Via della Rena/Raing near Piazza Walther (Mon–Fri 8:30–19:30, Sat 8:00–18:00, closed Sun; from Piazza Walther, facing TI, take street to the left for 2 blocks, supermarket is at bottom of stairs on your left).

TRANSPORTATION CONNECTIONS

From Bolzano by Train to: Milan (about hrly with a change in Verona, 3.5 hrs), **Verona** (about hrly, 90 min), **Trento** (about hrly, 50 min), **Venice** and **Florence** (about hrly, via Verona, 3–6 hrs), **Innsbruck** (every 2 hrs, 2 hrs).

By Bus to: Castelrotto (2/hr, every 2 hrs on Sun, 50 min, leaves Bolzano at :10 and :40, pick up free schedule at bus station, tel. 800-846-047). The bus leaves from Bolzano's bus station (1 block west of train station). Buy a €6 round-trip ticket from bus station ticket window or driver. If you are heading directly to **Alpe di Siusi,** take the same bus, get off just before the village of Siusi, and ascend on the cable car (tell driver you want to get off at the *cabinovia* or Seiseralm Bergbahn). For more on Alpe di Siusi, see page 177.

Castelrotto
(Kastelruth)

The ideal home base for exploring the Alpe di Siusi, Castelrotto (town population: 2,000, district population: 6,000, altitude: 3,475 feet) has more village character than any other town I know of in the region. With its traffic-free center, a thousand years of history, oversized and hyperactive bell tower, and traditionally clad locals, it seems lost in another world. Against a backdrop of mountains, Castelrotto conveys the powerful message that simple pleasures are enough.

ORIENTATION

Tourist Information
The TI is on the main square, Piazza Kraus (mid-May–Oct Mon–Sat 8:30–12:30 & 14:00–18:00, Sun 10:00–12:00, shorter hours and closed Sun off-season, tel. 0471-706-333, www.kastelruth.com). If you plan to do any hiking, pick up the TI's list of suggested hikes, including estimated walking times and trail numbers.

Arrival in Castelrotto
The bus station is a few steps below the town's main square. The bus parking lot has a little building with an ATM, WC, and phones; take the stairs to the right of this building to get to the main square and TI. Another cash machine is to the left of the TI.

Drivers can park near the *bushof* (bus station). Each of the recommended hotels has free parking. For Albergo Torre and Hotel Cavallino d'Oro, go right through the traffic-free town center (very likely with a police escort); under the bell tower, drive through the white arch to the right of the TI, and park in the lot opposite Albergo Torre. For Hotel al Lupo, park in the bus parking lot; it's behind the hotel. All three recommended private homes have free and easy parking.

SELF-GUIDED WALK

Welcome to Castelrotto

Castelrotto is tiny, with very little to distract you other than the surrounding mountains and hikes. The **main square**, Piazza Kraus, is named for the family who ruled the town from 1550–1800. Their palace, now the City Hall and TI, overlooks the square and sports the Kraus family coat of arms.

Castelrotto uses its square well. The farmers' market takes place here Friday mornings in the summer (June–Oct) and a clothing market fills the square most Thursday mornings. While touristy, Castelrotto is not a full-blown resort; if you're on the square weekdays at 14:45, you'll see local moms gather their pre-schoolers, chat, then stop by the playground on Plattenstrasse. Before and after Sunday Mass, the square is crowded with villagers and farmers (who fill the church). The main Mass (at 9:00 or 9:30) is in German, and another Mass takes place in Italian throughout tourist season (at 10:30) for visitors.

The 250-foot **bell tower** dominates the town. It was once attached to a church, which burned in 1753. While the bell tower was quickly rebuilt, the present-day church was constructed a century later next to the gutted church (which was then torn down to make space for the square). The wire between the church and tower connects the noisy bells. The sacristan can easily ring them using an electric switch.

The bells of Castelrotto—a big part of the town experience—ring on the hour throughout the day and night. While tourists wonder why they clang through the wee hours, locals—who grew up with the chimes—find them comforting. The bells mark the hours, summon people to Mass, announce festivals, and warn when storms threaten. In the days when people used to believe that thunder was the devil approaching, the bells called everyone to pray. Townspeople say that their sound cleared the clouds. Bells ring big at 7:00, noon, and 19:00. The biggest of the eight bells (7,500 pounds) peals only on special days. On Fridays, the bells ring at 15:00, commemorating Christ's sacrifice. The colorful **poles** in front of the church (yellow and white for the Vatican, red and white for Tirol) fly flags on festival days.

Before entering the church, notice the plaque commemorating this tiny community's WWI dead—*Dorf* means from the village itself and *Fraktion* is from an outlying district. Stepping into the church, you're surrounded by art from about 1850. The church is dedicated to Saints Peter and Paul. Paintings that flank the high altar show how each was martyred (crucifixion and beheading). The pews are carved of walnut wood.

Castelrotto

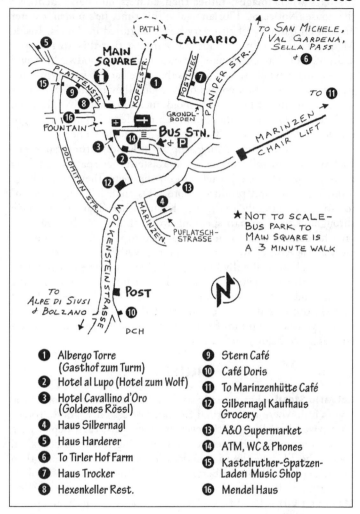

① Albergo Torre
(Gasthof zum Turm)

② Hotel al Lupo (Hotel zum Wolf)

③ Hotel Cavallino d'Oro
(Goldenes Rössl)

④ Haus Silbernagl

⑤ Haus Harderer

⑥ To Tirler Hof Farm

⑦ Haus Trocker

⑧ Hexenkeller Rest.

⑨ Stern Café

⑩ Café Doris

⑪ To Marinzenhütte Café

⑫ Silbernagl Kaufhaus
Grocery

⑬ A&O Supermarket

⑭ ATM, WC & Phones

⑮ Kastelruther-Spatzen-
Laden Music Shop

⑯ Mendel Haus

Back outside, belly up to the **fountain** (opposite the bell tower). It dates from the 19th century. St. Florian, the protector against fires, keeps an eye on it today as he did when villagers (and their horses) first came here for a drink of water. With your back to the bell tower, look to see a finely frescoed house half a block down the lane.

Mendel Haus has a traditional facade and a wood carvers' shop. Its frescoes (from 1886) include many symbolic figures, as well as an emblem of a carpenter above the door—a relic from the days when images, rather than address numbers, identified the house. Notice St. Florian again; this time, he's pouring water on a small painting of this very house engulfed in flames. Inside Mendel Haus are fine carvings, a reminder that this area—especially nearby Val Gardena—is famous for its woodwork. You'll also see many witches, folk figures that date back to when this area was the Salem of this corner of Europe. They burned women as witches who didn't fit society's mold, including midwives, healers, redheads, and so on. Walk around behind Mendel Haus, turn right on Dolomitenstrasse, and find a house of hometown heroes.

For the Beatles of yodeling, stop by the **Kastelruther–Spatzen-Laden** shop. The folk-singing group Kastelruther Spatzen is a gang of local boys who put Castelrotto on the map. They have a huge following here, and produce "more CDs than Michael Jackson" (or so I was proudly told). The Kastelruther–Spatzen are huge throughout the German-speaking world. Each October they put on a hometown concert, filling Castelrotto with fans from as far away as the Alsace, Switzerland, and the Netherlands. This shop—where you'll undoubtedly hear their imitable music—is a yodelers' Carnaby Street. Downstairs is a small museum slathered with gifts, awards, and gold records (Mon–Fri 9:00–12:00 & 14:00–18:00, Sat 9:00–12:00, closed Sun). For more of this Kastelruther–Spatzen mania, you can drop into the Hexenkeller (their fan club beer cellar, described below) for a drink.

SIGHTS

Calvario Stroll—For a scenic stroll, take a short walk around the town's hill, where the original Roman fortress once stood. Today, it's a paved lane lined with seven little chapels, each depicting a scene from Christ's Passion and culminating in the Crucifixion. Facing the TI, take the road under the arch to the right, and then follow signs to Kalvarienberg/Calvario. This 15-minute stroll is great after dark—romantically lit and under the stars.

Marinzen Lift—The little Marinzen cable car zips you up the mountain to the Marinzenhütte café, which has an animal park for kids (March–Oct daily 9:00–17:00, closed Nov–March, tel. 0471-707-158). The cable car runs only during the warmer months (€4.50 one-way, €6.50 round-trip, end of May–Oct daily 9:15–16:45, closed off-season and rainy mornings, tel. 0471-707-160; from the town square, head downhill toward Wolkensteinstrasse, turn left and go another 50 yards down the road towards San Michele, find the chairlift a few steps off the road on the right). You can hike down from Marinzen (1 hr) or return on the lift.

SLEEPING

(€1 = about $1.20, country code: 39)

$$$ **Albergo Torre** (in German, **Gasthof zum Turm**) is comfort-able, clean, and alpine-traditional, with great beds and modern bathrooms (small Db-€60–96, big Db-€80–122 depending on sea-son—price peaks in August, Tb-€94–165, includes breakfast, €4 extra for 1-night stays, closed April and Nov, elevator, behind TI at Kofelgasse 8, tel. 0471-706-349, fax 0471-707-268, www.zumturm .com, info@zumturm.com, Gabi and Günther).

$$ **Hotel al Lupo** (in German, **zum Wolf**) is pure Tirolean, with all the comforts in 23 neat-as-a-pin rooms, most with balconies (Sb-€35–50, Db-€56–85, prices vary with season and view, includes buffet breakfast, non-smoking rooms, elevator, free parking, closed April–mid-May and Nov–mid-Dec, a block below main square at Wolkensteinstrasse 5, tel. 0471-706-332, fax 0471-707-030, www .hotelwolf.it, info@hotelwolf.it, Arno).

$$ **Hotel Cavallino d'Oro** (in German, **Goldenes Rössl**), on the main square, has plenty of Tirolean character and plush, welcom-ing public rooms. Run by friendly and helpful Stefan and Susanne, the entire place is dappled with artistic woodsy touches and historic photos. If you love antiques by candlelight, this 650-year-old hotel is the best in town (Sb-€50–70, Db-€85–105 depending on season, discount for 3-night stay, no elevator, Krausplatz 1, tel. 0471-706-337, fax 0471-707-172, www.cavallino.it, cavallino@cavallino.it). Stefan converted his wine cellar into a spa and sauna, complete with heated tile seats, solarium (for tanning), and tropical plants (free and private for guests, great after a hike, just book an hour).

$$ **Haus Silbernagl** has 12 cozy and tranquil rooms with balconies and views, a heated indoor swimming pool, wet and dry saunas (in summer by request only), sun chairs, and free parking (Sb-€31–43, Db-€62–86, cash only, Puflatschstrasse 1, tel. 0471-706-699, fax 0471-710-004, www.garni-silbernagl.com, gsilber@tin.it, helpful Petra). It's a five-minute walk from the town center (from the main road, head out to Wolkensteinstrasse and up Marinzenstrasse).

$ **Haus Harderer,** below Hotel Kastelruth (take the middle road where it forks), rents an apartment for two to three people (€20–25/person, cash only, min 2-night stay in summer, Platten-strasse 20, tel. 0471-706-702, harderer@gmx.net, run by Inge, plus Oswald, Heinz, Ida, and Maunz the cat).

$ **Haus Trocker** is a modern home where Frau Trocker, who doesn't speak English, rents two simple rooms at the edge of town (D-€50, follow steps from bus station 50 yards below Hotel Kastel Seiseralm to Fostlweg 6, tel. 0471-707-087).

$ **Tirler Hof,** the storybook Jaider family farm, has 45 cows, one friendly *Hund,* four Old World-comfy guest rooms, and a great mountain view (D-€42, Db-€45, discount for stays longer than 1 night, includes breakfast, cash only, practical only for drivers, it's the first farm a half-mile outside of town on the right on road to San Michele, Paniderstrasse 44, tel. & fax 0471-706-017, jaider .klaus@rolmail.net, Paola). The ground-floor double has a private bath. The top-floor rooms share a bathroom and a great balcony. Take a stroll before breakfast.

EATING

Cavallino d'Oro Hotel Restaurant offers a variety of beautifully presented homemade Tirolean cuisine—including wild game, *canederli* dumplings, and strudel—in a dressy but relaxed and woodsy ambience. The head waiter, Marco, is very helpful; quiz him before you order (€25 meals, daily 12:00–14:00 & 18:00–21:00).

Albergo Torre's Restaurant, homier and a bit less expensive, has the best terrace in town and is another fine option for traditional and international dishes (Thu–Tue 12:00–14:00 & 18:00–21:00, closed Wed, April, and Nov).

The **Hexenkeller** ("Witches' Cellar") dishes up inexpensive and basic German and Italian grub in the liveliest venue in town. This is the clubhouse for the local superstar folk band (described above) so you'll be surrounded by their platinum records, photos, and music. If you need air, they have a simple back terrace (Mon–Sat 17:00–24:00, closed Sun; a half-block from TI on Plattenstrasse—facing TI, go left through arch; tel. 0471-707-393).

For strudel, locals like the no-nonsense **Stern** café (Tue–Sun 7:30–19:00, closed Mon, tel. 0471-706-382, on Plattenstrasse; facing TI, go left through arch) and **Café Doris** (Wed–Mon 12:00–23:00, closed Tue, on main road at Wolkensteinstrasse 29, tel. 0471-706-340); both have terraces.

Castelrotto has two groceries: **Silbernagl Kaufhaus** (Mon–Sat 8:00–12:00 & 15:00–19:00, closed Sat afternoons off-season and Sun, on Wolkensteinstrasse) and the smaller **A&O Supermarket,** two blocks away, also on the main drag (Mon–Sat 8:00–12:00 & 15:00–18:30, closed Sun, off-season closed Sat afternoon as well, Via Panider Strasse).

TRANSPORTATION CONNECTIONS

From Castelrotto by Bus to: Bolzano (€6 round-trip, 2/hr, every 2 hrs on Sun, 50 min, runs 6:50–19:10), **Vigo di Fassa** and **Canazei** (late June–mid-Sept only, 4/day, 2 hrs), and **Ortisei/St. Ulrich** and **St. Cristina** (6/day in summer, 4/day off-season, 30 min to Ortisei, 40 min to St. Cristina). Get bus schedules at the TI, call toll-free 800-846-047 or 0471-706-633, or check www.sii.bz.it. For **Alpe di Siusi** connections, see below.

Alpe di Siusi
(Seiser Alm)

Europe's largest high-alpine meadow, Alpe di Siusi separates two of the most famous Dolomite ski-resort valleys. Measuring eight by 20 miles and soaring up to 6,500 feet high, Alpe di Siusi is dotted by farm huts and wildflowers (mid-June–July), surrounded by dramatic—if distant—Dolomite peaks and cliffs, and much appreciated by hordes of walkers.

Compatsch, the little tourist town at the entrance of the meadow, has a TI, food, and services (described below). The Sasso Lungo mountains ("Langkofel" in German, "Long Stone" in English) at the head of the meadow provide a storybook Dolomite backdrop, while the spooky Schlern peak stands boldly staring into the haze of the peninsula. The Schlern, looking like a devilish *Winged Victory,* gave ancient peoples enough willies to spawn legends of supernatural forces. The Schlern witch, today's tourist-brochure mascot, was the cause of many a broom-riding medieval townswoman's fiery death.

Alpe di Siusi is my recommended one-stop look at the Dolomites because of Castelrotto's charm as a home base, its easy accessibility for those with and without cars, its variety of walks and hikes, and its quintessentially Dolomite mountain views.

The meadow is famous for its wildflowers—a fragrant festival (best in June) blooming with flowers that grow only between 1,800 and 2,200 meters above sea level. The cows munching away in this vast meadow produce 2.5 million gallons of milk annually, much of which is sent to Bolzano to make cheese. After tourism, dairy is the leading industry here. While cows winter in Castelrotto, they summer in Alpe di Siusi. The meadow is also dotted with small, idyllic hotels and chalet restaurants. It's extremely family-friendly, with playgrounds at each stop and plenty of animals to pet.

ORIENTATION

Getting to Alpe di Siusi

By Car: A natural preserve, Alpe di Siusi is closed to cars during the day (9:00–17:00) unless you're staying in one of the area hotels. (Show your reservation confirmation as proof.) Parking at Compatsch (€9/day) requires that you arrive before the road closes at 9:00 in the morning, though you can drive back down at any time. Or you can use the free parking lot located just 200 yards

Alpe di Siusi

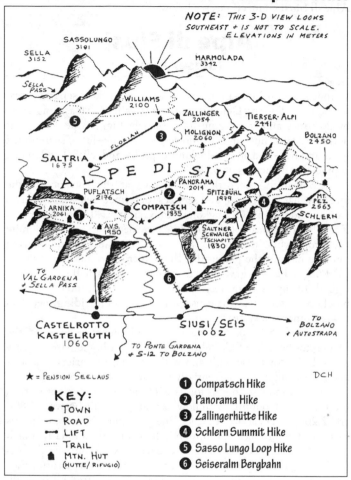

NOTE: THIS 3-D VIEW LOOKS SOUTHEAST & IS NOT TO SCALE. ELEVATIONS IN METERS

SELLA 3152
SELLA PASS
SASSOLUNGO 3191
WILLIAMS 2100
ZALLINGER 2054
MARMOLADA 3342
TIERSER·ALPI 2441
BOLZANO 2450
FLORIAN
SALTRIA 1675
MOLIGNON 2060
A L P E · D I · S I U S I
PUFLATSCH 2176
PANORAMA 2014
SPITZBÜHL 1979
MT. PEZ 2563
ARNIKA 2061
COMPATSCH 1835
SCHLERN
A.V.S. 1950
SALTNER SCHWAIGE ·TSCHAPIT 1830
TO VAL GARDENA & SELLA PASS
CASTELROTTO KASTELRUTH 1060
SIUSI/SEIS 1002
TO BOLZANO & AUTOSTRADA
TO PONTE GARDENA & S-12 TO BOLZANO

★ = PENSION SEELAUS
DCH

KEY:
- • TOWN
- — ROAD
- ⊷ LIFT
- ⋯ TRAIL
- ▲ MTN. HUT (HUTTE/ RIFUGIO)

1. Compatsch Hike
2. Panorama Hike
3. Zallingerhütte Hike
4. Schlern Summit Hike
5. Sasso Lungo Loop Hike
6. Seiseralm Bergbahn

outside the village of Siusi, on the road from Bolzano; park your car and take the cable car to get to Compatsch

By Cable Car from Siusi up to Alpe di Siusi: A cable car (*cabinovia*/Seiseralm Bergbahn) runs hikers and skiers from the village of Siusi to Compatsch, the gateway to the meadow (€9 one-way, €11 round-trip, 15-min ride to the top, daily June–mid-Oct 8:00–19:00, off-season 8:00–18:00—confirm times locally before making the trip to Siusi, www.seiseralm-bergbahn.com); from Compatsch you can take a shuttle bus farther into Alpe di Siusi to Saltria. A free shuttle-bus service connects the cable-car lift with Castelrotto (see below).

By Bus from Castelrotto: Buses shuttle hikers from Castel-rotto's bus station *(bushof)* to the base of the cable car (Seiseralm

Bergbahn) near the village of Siusi. Cable-car shuttle buses—from Castelrotto to Siusi are free (3/hr in season, daily 8:10–19:35, fewer mid-day), though the cable car costs money (see above).

Other regional buses (such as the one to and from Bolzano) also stop at Siusi (frequent in summer, 4/day in each direction off-season, tell driver you want to get off at the *cabinovia* or Seiseralm Bergbahn).

There is also the Alpe di Siusi Express, a shuttle bus that runs from Castelrotto to Compatsch (€9 one-way, €11 round-trip, 6/day, 25 min, see www.silbernagl.it for schedules).

For a longer stay, consider the Combi-Card (€27/3 days, €39/6 days, covers Alpe di Siusi Express, cable car, and Compatsch-Saltria shuttle bus, 1 round-trip on Marinzen lift, valid for 7 days from time stamp).

Getting Around Alpe di Siusi

Shuttle Buses: As the meadow is essentially car-free, the park's buses shuttle visitors to and from key points along the tiny road all the way from Compatsch, at the entry to the meadow, to the end of the line at Saltria, at the foot of the postcard-dramatic Sasso peaks (€4 round-trip, 50 percent discount if you have a cable-car ticket, runs every 20 min from 9:00–18:45, 40 min). The road to Alpe di Siusi is closed to drivers 9:00–17:00.

Cable Cars and Chair Lifts: The entire meadow is served by various lifts (marked on maps). These are worth the roughly €6 per ride to get you into the higher and more scenic hiking areas—or back to the shuttle buses quickly. Keep in mind that lifts and shuttle buses stop running fairly early (often around 17:30).

Compatsch

This tourist village (6,135 feet) at the entrance to the meadow is served by cable car from the town of Siusi. You can drive here if you are staying at a hotel in Alpe di Siusi (or if you arrive very early or leave very late, outside of park opening hours). Parking costs €9 per day.

Compatsch has a **TI** (Mon–Sat 9:00–17:00, Sun 9:00–12:00; off-season Mon–Sat 9:00–13:00, closed Sun; WCs at cable-car station, tel. 0471-727-904).

You'll also find a grocery store (open mid-June–mid-Oct), ATM, hotels, restaurants, and shops.

You can rent mountain bikes here; there is a world of tiny paved and gravel lanes to pedal on (€6.75/1 hr, €17/4 hrs, 50 yards from TI in strip mall, tel. 0471-727-824).

Trocker rents horses and provides guides (€15/1 hr, €30/2 hrs, €42/3 hrs, open June–Oct, closed Nov–May, next to Compatsch TI and near cable-car station, tel. 0471-727-807, no English spoken).

Sleeping Near the Park Entrance: $$$ Pension Seelaus, a 10-minute walk downhill from Compatsch, is a cozy, friendly, family-run place with a Germanic feel and down comforters. Its Wellness Center has a sauna, hydro-massage, and mini-pool (Sb-€55–90, Db-€108–178, prices vary with season and type of room; includes buffet breakfast, hearty dinner, free, easy parking and use of Wellness Center; Via Compatsch 8, tel. 0471-727-954, fax 0471-727-835, www.hotelseelaus.it, info@hotelseelaus.it, Roberto). There are many more chalets and huts with rooms for rent in Alpe di Siusi (which generally cost as much as a normal hotel; see TI for details).

ACTIVITIES

Hikes in Alpe di Siusi

Easy meadow walks abound, giving tenderfeet classic Dolomite views from baby-stroller trails. Experienced hikers should consider the tougher and more exciting treks. Before attempting a hike, call or stop by the local TI to confirm your understanding of the time and skills required. As always, when hiking in the mountains, assume weather can change quickly. Many lifts operate mid-June through mid-October and during the winter ski season. The Panorama and Puflatsch lifts (both near Compatsch) run further into the off-season. Meadow walks, for flower-lovers and strollers, are pretty—or maybe pretty boring. Chairlifts are springboards for more dramatic and demanding hikes. Trails are very well marked, and the brightly painted numbers are keyed into local maps. For simple hikes, you can basically string together three or four hut names. For anything more serious, invest in a good map. The Kompass Bolzano map #54 covers everything in this chapter (scale 1:50,000, €4.10). The Wanderkarte map of Alpe di Siusi (produced by Tabacco) offers more detail and focuses on just Alpe di Siusi (scale 1:25,000, €4.40).

Walks and Hikes from Compatsch

Panorama to Zallingerhütte—This is the basic four-hour, mostly level walk, giving you fine vistas from both ends of the meadow, fun stops along the way, and lifts up and down on each end. Ride the €5 lift to Panorama (6,500 feet), then hike 75 minutes to Molignonhütte (6,725 feet), and continue 2.5 hours (fairly level, follow trails #2 and then #7) to Zallingerhütte (6,725 feet). After 10 minutes, head to Williams Hütte, where you catch the €7 lift back to Saltria and the bus stop. Both Molignonhütte and Zallingerhütte have great restaurants for a drink or meal. For shorter or cheaper versions, you can ride the lift up and stroll back down. For a more thrilling extension from Zallingerhutte, take a short-but-steep trail that leads to a ridge (get local advice before starting out).

Summit Hike of Schlern (Sciliar)—For a challenging 12-mile, six-hour hike—with a possible overnight in a traditional mountain refuge (generally open mid-June–mid-Oct)—consider hiking to the summit of Schlern and spending a night in Rifugio Bolzano/Schlernhaus. Start at the Spitzbühl chairlift (5,659 feet, free parking lot, first bus stop in park), which drops you at Spitzbühl (6,348 feet). Trail #5 takes you through a high meadow, down to the Saltner Schwaige dairy farm (6,004 feet—you want the dairy farm at Tschapit, not the one near Zallingerhütte), across a stream, and steeply up the Schlern mountain. About three hours into your hike, you'll meet trail #1 and walk across the rocky tabletop plateau of Schlern to the mountain hotel **Rifugio Bolzano/Schlernhaus** (8,038 feet, 130 beds available, D-€40, dorm beds-€17, breakfast-€6, tel. 0471-612-024, call for reservation, closed mid-Oct–mid-June). From this dramatic setting, you can enjoy a meal and get a great view of the Rosengarten range. Hike 20 more minutes up the nearby peak (Mount Pez, 8,399 feet) for a 360-degree alpine panorama. From Rifugio Bolzano/Schlernhaus, you can hike back the way you came or walk farther along the Schlern (7 miles, 2.5 hrs, past **Rifugio Alpe di Tires**, €18.50 beds, €10 bunks, tel. 0471-727-958, 8,005 feet) and descend back into Alpe di Siusi, to the road where the bus or cable car will return you to your starting point or hotel. This is popular with serious hikers as the best hike in the region.

The "Trail of the Witches"—Take a lift from Compatsch to Puflatsch for the two-hour loop north to Arnikahütte (with a café) and back (elevation gain about 660 feet). Walking among the legendary stone seats of witches, you'll enjoy fine views of the valley all the way down to Castelrotto.

Loop around Sasso Lungo—Another dramatic but easy hike is the eight-hour walk around the Sasso Lungo (Langkofel) mountains. You can ride the bus to Saltria (end of the line), take the chairlift to Williamshütte, walk past the Zallingerhütte (overnight possible, Db-€90–122, includes breakfast and dinner, open mid-May–mid-Oct, tel. 0471-727-947), and circle the Sasso Lungo group. (Get details and advice from the TI.)

MORE SIGHTS IN THE DOLOMITES

▲▲**Great Dolomite Road**—This is the definitive Dolomite drive: Belluno–Cortina–Pordoi Pass–Sella Pass–Val di Fassa–Bolzano. Connecting Venice with Bolzano this way (the Belluno–Venice autostrada is slick) takes three hours longer than the direct Bolzano–Verona–Venice autostrada. No public transit does this trip. In spring and early summer, passes labeled "closed" are often bare, dry, and, as far as local drivers are concerned, wide open. Call

0471-200-198 for road conditions (in Italian or German only).

▲▲**Abbreviated Dolomite Loop Drive**—See the biggies in half the miles (allow 4 hrs, Bolzano–Castelrotto–Val Gardena–Sella Pass–Val di Fassa–Bolzano). Val Gardena (Grodner Tal) is famous for its skiing and hiking resorts, traditional Ladin culture, and wood-carvers (the wood-carving company ANRI is from the Val Gardena town of St. Cristina). It's a bit overrated, but even if its culture has been suffocated by the big bucks of hedonistic European fun-seekers, it remains a good jumping-off point for trips into the mountains. Within an hour, you'll reach Sella Pass (7,349 feet). After a series of tight, hairpin turns a half-mile or so over the pass, you'll see some benches and cars. Pull over and watch the rock climbers. Val di Fassa is Alberto Tomba (Tomba la Bomba) country.

The town of Canazei, at the head of the valley and the end of the bus line, has the most ambience and altitude (4,642 feet). From there, a lift (€5.30 one-way, €8 round-trip) or gondola (€8 one-way, €11.50 round-trip, Easter–Oct daily 8:45–12:30 & 14:00–18:00, closed Oct–Easter for both) takes you to Col dei Rossi Belvedere, where you can hike the Bindelweg trail past Rifugio Belvedere along an easy but breathtaking ridge to Rifugio Viel del Pan (Canazei TI for lift info: tel. 0462-601-113). This three-hour round-trip hike has views of the highest mountain in the Dolomites—the Marmolada—and the Dolo-mighty Sella range.

▲▲**Reifenstein Castle**—For one of Europe's most intimate looks at medieval castle life, let the friendly lady of Reifenstein (Frau Blanc) show you around her wonderfully preserved castle. She leads tours on the hour, in Italian and German, squeezing in whatever English she can (€5, open Easter–Oct; tours Sat–Thu at 10:30, 14:00, and 15:00; mid-July–mid-Sept also at 16:00, closed Fri, picnic spot at drawbridge, tel. 0472-765-879).

To drive to the castle, exit the autostrada at Vipiteno (Sterzing) and follow signs toward Bolzano. The castle is just west of the freeway; park at the base of the castle's rock. Of the two castles here, Reifenstein is the one to the west. While this is easy by car, it's probably not worth the trouble by train (from Bolzano, 6/day, 70 min).

▲**Glurns**—Drivers connecting the Dolomites and Lake Como by the high road via Meran and Bormio should spend the night in the amazing little town of Glurns (45 min west of touristy Meran, between Schluderns and Taufers). Glurns still lives within its square wall on the Adige River, with a church bell tower that has a thing about ringing, and real farms, rather than boutiques, filling the town courtyards. There are several small hotels in the town, but I'd stay in a private home (such as Family Hofer, 6 rooms, €25/person with breakfast, less for 3 nights, cash only, 100 yards from town square, near church, just outside wall on river, Via Adige 1, tel. 0473-831-597, fax 0473-835-864).

THE LAKES

Commune with nature where Italy is welded to the Alps, in the lovely Italian lakes district. In this land of lakes, the million-euro question is: Which one? For the best mix of accessibility, scenery, and offbeat-ness, Varenna on Lake Como is my top choice, followed by Stresa on Lake Maggiore. You'll get a complete dose of Italian-lakes wonder and aristocratic-old-days romance. Bustling Milan, just an hour away from either lake, doesn't even exist. Now it's your turn to be *chiuso per restauro* (closed for restoration). If relaxation's not on your agenda, the lakes shouldn't be either. If choosing between Lake Como or Maggiore, Lake Como is a better place to linger and Lake Maggiore makes a good day-trip from Milan.

Lake Como
(Lago di Como)

Planning Your Time

Lake Como is Milan's quick getaway, and the sleepy midlake village of Varenna is the gateway to the lake and the handiest base of operations. With good connections to Milan, Malpensa Airport, and midlake destinations, Varenna is my favorite home base for the lakes. Even though there are no essential activities, plan for at least two nights so you'll have an uninterrupted day to see how slow you can get your pulse.

Lake Como, lined with elegant, 19th-century villas, crowned by snowcapped mountains, and busy with ferries, hydrofoils, and little passenger ships, is a good place to take a break from the

The Italian Lakes

intensity and obligatory-turnstile culture of central Italy. It seems half the travelers you'll meet have tossed their itineraries into the lake and are actually relaxing.

Today the hazy, lazy lake's only serious industry is tourism. Thousands of lakeside residents travel daily to nearby Lugano, in Switzerland, to find work. The lake's isolation and flat economy have left it pretty much the way the 19th-century Romantic poets described it.

Getting Around Lake Como

By Boat: Lake Como is well-served by boats and hydrofoils. The lake service is divided into three parts: south–north from Como to Colico; midlake between Varenna, Bellagio, Menaggio, Tremezzo,

---

Boat Schedule Literacy Tips

Feriale = Monday–Saturday
Festivo = Sunday and holidays
Partenze da = Departing from

Autotraghetto = Car ferry
Aliscafo = Hydrofoil
Battello navetta =
    Passenger-only ferry

Central Lake Como

and Cadenabbia (Villa Carlotta); and the southeastern arm to Lecco. Unless you're going through Como, you'll probably limit your cruising to the midlake service (boat info: tel. 031-579-211 or toll-free 800-551-801). Boats go about hourly between Varenna, Menaggio, and Bellagio (€2.80 per hop, 15 min, daily approximately 7:00–21:00, confirm return trip when you disembark). Stopovers aren't allowed and there's no break for round-trips, so buy individual tickets for each ride. The one-day, €8 midlake pass saves you money if you make three rides.

The free schedule (available at TIs, hotels, and boat docks) lists prices and times. Confusingly, the schedule requires you to scan four different timetables to know all the departures: the all-lake service; the hydrofoil (*aliscafo-servizio rapido,* costs a third more, enclosed, stuffy, speedy, less scenic); the midlake-only passenger ferry *(battello navetta)* and the midlake car ferry (*autotraghetto;* also takes foot passengers). This aggravation is compounded by a ferry workforce that seems to have a disdain for English. To simplify matters, I'd just consider the timetables for the two main midlake services: the passenger ferry and the car ferry. Review these and jot down your possible connections before you set out (with the help of your hotelier) so you can pace your day smartly. It's a shame to miss a boat and lose out a hike or an eagerly anticipated meal because of confusing timetables.

By Car: With the parking problems, constant traffic jams, and expensive car ferries, this is no place to drive if you don't have to. While you can drive around the lake, the road is narrow, congested, and lined by privacy-seeking walls, hedges, and tall fences.

You can arrange a rental car for when you leave Varenna (contact the I Viaggi del Tivano travel agency in Varenna, listed below), but you'll have to get to Lecco or another larger town to pick up your car. It costs €7 including driver (plus €2.80 for each passenger) to take your car onto a ferry.

Parking is rarely easy where you need it, especially in Bellagio. Keep your car in Varenna and cruise. Parking is free Monday through Friday near Albergo Beretta (limited to 1 hour Sat–Sun, use the *discorario*—circular cardboard parking meter—usually in the glove compartment of the rental car) and at the train station (pay by the hour Sat–Sun 8:00–19:00, after that it's free—feed coins into meter at center of the lot and put the printed ticket on the dashboard).

In Varenna, white lines on the pavement indicate free parking (find spaces on road past Villa Monastero and a few near the harbor), yellow lines mean residents only, and blue lines mean you need to buy a ticket during peak times (€1/hr, 2 hrs maximum, payment times vary—often 8:00–12:00 & 14:00–19:00 on weekends, holidays, and during Aug, otherwise free). Buy tickets from the newsstand on the main square, the tobacco shop just south of the square, Baretta Bar on the way to the station, or Bar Cambusa near the ferry dock (scratch off the date and time you'll be parked and leave the ticket on your dashboard, overnight plus 2 hours is OK). Upon arrival in Varenna, you might find it easiest to park on the main square and find your hotel on foot.

Varenna

This town of 800 people offers the best of all lake worlds. Easily accessible by train, on the less-driven side of the lake, Varenna has a romantic promenade, a tiny harbor, narrow lanes, and its own villa. It's the right place to savor a lakeside cappuccino or *aperitivo*. There's wonderfully little to do here, and it's very quiet at night. The *passerella* (lakeside walk, unlit but safe after dark) is adorned with caryatid lovers pressing silently against each other in the shadows.

Varenna

(TRAIN STN. TO CHURCH IS A 10 MIN. WALK)

---- PASSERELLA (LAKESIDE WALK)
IIII STEPPED STREETS

TRAIN STATION
TRAIL TO CASTLE VEZIO
TRAIN TUNNEL
TRAIN TUNNEL
TO MILAN
TRAVEL AGENCY
TO TIRANO
MAIN ROAD
BANK
WC
CHURCH
TRAIL TO FIUMELATTE
MAIN RD. TO LECCO
PASSENGER BOAT DOCK + TICKETS
CAR FERRY DOCK
HARBOR
PIAZZA SAN GIORGIO
BANK
GARDENS
POST
L A K E
C O M O
TO MENAGGIO
TO BELLAGIO + COMO
DCH

① Albergo Olivedo
② Albergo Milano & Ristorante la Vista
③ Hotel/Ristorante Montecodeno
④ Albergo Beretta
⑤ Villa Elena
⑥ La Torretta B&B
⑦ Villa Cipressi
⑧ Hotel du Lac
⑨ To Hotel Eremo Gaudio
⑩ Ristorante del Sole
⑪ Rist. il Cavatappi
⑫ Vecchia Varenna
⑬ Nilus Bar & La Frulleria
⑭ Gelateria la Giazzera
⑮ Grocery Stores (3 locations)
⑯ Christ of the Lake (underwater statue)

ORIENTATION

Tourist Information

Varenna's TI (Pro Varenna) is up the street from the biggest church on the main square, across from the tobacco shop on Via IV Novembre (May–Oct Tue–Sat 10:00–12:00 & 15:00–17:00, Sun 10:00–12:00, closed Mon; Nov–April Sat–Sun 10:00–12:00 only, closed Mon–Fri; tel. 0341-830-367, www.varennaitaly.com).

Arrival in Varenna

From Milan, zip directly to Varenna by train. On arrival, set up, and limit your activities to the scenic midlake area (Varenna and Bellagio).

Here are the specifics: Leaving from Milan's central station, catch a train heading for Sondrio or Tirano—often confused with Torino...wrong city. (And, if you're heading for Varenna, be sure you don't end up in Verona.) All Sondrio trains stop in Varenna; the fine print on the *Partenze* (departures) schedule posted at Milan's train station will list Varenna as a stop. Trains leave about hourly (usually at :15 past the hour; approximate schedules listed in "Transportation Connections," page 196). Sit on the left for maximum lakeview beauty. Get off at Varenna-Esino. Note that the name "Varenna-Esino" appears only at the train station, even though train schedules list simply "Varenna." Same place.

Know what time you're supposed to arrive in Varenna so you can be ready to disembark with luggage in hand; the train stops for only one minute (literally). You may have to open the train door yourself. Otherwise you'll be carried to the next town and have to backtrack. And, because the trains can be longer then the station, your car may actually stop before it reaches the platform (causing you to mistakenly think that you're not there yet). Look out the window. If part of the train's at the station, you'll need to get out and walk to the platform.

You can also get to Varenna from Milan via the town of Como. Trains take you from Milan to Como (30-min rides usually leave at :25 past each hour), where you can catch a boat for the one-hour (if by hydrofoil) or two-hour ride up the lake to Varenna (about every 2 hrs, more frequent if you change in Menaggio, last departure at about 19:00, €7–10).

Helpful Hints

Money: A bank with a cash machine is near Varenna's main square, and another is near the boat dock (see town map).

Internet Access: To quote a local, "Internet access varies with the humor of the people." A phone-card-operated Internet point is in a kiosk next to the boat ticket office (buy €5/1 hour or €10/2 hours phone cards from the boat ticket office, break off the corner, insert into machine).

Post Office: It's just off the main square (Mon–Fri 8:30–14:00, Sat 8:30–12:30, closed Sun).

Travel Agency: For bus and boat tours, consider Varenna's travel agency, I Viaggi del Tivano, next to Albergo Beretta, a block below the train station. They book planes, trains, and automobiles and can offer half-day and day-long tours of the region and into Switzerland May–Sept; book tours by noon the day before (office open Mon–Fri 8:30–12:30 & 15:00–19:00, Sat 9:00–12:00, closed Sun, credit cards accepted but not for train tickets, Via Esino 3, tel. 0341-814-009, www.tivanotours.com, helpful Silvia and Luana speak English).

SELF-GUIDED WALK

Hello, Varenna

Since you came here to relax, this short walk gives you just the town basics.

Bridge near Train Station: This main bridge, just below the train station, spans the tiny Esino River. The river divides two communities: Perledo (which sprawls up the hill—notice the church spire high above) and the old fishing town of Varenna (huddled around its harbor). The train station is called Varenna-Esino, named for a third community eight miles higher in the hills. Follow the river down to the lakeside promenade by the ferry dock. The town's public beach (or *lido*) is just over the cute pedestrian bridge (free, rentable lounge chairs). Albergo Olivedo greeted ferry travelers back in the 19th century. It's named for the olive groves you can see halfway up the hill. Locals claim this is the farthest north olives grow in Europe.

• *Across from Albergo Olivedo is Varenna's...*

Ferry Landing: Since the coming of the train in 1892, Varenna has been *the* convenient access point from "midlake" (the communities of Bellagio, Menaggio, and Varenna) to Milan. From this viewpoint, you can almost see how Lake Como is shaped like a man. The head is the north end (to the right, up by the Swiss Alps). Varenna is the left hip. Menaggio, across the lake, is the right hip. And Bellagio (hiding behind the wooded hill) is where the legs come together—you can see the point (Punta Spartivento—literally, "point that divides the wind"). In a more colorful description, a local poem says, "Lake Como is a man, with Colico the head, Lecco and Como the feet, and Bellagio the testicles." (In the local dialect, this rhymes—ask a local to say it for you.)

The ridges high above the right hip are the border of Switzerland. The region's longtime poverty shaped the local character (much like the Great Depression shaped the outlook of a generation of Americans). Many still remember that this side of the lake was the poorest, because those on the other (Menaggio) side controlled the lucrative cigarette-smuggling business over the Swiss border. Today the entire region is thriving—thanks to tourism.

• *Walk past the ferry dock to Varenna's elevated shoreline walk, called the...*

Passerella: A generation ago, Varenna built this elegant lakeside promenade, which connects the ferry dock with the old town center. Strolling this lane, you'll come to the tiny two-dinghy concrete breakwater of a local villa. Lake Como is lined with swanky 19th-century villas. Their front doors faced the lake to welcome boats. At this point, the modern *passerella* cuts between this villa's water gate and its private harbor. Around the next corner and over the hump (which allows boats into a covered moorage), look up at another typical old villa—with a private *passerella*, a veil of serious wisteria, and a prime lakeview terrace. Many of these villas are owned by the region's "impoverished nobility." They were bred and raised not to work and, therefore, are now unable to pay for the upkeep of their sprawling houses. Lately, these villas are being bought by the region's nouveau riche.

• *About halfway down the* passerella *is a plaque marking* Il Signore del Lago, *which means...*

The Christ of the Lake: The local divers' association placed this crucifix (floodlit after dark) about 10 feet underwater, declaring, "We are committing ourselves to love, because this is the only certainty." From here, enjoy a good Varenna town view. These buildings are stringently protected. You can't even change the color of your paint.

• *Walk past the community harbor and under the old-time arcades to the fishermen's pastel homes, which face the harbor.*

Varenna Harborfront: Notice there are no streets in the old town...just characteristic stepped lanes called *contrade*. Varenna was originally a fishing community. Even today, old-timers enjoy Lago di Como's counterpart to lutefisk: *missoltino*, air-dried and salted lake "sardines." They're served with the region's polenta (different from Venice's because buckwheat is mixed in with the corn).

Imagine the harbor two hundred years ago—busy with coopers expertly fitting their chestnut and oak into barrels, stoneworkers carving and shipping the black marble quarried just above town, and fishing boats dragged onto the slopping beach. The little stone harbor dates from around 1600.

At the south end of the harbor (across from the gelato shop), belly up to the banister for another pastel-hued town view. Another local ditty goes, "If you love Lake Como, you know Bellagio is the pearl...but Varenna is the diamond."

• *Continue straight, leaving the harbor. A lane leads around past Hotel du Lac (its fine lakeside terrace welcomes nonresidents for a drink) to the tiny, pebbly town beach. From here, climb uphill to the town square, called...*

Piazza San Giorgio: Four churches face Varenna's town square. The main church dates from the 13th century. Romantic Varenna is an understandably popular spot for weddings—rice litters the church's front yard. Stepping inside, you'll find a few humble but centuries-old bits of carving and frescoes. The black floor and chapels are made from black marble quarried here. Outside, past the WWI monument, is the TI.

The Royal Victoria Hotel, also on the main square, recalls the 1839 visit of Queen Victoria, who registered herself as the Countess of Clare to stay anonymous. The trees are planted to make a V for Varenna. The street plan survives from Roman times, when gutters flowed down to the lake. The little church at the lake-side of the square is the baptistery. Dating from the ninth century, it's one of the oldest churches on the lake.

As you wander the lanes of Varenna, you'll notice plastic water bottles left out by the door. Locals believe that these keep cats from peeing on their doorstep (something about seeing their reflection causes them to get self-conscious).

Your walk is over. From this square, you can head south to the gardens, north to go to the train station, or hike up to reach the castle.

SIGHTS

In Varenna

Castle—A steep trail leads to Varenna's ruined hilltop castle, Castello di Vezio, located in a peaceful, traffic-free, one-chapel town. Start at the stairs to the left of Hotel Montecodeno and figure on a 20-minute walk one-way. The castle is pretty barren, though a falconry training center livens it up (€4, April–Oct daily from 10:00, closes at sunset, off-season weekends only, closed Jan and when rainy, sleepy café at entrance, mobile 335-465-186).

Gardens—Two manicured lakeside gardens—Villa Cipressi and the adjacent Villa Monastero—are tourable for a €4 combo-ticket (or pay €2.50 apiece, March–Oct daily 9:00–19:00, closed Nov–Feb).

Near Varenna

Fiumelatte—This town, about a half mile south of Varenna, was named for its milky river. It's the shortest river in Italy (at 800 feet) and runs—like most of the local tourist industry—only from April through September. The *La Sorgente del Fiumelatte* brochure, available at Varenna's TI, lays out a walk from Varenna to the Fiumelatte to the castle and back. It's a 30-minute hike to the source *(sorgente)* of the milky river (at Varenna's monastery, take high road, drop into peaceful and evocative cemetery, and climb steps to the wooded trail leading to peaceful and refreshing cave from which the river sprouts). For a longer lakeside hike, ask the TI about the *Sentiero del Viandante* (hike one-way up the lake, about 90 min, much more level than the hike to the castle, return by train).

SLEEPING

The area is tight in August, snug in July, and wide open most of the rest of the year. Many places close in winter. All places listed are family-run and have lakeview rooms, and some English is spoken. If you're expecting friendliness, especially during peak season, you'll likely be disappointed. Enjoy the view. View rooms are given (sometimes for no extra cost) to those who telephone for reservations and request a *"camera con vista."* Prices get soft off-season (Nov–May). Varenna's TI, across from the tobacco shop down the street from the main square, has a list of private rooms (tel. 0341-830-367).

$$$ Hotel du Lac, with 16 stylish, sleek, air-conditioned rooms, overlooks the water. Their secluded lakeside bar and terrace is jet-set cool (Db without view-€155, Db with view and balcony-€180, Db suite-€220, parking-€11/day, Via del Prestino 4, tel. 0341-830-238, fax 0341-831-081, www.albergodulac.com, albergodulac@tin.it).

$$ Albergo Milano, located right in the old town, is graciously run by Egidio and his Swiss wife, Bettina. Fusing the best of Italy with the best of Switzerland, the place manages to be both very well-run and romantic. Most of its eight comfortable rooms offer extravagant views, balconies, or big terraces (Sb-€100–110, Db-€135, €5 extra for view terrace, small discount for paying cash, confirm arrival the day before; from the station, take main road to town and turn right at steep alley where sidewalk and guardrail break, Via XX Settembre 29; tel. 0341-830-298, fax 0341-830-061, U.S. fax 781/634-0094, www .varenna.net, hotelmilano@varenna.net). For €25 per person, enjoy a three-course dinner made of seasonal produce and fresh lake fish (Mon and Wed–Sat). This place whispers *luna di miele*—honeymoon (see Web site for a 3-night honeymoon deal).

Sleep Code

(€1 = about $1.20, country code: 39)
S = Single, **D** = Double/Twin, **T** = Triple, **Q** = Quad, **b** = bathroom, **s** = shower only. Unless otherwise noted, you can assume breakfast is included, credit cards are accepted, and English is spoken.

To help you sort easily through these listings, I've divided the rooms into three categories based on the price for a standard double room with bath:

$$$ **Higher Priced**—Most rooms €150 or more.
$$ **Moderately Priced**—Most rooms between €100–150.
$ **Lower Priced**—Most rooms €100 or less.

$$ Albergo Olivedo, facing the ferry dock, is a romantic Old World hotel with antique furniture and classy parquet (Venetian *pavimento*) floors. Most of the rooms have tiny, glorious lakeview balconies. It's a fine place to practice the art of *la dolce far niente* and watch the children, boats, and sun come and go. The brisk, hardworking manager Laura doesn't smile a lot, and runs a very tight ship (prices vary with season and views: S-€50–60, Db-€130, half-pension required May–mid-Oct—see below, cash only, air-con, closed mid-Nov–mid-Dec, tel. & fax 0341-830-115, www.olivedo.it, olivedo@aruba.it). Laura's excellent dinner (€27 per person, required for guests May–mid-Oct) adds €54 to the price of double room per day and doesn't include drinks.

$$ Villa Cipressi is a sprawling, centuries-old lakeside mansion with 32 plain, modern rooms. It sits in a huge, quiet, terraced garden that non-guests pay to see (Sb-€95, non-view Db-€110, view Db-€130, extra cot-€15, rooms without views face the street and are noisier, elevator, Internet in lobby, garden access, mountain bike rental for guests, Via IV Novembre 18, tel. 0341-830-113, fax 0341-830-401, www.hotelvillacipressi.it, info@hotelvillacipressi.it, Davide).

$$ Eremo Gaudio stands in isolation halfway up the hill, with a commanding lake view high above Varenna. Once an orphanage, it became a hermitage run by the Church, and then—since 2000—a hotel accessed by a funky private funicular. Perfect for monks with champagne tastes, it's peaceful, with awe-inspiring view balconies and a breakfast terrace. There are 13 bright, comfy, air-conditioned rooms in the main building and 10 nice but less dramatic and non-air-conditioned rooms below (at the foot of the funicular) in a section that still feels like a priests' dorm (open Easter–Oct only, upper rooms: Sb-€90, Db-€110, Db with balcony-€120; lower rooms: Db-€95; all rooms have lake views, taxi from station about €10, 400 yards south of Varenna's main square at Via Roma 11, tel. 0341-815-301, fax 0341-815-314, www.eremogaudio.it, eremogaudio@yahoo.it). They give a 7 percent discount if you pay with cash (and the erratic management has an aggressive way of getting you a bad rate if you use a credit card)—so pay with cash. Light suppers are served on the lower terrace, weather permitting.

$$ La Torretta B&B, managed by Laura of Albergo Olivedo, is a restored Liberty-style villa just across from the ferry dock. It features five view rooms (some with terraces), a Jane Austen lounge, and a tiny manicured garden with tables for picnics or relaxing (Db-€130 with this book in 2006, cash only, closed Nov–April, tel. & fax 0341-830-115, www.olivedo.it, olivedo@aruba.it, check in at Albergo Olivedo—see above). This would be an awesome little palace for a party of eight to take over. Unlike at Albergo Olivedo, half-pension is not required here.

$ Hotel Montecodeno, with 11 decent rooms and no views, is a functional concrete box just off the main road between the train station and lake (2 Sb-€70, Db-€90, extra bed-€16, cheaper off-season, 10 percent discount for 3 nights, air-con, attached restaurant serves fresh fish and a €23 "Rick Steves" *menu*—see "Eating," below, Via della Croce 2, tel. 0341-830-123, fax 0341-815-227, www.hotelmontecodeno.com, ferrcas@tin.it, Marina Castelli).

$ Albergo Beretta, on the main road a block below the station, has 10 pleasant rooms, several of them with balconies (and street noise). The rooms on the second floor are quietest. This place, above a mundane coffee shop, feels homey and lacks any lakeside glamour (D-€58, Db-€68, extra bed-€12, breakfast-€6, Via per Esino 1, tel. & fax 0341-830-132, hotelberetta@iol.it, Signora Tosca does not speak English, Laura and daughter Julia do). This place reportedly tends to overbook—it's essential to reconfirm your reservation.

$ Villa Elena, a grandmotherly, low-energy place on the main square, offers the best budget beds in town. English-speaking Signora Vitali rents her four rooms at the same price—room #1 has a shabby bathroom and view terrace, while the others don't even have sinks (D-€40 with or without bath, cash only, it's the vine-covered facade at Piazza San Giorgio 9 near Via San Giovanni, tel. 0341-830-575).

EATING

On the Waterfront

Ristorante La Vista, at the recommended hotel Albergo Milano, serves up a fine fish dinner to guests and non-guests alike. Bettina and Egidio treat you well. Egi (pronounced "edgy") offers a very limited selection. I'd go with his €25 three-course *menu* (Mon and Wed–Sat 19:30–22:00, closed Sun and Tue, reservations recommended, Via XX Settembre 29, tel. 0341-830-298).

Albergo Olivedo's restaurant, across from the ferry dock, serves candlelit meals with no-nonsense service, making sure everything is properly done. Depending on the weather, you may be seated under a lakefront awning (with a view) or in a classy Old World dining hall. While Laura and her capable staff serve simple homemade pasta or one-course lunches, evening meals are a mandatory two-course affair. Try the local lake fish and handmade ravioli (€25–35 dinner, daily 12:15–14:00 & 19:30–21:15, stop by the hotel and reserve dinner in advance, tel. 0341-830-115).

Vecchia Varenna, on the harbor, is respected, pricey, and romantic. The menu features traditional cuisine and lake specialties (€11 pastas, €13 *secondi*, Tue–Sun 12:30–14:00 & 19:30–21:30, closed Mon, also closed Tue in winter, dressy indoors or on harborside deck, reservations smart, tel. 0341-830-793).

The **Nilus Bar,** with a stainless-steel-diner interior and the best harborfront seating in town, is *the* place for a light meal. The young waitstaff serves dinner crêpes, pizzas, salads, hot sandwiches, and cocktails with a smile (daily in summer 10:00–23:00, in spring and fall 12:00–23:00, closed Dec–Feb, tel. 0341-815-228, Fulvia and Giovanni).

Dessert: **La Frulleria** is a youthful place serving cold, sweet, and fruity treats from a fun menu. They have great harborfront seating—if you're eating dinner elsewhere without a lake view, consider skipping dessert and coming here for your finale (May–Oct Tue–Sun 12:00–24:00, closed Mon and Nov–April, 2 doors down from Nilus Bar, Claudia). To take a lakeside table, you need to order from the menu (items start at €2.50). **Gelateria la Giazzera,** also facing the harbor, is great for a cup or cone to go. English-speaking Eros makes his gelato fresh daily.

Off the Water, on or near Piazza San Giorgio

Ristorante del Sole, facing the town square, serves edible meals and Naples-style pizzas (€5–9). Making few concessions to the tourist crowds, this restaurant caters to locals, providing a fun atmosphere and a garden in back (daily 12:00–15:00 & 19:00–23:00, closed Wed off-season, Piazza San Giorgio 21, tel. 0341-815-218).

Ristorante il Cavatappi, a five-table place on a quiet lane 100 feet off the town square, is the new place in town. Helpful owner-chef Mario serves old-time specialties, such as *missoltino* (the air-dried lake fish that locals like more than tourists do) as an antipasto. Mario is serious about his wine. Plan on spending €25 plus wine (daily 12:30–14:30 & 19:00–22:30, closed Wed off-season, tel. 0341-815-349). Reservations are required for dinner, as Mario usually does evening meals in two seatings: 19:00 and 21:00.

Ristorante Montecodeno is on the main road, without a hint of lake ambience. This humble place, run by a hardworking family, serves a special "Rick Steves" *menu* designed to give visitors a sampler of lake cuisine. For €23, you get eight different fishy appetizers caught from Lake Como (including the salty run-over-by-a-car *missoltino,* described above), a *secondo* with another array of local fish, seasonal vegetables or a salad, dessert, and a carafe of wine. Other options are also possible (daily 12:00–14:00 & 19:00–21:00, Via della Croce 2, tel. 0341-830-123).

Picnics: Varenna's three little grocery stores, on and just off the main square, have all you need for a classy balcony or breakwater picnic dinner (they're all open roughly Tue–Sun 7:30–12:30 & 15:30–19:30, Mon 7:30–12:30 only).

TRANSPORTATION CONNECTIONS

From any destination covered in this book, you'll get to Lake Como via Milan. The quickest Milan connection to any point midlake (Bellagio, Menaggio, or Varenna) is via the train to Varenna. If leaving Varenna by train, purchase your train ticket from the ticket machine at the train station, the tobacco shop off the main square, or the travel agency, I Viaggi del Tivano, next door to the Albergo Beretta. Stamp your ticket in the yellow machine at the station before boarding. If both places are closed, win the sympathy of the conductor and buy your ticket on board (costs extra).

Milan to Varenna: Catch a train at Milano Centrale (€4.70; likely schedule: 8:15, 9:15, 12:15, 14:15, 16:15, 18:00, 19:10, 20:15, and 21:10; trip takes 1 hr). For tips on using the train, see "Arrival in Varenna," above.

Varenna to Milan: Trains leave Varenna for Milano Centrale at 6:18, 7:24, 8:23, 10:19, 12:21, 14:22, 16:22, 18:22, 20:20, and 22:30 (trip takes 1 hr). Confirm these times. If you take a train not listed here, it's likely a local milk-run train taking twice as long. Varenna makes a comfy last stop before catching the shuttle from Milan's train station to the airport.

Malpensa Airport to Varenna: Two buses a day (but not always on Sun) go directly to Varenna (€16.50, departs Terminal 1 at 11:00 and 20:40, 2 hrs). As you must reserve in advance (tel. 0342-216-220) and they go only with demand, this is not very workable. The alternatives are coughing up €150 for a taxi, or taking a train into Milan, then transferring to a Varenna-bound train (see "Transportation Connections" at end of Milan chapter).

Varenna to Malpensa Airport: Two buses a day go directly to Malpensa Airport (€18, departs Varenna at Albergo Beretta and Piazza San Giorgio at 5:30 and 16:30, 2.25 hrs). You must reserve and purchase tickets at least a day ahead at Varenna's travel agency, I Viaggi del Tivano (Mon–Fri 8:30–12:30 & 15:00–19:00, Sat 9:00–12:00, closed Sun, Via Esino 3, tel. 0341-814-009, www .tivanotours.com).

Varenna to Stresa: About every two hours, 2.75 hrs, transfer in Milan.

Varenna to St. Moritz in Switzerland: From Varenna, you have fantastic access to the Bernina Express scenic train to St. Moritz. First take the train to Tirano, and then transfer to St. Moritz (3/day, allow 6 hrs with transfer). For information on this route, stop by I Viaggi del Tivano travel agency (see above), or ask your hotelier if they have the handy tourist information book produced by the travel agency.

Bellagio

The self-proclaimed "Pearl of the Lake" is a classy combination of tidiness and Old World elegance. If you don't mind that "tramp in a palace" feeling, it's a fine place to shop for ties and umbrellas, while surrounding yourself with the more adventurous posh travelers. The heavy curtains between the arcades keep the visitors and their poodles from sweating. Thriving yet still cute, Bellagio is a much more substantial town than Varenna (which has almost no shops).

ORIENTATION

The **TI** is right downtown, at the passenger boat dock (daily 9:00–12:00 & 15:00–18:00, Nov–March closed Sun and Tue, tel. 031-950-204, prombell@tin.it). Also at the dock, you'll find the **boat-ticket office**, and next door, an **Internet access point** (to operate machine, buy phone cards from boat-ticket office).

The **Docks:** Bellagio has two docks, a few minutes' walk apart. The northern dock is for the passenger-only ferry *(battello navetta)* and the hydrofoil *(aliscafo-servizio rapido)*; the southern dock is for the car ferry *(autotraghetto)*, which also takes foot passengers. To make sure you're waiting at the right dock for the boat you want to take, check the boat schedule carefully (posted near dock, free brochure from kiosk at dock). Remember that if you want to know all your departure options, you need to study four different time-tables (see "Getting Around Lake Como," page 184). Confirm your intentions at the kiosk near either dock.

SIGHTS AND ACTIVITIES

Villa Serbelloni Park—If you need a destination, you can visit this park—overlooking the town—with a guide (€6.50, April–Oct 2 tours/day at 11:00 and 16:00 except Mon and when rainy, 90 min, must show up at the medieval tower in Piazza della Chiesa 30 min before tour time to buy tickets, confirm time at TI).

Strolling—Explore the steep-stepped lanes rising from the harborfront. While Johnny Walker and jewelry sell best at lake level, the locals shop up the hill. Piazza Chiesa, near the top of town, has a worth-a-look church. The TI produces a free little town walk flier in English.

The administrative capital of the midlake region, Bellagio is located where the two southern legs of the lake split off. For an easy break in a park with a great view, wander right on out to the crotch. Meander past the rich and famous Hotel Villa Serbelloni, and walk five minutes to Punta Spartivento ("point that divides the

Bellagio

NOT TO SCALE
PASSENGER DOCK
TO CHURCH IS A
5 MINUTE WALK
UPHILL.

- ❶ Hotel du Lac
- ❷ Hotel Florence
- ❸ Hotel/Rist. Metropole
- ❹ Grand Hotel Villa Serbelloni
- ❺ Albergo Europa
- ❻ Hotel Suisse
- ❼ Hotel Giardinetto
- ❽ Hotel Bellagio
- ❾ Il Borgo Apartments
- ❿ Locanda Barchetta
- ⓫ Ristorante Bilicus
- ⓬ Trattoria S. Giacomo
- ⓭ Pizzeria Carillon
- ⓮ To La Punta Ristorante
- ⓯ Gilardoni Alimentari

wind"). You'll find a Renoir atmosphere complete with an inviting bar/restaurant, a tiny harbor, and a chance to sit on a park bench and gaze north past Menaggio, Varenna, and the end of the lake to the Swiss Alps.

For another stroll, head south from the car-ferry dock down the tree-shaded promenade. Ten minutes later, you'll hit Bellagio's beach. The Lido di Bellagio has a chilly pool, lounge chairs, and a diving board into the lake (€5, daily in summer 10:00–19:00, tel. 031-950-597). The public beach is a long walk farther south from there.

Biking—Bikers could enjoy a downhill mountain-bike run. Cavalcalario Club shuttles you uphill, then lets you go (€30 includes bike rental, several itineraries, reservations necessary at least a day ahead, tel. 031-964-814, mobile 339-530-8138, www.bellagio-mountains.it, cavalcalarioclub@tiscalinet.it). They also offer horseback riding (€21/hr), paragliding, canoeing, kayaking, sailboat rentals, and supplies for trekking.

SLEEPING

(€1 = about $1.20, country code: 39)

This is a "boom or bust" lake resort, with high-season prices (those listed here) straight through from May through October, plus a brief shoulder season (with discounted prices) in November and April. Off-season (Dec–March), nearly everything is literally closed down.

$$$ Hotel du Lac, a good waterfront splurge, comes with 43 rooms, a roof terrace, and a classic ambience with no loss of comfort (Sb-€95–110, Db-€170–180, prices depend on view, plush superior Db-€210, 8 percent discount with cash, air-con, parking-€8, includes access to Bellagio Sporting Club's swimming pool outside town—a long walk or shuttle-bus ride away, Piazza Mazzini 32, tel. 031-950-320, fax 031-951-624, www.bellagio.info, dulac@tin.it, Leoni family). They have a fine restaurant, making the €15 supplement per person for optional half-board a great dinner value.

$$$ Hotel Florence, a few doors away and 150 years old, is family-run, with 30 rooms, hardwood, pastels, and a rich touch of Old World elegance (Sb-€103–120, Db-€135–195, Db suite-€220–250, prices depend on view and balcony, closed Nov–March, handheld showers only, fans on request, elevator, tel. 031-950-342, fax 031-951-722, www.hotelflorencebellagio.it, hotflore@tin.it, Ketzlar family).

$$$ Grand Hotel Villa Serbelloni, a famous 19th-century palace, comes with history, doormen, two pools (indoor and out), a fitness center, a garden, an elite clientele, and sky-high prices. While the grounds and public spaces are fancy, their 81 rooms don't merit the extra cost (standard Db-€370, deluxe Db-€480, executive Db-€630; pricier rooms have views, air-con and all the comforts; closed Nov–April, tel. 031-950-216, fax 031-951-529, www.villaserbelloni.com, inforequest@villaserbelloni.com). Sitting by the pool at the Villa Serbelloni gives you the ultimate lakeside resort experience.

$$ Hotel Bellagio, run by the Leoni family of the Hotel du Lac (described above), is a new two-star place with 29 rooms two blocks off the harborfront. Completely renovated in 2005, it's a good bet for modern comfort in the old center (non-view Db-€120, view Db-€140, extra bed-only €10, air-con, includes access to Bellagio Sporting Club's swimming pool outside town—a long walk or shuttle-bus ride away, Salita Grandi 6, tel. 031-950-424, fax 031-951-966, www.bellagio.info, hotelbellagio@virgilio.it).

$$ Hotel Metropole, a tired but grand old place, dominates Bellagio's waterfront with plush public spaces, sagging floors, and 42 spacious, dog-eared rooms (Db-€129, €10–20 more for view balcony or terrace, fans, elevator, tel. 031-950-409, fax 031-951-534, www.albergometropole.it, info@albergometropole.it).

$ Albergo Europa, run with low energy, is in a concrete annex behind a restaurant, away from the waterfront. Its 10 rooms have no charm but are reasonably comfortable (Db-€86, breakfast extra, balconies lack views but overlook quiet courtyard, free parking, Via Roma 21, tel. & fax 031-950-471, albeuropa@tiscali.it, family Marchesi).

$ Hotel Suisse, the cheapest and most neglected place on the waterfront, has 10 simple rooms, hardwood floors, dim lights, almost no service, unpredictable beds, and some great views and balconies. The only thing this place has going for it is price and location (Db-€75 through 2006 with this book, view rooms-€5 extra, breakfast-€10, 12 percent discount in hotel restaurant with this book, Piazza Mazzini 8/10, tel. 031-950-335, fax 031-951-755, www.suissehotel.it, Guido).

$ Hotel Giardinetto, at the top of town near the TI (100 steps above the waterfront), is a homey, laidback place renting 13 cheap, squeaky-clean, and spartan rooms. The rooms are stark, but the breezy, peaceful garden is a joy—and good for picnics (Sb-€40, non-view Db-€52, view Db-€55, Tb-€70, breakfast-€6, cash only, Via Roncati 12, tel. 031-950-168, tczgne@tiscali.it, Eugene and Laura Ticozzi).

$ Il Borgo Apartments rents six modern *Better Homes and Gardens*-quality apartments in the old center at great prices. This option is far better than a hotel room, but you don't get a reception desk—pick up your key from the art gallery downstairs (Db-€75, 2 bigger apartments for up to 5 people—€95, no breakfast, 2-night minimum preferred, air-con, Salita Plinio 4, tel. 031-952-497, mobile 338-193-5559, fax 031-951-585, residenceilborgo@libero.it, www.bellagio.co.nz/ilborgo, Flavio).

$ Locanda Barchetta rents four new rooms high above a chaotic restaurant. The rooms are great, but they're an afterthought to the restaurant (Db-€80, air-con, Salita Mella 13, tel. 031-951-030).

EATING

Ristorante Bilicus, up a steep lane from the waterfront, is a dressy place serving regional and lake cuisine with passion. While a little pricey, the restaurant is famous for value and quality cooking (€9 pastas, €12 *secondi*, April–Oct Tue–Sun 12:00–14:30 &

18:30–22:00, closed Mon and Nov–March, indoor/outdoor garden seating, Salita Serbelloni 30, tel. 031-950-480).

Trattoria S. Giacomo, across the street and less expensive, is respected for its traditional cuisine, such as *riso e filetto di pesce*—rice and fish fillet. It has daily themed, inviting *menu*s (€13 and €16) based on the specialties of Italy's regions (Mon–Thu 12:00–14:30 & 19:00–21:30, Fri–Sun open later midday and evenings, closed Tue, Salita Serbelloni 45, tel. 031-950-329).

Hotel Metropole Ristorante's terrace offers the best waterfront view. Even though the restaurant is a mediocre food value, I'd eat here to savor the lakeside setting (€10 pastas, €12 *secondi*, April–Oct daily 12:00–14:30 & 19:00–21:30, closed Nov–March, tel. 031-950-409; also see "Sleeping," above).

Pizzeria Carillon, the local choice for pizza, is a nondescript place with a shady terrace just across the parking lot from the ferry dock (Lungolago Manzoni 8, tel. 031-950-212).

Picnics: You'll find benches at the park, along the waterfront in town, and lining the promenade south of town. Pick up your picnic supplies at **Gilardoni Alimentari**. They have roast chicken, ribs, and focaccia, and are happy to make fresh sandwiches to your order (Tue–Sat 7:30–13:00 & 15:00–19:00, Sun 7:30–13:00 only, closed Mon, shorter hours off-season, on corner of Via Garibaldi and Salita Cavour, tel. 031-951-815).

Punto Spartivento: This dramatic park, a five-minute walk north of town (see "Strolling," page 197), is a great place for either a picnic or a meal at **La Punta Ristorante** (€8 pastas, €12 *secondi*, daily 12:00–14:30 & 19:00–22:00, bar open 9:00–22:00 for snacks only, tel. 031-951-888).

Menaggio

Menaggio has more urban bulk than its neighbors. Since most visitors find Lake Como too dirty for swimming, consider spending time in Menaggio's fine public pool. This is the starting point for a few hikes. Only a few decades ago, these trails were used by cigarette smugglers, sneaking at night from Switzerland back into Italy with their tax-free booty. The hostel has information about mountain biking and catching the bus to trailheads on nearby Mount Grona.

SLEEPING

(€1=about $1.20, country code: 39)

$ La Primula Youth Hostel (Ostello la Primula) is a rare area hostel. Run by Alberto, it caters to a quiet, savor-the-lakes crowd.

Located about 300 yards south of the Menaggio dock, it has a view terrace, games galore, Internet access, and a washing machine, as well as bike, canoe, and kayak rentals (€14/person in dorm bed, €15/person for 4- to 6-bed room with private bath, €2.60 extra for nonmembers, includes breakfast, sheets and towels extra, cash only, easy parking nearby, reception and bar open 8:00–24:00, rooms closed 10:30–15:00, hotel closed Nov–mid-March; hearty dinners with drinks for €12—reserve dinner by 18:00, served at 20:00; Via IV Novembre 106, tel. & fax 0344-32356, www.menaggiohostel .com, menaggiohostel@mclink.it). Show this book for a free half hour of Internet access, and ask Alberto for ideas about hikes and bike rides in the area.

$ **La Marianna B&B** is run by a husband-and-wife team, Ty and Paola. They rent eight rooms and run a fine restaurant in Cadenabbia, about a mile south of Menaggio on a busy road (Db with view-€80, lakeside terrace at restaurant, air-con, tel. 0344-43095, www.la-marianna.com, inn@la-marianna.com). The hourly Como–Menaggio bus #C-10 stops here.

TRANSPORTATION CONNECTIONS

From Malpensa Airport to Menaggio: Buses run between Milan's Malpensa Airport and Como, where you change to local bus #C-10 to get to Menaggio.

From Menaggio to Milan: It's a 20-minute ferry to Varenna, where trains connect to Milan (70 min, every 2 hrs).

MORE SIGHTS ON LAKE COMO

Villa Carlotta—If you plan to tour one of Lake Como's famed villas, this is the best (€7, daily April–Sept 9:00–18:00, Oct 9:00–11:30 & 14:00–16:30, closed Nov–March, tel. 034-440-405). I see the lakes as a break from Italy's art, but if you're in need of a place that charges admission, Villa Carlotta offers an elegant neoclassical interior, a famous Canova statue, and a garden (its highlight, best in spring). Nearby Tremezzo and Cadenabbia are pleasant lakeside resorts an easy walk away. Boats serve both places (5-min walk from either dock to the villa).

Isola Comacina—This remote little island (just south of Bellagio) offers peace, ancient church foundations, goats, sheep, and a lovely view of Lago di Como. It takes 30 minutes to walk around the island, but longer to savor it. Bring a picnic or try the snack bar at the dock. Look for trips to Isola Comacina on the Colico–Como schedule (listed in Lago di Como boat timetable brochure, free at ticket booths at ferry docks). The *isola* is accessible from Varenna

(1 hour), Menaggio (45 min), or Bellagio (30 min). Check return times carefully (Como–Colico direction) and don't miss your boat. Usually only one trip a day each way works out for a visit.

Como—On the southwest tip of the lake, Como has a good, traffic-free old town, an interesting Gothic/Renaissance cathedral, and a pleasant lakefront with a promenade (**TI** open Mon–Sat 9:00–13:00 & 14:30–18:00, closed Sun, tel. 031-269-712). It's an easy walk from the boat dock to the train station (from Milan in 30 min, usually leaving at :25 past each hour). Boats leave Como about hourly for midlake (ferries-€6–7, 2 hrs; hydrofoils-€9–10, 45 min, departures 7:30–19:10, tel. 031-579-211).

Sleeping in Como: For a cheap overnight, try the **$ Villa Olmo Hostel** (€13.50, includes breakfast and sheets, €3 extra for non-members, €9–11 dinners, bike rental and laundry service available, reception open 7:00–10:00 & 16:00–22:00, lockout during the day, 23:30 curfew, closed Dec–Feb, Via Bellinzona 2, tel. & fax 031-573-800, ostellocomo@tin.it).

Lake Maggiore

Lake Maggiore is ringed by mountains, snow-capped in spring and fall, and lined with resort towns such as Stresa. While crassly touristic, the town of Stresa is a handy base from which to explore the exotic garden islands of Lake Maggiore. And many consider it a pleasant last stop before flying home from nearby Malpensa Airport.

A visit to this region is worth the trouble for its two islands—each with exotic gardens and Borromeo family villas. The Borromeo family—over many generations since 1630—lovingly turned their islands into magical retreats with elaborate villas and fragrant gardens. Isola Bella has the palace and terraced garden; Isola Madre has a villa and sprawling English-style (rougher) garden. A third island, Isola Pescatori, is simply small, serene, and residential. The Borromeos, who made their money from trade and banking, enjoyed the arts—from paintings (hung in lavish abundance throughout the palace and villa) to plays (performed in an open-air theater on Isola Bella) and marionette shows (you'll see the puppets that performed here).

Tourists flock to the lakes in May and June, when flowers are in bloom, and in September. Concerts held in scenic settings draw music-lovers, particularly during the Musical Weeks in August (get details from Stresa TI). For fewer crowds, visit in April, July, and August (when Italians prefer the Mediterranean beaches), and October. In winter, the snow-covered mountains (with resorts a 90-min drive away) attract skiers.

Planning Your Time

This region is best visited on a sunny day, when the mountains are clear, the lake is calm, and the heat of the sun brings out the scent of the blossoms. The two top islands for sightseeing are Isola Bella and Isola Madre. Isola Pescatori has no sights but is a peaceful place for lunch.

Day Trip from Milan: Catch an early train from Milan to Stresa (take a 1-hour fast train). Upon arrival in Stresa, walk 10 minutes downhill to the boat dock, and catch a boat to Isola Madre. Then work your way back to Isola Pescatori for a lazy lunch, and on to Isola Bella for the afternoon, before returning to the town of Stresa and back to Milan.

Overnight: Small, touristy Stresa makes a fine first or last stop in Italy—its connections with Milan's airport, which is located about halfway between Stresa and Milan, don't involve a transfer in big Milan (see "Transportation Connections," page 211).

Getting Around Lake Maggiore

Boats link the islands and Stresa, running about twice hourly. Allow roughly 10 minutes between stops. Since short round-trip hops add up to the same cost as a day pass, it's easiest to simply buy the all-day pass: €7 for two islands (Bella and Pescatori); or €10 for all the islands, plus Pallanza (a town on the opposite shore) and Villa Taranto.

If you're planning to tour Isola Bella and Isola Madre, you'll save a couple of euros by buying a boat pass with the admission fee *(ingresso)* included—you'll need to ask for it (€25 for all-day boat pass plus villas on Isola Bella and Isola Madre; this combo-ticket available only from boat ticket office, not once you get to villas).

Boats run daily March through October. The map on page 205 shows the route: Stresa, Carciano/Lido, Isola Bella, Isola Pescatori, Baveno (lakeside town), Isola Madre, Pallanza, and Villa Taranto. This route is part of a longer one. To follow the boat schedule (free, available at boat docks, TI, and maybe your hotel), look at the Arona–Locarno timetable for trips from Stresa to the islands, and the Locarno–Arona timetable for the return trip to Stresa.

Buy boat tickets directly from the dock ticket booth. Private taxi-boat drivers and their little sales booths will try to talk you into paying way too much (boat info: tel. 800-551-801).

Stresa

Stresa—which means "thin stretch"—was named for the original strip of fishermen's huts that lined the shore. Today grand old hotels run along that same shore. The old town—basically a traffic-free

Stresa and the Borromeo Islands

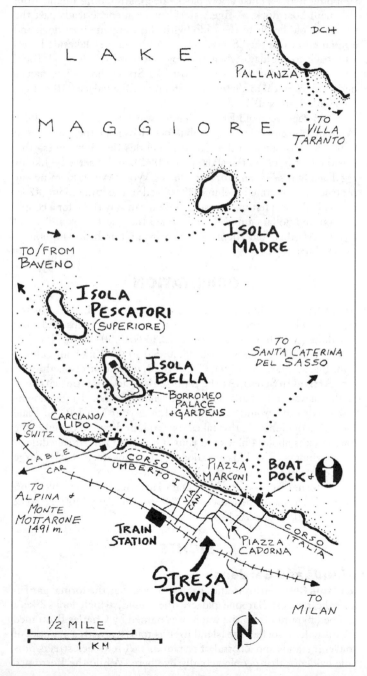

LAKE

MAGGIORE

DCH

PALLANZA

TO VILLA TARANTO

ISOLA MADRE

TO/FROM BAVENO

ISOLA PESCATORI (SUPERIORE)

ISOLA BELLA

TO SANTA CATERINA DEL SASSO

BORROMEO PALACE + GARDENS

CARCIANO/ LIDO

TO SWITZ.

CABLE CAR

TO ALPINA & MONTE MOTTARONE 1491 m.

CORSO UMBERTO I

VIA CAN.

PIAZZA MARCONI

BOAT DOCK & ℹ

CORSO ITALIA

TRAIN STATION

PIAZZA CADORNA

STRESA TOWN

TO MILAN

½ MILE

1 KM

N

shopping mall—is just a few blocks deep, stretching inland from the main boat dock. A fine waterfront promenade leads past the venerable old hotels to the Lido (with the Carciano boat dock and a mountain cable car). Stresa's stately 19th-century lakeside hotels date back to the days when this town was on the "Grand Tour" circuit. In any Romantic-age resort like Stresa, hotels had names designed to appeal to Victorian aristocrats...like Palace (rather than Palazzo), Astoria, Bristol, and Victoria.

Nineteen-year-old Ernest Hemingway first came here in 1918. Wounded in Slovenia as an ambulance driver for the Italian Red Cross, he was taken to the Grand Hotel des Iles Borromees. This was the first hotel on the shore (from 1862), and it served—like its regal neighbors—as an infirmary during World War I. Hemingway returned to the same hotel in 1948, stayed in the same room (#205, now called the "Hemingway suite"—you can stay there for a couple of thousand dollars a night), and signed the guest book as "an old client." Another "old client" was Winston Churchill, who honeymooned here.

ORIENTATION

Tourist Information: The helpful TI, located to the right of the ticket window at the boat dock, gives out free maps and boat schedules (March–Oct daily 10:00–12:30 & 15:00–18:30; Nov–Feb Mon–Fri 10:00–12:30 & 15:00–18:30, Sat 10:00–12:30 only, closed Sun; Piazza Marconi 16, tel. 0323–30150, www.distrettolaghi.it).

Arrival in Stresa: At the train station, ask for a free city map at the newsstand (marked *Libri Giornali Riviste*). To get downtown, exit right from the station and take your first left (on Viale Duchessa di Genova). This takes you straight down to the lake (the boat dock is about 4 blocks to your right; ask for boat schedule at ticket window). The TI is next door on the same dock. Taxis charge a fixed rate of €7 for even the shortest ride in town.

Internet Access: The **New Data Internet Point** is a block off Piazza Cadorna in the old center (€4/30 min, daily 9:00–12:30 & 15:00–19:00, Via de Vit 15A).

SIGHTS

Islands and Gardens
▲▲**Isola Bella**—This island, nearest Stresa, has the formal garden and the fanciest Baroque palace. The island, which looks like a stepped pyramid from the water, was named by Charles Borromeo for his wife, Isabella. The island itself is touristy, with a gauntlet of souvenir stands and a corral of restaurants. A few back streets provide evidence that people actually live here. While the Borromeo

family now lives in Milan, they spend a few weeks each summer on Isola Bella (when their blue-and-red family flag flies from the top of the garden).

Your visit is a one-way tour, starting with the palace and finishing with the garden. (There's no way to see the garden without the palace.) In the lavishly decorated Baroque palace, stairs lead to stucco crests of Italy's top families (balls signify the Medici, bees mean the Barberini, and a unicorn symbolizes the Borromeo's motto: Humility). The next room shows a portrait of the first Borromeo. The richly stuccoed grand hall, with its 80-foot-high dome, features an 18th-century model of the villa, including a grand entry that never materialized. Next, the room with the musical instruments was the site of the 1935 Stresa Conference, in which Mussolini met with British and French diplomats in a united attempt to scare Germany out of starting World War II. This "Stresa Front" soon fizzled when Mussolini attacked Ethiopia and joined forces with Hitler. A photocopy of the treaty with Mussolini's signature is on the wall. Napoleon's bedroom comes with an engraving showing his 1797 visit. (Napoleon is on a bench with his wife and sister enjoying festivities in his honor.) The last rooms display souvenirs and gifts that the Borromeo family picked up over the generations.

Downstairs, the 18th-century grotto, decorated from ceiling to floor with shell motifs and black-and-white stones, still serves its original function of providing a cool refuge from Italy's heat. Many of the famous Borromeo marionettes are on display here—with fine details, from beautiful to grotesque. (A larger collection is on Isola Madre.) The dreamy marble statues are by Gaetano Monti, a student of Canova. Climbing out of the basement, look up at the unique cantilevered stairs; they're from a 16th-century fortress that predates this building.

The ornate hall of 16th-century Flemish tapestries leads to the finale of this island visit: the garden, complete with Chinese white peacocks to give it all an exotic splash. Baroque—which is exactly what you see here—is all about controlling nature. The terraced gardens are crowned by the Borromeo family unicorn.

A fine €2.50 audioguide (€4 for 2 headsets) describes the villa (admission for the palace and garden-€9, €15 combo-ticket includes Isola Madre, April–mid-Oct daily 9:00–18:30, last entry 1 hour before closing, closed mid-Oct–March, English descriptions in palace, WC at entrance to garden, tel. 0323-30556). Note there are two docks on this island (one for each direction). Departure times are indicated by clocks at each dock. Picnicking is not allowed in the garden, but you can picnic at the point of the island (free and open to the public); take the mosaic sidewalk to the left of the palace entrance.

▲**Isola Pescatori**—This sleepy island—home to 35 families—is the smallest and most residential of the three. It has a couple of good seafood restaurants, picnic benches, views, and, blissfully, nothing to do—under arbors of wisteria. A delight for photographers and painters, the island is never really crowded, except at lunchtime.

▲▲**Isola Madre**—Don't come here unless you intend to tour the sight, because that's all there is: an interesting, furnished villa and a lovely garden filled with exotic birds and plants. Visiting is a one-way affair, starting with a long stroll through the garden and finishing with the villa. Eight gardeners (with the help of water continually pumped from the lake) keep this English-style garden paradise lush and a joy even for those bored by gardens. You'll see trees from around the world, a menagerie, and exotic silver pheasants. In front of the villa, a magnificent Himalayan cypress tree paints your world a streaky green. The 16th-century villa is the first of the Borromeo palaces. A century older than the other, it's dark, somber, and Renaissance. The clever angled hinges keep the doors from flapping in the lake breeze. The family's huge collection of dolls, marionettes, and exquisite 17th-century marionette theater sets—painted by a famous La Scala opera set designer—fill several rooms. A corner room is painted to take you into an 18th-century Venetian Rococo sitting room under a floral green house. You'll see some of the garden's best flowers immediately after leaving the villa.

The sightseeing route is clearly signed for you, taking you through the gardens and villa, and ending at the chapel (€9.50, €15 combo-ticket includes Isola Bella, daily 9:00–17:30, no photos in villa, WC next to chapel, tel. 0323-31261). The €2.50 audioguide here (€4 for 2 headsets) is devoted almost entirely to the garden—a good investment to properly appreciate the plantings.

While eating is best on Isola Pescatori, Isola Madre has one eatery: **La Piratera Ristorante Bar** (€20 tourist *menu,* daily 8:00–17:00, sit-down meals from 12:00–15:00 and simple sandwiches to go anytime, picnic at rocky beach a minute's walk from restaurant, tel. 0323-31171).

▲**Villa Taranto Botanical Gardens**—Garden-lovers will enjoy this large landscaped park, located on the mainland a 10-minute boat ride beyond Isola Madre (across the lake from Stresa). The gardens are a Scotsman's labor of love. Starting in the 1930s, Neil MacEacharn created this garden of delights—bringing in thousands of plants from all over the world—and here he stays, in the small mausoleum. The park's highlight is the terraced garden with a series of cascading pools. Villa Taranto is directly across the street from the boat dock (€8, April–Oct daily 8:30–19:30, ticket office closes at 18:30, closed Nov–March, tel. 0323-404-555).

Mountain Cable Car—From Stresa's Lido, a cable car takes you up—in two stages and a 20-minute ride—to the top of Mount

Mottarone (about 5,000 feet). From here, you get great views of neighboring peaks and, by taking a short hike, a bird's-eye view of the small, neighboring Lake Orta. The cable car runs April through October (€13 round-trip, €7 one-way, daily 9:30–12:30 & 13:30–17:40, 3/hr, tel. 0323-30295).

To visit the **Alpine Gardens**, get off at the midway Alpina stop, where a 10-minute walk leads to the gardens (turn left as you leave; €2, included in price of round-trip cable-car ticket, April–mid-Oct daily 9:30–18:00, closed mid-Oct–March). The gardens come with great lake views and picnic spots, but can't compare to what you'll see on the islands.

If **hiking** down, bring a good map and allow 3.5 hours from the top of Mount Mottarone, or 1.5 hours from the Alpine Gardens.

You can rent a **bike** at the base of the cable-car lift (full-suspension mountain bike-€26/day, €21/half-day, €5.50/hr, helmet included, tel. 338-839-5692) and bring it on the cable car with you (€8 extra). It's a treacherous ride, enjoyable only for serious bikers. While the ride is nice on top, you'll fight traffic on congested, rough, and windy roads for the rest of the trip.

Day Trips from Stresa

▲**Scenic Boat and Rail Trip to Locarno and Centovalli**—This enjoyable all-day excursion from Stresa involves three segments. Confirm all times, particularly the departure of the last boat from Locarno, before you embark on the trip. Take the train from Stresa to Domodossola, then catch the "Centovalli" train for a 90-minute ride that links together remote mountain villages on your way to Locarno, in the Italian-speaking Swiss canton of Ticino (bring your passport). Spend an hour or so exploring this town, on the far end of Lake Maggiore. Then take the boat past loads of small lakeside hamlets back to Italy. As a relaxing finale, you'll cruise into your home port of Stresa. The trip can also be done in reverse (with the boat trip first). A special €24 ticket covers both the train and boat tickets (you must reserve in advance, fax 0322-249-530—indicate the date you'll travel, number of passengers, and a return fax number, call 800-551-801 or 0322-233-200 for info).

▲**Lake Orta**—Just on the other side of Mount Mottarone is the small lake of Orta. The lake's main town, Orta San Giulio, has a beautiful lakeside piazza ringed by picturesque buildings. The piazza faces the lake with a view of Isola San Giulio. Taxi boats (€3 round-trip) make the five-minute trip throughout the day. The island is worth a look for the church of San Giulio and the circular "path of silence" that takes about 10 minutes. In peak season, Orta is anything but silent, but off-season or early or late in the day, this place is full of peace and magic (**TI** tel. 0322-905-163, April–Sept Wed–Thu 10:00–13:00 & 15:00–18:30, Fri–Sun

9:00–13:00 & 15:00–19:00, Tue 10:00–13:00, closed Mon, shorter hours Oct–March, located on Via Panoramica next to the parking lot downhill from the train station).

The train ride from Stresa to Orta-Miasino (a short walk from the lakeside piazza) takes 1.5–2 hrs and requires a change or two (4/day).

SLEEPING

(€1 = about $1.20, country code: 39)
Because Stresa town is just a resort, I'd day-trip from Milan. But here are good options if you'd like to stay.

$$ Hotel Milan Speranza is an impersonal, four-star, corporate-style hotel that caters mostly to tour groups, with 170 predictably comfortable rooms across from the boat dock (Db-€100-150 depending on season and view, €20–30 extra for lake views, air-con, elevator, tel. 0323-31178, fax 0323-32729, www.milansperanza.it, hotmispe@tin.it).

$$ Hotel Moderno offers 54 pastel rooms on a pedestrian street a block from the main square (Db-€130, closed Nov–mid-March, air-con, elevator; Via Cavour 33, from Piazza Matteotti, with your back to the lake, go right—up small street; tel. 0323-933-773, fax 0323-933-775, www.hms.it, moderno@hms.it).

$ Hotel Saini Meublè is a cozy place located in a pedestrian zone in the old center. Its 14 rooms are big and modern, with hardwood floors (Sb-€75, Db-€95, lower prices off-season, ask for 5 percent discount with this book in 2006, elevator, Via Garibaldi 10, from Piazza Matteotti head up Via Mazzini and turn left on Via Garibaldi, tel. 0323-934-519, fax 0323-31169, www.hotelsaini.it, info@hotelsaini.it).

$ Hotel Primavera, next door to Hotel Moderno, rents 34 decent rooms, many with terraces (Db-€75–95, tel. 0323-31286, fax 0323-33458, www.stresa.it, hotelprimavera@stresa.it).

$ Albergo Luina is a cheap sleep, with seven clean and basic rooms above a restaurant (Sb-€30–46, D/Db-€50–70, breakfast extra, cash only, ask for Rick Steves discount; Via Garibaldi 21, 2 blocks off Piazza Matteotti—with back to lake, go left up small street; tel. 0323-30285, luinastresa@yahoo.it).

$ Albergo Meuble Orsola di Gallia Cinzia is a humble and homey little place two blocks from the train station and just far enough off the tracks (only one train goes by in the middle of the night). It offers time-warp rooms—well-worn, not particularly clean...but the cheapest in town (S-€20, Sb-€25, D-€40, Db-€50, 2-min walk from station at Via D di Genova 45, tel. 0323-31087, fax 0323-933-121, e-mail: what's that?).

EATING

Osteria degli Amici serves up tasty risotto, pastas, and pizzas with fast and friendly service under a canopy of grape and kiwi leaves (daily 12:00–14:00 & 19:00–22:30, closed Wed Sept–May, deep in the old town past Piazza Cadorna at Via Bolongaro 33, tel. 0323-30453).

Le Botte offers a variety of Piedmont's regional specialties in a casual atmosphere (daily 12:00–15:00 & 18:30–23:00 in summer, closed Thu Oct–April and all of Dec–March, Via Mazzini 6/8, tel. 0323-30462).

La Rosa dei Venti is the locals' favorite pizzeria, located on the main drag (Wed–Mon 12:00–14:30 & 19:00–22:30, closed Tue, 2 blocks south of the boat dock at Corso Italia 50, tel. 0323-31431).

The main square, **Piazza Cadorna,** is a carnival of locals selling things to tourists. Still, at night it has a certain charm. It seems anyone who claims to be a musician can get a gig singing for eaters. The **Pizzeria Centrale** (on a platform in the center) is a good place to enjoy the ambience with decent pizzas, but don't order any serious food here.

TRANSPORTATION CONNECTIONS

From Stresa by Train to: Milan (nearly hrly, 1-hr fast train, 1.25-hr slow train), **Varenna** (nearly hrly, 2.75 hrs, transfer in Milan), **Venice** (1/day direct, many more with changes in Milan, 4 hrs), **Domodossola** (on the French border, hrly, 30 min).

To Malpensa Airport: For a **train/bus combination,** take the train toward Milan (hrly) and get off at Gallarate (about 40 min from Stresa), where frequent, cheap shuttle buses run to Malpensa's Terminal 1 (€1.50, pay driver, about 2/hr, 10 min, from Gallarate the bus departs from train station and runs 6:00–20:15, from Malpensa's Terminal 1 the bus runs 5:35–19:50, tel. 0331-230-830).

Airport buses run directly between Stresa and Malpensa (€8, 50 min, leaves airport at 7:30, 10:30, 14:30, 17:30, and 20:30; leaves Stresa at 6:30, 9:30, 13:30, 16:30 and 19:30; confirm schedule, must reserve by noon the previous day, tel. 0323-552-172, verbania@safduemila.com).

Taxis to the airport cost €90 (1–4 people, or €115 for mini-van seating up to 8 people) and take about an hour; your hotel can arrange the taxi for you, but may charge you for it. It's easy to arrange a taxi on your own at the train station's taxi stand. Franco and Tiziano Ferrara's Taxi and Minibus Rental is reliable (tel. 0323-31000, mobile 335-644-5319, ferrara.t@libero.it).

MILAN

(Milano)

For every church in Rome, there's a bank in Milan. Italy's second city and the capital of Lombardy, Milan is a hardworking, fashion-conscious, time-is-money city of 1.3 million. It's a melting pot of people and history. Milan's industriousness may come from the Teutonic blood of its original inhabitants, the Lombards, or from the region's Austrian heritage. Milan is Italy's industrial, banking, TV, publishing, and convention capital. The economic success of modern Italy can be blamed on this city of publicists and pasta power lunches.

As if to make up for its shaggy parks, blocky fascist architecture, and recently bombed-out feeling (World War II), its people are works of art. Milan is an international fashion capital with a refined taste. Window displays are gorgeous, cigarettes are chic, and even the cheese comes gift-wrapped. Yet, thankfully, Milan is no more expensive for tourists than other Italian cities.

Three hundred years before Christ, the Romans called this place Mediolanum, or "the central place." By the fourth century A.D., it was the capital of the western half of the Roman Empire. It was from here that Emperor Constantine issued the Edict of Milan, legalizing Christianity. After some barbarian darkness, medieval Milan rose to regional prominence under the Visconti and Sforza families. By the time of the Renaissance, it was called "the New Athens" and was enough of a cultural center for Leonardo to call home. Then came 400 years of foreign domination (Spain, Austria, France, more Austria). Milan was a center of the 1848 revolution against Austria and helped lead Italy to unification in 1870.

Mussolini left a heavy fascist touch on the city's architecture (such as the central train station). His excesses also led to the

Greater Milan

TO COMO & MALPENSA AIRPORT

TO ALMOST EVERYWHERE

N

CORSO

SEMPIONE

MONUMENTAL CEMETERY ■

PORTA GARIBALDI STATION Ⓜ

CENTRAL STATION

PIRELLI TOWER

AIRPORT BUSES
V. A. DORIA

Ⓜ

VIA LIB.

VIA PISANI

VIA VITRUVIO

VIA LIMA

TO FIERA DI MILANO TRADE FAIR

SEE CENTRAL MILAN DETAIL

VIA TURATI

Ⓜ REPUB-BLICA

CORSO BUENOS AIRES

BRANCA TOWER

SFORZA CASTLE

LAST SUPPER
S. MARIA D. GRAZIE

NORD STN. Ⓜ

BRERA GALLERY

Ⓜ TURATI

MONTE-NAPOLEONE

Ⓜ PORTA VENEZIA

CONC. Ⓜ

CORSO

MAGENTA

CADORNA

LA SCALA

VIA MONTE-NAPOLEONE

TO LEONARDO'S HORSE & MEAZZA STADIUM

TRAM #16 STOP

V. MERAVIGLI

DUOMO

Ⓜ Ⓜ **Duomo**

RING ROAD

Ⓜ S. AMB

VIA TORINO

VELASCO TOWER

NATIONAL SCIENCE MUSEUM

Ⓜ MISSORI

VIA

P. ROMANA

PORTA GENOVA STATION Ⓜ

CORSO

PORTA TICINESE

CORSO ITALIA

CORSO

VIALE CALDARA

VIALE B. D'ESTE

Ⓜ PORTA ROMANA

NAVIGLI DISTRICT

¼ MILE

400 METERS

DCH

Ⓜ METRO STOPS (NOT ALL SHOWN)

WWII bombing of Milan. But Milan rose again. The 1959 Pirelli Tower (the skinny skyscraper in front of the station) was a trendsetter in its day. Today, Milan is people-friendly, with a great transit system and inviting pedestrian zones.

Many tourists come to Italy for the past. But Milan is today's Italy, and no Italian trip is complete without visiting it. While it's not big on the tourist circuit, Milan has plenty to see. And fortunately, seeing Milan—so manageable and well-organized—is not difficult.

For pleasant excursions from the city, consider visiting Lake Como or Lake Maggiore—both are about an hour from Milan by train (see The Lakes chapter).

Planning Your Time

OK, it's a big city, so you probably won't linger. Compared to Rome and Florence, Milan's art is mediocre, but the city does have unique and noteworthy sights: the Duomo and Galleria, La Scala Opera House, Brera Gallery, Michelangelo's last *Pietà* in Sforza Castle, and Leonardo's *Last Supper* (reserve at least a month in advance). To maximize your time, use the Metro and note which places stay open through the siesta.

With two nights and a full day, you can gain an appreciation for the town and see the major sights. (Note that about half of Milan's sights close on Monday.) With 36 hours, I'd sleep in Milan and focus on the center. Tour the Duomo, hit what art you like, browse through the elegant shopping area and the Galleria, and try to see an opera. Technology buffs like the Science and Technology Museum, while medieval art buffs dig the city's early Christian churches. People-watchers and pigeon-feeders could spend their entire visit never leaving sight of the Duomo. And if you dig burial grounds, rattle through Milan's evocative Monumental Cemetery.

Since Milan is a cold Italian plunge, and most flights to the United States leave Milan early in the morning, you could save Milan for the end of your trip and start your journey softly by going directly from Milan to Lake Como (1-hr train ride to Varenna), Lake Maggiore (about an hour by train to Stresa—see page 204), or the Cinque Terre (4 hrs to Vernazza). Then spend a night or two in Milan at the end of your trip before flying home.

A Three-Hour Tour: If you're just changing trains in Milan (as, sooner or later, you will), consider this blitz tour: Check your bag at the station, pick up a city map at the station TI, ride the subway to the Duomo (see "Arrival," below, for specifics), peruse the square, explore the cathedral's rooftop and interior, have a scenic coffee in the Galleria, spin on the floor mosaic of the bull for good luck, see a museum or two (most are within a 10-min walk of the main square), and return by subway to the station. Art fans could make time for *The Last Supper* (if they've made reservations at least a month in advance; Metro: Cadorna or Conciliazione, or tram #16, direction San Siro), the Michelangelo *Pietà* in Sforza Castle (no reservations necessary, Metro: Cairoli), the Brera Art Gallery (Metro: Lanza), or the Duomo Museum (Metro: Duomo; likely closed in 2006).

ORIENTATION

My coverage focuses on the old center. Most sights and hotels are within a 10-minute walk of the cathedral (Duomo), which is a straight eight-minute Metro ride from the train station.

Rome vs. Milan: A Classic Squabble

In Italy, the North and South bicker about each other, hurling barbs, quips, and generalizations. All the classic North/South traits can be applied to Rome (the government capital) and Milan (the business capital). Although the differences have become less pronounced lately, the sniping continues.

The Milanese say the Romans are lazy. Roman government jobs come with short hours—cut even shorter by too many coffee breaks, three-hour lunches, chats with colleagues, and phone calls to friends and relatives. Milanese contend that *Roma ladrona* (Rome the big thief) is a parasite that lives off the taxes of people up North. Until recently, there was a strong Milan-based movement seriously promoting secession from the South.

Romans, meanwhile, dismiss the Milanese as uptight workaholics with nothing else to live for—gray like their foggy city. Romans do admit that in Milan, job opportunities are better and based on merit. And the Milanese grudgingly concede the Romans have a gift for enjoying life.

While Rome is more of a family city, Milan is the place for high-powered singles on the career fast track. Milanese yuppies mix with each other...not the city's long-time residents. Milan is seen as wary of foreigners and inward-looking, and Rome as fun-loving, tolerant, and friendly. In Milan, bureaucracy (like social services) works logically and efficiently, while in Rome, accomplishing even small chores can be exasperating. In Rome, everything—from finding a babysitter to buying a car—is done through friends. In Milan, while people are not as willing to discuss their personal matters, they are generous and active in charity work.

Milanese find Romans vulgar. The Roman dialect is considered one of the coarsest in the country. Much as they try, Milanese just can't say, "Damn your dead relatives" quite as effectively as the Romans. Still, Milanese enjoy Roman comedians and love to imitate the accent.

The Milanese feel that Rome is dirty and Roman traffic nerve-wracking. But despite the craziness, Rome maintains a genuine village feel. People share family news with their neighborhood grocer. Milan lacks people-friendly piazzas, and entertainment comes at a high price. But in Rome, *la dolce vita* is as close as the nearest square, and a full moon is enjoyed by all.

Tourist Information

Milan's main TI is in the central train station (Mon–Sat 9:00–13:00 & 14:00–18:00, Sun 9:00–13:00 & 14:00–17:00, tel. 02-7252-4360, www.milanoinfotourist.com). At track level (with your back to the tracks), look for "APT Tourist Information" sign near the blinking orange-and-white T. The TI is down a corridor next to a Telecom telephone center (Internet access with phone card, daily 9:00–20:00). Another TI has just opened in front of Sforza Castle (Mon–Sat 9:00–18:00, closed Sun, Piazza Castello 1, corner of Beltrami, tel. 02-8058-0614). A TI may also be on Piazza Duomo (likely on Via Silvio Pellico; facing the cathedral, it's to your left).

At the TI, confirm your sightseeing plans and pick up a free map. For a list of Milan's sights (including hours, prices, and directions), events, concerts, films in English, expatriate groups, and cultural insights, ask for the free *Hello Milano* monthly newspaper (www.hellomilano.it) or the less-helpful, Italian-only *Milano Mese* (events are listed by category rather than date).

While I've listed enough sights to keep you hectically busy for two days, there's much more to see in Milan. Its many thousand-year-old churches make it clear that Milan was an important beacon in the Dark Ages. The TI and local guidebooks and newspapers can point you in the right direction if you have more time.

Arrival in Milan

By Train: The huge, sternly decorated, fascist-built (in 1931) train station is a city and a sight in itself. You'll get off the train and enter the lobby at track level; another floor is downstairs.

Orient from the track-level lobby with your back to the tracks. On your right: **train information** (daily 7:00–21:00, validate railpasses here at any window), **baggage check** (€4/5 hrs, €10/24 hrs, daily 6:00–24:00), and a 24-hour **pharmacy** (*farmacia,* look for green neon cross). At your back between the two clocks facing the tracks is the **365 Travel Agency** (Mon–Fri 8:00–20:00, Sat–Sun 9:00–18:00, sells train tickets, supplements, and *cuccetta* reservations without a commission, tel. 02-6749-3147). On your left are **cash machines** (near track 14) and the **TI** (see above, look for blinking orange T). Out the side exit on the left (down the escalator under the "Gran Bar" sign), you'll find **airport shuttle buses** to Malpensa and Linate airports (run by STAM). Past those buses is another 365 Travel Agency with fewer crowds (Mon–Fri 8:00–20:00, Sat–Sun 9:00–17:50, Piazza Luigi di Savoia 1, tel. 02-669-1351).

From the track level, go downstairs straight ahead to find train-ticket windows, Hertz/Avis/Europcar offices, and a great and huge supermarket/cafeteria that's hidden away (daily 8:00–23:00 year-round; after you descend stairs from track-level lobby, go right to the far end, enter Pellini bar, and snake your way through the cafeteria to the Super Centrale market, also called Supermercato Sigma). Just outside the front of the station is the taxi stand (figure €8 to Duomo) and escalators, which take you down into the Metro system (€1 to Duomo, faster than a taxi).

Station change offices are a rip-off. Use a cash machine in the train station (from track 14, enter the lobby—you'll find a *Bancomat* cash machine to your left, and another a few more steps to the left down the hall; yet another one is at the station post office), or exit the station straight ahead and cross the square to Banca Intesa (Mon–Fri 8:30–13:30 & 15:00–16:00, closed Sat–Sun).

If you need to buy tickets, avoid the language barrier and long lines by visiting a travel agency or by buying tickets from the user-friendly yellow machines on the ground floor of the station (see page 21).

Taking the Metro to the Duomo and Back: For most quick visits, the giant city is one simple axis from the train station to the Duomo. To get to the Duomo, go straight into the Metro (look for red *M*) and buy a €1 ticket from the underground ticket office at the Metro stop (with all prices listed in English over the window) or from a machine (push green button marked *rete urbana di Milano*). Follow signs for line 3 (yellow), direction San Donato, and in eight minutes (4 stops) you'll be facing the cathedral. To return to the station, take the yellow line 3, direction Maciachini. After one trip on the Metro, you'll dream up other excuses to use it.

By Car: Driving is bad enough in Milan to make the €20/day fee for a downtown garage a blessing. If you're driving, do Milan (and Lake Como) before or after you rent your car, not while you're renting it. If you have a car, use the well-marked suburban *parcheggi* (parking lots), which offer affordable (€1/day) and safe parking at city-edge subway stations.

By Plane: Frequent shuttle trains and buses connect the airports and train station. See "Transportation Connections," page 248.

Helpful Hints

Theft Alert: Be on guard. Milan's thieves target tourists. At the station and around the Duomo, thieves roam dressed as beggars, sometimes in gangs of several too-young-to-arrest children. Watch out for ragged people carrying newspaper and cardboard; they thrust it at you while they pick your pocket. If you're ripped off, ask the police to fill out a report. It's necessary if you plan to file a claim with your insurance company (Police Station, "Questura," Via Fatebenefratelli 11, Metro: Turati, tel. 02-62261, or Piazza San Sepolcro 9 behind Pinacoteca Ambrosiana near Duomo, tel. 02-806-051). For police emergencies, call 113. For lost or stolen credit cards, see page 13.

U.S. Consulate: It's at Via Principe Amedeo 2/10 (Mon–Fri 8:30–12:30 & 13:30–17:30, closed Sat–Sun, Metro: Turati, tel. 02-290-351 for recorded info and phone tree, http://milan .usconsulate.gov).

Scheduling: Monday is a terrible sightseeing day, since many museums are closed. August is rudely hot and muggy. Locals who can, vacate, leaving the city pretty quiet. Those visiting in August find the nightlife sleepy; many shops, restaurants, and some hotels closed; and the hotels that are open, empty and discounted. I've indicated which recommended hotels offer air-conditioning, a splurge worth the money for a summer visit.

Medical Help: A 24-hour pharmacy is in the central train station; look for the neon-green cross. Several international medical clinic/emergency care facilities are in Milan: at Via Cerva 25 (Mon–Thu 9:00–19:00, Fri 9:00–18:00, closed Sat–Sun; if calling outside office hours, English message gives you number for 24-hr emergency doctor; Metro: San Babila, tel. 02-7601-6047); in Galleria Strasburgo #3 (between Via Durini and Corso Europa, 3rd floor, Metro: San Babila, tel. 02-763-407-20); and at Via Mercalli 11 (Metro: Missori or Crocetta, call for appointments, tel. 02-5831-9808, Mon–Fri 9:00–17:00, English message with emergency number during off hours). Dial 118 for medical emergencies.

Street Markets: Milan has two very popular flea markets. **Fiera di Sinigallia** spills down Viale d'Annunzio every Saturday 8:30–17:00 (later in summer, Metro: San Agostino). If you continue along Viale d'Annunzio to Viale Papiniano, you'll run into the **Papiniano** market (Tue and Sat). Small street markets are held every morning except Sunday in various neighborhoods; *Hello Milano* has a complete listing (free at TI). Be wary of pickpockets at any street market.

Internet Access: Major phone offices (e.g., at central train station) have phone card-operated computers that work well (daily 9:00–20:00). Two Internet Point shops are just off Via Torino, near the Duomo: at Via Medici 6, near Largo Carrobbio (Mon–Sat 10:00–24:00, Sun 14:00–20:00, tel. 02-866-800) and at Via Valpetrosa 5 (daily 8:30–20:30, tel. 02-4547-8874).

Bookstores: The handiest major bookstore is **Libreria Feltrinelli,** under the Galleria Vittorio Emanuele. The books in English—fiction and guidebooks—are at opposite ends of the store (Mon–Sat 10:00–23:00, Sun 10:00–20:00; store is huge and entrances are subtle—either enter at Ricordi Mediastore next to McDonald's in center of Galleria and go downstairs, or enter through Autogrill restaurant on Piazza Duomo, store is in the basement level; also sells maps; tel. 02-8699-6903). The **American Bookstore** is at Via Camperio 16, near Sforza

Castle (Mon 13:00–19:00, Tue–Sat 10:00–19:00, closed Sun, tel. 02-878-920).

Travel Agencies: You can buy train tickets and reserve an overnight berth (*cuccetta,* koo-CHEH-tah) at the **365 Travel Agency** at the train station at no extra cost and without the lines (see their two offices listed in "Arrival in Milan by Train," above) or at a downtown travel agency such as **American Express,** near the Duomo (Mon–Fri 9:00–17:30, train tickets not for sale 13:00–14:00, closed Sat–Sun, pay cash or use AmEx credit card, at Via Larga 4, 2 blocks southeast of Duomo, tel. 02-721-041).

Getting Around Milan

Use Milan's great subway system. The clean, spacious, fast, and easy three-line Metro zips you nearly anywhere you may want to go, and trams and city buses fill in the gaps. The handiest Metro line for a quick visit is the yellow line (3), connecting the train station to the Duomo. The other lines are red (1) and green (2).

A **ticket,** valid for 75 minutes, can be used for one subway, tram, or bus ride, plus a transfer (€1, sold at newsstands, many *tabacchi* shops, and at machines in subway station—push green *rete urbana di Milano* button; note that some machines sell only the €1 ticket and offer no other options—just feed in the money).

Milan's Metro

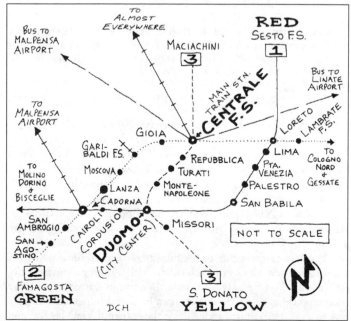

Milan at a Glance

▲▲Duomo Milan's showpiece cathedral on the main square (facade covered with scaffolding through 2006). You can walk on its roof amid a forest of spires. **Hours:** Daily 7:00–19:00.

▲▲Duomo Museum Provides insight to the Duomo and a chance to see its original art. **Hours:** Daily 10:00–13:15 & 15:00–18:00. Likely closed through 2006.

▲▲Galleria Vittorio Emanuele Glass-domed arcade on the main square, perfect for window-shopping and people-watching. **Hours:** Always open.

▲▲La Scala Opera House and Museum The world's most prestigious opera house, recently re-opened after a lengthy renovation. **Hours:** Museum daily 9:00–12:30, 13:30–17:30.

▲Brera Art Gallery World-class collection of Italian paintings (13th-20th centuries), including Raphael, Caravaggio, Gentile da Fabriano, Piero della Francesca, Mantegna, and the Bellini brothers. **Hours:** Tue–Sun 8:30–19:15, closed Mon.

▲*The Last Supper* Leonardo da Vinci's masterpiece, viewable only with a reservation—book at least a month in advance. **Hours:** Tue–Sun 8:15–18:45 (last visit), closed Mon.

▲Leonardo da Vinci National Science and Technology Museum Leonardo's designs illustrated in wooden models, plus a vast collection of historical, scientific bric-a-brac. **Hours:** Tue–Fri 9:30–17:00, Sat–Sun 9:30–18:30, closed Mon.

Other options include: a *carnet* (€9.20 for 10 rides; you get 5 tickets that can be used twice—flip over to use a second time; these can be shared); a **24-hour pass** (€3, worthwhile if you take 4 rides; can usually cover a journey the following morning since it's a 24-hour rather than a 1-day pass); and a **48-hour pass** (€5.50). Transit info: toll-free tel. 800-808-181 (underground transit system office—called ATM Point—at Duomo stop near Arengario exit, can access from square, entrance to the right of Duomo as you face it, Mon–Sat 7:45–19:00, closed Sun).

I've keyed sightseeing to the subway system. While most sights are within a few blocks of each other, Milan is an exhausting city for walking. You'll rarely wait more than five minutes for a subway train, and the well-marked trams can be useful (especially for getting to *The Last Supper*: catch #16 on the corner of Via Mazzini and

▲Sforza Castle Milan's castle containing a museum whose highlight is an unfinished Michelangelo *Pietà*. **Hours:** Tue–Sun 9:00–17:30, closed Mon.

▲Risorgimento Museum History of Italian unification. **Hours:** Tue–Sun 9:00–13:00 & 14:00–17:30, closed Mon.

▲Via Dante Human traffic buzzes to the tune of lilting accordions on one of Europe's longest pedestrian-only boulevards. **Hours:** Always open.

▲Monumental Cemetery An evocative outdoor art gallery with tombs showcasing expressive art styles from 1870 to 1930. **Hours:** Tue–Sun 8:30–17:30, closed Mon.

Pinacoteca Ambrosiana Oldest museum in Milan, with works by Raphael, Leonardo, Botticelli, Titian, and Caravaggio. **Hours:** Tue–Sun 10:00–17:30, closed Mon.

Poldi Pezzoli Museum Italian paintings (15th–18th centuries), weaponry, and decorative arts. **Hours:** Tue–Sun 10:00–18:00, closed Mon.

Bagatti Valsecchi Museum 19th-century Italian Renaissance furnishings. **Hours:** Tue–Sun 13:00–17:45, closed Mon.

Church of Santa Maria presso San Satiro Pilgrim church with impressive 3-D paintings. **Hours:** Daily 7:30–11:30 & 15:30–18:30.

Via Dogana, just off Piazza del Duomo, see page 236).

Small groups go cheap and fast by **taxi** (drop charge-€3.10, €0.70 per km, additional supplements for luggage and on Sun and holidays). It's often easier to walk to a taxi stand than to flag down a cab.

TOURS

Bus Tours—The three-hour **Autostradale** city bus tour is a good value, has a live guide, and guarantees you'll see Leonardo's *The Last Supper* (useful if you haven't booked ahead for this sight). The jam-packed itinerary also includes visits to the Duomo, Galleria, Sforza Castle, and La Scala Opera House (€47, departures daily at 9:00, Tue and Fri–Sun also at 15:00, depart from Piazza Duomo—next

Milan

- **1** Tram #16 (To *Last Supper*, Leonardo's Horse & Meazza Stadium)
- **2** City Museum Entrance

to taxi stand at far end of square from church, book in advance at TI by calling 02-7252-4301 or show up 30 min early to ensure you get a seat; to confirm details call 02-3391-0794 or 02-720-01304 or visit www.autostradale.it). **Zani Viaggi** does simpler, cheaper city tours—without Leonardo—daily at 14:00 (€26, 3 hrs, bus and walking tour with live guide, tel. 02-7060-3685).

Vintage Tram Tour—The **Ciao Milano** vintage tram does a two-hour, figure-eight trip around the city with a taped spiel (recorded back before the euro replaced the lira). While an appealing concept, the slow pace and uninteresting commentary make it worth neither the time nor the €20 (3/day, departs at roughly 11:00, 13:00, and 15:00 from Piazza Castello at Via Beltrami, Metro: Carioli, tel. 02-720-01304).

Private Guide—Lorenza Scorti is a hardworking young woman who knows her local history and how to teach it. She can be booked well in advance (necessary in May and Sept) or on short notice (€100/3-hr tour, eves OK, €200/full day, price identical for individuals or groups, tel. 02-4801-7042, lorenza.scorti@libero.it).

SIGHTS

Milan's Cathedral and Museum

To get the most out of your cathedral visit, start by visiting the adjacent Duomo Museum (see page 225; unfortunately, likely to be closed through 2006), located just outside the church, around to the right, directly across from the south transept.

▲▲Duomo (Cathedral)—The city's centerpiece is the fourth-largest church in Europe—after the Vatican's, London's, and Sevilla's. Back when Europe was fragmented into countless tiny kingdoms and dukedoms, the dukes of Milan wanted to impress their counterparts in Germany and France. Their goal was to earn Milan recognition and respect from both the Vatican and the kings and princes of northern Europe by building a massive, richly ornamented cathedral. Even after Renaissance-style domes were in vogue elsewhere in Italy, conservative Milan's cathedral stayed on Gothic target. The dukes—thinking northerners would relate better to Gothic—loaded it with pointed arches and spires. For good measure, the cathedral was built not of ordinary stone but of marble—pink marble of Candoglia, from top to bottom—rafted across Lake Maggiore from a quarry about 60 miles away to a canal port at the cathedral. (Note: The glorious facade is covered with scaffolding through 2006.)

Cost, Hours, Location: Free, daily 7:00–19:00, Metro: Duomo.

Audioguide: €3 for 45-min audioguide, €5 for two audioguides (available from kiosk located inside to right of entrance, kiosk open daily 9:30–17:30, ID required).

Dress Code: Modest dress is required. Don't wear shorts or sleeveless shirts. Even kids with exposed shoulders or knees are likely to be turned away at the door.

Interior: At 525 by 300 feet, with 52 100-foot-tall, sequoia-sized pillars and more than 2,000 statues inside, the place is immense. If you do two laps, you've done your daily walk.

Built from 1386 to 1810, this construction project originated the Italian phrase meaning "never-ending": "like building a cathedral." It started Gothic (best seen in the apse behind the altar) and was finished in the early 1800s under Napoleon (particularly the noteworthy west facade, which is wonderful—when not covered in scaffolding—late in the day, with the sun low in the sky). While the church is a good example of the flamboyant, or "flamelike," overripe final stage of Gothic, architectural harmony is not its forte.

Walk around the entire church exterior and notice the statues, all made between the 14th and 20th centuries by sculptors from all over Europe. There are hundreds of these statues—each different and quite creative. Notice the statues on the tips of the many spires...they seem so relaxed, like they're just hanging out, waiting for their big day. The 96 fanciful gargoyle monsters, functioning as drain spouts, are especially imaginative.

Standing inside (at the back rear), notice two tiny lights: The little red one above the altar marks where a nail from the cross of Jesus is kept. This relic was brought to Milan by St. Helen (Emperor Constantine's mother) in the fourth century, when Milan was the capital of the Western Roman Empire. It's on display for three days a year (in mid-Sept). Now look high to the right and find a tiny pinhole of white light. This is designed to shine a 10-inch sunbeam onto the bronze line running across the floor at noon, indicating where we are on the zodiac (but local guides claim they've never seen it work).

Wander deeper into the church up the right aisle. Notice the windows. Those on the right are 15th-century; these mosaics of colored glass are brilliant and expensive, bought by wealthy families seeking the Church's favor. Many on the left date from the time of Napoleon and are dimmer, cheaper painted glass.

Belly up to the bar facing the high altar. While the church is Gothic, the area around the altar was made Baroque—the style of the Vatican in the 1570s (a Roman Catholic statement to counter the Protestant churches of the north, which were mostly Gothic). Now look to the rear up at the ceiling and see the fancy "carving" (between the ribs)...nope, that's painted. It looks expensive, but paint is more affordable than carved stone.

Look down at the fine 16th-century inlaid marble floor. The pieces around the altar are original...and you can tell that the black marble is harder then the rest. A grotesque 16th-century statue of St. Bartolomeo, a martyr skinned alive by the Romans, stands in the south transept near the side (right) exit. Walk behind the poor guy wearing his skin like a robe to see his face, hands, and feet.

Treasury: The treasury, or *tesoro,* to the right under the altar, thrills pilgrims with reliquaries containing thorns from Jesus' crown and the "Tree of Apostles" with bones, fingernails, and hair from each of the 12 apostles (€1, covered by Duomo Museum ticket, daily 9:30–13:30 & 15:00–18:00).

Paleo-Christian Baptistery: In the rear of the church (buy €1.50 ticket at kiosk, daily 9:30–17:00), you can climb down into the church that stood here long before the present one. Milan was an important center of the early Christian Church. In Roman times, Mediolanum's street level was 10 feet below today's level. You'll see the scant remains of an eight-sided Baptistery (where saints Augustine and Ambrose were baptized) and a little church. Back then, since you couldn't enter the church until you were baptized, which didn't happen until age 18, churches had a little "holy zone" just outside for the unbaptized. This included a Baptistery.

Cathedral Rooftop: This is the most memorable part of a Duomo visit. You'll wander through a fancy forest of spires with great views of the city, the square, and—on clear days—the crisp and jagged Italian Alps. And, 330 feet above everything, La Madonnina overlooks it all. This 15-foot-tall gilt Virgin Mary is a symbol of the city.

Climb the stairs for €4, or ride the elevator for €6 (€8 combo-ticket includes elevator and Duomo Museum; daily mid-Feb–mid-Nov 9:00–17:50, mid-Nov–mid-Feb 9:00–16:50). Enter outside from the north transept (clue: old European churches face roughly east). The stair entrance is across from Rinascente department store, and the elevator is further ahead toward the back of the church (be prepared to climb a few more stairs once you reach the lowest level of the roof by elevator).

▲▲Duomo Museum (Museo del Duomo)—This fine museum will likely be closed through 2006 for renovation. When open, it offers an excellent opportunity to really understand Milan's cathedral and enjoy a chance to see its original art close up. While the admission is €6 (includes treasury), their discounted €8 combo-ticket (which includes the treasury plus the elevator to church rooftop) is an even better deal (daily 10:00–13:15 & 15:00–18:00, in Ducal Palace next to south side of Duomo, Piazza Duomo 14, Metro: Duomo, tel. 02-860-358). Here's a tour:

Room 1: After you buy your ticket, look up. Greeting you, as he did pilgrims 500 years ago, is God the Father, made of wood, wrapped in copper, and gilded. In 1425, this covered the keystone connecting the tallest arches directly above the high altar of the Duomo.

Room 2: Meet St. George. Among the oldest cathedral statues, it once stood on the front spire and shows nearly 600 years of pollution and aging. Some think this is the face of Duke Visconti—the man who started the cathedral. The museum is filled with originals like this. On the right, finger a raw piece of *marmo di Candoglia*—the material of the church, spires, and statues. The duke's family gave the entire Candoglia quarry (near Stresa) to the church for all the marble it would ever need.

Room 3: This room (which used to be the stable for the Duke's horses) shows how Gothic was an international style. Gothic craftsmen, engineers, and artists roamed across Europe to work on huge projects such as Milan's cathedral. The statues in this room show the national differences: Peter (near the door, showing off his big keys) is Italian. His expressive face is made even more expressive by his copper-button pupils. The smaller statues behind glass (which were models for the big ones) are German (showing inner strength) and French (more graceful). Pope Martino V, overlooking the room from his perch at the end (to the left as you enter), celebrated the first Mass in the cathedral in 1418. Study the 15th-century stained-glass windows close up. The grotesque gargoyles (originals), protruding over the door you entered, served two purposes: to scare away evil spirits and to spew rainwater away from the building. Leaving the room, you'll walk under a stylized sun—a symbol of both Jesus and the Visconti family.

Room 5: A lit panel shows how the church was built in stages from 1386 to 1774. Building resumed whenever the community had the money.

Room 6: The brick backdrop reminds us what the church would have looked like if not for the 15th-century dandy with the rolled-up contract in his hand. That's Visconti's descendant, Galeazzo Sforza, making it official—the church now owns the marble quarry (and it makes money on it to this day). A photo of the contract is opposite.

Room 7: The Byzantine-style crucifix (again, copper-sheet gilded with real gold nailed onto wood) is 900 years old. It hung in the church that stood here previously, as well as in today's cathedral. The two-sided miniature altar painting has been carried through the city on festival days for 500 years.

Room 8: These statues, from around 1500, are originals. Copies now fill their niches in the church. St. Paul the Hermit (in front of the blue curtain) got close to God by living in the desert. While wearing only a simple robe, he's filled with inner richness. The intent is for pilgrims to stare into his eyes and feel at peace (but I couldn't stop thinking of the Cowardly Lion). Check out the interactive computer detailing restoration techniques and works in progress on the cathedral.

Room 9: Five hundred years ago, this sumptuous Flanders-style tapestry—woven of silk, silver, and gold—hung from the high altar. In true Flemish style, it shows fun details of everyday life woven into the theology. It tells the story of the Crucifixion by showing three scenes at once. Note the exquisite detail, down to the tears on Mary's cheeks. (A discreet WC hides behind the wooden door.)

Room 10: The sketchy red cartoons were designs for huge paintings (see an actual painting and photographs of others nearly opposite) that still hang between the cathedral pillars

(Oct–Christmas). Notice the inlaid 16th-century marble floor. The black (from Lake Como) and red (from Verona) marble is harder. Go ahead, wear down the white a little more.

Room 12: Enter the long room 12 and turn around to see the artwork lining the wall. The terra-cotta was clay—worked in a creative frenzy and then baked. Study the quick design below the careful marble originals (flanking the doorway you entered). Notice what 300 years of acidic pigeon droppings do to marble.

The statues all around this room (c. 1600) were sculpted 100 years later than the statues in room 8, and therefore are more expressive.

Find the painting of St. Carlo Borromeo in the black robe (high up, on your right). The 16th-century saint carries a cross showing the holy nail (the church's top relic) as he leads the plague out of Milan. In the background, see the previous 13th-century facade with today's church—before spires—behind it.

Circle the room clockwise. Crespi's monochrome painting of the *Creation of Eve (Creazione di Eva)* came first (1628). From that, the terra-cotta model was made (1629), and this served as the model for the marble statue that still stands above the center door on the church's west portal (1643). Three other sets line the wall.

Opposite *Eve,* see the swirling *Dance of Angels* and its terra-cotta model. This is the original, which decorated the ceiling over the door.

Room 20: This room (off room 12) displays vestments on loan from the treasury. Showing off rich red robes with lavish gold brocade, it's like a priestly fashion show from the 16th through 20th centuries.

Go back through Room 12, and at the far end, enter...

Room 13: Standing like a Picasso is the original iron frame (1772) for the statue of the Virgin Mary that still crowns the cathedral's tallest spire. In 1967, a steel replacement was made for the 33 pieces of gilded copper bolted to the frame. The carved wood face of Mary (in the corner) is the original mold for Mary's cathedral-crowning copper face.

Go back into Room 12 once more, and enter the nearby tunnel-like hall, into...

Room 15: Along the left wall, diagrams show competition designs proposing possible facades for the cathedral. A photo of the actual west portal is at the end of the hall.

Room 16: This huge wooden model of the cathedral was the actual model—necessary in that pre-computer age—used in the 16th century by the architects and engineers to build the church. This version of the facade wasn't actually built. Climb around the back to see the spire-filled rooftop, which you'll explore later if you like.

Room 17: The art here seems a mix of old and new, but it's all 20th-century. Notice the vibrant Pope Martin V popping out of the wall (bronze panel to the left as you enter; by artist Lucio Fontana). On the opposite wall (between the windows), Fontana's *Assumption of Mary (Maria Assunta)* is making a jump shot into heaven. Her veil looks like flowing hair, like the wings of an angel.

The last rooms are technical, showing the recent restoration work and the stabilization and reinforcement of the main pylons. To exit, retrace your steps.

Near the Duomo

▲Piazza Duomo—Milan's main square is a classic European scene and a popular local gathering point. Professionals scurry, fashion-conscious kids loiter, young thieves peruse.

Standing in the square (midway between the statue and the Galleria), you're surrounded by history. The statue is Victor Emmanuel II, first king of Italy. He's looking at the grand Galleria named for him. The words above the triumphal arch entrance read: "To Victor Emmanuel II, from the people of Milan."

Behind the statue (opposite the cathedral) is the center of medieval Milan—Piazza Mercanti. The medieval city hall (look for its red brick arches), dating from 1220, marked the center of town back when the entire city stood within its immense fortified walls. The merchant's square is a strangely peaceful place today, with a fine smattering of old-time Milano architecture.

Opposite the Galleria are twin fascist buildings. Mussolini made grandiose speeches from their balconies. Study the buildings' relief panels telling—with fascist drama—the history of Milan. Between these buildings and the cathedral (set back a bit) is the historic ducal palace, Palazzo Reale. This building, now a venue for temporary art exhibits, was redone in the neoclassical style by Maria Theresa in the late 1700s, when Milan was ruled by the Austrian Hapsburgs. For a fine view of the Duomo and the piazza, climb the steps to the balcony of the skinny, fascist-style building closest to the cathedral (can be closed for frequent *manifestazioni*—demonstrations—or any other perceived security threat). Behind the Duomo is a vibrant pedestrian shopping zone along Corso Vittorio Emanuele.

▲▲Galleria Vittorio Emanuele—A symbol of Milan is its great four-story, glass-domed arcade on the cathedral square. Built during the heady days of Italian unification (c. 1870), it was the first building in town to have electric lighting. Here you can turn an expensive cup of coffee into a good value by enjoying Europe's best people-watching (or get the same view for peanuts from the strategically placed McDonald's).

The venerable **Bar Zucca** (at the entry), with a friendly staff and an Art Deco interior typical of the 1920s, is the former haunt of famous opera composer Giuseppe Verdi and conductor Arturo Toscanini, who used to stop by after their performances at La Scala. It's a fine place to enjoy a drink and people-watch (€2.80 per cup is a great deal if you relax and enjoy the view). Once called the Campari café, this is considered the birthplace of the famous Campari bitter. Now a bitter apéritif, Zucca, is their signature drink (€3.30 standing or €8 seated, Tue–Sun 7:30–20:30, closed Mon, tel. 02-8646-4435).

Wander around the gallery. Its art celebrates the establishment of Italy as an independent country. Around the central dome, patriotic mosaics symbolize the four major continents. The mosaic floor is also patriotic. The white cross in the center represents the king. The she-wolf with Romulus and Remus (on the south side—facing Rome) honors the city that, since 1870, has been the national capital. On the west side (facing Torino, the provisional capital of Italy from 1861–1865), you'll find that city's symbol: a *torino* (little bull). For good luck, locals step on his irresistible little testicles. Two local girls explained to me that it works better if you spin. Find the poor little bull and observe for a few minutes...it's a cute scene. With so much spinning, the mosaic is replaced every few years.

Piazza della Scala—This smart, little, traffic-free square, out the back between the Galleria and the opera house, is dominated by a statue of Leonardo da Vinci. The statue (from 1870) is a reminder that Leonardo spent many years in Milan working for the Sforza family (who dominated Milan as the Medici family dominated Florence). Under the great Renaissance genius stand four of his greatest "Leonardeschi." (He apprenticed a sizable group of followers.) The reliefs show his various contributions—painter, architect, and engineer. Leonardo, wearing his hydro-engineer hat, re-engineered Milan's canal system complete with locks. (Until the 1920s, Milan was one of Italy's major ports, with canals connecting the city to the Po River and Lake Maggiore.)

▲▲La Scala Opera House and Museum—Behind the Galleria is a statue of Leonardo. He's looking at a plain but famous neoclassical building, possibly the world's most prestigious opera house: Milan's Teatrale alla Scala. La Scala opened in 1778 with an opera by Antonio Salieri (of *Amadeus* fame).

At Milan's famous opera house and its adjacent museum, which have both undergone a lengthy restoration, opera buffs can see the museum's extensive collection, and get a glimpse of the theater.

Museum: The collection—well-described in English—features things that mean absolutely nothing to the hip hop crowd: Verdi's top hat, Rossini's eyeglasses, Toscanini's baton, Fettuccini's pesto, and original scores, diorama stage sets, costumes, busts, portraits, and death masks of great composers and musicians. The museum allows you to peek into the actual theater. The stage is as big as the seating area on the ground floor. The royal box is just below your vantage point, in the center rear. Notice the massive chandelier made of Bohemian crystal (€5, daily 9:00–12:30 & 13:30–17:30, Piazza della Scala, tel. 02-88791).

Opera: The show goes on at the world-famous La Scala Opera House. Schedules vary, but the opera season is nearly year-round (show time 20:00), and ballet and classical concerts are held from October through June. No performances are held in August (for information and booking call Scala Infotel Service, daily 12:00–18:00, tel. 02-7200-3744—live; or tel. 02-860-775—automated booking, press 2 for English; or book online at La Scala's fine Web site: www.teatroallascala.org). While tourists are usually keen on seeing an opera in La Scala, note that many of the performances are actually in a second hall, the Arcimboldi Theater. On the opening night of an opera, a dress code is enforced for men (suit and tie).

Tickets generally go on sale two months before a performance. Seats sell out quickly. At noon on the day of the show, any remaining seats (usually in the affordable, sky-high gallery) are sold at a 30 percent discount at the box office; at another handy ticket office in the Duomo Metro station (daily 12:00–18:00, entrance is to right of Duomo as you face it, underground, follow the signs to ATM Point); and on the Internet (Web sales cease 1 hour before show time).

La Scala has historically reserved about 100 seats at each performance for struggling artists and students, selling them at dirt-cheap prices the day of the performance. These discounted tickets are now in high demand and getting one is pretty tough, especially considering the arcane system they use to allot the seats. Usually at around 10:00 the morning of the performance, a man with an *Accordo* badge (*Accordo* is the name of the association providing this "service") loiters outside the opera house, collecting names from anyone who wants a ticket (1 name per person). Then, three hours before show time, he returns with the names of the lucky recipients of the tickets. Those who make the cut go to the theater ticket office and buy their cheap ticket (€5 for concerts, €10 for ballet, €15 for opera). Realistically, the way most tourists snare a ticket is to book via the Web long in advance and pay the high price.

▲**Via Speronari**—A block off Piazza Duomo, this is one of Milan's oldest streets and the most charming street in the old center. Via Speronari—named for the spurs once made and sold here—is worth a wander. Streets around here recall their medieval crafts: *speronari*—spurs, *spadari*—swords, *armorari*—armor. The weaponry made on these streets was high fashion among Europe's warrior class...like having an Armani dagger. While right in the city center, the neighborhood feels vital. That's because it's also a residential street. Banks of doorbells indicate that families live above the shops. Start at the recommended Hotel Speronari, formerly a dorm for monks from the church across the street. The classy Vino Vino wine shop next door welcomes tasters (about €2/glass—daily specials posted at the tasting bar in the middle, Tue–Sat 9:00–19:30, closed Sun–Mon, tel. 02-8646-4055). The sign next door—*L'Ortolan Pusae Vecc de Milan*—brags in the old Milanese language that this is the oldest fruit and veggie store in the city. The neighboring Princi bakery is understandably popular. Its brioches are rarely more than a few minutes old.

Where Via Speronari hits Via Torino, go 20 yards to the left to find the **Church of Santa Maria presso San Satiro** (Church of St. Mary at St. Satiro) hiding behind its Baroque facade (daily 7:30–11:30 & 15:30–18:30, tel. 02-874-683). It was the scene of a temper tantrum in 1242, when a losing gambler vented his anger by hitting the baby Jesus in the Madonna-and-Child altarpiece. Blood "miraculously" spurted out, and the beautiful little church has been on the pilgrimage trail ever since. While I've never seen any blood, I'd swear I've seen a 3-D background behind the basically flat altar (a *trompe l'oeil* illusion by Bramante—only about a foot deep). This church—squeezed between the earlier church of San Satiro and a street—had no room for a real apse, so, with the help of math, the Renaissance architect Bramante made what looks like an apse. In the north transept, you'll find that original ninth-century church of San Satiro (brother of St. Ambrogio, patron saint of Milan). This tiny church—with surviving bits of Byzantine fresco—predated the rest. From this chapel, look back at the main altar to see Bramante's 3-D work collapsed. On the opposite side (near entry)—with dimensions mirroring this old chapel—an eight-sided Baptistery by Bramante from the 1480s shows the mathematically based values of the Renaissance. If you have a prayer in need of an extra boost, pop a coin into the box and "light" an electric candle.

Pinacoteca Ambrosiana—This oldest museum in Milan was inaugurated in 1618 to house Cardinal Federico Borromeo's painting collection. It began as a teaching academy, which explains the many replicas, some of which you may recognize (including a painting of Leonardo's faded *The Last Supper* where you buy your ticket and some famous statues along the stairway). In this prestigious collection, look for these highlights: Leonardo da Vinci's *Portrait of a Musician* (like the *Mona Lisa*, Leonardo has you wondering, "What's he thinking?" "What's he listening to?" and "Where's his iPod?"); Leonardo's *Codex Atlanticus* (collection of his writings—originals locked up in their vault, only copies on display); works by Botticelli and Caravaggio; and a room (#7) full of Flemish paintings—including delightful works by Jan Brueghel (study the wonderful detail in *Allegory of Fire* and *Allegory of Water*). You'll see lots of art that looks like da Vinci's but was actually done by his followers, such as Bernardino Luini. Titian was a favorite of Cardinal Borromeo, so you'll see plenty of work by this Venetian master and his followers.

Perhaps the highlight of the collection is the Raphael cartoon—the original charcoal-on-canvas design that Raphael drew as an outline for the famous *School of Athens* fresco. While the Vatican's much-adored fresco is attributed to Raphael, it was actually mostly painted by his students; it's safe to say, however, that this cartoon version was wholly sketched by the hand of Raphael. To make the fresco, they riddled this cartoon with pin pricks along the outlines of the characters, stuck it to the wall of the pope's study, and then applied a colored powder. When they removed the cartoon, the characters' shapes would be marked on the wall, and completing the fresco was a lot like a coloring a coloring book (€7.50, no English descriptions but small English guidebook for €6.20 covers museum's highlights nicely, Tue–Sun 10:00–17:30, last entrance 1 hour before closing, closed Mon, a couple of blocks from Piazza Duomo at Piazza Pio XI 2, tel. 02-8069-2225, free WC behind ticket desk to the right and downstairs).

In the Brera Neighborhood

▲Brera Art Gallery—Milan's top collection of Italian paintings (13th–20th centuries) is world class, but it can't top Rome's or Florence's. Established in 1809 to house Napoleon's looted art, it fills the first floor above a prestigious art college.

Enter the grand courtyard of a former monastary, where you'll be greeted by the nude *Napoleon with Tinkerbell* (by Canova). Climb the stairway, past all the art students, following signs to *Pinacoteca*, and buy your ticket.

The gallery's highlights include works by Gentile da Fabriano, hinting at the realism of the coming Renaissance (check out the lifelike flowers and realistic, bright gold paint—he used real gold powder, Room IV). Mantegna's *The Dead Christ* is a textbook example of feet-first foreshortening (Room VI). In Room XXI, notice how Crivelli employs Renaissance technique (he was a contemporary of Leonardo) yet clings to the mystique of the Gothic Age (that's why I like him so much). Find three Crivellis. Also, don't miss Raphael's *Wedding of the Madonna*, Piero della Francesca's *Madonna and Child with Four Angels* (Room XXIV), and the gritty-yet-intimate realism of Caravaggio's *Supper at Emmaus* (Room XXIX). There's often a glass-enclosed restoration lab set up right in the gallery, allowing you to see the restoration work in progress.

Cost, Hours, Location: €5, more during special exhibits, open Tue–Sun 8:30–19:15, last entry 45 min before closing, closed Mon, Via Brera 28, Metro: Lanza or Montenapoleone, tel. 02-722-631, www .brera.beniculturali.it. Since there are no English descriptions, consider the audioguide (€3.50, or €5.50 for 2 headsets), or pick up the fine *Guide to the Galleries* (€8.20) in the bookshop. Java junkies will seek out the great, cheap cappuccino machine: Go through Napoleon's courtyard and straight through the art school to the end of the long hall; the machine's on your left. It's fun to explore the art school on the ground floor, mill about among the many young students, and wonder if there's a 21st-century Leonardo in your midst.

▲**Risorgimento Museum**—With a quick 30-minute swing through this quiet, one-floor museum thoughtfully described in English, you'll learn the interesting story of Italy's rocky road to unity: from Napoleon (1796) to the victory in Rome (1870). It's just around the block from the Brera Art Gallery at Via Borgonuovo 23 (€2, Tue–Sun 9:00–13:00 & 14:00–17:30, closed Mon, tel. 02-8846-4176, Metro: Montenapoleone).

Near Montenapoleone

Poldi Pezzoli Museum—This classy house of art features top Italian paintings of the 15th through 18th centuries, old weaponry, and lots of interesting decorative arts, such as a roomful of old sundials and compasses (€6; Tue–Sun 10:00–18:00, closed Mon, not a word of English but free English audioguides, ID required; Via Manzoni 12, Metro: Montenapoleone; tel. 02-796-334).

Bagatti Valsecchi Museum—This unique 19th-century collection of Italian Renaissance furnishings was assembled by two aristocratic brothers who spent a wad turning their home into a Renaissance mansion. Museum guards pack flashlights for closer examination of fine wood carvings (€6, more if there are special exhibits, half-price on Wed, Tue–Sun 13:00–17:45, closed Mon, good English descriptions, Via Gesu 5, Metro: Montenapoleone, tel. 02-7600-6132).

Sforza Castle and Nearby

▲**Sforza Castle (Castello Sforzesco)**—The castle of Milan tells the story of the city in brick. Built in the late 1300s as a military fortress, it guarded the gate to the city wall and defended the city from enemies "within and without." It was beefed up by the Sforza duke in 1450 in anticipation of a Venetian attack. Later, it was the Renaissance palace of the Sforza family and was even home to their in-house genius, Leonardo. During the centuries of foreign rule (16th–19th), it was a barracks for occupying Spanish, French, and Austrian soldiers. Today, it houses several museums (€3, Tue–Sun 9:00–17:30, closed Mon, free for those entering 16:30–17:00, English info fliers throughout, Metro: Cairoli, tel. 02-8846-3700).

The **gate** stands above the ditch once filled with water. A relief celebrates Umberto I, the second king of Italy. Above that, a statue of St. Ambrosius, the patron of Milan (and a local bishop in the

4th century), oversees the action. Notice the chart, just outside the gate, showing how the city was encircled first by a crude medieval wall, and then by a state-of-the-art 16th-century wall—of which this castle was a key element. It's apparent from the enormity of these walls that Milan was a strategic prize. Today the walls are gone, giving the city two circular boulevards.

This immense, much-bombed-and-rebuilt brick fortress— exhausting at first sight—can only be described as heavy. But its courtyard has a great lawn for picnics and siestas, and its main museum, the **City Museum** (Museo di Civici di Milano) is fascinating, unlike the other museums in the castle. Passing under the first gate, you enter the museum from inside the second gate (on the right). It fills the old Sforza family palace with interesting medieval armor, furniture, early Lombard art, an Egyptian collection, and, most important, Michelangelo's unfinished *Pietà Rondanini*.

Michelangelo died while still working on this piece—his fourth *Pietà*. A *pietà*, by definition, portrays a dead Christ with a sorrowful Virgin Mary. This unfinished statue is unique in that it shows the genius of Michelangelo midway through a major rework—Christ's head is cut out of Mary's right shoulder and an earlier arm is still just hanging there. But there's a certain power to this rawness. Walk around the back to see the strain in Mary's back (and Michelangelo's rough chisel work) as she struggles to support her son. The sculpture's elongated form hints at the Mannerist style that would follow. Notice the ancient Roman altar underneath the *Pietà*. This sculpture was owned by the Rondanini family until just after World War II. This is a rare opportunity to enjoy a Michelangelo with no crowds.

At the far end of the castle's grounds is the monumental Arco della Pace, a triumphal arch. They built the arch facing Paris to welcome Napoleon's rule, because locals believed he would bring with him the ideals of the French Revolution. When they learned he was just another megalomaniac, they turned the horses around, their tails facing France.

Branca Tower—The tower, a five-minute walk from Sforza Castle, offers perhaps the best view in Milan. For €3, a lift takes you as high as the Mary crowning the Cathedral (hours are crazy, roughly Tue and Thu 20:30–24:00, Wed and Sat–Sun 10:00–24:00, Fri 14:30–24:00, frequent breaks during day, closed Mon, tel. 02-331-4120, trendy bar at ground level).

▲**Via Dante**—This grand pedestrian boulevard leads from Sforza Castle toward the town center and the Duomo. Since Via Dante was carved out of a medieval tangle of streets to celebrate Italian unification (c. 1870), all the facades lining it are relatively new. Over the vigorous complaints of merchants, the street became traffic-free in 1995. Today, they'd have it no other way. Enjoy strolling this beautiful people zone, where, instead of traffic noise, you'll hear the whir of bikes and the lilting melodies of accordion players. In front of Sforza Castle, a commanding statue of Giuseppe Garibaldi, one of the heroes of the unification movement, looks down one of Europe's longest pedestrian zones. From here you can walk to the Duomo and beyond (about 1.5 miles), nearly all traffic-free.

The Last Supper and Nearby

▲**Leonardo da Vinci's** *The Last Supper (Cenacolo)*—You must have a reservation to see this Renaissance masterpiece in the Church of Santa Maria delle Grazie.

Because of Leonardo's experimental fresco technique, deterioration began within six years of its completion. The church was bombed in World War II, but—miraculously, it seems—the wall holding *The Last Supper* remained standing. The 21-year restoration project (completed in 1999) peeled 500 years of touch-ups away, leaving a faint but vibrant masterpiece. In a big, vacant, whitewashed room, you'll see faded pastels and not a crisp edge. The feet under the table look like negatives. But the composition is dreamy—Leonardo captures the psychological drama as the Lord says, "One of you will betray me," and the apostles huddle in stressed-out groups of three, wondering, "Lord, is it I?" Some are scandalized. Others want more information. Simon (on the far right) gestures as if to ask a question that has no answer. In this agitated atmosphere, only Judas (fourth from left and the only one with his face in shadow)—clutching his 30 pieces of silver and looking pretty guilty—is not shocked.

The circle meant life and harmony to Leonardo. Deep into a study of how life emanates in circles—like ripples on a pool hit by a pebble—Leonardo positioned the 13 characters in a semicircle. Jesus is in the center, from whence the spiritual force of God emanates.

The room depicted in the painting seems like an architectural extension of the church. The disciples form an apse, with Jesus as the altar—in keeping with the Eucharist. Jesus anticipates his sacrifice—his face sad, all-knowing, and accepting. His feet even foreshadowed his death by crucifixion. Had the door, which was cut out in 1652, not been added, you'd see how Leonardo placed Jesus' feet atop each other, ready for the nail.

The room was a refectory or dining room for the Dominican friars. Traditionally, they'd gather here to eat with a Last Supper scene on one wall facing a Crucifixion scene on the opposite wall.

The perspective is mathematically correct. In fact, restorers found a tiny nail hole in Jesus' right ear, which anchored the strings Leonardo used to establish these lines. The table is cheated out to show the meal. Notice the exquisite lighting. The walls are lined with tapestries (as they would have been) and the one on the right is brighter—to fit the actual lighting in the refectory (with windows on the left). With the extremely natural effect of the light and the drama of the faces, Leonardo created an effective masterpiece.

Reservations are mandatory. These days, because of the hype surrounding Dan Brown's blockbuster novel *The Da Vinci Code*, spots are booked at least a month in advance—so plan ahead. To minimize the humidity problem—even though the damage has already been done—only 25 tourists are allowed in every 15 minutes for exactly 15 minutes. Prior to your appointment time, you wait in several rooms, while doors close behind you and open up slowly in front of you. The information posted on Leonardo is mainly in Italian.

For a reservation, call 02-8942-1146 (or from the U.S., dial 011-39-02-8942-1146, number is often busy, keep trying; booking office open Mon–Fri 9:00–18:00, Sat 9:00–14:00, closed Sun). Getting the reservation is a two-minute process, and you'll hang up with an appointed entry time and a number (€8 entry includes €1.50 reservation fee, cash only, pay upon arrival, if booking more than 2 tickets you'll need to pay in advance with credit card, visits scheduled at 9:30 and 15:30 cost €3.25 extra for guided English tour). While "reservations are required," if spots are available (more likely on weekdays and late) you can book one at the desk (even if "Sold Out" sign is posted). If fewer than 25 people show up for a particular time slot, you can get lucky. But those who show up without a reservation generally kill lots of time waiting around. Note that the Autostradale city bus tour (see "Tours" page 221) includes entry to *The Last Supper*. In a pinch, you might be able to buy tickets from Autostradale without going on their tour. They book out the 12:00 and 12:15 slots, speculating that they'll fill their buses. If they don't, they release these extra tickets each morning. You can try to nab one by showing up at the Church of Santa Maria delle Grazie at 10:00.

Hours of *The Last Supper*: Tue–Sun 8:15–18:45 (last visit), always closed Mon. You'll be asked to show up 20 minutes before your scheduled time. When an attendant calls your time, get up and move into the next room. Consider the fine €2.50 audioguide (€4.50 with 2 headphones). Its spiel fills every second of the time you're in the room—so try to start listening just before you enter. You might want to listen to it in the waiting room while studying the reproduction of the actual *The Last Supper* there until you're let in. No photos are allowed.

Getting There: Take the Metro to Cadorna or Conciliazione (plus a 5-min walk), or hop on tram #16 (catch it just off Piazza Duomo on corner of Via Mazzini and Via Dogana), which drops you off in front of the Church of Santa Maria delle Grazie. The Science Museum (see below) is two blocks away.

▲**Leonardo da Vinci National Science and Technology Museum (Museo Nazionale della Scienza e Tecnica "Leonardo da Vinci")**—The spirit of Leonardo lives here. Most tourists visit for the hall of Leonardo designs illustrated in wooden models, but Leonardo's mind is just as easy to appreciate by paging through a coffee-table edition of his notebooks in any bookstore. The rest of this immense collection of industrial cleverness is fascinating, with planes, trains, and automobiles, ships, radios, old musical instruments, computers, batteries, telephones, chunks of the first transatlantic cable, interactive science workshops, and on and on. Some of the best exhibits (such as the Marconi radios) branch off the Leonardo hall. Ask for a museum map from the ticket desk—you'll need it (€7, Tue–Fri 9:30–17:00, Sat–Sun 9:30–18:30, closed Mon, Via San Vittore 21, bus #50 or #58 from Duomo, or Metro: Sant'Ambrogio or Cadorna, tel. 02-4855-5200). Complain politely about the lack of English descriptions.

Away from the Center

Leonardo's Horse—This largest equestrian monument in the world is a modern reconstruction of a model created in 1482 by Leonardo da Vinci for the Sforza family. The model was destroyed in 1499 by invading French forces, who used it for target practice. In 1999, American Renaissance art collector Charles Dent decided to build the 15-ton, 24-foot-long statue from Leonardo's design. He presented it to the Italians in appreciation for their role in the Renaissance and in homage to Leonardo's genius. The exhibit, described in English, includes statue casts and photos of the construction (free, daily 9:30–18:30, located on outskirts near Meazza soccer stadium and San Siro racetrack; from corner of Via Mazzini and Via Dogana, take tram #16, direction San Siro, to Stratico Palatino stop—ask conductor when to get off, then head right on Via Palatino, and left on Piazzale dello Sport to #9; or you can walk from Metro: Lotto).

Soccer—The Milanese claim that their soccer (*football* or *calcio* in Italian) team is the best in Europe. For a dose of Europe's soccer mania (which many believe provides a necessary testosterone vent to keep Europe out of a third big war), catch a match in Milan. Inter and A.C. Milan are the ferociously competitive home teams (tickets-€15–115, A.C. Milan tickets sold at Cariplo banks—one at Via Verdi 8, Mon–Fri 8:45–13:45 & 14:45–15:45, closed Sat–Sun—or through www.acmilan.com; Inter tickets at Banca Popolare di Milano—Piazza Meda 4, Metro: San Babila, Mon–Fri 8:45–13:45 & 14:45–15:45, closed Sat–Sun—or visit www.ticketone.it). Games are held in the 85,000-seat Meazza stadium most Sunday afternoons from September to June (Metro: Lotto, or tram #16—catch it just off Piazza del Duomo, on corner of Via Mazzini and Via

Dogana, direction San Siro, take it to last stop, where you'll find stadium; stadium info tel. 02-4870-7123). For more on the Italian passion for soccer, see page 706.

▲Monumental Cemetery (Il Monumentale Cimitero)— Europe's most artistic and dreamy cemetery experience, this grand place was built just after unification to provide a suitable final resting place for the city's "famous and well-deserving men." Any cemetery is evocative, but this one—with its super-emotional portrayals of the deceased and their heavenly escorts (in art styles c. 1870–1930)—is in a class by itself. It's a vast garden art gallery of proud busts and grim reapers, heartbroken angels and weeping widows, too-young soldiers and countless old smiles, frozen on yellowed black-and-white photos (free, Tue–Sun 8:30–17:30, closed Mon, a long walk from Metro: Garibaldi FS, or tram #3, #4, #11, #12, or #14).

SHOPPING

World-Class Window-Shopping

The "Quadrilateral," an elegant, high-fashion shopping area around Via Montenapoleone, is fun for shoppers. This was the original Beverly Hills of Milan. In the 1920s, the top fashion shops moved in, and today it remains *the* place for designer labels. Most places close Sunday and for much of August. On Mondays, stores open only after 16:00. In this land where fur is still prized, the people-watching is as entertaining as the window-shopping. Notice also the exclusive penthouse apartments with roof gardens high above the scene. Via Montenapoleone and the pedestrianized Via Spiga are the best streets.

Whether you're gawking or shopping, here's the best route: From La Scala, walk up Via Manzoni to the Metro stop at Montenapoleone, browse down Via Montenapoleone, cut left on Via Santo Spirito (lined with grand aristocratic palazzos—peek into the courtyard at #7), turn right to window-shop down Via Spiga, turn right on San Andrea and then left, back onto Montenapoleone, which leads you through a finale gauntlet of temptations to Piazza San Babila. Then (for less expensive shopping thrills), walk back to the Duomo down the pedestrian-only Corso Vittorio Emanuele. La Rinascente, next to the Duomo, is a Nordstrom-type department store with reasonable prices (Mon–Sat 9:00–22:00, Sun 10:00–20:00, good toy selection, faces north side of Duomo on Piazza Duomo, VAT refund kiosk at top of escalator on 7th floor) and recommended restaurants (see page 244).

NIGHTLIFE

For evening action, check out the artsy, student-oriented Brera area in the old center and Milan's formerly bohemian, now gentrified "Little Venice," the Navigli neighborhood (Metro: Porta Genova). Specifics change quickly, so it's best to rely on the entertainment information in periodicals from the TI.

SLEEPING

I've tried to minimize traffic-noise problems in my listings. All are within a few minutes' walk of Milan's subway system. With Milan's fine Metro, you can get anywhere in town in a flash. Anytime in March, April, September, and October, the city can be completely jammed by conventions, and hotel prices jump way up. I've listed high-season prices, but not convention-gouging prices. (For the convention schedule, see www.fieramilano.it.) Summer is usually wide open and prices are discounted, though many hotels close in August for vacation. Hotels cater more to business travelers than to tourists, so Fridays and Saturdays are generally cheaper and wide open.

Near the Duomo

The Duomo area is thick with people-watching, reasonable eateries, and the major sightseeing attractions. From the central train station to the Duomo, it's just four stops on a direct Metro line (yellow line 3, direction San Donato) to Metro: Duomo.

$$$ Hotel Grand Duca di York, with 33 pleasant, newly-refurbished rooms and lavish public spaces, is oddly stuck in the middle of banks and big-city starkness three blocks southwest of

---

Sleep Code

(€1 = about $1.20, country code: 39)
S = Single, **D** = Double/Twin, **T** = Triple, **Q** = Quad, **b** = bathroom, **s** = shower only. Unless otherwise noted, credit cards are accepted, English is spoken, and breakfast is included.

To help you sort easily through these listings, I've divided the rooms into three categories based on the price for a standard double room with bath:

$$$ **Higher Priced**—Most rooms €150 or more.
$$ **Moderately Priced**—Most rooms between €110–150.
$ **Lower Priced**—Most rooms €110 or less.

Milan's Center

1 Hotel Grand Duca di York
2 Hotel Spadari & Peck Deli
3 Hotel Gritti
4 Hotel Santa Marta
5 Hotel Speronari & Princi Bakery
6 Hotel Star
7 London Hotel
8 Antica Locanda dei Mercanti & Alle Meraviglie
9 Trattoria Milanese
10 Ristorante Bruno
11 Ristorante al Mercante
12 Peck Italian Bar
13 La Rinascente Dept. Store: Bistrot & Brunch
14 Latteria Cucina Veg. & Pizzeria Calafuria Unione

15 Pastarito Pizzarito
16 Rist./Pizzeria Al Dollaro
17 Luini Panzerotti
18 Agnello Pizzeria
19 Autogrill/Ciao Cafeteria (2 Locations)
20 Ristorante Rita
21 To Le Briciole Ristorante
22 Garbagnati Cafeteria
23 Odeon Gelateria
24 Standa Superfresco Supermarket
25 Bar Zucca, McDonald's, Torino Mosaic
26 Elevator to Duomo Roof
27 Stairs to Duomo Roof
28 Pinacoteca Ambrosiana (Museum)

Piazza Duomo (Sb-€98, Db-€178, some rooms with balconies, includes breakfast, air-con, elevator, closed Aug, near Metro stops: Piazza Cordusio or Duomo, Via Moneta 1/A, tel. 02-874-863, fax 02-869-0344, www.ducadiyork.it, info@ducadiyork.it).

$$$ **Hotel Spadari** boasts an Art Deco interior designed by the Milanese artist Gio Pomodoro (Joe Tomato in English). The 40 rooms have billowing drapes, big paintings, and designer doors. It's next door to the recommended Peck deli (see "Eating," below), and two blocks from the Duomo (standard Db-€208, deluxe Db–268, no need for pricier suites, includes breakfast, Via Spadari 11, tel. 02-7200-2371, fax 02-861-184, www.spadarihotel .com, reservation@spadarihotel.com).

$$ **Hotel Santa Marta,** a shiny little hotel on a small street, has 15 fresh, tranquil, and basic rooms (Db-€130, includes breakfast, air-con, elevator, closed Aug, Via Santa Marta 4, tel. 02-804-567, fax 02-8645-2661, www.hotel-santamarta.it, info@hotel-santamarta.it).

$$ **Hotel Gritti,** facing a peaceful square just off Via Torino, is a three-star hotel that comes with 48 classy rooms. It has just been sold and as of mid-2005, its future is uncertain (2 blocks southwest of Piazza Duomo, Piazza S. Maria Beltrade 4, tel. 02-801-056, fax 02-8901-0999, www.hotelgritti.com, info@hotelgritti.com).

$ **Hotel Speronari** is well-located, with 32 decent rooms on a great pedestrian street full of fun delis. Enjoy a free hot or cold drink upon arrival. If you need an elevator, air-con, and more comfort, spend more money and go elsewhere; this is a very simple, friendly, and cheap one-star place. It gets complaints from people who don't understand that it's dirt cheap for Milan and a fine value even with its rough edges (S-€50, Ss-€62, D-€76, Db-€96, T-€88, Tb-€130, Qb-€145, prices promised in 2006 with this book—mention it when you reserve, €3/person/night discount with cash, lots of stairs, no breakfast, ceiling fans, 200 yards off Piazza Duomo, Via Speronari 4, tel. 02-8646-1125, fax 02-7200-3178, hotelsperonari@inwind.it, run by friendly Isoni family: father Paolo, Carla, and Adam).

Between La Scala and Sforza Castle

$$$ **Hotel Star** is a comfortable, modern 30-room place that prefers guests who stay a minimum of two nights (Sb-€125, Db-€170, includes breakfast, closed Aug, air-con, fridge, Via dei Bossi 5, tel. 02-801-501, fax 02-861-787, www.hotelstar.it, reception@hotelstar.it).

$$ **London Hotel,** a 30-room hotel with all the amenities, is tucked away on a quiet street just off vibrant Via Dante. It's warmly run by the friendly Gambino family: mom and pop Elda and Franco don't speak English, but daughters Tanya and Licia do (S-€90, Sb-€100, D-€140, Db-€150, Tb-€200, skip their €8 breakfast and grab something on Via Dante, cheaper in July and Aug, 10 percent off with cash, air-con, elevator, near Metro: Cairoli at Via Rovello 3,

on relatively quiet side street, tel. 02-7202-0166, fax 02-805-7037, www.hotel-london-milan.com, info@hotel-london-milan.com).

$$ Antica Locanda dei Mercanti feels like a library in heaven, well-located and seriously quiet (no TVs, lots of books). It lacks public spaces and a breakfast area but comes with fresh flowers in each of its 14 rooms (Db-€155, Db with air-con and garden terrace-€255, optional €9 breakfast served in room, no credit cards except to hold room, fans, elevator, no very young children, Via San Tomaso 6 Metro: Cordusio; tel. 02-805-4080, fax 02-805-4090, www.locanda .it, locanda@locanda.it, Alex speaks English).

$$ Alle Meraviglie, another luxurious haven, offer six spacious, elegant, lovingly-maintained rooms with down comforters, marble baths, and velvety carpets or parquet floors (Db-€145, pricier suites available, air-con, elevator, Via San Tomaso 8, tel. 02-805-1023, fax 02-805-4090, www.allemeraviglie.it, info@allemeraviglie .it, Bruce).

Near the Train Station

If you like to stay near the station, this is a handy, if dreary, area. The neighborhood between the train station and Corso Buenos Aires, in spite of its shady characters in the park and 55-year-old prostitutes after dark, is reasonably safe. Many soulless business hotels have desperately discounted prices for those who drop in during slow times. Just walk down Via Scarlatti (with the tracks to your back, leave the station's upper hall to the left, cross the parking lot, and take the street to the left of the tallest building).

Here are some decent options:

$ "The Best" Hotel, a five-minute walk from the station, rents 25 spartan rooms with dim lights and offers a peaceful garden terrace in the middle of the bustling city. While it's a bit rundown, the staff is hardworking and the price is great, making this a fine value (Sb-€45–55, Db-€65–85, includes breakfast, Via B. Marcello 83, tel. 02-2940-4757, fax 02-201-966, thebesthotel@tiscalinet.it; helpful, friendly Filippo and Riccardo). From Via Scarlatti (see above), turn right onto Via B. Marcello and follow it a half-block down.

$ Hotel Valley is family-run, homey, small (just 12 rooms), dark, and inexpensive (Ss-€35, Sb-€40, Ds-€50, Db-€60, Tb-€80, cheaper Ds rooms available, Via Soperga 19, tel. & fax 02-6698-7252, www.hotelvalley.it, info@hotelvalley.it, Umberto). It's 300 yards from the station: at Via Lepetit turn left. Via Lepetit turns into Via Soperga.

$ Hotel Andreola Central, a four-star, 83-room business hotel—the kind with a big revolving glass door—is a particularly good value if they're offering their occasional door-breaker prices (e.g., as low as Db-€99 on some weekends instead of midweek

---

Milanese Specialties

Milan's signature dishes (often served together as a *piatto unico,* or "single dish") are *risotto alla Milanese* and *ossobuco.* The risotto is flavored with saffron, which gives it its intense yellow color. It's said that a 16th-century Belgian glassworker first stumbled on the use of saffron as a spice. Initially, he used saffron to tint the glass mixture he used to complete the stained-glass windows of the Duomo in 1574. His master joked that he'd end up adding the precious spice to his food as well. On the day of his master's daughter's wedding, the glassworker persuaded the chef to add saffron to the rice cooked for the reception. After the guests got over their initial surprise, the dish was a great success, and has been a staple on Milan's menus ever since. The subtle flavor of the saffron pairs nicely with the *ossobuco* (meaning "hole in the bone" of the veal shank). The prized marrow is extracted with special little forks and considered the best part of the meal.

€150 rate, Via Scarlatti 24, tel. 02-670-9141, www.andreolahotel.it, info@andreolahotel.it).

Hostels in Milano

For beds around €20, consider Milan's hostels. Most are away from the center, but I've listed one (La Cordata) closer to town. **$ AIG Piero Rotta** offers cheap, basic accommodation with a simple breakfast (€18.50 beds in 6- to 8-bed dorms, €22 beds in 3- to 4-bed dorms, hostel membership required, non-members pay more, near Metro: Lotto at Viale Salmoiraghi 1, tel. 02-392-67095, www.ostellionline.org, milano@ostellionline.org). Smaller **$ Ostello La Cordata** is another good choice (€18 for beds in 6-, 10-, and 16-bed dorms, reserve ahead, check in 14:00–23:30, Via Burigozzo 11, tel. 02-583-14675, www.lacordata.it/ostelli, ostello@lacordata.it).

EATING

This is a fast-food city, but fast food in a fashion capital isn't a burger and fries. Milan's bars, delis, *rosticcerìe,* and self-service cafeterias cater to people with plenty of taste and more money than time. You'll find delightful eateries all over town (but many close in Aug for vacation).

I find the price difference between basic and classy restaurants to be negligible (e.g., pastas-€7–10, *secondi*-€8–12, cover-€1–2), so it's worth springing for the places giving the best experience. To eat mediocre food on a famous street with great people-watching, choose an eatery on the pedestrian-only Via Mercanti or Via Dante. To eat with students in trendy little trattorias, explore the Brera neighborhood. To eat well near the Duomo, consider the recommended places below.

Locals like to precede a lunch or dinner with an apéritif (while Campari made its debut in Milan, a simple glass of *vino bianco* or *prosecco,* the Italian champagne, is just as popular). Bars fill their counters with inviting baskets of munchies, which are served free with these drinks. A cheap drink (if you're either likable or discreet) can become a light meal. For example, check out the wonderful buffet spread at Bar Brera (see page 247).

Breakfast is a bad value in hotels and fun on Via Dante or in bars. It's OK to quasi-picnic. Bring in a banana (or whatever) and order a toasted ham-and-cheese sandwich (called and pronounced *tost*) or brioche with your cappuccino.

Near the Duomo

Dining with Class

Trattoria Milanese, sophisticated and family-run, is a splurge. It has an enthusiastic and local clientele—the restaurant didn't even bother to get a phone until 1988. Expect a Milanese ambience and quality, traditional local cuisine (Wed–Mon 12:30–15:00 & 19:30–23:00, closed Tue and mid-July–Aug, air-con, Via Santa Marta 11, 5-min walk from Duomo, near Pinacoteca Ambrosiana, tel. 02-8645-1991).

Ristorante Bruno serves Tuscan cuisine with a passion for fresh fish. This place impresses with its dressy waiters, hearty food, inexpensive desserts, and a fine self-serve antipasto buffet (a plate full of Tuscan specialties for €7.50). You can eat inside or on the sidewalk under fascist columns (Sun–Fri 12:00–14:45 & 19:00–22:45, closed Sat and Aug, moderate prices, air-con, Via M. Gonzaga 6, reservations wise, tel. 02-804-364). Giuseppe (from Volterra) and Graziella take good care of their eaters.

Ristorante al Mercante is a tourist trap but a decent place to dine elegantly—inside or outside, under historic arches, in a peaceful square a block from the cathedral. The only locals are the servers and you'll pay extra for the location, but the food is good. Make a meal out of their extensive antipasto buffet featuring fresh sliced prosciutto, *mozzarella di bufala,* grilled and marinated vegetables, and more for €6–13 (moderately expensive, €18 *secondi,* Mon–Sat 12:00–14:30 & 19:00–22:30, closed Sun, reservations smart, near Piazza Cordusio at Piazza Mercanti 17, follow Via Mercanti away from Duomo and turn left just after passing covered market square, tel. 02-805-2198).

Duomo Views on a Terrace: The seventh floor of La Rinascente, alongside the Duomo, has three rooftop eateries, each with a terrace overlooking the ornate top of the cathedral (terrace dining only May–Sept). **Bistrot** is an upscale restaurant serving modern Mediterranean cuisine (Tue–Sat 12:00–15:00 & 19:00–22:00, Mon 19:00–22:00, closed Sun, tel. 02-877-120). The **Brunch** is a cafeteria with a much simpler, cheaper menu (daily 12:00–15:30). Anyone can pop up to the **bar** for a look at the cathedral. While you can go through the department store taking escalators to the top, it's faster to take the elevator (just inside the side entrance—on the Galleria Vittorio Emanuele side—there's a direct elevator to the 6th floor, where you can ride the escalator to the 7th).

Eating Simply

Latteria Cucina Vegetariana serves a good vegetarian Italian lunch. This busy joint is actually a tiny grocery store overrun with dining tables, where local workers enjoy soup, salads, pasta dishes, and affordable prices (€5–15 meals, Mon–Sat 11:30–16:30, closed Sun, just off Via Torino at Via dell'Unione 6, 2 blocks southwest of Duomo, tel. 02-874-401). Judging from his happy scrapbook walls, Giorgio is a hit with camera-toting eaters.

Pastarito Pizzarito is a pasta-and-pizza chain with a wonderful formula. In a bright atmosphere under literal walls of pasta, you can choose from 10 fresh pastas and lots of sauces to create a huge dish (€5–10)—splitting is welcome. Pizzas run €3–10 (daily 12:00–14:30 & 19:30–23:30, air-con, 4 blocks from Duomo, a block behind opera house at Via Verdi 6, tel. 02-862-210).

Ristorante Pizzeria Calafuria Unione serves tasty €5–10 pizzas and pastas in a non-smoking room (Mon–Sat 12:00–15:00 & 19:00–24:00, closed Sun and Aug, near where Via Falcone hits Via dell'Unione at Via dell'Unione 8, 2 blocks southwest of Duomo, tel. 02-866-103).

Ristorante/Pizzeria Al Dollaro is a mod, happy place with well-fed locals (Mon–Fri 12:00–16:00 & 18:00–23:00, Sat 18:00–23:00, closed Sun and Aug, air-con, 4 blocks south of Duomo at Via Paolo da Cannobio 11, tel. 02-869-2432).

Peck Italian Bar is a hit with the sophisticated office crowd, who mob the place at lunch for its fast, excellent meals. It's owned by the same people who run the high-end Peck deli (see next page), so be prepared to spend—this place's classiness alone makes it worth the money. And any time you find yourself among such a quality-conscious group of Milanese, you know you're getting good food (€11 pastas, €18 *secondi*, Mon–Sat 11:30–20:00, closed Sun, Via Cantu 3, tel. 02-869-3017).

Agnello Pizzeria, less than a block off Piazza del Duomo, has a dressy Art Nouveau interior and makes made-to-order pizzas and fresh pastas for reasonable prices (daily 12:00–14:30 & 19:00–23:00, closed Aug, Via Agnello 8, tel. 02-8646-1654).

Ciao, a self-service cafeteria, offers a low-stress, affordable meal above a fast-food arcade on Piazza Duomo (daily 11:30–23:00, on second floor, inexpensive pasta and good salad bar, easy public WC).

Ristorante Rita, a block behind Ciao, is a classier budget option without the Italian fast-food feel. While the downstairs has a take-out place, there's a sleek, modern restaurant upstairs with good food and cafeteria prices (Mon–Sat 12:00–14:30, closed Sun, Via Marconi between Piazza Duomo and Piazza Diaz, tel. 02-8699-7387).

Fast-food cheapskates enjoy the best people-watching in Milan inside the Galleria at **McDonald's** (long hours daily, salad/pasta plate and tall orange juice for €5).

Gelato: Floodlit Mary gazes down from the top of the Duomo on the **Odeon Gelateria** for good reason (next to McDonald's on Piazza Duomo, on far side of square opposite Duomo facade, open nightly until 24:00).

Picnics

For a fun adventure, assemble an elegant dinner picnic by hitting the colorful deli, cheese, and produce shops on Via Speronari. The **Princi bakery** is mobbed with locals vying for focaccia, olive breadsticks, and luscious pastries. For most pastry items (like the brioche), pay the cashier first; for items sold by weight (such as pizza and cake), get it weighed before you pay (Mon–Sat 7:00–20:00, closed Sun, on Via Speronari, off Via Torino, a block southwest of Piazza Duomo). At the small bar in the back, you get free, fresh munchies with your drink, or you can try a cheap meal (about €5 per plate, 12:00–14:00 only).

Peck is an aristocratic deli with a fancy coffee/pastry/gelato shop upstairs, a gourmet grocery and *rosticceria* on the main level, and an *enoteca* wine cellar in the basement. Even if all you can afford is the aroma, peek in. Check out the gourmet assembly-line action in the kitchen in the back (Mon 15:00–19:30, Tue–Sat 8:45–19:30, closed Sun, Via Spadari 9, tel. 02-802-3161). The *rosticceria* serves fancy food to go for a superb picnic dinner in your hotel. It's delectable, beautiful, sold by weight (order by the *etto*—100-gram unit, 250 grams equals about a half-pound), and pricey. Try the risotto.

Luini Panzerotti serves up piping-hot mini-calzones (*panzerotti*) stuffed with mozzarella, tomatoes, ham, or whatever for €4–5 (Tue–Sat 10:00–20:00, Mon 10:00–15:00, closed Sun and Aug, Via S. Radegonda 16, tel. 02-8646-1917). From the back of the Duomo, head north and look for the lines of hungry locals out front. Traditionally, Milanese munch their hot little meals on nearby Piazza San Fedele.

Standa Superfresco supermarket is within a few blocks of the Duomo (Mon–Sat 8:00–20:30, Sun 9:00–20:00, small deli on ground level, big supermarket in basement, on Via Torino at intersection with San Maurilio).

Near Sforza Castle

Le Briciole, run by the Campenella family, is small and dressy, drawing a local crowd for its quality Ligurian cuisine (pesto, seafood) and friendly family feel (self-serve *antipasti* buffet-€8, homemade pastas-€10, Tue–Sun 12:15–14:30 & 19:15–22:30, closed Mon and Aug, Via Camperio 17, a block in front of castle, on small street at end of Via Dante, tel. 02-877-185).

Garbagnati is a tasty self-service cafeteria on Via Dante 13, near several recommended hotels and a couple of blocks in front of the castle. This is *the* place to enjoy elegant boulevard seating at self-service prices. For half the price of a lousy hotel breakfast, you can eat here and have a truly memorable morning meal. At lunch (daily 12:00–15:00), join the local workers on the cafeteria line (daily 17:30–20:00, tel. 02-8646-0672).

The **Princi** bakery near the castle works the same as the one on Via Speronari (listed in "Sights," page 230); get pizza, sandwiches, or pastries to go, or eat at their tables (Mon–Sat 7:00–20:00, closed Sun, Via Ponte Vetero 10, tel. 02-7201-6067). At lunchtime, they serve up delicious homemade €5 *primi* and €5–7 *secondi* courses to in-the-know locals (12:00–15:00 only, can take out, prices slightly higher for full table service).

A **Ciao Autogrill** cafeteria is on Via Dante, just off Piazza Cordusio, with outdoor seating on the pedestrian-only street (daily 11:30–22:30).

In the Brera Neighborhood

The Brera neighborhood surrounding the Church of St. Carmine is laced with narrow, inviting pedestrian streets. Find your own *ristorante* or consider **Al Pozzo,** which offers Tuscan cuisine (Tue–Fri and Sun 12:00–14:30 & 19:00–23:30, Sat 19:00–23:30, closed Mon, Via S. Carpoforo 7, tel. 02-877-775). **Bar Brera,** across the street from the Brera Art Gallery, serves salads, sandwiches, and pastas to throngs of art students. During happy hour (daily 17:00–21:00), the bar offers a buffet with a generous variety of *antipasti,* from marinated veggies to prosciutto (buffet is free if you buy drinks, otherwise €5; bar open daily 6:00–2:00, great street-side seating, Via Brera 23, tel. 02-877-091). **Caffè Vecchia Brera** dishes up tempting sandwiches, savory and sweet crêpes from €4–7, and has full restaurant service (*primi*-€6.50, *secondi*-€8–13, Mon–Sat 8:00–24:00, closed Sun, Via dell'Orso 20, tel. 02-8646-1695).

Eating Cheaply near Montenapoleone

For inexpensive, healthy food near the classy shopping street, **Brek** cafeterias are good. One Brek is near one end of Montenapoleone (daily 11:30–15:00 & 18:30–22:30; Via dell'Annunciata 2, 2 blocks from Montenapoleone; tel. 02-653-619), and another is near the other end, a half-block off Piazza San Babila (daily 11:30–15:00 & 18:30–22:30, Piazza Giordano 1, on Piazza Babila; with back to "egg monument" and facing fountain, Brek is through arch in building on right; tel. 02-7602-3379). The Brek chain is moving toward having full table service in the evenings (same food, but more expensive; most likely at Piazza Babila location).

Near the Train Station

A good **self-serve cafeteria** is in the station (open daily long hours, lower level of station, with back to the tracks, it's on far right between Pellini bar and the Super Centrale Market). And, just a block away, the big **Brek Cafeteria** serves food that's reasonably priced and fast (Mon–Sat 11:30–15:00 & 18:30–22:30, closed Sun; with back to tracks, exit station to left, Via Lepetit 20, tel. 02-670-5149).

TRANSPORTATION CONNECTIONS

From Milan by Train to: Venice (departures :05 after each hour, 3 hrs), **Florence** (hrly, 3 hrs, also check schedule for trains going to Rome and Naples—these stop in Florence), **Genoa** (about hrly, also look for trains heading for La Spezia or Livorno, which stop at Genoa, 2 hrs), **Rome** (hrly, 4.5 hrs), **Brindisi** (8/day, 9–12 hrs, many with changes), **Cinque Terre** (about hrly, 2 hrs to Genoa, then hrly, 2 hrs to Monterosso, some direct trains to Monterosso; trains from La Spezia to the villages go nearly hrly), **Varenna** on Lake Como (small line to Lecco/Sondrio/Tirano leaves about every 2 hrs for the 1-hr trip to Varenna, roughly 8:15, 9:15, 12:15, 14:15, 16:15, 17:05, 18:00, 19:10, and 20:15), **Stresa** (hrly, 50–75 min, faster trains require reservations; trains going to Domodossola and some international destinations stop at Stresa), **Como** (around :25 after each hour, 30 min, ferries go from Como to Varenna until 19:00).

International Destinations: Amsterdam (6/day, 14 hrs, changes required), **Barcelona** (1/day with no changes, 13 hours, or several with 2–5 changes, 12–22 hrs—before paying extra for Pablo Casals express, consider flying), **Bern** (7/day with change in Brig, 3–4 hrs), **Frankfurt** (5/day, 9 hrs with change in Basel, Switzerland), **London** (4/day, 12–18 hrs with change in Paris), **Munich** (9/day, 8–10 hrs with changes), **Nice** (5/day, 6 hrs), **Paris** (3/day, 7 hrs), **Lyon** (7/day, 6 hrs), **Vienna** (4/day, 11–14 hrs with changes).

Train Connections from Milan

Airports

To get flight information for either airport or the current phone number of your airline, call 02-74851 or 02-7485-2200.

Malpensa Airport

Most international flights land at the manageable Malpensa Airport, 28 miles northwest of Milan. Customs guards fan you through, and even the sniffing dog seems friendly. You'll most likely land at Terminal 1 (international flights) rather than Terminal 2 (charter flights); buses connect the two. Both have cash machines (at Terminal 1, near exit 4 at Banca Nazionale del Lavoro), banks, and change offices. Terminal 1 has a pharmacy, eateries, and a hotel reservation service disguised as a TI (daily 7:00–23:00; when you exit the baggage-carousel area, go right to reach services and exit; tel. 02-5858-0080). At the *tabacchi* shop, buy a phone card and confirm your hotel reservation.

You have three easy ways to get to downtown Milan: by train, shuttle bus, or taxi.

By Train: The Malpensa Express zips between Malpensa Airport and Milan's Cadorna station, which is both a Metro stop and a small train station, closer to the Duomo than the central train station (€9, 40 min, 2/hr; departing airport at :23 and :53 past the hour from 6:45–21:45, departing Cadorna at :27 and :57 past the hour from 5:50–20:20, not covered by railpasses, tel. 02-20222, www.ferrovienord.it/webmxp). At the airport, as you pop out through customs, you'll see a "Treno per Malpensa" kiosk selling tickets and a big electric reader board on the wall indicating how many minutes until the next departure. Follow signs (*Treni* and *Malpensa Express*) down the stairs to the tracks. If you're leaving Milan to go to the airport, take the Metro to the Cadorna stop, surface, and buy a ticket at the Malpensa Express office in the station or from ticket windows in front of track 8. Purchase your ticket before you board, or you'll pay €2.50 extra to buy it on the train. Note that some earlier and later departures from Cadorna are by bus—ask when you buy your ticket. If your departure is by bus, the stop is outside the station; head left as you exit and the stop is 50 yards to the left on Via Paleocapa.

By Bus: Two bus companies offer virtually identical, competing services between Malpensa Airport and Milan's central train station. They each charge about €5 for the 50-minute trip (buy ticket from driver) and depart from the same places: in front of the airport (outside exit 5, at stops 2 and 3) and from Piazza Luigi di Savoia (east side of Milan's train station). You'll generally find a bus leaving about every 15 minutes, every day, nearly all day (from downtown roughly 5:00–22:30 and from the airport roughly 6:30–23:00, tel. 02-5858-3185, www.malpensa-shuttle.com).

By Taxi: Taxis into Milan cost €80 (more if there's heavy traffic, insist on meter, you'll pay supplements on Sun and holidays, avoid hustlers in airport halls, catch outside exit 6). Considering how far the city is from the airport and how good the train and bus services are, Milan is the last place I'd take a taxi to the airport. I taxi to the Cadorna station and then catch the Malpensa Express train.

Sleeping near Malpensa: **$ Hotel Cervo** offers newly renovated rooms and transport to and from the nearby airport for €3/person (Sb-€62, Db-€93, air-con, restaurant open Mon–Fri 20:00–22:00, parking, Via de Pinedo 1, Somma Lombardo, Fraz. Case Nuove, Malpensa, tel. 0331-230-821, fax 0331-230-156, www.hotelcervo.it, hotelcervo@malpensa.it).

Getting between Malpensa and Linate: The Malpensa Shuttle company runs a bus between the airports about hourly (€8, runs 4:30–22:30, 75 min, catch bus outside Malpensa's exit 4, stops 20 and 21, buy tickets from Thomas Cook or Airport 2000 offices; coming from Linate, bus stops at Malpensa's Terminal 1—you must request stop if you need Terminal 2; tel. 02-5858-3185 for English recording).

Linate Airport

Most European flights fly into Linate, five miles east of Milan. The airport has a bank (just past customs, cash machine, decent rates) and a hotel-finding service disguised as a TI (daily 7:30–22:30, tel. 02-7020-0443).

You can get to downtown Milan by bus or taxi (or to Malpensa Airport by bus; see above).

By Bus: Two different buses—STAM and ATM—take you from Linate Airport to downtown. The STAM bus zips you to the central train station (buy €2.50 ticket from driver, 3/hr, 20 min, bus runs from airport 6:05–23:35, from station 5:40–21:35, leaves from east side of station at Piazza Luigi di Savoia, tel. 02-717-106). The cheaper ATM city bus gets you to the San Bibila Metro stop (specifically to Corso Europa, just around the corner from Piazza San Babila and its Metro station; from here it's 1 stop to Duomo, red line 1, direction Molino Dorino or Bisceglie). The bus costs €1, departs every 10 minutes, and takes 20 minutes (departures leaving city center 5:35–24:35, from airport 6:05–24:55). Either bus company works fine. Wait for the one handier to your hotel, or hop on the first one that shows up; from where it drops you off, take the Metro or a taxi to your hotel. Both buses leave from outside the arrival hall.

By Taxi: Taxis from Linate to the Duomo cost about €18.

THE CINQUE TERRE

The Cinque Terre (CHINK-weh TAY-reh), a remote chunk of the Italian Riviera, is the traffic-free, lowbrow, underappreciated alternative to the French Riviera. There's not a museum in sight. Just sun, sea, sand (pebbles), wine, and pure, unadulterated Italy. Enjoy the villages, swimming, hiking, and evening romance of one of God's great gifts to tourism. For a home base, choose among five *(cinque)* villages, each of which fills a ravine with a lazy hive of human activity—callused locals, sunburned travelers, and no Vespas. While the Cinque Terre is now discovered (www.cinqueterre.it), I've never seen happier, more relaxed tourists.

The chunk of coast was first described in medieval times as "the five lands." In feudal times, this land was watched over by castles; tiny communities grew up in their protective shadows, ready to run inside at the first hint of a Turkish Saracen pirate raid. Many locals were kidnapped and ransomed or sold into slavery. As the threat of pirates faded, the villages grew, with economies based on fish and grapes. Until the advent of tourism in this generation, the towns were remote. Even today, traditions survive, and each of the five villages comes with a distinct dialect and its own proud heritage. The region has become a national park, and its natural and cultural wonders will be carefully preserved.

Over the next decade, Italy has ambitious plans for the Cinque Terre. In Vernazza, for example, there's a new waterfront piazza, the church is being refurbished, and a disabled-access elevator is being installed at the train station.

Sadly, a few ugly, noisy Americans are giving tourism a bad name here. Even hip, young locals are put off by loud, drunken tourists. They say, and I agree, that the Cinque Terre is an exceptional

The Cinque Terre

place. It deserves a special dignity. Party in Viareggio or Portofino, but be mellow in the Cinque Terre. Talk softly. Help keep it clean. In spite of the tourist crowds, it's still a real community, and we are guests.

In this chapter, I cover the five towns in order from east to west, from Riomaggiore to Monterosso. Since I still get the names of the towns mixed up, I think of them by number: #1. Riomaggiore (a workaday town), #2. Manarola (picturesque), #3. Corniglia (on a hilltop), #4. Vernazza (the region's cover girl, the most touristy and dramatic), and #5. Monterosso (the closest thing to a beach resort of the five towns).

Planning Your Time

The ideal minimum stay is two nights and a completely uninterrupted day. The Cinque Terre is served by the local train from Genoa and La Spezia. Speed demons arrive in the morning, check their bags in La Spezia, take the five-hour hike through all five towns, laze away the afternoon on the beach or rock of their choice, and zoom away on the overnight train to somewhere back in the real world. But be warned: The Cinque Terre has a strange way of messing up your momentum. Frankly, anything less than two nights is a mistake that you'll likely regret.

The towns are just a few minutes apart by hourly train or boat. There's no checklist of sights or experiences—just a hike, the towns themselves, and your fondest vacation desires. Study this chapter in advance and piece together your best day, mixing hiking, swimming, trains, and a boat ride. For the best light and coolest temperatures, start your hike early.

Market days perk up the towns from 8:00 to 13:00 on Tuesday in Vernazza, Wednesday in Levanto (see page 297, next chapter), Thursday in Monterosso, and Friday in La Spezia (see page 318, next chapter). The winter is really dead—most hotels close in December and January. Easter (April 16 in 2006) and July through August is peak of peak, the only tough time to find rooms.

The Cinque Terre National Park

Now that the region is a national park, there are tighter restrictions on development, a push for sensitive management of the environment, and money for maintenance and improvement of the area. The director of the park (famous for his grandiose visions) is doing impressive things. There are well-staffed information offices in each town (generally offering baggage check, Internet access, maps, hiking tips, souvenirs, and various passes for sale). At the mountain station above Riomaggiore, you can rent mountain bikes and arrange horse rides. For all the latest, see www.parconazionale5terre.it or stop by a local TI.

Cinque Terre Cards and Passes

Visitors hiking between the towns need to pay a **park entrance fee.** This fee keeps the trails safe and open, and pays for building fine viewpoints, picnic spots, WCs, and more. The popular coastal trail generates enough revenue to subsidize the development of trails and outdoor activities higher in the hills.

You have several options (all valid until midnight of the expiration date):

The **Hiking Pass** costs €3 (comes with map, kids under 4 free). It's valid for one day and covers all trails (but no buses or trains). Buy it at trailheads, at national park offices, and usually at train stations (no validation required).

The **Cinque Terre Card** combines hiking privileges with free transportation. It covers the park entrance fee, local trains (from Levanto to La Spezia, including all Cinque Terre towns), and shuttle buses (see page 257). It's sold at TIs inside train stations, but not at trailheads (€5.40/1 day, €13/3 days, €20.60/week, kids 4–11 half-price, under 4 free). The card comes with a map, information brochure, and train schedule. Validate your Cinque Terre Card at a

2006 Events in the Cinque Terre

For more festival information, check www.cinqueterre.it and www.5terre.com.

May	Monterosso: Lemon Festival
June 18	Monterosso: Feast of Corpus Domini (procession on carpet of flowers at 18:00)
June 24	Riomaggiore and Monterosso: Festival in honor of St. John the Baptist (procession and fireworks; big fire on old town beach the day before)
June 29	Corniglia: Festival of St. Peter and St. Paul
July 20	Vernazza: Festival for patron saint, St. Margaret
Aug 10	Manarola: Festival for patron saint, St. Lawrence
Aug 15	All towns: Assumption of Mary
Sept 8	Monterosso: Maria Nascente, or "Birth of Mary" (fair with handicrafts)

train station by punching it in the yellow machine. The pass pays for itself if you hike, ride a train, and use a shuttle bus in a single day.

The **Cinque Terre Card Plus Boats** includes all of the above, plus unlimited passage on Cinque Terre boats (€13.60/1 day; skip the boats-only pass).

For most travelers, the best option is to buy the Cinque Terre Card and pay out of pocket for boat trips.

Getting Around the Cinque Terre

Within the Cinque Terre, you'll get around the villages more cheaply by train, but more scenically by boat.

By Train: At La Spezia, the gateway to the Cinque Terre, you'll transfer to the milk-run Cinque Terre train. Don't bother with the TI in La Spezia. At the station, buy your train ticket (€1.10) or Cinque Terre Card, and take the half-hour train ride into the town of your choice. To orient yourself, remember that directions are "*per* (to) Genova" (the Italian spelling of Genoa) or "*per* La Spezia." Assuming you're on vacation, accept the unpredictability of Cinque Terre trains (you're often early, they're often late). Relax while you wait—buy a cup of coffee at a station bar. When the train comes (know which direction to look for), casually walk over and hop on. This is especially easy in Monterosso, with its fine café-with-a-view on track #1 (direction Milano/Genova).

By train, the five towns are several minutes apart. Know your stop. After the train leaves the town before your destination, go to the door and get ready to slip out before mobs pack in. Words to the wise for novice tourists, who often miss their stop: The stations are small and the trains are long, so you might have to get off deep in a tunnel. The doors don't open automatically—you might have to flip open the handle of the door yourself.

It's cheap to buy individual train tickets to travel between the towns. Since a one-town hop costs the same as a five-town hop (around €1) and every ticket is good for six hours with stopovers, save money and explore the region in one direction on one ticket. Stamp the ticket at the station machine before you board. If you have a Eurailpass, don't spend one of your valuable flexi-days on the cheap Cinque Terre.

Cinque Terre Train Schedule: Since the train is the Cinque Terre's lifeline, many shops and restaurants post the current schedule. Carry a copy of it—it'll come in handy (comes with Cinque Terre Card). Note that many trains leaving La Spezia zip right through the Cinque Terre, or stop only in Monterosso. But the trains on the following schedule will stop at all five Cinque Terre towns. All of the below times are accurate as of 2005; most are daily and a few run daily except Sunday, while others (not listed here) operate only on Sundays.

Trains leave La Spezia for the Cinque Terre villages at 7:12, 8:15, 10:00, 11:15, 12:29, 13:19, 14:29, 15:02, 16:28, 17:20, 18:12, 19:03, 20:20, 21:11, 22:30, and 00:20.

Going back to La Spezia, trains leave Monterosso al Mare at 6:31, 8:11, 9:21, 10:18, 10:49, 12:04, 13:00, 14:12, 15:19, 16:16, 17:18, 18:40, 19:14, 20:27, 22:32, 23:20, and 23:58 (same trains depart Vernazza about 4 min later).

By Boat: From Easter through October (into Nov if weather's good), a daily boat service connects Monterosso, Vernazza, Manarola, Riomaggiore, and Portovenere. Boats provide a scenic way to get from town to town and survey what you just hiked. And boats offer the only efficient way to visit the nearby resort of Portovenere (see next chapter; the alternative is a tedious train/bus connection via La Spezia). In peaceful weather, the boats can be more reliable than the trains, but if seas are rough, they don't run at all. Because the boats nose in and tourists have to gingerly disembark along little more than a plank, even a small chop can cancel some or all of the stops.

I see the tour boats as a syringe, injecting each town with a boost of euros. The towns are addicted, and they shoot up hourly through the summer. (Between 10:00 and 15:00—especially on weekends—masses of gawkers unload from tour buses and cruise ships, inundating the villages and changing the tenor of the region.)

Boats depart Monterosso about hourly (10:30–18:00), stopping at the Cinque Terre towns (except at Corniglia) and ending an hour later in Portovenere. (The Portovenere–Monterosso boats run 9:00–17:00.) Single hops cost about €3 per town. Some towns are also connected by smaller boats and may honor the same tickets—ask.

You can buy tickets at little stands at each town's harbor (tel. 0187-732-987 and 0187-818-440). An all-day boat pass, which covers the Cinque Terre towns, costs around €12 (price depends on time of year; the Cinque Terre Card Plus Boats pass is a better value—sold only at TIs, see page 255). Boat schedules are posted at docks, harbor bars, Cinque Terre park offices, and hotels.

By Shuttle Bus: Shuttle buses connect each Cinque Terre town with distant parking lots and various points in the hills (for example, from Corniglia's beach and train station to its hilltop town center). Most rides cost €1.50—pick up schedules from a Cinque Terre park office.

Hiking the Cinque Terre

All five towns are connected by good trails. You'll experience the area's best by hiking all the way from one end to the other. While you can detour to dramatic hilltop sanctuaries, I'd keep it simple by following the easy red-and-white-marked low trail between the villages. This entire seven-mile hike can be done in about four hours, but allow five for dawdling. Germans (with their task-oriented *Alpenstock*—walking sticks) are notorious for marching too fast through the region. (The non-German record for the entire five-town hike is by one of my tour guides: 1 hour, 52 minutes.)

Trails can be closed in bad weather or because of landslides. Remember that hikers need to pay a fee to enter the trails (see "Cinque Terre Cards and Passes," page 254). If hiking the entire five-town route, consider that the trails between towns Riomaggiore (#1), Manarola (#2), and Corniglia (#3) are easiest. The trail from Vernazza (#4) to Monterosso (#5) is the most challenging. You might want to start in Monterosso in order to tackle the toughest section while you're fresh.

Maps aren't necessary for the basic coastal hike described here. But for the expanded version of this hike (12 hrs, from Portovenere to Levanto) and more serious hikes in the high country, pick up a good hiking map (about €5, sold everywhere). To leave the park cleaner than when you found it, request a plastic bag *(sacchetto di plastica)* at any park information booth and pick up a little trail trash along the way. It would be great if American visitors—who get so much joy out of this region—were known for this good deed.

Riomaggiore-Manarola (20 min): Facing the front of the train station in Riomaggiore (#1), go up the stairs to the right, following signs for the Via dell'Amore. The film-gobbling promenade—wide enough for baby strollers—leads down the coast to Manarola (#2). While there's no beach here, stairs lead down to sunbathing rocks. A long tunnel and mega-nets protect hikers from mean-spirited rocks. There's a classy, park-run Bar & Vini wine bar at the Riomaggiore trailhead (light meals, awesome town views, clever boat storage under train tracks) and a scenic and peaceful bar midway.

Manarola-Corniglia (45 min): The walk from Manarola (#2) to Corniglia (#3) is a little longer and more rugged than that from #1 to #2. To avoid the last stretch (the corkscrew stairs leading up to the hill-capping town of Corniglia), you could catch the shuttle bus from Corniglia's train station (€1.50, free with Cinque Terre Card, 2/hr, usually timed to meet the trains).

Corniglia-Vernazza (90 min): The hike from Corniglia (#3) to Vernazza (#4)—the wildest and greenest of the coast—is most rewarding. From the Corniglia station and beach, zigzag up to the town (via the steep corkscrew stairs, the longer road, or the shuttle bus). Ten minutes past Corniglia, toward Vernazza, you'll see Guvano beach far beneath you (the region's nude beach, see page 270). The trail leads past a bar and picnic tables, through lots of fragrant and flowery vegetation, scenically into Vernazza. If you need a break before reaching Vernazza, Franco's Ristorante "La Torre" has a small menu, but big views (between meal times, only drinks are served).

Vernazza-Monterosso (90 min): The trail from Vernazza (#4) to Monterosso (#5) is a scenic, up-and-down-a-lot trek. Trails are rough (some readers report "very dangerous") and narrow, but easy to follow. Locals frown on camping at the picnic tables located midway. The views just out of Vernazza are spectacular.

Longer Hikes: Above the trails that run between the towns, higher-elevation hikes crisscross the region. Shuttle buses make the going easier, connecting villages and trailheads in the hills. Ask locally about the more difficult six-mile inland hike to Volastra. This tiny village, perched between Manarola and Corniglia, hosts the 5-Terre wine co-op. The Cantina Sociale is a third of a mile away from Volastra, in the hamlet of Groppo. If you take this high road between Manarola and Corniglia, allow two hours one-way. In return, you'll get sweeping views and a closer look at the vineyards. Shuttle buses run about hourly to Volastra from Manarola and Corniglia (€2.50 or free with Cinque Terre Card, pick up schedule from park office); consider taking the bus up and hiking down.

Swimming and Kayaking

Every town has a beach. Monterosso has the biggest and sandiest, with paddleboats, beach umbrellas, and beach-use fees (but it's free where there are no umbrellas). Vernazza's is tiny—better for sunning than swimming. Manarola and Riomaggiore have the worst beaches (no sand), but Manarola offers the best deep-water swimming.

Wear your walking shoes and pack your swim gear. Several of the beaches have showers (no shampoo, please). Underwater sightseeing is full of fish—goggles are sold in local shops. Sea urchins can be a problem if you walk on the rocks.

You can rent kayaks in Riomaggiore, Vernazza, and Monterosso (details listed below per town). Mountain biking and horseback riding are possible (park info booths have details on rentals and a map with trails high above the coast).

Tours

Paola Tommarchi, a local guide, leads hiking, wine tasting, and town tours throughout the Cinque Terre for individuals or groups (€100/ half-day tour, €165/day, mobile 333-798-7728, paolatomma1966 @libero.it).

Riomaggiore
(Town #1)

The most substantial non-resort town of the group, Riomaggiore is a disappointment from the train station. But walk through the tunnel next to the train tracks (or ride the elevator through the hillside to the top of town), and you land in a fascinating tangle of pastel homes leaning on each other as if someone stole their crutches.

ORIENTATION

Tourist Information

The TI is inside the train station (daily 6:30–20:00 in winter, until 22:00 in summer, tel. 0187-920-633). If the TI is crowded, buy your hiking pass at the Cinque Terre park office next door to the TI, or at the kiosk next to the stairs leading to the Via dell'Amore trail (park office open daily 8:00–23:00 in summer, until 20:00 in winter, Internet access, no baggage deposit). A less formal information source is friendly and helpful Ivo, who runs the Bar Centrale (see "Eating," page 265).

Helpful Hints

Laundry: A self-service launderette is on the main street (daily 8:00–22:00, €3.50 wash, €3.50 dry, next to Edi's Rooms on Via Columbo 111).

Bus Service: The bus shuttles locals and tourists up and down Riomaggiore's steep main street and continues to the parking lot outside of town. It runs twice an hour—just flag it down as it passes (€1.50, €2.50 round-trip, free with Cinque Terre Card). The bus heads into the hills, where you'll find the region's top high-country activities (see below). Pick up a schedule from the Cinque Terre park office.

SELF-GUIDED WALK

Welcome to Riomaggiore

Here's an easy loop trip that maximizes views and minimizes uphill walking. Start at the train station (if you arrive by boat, take the tunnel alongside the tracks to get to the station). From the station, walk past the colorful murals glorifying the nameless workers (modeled after real-life Riomaggiorians) who constructed the nearly 300 million cubic feet of dry stone walls (without cement) throughout the Cinque Terre, giving the region its characteristic *muri a secco* terracing for vineyards and olive groves. The murals, done by Argentinean artist Silvio Benedetto, are well-explained in English.

At the entrance of the railway tunnel, ride the elevator to the top of town (€0.50 or €1 family ticket, free with Cinque Terre Card, daily 8:00–19:45). At the top, go right, following the walkway—with spectacular sea views—around the cliff. Ignore the steps marked *Marina Seacoast* (harbor). Instead, continue along the path; it's a five-minute, slightly inclined stroll to the church. While the church was rebuilt in 1870, it originally dates from 1340. When it was built, the disparate hamlets of this stretch of coastline coalesced into what is today known as Riomaggiore. Continue past the church and then take a right, down a stepped lane to Via Colombo, Riomaggiore's main street.

Stroll down Via Colombo. Just past the WC, you'll see flower boxes on the street, which sometimes block it—these slide back electronically to let the shuttle bus get past. On your way down the hill, you'll pass colorful, small shops, including a bakery, a couple of grocery shops, and the self-service laundry. There's homemade gelato next to the Bar Centrale. When Via Colombo dead-ends, on your left you'll find the stairs down to "The Marina" neighborhood, with the harbor, the boat dock, a 200-yard trail to the beach *(spiaggia)*, and an inviting little art gallery (Galleria d'Arte Sciaccheart, with local scenes, Via Giacomo 51). To your right is the tunnel, running alongside the tracks, which takes you directly back to the station and the trail to the other towns. From here, you can take a train, hop a boat, or hike to your next destination.

ACTIVITIES

Beach—Riomaggiore's "beach" is rocky, but it's clean and peaceful. Take a two-minute walk from the harbor: Face the harbor, then follow the path to your left. At the La Conchiglia bar, go down the stairs to the right and stay on the path to the beach.

Kayaks and Water Sports—Mar Mar rents kayaks (€4/hr for 1-person kayak, €10/hr for 2-person kayak) and offers boat excursions

Riomaggiore

VIA DELL'AMORE
TO MANAROLA

MURALS

ELEVATOR TO
HIGH ROAD

S. GIO.
CHURCH

TRAIN
STATION

V. GASPERI

VIA SANT.

CINQUE
TERRE
INFO

PED.
TUNNEL

COLOMBO

LIGURIAN
SEA

VIA

(NOT TO SCALE)

HARBOR

BOAT DOCK

SWIMMING
+ SHOWERS

DCH

1. Edi's Rooms & Launderette
2. La Dolce Vita Rooms
3. Mar Mar Rooms
4. Fazioli Brothers' Rooms
5. Locanda dalla Compagnia
6. Locanda del Sole
7. Anna Michielini Apartments
8. Ristorante la Lampara
9. La Lanterna Ristorante

10. Te La Do Io La Merenda Snack Bar
11. Gigi's Veciu Muin Pizzeria
12. Bar Centrale & Gelateria
13. Dau Cila Bar
14. Bar & Vini
15. Boat Dock & Slippery Launch
16. Boat Tickets

(fishing or cruising, €30/day per person for up to 8 people, see their listing under "Sleeping," below). The town also has a diving center (scuba, snorkeling, boats, and kayaks; office under the tracks on Via San Giacomo, tel. 0187-920-011).

Hikes—Consider the cliff-hanging trail that leads from the beach to old WWII bunkers and a hilltop botanical garden (free entry with Cinque Terre Card). Another trail climbs scenically to the Madonna di Montenero sanctuary, high above the town. If you don't feel like hiking, take the green shuttle-bus up. The bus departs from the starting point of the oversized *trenino* (grape-pickers train), then shuttles you up to the sanctuary (12-min trip, details at park office). The park center and bar up top also offer horse rides and bike rentals.

SLEEPING

Riomaggiore has arranged its private-room rental system better than its neighbors. But with organization (and middlemen) come higher prices. Several agencies—with regular office hours, English-speaking staff, and e-mail addresses—line up within a few yards of each other on the main drag. Each manages a corral of local rooms for rent. These offices can close unexpectedly, so it's smart to settle up the day before you leave in case they're closed when you have to depart. Expect lots of stairs. To avoid ripoffs, see my "New Ethic," below in the "Sleep Code."

Room-Finding Services

$$$ **Locanda del Sole** has 10 basic but sparkling-clean rooms with shared terraces. At the utilitarian edge of town, it's a five-minute

---

Sleep Code

(€1 = about $1.20, country code: 39)

S = Single, **D** = Double/Twin, **T** = Triple, **Q** = Quad, **b** = bathroom, **s** = shower only. Unless otherwise noted, credit cards are accepted, English is spoken, and breakfast is included.

To keep my readers from being overcharged, I've established a **"New Ethic"** (Nuova Etica), which means that my Cinque Terre recommendations will charge no more in 2006 than the prices listed in this book. Each place understands if they exceed this agreed-upon price, my readers will let me know, and they will lose their place in next year's edition of this book. I've listed only peak-season prices—off-season can be cheaper. Please help me enforce this practice. (E-mail me at rick@ricksteves.com if someone overcharges you. Seriously.) Hoteliers have also agreed to be honest in what they promise—for example, providing a view room if one is reserved. Honest hosts think it's a wonderful idea. The others wiggle and squirm.

To help you sort easily through these listings, I've divided the rooms into three categories based on the price for a standard double room with bath:

$$$ **Higher Priced**—Most rooms €100 or more.
$$ **Moderately Priced**—Most rooms between €50–100.
$ **Lower Priced**—Most rooms €50 or less.

Sleeping in the Cinque Terre

If you think too many people have my book, avoid Vernazza. Monterosso is a good choice for the younger crowd (more nightlife) and rich, sun-worshipping softies (who prefer the comfort and ease of a real hotel). Hermits, anarchists, wine-lovers, and mountain goats like Corniglia. Sophisticated Italians and Germans choose Manarola. Riomaggiore is bigger than Vernazza and less resorty than Monterosso.

While the Cinque Terre is too rugged for the mobs that ravage the Spanish and French coasts, it's popular with Italians, Germans, and in-the-know Americans. Hotels charge more and are packed on holidays, mid-May through mid-June, in August, and on Fridays and Saturdays all summer. August weekends are worst. But €65 doubles abound throughout the year. For a terrace or view, you might pay an extra €20 or more.

Book ahead if you'll be visiting in July, August, on a week-end, or around a holiday, especially Easter (April 16 in 2006), April 25 (Liberation Day), May 1 (Labor Day), and the Feast of Corpus Domini (June 18 in 2006). At other times, you can land a double room on any day by just arriving in town (ideally by noon) and asking around at bars and restaurants, or simply by approaching locals on the street. Many travelers enjoy the opportunity to shop around a bit and get the best price by bargaining. Private rooms—called *affitta camere*—are no longer an intimate stay with a family. They are generally comfortable apartments (often with small kitchens) where you get the key and come and go as you like, rarely seeing your landlord. Often landowners rent the buildings by the year to local managers, who then attempt to make a profit by filling them night after night with tourists.

For the best value, visit three private rooms and snare the best. Going direct cuts out a middleman and softens prices. Plan on paying cash. Private rooms are generally bigger and more comfortable than those offered by the pensions and they offer the same privacy as a hotel room.

If you want the security of a reservation, make it at a hotel long in advance (small places generally don't take reservations that far ahead). If you don't get a reply to your faxed request for a room, assume the place is fully booked. If you do reserve, honor your reservation (or, if you must cancel, do it as early as possible). Since people renting rooms usually don't take deposits, they lose money if you don't show up. Cutthroat room hawkers at the train stations might try to lure you away with offers of cheaper rates from a room that you've already reserved. Don't do it. You owe it to your hosts to stick with your original reservation.

walk to the center. The easy parking (€10/day in high season but soft otherwise) makes this especially appealing to drivers (Db-€110, includes breakfast, Via Santuario 114, tel. & fax 0187-920-773, mobile 340-983-0090, www.locandadelsole.net, info @locandadelsole.net, cheerful Enrico speaks English).

$$ **Edi's Rooms** has 20 fine rooms and apartments—most with views. Edi and her partner Luana get my "best business practices" award for this town (Db-€52, apartment Db-€70–80, apartment Qb-€120, these prices promised to readers through 2006, office open daily 9:00–20:00 in summer, otherwise 9:00–13:00 & 14:00–19:00, Via Colombo 111, tel. 0187-760-842, tel. & fax 0187-920-325, edi-vesigna@iol.it).

$$ At **Mar Mar Rooms,** Mario rents 12 rooms, 10 apartments, and a mini-hostel, with American expat Amy smoothing communications (dorm bed-€20 per person, Db-€60–90 depending on view, reception open 9:00–19:00 in season, 30 yards above train tracks on main drag next to Lampara restaurant, Via Malborghetto 4, tel. & fax 0187-920-932, www.5terre-marmar .com, marmar@5terre.com). Mar Mar also rents kayaks and runs fishing trips.

$$ **La Dolce Vita,** across from Edi's, offers five rooms and eight apartments (€20–30 per person; open daily 9:30–19:30—if they're closed, they're full; Via Colombo 120, tel. & fax 0187-760-044, mobile 349-326-6803, agonatal@tin.it, Giacomo and Simone speak English).

$$ **Luciano and Roberto Fazioli** rent nine rooms and also run a basic eight-bed mini-hostel (dorm bed-€20, €25 on Fri–Sat or for 1-night stays; D-€50–70, Db-€50–80, cash only, office open daily 9:00–20:00, Via Colombo 94, tel. 0187-920-904, robertofazioli@libero.it). The apartments are overpriced and the rooms vary in quality—ask to see a room before you commit.

Private Rooms and Hotels on Riomaggiore's Main Drag

$$ **Locanda dalla Compagnia** rents five modern rooms—each with air-conditioning, a mini-fridge, and no view—at the top of town, just 300 yards below the parking lot and the little church. All rooms are on the same airy ground floor, sharing an inviting lounge. Franca runs it with the help Monica (Db-€75, includes breakfast, Via del Santuario 232, tel. 0187-760-050, fax 0187-760700, lacomp@libero.it).

$$ **Anna Michielini** rents five attractive apartments in the center—they lack sea views, but some have views of the *castello* above town. Two apartments have kitchens and can connect to sleep up to

six (Db-€56-66, Tb-€99, Qb-€110, cheaper Oct–mid-April and for longer stays, 2 nights preferred June–Sept, reserve with credit card but pay cash, across from Bar Centrale at Via Colombo 143, ring bell to open door, friendly Daniela speaks good English—mobile 328-131-1032—and her mother speaks *solo Italiano*—tel. & fax 0187-920-411, michielinis@yahoo.it).

EATING

Ristorante la Lampara, decorated like a ship, serves a *frutti di mare* pizza, *trenette al pesto,* and the aromatic *spaghetti al cartoccio*—spaghetti with mixed seafood cooked in foil (daily 12:00–15:00 & 18:30–22:30, closed Tue in winter, on Via Malborghetto 10 just above tracks off Via Colombo, tel. 0187-920-120).

La Lanterna is dressier and more expensive, with better food. It's wedged into a niche in the Marina, overlooking the harbor under the tracks (daily 12:00–22:00, tel. 0187-920-589).

For a snack or good takeout, try **Te La Do Io La Merenda** ("I'll Give You A Snack"). Their counter is piled with an assortment of munchies, and they have pastas, roasted chicken, and focaccia sandwiches to go (daily 8:30–21:30, tel. 0187-920-148, Via Colombo 171). For cheap sit-down pizza, try **Gigi's Veciu Muin** (daily 12:00–14:30 & 18:30–23:00, closed Mon off-season, at Via Colombo 83, tel. 0187-920-487). **Bar & Vini,** at the trailhead on the Manarola end of town, is great for a scenic light meal or quiet drink at night. **Groceries and delis** on Via Colombo sell food to go, including pizza slices, for a picnic at the harbor or beach.

Bar Centrale, run by sociable Ivo and his gang, is a good stop for breakfast, Internet access, and music. Ivo lived in San Francisco and speaks good English. He fills his bar with only the best San Franciscan rock and hosts a big party on the Fourth of July. During the day, Bar Centrale is a shaded place to relax with other travelers. At night, it offers younger travelers the liveliest action in town. Ivo makes "better mojitos than you can get in Cuba," plucking fresh mint leaves for your drink from a plant growing on the counter (daily 7:30–24:00, closed Mon in winter, Via Colombo 144, tel. 0187-920-208, barcentrale1969@libero.it). For the best gelato in town, go next door.

While the late-night fun is at Ivo's Bar Centrale, take a walk down to the harborside **Dau Cila Bar** for jazz, nets, and mellow *limoncino* (called *limoncello* elsewhere in Italy)—a drink of lemon juice, sugar, and pure alcohol (Wed–Mon 10:30–24:00, closed Tue, tel. 0187-760-032).

Manarola
(Town #2)

Like Riomaggiore, Manarola is attached to its station by a 200-yard-long tunnel. During WWII air raids, these tunnels provided refuge and a safe place for rattled villagers to sleep.

The town is tiny and picturesque, a tumble of buildings bunny-hopping down its ravine to the fun-loving harbor. Notice how the I-beam crane launches the boats.

Facing the harbor, look at the hillside to your right, dotted with a bar in the middle. It's Punta Bonfiglio, an entertaining park/game area/bar with the best view playground on the coast. From here you can get poster-perfect views of Manarola (2-min walk from the harbor on path to Corniglia) while you sip a coffee or munch a light lunch. The gate farther up the hillside is the entrance to the cemetery. At the top of the town, you'll find great views, the church, and a cluster of accommodations, including a super hostel.

The simple, wooden religious scenes that you'll likely see on the hillside are the work of local resident Mario Andreoli. Before

Manarola

1. Albergo ca' d'Andrean
2. Marina Piccola
3. Affitta Camere de Baranin
4. La Torretta Rooms
5. Ostello 5-Terre
6. Casa Capellini
7. Trattoria Il Porticciolo
8. Shuttle Bus to Parking Lot & Volastra

his father died, Mario promised him he'd replace the old cross on the family's vineyard. Mario's been adding figures ever since. After recovering from a rare illness, he redoubled his efforts. On religious holidays, everything's lit up: the Nativity, the Last Supper, the Crucifixion, the Resurrection, and more. The scenes are sometimes left up year-round.

ORIENTATION

Helpful Hints

Park Info: The Cinque Terre park office is in the train station (daily 7:00–20:00, €0.50/hr, limited bag storage, tel. 0187-760-511). WCs are on the opposite side of the building from the park office entrance.

Bus Service: A shuttle bus runs between the low end of the main street (at *tabacchi* shop and newsstand) and the parking lot (€1.50 one-way, €2.50 round-trip, free with Cinque Terre Card, 2/hr, just flag it down).

Boats: Find the steps to the left of the harbor view—they lead down to the ticket kiosk. Continue around the left side of the cliff (as you're facing the water) to catch the boats to other Cinque Terre towns.

ACTIVITIES

Beach—Manarola has no sand, but offers the best deep-water swimming in the area. The first "beach" has a shower, ladder, and wonderful rocks. The second has tougher access and no shower, but feels more remote and pristine (follow paved path toward Corniglia just around the point).

SLEEPING

(€1 = about $1.20, country code: 39)

Manarola has plenty of private rooms. Ask in bars and restaurants. There's a modern, three-star place halfway up the main drag, a pricey hotel on the harbor, and a cluster of options around the church at the peaceful top of the town (a 5-min hike from the train tracks). Manarola's handy shuttle-bus service makes it easy to get to and from your car (see above). To ensure honest prices, see my "New Ethic" in the "Sleep Code" on page 262.

$$ Albergo ca' d'Andrean is quiet, comfortable, modern, and like a normal hotel. It has 10 big, sunny, air-conditioned rooms and a cool garden oasis, complete with lemon trees (Sb-€67, Db-€90, breakfast-€6, cash only, send personal or traveler's check to reserve or call if you're already traveling, closed Nov–Christmas, up the hill at Via A. Discovolo 101, tel. 0187-920-040, fax 0187-920-452, www.cadandrean.it, cadandrean@libero.it, Simone speaks English).

$$ Marina Piccola offers 13 bright, slick rooms on the water—so they figure a warm welcome is unnecessary (Db-€90, no breakfast, 3-night minimum July–Aug, air-con, Via Birolli 120, tel. 0187-920-103, fax 0187-920-966, www.hotelmarinapiccola.com, info@hotelmarinapiccola.com).

$$ These two places have a complex pricing system for their pricey rooms: **La Torretta** (cancellations incur 1-2 night charge, Piazza della Chiesa, Vico Volto 20, tel. 0187-920-327, fax 0187-760-0284, www.torrettas.com, torretta@cdh.it), and **Affitta Camere de Baranin** (Via Rollandi 29, tel. & fax 0187-760-954, www.baranin.com; Sara, Silvia, and Andrea).

$ Casa Capellini rents four fine rooms. One has a view balcony, another a 360-degree terrace (Db-€48; €65 for the *alta camera* on the top, with a kitchen, private terrace, and knockout view; 2 doors down the hill from the church; with your back to the church, it's at 2 o'clock; Via Ettore Cozzani 12; tel. 0187-920-823 or 0187-736-765, www.casacapellini-5terre.it, casa.capellini@tin.it, Gianni and Franca don't speak English).

$ Ostello 5-Terre, Manarola's modern and well-run hostel, stands like a Monopoly hotel behind the church square. It's smart to reserve well in advance in high season. You book with your credit-card number; if you cancel with less than three days' notice, you'll be charged for one night. This is not a party hostel—quiet is greatly appreciated (May–Sept dorm beds-€23, Qb-€92; off-season dorm beds-€18, Qb-€72; closed Dec–mid-Feb, 48 beds in 4- to 6-bed rooms, not co-ed except for couples and families, optional €3.50 breakfast and €6 dinner; in summer, office closed 13:00–17:00, rooms closed 10:00–17:00, curfew-1:00; during off-season, office and rooms closed until 16:00, curfew at 24:00; open to all ages, laundry, safes, phone cards, Internet, book exchange, elevator, great roof terrace and sunset views, Via B. Riccobaldi 21, tel. 0187-920-215, fax 0187-920-218, www.hostel5terre.com, ostello@cdh.it, well-managed by Nicola).

EATING

Many hardworking places line the main drag. I liked the Botto family's friendly **Trattoria Il Porticciolo** (€6 pastas, Thu–Tue 12:00–15:00 & 18:00–22:30, closed Wed, just below the train tracks at Via R. Birolli 92, tel. 0187-920-083). For harborside dining, **Marina Piccola** is the winner. While less friendly and a little more expensive, it's worth it for the setting (Wed–Mon 12:30–15:30 & 18:30–22:00, closed Tue, tel. 0187-920-103). The bar in the Punta Bonfiglio park offers light meals and the best views of Manarola.

Corniglia
(Town #3)

This is the quiet town—the only one of the five not on the water—with a mellow main square. From the station, a footpath zigzags up nearly 400 stairs to the town. Or take the shuttle bus, which is generally timed to meet arriving trains (€1.50, free with Cinque Terre Card, 2/hr).

Originally settled by a Roman farmer who named it for his mother, Cornelia (how Corniglia is pronounced), the town and its ancient residents produced a wine so famous that—according to legend—vases found at Pompeii touted its virtues. Today, wine is still its lifeblood. Follow the pungent smell of ripe grapes into an alley cellar and get a local to let you dip a straw into a keg. Remote and less visited than the other Cinque Terre towns, Corniglia has fewer tourists, cooler temperatures, a few restaurants, a windy overlook on its promontory, and plenty of private rooms for rent (ask at any bar or shop).

SELF-GUIDED WALK

Welcome to Corniglia

1. Bus Stop/Town Square: The gateway to this community of 240 people is "Ciappa" square, with an ATM, phone booth, and bus stop. The national park designation has sparked a revitalization of the town, and Corniglia's young generation is now staying put rather than migrating into big cities.

2. Main Street: Stroll the spine of Corniglia, Via Fieschi. In the fall, the smell of grapes (on their way to becoming wine) wafts from busy cellars. At the Butiega shop (#142), Vincenzo and Lorenzo sell organic local specialties (daily 8:00–20:00). For picnickers, they offer €2.50 made-to-order sandwiches and a fun €3.50 *antipasto misto* to go.

The enjoyable wine bar Enoteca Il Purin, named for the odd, old-fashioned pitcher used to pour (and drink) wine, is located in a cool cantina at #115 on Via Fieschi (open daily, tel. 0187-812-315). Sample any of the 30 local or national wines that friendly Mario offers by the glass, and have a light appetizer or salad. Mario doesn't speak English, but he tries.

3. Main Square: On Largo Taragio, tables from two bars and a trattoria spill around a memorial to World War I and the town's old well, which once piped in natural spring water from the hillside to locals living without plumbing. What looks like a church is the Oratory of Santa Caterina. (An oratory is a kind of a spiritual clubhouse for a service group doing social work in the name of the

Corniglia

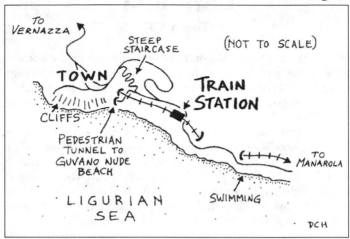

Catholic Church. For more information see "Oratory of the Dead" on page 289.) Behind the oratory is a soccer field with benches and a viewpoint, a peaceful place for a picnic (less crowded than end-of-town viewpoint, below). Opposite the oratory, steps lead steeply down on Via alla Marina to Corniglia's non-beach, a five-minute paved climb to sunning rocks, a shower, and a small deck (with a treacherous entry into the water). Continue down Via Fieschi, past Alberto and Cristina's *gelateria* (the only—and therefore best—in town). Before ordering, get a free taste of Alberto's *miele di Corniglia* (made from local honey).

4. End-of-Town Viewpoint: The Santa Maria Belvedere, named for a church that once stood here, marks the scenic end of Corniglia. This is a super picnic spot. From here, look high to the west, where the village of San Bernardino straddles a ridge (a good starting point for a hike; accessible by shuttle bus or long uphill hike from Vernazza). Below is the tortuous harbor, where locals hoist their boats onto the cruel rocks.

ACTIVITIES

Beaches—This hilltop town has rocky sea access below its train station (toward Manarola). It's clean and uncrowded, but has no cafés, WCs, or showers.

The nude Guvano (GOO-vah-noh) beach is in the opposite direction (toward Vernazza). Guvano made headlines in Italy in the 1970s, as clothed locals in a makeshift armada of dinghies and fishing boats retook their town beach. But big-city nudists still work on all-over tans in this remote setting. To reach the beach from the Corniglia train station, follow the road north, go over the tracks, and then zigzag below the tracks, following signs to the tunnel in the cliff (walk past the *proprietà privata* sign). When you buzz the intercom, the hydraulic *Get Smart*-type door is opened from the other end. After a 15-minute hike through a cool, moist, and dimly lit and unused train tunnel, you'll emerge at the Guvano beach—and get charged €5. The beach has drinking water, but no WC. A steep (free) trail leads from the beach up to the Corniglia-Vernazza trail. The crowd is Italian counterculture: pierced nipples, tattooed punks, hippie drummers in dreads, and exhibitionist men. The ratio of men to women is about three to two. About half the people on the pebbly beach keep their swimsuits on. With new national park standards, the future of Guvano is in doubt.

SLEEPING

(€1 = about $1.20, country code: 39)
Perched high above the sea on a hilltop, Corniglia has plenty of private rooms (generally Db-€60). To get to the town from the station, catch the shuttle bus or take a 15-minute uphill hike. The town—riddled with meager places charging too much for their rooms—is almost never full. To keep prices under control, see my "New Ethic" in the "Sleep Code" on page 262.

$$ Cristiana Ricci (not the movie star) rents four small, clean, and peaceful rooms—three with kitchens and one with a terrace and sweeping view—just inland from the bus stop (Db-€60, Qb-€90, mobile 338-937-6547, tel. 0187-812-541, fax 0187-812-345, cri_affittacamere@virgilio.it). She works at Bar Matteo, on the main square, and can meet you there. Her mom rents a few places in town for same price. Cristiana gives guests with this year's book a free coffee-and-brioche breakfast along with their room.

$$ Villa Cecio, more like a hotel, rents eight well-worn rooms on the outskirts of town, all with no character or warmth (Db-€65, cash preferred, views, on main road 200 yards toward Vernazza, tel. 0187-812-043, fax 0187-812-138, www.cecio5terre.com).

$$ Pellegrini, on a quiet side street, offers three rooms (1 with balcony) and a rooftop terrace. You are actually taking a room in someone's home here (D-€60; going up Via Fieschi, take a left at Via Solferino, then go right, immediately left, and left again to find #34; tel. 0187-812-184 or 0187-821-176, Romina).

$$ Il Girasole, run by Stefano, has four rooms to rent—two with a shared bathroom and kitchen (D-€45, Db-€55–60, Via Fieschi 93, tel.0187-812-551, mobile 338-209-3565, www.corniglia.com).

$$ La Lanterna, a bar on the main square, rents 12 sleepable rooms. It's a last resort (D-€60, Db-€70, tel. 0187-812-291, Via Fieschi 164).

EATING

Corniglia has three decent restaurants. **Cecio,** above the town, known for its homemade pasta and fresh pesto, has terrace seating with a view of the sea. The trattoria **La Lantera,** on the main square, is most atmospheric. Neither come with particularly charming service. At **Bar Matteo,** Cristiana and Stefano offer light meals and Internet access (also on the main square).

Vernazza
(Town #4)

With the closest thing to a natural harbor—overseen by a ruined castle and an old church—Vernazza is the jewel of the Cinque Terre. Only the occasional noisy slurping up of the train by the mountain reminds you of the modern world.

The action is at the harbor, where you'll find outdoor restaurants, a bar hanging on the edge of the castle, a breakwater with a promenade, and a tailgate-party street market every Tuesday morning. In the summer, the beach becomes a soccer field, where teams fielded by local bars and restaurants provide late-night entertainment. In the dark, locals fish off the promontory, using glowing bobs that shine in the waves.

The town's 500 residents, proud of their Vernazzan heritage, brag, "Vernazza is locally owned. Portofino has sold out." Fearing the change it would bring, keep-Vernazza-small proponents stopped the construction of a major road into the town and region. Families are tight and go back centuries; several generations stay together. In the winter, the population shrinks, as many people move to more comfortable big-city apartments.

Leisure time is devoted to the *passeggiata*—strolling lazily together up and down the main street. Sit on a bench and study the passersby. Explore the characteristic alleys, called *carugi*. Learn—and live—the phrase, *"vita pigra di Vernazza"* (the lazy life of Vernazza).

ORIENTATION

Tourist Information
The TI/park information booth is in the train station (daily 6:30–22:00 in summer, until 19:30 off-season, baggage-check sometimes available for €0.50/hour, tel. 0187-812-533). Public WCs are on the opposite side of the park office from the entrance.

Helpful Hints

Money: The town has two ATMs (in center and top of town) and a bank.

Internet Access: The slick **Internet Point,** run by Alberto and Isabella, is in the village center (daily 9:30–20:00, until 23:00 in summer, high-speed line, will burn CDs for a back-up of your digital photos for €8, sells international phone cards, tel. 0187-812-949). The **Blue Marlin Bar,** run by Massimo and Carmen, offers Internet access as well (Fri–Wed 7:00–24:00, closed Thu, see "Eating," page 282).

Laundry: The Blue Marlin Bar on the main drag runs a self-service laundry. Buy tokens at the bar (€5 wash, €5 dry, Fri–Wed from 8:00, last load at 22:00, closed Thu—but if you buy your tokens the day before, Carmen will open the laundry for you on Thu, English instructions, 30 yards below train station).

Parking: Driving to Vernazza is a reasonable option because of the parking lot (€1.50/hr, €12/24 hrs, about 500 yards above town) and the hardworking shuttle service (connects the lot to the top of town every 15 min).

Bus Service: A shuttle bus, generally with friendly English-speaking Beppe or Simone behind the wheel, runs from the top of the main street to the non-resident parking lot about 500 yards above Vernazza (€1.50 or free with Cinque Terre Card, runs 7:20–19:30, 4/hr). You can also catch the bus to the two sanctuaries in the hills above town (€2.50 each way or free with Cinque Terre Card, 5/day, find schedule at park office and posted in train station). This high-country 40-minute loop gives you lots of scenery without having to hike.

Best Views: A steep five-minute hike in either direction from Vernazza gives you a classic village photo op (for the best light, head toward Corniglia in the morning, toward Monterosso in the evening). Ristorante "La Torre," with a panoramic terrace, is at the tower on the trail toward Corniglia.

Rick Steves' Cinque Terre Public TV Show: The industrious Blue Marlin Bar (see above) has a DVD player and welcomes travelers to drop by to enjoy a video introduction to the region (with no pledge breaks).

SELF-GUIDED WALKS

Welcome to Vernazza

Walk uphill until you hit the parking lot, with a bank, a post office, and a barrier that keeps out all but service vehicles. Vernazza's shuttle buses run from here to the parking lot and into the hills. The tidy modern square is called **Fontana Vecchia,** after a long-gone fountain. Older locals remember the river filled with townswomen

Vernazza

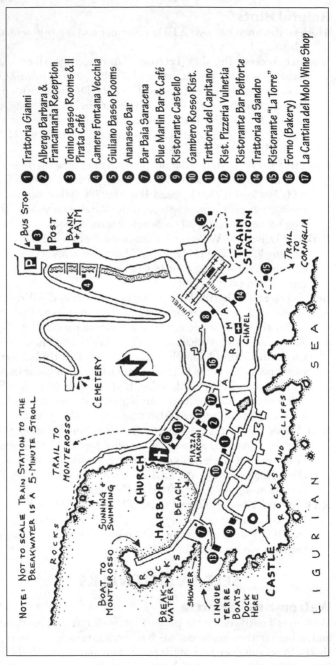

1. Trattoria Gianni
2. Albergo Barbara & Francamaria Reception
3. Tonino Basso Rooms & Il Pirata Café
4. Camere Fontana Vecchia
5. Giuliano Basso Rooms
6. Ananasso Bar
7. Bar Baia Saracena
8. Blue Marlin Bar & Café
9. Ristorante Castello
10. Gambero Rosso Rist.
11. Trattoria del Capitano
12. Rist. Pizzeria Vulnetia
13. Ristorante Bar Belforte
14. Trattoria da Sandro
15. Ristorante "La Torre"
16. Forno (Bakery)
17. La Cantina del Molo Wine Shop

NOTE: NOT TO SCALE TRAIN STATION TO THE BREAKWATER IS A 5-MINUTE STROLL

doing their washing. Now they enjoy checking on the baby ducks. The trail leads up to the cemetery. Imagine the entire village trudging sadly up here during funerals. Glad to be here in happier times, begin your saunter downhill to the harbor.

Just before the Pensione Sorriso sign, you'll see the **ambulance** barn (big brown wood doors) on your right. A group of volunteers is always on call for a dash to the hospital, 40 minutes away in La Spezia. Opposite from the barn is a big, empty lot. Like many landowners, the owner of Pension Sorriso had plans to expand, but since the 1980s, the government said no. While some landowners are frustrated, the old character of these towns survives.

A few steps farther along (past the town clinic and library), you'll see a **monument** dedicated to those killed in the World Wars (marble plaque in the wall to your left). Not a family here was spared. Study this sight: On the left are soldiers *morti in combattimento,* who died in World War I; on the right is the World War II section. Some were deported to *Germania;* others—labeled *Part* (stands for *partigiani,* or "partisans")—were killed while fighting against Mussolini. Cynics considered partisans less than heroes. After 1943, Hitler called up Italian boys over 15. Rather than die on the front for Hitler, they escaped to the hills. They become "resistance fighters" in order to remain free.

Perhaps your knees are pressing against the track of the tiny monorail *trenino.* The little train is kept up on the wall on your right, except in September and October, when it's busy helping locals bring down the grapes. (Sorry, no rides for the public.) After the harvest, the cantinas in Vernazza are draped with drying grapes. The path to Corniglia leaves from here (behind and above the plaque). Behind you is a tiny square and playground, decorated with three millstones, which no longer grind local olives into oil. From here, Vernazza's tiny river goes underground. Until the 1950s, Vernazza's river ran openly through the center of town. Old-timers recall the days before the breakwater, when the river cascaded down and the surf crashed along Vernazza's main drag. Back then, the town was nicknamed "Little Venice."

Before the tracks (on the left), the wall has 10 spaces, one reserved for each party's political ads during elections—a kind of local pollution control. The **map** on the right, under the railway tracks, shows the region's hiking trails. Number two is the basic favorite. The second set of tracks (nearer the harbor) was recently renovated to lessen the disruptive noise, but locals say it made no difference. Follow the road downhill.

Wandering through this main business center, you'll pass many locals doing their *vasca* (laps) past the entrepreneurial Blue Marlin Bar and the tiny **Chapel of Santa Marta** (the small stone chapel with iron grillwork over the window), where Mass is celebrated only on special Sundays. Next you'll see a grocery, *gelateria*, bakery, pharmacy, another grocery, and another *gelateria*.

On the left, in front of the second *gelateria*, an arch leads to what was a beach, where the town's stream used to hit the sea. Continue down to the **harbor square** and breakwater. Vernazza, with the only natural harbor of the Cinque Terre, was established as the sole place boats could pick up the fine local wine. Peek into the tiny street (behind the Vulnetia restaurant) with the commotion of arches. Vernazza's most characteristic side streets, called *carugi*, lead up from here. The trail (above the church, toward Monterosso) leads to the classic view of Vernazza (see "Best Views," above).

The Burned-Out Sightseer's Visual Tour of Vernazza

Sit at the end of the harbor breakwater (perhaps with a glass of local white wine or something more interesting from a nearby bar—borrow the glass, they don't mind), face the town, and see...

The Harbor: In a moderate storm, you'd be soaked, as waves routinely crash over the *molo* (breakwater, built in 1972). Waves can even wash away tourists squinting excitedly into their cameras. (I've seen it happen.) Enjoy the new waterfront piazza—carefully.

The train line (to your left), constructed 130 years ago to tie together a newly united Italy, linked Turin and Genoa with Rome. A second line (hidden in a tunnel at this point) was built in the 1960s. The yellow building alongside the tracks was Vernazza's first train station. You can see the four bricked-up alcoves where people once waited for trains.

Vernazza's fishing fleet is down to just a couple of fishing boats (with the net spools). Vernazzans are more likely to own a boat than a car. Boats are on buoys, except in winter or when the red flag on the pole indicates stormy seas (in which case, they're allowed to be pulled up onto the square—usually reserved for restaurant tables). In the 1970s tiny Vernazza had one of the top water polo teams in Italy, and the harbor was their "pool." Later, when the league required a real pool, Vernazza dropped out.

The Castle: On the far right, the castle, which is now a grassy park with great views, still guards the town (€1, daily 10:00–19:00; from harbor, take stairs by Trattoria Gianni and follow signs to Castello restaurant, tower is a few steps beyond; see the photo and painting gallery rooms). It was the town's lookout back in pirate days. The highest umbrellas mark the recommended Ristorante Castello (see page 284). The squat tower on the water is great for a glass of wine or a bite to eat. Follow the rope to the Ristorante Bar Belforte (see page 284), and pop inside the submarine-strength door. A photo of a major storm shows the entire tower under a wave.

The Town: Vernazza has two halves. *Sciuiu* (literally, "flowery") is the sunny side (on the left), and *luvegu* (literally, "dank") is the shady side (on the right). The houses below the castle were connected by an interior arcade—ideal for fleeing attacks. The "Ligurian pastel" colors are regulated by a commissioner of good taste in the community government. The square before you is locally famous for some of the region's finest restaurants. The big, red, central house—on the site where Genoan warships were built in the 12th century—used to be a kind of guardhouse. Gaze across the windows and notice inhabitants quietly gazing back.

Above the Town: The small, round tower above the guardhouse—another part of the city fortifications—reminds us of Vernazza's importance in the Middle Ages, when it was a key ally of Genoa (whose archenemies were the other maritime republics, especially Pisa). Ristorante "La Torre," just behind the tower, welcomes hikers finishing, starting, or simply contemplating the Corniglia–Vernazza hike, with great town views (between meal times, only drinks are served). Vineyards fill the mountainside beyond the town. Notice the many terraces. Someone—probably after too much of that local wine—calculated that the vineyard terraces of the Cinque Terre have the same amount of stonework as the Great Wall of China. Wine production is down nowadays, as the younger residents choose less physical work. But locals still maintain their plots and proudly serve their family wines. A single steel train line winds up the gully behind the tower. This is for the vintner's *trenino,* the tiny service train. Play "Where's *trenino*?" and see if you can find two. The vineyards once stretched as high as you can see, but since fewer people sweat in the fields these days, the most distant terraces have gone wild again.

The Church, School, and City Hall: Vernazza's Ligurian Gothic church, built with black stones quarried from Punta Mesco (the distant point behind you), dates from 1318. The gray-and-red house above the spire is the local elementary school (which about 25 children attend). High-schoolers go to the "big city," La Spezia. The red building to the right of the schoolhouse, a former monastery, is the city hall. Vernazza and Corniglia function as one community. Through most of the 1990s, the local government was communist. In 1999, they elected a coalition of many parties working to rise above ideologies and simply make Vernazza a better place. Finally, on the top of the hill, with the best view of all, is the town cemetery.

ACTIVITIES

Beach—The harbor's sandy cove has sunning rocks and showers by the breakwater. There's also a ladder on the breakwater for deep-water access. There's a tiny *acqua pendente* (waterfall) cove, between

Vernazza and Monterosso, which is accessible by boat—when the service is available (ask at TI). Locals call it their *laguna blu*.

Kayaks—At the harbor, one- or two-person kayaks are rentable by the hour (June–Sept only, €4/hr for 1, €8/hr for 2), as well as dinghy and motorboats.

Massage—Seven years ago, Kate Allen moved her massage table from London to the Cinque Terre. She provides a good therapeutic rub-down for €50 an hour. Head to the clinic across from Pensione Sorriso (100 yards above Vernazza's train tracks) or, for women, arrange for an in-room massage at your hotel rooms while in Vernazza or Monterosso (call for an appointment, cash only, 0187-812-537, katarinaallen@hotmail.com).

SLEEPING

(€1 = about $1.20, country code: 39)
Vernazza, the essence of the Cinque Terre, is my top choice for a home base. There are two recommended pensions and piles of private rooms for rent.

These days, with so many rooms available, you can generally arrive without a reservation and find a place (except holidays such as Easter, weekends, and July–Aug). In fact, you'll save money this way—or gain the chance to shop around and land a place with a terrace and a view for less. Drop by any shop or bar and ask; most locals know someone who rents rooms.

Anywhere you stay here requires some climbing. Night noises can be a problem if you're near the station. Rooms on the harbor come with church bells (but only from 7:00–22:00). Prices do not include breakfast unless otherwise noted. For details on "Sleeping in the Cinque Terre," see page 263.

Be aware of—and help me enforce—my "New Ethic" system, which keeps hoteliers honest and guarantees you these prices for 2006 (see page 262).

Pensions

$$ Trattoria Gianni rents 23 small rooms just under the castle. The funky ones are artfully decorated à la shipwreck and are up a hundred tight, winding, spiral stairs. Most have tiny balconies and grand views. The new, comfy rooms lack views but have modern bathrooms and a super-scenic, cliff-hanging private garden. Steely Marisa, who rarely smiles at anyone (not just you), requires check-in before 16:00 (or a phone call to explain when you're coming). Her staff, Giovanni and Simona, both smile and speak a little English (S-€42, D-€60, D with small balcony-€65, Db-€80, Tb-€100, 10 percent discount in 2006 with this book and cash payment—request when you reserve, cancellations required 48 hrs in advance or you'll be charged 1 night deposit, Piazza Marconi 5, closed Jan–Feb, tel. & fax 0187-812-228, tel. 0187-821-003, www.giannifranzi.it, info @giannifranzi.it). Pick up your keys at Trattoria Gianni's restaurant/reception on the harbor square and hike up scores of steps to #41 (funky but with sea view, *con vista sul mare*) or #47 (new, *nuovo*) at the top. If you arrive on Wednesday, when the restaurant is closed, pick up your keys at the big *gelateria* by the grotto.

$$ Albergo Barbara, on the harbor square, is run by kindly, English-speaking Giuseppe and his Swiss wife, Patricia. They're planning to remodel for 2006, and most of their clean, modern rooms will soon have private baths (D-€48, Db-€55–60, big Db with view-€80; fax or e-mail credit-card information to hold room, but pay cash; 2-night stay preferred, closed Dec–Feb, fans, Piazza Marconi 30, tel. & fax 0187-812-398, mobile 338-793-3261, www .albergobarbara.it, albergobarbara@libero.it). The two big doubles on the main floor come with grand harbor views (top-floor doubles have small windows and small views). The office is on the top floor of the big, red, vacant-looking building facing the harbor.

Private Rooms *(Affitta Camere)*

The town is honeycombed year-round with private rooms, offering the best values in Vernazza. The owners may be reluctant to reserve rooms far in advance. It's easiest to call a day or two ahead or simply show up in the morning and look around. Doubles cost €45–70, depending on the view, season, and plumbing. Most places accept only cash. Some have killer views, come with lots of stairs, and cost the same as a small dark place on a back lane over the train tracks. Little English is spoken at many of these places. If you call to let them know your arrival time (or call when you arrive, using the pay phone just below the station), they'll meet you at the train station.

Especially Well-Managed and Well-Appointed
Rooms at the Top of Town

$$$ Tonino Basso rents four super, clean, modern rooms, each with its own computer for free Internet access. He's located near the post office, in the only building in Vernazza with an elevator. You get tranquility and air-conditioning, but no views. This is the only *affita camere* that takes credit cards (Sb-€60, Db-€100, Tb-€120, Qb-€150, mention this book when you reserve to get these prices in 2006, call Tonino's mobile number upon arrival and he'll meet you, mobile 335-269-436, tel. 0187-821-264, fax 0187-821-260, toninobasso@libero.it). If you can't locate Tonino, his wife Tania works at the harborside Gambero Rosso restaurant.

$$ Camere Fontana Vecchia is a delightful place, with four bright, spacious, quiet rooms near the post office (no view). It's the only place in Vernazza with almost no stairs to climb (D-€50–60, Db-€60–70, T-€90, Tb-€110, fans and heat, open year-round, Via Gavino 15, tel. & fax 0187-821-130, mobile 333-454-9371, m.annamaria@libero.it, youthful and efficient Annamaria speaks English).

$$ Giuliano Basso rents four fine rooms that share a large view balcony, allowing you to survey the whole town and Giuliano's own terraced gardens below (but no sea views). Straddling a *trenino* line among orange trees, it's an artfully decorated, Robinson Crusoe-chic wonderland, proudly built out of stone by Giuliano (Db-€70, optional breakfast-€5/person, one family room, open year-round, fridge access, above train station—and therefore with more train noise than others, mobile 333-341-4792, or have the Blue Marlin bar—see "Eating," below—contact him, www.cdh.it /giuliano, giuliano@cdh.it). If you call to let him know what time you'll arrive, he'll meet you at the station. From Pensione Sorriso, hike up the trail at the sign to Corniglia; 100 yards later, at the second Corniglia sign, follow the narrow lane left.

Other Reliable Places Scattered through Town and Harborside

$$$ Egi Rooms, run by friendly, English-speaking Egi Verduschi (pronounced "edgy"), offers three rooms right in the center on the main drag (S-€70, D-€90, plush and designer Db-€115, Tb-€150, across the street from *gelateria* just before harbor square on main drag at Via Visconti 9, mobile 338-822-3202, tel. 0187-703-905, egidioverduschi@libero.it).

$$ Memo Rooms offers three newly-renovated, immaculate rooms overlooking the main street, in what feels like a miniature hotel. Enrica will meet you if you call upon arrival (Db-€65, Via Roma 15, tel. 0187-812-360, mobile 338-285-2385).

$$ Martina Callo rents four rooms overlooking the square, up plenty of steps near the silent-at-night church tower (room #1: Qb with harbor view-€110; room #2: huge Qb family room with no view-€110; room #3: Db with grand view terrace-€70; room #4: roomy Db with no view-€55; ring bell at Piazza Marconi 26, tel. & fax 0187-812-365, mobile 329-435-5344, www .roomartina.com, roomartina@supereva.it).

$$ Elisabetta's Villino Azzurro has three ramshackle rooms with views. The lower room has a small window with a sea view; the two rooms upstairs come with view terraces; and the uppermost terrace has 360-degree views of town, the *castello*, the terraced hills, and the sea (Db-€50–62, Via Carattino 62, tel. 0187-458-437, mobile 347-451-1834, www.elisabettacarro.it, carroelisabetta@hotmail.com).

$$ Nicolina rents four decent rooms: a large one with a view, two overlooking Vernazza's main drag (one comes with frescoed ceiling plus a washing machine she'll let you use), and one without any view. Inquire at Pizzeria Vulnetia on the harbor square or reserve in advance by phone (Db-€70, Qb with terrace and view-€130, Piazza Marconi 29, tel. & fax 0187-821-193, www.camerenicolina .it, camerenicolina.info@cdh.it).

$$ Rosa Vitali rents two apartments overlooking the main street. One, for up to three people, has a terrace and fridge (top floor); the other, for four, has windows and a full kitchen (Db-€75, Tb-€100, Qb-€120, reception at Via Visconti 10 next to *gelateria* near the grotto, tel. 0187-821-181, mobile 340-267-5009, rosa .vitali@libero.it, speaks English).

$$ Francamaria rents four sharp, comfortable rooms and has only a few stairs to climb. The two rooms above Trattoria Gianni's bar can be noisy in the evenings until 23:30 (Db-€60–100, Qb-€100–145, prices depend on view and season, Piazza Marconi 30, tel. 0187-812-002, fax 0187-812-956, mobile 328-711-9728, www.francamaria.com, francamaria@francamaria.com). Son Giovanni has three rooms of his own to rent (same prices but no views, 1 with no window).

$$ Tilde's cheery and clean little room has a sea view (Db-€70, up Via Mazzini 9, mobile 339-298-9323).

$$ Daria Bianchi offers three clean, spacious, and comfortable rooms near the station. Each has bright colors, worn carpeting, and either overlooks the main street or the inland hills (Db-€70, Qb-€100, mobile 338-581-4688, tel. 0187-812-151, www .vernazzarooms.com).

$$ Affitta Camere da Annamaria offers six basic rooms (avoid the 2 viewless rooms) with barnacled ambience up a series of comically-tight spiral staircases (Db-€75 with town views and terrace, Db-€85 for top room with sea-view terrace, at pharmacy climb Via Carattino to #64, mobile 349-887-8150, tel. 0187-821-082).

Other Private Rooms in Vernazza

Many of these places claim to agree to my "New Ethic" system, but I can't say for sure how committed they are—confirm these prices when reserving and let me know about violations. Consider these options only if the places above are booked up: **Filippo Rooms** (lots of rooms, D-€65, tel. 0187-812-244), **Eva's Rooms** (Db-€50–60, air-con, tel. 0187-821-134, massimoeva@libero.it), **Sergio Callo Rooms** (apartment sleeps up to three, Db-€70, Tb-€90, tel. 0187-812-284, gemmina@5terre.com), **Armanda** (€75, no view but has small kitchen, near castle, Piazza Marconi 15, tel. 0187-812-218, mobile 347-306-4760), **Manuela Moggia** (Qb-€110, extra €10 to use kitchen, top of town, Via Gavino 22, tel. 0187-812-397, mobile 333-413-6374), **Patrizia** (Db-€65–75, Qb-€100, all with kitchens, on main street, tel. 0187-821-231, mobile 335-653-1563, fax 0187-812-907, bemili@libero.it), and **Villa Antonia** (Db-€70, on main drag, tel. 0187-821-143).

EATING

Breakfast

Locals take breakfast about as seriously as flossing. A cappuccino and a pastry or a piece of focaccia does it. No accommodations come with breakfast. Instead, you have several fun options.

The two harborfront bars offer the most ambience. **Ananasso Bar** feels Old World, with low energy but a great location (toasted *panini*, pastries). Eat a bit cheaper at the bar (you're welcome to picnic on a bench or rock) or enjoy the best-situated tables in town (Fri–Wed 8:00–late, closed Thu). **Bar Baia Saracena** has a chalkboard explaining their various breakfast *menus* for €5–7. Luca, the owner, promises a free slice of *bucellato* (the local coffee cake) for breakfast as a bonus for anyone with this year's book taking a breakfast here (opens 7:30, located out on the breakwater, tel. 0187-812-113).

The **Blue Marlin Bar** (mid-town) serves a good array of clearly-priced à la carte items (Fri–Wed 7:00–24:00, closed Thu, open daily in Aug, just below station, tel. 0187-821-149). If awaiting a train, its outdoor seats beat the platform. The nearby bakery opens early, offering freshly-made focaccia.

At **Il Pirata delle Cinque Terre,** dynamic Sicilian duo Gianluca and Massimo—and their trusty sidekick Sonia—enthusiastically offer a great assortment of handcrafted, authentic-Sicilian pastries. Gianluca is a pastry artist, hand-painting fanciful sculptured marzipan. Their sweet pastry breakfasts are a hit, with a stunning array of hot-out-of-the-oven treats like *panzerotto*, made of ricotta, cinnamon, and vanilla (€1.50). Other favorites include their *granitas*, slushees made from fresh fruit and garnished with thick whipped cream (daily 6:30–24:00, serves simple lunches and tasty dinners, by post office at top of town, Via Gavino 36, tel. 0187-812-047). While the atmosphere of the place seems like suburban Milano, it has a curious charisma among its customers—bringing Vernazza a welcome bit of Sicily.

Lunch and Dinner

If you enjoy Italian cuisine, Vernazza's restaurants are worth the splurge. All take pride in their cooking and have similar prices. Wander around at about 20:00 and compare the ambience, but don't wait too late to eat—most kitchen staff have to catch the last train back home to La Spezia at 22:30. To get an outdoor table on summer weekends, reserve ahead. Expect to spend €8 for pastas

Cinque Terre Cuisine 101

Local Specialities: *Acciughe* (ah-CHOO-gay) are anchovies, a local specialty—always served the day they're caught. If you've always hated anchovies (the harsh, cured-in-salt American kind), try them fresh here. *Tegame alla Vernazza* is the most typical main course in Vernazza: anchovies, potatoes, tomatoes, white wine, oil, and herbs. *Pansotti* are ravioli with ricotta and spinach, often served with a hazelnut or walnut sauce... delightful and filling. While antipasto means cheese and salami in Tuscany, here you'll get *antipasti frutti di mare,* a plate of mixed "fruits of the sea" and a fine way to start a meal. For many, splitting this and a pasta dish is plenty. Try the fun local dessert: *torta della nonna* (grandmother's cake), with a glass of *sciacchetrà* for dunking (see "Wine," below).

Pesto: This region is the birthplace of pesto. Basil, which loves the temperate Ligurian climate, is mixed with cheese (half *Parmigiano* cow cheese and half pecorino sheep cheese), garlic, olive oil, and pine nuts, and then poured over pasta. Try it on spaghetti, *trenette,* or *trofie* (made of flour with a bit of potato, designed specifically for pesto to cling to). Many also like pesto lasagna. If you become addicted, small jars of pesto are sold in the local grocery stores (you can take it home or spread it on focaccia here).

Focaccia: This tasty bread also originates from here in Liguria. Locals say the best focaccia is made between the Cinque Terre and Genoa. It's simply flatbread with olive oil and salt. The baker roughs up the dough with finger holes, then bakes it. Focaccia comes plain or with onions, sage, and olive bits, and is a local favorite for a snack on the beach. Bakeries sell it in rounds or slices by the weight (a portion is about 100 grams, or *un etto*).

Wine: The *vino delle Cinque Terre,* respected throughout Italy, flows cheap and easy throughout the region. It's white—great with the local seafood. *D.O.C.* is the mark of top quality. Red wine is better elsewhere. For a sweet dessert wine, the local *sciacchetrà* wine is worth the splurge (€3 per glass, often served with a cookie). While 10 kilos of grapes yield seven liters of local wine, *sciacchetrà* is made from near-raisins, and 10 kilos of grapes make only 1.5 liters of *sciacchetrà*. The word means "push and pull"—push in lots of grapes, pull out the best wine. If your room is up a lot of steps, be warned: *sciacchetrà* is 18 percent alcohol, while regular wine is only 11 percent. In the cool, calm evening, sit on the Vernazza breakwater with a glass of wine and watch the phosphorescence in the waves.

and €12 for *secondi*. Harborside restaurants and bars are easygoing. You're welcome to grab a cup of coffee or glass of wine and disappear somewhere on the breakwater, returning your glass when you're done.

Ristorante Castello is run by gracious and English-speaking Monica, her husband Massimo, kind Mario, dashing Francesco, and the rest of her family (you won't see mamma—she's busy personally cooking each *secondo*). Hike high above town to just below the castle for great seafood and regional specialties with commanding views (Thu–Tue 12:00–15:00 for lunch, 15:00–19:00 for drinks and snacks on cliff-hugging terrace, 19:30–22:00 for dinner, closed Wed and Nov–April, tel. 0187-812-296). Their *lasagna al pesto* and *ravioli di pesce* are time-honored family specialties.

Four places fill the harborfront with happy eaters: **Gambero Rosso,** considered Vernazza's best restaurant, feels classy and costs only a few euros more than the others (Tue–Sun 12:00–15:00 & 19:00–22:00, closed Mon and Dec–Feb, Piazza Marconi 7, tel. 0187-812-265). **Trattoria del Capitano** might serve the best food for the money, including *tagliolini sul pesce*—white fish and delicate pasta—and their *zuppa provenzale,* a hearty Ligurian bouillabaisse (Wed–Mon 12:00–15:00 & 19:00–22:00, closed Tue except in Aug, closed Dec–Jan, tel. 0187-812-201; Paolo, his American wife Julia, and Barbara speak English, grandpa Giacomo doesn't need to). **Trattoria Gianni** is an old standby for locals and tourists alike, especially for well-prepared seafood (Thu–Tue 12:00–15:00 & 19:30–22:00, closed Wed except July–Aug, tel. 0187-812-228). **Ristorante Pizzeria Vulnetia** serves regional specialties and pizza (Tue–Sun 12:00–15:00 & 18:30–22:00, closed Mon, Piazza Marconi 29, tel. 0187-821-193).

From the breakwater, a rope leads up and around to the little **Ristorante Bar Belforte,** embedded in the lower part of the old castle. While they serve meals, it's a good spot outside of mealtime for a romantic and/or late-night drink (Wed–Mon 12:00–22:00, closed Tue and Nov–March, limited menu between mealtimes, drinks served until late, Seattleite Ryan married into the town and now works here).

Several inland places, without the harbor ambience, manage to compete: **Trattoria da Sandro,** on the main drag, mixes Genovese and Ligurian cuisine with friendly service. It can be a peaceful alternative to the harborside scene (Wed–Mon 12:00–15:00 & 19:00–22:00, closed Tue, just below train station, Via Roma 62, tel. 0187-812-223, Gabriella speaks English). **Il Pirata delle Cinque Terre,** a haven of heavenly pastry, is popular for good meals at dinner (only sandwiches for lunch), and offers more than a dozen homemade desserts and drinks until late (see listing under "Breakfast," above).

For a grand view and perfect peace, hike to Franco's **Ristorante "La Torre"** for a dinner at sunset (Wed–Mon 12:00–21:30, sometimes also open Tue, kitchen closes from 15:00–19:30 but drinks are served, drink-only service during mealtimes is sporadic, on trail toward Corniglia, mobile 338-404-1181, tel. 0187-821-082).

The waiters at **Bar Baia Saracena** ("Saracen Bay") take the pirate theme to heart, swinging in with earrings that blow in the wind. The bar has a dozen plastic tables on the breakwater and serves light meals throughout the day (€5–7 salads, €8 pizza, €4 glasses of *sciacchetrà*—sweet dessert wine; also see listing under "Breakfast," above).

The main street is creatively filling tourists' needs. The **Blue Marlin** bar offers a good selection of bruschetta, salad, and sandwiches. The **Forno** bakery has good focaccia and veggie tarts, and several bars sell sandwiches and pizza by the slice. **Grocery stores** also make inexpensive sandwiches to order (Mon–Sat 8:00–13:00 & 17:00–19:30, Sun 7:30–13:00). The town's two *gelaterias* are good.

La Cantina del Molo, the wine shop, will uncork the bottle you buy and supply cups to go (daily 10:30–20:00, until 22:00 in summer, owner makes 5 of the wines).

Monterosso al Mare
(Town #5)

This is a resort with cars, hotels, rentable beach umbrellas, crowds, and a thriving late-night scene. Monterosso has two parts: A new town (called Fegina) with a parking lot, train station, and the TI; and an old town *(centro storico)*, cradling the Old World charm with small, crooked lanes, hole-in-the-wall shops, pastel townscapes, and a new generation of creative small businesspeople eager to keep their visitors happy. A pedestrian tunnel connects the old with the new.

Strolling the waterfront promenade, you can pick out each of the Cinque Terre towns decorating the coast. After dark they sparkle. This town is the most enjoyable of the five for young travelers wanting to connect with other young travelers and looking for a little action after dark. Even still, Monterosso is not a full-blown Portofino-style resort—and locals appreciate quiet, sensitive guests.

ORIENTATION

Tourist Information

The TI Proloco is next to the train station (Easter–Oct daily 9:30–18:30, closed Nov–Easter, exit station and go left a few doors, tel. 0187-817-506). The Cinque Terre has park offices on Piazza Garibaldi in the old town and in the train station in the new town (daily 8:00–22:00, until 20:00 in winter, baggage check-€0.50/hr, tel. 0187-817-059, www.parconazionale5terre.it, parconazionale5terre @libero.it).

Arrival in Monterosso al Mare

Monterosso is 30 minutes off the freeway (exit: Carrodano). Parking is easy (except July, Aug, and summer weekends) in the huge beachfront guarded lot (€12/day). As you approach, save six miles of needless driving by deciding ahead of time whether to head into the old or new town. Pay attention to the fork that pops up three miles above town, directing cars to *Centro Storico* (old center, no parking available except for Villa Steno guests) or Fegina (the new town, parking, most likely where you want to go). Train travelers arrive in the new town, where it's a scenic 10-minute stroll to all the old-town action (leave station to the left, but for hotels in the new town, turn right out of station).

Helpful Hints

Bus Service: Shuttle buses run along the waterfront between the old town (Piazza Garibaldi, just beyond the tunnel), the train station, and the parking lot at the end of Via Fegina (Campo Sportivo stop). While the buses can be convenient, saving you a 10-minute schlep with your bags, they only go once an hour and are likely not worth the trouble (€1.50, free with Cinque Terre Card).

Medical Help: The town's bike-riding, leather-bag-toting doctor is Dr. Vitone (mobile 338-853-0949).

Internet Access: The Net, a few steps off the main drag (Via Roma) on Via Vittorio Emanuele has 10 high-speed comput-ers, and classical music (if Renato's on duty). Renato and Enzo happily provide information on the Cinque Terre, helping visi-tors book accommodations and schedule tours or scuba-div-ing excursions (daily 10:00–24:00, off-season until 19:30, Via Vittorio Emanuele 55, tel. 0187-817-288, www.monterossonet .com). To view my Cinque Terre public television show on their DVD player for free, show them this year's book.

Laundry: A self- and full-service launderette is at Via Mazzini 4 (full-service 13 pounds wash and dry for €11, allow 2 hrs, daily 9:30–13:00 & 15:00–20:00, June–Aug until 24:00, just off main drag below L'Alta Marea restaurant, call 333-525-7416 if it's closed during business hours and they'll come open it for you).

Boats: From the old-town harbor, boats run nearly hourly (10:30–17:00) to Vernazza, Manarola, Riomaggiore, and Portovenere. Schedules are posted in Cinque Terre park offices (for details, see page 256).

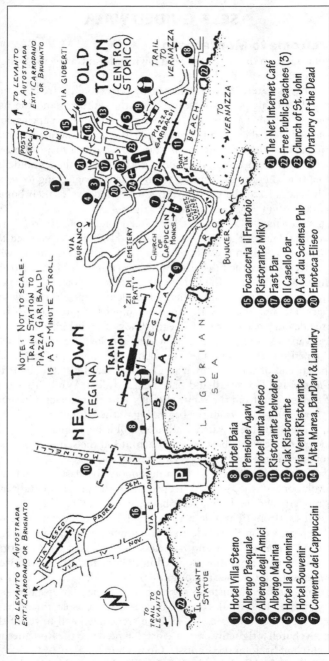

Monterosso al Mare

NEW TOWN (FEGINA)

OLD TOWN (CENTRO STORICO)

TRAIN STATION

LIGURIAN SEA

NOTE: NOT TO SCALE · TRAIN STATION TO PIAZZA GARIBALDI IS A 5-MINUTE STROLL

TO LEVANTO & AUTOSTRADA EXIT: CARRODANO OR BRUGNATO

TO LEVANTO & AUTOSTRADA EXIT: CARRODANO OR BRUGNATO

TRAIL TO VERNAZZA

TO VERNAZZA

IL GIGANTE STATUE

TRAIL TO LEVANTO

VIA GIOBERTI
VIA BURANCO
VIA FEGINA
VIA E. MONTALE
VIA MESCO
VIA PADRE SEM.
VIA IV NOV.
"ZII DI FRATI"
Cemetery
Church of Cappuccin Monks
PEDEST. TUNNEL
BOAT TIX
BUNKER
BEACH
ROCKS
POST
GROC.

1 Hotel Villa Steno
2 Albergo Pasquale
3 Albergo degli Amici
4 Albergo Marina
5 Hotel la Colonnina
6 Hotel Souvenir
7 Convento dei Cappuccini

8 Hotel Baia
9 Pensione Agavi
10 Hotel Punta Mesco
11 Ristorante Belvedere
12 Ciak Ristorante
13 Via Venti Ristorante
14 L'Alta Marea, BarDavi & Laundry

15 Focacceria il Frantoio
16 Ristorante Miky
17 Fast Bar
18 Il Casello Bar
19 A Ca' du Sciensa Pub
20 Enoteca Eliseo

21 The Net Internet Café
22 Free Public Beaches (3)
23 Church of St. John
24 Oratory of the Dead

SELF-GUIDED WALK

Welcome to Monterosso

Hike out from the dock in the old town and climb a few rough steps to the very top of the...

Breakwater: If you're visiting by boat, you'll start here anyway. From this point, you can survey the old town and the new town (stretching to the left, with train station and parking lot). The little fort above is a private home. The harbor now hosts more paddleboats than fishing boats. Sand erosion is a major problem here. While old-timers remember a vast beach, their grandchildren truck in sand each spring to give tourists something to lie on. (The Nazis liked the Cinque Terre, too—find two of their bomb-hardened bunkers, near left and far right.)

The fancy €300-a-night, four-star Hotel Porto Roco (on the far right) marks the trail to Vernazza. High above, you see the costly road built in the 1980s to connect Cinque Terre towns with the freeway over the hills. The two capes (Punta di Montenero and Punta Mesco) define the Cinque Terre region—you can just about make out the towns from here. The closer cape, Punta Mesco, marks an important sea-life sanctuary, home to a rare sea grass that provides an ideal home for fish eggs. Buoys keep fishing boats away. The cape was once a quarry, providing employment to locals who chipped out the stones used to cobble the streets of Genoa. On the far end of the new town you can just see the statue named *Il Gigante*. It's 45 feet tall and once held a trident. While it looks as if it was hewn from the rocky cliff, it's actually made of reinforced concrete and dates from the beginning of the 20th century.

From the breakwater, walk to the old-town square (just past the train tracks and beyond the beach). Find the statue of a dandy holding what looks like a box cutter in...

Piazza Garibaldi: The statue honors the dashing firebrand revolutionary who, in 1870, helped unite the people of Italy into a modern nation. Facing Garibaldi, with your back to the sea, you'll see (from right to left) the City Hall (with the now-required European Union flag aside the Italian one), a big home and recreation center for poor and homeless elderly, and a park information center (in a building bombed in 1945 by the Allies, who were attempting to take out the train line). You'll also see the A Ca' du Sciensa pub (with historic town photos inside and upstairs—see "Nightlife," page 290), covered arcades where the old-timers hang out (they know and see all), and the crenellated bell tower of the town church (originally part of a fort that predated the Romanesque Church of St. John the Baptist). Go to church.

Church of St. John the Baptist: This black-and-white church, with marble from Carrara, is typical of this region's Romanesque style. The church dates from 1307—the proud inscription on the middle column inside reads "MilleCCCVII." Leaving the church, turn immediately left and go to church again.

Oratory of the Dead: During the Counter-Reformation, the Catholic Church offset the rising influence of the Lutherans by creating brotherhoods of good works. These religious Rotary clubs were called "confraternities." Monterosso had two, nicknamed White and Black. This building is the oratory of the Black group, whose mission—as the macabre decor indicates—was to arrange for funerals and take care of widows, orphans, the shipwrecked, and those who ignore the request for a €1 donation. It dates from the 16th century, and membership has passed from father to son for generations. Notice the fine 17th-century carved choir stalls just inside the door.

Return to the beach and find the brick steps leading up to the hill-capping convent (starting between the train tracks and the pedestrian tunnel).

The Switchbacks of the Monks: Follow the yellow brick road (OK, it's orange...but I couldn't help singing as I skipped skyward). Go constantly uphill until you reach a convent church, then a cemetery, in a ruined castle at the summit. The lane (Salita dei Cappuccini) is nicknamed "Zii di Frati" (switchbacks of the monks). Midway up the switchbacks, you'll see a statue of St. Francis and a wolf enjoying a grand view. From here, backtrack 20 yards and continue uphill. When you reach a gate marked "Convento e Chiesa Cappuccini" you have arrived. Go to church.

Church of the Cappuccin Monks: The convent is once again owned by monks. Before stepping inside, notice the church's striped Romanesque facade. It's all fake. Tap it—no marble, just cheap 18th-century stucco. Sit in the rear pew. The high altarpiece painting of St. Francis can be rolled up on special days to reveal a statue of Mary, which stands behind it. Look at the statue of St. Anthony to the right and smile (you're on convent camera). Wave at the security camera—they're nervous about the precious painting to your left.

This fine painting of the Crucifixion is attributed to Antony Van Dyck, the Flemish master who lived and worked for years in nearby Genoa. When Jesus died, the earth went dark. Notice the eclipsed sun in the painting, just to the right of the cross. Do the electric candles work? Pick one up, pray for peace, and plug it in. (Leave €0.50, or unplug it and put it back.) From the church, hike uphill to the cemetery that fills the remains of the castle, capping the hill. Look out from the gate and enjoy the view.

Cemetery: In the Dark Ages, the village huddled within this castle. Slowly it expanded. Notice the town view from here—no sea. You're looking at the oldest part of Monterosso, huddled behind the hill, out of view of 13th-century pirates. Explore the cemetery, but remember that cemeteries are sacred and treasured places (as is clear by the abundance of fresh flowers). Ponder the B&W photos of grandparents past. Q.R.P. is *Qui Riposa in Pace* (a.k.a. R.I.P.). Rich families had their own little tomb buildings. Climb to the very summit—the castle's keep, or place of last refuge. Priests are buried in a line of graves closest to the sea, but facing inland—the town's holy sanctuary high on the hillside (above the road, hiding behind trees). Each Cinque Terre town has a lofty sanctuary, dedicated to Mary and dear to the village hearts. From here, your tour's over—any trail leads you back into town.

ACTIVITIES

Beaches—Monterosso's beaches, immediately in front of the train station, are easily the Cinque Terre's best and most crowded. This town is a sandy resort with everything rentable: lounge chairs, umbrellas, and paddleboats. Beaches are free only where you see no umbrellas. It's often worth the euros to enjoy a private beach. The local hidden beach (free and generally less crowded) is tucked away under Il Casello restaurant at the east end of town (near Vernazza trailhead).

Kayaks—Bagni Stella Marina, next to the parking lot in the new town (train station side), rents kayaks (€8/hr, tel. 0187-817-209).

Shuttle Buses for High-Country Hikes—Monterosso's bus service (described in "Helpful Hints," above) continues beyond the town limits. They do the heavy lifting, taking hikers to interesting trailheads in the nearby hills. They also go to Colle di Gritta, where you can hike back down to Monterosso via the Sanctuary of Soviore (1 hr, easy) or to Levanto via Punta Mesco (2.5 hrs, strenuous). Rides cost €1.50 (free with Cinque Terre Card, pick up schedule from park office). For hiking details, ask at either park info booth (at the train station or Piazza Garibaldi).

NIGHTLIFE

Wander up to **Il Casello** for nightlife with a sea view. It's the best on-the-beach drinking spot—inexpensive and hip—with a creative and fun drink list. Built in about 1870 as the town's first train station, it overlooks the beach on the road toward Vernazza, with outdoor tables sandwiched between the old-town beaches. It's also a great place for a salad or sandwich during the day (Wed–Mon 10:30–3:00, closed Tue and Oct–March, shorter hours outside June–Aug, tel. 0187-818-330).

A Ca' du Sciensa (The House of Sciensa) fills an old mansion with an antique dumbwaiter—a remnant from the days when servants toiled downstairs while the big shots wined and dined up top. This classy-yet-laid-back pub offers breezy square seating, bar action on the ground level, an intimate lounge upstairs, and discreet balconies overlooking the square to share with your best travel buddy. It's a good place for light meals (until 23:00) and plenty of drinks. Luca and Diego encourage you to wander around the place and enjoy the old Cinque Terre photo collection (daily 10:30–24:00, closed Wed off-season, Piazza Garibaldi 17, tel. 0187-818-233).

Enoteca Eliseo, the first wine bar in town, comes with operatic ambience. Eliseo and his wife Mary love music and wine. You can select a fine bottle from their shop shelf, and for €6 extra, enjoy it and the village action from their cozy tables. They serve munchies and light snacks. Wines sold by the glass *(bicchiere)* are posted (closed Tue in winter, Piazza Matteotti 3, a few blocks inland behind church, tel. 0187-817-308).

BarDavi showcases owners Daniele's and Valeria's stylish knack for delicious entertainment. Each day after 17:00, they offer an amazing "cocktails *con tapas*" deal: Buy a €6 drink or glass of wine and get a light meal's worth of good, local appetizers for free (daily 7:30–22:00, closed Tue Sept–June, under the arch on main drag, Via Roma 34, tel. 0187-817-019).

Fast Bar, where young travelers and night owls gather, is located on Via Roma in the old town. Customers mix travel tales with big, cold beers, and the crowd gets noisier as the night rolls on (sandwiches and snacks served until midnight, open nightly until 2:00, closed Thu Oct–May).

SLEEPING

(€1 = about $1.20, country code: 39)
Monterosso al Mare, the most beach-resorty of the five Cinque Terre towns, offers maximum comfort and ease. The TI (Proloco) just outside the train station can give you a list of €30–35 per-person double rooms. You can also check with The Net Internet café in town (see page 286). Room-hawkers at the train station offer poor-quality rooms and are a last resort.

Recommended hotels are listed for the old town and the new town, with a convent-run place in between. Prices are promised through 2006 (see "New Ethic" on page 262). To locate the hotels, see the map on page 287. To get to the old town from the station, exit left, walk along the waterfront, and go through the tunnel.

In the Old Town

$$$ Hotel Villa Steno is lovingly managed and features great view balconies, private gardens off some rooms, air-conditioning, and the friendly help of English-speaking Matteo and his wife Carla.

Of their 16 rooms, 12 have view balconies (Sb-€90, Db-€140, Tb-€160, Qb-€180, includes hearty buffet breakfast, €10 discount through 2006 if you pay cash and show this book, Internet, self-service laundry for guests, Via Roma 109, tel. 0187-817-028 or 0187-818-336, fax 0187-817-354, www.pasini.com, steno@pasini.com). It's a 10-minute hike (or €7 taxi ride) from the train station to the top of the old town. Readers get a free Cinque Terre info packet and a glass of the local sweet wine, *sciacchetrà,* when they check in—ask for it. They have my Cinque Terre public television show and other Italy episodes for their lobby DVD player. The Steno has a tiny parking lot (free, but call to reserve a spot).

$$$ **Albergo Pasquale** is a modern, comfortable place, run by the same family that owns Hotel Villa Steno (see above). It's just a few steps from the beach, boat dock, tunnel entrance (to new town), and train tracks. Noise is not a problem (same prices, welcome drink, and Italy DVD as Villa Steno, above; air-con, all rooms with sea view, Via Fegina 8, tel. 0187-817-550 or 0187-817-477, fax 0187-817-056, pasquale@pasini.com, Felicita and Marco speak English).

$$$ Two places, next door to each other on a quiet street, both push half-pension by bloating their B&B prices and offering dinner for just a few euros more. The fancy **Albergo degli Amici** has 40 modern rooms (Db-€100–137, includes breakfast, Db with optional half-pension-€150; no views from rooms, but peaceful above-it-all view garden with "sun beds"—lawn chairs with movable sun shades; Via Buranco 36, tel. 0187-817-544, fax 0187-817-424, www.hotelamici.it, amici@cinqueterre.it). The less-fancy **Albergo Marina** has 23 decent rooms and a garden with lemon trees (Db-€108–131, €140 with optional dinner July–Aug, 5 percent discount with cash, elevator, air-con; free mountain bike, kayak, and snorkel equipment; next door at Via Buranco 40, tel. & fax 0187-817-242 or 0187-817-613, www.hotelmarinacinqueterre.it, marina@cinqueterre.it). To get there from the old-town harbor, go to the left of the arcaded building with the bell tower, walk a block, and turn left.

$$$ **Hotel la Colonnina,** a comfy, modern place with big rooms, is on a sleepy side street (Db-€90–120, can be higher on weekends July–Aug, cash only, breakfast extra, air-con, elevator, rooftop terrace, garden, Via Zuecca 6, tel. 0187-817-439, fax 0187-817788, www.lacolonninacinqueterre.it, info@lacolonninacinqueterre.it) The hotel is in the old town by the train tracks, directly behind the statue of Garibaldi (take street to left of A Ca' du Sciensa one block up, hotel is to the right).

$$ **Hotel Souvenir** is Monterosso's cash-only backpacker's hotel. It has two buildings, each utilitarian but comfortable (one more stark than the other). The first is for students (S-€25, Sb-€30,

D-€50, Db-€60, T-€75, no breakfast); the other one is nicer and pricier, with a lounge and pleasant, leafy courtyard (Sb-€40, Db-€80, Tb-€120, includes breakfast). Walk three blocks inland from the main old-town square to Via Gioberti 24 (tel. 0187-817-822, tel. & fax 0187-817-595, www.monterossonet.com, hotel_souvenir @yahoo.com).

$ **Casa Manuel B&B** is a ramshackle place run by a ramshackle artist with five big, basic youth-hostel-type rooms and a good view (€25 per person in Sb, Db, and Tb; family and student deals, cash only, includes self-serve breakfast, Manuel has an honor-system bar of beer and wine, €5/liter; in old town, up stepped lane, behind church at top of town, Via San Martino 39; to reserve, contact Kate at kate@fishnet.it or through The Net Internet café—see "Helpful Hints," above).

Between the Old and New Towns

$$ **Convento dei Cappuccini,** which might close in 2006, rents 16 spartan rooms on the hill that divides the old and new parts of Monterosso. The terrace, overlooking the garden, has a tremendous panoramic view. Meals are served in a stark old refectory, surrounded by musty, faith-bolstering paintings. It's a long, steep, 15-minute hike from the station (follow the signs from just before the tunnel). You can taxi to within 200 yards (the cemetery) for €7. Rooms, named for monks, come with killer views, a 23:00 curfew, and angelic twin beds. The gardens, cloisters, views, and rustic elegance all contribute to the dreamy-retreat atmosphere Sergio and Jerri Redaelli like to give their guests (S-€35, D-€70, Db-€80, all twin beds, includes breakfast, occasional optional dinners served at 19:30-€15, reserve by leaving credit card number but pay cash, 2-night minimum, parking about 300 yards from convent-€8/day, tel. 0187-817-531, monterosso.convento@libero.it).

In the New Town

To reach the following listings, turn right as you leave the station. The first two are on the beach, with great views.

$$$ **Hotel Baia** (by-yah), overlooking the beach near the station, has appealing, high-ceilinged rooms, darkly-painted hallways, and impersonal staff. Of the hotel's 28 rooms, the best little two-chair view balconies are on top floors. No matter what, request a view room, since it's the same price (Db-€100–150, includes breakfast, slow elevator, Via Fegina 88, tel. 0187-817-512, fax 0187-818-322, www.baiahotel.it, info@baiahotel.it).

$$$ **Pensione Agavi** has 10 bright, airy, tranquil, and quiet rooms overlooking the beach near the big rock—this is not a place to party (S-€35, Sb-€60, D-€80, Db-€100, couples preferred, no breakfast, refrigerators, turn left out of station to Fegina 30,

tel. 0187-817-171, fax 0187-818-264, mobile 333-697-4071, www
.paginegialle.it/hotelagavi, agavi@libero.it, spunky Hillary speaks
English).

$$$ Hotel Punta Mesco has 17 quiet, modern rooms without
views, but 10 have little terraces (Db-€120, includes breakfast, 5
percent discount with cash, air-con, free bike loan, free parking;
exit right from station, take first right to Via Molinelli 35; tel. & fax
0187-817-495, www.hotelpuntamesco.it, info@hotelpuntamesco.it).

EATING

Ristorante Belvedere is *the* place for a good-value meal on the har-
borfront. Their *amfora bel vedere*—mixed seafood stew—is huge,
and can easily be shared by up to four (€43/2 people, extra for
antipasti or pasta). It's energetically run by Fredrico and Roberto
(Wed–Mon 12:00–14:30 & 19:00–22:00, closed Tue off-season, on
the harbor in the old town, tel. 0187-817-033).

L'Alta Marea offers a specialty fish ravioli, the catch of the
day, and huge crocks of fresh, steamed mussels. The young chef
Marco cooks with charisma, while his wife Anna takes good care
of the guests (Thu–Tue 12:00–15:00 & 18:30–22:00, open later in
summer, closed Wed, Via Roma 54, tel. 0187-817-170). This place
is quieter, buried in old town two blocks off the beach, and has
covered tables out front for people-watching.

Nearby, spendier **Ciak** is ideally located on the main drag
at the bottom of Via Roma. They are known for their three huge
terra-cotta crocks for two, crammed with the day's catch and
either accompanied by risotto or spaghetti, or swimming in a soup
(zuppa). Another popular choice is the seafood antipasto Lampara.
Stroll a couple of paces past the outdoor tables up Via Roma to see
what Ciak's got on the stove (Thu–Tue 12:00–14:00 & 19:00–21:30,
closed Wed, tel 0187-817-014).

Via Venti is a mod little trattoria, buried on an alley deep in the
heart of the old town, where Papa Ettore creates imaginative seafood
dishes using the day's catch and freshly-made pasta. Son Michele and
Ilaria serve up delicate and savory *gnocchi* (tiny potato dumplings) with
crab sauce, tender ravioli stuffed with fresh fish in a swordfish sauce,
and unusual vegetarian items such as *risotto alle fragole* (strawberry
risotto). From Piazza C. Colombo at the bottom of Via Roma, head
down Via XX Settembre and follow it to the end to #32 (Wed–Mon
11:30–14:30 & 18:30–22:00, closed Tue, tel. 0187-818-347).

Miky is packed with locals who know their seafood and want
to eat in a classy environment, but don't want to spend a fortune. For
great food, this could be the best value in the entire Cinque Terre.
It's clearly a family operation: Miky (dad), Simonetta (mom), and
charming Sara (the daughter) all work hard. All their pasta is "pizza

pasta"—cooked normally but finished in a bowl that's encased in a thin pizza crust. They cook the concoction in a wood-fire oven to keep in the aroma. This place also has the best wine list in the area, with most available by the glass if you ask (pastas-€10, *secondi*-€18, sweets-€5, Wed–Mon 12:00–15:00 & 19:00–23:00, closed Tue, reservations wise in summer, in the new town, 100 yards north of train station at Via Fegina 104, tel. 0187-817-608).

Light Meals, Take-Out Food, and Breakfast

Lots of shops and bakeries sell pizza and focaccia for an easy picnic at the beach or on the trail. At **Il Frantoio,** Simone makes tasty pizza to go or to munch perched on a stool (daily 9:00–14:00 & 16:00–20:00 but closed Thu in winter, Via Gioberti 1, just off Via Roma, tel. 0187-818-333). For a fun, light meal on a terrace overlooking the beach, try **Il Casello** (see "Nightlife," page 290).

BarDavi serves the best breakfast in town. For a light lunch or dinner, try their great €10 "international" buffet, or dine à la carte (see page 291).

TRANSPORTATION CONNECTIONS

Trains

The five towns of the Cinque Terre are on a pokey, milk-run train line (described in "Getting Around the Cinque Terre," page 255). Hourly trains connect each town with the others, La Spezia, and Genoa. While a few of these local trains go to more distant points (Milan or Pisa), it's much faster to change in La Spezia or Monterosso to a bigger train. Local train info tel. 0187-817-458.

From La Spezia by Train to: Rome (10/day, 4 hrs), **Pisa** (hrly, 1 hr, direction: Livorno, Rome, Salerno, Naples, etc.), **Viareggio** (3–4/hr, 30–60 min), **Florence** (nearly hrly, 2.5 hrs, change in Pisa), **Milan** (hrly, 3 hrs direct or 4 hrs with change in Genoa), **Venice** (2/day, 6 hrs, with change in Pisa and Florence; or 2/day, 6 hrs, with change in Milan; or 1 direct/day, in summer only).

From Monterosso by Train to: Venice (2/day, 5.5 hrs, with change in Florence and Pisa; or 2/day, 6 hrs, with change in Milan), **Milan** (11/day, 3 hrs, with change in Genoa), **Genoa** (hrly, 1.25 hrs), **Turin** (7/day, 3 hrs), **Pisa** (8/day, 1.5 hrs), **Sestri Levante** (hrly, 15 min, most trains to Genoa stop here), **La Spezia** (nearly hrly, 20 min), **Levanto** (nearly hrly, 6 min).

Driving in the Cinque Terre

Milan to the Cinque Terre (130 miles): Drivers speed south by autostrada A7 from Milan, skirt Genoa, and drive some of Italy's most scenic and impressive freeways toward the port of La Spezia (A12). The road via the city of Parma is 30 miles longer and less scenic, but faster.

Each Cinque Terre town has a parking lot and a shuttle bus to get you into town (except Corniglia, where parking is free and easy). Monterosso's guarded beachfront lot fills up only in August and on weekends (€12/day).

For Monterosso or Vernazza, exit the autostrada at Uscita (exit) Carrodano, west of La Spezia. Monterosso is 30 minutes from the autostrada. Note that three miles above Monterosso, a fork directs you to *Centro Storico* (a dead-end with no parking, only for Villa Steno clients) or Fegina (where you'll find cheap and easy parking for the town). Vernazza is 45 minutes from the autostrada. The drive down to Vernazza is scenic, narrow, and scary. On busy weekends and in July and August, Vernazza fills up, and police at the top of town will deny entry to anyone without a hotel reservation. It's smart to have a confirmation in hand. If you don't, insist (politely) that they allow you to enter—but only if you actually have a room reserved (the police might call your hotel to check your story). To drive to Riomaggiore, Corniglia, or Manarola, leave the freeway at La Spezia.

You can park your car near the train stations in La Spezia or Levanto (the first town past Monterosso; see parking specifics on page 298). Confirm that parking is OK and leave nothing inside to steal. In La Spezia, cheap parking is a few blocks west of the station at the end of Via XV Giugno in Piazza d'Armi and along Viale Amendola.

RIVIERA TOWNS
near the CINQUE TERRE

The Cinque Terre is tops, but several towns to the north have a breezy beauty and more beaches. Towns to the south offer a mix of marble, trains, and yachts.

Levanto, the northern gateway to the Cinque Terre, has a long beach and a scenic, strenuous two-hour trail to Monterosso. Sestri Levante, on a narrow peninsula flanked by two beaches, is for sun-seekers. Santa Margherita Ligure is more of a real town, with actual sights, beaches, and easy connections with Portofino by trail, bus, or boat. All three towns are a straight shot to the Cinque Terre by train.

South of the Cinque Terre, you'll likely pass through (don't stay unless desperate) the work-a-day town of La Spezia, the southern gateway to the Cinque Terre. Carrara is a quickie for marble-lovers who are driving between Pisa and La Spezia. The picturesque village of Portovenere, near La Spezia, has scenic boat connections with Cinque Terre towns.

North of the Cinque Terre

Levanto

Graced with a long, sandy beach, Levanto is packed in summer. The rest of the year, it's just a small, sleepy town, with less colorful charm and fewer tourists than the Cinque Terre. With quick connections to Monterosso (6 min by train), Levanto makes a decent home base if you can't snare a room in the Cinque Terre.

Levanto has a new section (gridded street plan) and a twisty

Riviera Towns near the Cinque Terre

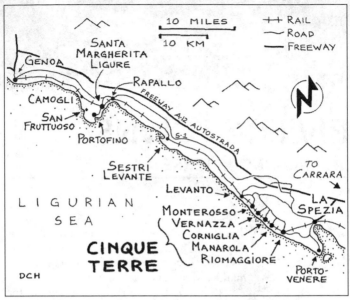

old town (bisected by a modern street), plus a few pedestrian streets and a castle (not open). From Levanto, you can take a no-wimps-allowed hike to Monterosso (2.5 hrs) or hop a boat to Cinque Terre towns and beyond.

ORIENTATION

Tourist Information: The TI is on Piazza Mazzini (Mon–Sat 9:00–13:00 & 14:30–19:00, Sun 9:30–12:30 & 16:00–19:00, shorter hours in winter, tel. 0187-808-125, www.comune.levanto.sp.it).

Arrival by Train or Car: It's a 10-minute walk from the Levanto train station to the TI in town (head down stairs in front of station, turn right, cross bridge, then follow Corso Roma to Piazza Mazzini).

Drivers can find cheap day parking in lots on either side of the train station, but because you have to pay each day (at the machines), long-term parking is difficult. The lots at Piazza Mazzini and to the west of the TI—while sometimes free during the off-season (Nov–April)—are expensive and geared toward long-term parking in high season. A better summer option is the lot near the hospital on the way into town (north of the church), which can be free during high season. Parking is always in flux, so confirm rates and availability with the TI.

Levanto

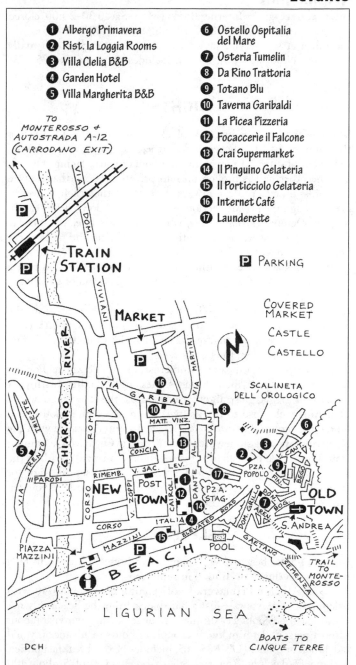

1. Albergo Primavera
2. Rist. la Loggia Rooms
3. Villa Clelia B&B
4. Garden Hotel
5. Villa Margherita B&B
6. Ostello Ospitalia del Mare
7. Osteria Tumelin
8. Da Rino Trattoria
9. Totano Blu
10. Taverna Garibaldi
11. La Picea Pizzeria
12. Focaccerìe il Falcone
13. Crai Supermarket
14. Il Pinguino Gelateria
15. Il Porticciolo Gelateria
16. Internet Café
17. Launderette

P PARKING

TO MONTEROSSO & AUTOSTRADA A-12 (CARRODANO EXIT)

TRAIN STATION

MARKET

COVERED MARKET
CASTLE
CASTELLO

SCALINETA DELL' OROLOGICO

VIA DOM.
VIA VIVIANI
VIA MARTIRI
VIA GARIBALDI
VIA ROMA
VIA TRENTO TRIESTE
GHIARARO RIVER
VIA PARODI

MATT. VINZ.
CONCIA
RIMEMB.
CORSO
V. NOPPI
V. JAC.
LEV.
CAIROLI
ITALIA
DANTE ALI.
V. GUAN.

NEW TOWN
POST TOWN
PZA. STAG.
PZA. POPOLO

OLD TOWN

S. ANDREA

CANT.
DOM. FIN.
BEGO
DOM. GRILLO
AREN.
BOG.
GAETANO SEMENZA

PIAZZA MAZZINI

MAZZINI

ELEVATED ROAD

POOL

B E A C H

TRAIL TO MONTEROSSO

L I G U R I A N   S E A

BOATS TO CINQUE TERRE

DCH

Helpful Hints

Internet Access: Try Internet Buffet (Mon–Sat 10:30–20:00, closed Sun, €3.60/30 min, Via Garibaldi 68, tel. 0187-804-025).

Laundry: A self-service laundry is at Piazza Staglieno 38 (daily 9:00–19:00, €5 wash, €5 dry, includes soap, mobile 335-653-5964).

SIGHTS

Beach—The beach is just two blocks away from the TI. During the summer, half the beach is free (the side closest to boathouse, to the left of Casinò Lido swimming pool as you're facing the sea), and the other half is broken up into private sections that require an admission fee. You can always stroll along the beach, however, even through the private sections—just don't sit down. Off-season, roughly October through May, when the sea is free, you can lay your towel anywhere on the entire beach. Facing the harbor, the boat dock is to your far left and the diving center is at your far right (rental boats available at either place in summer). You can rent a kayak or canoe on the beach, just below the east end of the Piazza Mazzini parking lot.

Old Town and Trailhead—The old town, several blocks from the TI and beach, clusters around Piazza del Popolo. Until 15 years ago, the town open-air market was held at the 13th-century loggia in the square. Explore the back streets.

To get to the trailhead to Monterosso: From Piazza del Popolo, head uphill to the striped church, Chiesa di S. Andrea (with your back to the loggia, go straight ahead—across the square and up Via Don Emanuele Toso to the church). From the church courtyard, follow the sign to the *castello* (castle), go around the castle with the blue windows and stonework, and turn left. Or, if you're coming from the seaside promenade (Via Gaetano Semenza), head up the stairs and follow the signs to the *castello*. You'll see the sign for Punta Mesco, the rugged tip of the peninsula. From here you can hike up to Monterosso (2.5 hrs).

SLEEPING

In this popular beach town, a number of hotels want you to take half-pension (lunch or dinner) in summer.

$$$ Albergo Primavera has 17 comfortable rooms—10 with balconies but no views—just a half-block from the beach. Owner Carlo is a good cook. Try dining here once during your visit (about €10 per person); let him know a couple of hours in advance if you'd like lunch or dinner (Db-€85–105, includes hearty breakfast buffet, parking-€5/day July–Aug, free off-season, Via Cairoli 5, about 100

Sleep Code

(€1 = about $1.20, country code: 39)
S = Single, **D** = Double/Twin, **T** = Triple, **Q** = Quad, **b** = bathroom, **s** = shower only. Unless otherwise noted, credit cards are accepted, English is spoken, and breakfast is included.

To help you sort easily through these listings, I've divided the rooms into three categories based on the price for a standard double room with bath:

$$$ **Higher Priced**—Most rooms €100 or more.
$$ **Moderately Priced**—Most rooms between €50–100.
$ **Lower Priced**—Most rooms €50 or less.

---

yards from the beach, tel. 0187-808-023, fax 0187-801-588, www .primaverahotel.com, info@primaverahotel.com, friendly Carlo and Daniela speak a little English).

$$$ Villa Margherita B&B is 300 yards out of town, but the shady gardens, seven characteristic tiled rooms (some with terraces), and tranquility are worth the walk (Db-€80–115, Tb-€85–130, elevator, free Internet in lobby, free parking, 10-min walk to town, 5-min walk to train station, free shuttle service from station if you tell them when you'll arrive, Via Trento e Trieste 31, tel. & fax 0187-807-212, mobile 328-842-6934, www.levanto.net, info@villamargherita.net). They also have apartments (some are central) for two to six people, rentable by the week.

$$ Ristorante la Loggia has four pleasant rooms perched above the old loggia on Piazza del Popolo (Db-€55–70, air-con, request balcony, quieter rooms in back, apartment available, Piazza del Popolo 7, tel. & fax 0187-808-107, www.tigulliovino.it /ristorantelaloggia.htm).

$$ Villa Clelia B&B has six peaceful, air-conditioned rooms (named for the winds—*scirocco*, *maestrale*, and so on) with minifridges and terraces in a garden courtyard just 50 yards from the sea (Db-€75–85, with loggia on your left it's straight ahead at Piazza da Passano 1, tel. 0187-808-195, mobile 328-797-6403, villa_clelia@libero.it). They also have three central apartments that each sleep up to four (€90/night).

$$ Garden Hotel offers 17 tidy, bright rooms, all with balconies (but no real views due to the seawall), a block from the beach on busy Corso Italia (Sb-€60–70, Db-€80-98, air-con, free Internet in lobby, free parking but not on-site—can unload bags and then park near the station, Corso Italia 6, tel. 0187-808-173, fax 0187-803-652, www.nuovogarden.com, francesca@nuovogarden.com).

$$ Erba Persa Agriturismo, run by friendly Grazio Lizza and her gardener husband, is about a 10-minute walk from the train station (Db-€35, Db with balcony and view-€70, buffet breakfast, 21 Via N. S. della Guardia, tel. 0187-801-376, fax 0187-801-376, erbapersa@aliceposta.it).

Hostel: **$ Ostello Ospitalia del Mare** has 62 beds, airy rooms, Internet access, an elevator, and a terrace in a well-constructed building a few steps from the old town (beds-€20–29 in 2-, 4-, 6-, and 8-bed rooms with private bath, includes breakfast and sheets, non-members welcome, co-ed unless you strenuously object, no curfew, office hours daily April–Sept 8:00–12:00 & 16:00–19:00, later weekend nights, Oct–March 10:00–12:00 & 16:00–18:00, Via San Nicolo 1, tel. 0187-802-562, fax 0187-803-696, www .ospitaliadelmare.it, ospitalia@libero.it).

EATING

Osteria Tumelin is more expensive than other options, but has great fresh seafood and ambience (Fri–Wed 12:00–14:30 & 19:00–23:30, closed Thu in winter, Via d. Grillo 32, across street from loggia, reservations recommended in summer, tel. 0187-808-379).

Da Rino, a small trattoria on a quiet pedestrian street, dishes up reasonably priced, fresh seafood and homemade Ligurian specialties prepared with care, including grilled *totani* (squid), *pansotti con salsa di noci* (cheese ravioli with walnut sauce), and *trofie al pesto* (local pasta with pesto sauce). Dine indoors, or at one of the few outdoor tables. With your back to the sea, turn right off Via Dante onto Via Garibaldi and follow the corner around to the right (daily mid-March–Oct 19:30–22:00, closed Nov–mid-March, Via Garibaldi 10, mobile 328-3890-350).

La Loggia, next to the old loggia, makes fine *gnocchi* with saffron sauce, *gattafini* (Levanto-style fritters filled with herbs and cheese), and daily fish specials served in a homey, wood-paneled dining room or on a little terrace overlooking the square (in summer Thu–Tue 19:30–22:00, closed Wed, in off-season daily 12:30–14:00 & 19:30–22:00, Piazza del Popolo 7, tel. 0187-080-107).

Totano Blu, in the old town, is a fine bet for affordable regional cuisine and wood-fired pizza (Fri–Wed 12:00–14:00 & 19:00–22:00, Thu 19:00–22:00, take out available, Via Molinelli 10/12, tel. 0187-808-714).

Taverna Garibaldi is a good-value, cozy place on the most characteristic street in Levanto, serving focaccia with various toppings, made-to-order *farinata* (savory chickpea crêpe), salads, and light meals (daily in summer 19:30–23:00, closed Tue Sept–June, Via Garibaldi 57, tel. 0187-808-098).

La Picea serves up wood-fired pizzas to go (Tue–Sun 11:30–14:30 & 17:00–21:30, closed Mon, dinner only off-season, Via della Concia 18, on the corner of Via Varego and Via della Concia behind the soccer field, tel. 0187-802-063).

Focaccerìe, rosticcerìe, and delis with take-out pasta abound on Via D. Alighieri. *Focaccerìe* **il Falcone** has a great selection of focaccia with different toppings (daily June–Sept 9:30–20:00, shorter hours off-season, Via Cairoli 19, tel. 0187-807-370).

For more picnic fare, try Levanto's modern, covered *mercato* (fish and produce market, Mon–Sat 8:00–13:00, closed Sun, between train station and TI, on Via del Mercato). On Wednesday morning, an **open-air market,** with clothes, shoes, and housewares, fills the street in front of the *mercato.* The **Crai supermarket** is on Via del Municpio, just off Via Jacopo da Levanto (Mon–Sat 8:00–13:00 & 17:00–20:00, Sun 8:00–13:00). Piazza C. Colombo, with its benches and sea view, makes an excellent picnic spot. For a shadier setting, lay out your spread on a bench in the grassy park at Piazza Staglieno.

For dessert, sample **Il Pinguino Gelateria** on Piazza Staglieno 2 (daily until late), or **Il Porticciolo Gelateria** at the end of Via Cairoli at Piazzetta Marina (daily in summer, closed Mon Sept–May, tel. 0187-800-954).

TRANSPORTATION CONNECTIONS

To get from Levanto to the Cinque Terre, take the **train** (nearly hrly, 6 min to Monterosso) or the **boat** (roughly 1–2/day March–Oct, more in summer, none Nov–Feb, stops at every Cinque Terre town except Corniglia before heading to Portovenere; €4.50 one-way to Monterosso, or €16 for half-day pass to Portovenere—departing Levanto around 14:30, with 1-hr stop before return to Levanto; as much as €22 for all-day weekend pass to Portovenere; 1 return boat/day from Portovenere departing around 17:00; pick up boat schedule and price sheet from TI or boat dock, or call tel. 0187-732-987 or 0187-777-727).

Sestri Levante

This peninsular town is squeezed as skinny as a hot dog between its two beaches. The pedestrian-friendly Corso Colombo, which runs down the middle of the peninsula, is lined with shops selling take-away pizza, pastries, and beach paraphernalia.

Hans Christian Andersen enjoyed his visit here in the mid-1800s, writing, "What a fabulous evening I spent in Sestri Levante!" One of the bays—Baia delle Favole—is named in his honor (*favole* means fairy tale). The last week of May is a street festival, culminating in a ceremony for locals who write the best fairy tales (four prizes for four age groups, from pre-kindergarten to adult). The "Oscar" awards are little mermaids. The small mermaid curled on the edge of the fountain (behind the TI) is another nod to the beloved Danish storyteller.

ORIENTATION

Tourist Information: From the train station, it's a five-minute walk to the TI to get a map (May–Sept Mon–Sat 9:30–12:30 & 15:00–19:30, Sun 9:30–12:30 & 16:30–19:30, Oct–April closes at 17:30 and on Sun; go straight out of station on Via Roma, turn left at fountain in park, TI at next square—Piazza S. Antonio 10; tel. 0185-457-011). No luggage storage is available at the station. **Market day** is Saturday at Piazza Aldo Moro (8:00–13:00).

ACTIVITIES

Stroll the Town—From the TI, take Corso Colombo (to the left of Bermuda Bar, eventually turns into Via XXV Aprile), which runs up the peninsula. Follow this street—lively with shops and eateries—until nearly the end (about 5 min). Just before you get to the large white church at the end, turn off for either beach (free Silenzio beach is on your left; see below). Or head uphill behind the church. You'll pass the evocative arches of a ruined chapel (bombed during World War II, and left as a memorial). Continue a few minutes farther to the Hotel Castelli and consider a drink at their view café (so-so view, reasonably priced drinks, café is at end of parking lot to your right). The rocky, forested bluff at the end of the town's peninsula is actually the huge, private backyard of this fancy hotel.

Beaches—These are named after the bays (*baia*) they border. The bigger beach, Baia delle Favole, is divided up much of the year (May–Sept) into sections that you pay to enter. The fees, which can soar up to €28 per day in August (no hourly rate), generally include chairs, umbrellas, and fewer crowds. There are several small free sections: at the ends and in the middle (look for *libere* signs, and ask "*Gratis?*" to make sure it's free). For less-expensive sections of beach (where you can rent less than the works), ask for *spiaggia libera attrezzata* (spee-AH-jah LEE-behr-ah ah-treh-ZAHT-tah). Bocce courts, boat rentals, sailing lessons, and the other usual beach-town activities are clustered along this *baia*.

The town's other beach, Baia del Silenzio, is narrow, virtually all free, and packed, providing a good chance to see Italian families at play. There isn't much more to do here than unroll a beach towel and join in. At the far end of Baia del Silenzio is Citto Beach bar, offering front-row seats of bay views (daily April–Oct 10:00–24:00, closed Nov–April).

SLEEPING

(€1 = about $1.20, country code: 39)

$$$ Hotel Due Mari, located in an old Genoese palazzo, has three stars, 65 fine rooms, and a rooftop terrace with a super view of both beaches. Ideally, reserve well in advance (Db-€110–140 depending on view and type of room, Db with half-pension required July–Aug-€174–180, includes buffet breakfast, some air-con, elevator, garden, outdoor and heated indoor seawater swimming pools, parking-€10/day, open off-season, take Corso Colombo to the end, hotel is behind church in Piazza Matteotti—take either alleyway flanking church, Vico del Coro 18, tel. 0185-42695, fax 0185-42698, www.duemarihotel.it, info@duemarihotel.it).

$$$ Hotel Helvetia, overlooking Baia del Silenzio, is another good three-star bet, with 21 bright rooms, a large sun terrace, and a peaceful atmosphere (Db-€145–160 depending on view/balcony, includes breakfast, air-con, elevator, off-site parking-€10/day with free shuttle service, from Corso Colombo turn left on Palestro and angle left at square, Via Cappuccini 43, tel. 0185-41175, fax 0185-457-216, www.hotelhelvetia.it, helvetia@hotelhelvetia.it).

$$$ Hotel Genova, run by the Bertoni family, is a shipshape hotel with 18 shiny-clean, bright, and cheery rooms, a rooftop sundeck, free loaner bikes, air-conditioning, elevator, and a good location just two blocks from Baia delle Favole (Sb-€48–60, Db-€68–110, Tb-€85–140, prices depend on season, includes buffet breakfast, ask for quieter room in back, elevator, parking available, Viale Mazzini 126, tel. 0185-41057, fax 0185-457-213, www.hotelristorantegenova.it, info@hotelristorantegenova.it).

$$ Hotel Elisabetta, less central, has 38 plain rooms on a busy street at the end of Baia delle Favole, a block from the beach (D-€65–75, Db-€75–90, prices depend on season, half-pension available but not required, double-paned windows, air-con, free parking; walk straight out of station, then turn right at park, 12-min walk to Via Novara 7; tel. 0185-41128, fax 0185-487-206, albergoelisabetta@libero.it, leetle English spoken).

$$ Villa Jolanda is a homey, kid-friendly, basic *pensione* with 17 simple rooms, five with little balconies but no views, all with new bathrooms, two apartments, and a garden courtyard with a small swimming pool—perfect for families on a budget (Db-€80, Qb-€120, free parking, Via Pozzetto 15, located near Baia del Silenzio, take alley just to the right of the church on Piazza Matteotti, tel. 0185-41354, www.villaiolanda.com, info@villaiolanda.com).

EATING

Everything I've listed is on classic Via XXV Aprile, which also abounds with *focaccerìe*, take-out pizza by the slice, and little grocery shops. Assemble a picnic or try one of the places below.

At **L'Osteria Mattana,** where everyone shares long tables in two dining rooms (second one is in the back, past the wood oven and brazier), you can mix with locals while enjoying traditional cuisine, listed on the chalkboard menus (Tue–Thu 19:30–23:00, Fri–Sun 12:30–14:30 & 19:30–23:00, closed Mon except July–Aug when it's open daily, cash only, take Corso Colombo from TI, turns into Via XXV Aprile, restaurant on right at #36, tel. 0185-457-633).

Polpo Mario is classier but affordable, with a fun people-watching location on the main drag (€30 tasting menu, Tue–Sun 12:15–14:30 & 19:30–22:30, closed Mon, cash only, Via XXV Aprile 163, tel. 0185-480-203).

Trattoria Mainolla offers big salads, focaccia sandwiches, and reasonably-priced pastas near Baia del Silenzio (daily in summer 12:00–15:00 & 19:00–22:00, closed Tue off-season, Via XXV Aprile 187, tel. 0185-42556).

Locals flock to **Gelateria Carrugio** on Via XXV Aprile 48—look for the pink ice-cream cart parked out front (long hours daily in summer, closed Mon off-season, tel. 0185-41370). **Crema e Cioccolato** *gelateria* has lots of flavors to choose from (open daily until late in summer, closed Mon off-season, Via XXV Aprile 126).

For stocking up on picnic supplies, **Co-op supermarket** is just to the left of the train station (Mon–Sat 8:30–13:00 & 15:30–19:30, closed Sun).

TRANSPORTATION CONNECTIONS

Sestri Levante is just 20 to 30 minutes away from Monterosso by **train** (hourly connections with Monterosso, nearly hourly with other Cinque Terre towns).

Boats depart to the Cinque Terre, Portofino, and San Fruttuoso from the dock *(molo)* on the peninsula. Pick up a schedule of departures and excursion options from the TI or ask at your hotel (boats run Easter-Sept; to get to the dock: facing the church in Piazza Matteotti, take the road on the right with the sea on your right, about halfway down Via P. Queriolo, tel. 0185-284-670).

Santa Margherita Ligure

If you need the movie star's Riviera, park your yacht at Portofino. Or you can settle down in the nearby and more personable Santa Margherita Ligure (15 min by bus from Portofino and 1 hr by train from the Cinque Terre). While Portofino's velour allure is tarnished by snobby residents and a nonstop traffic jam in peak season, Santa Margherita tumbles easily downhill from its train station. The town has a fun resort character and a breezy promenade.

On a quick day trip, walk the beach promenade, see the small old town, and catch the bus (or boat) to Portofino to see what all the fuss is about. With more time, Santa Margherita makes a fine overnight stop.

ORIENTATION

Tourist Information: Pick up a map at the TI (Mon–Sat 9:30–12:30 & 15:00–19:30, shorter hours on Sun, in winter Mon–Sat 9:30–12:30 & 14:30–17:30, closed Sun, Via XXV Aprile 2b, tel. 0185-287-485, www.apttigullio.liguria.it).

Arrival by Train: To get to the city center from the station, take the stairs marked *Mare* (sea) down to the harbor. The harbor-front promenade is as wide as the skimpy beach. (The real beaches, which are pebbly, are a 10-min walk farther on, past the port.)

To reach the pedestrian-friendly old town and the TI, take a right at Piazza Veneto (with the roundabout, flags, and park) onto Largo Antonio Giusti. For the TI, angle left on Via XXV Aprile. For the old town (a block off Piazza Veneto), head toward the TI, but turn left on Via Torino, which opens almost immediately onto Piazza Caprera, a square with a church and morning fruit vendors in the midst of pedestrian streets.

Helpful Hints

Internet Access: Internet Point gives readers with this book a free additional 30 minutes in 2006 (€3.50 for the first 30 min, Mon, Wed, and Fri 9:30–12:30 & 15:00–19:00, Tue and Thu 14:00–19:00, Sat 10:00–12:30 & 15:00–19:00, closed Sun, Via Guincheto 39, off Piazza Mazzini, tel. 0185-293-092, run by owners of recommended Hotel Fasce).

Baggage Storage: Day-trippers arriving by train can stash their bags at the station's café/bar (€2.50/day per piece, daily 5:00–20:00).

Local Guide: Raffaella Cecconi communicates clearly in English and knows the region's history better than anyone I've met (€100/half-day, €165/day, tel. & fax 0185-41023, mobile 339-630-9908, info@terra-mare.it).

SELF-GUIDED WALK

Welcome to Santa Margherita Ligure

Explore Santa Margherita Ligure on the following self-guided stroll. To begin, walk out to the tip of the **dock** (from Piazza Libertà). Find the statue of "Santa Margherita virgin martyr." Survey the town from here: the villas dotting the hills, the castle built in the 16th century (closed except for special exhibitions), the exclusive hotels.

Wander along the harborfront (down Corso Marconi) past the castle to the marina and what's left of the town's fishing fleet. The fishing industry survives here, drag-netting octopus, shrimp, and miscellaneous "blue fish"—plus mountains of anchovies attracted to midnight lamps. The fish market (burgundy-colored stalls across the street) wiggles daily at around, oh, maybe 16:00 or so. Residents complain it's easier to buy their locally-caught fresh fish in Milan than here.

Behind the fish market stands a small church, the **Oratory of San Erasmo.** St. Erasmus is the protector of the fishermen. Notice the fine and typically local black-and-white pebble mosaic *(riseu)* in front of the church (with maritime themes). The church is actually an "oratory," where a brotherhood of faithful men who did anonymous good deeds congregated and worshipped. It's decorated with ships and paintings of storms that—thanks to St. Erasmus—the local sailors survived. The huge crosses are carried through town on special religious holidays (church supposedly only open during Mass, but often open at other times, too).

Next, climb the stairway (Via Tre Novembre) to the church that stands overlooking the bay, the **Church of St. James** (Giacomo, daily 7:30–12:00 & 15:00–18:00). Even though this is a secondary church in a secondary town, it's impressively lavish. The region's aristocrats amassed wealth from trade in the 11th to 15th centuries. When Constantinople fell to the Turks, free trade in the Mediterranean stopped and Genovese traders became bankers—making even more money. A popular saying of the day: "Silver is born in America, lives in Spain, and dies in Genoa." Bankers here served Spain's 17th-century royalty and aristocracy, and the accrued wealth paid for a golden age of art. Wander the church, noticing the inlaid marble floors and chapels.

Step out of the church and enjoy the sea view. Then turn left and step into **Durazzo Park** (Parco Comunale Villa Durazzo). This park was an abandoned shambles until 1973, when the city took it over (free, daily 9:00–19:00, until 20:00 July–Aug, until 17:00 in winter). Today it's a delight, with a breezy café enjoyed mostly by locals (closed Mon, open only weekends in winter). The garden has two distinct parts: the carefully-coiffed Italian garden (designed

Santa Margherita Ligure

1. Hotel Laurin
2. Hotel Jolanda
3. Hotel Fasce
4. Hotel Fiorina
5. Hotel Nuova Riviera
6. Nuovo Hotel Garden
7. Hotel Conte Verde
8. Hotel Mediterraneo
9. To Rist. A' Lampara & Via Tommaso Bottaro eateries
10. Ristorante il Nostromo
11. Da Pezzi Ristorante
12. Gelateria Centrale
13. Gelateria il Portico
14. Seghezzo Deli
15. D'Oro Centry Supermarket
16. Internet Café
17. Main Bus Stop for Portofino

to complement the villa's architecture) and the calculatedly wild "English garden" below. The Italian garden is famous for its collection of palm trees—each one is different.

In the park, you'll see **Villa Durazzo.** The building is typical of the region, with some period furniture, several grand pianos, chandeliers, and paintings strewn with cupids on the walls and ceilings. It's not worth the entry fee for most (€5.50, summer Tue–Sun 9:30–18:30, winter Tue–Sun 9:30–16:30, closed Mon, WC opposite entry on left, tel. 0185-205-449). Classical music concerts are held here from May through September (ask at TI or villa ticket desk, or call 340-714-7802).

Your self-guided walk is over. Enjoy the park.

SIGHTS

Church of Santa Margherita (Basilica di Nostra Signora)—The town's main church is textbook Italian Baroque. Its 18th-century facade hides a 17th-century interior. The chapels to the right of the high altar contain religious "floats" used in local festival parades. The wooden groups in the niches higher up used to be part of the processions, too. The altar is typical of 17th-century Ligurian altars—shaped like a boat, with lots of shelf space for candles, flowers, and relics. Remember, Baroque is like theater. After Vatican II in the 1960s, priests faced their flock, turning their back on the old altars rather than the people. For this reason, all over the Catholic world, modern tables serving as post-Vatican II altars stand in front of earlier altars that are no longer the center of attention during the Mass (daily 7:00–12:00 & 15:00–19:00).

Via Palestro—This promenade (a.k.a. *caruggio*—"the big street" in local dialect) is *the* strolling street for window-shopping, people-watching, and studying the characteristic Liberty Style house painting from about 1900. Before 1900, people distinguished their buildings with pastel paint and distinctive door and window frames. Then they decided to get fancy and paint entire exteriors with false balconies, weapons, saints, beautiful women, and 3-D Gothic concentrate.

As you wander from the Church of Santa Margherita inland, pop into the fanciest grocer/deli in town—**Seghezzo** (immediately to the right of the church on Via Cavour, closed Wed). Locals know that this venerable institution has whatever odd ingredient the toughest recipe calls for.

Farther up Via Palestro, you might drop into the traditional old **Panificio** (bakery, open daily) for a slice of fresh focaccia. Saying *"Vorrei un etto di focaccia"* will get you a Ligurian olive-oily, 100-gram, €1 hunk of every kid's favorite beach munchie. Locals claim the best focaccia in Italy is made along this coast.

Markets—Around 16:00 on weekdays, fishing boats dock at the fish market to unload their catch, which is then sold to waiting customers. The market—Mercato del Pesce—is the rust-colored building with arches and columns on Via Marconi, on the harbor, just past the castle. The open-air market, a commotion of clothes and produce, is held every Friday morning on Corso Matteotti (8:00–13:00). Piazza Caprera (facing the main church) daily hosts a few farmers selling their produce from stalls.

Rise of a Resort:
The History of Santa Margherita Ligure

This town, like the entire region (from the border of France to La Spezia), was once ruled by the Republic of Genoa. In the 16th century, when Arab pirates from North Africa plagued the entire coastal area, Genoa had castles built in the towns and lookout towers in the neighboring hills.

Santa Margherita was actually two bickering towns—each with its own bay. In 1800, Napoleon came along, took over the Republic of Genoa, and made it one city—naming it Porto Napoleone. When Napoleon fell in 1815, the town stayed united and took the name of the patron saint of its leading church, Santa Margherita.

In 1850, residents set to work creating a Riviera resort. They imported palm trees from North Africa and paved a fine beach promenade. Santa Margherita and the area around it was studded with fancy villas built by the aristocracy of Genoa (which was controlled by just 35 families). English, Russian, and German aristocrats also discovered the town in the 19th century. Mass tourism only hit in the last generation. Even with the increased crowds, the town decided to stay chic and kept huge developments out. Its neighbor, Rapallo, chose the extreme opposite—giving Italian its word for uncontrolled growth ruining a once-cute town: *Rapallizzazione*.

Beaches—The handiest Santa Margherita beaches are just below the train station. But the best are on the Portofino side of town. Among these, I like "Gio and Rino beach" (just before Covo di Nord Est)—not too expensive, with fun and creative management; and the beach on the Portofino side of Hotel Miramare (free entry, rentable chairs and umbrellas; take bus from either the train station or Piazza V. Veneto, €0.80 each way, buy tickets from kiosk, newsstands, or *tabacchi* shops). Paraggi beach, which is halfway to Portofino (with an easy bus connection, see below), is better than any Santa Margherita beach, but it's very expensive (€50–80/day in July–Aug, €30 in spring and fall, you can't pay by the hour) and generally booked up by big shots from Portofino who have no beach—although there is a skinny stretch that's free (on the Portofino end).

Side-Trip to Portofino

Santa Margherita Ligure, with its aristocratic architecture, hints at old money, whereas Portofino, with its sleek shops, reeks of new money. Fortunately, a few pizzerias, *focaccerìe*, bars, and grocery shops are mixed in with Portofino's jewelry shops, art galleries, and *haute couture* boutiques, making the town affordable. The *piccolo* harbor, classic Italian architecture, and wooded peninsula can even turn glitzy Portofino into an appealing package. For an artsy break, stroll around **Museo del Parco**—a park littered with modern statues just above the harbor (€5, June–Sept daily 10:00–13:30 & 15:00–19:30, closed Oct–May and in bad weather, mobile 337-333-737).

Ever since the Romans founded Portofino for its safe harbor, it has had a strategic value (appreciated by everyone, from Napoleon to the Nazis). In the 1950s, *National Geographic* did a beautiful exposé on the idyllic port, and locals claim that's when the Hollywood elite took note. Liz Taylor and Richard Burton came here annually. During one famous party, Rex Harrison dropped his Oscar into the bay (it was recovered). Ava Gardner came down from her villa each evening for a drink—sporting her famous fur coat. Greta Garbo loved to swim naked in the harbor, not knowing that half the town was watching. Truman Capote called Portofino home. But VIPs were here a century earlier. Nietzsche claimed he strolled with Zarathustra on the path between Portofino and Santa Margherita.

My favorite Portofino plan: Visit for the evening. Leave Santa Margherita on the bus around 17:00, hike the last 20 minutes from Paraggi beach, explore Portofino, splurge for a drink and then dinner on the harborfront, and return to Santa Margherita by bus (confirm late departures).

Portofino's snooty **TI,** downhill from the bus stop, on your right under the portico, reluctantly gives out information (daily in summer 10:30–13:30 & 14:30–19:30, in winter Tue–Sun 10:30–13:30 & 14:30–17:30, closed Mon, Via Roma 35, tel. 0185-269-024). Pick up a free town map and a rudimentary hiking map.

For **hikers,** the best thing about Portofino is leaving it. One option is the well-trodden path that leads out to the lighthouse *(faro)* at the point (20 min, medieval castle en route—Castello Brown, a fence blocks most views until end; lighthouse-€3.50, daily 10:00–19:00, shorter hours in winter, tel. 0185-267-101). You can also take the pedestrian promenade from Portofino to Paraggi (20 min, path starts to the right of yellow-and-gray-striped Divo Martino church—look for clock tower, parallels main road, ends at ritzy beach where it's easy to catch bus back to Santa Margherita Ligure). Or you can hike out to San Fruttuoso Abbey (see below, 2.5 hrs, steep at beginning and end, trail starts on the inland-most point of town in Santa Margherita past Piazza della Libertà; from Portofino, pick up the trailhead at the top of town, near the Carabinieri).

The 11th-century **San Fruttuoso Abbey,** accessible only by foot or boat (from Portofino or Santa Margherita), isn't the main

Near Santa Margherita Ligure

attraction. The intriguing draw is the statue *Christ of the Abyss (Cristo degli Abissi),* 60 feet underwater. For a small fee, boats run from the abbey to the statue, where you can look down to see the arms of Jesus—outstretched, reaching upward (round-trip by boat 15 min; abbey-€4, more for special exhibits, May–Sept daily 10:00–18:00, March–April and Oct–Nov Tue–Sun 10:00–16:00, closed Mon, open Sun only Dec–Feb, tel. 0185-772-703).

Getting to Portofino from Santa Margherita: Portofino is an easy day trip by bus, boat, or foot.

Catch **bus** #82 or #882 from Santa Margherita's train station or at bus stops along the harbor (€0.80 to Paraggi, €1 to Portofino, 2–3/hr, 15 min). Buy tickets at the bar in the station, at Piazza Veneto's bus kiosk (daily 7:05–19:35), from the blue machine in front of the kiosk, or at any shop that displays a *Biglietti Bus* sign. In Portofino, get tickets at the newsstand or from the blue machine next to the bus stop (above newsstand, on right side of piazza as you go uphill, directions in English).

The **boat** makes the trip with more class and without the traffic jams (€4.50 one-way, €7 round-trip, €0.50 more on Sun and holidays; nearly hourly April–Sept 10:15–16:15, May–Sept also at 9:15 on Sun and daily in Aug, in winter only Sun at 10:15 and 14:15, dock is off Piazza Martiri della Libertà, a 2-min walk from Piazza Veneto, call to confirm or pick up schedule from TI, tel. 0185-284-670, www.traghettiportofino.it). The boats run between Rapallo and the San Fruttuoso Abbey, stopping in between at Santa Margherita Ligure and Portofino. (Another boat line runs from Camogli to the Abbey.)

To **hike** the entire distance from Santa Margherita Ligure to Portofino, you have two options: You can follow the sidewalk along the sea (1 hr, 2.5 miles)—although traffic can be noisy and, in a couple of places where the sidewalk ends, even scary. Or, if you're able and ambitious, you can leave Santa Margherita at Via Maragliano and follow the Ligurian symbol trail markers (look for red-and-white stripes—they're not always obvious, sometimes numbered according to the path you're on, usually painted on rocks or walls, especially at junctions). This trail climbs high into the hills. Keep left after Cappelletta delle Gave, then several blocks past a castle you'll drop down into Paraggi, where you'll take the Portofino trail the rest of the way. TIs have maps of the trails in the area.

For a **shorter hike** (20 min) into Portofino, ride bus #82 or #882 only as far as the ritzy Paraggi beach. At the far end of the beach, cross the street and follow the paved trail marked *Pedonali per Portofino* high above the road. Twenty minutes later, you'll enter Portofino at a yellow-and-gray-striped church labeled "Divo Martino"—which I figure means "the divine Martin" and has something to do with Dean Martin giving us all *Volare* (which I couldn't get out of my head for the rest of the day).

SLEEPING

(€1 = about $1.20, country code: 39)
To locate these Santa Margherita Ligure hotels, see map on page 309.

$$$ Hotel Laurin is a slick, air-conditioned, modern place fixated on its harborfront views. All of its 43 rooms face the sea, most have terraces, and there's a heated pool, sundeck, gym, and wet sauna. Though it's a Best Western, it's still family-run (Sb-€88–135, Db-€129–190, prices depend on season, 10 percent discount with this book when you reserve but only if you book directly through hotel, air-con, double-paned windows, elevator, Lungomare G. Marconi 3, past the castle, 15-min walk from station, tel. 0185-289-971, fax 0185-285-709, www.laurinhotel.it, info@laurinhotel.it).

$$$ **Hotel Jolanda** is a solid, well-run hotel with 50 rooms, a revolving door, lavish public spaces, a friendly staff, fine air-conditioned rooms (Db-€130, superior Db-€140, 10 percent discount if you show this book upon arrival, about 20 percent less off season, Internet access available, free use of small weight room, dry and wet sauna cost extra, 2 blocks from TI at Via Luisito Costa 6, tel. 0185-287-512, fax 0185-284-763, www.hoteljolanda .it, desk@hoteljolanda.it). They have 10 free loaner bikes parked at the front door.

$$$ **Hotel Fiorina,** with 44 airy rooms decorated in a light-and-dark color scheme, is on a busy square with quieter rooms in the back. It's family-run with pride and care (Db-€95–125 depending on season, fans in every room, some rooms with balconies, sun terrace but no views, Piazza Mazzini 26, 2 blocks inland from pedestrian Piazza Caprera, tel. 0185-287-517, fax 0185-281-855, www.hotelfiorina.com, fiorinasml@libero.it).

$$$ **Hotel Mediterraneo,** run by the Melegatti family, offers 30 spacious rooms (a few with balconies or sun terraces) in a friendly, comfy-cozy palazzo a five-minute walk from Piazza Veneto (Sb-€71–95, Db-€100–140, Tb-€130–165, closed Jan–March, includes breakfast, sun garden with lounge chairs, free parking, free loaner bikes, take street immediately to the right of Church of Santa Margherita and find hotel straight ahead at Via della Vittoria 18/A, tel. 0185-286-881, fax 0185-286-882, www.sml-mediterraneo.it, info@sml-mediterraneo.it, Finnish Pia speaks English).

$$ At **Hotel Nuova Riviera,** a stately old villa, the Sabini family rents 12 non-smoking rooms (Db-€98, Tb-€122, Qb-€152, these prices promised with this book through 2006, plus 5 percent discount with cash, helpful Cinque Terre info packet—including maps and train schedules—given to guests upon arrival, strict 30-day cancellation policy, fans in every room, some balconies, Internet access, free parking, peaceful garden, 2-room apartment available for longer stays, 10-min walk from station, walking or driving, follow signs to hospital, on Piazza Mazzini see hotel signs, Via Belvedere 10, tel. & fax 0185-287-403, www.nuovariviera .com, info@nuovariviera.com, pleasant daughter Cristina and son Giancarlo speaks English). Cristina also runs a nearby annex (3 nights preferred, D-€65, T-€95, Q-€110, 4 rooms share 2 bathrooms, cash only, tel. 329-982-2689).

$$ **Hotel Fasce** is a hardworking 16-room hotel run enthusiastically by intense Englishwoman Jane Fasce and her husband, Aristide. Jane gets mixed reviews from my readers—some find her helpful, while others find her rules too strict...my advice is to toe the line (Sb-€90, Db-€100, Tb-€126, Qb-€146, a couple rooms have private bathrooms but across the hall, includes English breakfast or

choose from other items from the menu, free happy-hour welcome drink, free round-trip train tickets to Cinque Terre for 3-night stays if you book room online, no-nonsense 21-day cancellation policy, free loaner bikes, English newspapers, rooftop garden, laundry service-€16, parking-€16/day, 10-min walk from station at Via Bozzo 3, taxi from station costs about €10, tel. 0185-286-435, fax 0185-283-580, www.hotelfasce.it, hotelfasce@hotelfasce.it).

By the Train Station

Expect a little train noise at these places.

$$$ Nuovo Hotel Garden is tucked away down a side street. From its 31 comfortable rooms to its restaurant, the hotel is high-quality (Db-€100, Qb-€200, higher in July–Aug, includes breakfast buffet, air-con, double-paned windows on train side, terrace, bar, free loaner bikes, parking-€11/day but only a few first-come, first-served spaces, Via Zara 13, a block from train station—instead of taking the stairs down to harbor, face stairs and go right, tel. 0185-285-398, fax 0185-290-439, www.nuovohotelgarden.com, info @nuovohotelgarden.com).

$$$ Hotel Conte Verde, on the same street, rents 31 rooms of varying quality and price. Ask if a room with a big terrace is available (Sb-€75, D-€65, Db-€110, price higher in July–Aug and for bigger rooms, includes breakfast, no air-con, fans available but shady rooms stay cool, exercise room, garden patio for picnics, free loaner bikes, big public areas, parking-€8–15/day, Via Zara 1, tel. 0185-287-139, fax 0185-284-211, www.hotelconteverde.it, info@hotelconteverde.it).

EATING

Ristorante "A' Lampara" is the locals' favorite for *casalinga* (home-cooked) Genovese cuisine, prepared by the endearing Barbieri family—Mamma Marialouisa, son Mario, and daughter Natalina. Try their specialties, such as *ravioli di pesce* (fish ravioli with tomato sauce) or *pansotti con salsa di noce*—cheese ravioli with walnut sauce (Fri–Wed 12:30–14:00 & 19:30–22:00, closed Thu, veggie options, follow Lungomare G. Marconi 3 blocks past the fish market, turn right onto Via Maragliano and find #33 a block and a half ahead on left, tel. 0185-288-926).

Ristorante il Nostromo, more central, also specializes in fish, offering a €20 *menu* plus à la carte options (daily in summer, closed Tue off-season, Via dell'Arco 6, a block off Piazza Veneto, take Via Gramsci and turn inland on Via dell'Arco, tel. 0185-281-390, run by Janet and Umberto).

Da Pezzi is a cheap and cheerful greasy spoon packed with workers at midday and locals at night, munching *farinata* (crêpe made from chickpeas) at the bar and enjoying pesto and fresh fish in the dining room (Sun–Fri 11:45–14:00 & 18:00–21:00, closed Sat, Via Cavour 21, tel. 0185-285-303).

Waterfront Dining: All along Via Tommaso Bottaro, you'll find restaurants, pizzerias, and bars serving food with a harbor view. The place above the fish market has the best views. The **pizzeria** next to Hotel Laurin is popular. **Bar Giuli**—the only place actually on the harbor—serves forgettable salads and sandwiches for a reasonable price.

Gelato: The best *gelateria* I found (with chocolate-truffle *tartufato*) is **Il Portico** (closed Mon off-season, under the castle, closest to the water at Piazza Libertà 48). **Gelateria Centrale,** just off Piazza Veneto near the cinema, serves up their specialty—*pinguino* (penguin), a cone with your choice of gelato dipped in chocolate (closed Wed off-season).

Groceries: **Seghezzo** is classiest (closed Wed Sept–May, immediately to the right of the church on Via Cavour). The **D'Oro Centry** supermarket, just off Piazza Mazzini, has better prices (Mon–Sat 8:30–13:00 & 15:30–19:30, Sun 8:30–12:30, across from Hotel Fiorina at Piazza Mazzini 38, tel. 0185-286-6470).

TRANSPORTATION CONNECTIONS

From Santa Margherita Ligure by Train to: Sestri Levante (hrly, 30 min), **Monterosso** (hrly, 1 hr), **La Spezia** (hrly, 60–90 min), **Pisa** (7/day, 2.5 hrs, more with transfer in La Spezia), **Genoa** (hrly, 45–60 min), **Milan** (5/day, 2.5 hrs, more with transfer in Genoa), **Ventimiglia** (1/day, 4 hrs, to French border, hrly with change in Genoa), **Venice** (6 hrs with changes in Milan or Genoa). For **Florence**, you'll transfer in La Spezia, Pisa, or both (allow 3.5–4 hrs). If heading for the **Cinque Terre** (as most visitors home-basing in Santa Margherita are), the schedule is confusing. It's a 60-minute trip, with hourly departures, but beware—some trains are much slower, the fastest trains stop only at Monterosso and Riomaggiore, and most trains run late. Look for the schedule on the train station wall specifically listing Cinque Terre trains.

From Santa Margherita Ligure by Boat to the Cinque Terre: Day-trip cruises from Santa Margherita to the Cinque Terre depart at 9:00, with lengthy stops in three Cinque Terre towns (Wed and Sat only July–Sept, €18 one-way, €29 round-trip). Some all-day trips include the Cinque Terre and Portovenere (depart at 9:00 Sun Easter–Sept and Tue and Thu July–Sept, €18 one-way, €29 round-trip). And there are half-day excursions to the Cinque Terre (depart at 13:30 Mon and Fri July–Sept, €15 one-way, €22 round-trip, tel. 0185-284-670).

South of the Cinque Terre

La Spezia

While just a quick train ride away from the fanciful Cinque Terre (20–30 min), La Spezia feels like reality Italy. The **TI** is a 20-minute walk from the station, near the waterfront (Mon–Sat 9:00–13:00 & 14:00–17:00, Sun 9:30–12:30, shorter hours in winter, Viale Mazzini 45, tel. 0187-770-900). There's usually a kiosk branch at the station in summer. If not, skip it. You can check your bags at the station (daily 8:00–22:00, €3/12 hrs, they'll photocopy your passport, baggage deposit isn't always manned—ring bell to left of doorway to call attendant, allow time to pick up baggage before departing). Buy your Cinque Terre Card (covers train ride to Cinque Terre; see page 254) at the park office in the train station (daily 7:00–20:00, to right of station bar, underground stairwell, and Internet Point).

Sights in La Spezia are slim. Each day, a colorful covered market sets up in Piazza Cavour from 8:00–13:00. On Fridays, a huge, all-day open-air market sprawls along Via Garibaldi (about 6 blocks from station). The pedestrian zone on Via del Prione to the gardens along the harbor makes a pleasant stroll. The nearly deserted **Museo Amedeo Lia** displays Italian paintings from the 13th to 18th centuries, including minor works by Venetian masters Titian, Tintoretto, and Canaletto (€6, Tue–Sun 10:00–18:00, closed Mon, last entry 30 min before closing, English descriptions on laminated sheets in most rooms, audioguide-€3, WCs across hall from ticket desk, no photos allowed, 10-min walk from station at Via Prione 234, tel. 0187-731-100, www.castagna.it/mal). To grab a meal while you wait for a train, see "Eating," below.

Stay on the Cinque Terre if you can, but if you're in a bind...

SLEEPING

(€1 = about $1.20, country code: 39)
The first five hotels are within a five-minute walk of La Spezia's station. The last two are for drivers only.

$$$ The grand, old, but newly restored **Hotel Firenze e Continentale** has 68 rooms with all the classy comforts (Sb-€80, Db-€115, these special prices valid only with this book in 2006, even cheaper during slow times, includes buffet breakfast, double-paned windows, air-con, some non-smoking rooms, elevator, parking-€13/day, Via Paleocapa 7, tel. 0187-713-200, fax 0187-714-930, www.hotelfirenzecontinentale.it).

$$$ Hotel Astoria, with 56 decent rooms, has a combination lobby and breakfast room as large as a school cafeteria. It's a fine backup if the hotels nearer the station are full (Db-€80–130, higher-end prices are for the 10 brand-new rooms with air-con and double-paned windows, includes breakfast, elevator, Via Roma 139, take Via Milano left of Albergo Parma then go 3 blocks and turn left on Via Roma, tel. 0187-714-655, fax 0187-714-425, hotelastoria@tiscali.it).

$$ Hotel Venezia, across the street from Hotel Firenze e Continentale, has a plain lobby, but its 19 rooms are modern (Db-€62–90, elevator, Via Paleocapa 10, tel. & fax 0187-733-465).

$$ Albergo Parma is tight, bright, and bleachy clean, with 36 rooms (D-€48, Db-€60, these prices promised through 2006 with this book, double-paned windows, hotel located just below station, down stairs to Via Fiume 143, tel. 0187-743-010, fax 0187-743-240, albergoparma@libero.it, some English spoken).

$$ Hotel Mary, just a few doors down from Albergo Parma, is sleepable but could be cleaner (Sb-€48, Db-€90, Tb-€115, prices soft, breakfast-€2, below station at Via Fiume 177, tel. 0187-743-254, fax 0187-743-375, info@hotelmary.it).

$$ Il Gelsomino, for drivers only, is a homey B&B in the hills above La Spezia overlooking the Gulf of Poets with three tranquil rooms: one with a bay-view terrace, one with hillside views, and a third that lacks views and a terrace (D-€66, Db-€74, Tb-€85, confirm arrival time 2 days in advance and cancel at least 24 hrs in advance, large breakfast, Via dei Viseggi 9, tel. & fax 0187-704-201, www.cinqueterreedintorni.it, ilgelsomino@inwind.it, gracious Carla and Walter Massi).

$ Santa Maria del Mare Monastery, a last resort for drivers, rents 15 comfortable rooms high above La Spezia in a scenic but institutional setting (for Db and dorm beds, €30/person donation requested; Castellazzo Stra, Via Montalbano, tel. 0187-711-332, mare@nse.it).

EATING

Ristorante Roma has better food than you'll find at the station and is reasonably priced, with a cool, leafy terrace to relax on while you await your train (just a few steps downhill—not downstairs—from the station, turn right as you exit station, across from Hotel Firenze e Continentale on Via Paleocapa 18, tel. 0187-715-921).

TRANSPORTATION CONNECTIONS

From La Spezia by Train to: Rome (10/day, 4 hrs), **Pisa** (hrly, 1 hr, direction: Livorno, Rome, Salerno, Naples, etc.), **Viareggio** (3–4/hr, 30–60 min), **Florence** (nearly hrly, 2.5 hrs, change in Pisa),

Milan (hrly, 3 hrs direct or 4 hrs with change in Genoa), **Venice** (2/day, 6 hrs, with change in Pisa and Florence; or 2/day, 6 hrs, with change in Milan; or 1 direct/day, in summer only).

Carrara

Perhaps the world's most famous marble quarries are just east of La Spezia in Carrara. Michelangelo himself traveled to these valleys to pick out the marble that he would work into his masterpieces. The towns of the region are dominated by marble. The quarries higher up are vast digs that dwarf their hardworking trucks and machinery. The Carrara museum allows visitors to trace the story of marble-cutting here from pre-Roman times until today.

For a guided visit, Sara Paolini is excellent (€80/half-day tour for the group, mobile 347-888-3833, sarapaolini@hotmail.com). She is accustomed to meeting drivers at the Carrara freeway exit, or she can pick you up at the train station.

Portovenere

While the gritty port of La Spezia offers little in the way of redeeming touristic value, the nearby resort of Portovenere is enchanting. This Cinque Terre-esque village clings to a rocky promontory jutting into the sea, protecting the harbor from the crashing waves. On the harbor, next to colorful bobbing boats, a row of restaurants—perfect for *al fresco* dining—feature local specialties such as *trenette* pasta with pesto and *spaghetti frutti di mare.* ·

Local boats take you on excursions to nearby islands or over to Lerici, the town across the bay. Lord Byron swam to Lerici (not recommended). Hardy hikers enjoy the five-hour (or more) hike to Riomaggiore, the nearest Cinque Terre town.

Portovenere is an easy day trip from the Cinque Terre by boat (Easter–Oct, nearly hourly 9:00–17:00), or take the bus from La Spezia (25 min, buy tickets at *tabacchi* shops or newsstands; to get from the train station to the bus stop, head downhill to the roundabout and continue onward to Piazza Garibaldi, then turn right at the fountain in the square onto Via Garibaldi—the bus stop for Portovenere buses is after the first stoplight on the right side of the street). In peak season, buses shuttle drivers from the parking lot just outside Portovenere to the harborside square.

Sleeping in Portovenere: If you forgot your yacht, try **Albergo Il Genio,** in the building where the main street hits the piazza (Db-€90–105, Piazza Bastreri 8, tel. & fax 0187-790-611, hotelgenioportovenere@interfree.it). If your *vita* is feeling *dolce*, consider **Grand Hotel Portovenere** (from €130 for a viewless double off-season to €295 for a view suite in summer with half-pension, tel. 0187-792-610, fax 0187-790-661, Via Garibaldi 5, www .portovenerehotel.it, ghp@village.it).

FLORENCE

(Firenze)

Florence, the home of the Renaissance and birthplace of our modern world, is a "supermarket sweep," and the groceries are the best Renaissance art in Europe.

Get your bearings with a Renaissance walk. Florentine art goes beyond paintings and statues—there's food, fashion, and handicrafts. You can lick Italy's best gelato while enjoying some of Europe's best people-watching.

Planning Your Time

If you're in Italy for three weeks, Florence deserves at least a well-organized day. Make reservations at least a month in advance for the Uffizi Gallery (best Italian paintings anywhere) and a few days in advance for the Accademia (Michelangelo's *David*). You can have your hotelier make these reservations for you—request this free service when booking your room (see page 349 for details).

For a day in Florence, see the Accademia, tour the Uffizi Gallery, visit the underrated Bargello (best statues), and do the Renaissance ramble (explained below).

Art-lovers will want to chisel out another day of their itinerary for the many other Florentine cultural treasures. Shoppers and ice cream-lovers may need to do the same.

Plan your sightseeing carefully. Some sights close Mondays and afternoons. While many spend several hours a day in lines, thoughtful travelers avoid this by making reservations or going late in the day. Places open at night are virtually empty.

Connoisseurs of smaller towns should consider taking the bus to Siena for a day or evening trip (75-min one-way, confirm when

Florence Overview

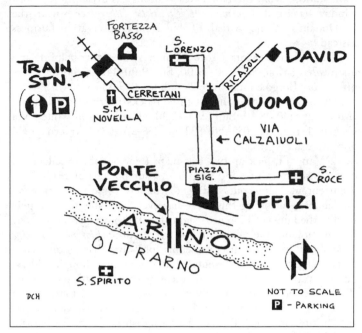

last bus returns). Siena is magic after dark. For more information, see the Siena chapter.

ORIENTATION

The best of Florence lies mostly on the north bank of the Arno River. The main historical sights cluster around the red-brick dome of the cathedral (Duomo). Everything is within a 20-minute walk of the train station, cathedral, or Ponte Vecchio (Old Bridge). The less impressive but more characteristic Oltrarno area (south bank) is just over the bridge. Though small, Florence is intense. Prepare for scorching summer heat, kamikaze motor scooters, slick pick-pockets, few WCs, steep prices, and long lines.

Tourist Information

There are three TIs in Florence: across from the train station, near Santa Croce Church, and on Via Cavour.

The TI across the square from the train station is most crowded—expect long lines (Mon–Sat 8:30–19:00, Sun 8:30–14:00; with your back to tracks, exit the station—it's across the square in wall near corner of church, Piazza Stazione, tel. 055-212-245). In the train station, avoid the Hotel Reservations "Tourist Information" window (marked *Informazioni Turistiche Alberghiere*) near the McDonald's; it's not a real TI, but a hotel-reservation business instead.

The TI near Santa Croce Church is pleasant, helpful, and uncrowded (Mon–Sat 9:00–19:00, Sun 9:00–14:00, shorter hours off-season, Borgo Santa Croce 29 red, tel. 055-234-0444).

Another winner is the TI three blocks north of the Duomo (Mon–Sat 8:30–18:30, Sun 8:30–13:30, closed Sun in winter, Via Cavour 1 red, tel. 055-290-832 or 055-276-0383, international bookstore across street).

At any TI, pick up two free maps (tear out the excellent old center inset from one and keep it in your pocket for ready use), a current museum-hours listing (extremely important, since no guidebook—including this one—has ever been able to accurately predict the hours of Florence's sights for the coming year), and any information on entertainment. The free monthly *Florence Concierge Information* magazine lists museums, plus lots that I don't: concerts, markets, sporting events, church services, shopping ideas, bus and train connections, and an entire similar section on Siena. *The Florentine* is a free weekly paper for expats and tourists that comes out every Thursday (in English; news, events, kids' activities, cultural insights). Both of these English-language freebies are available at TIs and hotels all over town.

Arrival in Florence

By Train: The station soaks up time and generates dazed and sweaty crowds. If you arrive by train, there's no need to linger at the station. Extremely user-friendly, coin-operated gray-and-yellow machines can display schedules, issue tickets, and even make reservations for railpass holders. Otherwise, get tickets and train information for your next destination from travel agencies away from the congested station (e.g., American Express, see page 328). The fake "Tourist Information" office in the station (next to McDonald's) is actually a room-booking service funded by the hotels. The real TI is across the square from the station (see page 323).

With your back to the tracks, look left to see a 24-hour pharmacy (*Farmacia Comunale*, near McDonald's), city buses, and the entrance to the underground mall/passage that goes across the square to the Church of Santa Maria Novella. (Note: Pickpockets frequent this tunnel, especially the surface point near the church.) Baggage check is near track 16.

By Car: If you're taking the autostrada (north or south) to Florence, get off at the Certosa exit and follow signs to *Centro*; at Porta Romana, go to the left of the arch and down Via Francesco Petrarca. After driving around and trying to park in Florence,

Greater Florence

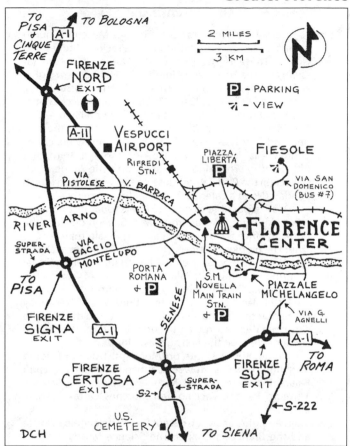

you'll understand why Leonardo never invented the car. Cars flatten the charm of the city.

Don't drive into the historic core of Florence. Every car entering the city is photographed. You must register your car with your hotel, whether you just drove in to drop off luggage or if you have parking reserved at your hotel. If you don't, a hefty fine will appear on your rental-car statement. If you go into the city beyond the ring road, even accidentally, you need to report your license-plate number to avoid the fine.

Non-residents are not allowed to park on the streets anywhere near or in the old center. Many hotels listed in this book have a few parking spots they can rent to guests in the center—most charge €15–20 per day. In addition, the city has plenty of **parking lots.** For a short stay, park underground at the train station (€2/hr). The best

Daily Reminder

Sunday: Today the Duomo's dome, Science Museum, Church of San Lorenzo, and Museum of Precious Stones are closed. These sights close early: Duomo Museum (at 13:40) and the Baptistery's interior (at 14:00). A few sights are open only in the afternoon: Duomo (13:30–16:45), Santa Croce Church (13:00–17:30), and Brancacci Chapel and the Church of Santa Maria Novella (both 13:00–17:00). The Museum of San Marco, which is open on the second and fourth Sunday of the month until 19:00, closes entirely—as does the Bargello—on the first, third, and fifth Sunday. The Medici Chapels and the Modern Art Gallery (in the Pitti Palace) close on the second and fourth Sunday. (Need a calendar? Look in the appendix.)

It's not possible to reserve tickets today by phone for the major sights (Accademia, Uffizi Gallery) because the booking office is closed; see page 331 for alternatives.

Monday: The biggies are closed, including Accademia *(David)* and Uffizi Gallery, as well as the Palatine Gallery/Royal Apartments in the Pitti Palace.

The Medici Chapels and the Modern Art Gallery (in the Pitti Palace) close on the first, third, and fifth Monday of the month. The Museum of San Marco and the Bargello close on the second and fourth Monday. The Boboli Gardens close on the first and last Monday.

Target these sights on Mondays: Duomo, Duomo Museum, Giotto's Tower, Baptistery, Medici-Riccardi Palace, Brancacci Chapel, Michelangelo's House, Science Museum, Palazzo Vecchio, and churches. Or take a walking tour.

Tuesday: All sights are open except for Michelangelo's House and the Brancacci Chapel. The Science Museum closes early (13:00). In July and August, the Accademia *(David)* may be open and free from 19:00–22:00.

Wednesday: All sights are open except for Medici-Riccardi Palace and Santo Spirito Church (closed in afternoon).

Thursday: All sights are open. These sights close early: Palazzo Vecchio (14:00) and the Duomo (15:30).

Friday: All sights are open. The Church of Santa Maria Novella opens only in the afternoon (13:00–17:00).

Saturday: All sights are open, but the Science Museum closes at 13:00. These sights close early on the first Saturday of the month: Duomo (15:30) and the Duomo's dome (16:00). The Museum of San Marco stays open until 19:00.

options for a longer stay are parking at Piazza della Libertà (€15/24 hrs, perhaps cheaper with hotel reservation, 4 long blocks east of Fortezza di Basso, on the inner ring road) and Porta Romana (exit A1 at Firenze-Certosa, follow signs to Porta Romana; €15 per day). For parking information, ask at your hotel or consult the useful Web site, www.firenzeparcheggi.it.

By Plane: Florence has its own airport and Pisa's is nearby. See "Transportation Connections" on page 366 for details.

Helpful Hints

Theft Alert: Florence has particularly hardworking thief gangs. They specialize in tourists and hang out where you do: near the train station, the station's underpass (especially where the tunnel surfaces), and major sights. Also be on guard at two squares frequented by drug pushers (Santa Maria Novella and Santo Spirito). American tourists—especially older ones—are considered easy targets.

Price Hike Alert: Italy's museums have found a clever way to squeeze more money out of their visitors. They host a special exhibit (which no tourist really cares to pay for) and require that you pay to see it along with the permanent collection. The result: Already steep admission fees jump by about €3.

Medical Help: To track down a doctor who speaks English, call 055-475-411 (they answer 24/7, reasonable house calls to your hotel—arriving within an hour for €100, only €45 if you go to the clinic at Via L. Magnifico 59, near Piazza Libertà when the doctor's in: 11:00–12:00 & 17:00–18:00, no appointment necessary). The TI has a list of English-speaking doctors. There are 24-hour pharmacies at the train station and near the Duomo on Borgo San Lorenzo.

Addresses: Street addresses list businesses in red and residences in black (color-coded on the actual street number and indicated by a letter following the number in printed addresses: r = red, no indication = black). *Pensioni* are usually black but can be either. The red and black numbers each appear in roughly consecutive order on streets but bear no apparent connection with each other. I'm lazy and don't concern myself with the distinction (if one number's wrong, I look for the other) and can easily find my way around.

Churches: Many churches now operate like museums, charging an admission fee to see their art treasures. Modest dress is required in some churches, and recommended for all of them—no short shorts (or short skirts) and no bare shoulders. Be respectful of worshippers; don't use a flash. Churches usually close from 12:30 to 15:00 or 16:00.

Chill Out: Schedule into your sightseeing several cool breaks where you can sit, pause, and refresh yourself with a sandwich, gelato, or coffee.

Internet Access: Internet Train is the dominant chain, with bright and cheery rooms, speedy computers, and long hours (daily 9:00–23:00). They have branches at the train station (Galleria Commerciale), Piazza della Repubblica (Via Porta Rossa 38 red), Piazza Santa Croce (Via de Benci 38 red), and Ponte Vecchio (Borgo San Jacopo 30 red). **Florence-email** is another good place (behind the Duomo at Via F. Portinari 15 red). An **easyInternetcafé** is just south of the Medici-Riccardi Palace (daily 9:00–23:00, Via Martelli 22).

Laundry: The **Wash & Dry Lavarapido** chain offers long hours and efficient, self-service launderettes at several locations (about €6.20 for wash and dry, daily 8:00–22:00, tel. 055-580-480). These are close to recommended hotels: Via dei Servi 105 (and a rival launderette at Via Guelfa 22 red, off Via Cavour; both near *David*); Via del Sole 29 red and Via della Scala 52 red (between train station and river); and Via dei Serragli 87 red (across the river in Oltrarno neighborhood).

Bookstores: Local guidebooks (sold at kiosks) are cheap and give you a map and a decent commentary on the sights. For brand-name guidebooks in English, try **Feltrinelli International** (Mon–Sat 9:00–19:30, closed Sun, Via Cavour 20 red, a few blocks north of the Duomo and across the street from the TI and the Medici-Riccardi Palace on Via Cavour, tel. 055-219-524), **Edison Bookstore** (daily 9:00–24:00, sells CDs and novels on Renaissance, facing Piazza della Repubblica, tel. 055-213-110), or **Paperback Exchange**, an Anglo-American Bookshop (cheaper but smaller selection, Mon–Fri 9:00–19:30, Sat 10:00–13:00 & 15:30–19:30, closed Sun, shorter hours in Aug, Via delle Oche 4 red, two blocks south of the south transept of the Duomo, tel. 055-293-460).

Travel Agency: Get train tickets, reservations, and supplements at travel agencies rather than at the congested train station. The cost is often the same, though sometimes there's a minimal charge. Ask your hotel for the nearest travel agency, or try American Express.

American Express offers all the normal services, but is most helpful as an easy place to get your train tickets, reservations, supplements (all the same price as at the station), or even just information on train schedules (Mon–Fri 9:00–17:30, closed Sat–Sun, 3 short blocks north of Palazzo Vecchio at Via Dante Alighieri 22 red, tel. 055-50981).

Florence

Getting Around Florence

I organize my sightseeing geographically and do it all on foot.

If you take **buses**, a €1 ticket gets you one hour (€1.80/3 hrs, €4/24 hrs, tickets not sold on bus before 21:00—buy in *tabacchi* shops or newsstands, validate on bus, after 21:00 buy tickets on bus, route map available at TI, info tel. 800-424-500). Multi-day passes are also available.

Florence requires a lot of walking. Its buses don't really cover the old center well. Fun little *elettrico* buses weave and circle around the old center from the train station and big buses rumble from the station and Piazza San Marco (near the Museum of San

Marco and many recommended hotels) to points beyond where most tourists go.

Of the many bus lines, here are the only ones I find helpful: *elettrico* #D (from train station to Ponte Vecchio, joy-riding through Oltrarno), *elettrico* #B (up and down the Arno River from Ognissanti to Santa Croce), lines #7, #31, and #32 (connecting the station, Duomo, and Piazza San Marco with #7 continuing on to Fiesole) and line #13 (from station to Porta Romana, up to Piazzale Michelangelo, and on to Santa Croce).

Hop-on, hop-off bus tours stop at the major sights (see "Tours," below).

The minimum cost for a **taxi** ride is €4 or, after 22:00, €5 (rides in the center of town should be charged as tariff #1). A taxi ride from the train station to Ponte Vecchio costs about €8. Taxi fares and supplements (e.g., €2 extra if you telephone a cab) are clearly explained on signs in each taxi.

TOURS

Note that big bus companies offer tours of Florence, but for most, the city is really best seen on foot. The outfits listed here are hard-working, creative, and offer a worthwhile array of organized sight-seeing activities. Nearly all have guides available for private hire. Study their Web sites for details.

Walking Tours of Florence—This company offers a variety of tours (up to 12/day year-round) featuring downtown Florence, Uffizi highlights, and Tuscany day trips. Their guides are native English-speakers. The three-hour "Original Florence" walk hits the main sights but gets offbeat to weave a picture of Florentine life in medieval and Renaissance times. Tours go rain or shine with as few as two participants. Advance booking is required (€25 for 3-hr Original Florence walk at 9:30 daily, office open Mon–Sat 8:30–18:00, Sun 8:30–13:30 but off-season closed on Sun and for lunch, tours depart from office, Via dei Sassetti 1, above Odeon Cinema on 2nd floor, on Piazza Davanzati, a couple blocks southwest of Piazza della Repubblica, tel. 055-264-5033, mobile 329-613-2730, www.italy.artviva.com, staff@artviva.com). For all the schedule details, pick up their extensive brochure in your hotel lobby.

Florentia—These top-notch, private walking tours—geared for thoughtful, well-heeled travelers with longer-than-average attention spans—are led by local scholars. The tours range from introductory city walks and museum visits to in-depth thematic walks such as the Golden Age of Florence, Medici Dynasty, and side-trips into Tuscany (half-day tours start at €175, reserve in advance, tel. 338-890-8625, U.S. tel. 510/549-1707, www.florentia .org, info@florentia.org).

Make Reservations to Avoid Lines

Florence has a reservation system for its top five sights—Uffizi, Accademia, Bargello, Medici Chapels, and the Pitti Palace. I highly recommended getting reservations for the Accademia (Michelangelo's *David*) and the Uffizi (Renaissance paintings). While you can generally get an entry time for the Accademia within a few days, the Uffizi is often booked up a month in advance. Your best strategy is to get reservations for both as soon as you know when you'll be in town. Hotels are accustomed to offering this service free when clients make a room reservation. Just request it with your hotel booking. After learning how easy this is and seeing hundreds of bored, sweaty tourists waiting in lines without a reservation, it's hard not to be amazed by their cluelessess.

If you want to make the booking yourself, dial 055-294-883 (Mon–Fri 8:30–18:30, Sat 8:30–12:30, closed Sun). An English-speaking operator walks you through the process and two minutes later you say *grazie,* with appointments (15-min entry window) and six-digit confirmation numbers for each of the top museums and galleries. The ticket phone number is often busy; be persistent. It's easier to get through if you call late. Some booking agencies offer reservations online for a fee (such as www.weekendafirenze.it).

Besides than these main attractions, the only other places you should book in advance are the Brancacci Chapel (to see the Masaccio frescoes; reservations required, in fact) and the Medici-Riccardi Palace (to see the sumptuous Chapel of the Magi). You do this direct (phone numbers are included in the sight listings) and spots are generally available a day in advance.

Context Florence—Started by the folks who run Context Rome in Rome, this is a group of graduate students and professors who lead "walking seminars," with a scholarly approach similar to Florentia's. Their tours include a three-hour Michelangelo Seminar, an in-depth study of the artist's work and influence (€50/person) and an evening orientation stroll called the Florence Evening Transect (€35/person; tel. 06-482-0911, U.S. tel. 888-467-1986, www.contextflorence.com, info@contextflorence.com, run by Lani Bevacqua and Paul Bennett).

Local Guides—Paola Migliorini offers museum tours, city walking tours, and Tuscan excursions by van. You (and your group) can tailor tours as you like. Paola's van can go anywhere in the center and allows slow walkers to enjoy the city nearly sweat-free (€50/hr or €65/hr with 8-seat van, Via S. Gallo 120, tel. 055-472-448, mobile 347-657-2611, www.florencetour.com, info@florencetour.com). Other good guides

Florence at a Glance

▲▲▲Uffizi Gallery Greatest collection of Italian paintings anywhere—reserve at least one month in advance. **Hours:** Tue–Sun 8:15–18:50, closed Mon.

▲▲▲Accademia Michelangelo's *David* and powerful (unfinished) *Prisoners*—reserve ahead. **Hours:** Tue–Sun 8:15–18:50, plus possibly Tue 19:00–22:00 in July and Aug, closed Mon.

▲▲▲Bargello Underappreciated sculpture museum (Michelangelo, Donatello, Medici treasures). **Hours:** Daily 8:15–13:50; closed first, third, and fifth Sun and second and fourth Mon of each month.

▲▲Museum of San Marco Best collection anywhere of frescoes and paintings by the early Renaissance master Fra Angelico. **Hours:** Mon–Fri 8:15–13:50, Sat–Sun 8:15–19:00; closed first, third, and fifth Sun and second and fourth Mon of each month.

▲▲Medici Chapels Tombs of Florence's great ruling family, designed and carved by Michelangelo. **Hours:** Daily 8:15–16:50; closed the second and fourth Sun and the first, third, and fifth Mon of each month.

▲▲Church of Santa Maria Novella 13th-century Dominican church with Masaccio's famous 3-D painting. **Hours:** Mon–Thu and Sat 9:30–17:00, Fri and Sun 13:00–17:00.

▲▲Santa Croce Church 14th-century Franciscan church with precious art, tombs of famous Florentines, and Brunelleschi's Pazzi Chapel. **Hours:** Mon–Sat 9:30–17:30, Sun 13:00–17:30; winter Mon–Sat 9:30–12:30 & 15:00–17:30, Sun 13:00–17:30.

▲▲Science Museum Fascinating collection of old clocks, telescopes, maps, and Galileo's finger. **Hours:** Mon and Wed–Fri 9:30–17:00, Tue and Sat 9:30–13:00, closed Sun.

▲▲Pitti Palace Three museums in lavish palace: Palatine Gallery (Raphael art), Modern Art Gallery, Grand Ducal Treasures (Medici treasure chest), plus sprawling Boboli Gardens. **Hours:** Palatine: Tue–Sun 8:15–18:50, closed Mon; Modern Art and Treasures: daily 8:15–13:50, closed second and fourth Sun and first, third, and fifth Mon; Boboli: daily 9:00–19:30 June–Aug, 9:00–18:30 fall and spring, 9:00–16:30 in winter, closed first and last Mon of month.

▲▲Brancacci Chapel Works of Masaccio, early Renaissance master who reinvented perspective. **Hours:** Mon and Wed–Sat

10:00–17:00, Sun 13:00–17:00, closed Tue. Reservations required.

▲▲**Duomo (Santa Maria del Fiore)** Gothic Cathedral with colorful facade, long nave, and the first dome built since ancient Roman times. **Hours:** Mon–Wed and Fri–Sat 10:00–17:00 except first Sat of month 10:00–15:30, Thu 10:00–15:30, Sun 13:30–16:45.

▲▲**Duomo Museum** Underrated cathedral museum with great sculpture. **Hours:** Mon–Sat 9:00–19:30, Sun 9:00–13:40.

▲**Climbing Duomo's Dome** Grand view into the cathedral, close-up of dome architecture, and after 463 steps, a glorious Florence vista. **Hours:** Mon–Fri 8:30–19:00, Sat 8:30–17:40 except first Sat of month 8:30–16:00, closed Sun. Long slow lines, no reservations accepted.

▲**Giotto's Tower** Bell tower with 50 fewer steps, fewer lines, and lesser views than Duomo climb. **Hours:** Daily 8:30–19:30.

▲**Baptistery** Bronze doors fit to be the gates of Paradise. **Hours:** Doors always viewable; Baptistery open Mon–Sat 12:00–19:00, Sun 8:30–14:00.

▲**Medici-Riccardi Palace** Lorenzo the Magnificent's home, with fine art, frescoed ceilings, and the lovely Chapel of the Magi. **Hours:** Tue–Thu 9:00–19:00, closed Wed.

▲**Palazzo Vecchio** Fortified palace once the home of the Medici family, wallpapered with mediocre art. **Hours:** Fri–Wed 9:00–19:00, Thu 9:00–14:00.

▲**Ponte Vecchio** Famous bridge lined with gold and silver shops. **Hours:** Bridge always open.

▲**Mercato Nuovo** Bustling market in *loggia*. **Hours:** Open daily.

▲**Michelangelo's House** Museum featuring early, lesser-known works of the master. **Hours:** Wed–Mon 9:30–14:00, closed Tue.

▲**Piazzale Michelangelo** Hilltop square in south Florence offering stunning view of city and Duomo. **Hours:** Always open.

▲**San Miniato Church** Gem of a basilica, with sumptuous Renaissance chapel and sacristy showing scenes of St. Benedict. **Hours:** Daily 9:00–19:00.

include: Paola Barubiani and her partners at Walks Inside Florence (tel. 335-526-6496, www.walksinsideflorence.it, pbarub@tin.it), and Alessandra Marchetti (tel. 055-654-9160, mobile 347-386-9839, aleoberm@tin.it).

Hop-on, Hop-off Bus Tours—Around town, you'll see big double-decker sightseeing buses double-parking at major sights. Tourists on the top deck can listen to brief recorded descriptions of the sights, snap photos, and enjoy an effortless drive-by look at the major landmarks. Tickets cost €20 (good for 24 hours, pay as you board, tickets include 2 bus lines—Blue is 1 hour with a trip up to Piazzale Michelangelo, Green is 2 hours with a side-trip to Fiesole). As the name implies, you can hop off when you want and catch the next bus. Hop-on stops include the train station, Duomo, and Pitti Palace.

Accidental Tourist—This tour company picks you up in a van for a day of hiking, biking, or cooking classes, and then drops you off back in Florence (prices vary, e.g., €80 for cooking class 9:30–17:00, book online in advance, allow 4 days for reply to e-mails, www .accidentaltourist.com, info@accidentaltourist.com).

SELF-GUIDED WALK

A Renaissance Walk through Florence

During the Dark Ages, it was especially obvious to the people of Italy—sitting on the rubble of Rome—that there had to be a brighter age before them. The long-awaited rebirth, or Renaissance, began in Florence for good reason. Wealthy because of its cloth industry, trade, and banking; powered by a fierce city-state pride (locals would pee into the Arno with gusto, knowing rival city-state Pisa was downstream); and fertile with more than its share of artistic genius (imagine guys like Michelangelo and Leonardo attending the same high school)—Florence was a natural home for this cultural explosion.

Take a walk through the core of Renaissance Florence by starting at the Accademia (home of Michelangelo's *David*) and cutting through the heart of the city to Ponte Vecchio on the Arno River.

At the Accademia, you'll look into the eyes of Renaissance man—humanism at its confident peak. Then walk to the cathedral (Duomo) to see the dome that kicked off the architectural Renaissance. Step inside the Baptistery to view a ceiling covered with preachy, flat, 2-D, medieval mosaic art. Then, to learn what happened when art met math, check out the realistic 3-D reliefs on the doors. The painter, Giotto, also designed the bell tower—an early example of a Renaissance genius excelling in many areas. Continue toward the river on Florence's great pedestrian mall, Via de' Calzaiuoli (or "Via Calz")—part of the original grid plan given to the city by the ancient Romans. Down a few blocks,

Renaissance Walk

N

200 YARDS
200 METERS

MUSEUM OF
SAN MARCO

P. S.
MARCO

START

ACCADEMIA

P.
S. S.
ANNUNZ.

V. GUELFA

CAVOUR

RICASOLI

MEDICI
CHAPELS

SAN
LORENZO

MEDICI-
RICCARDI
PALACE

FOUNDLING
HOSP.

V. SERVI

V. ALF.

TO
TRAIN
STN.

MKT.

B. S. LOR.

VIA PUCCI

VIA

V. PANZ.

CERRETANI

DUOMO

DUOMO
MUSEUM

AGLI

BAPT.

CAMP.

ORIUOLO

SOLO

STROZZI

P.
REP.

CORSO

DANTE'S
HOUSE

BARGELLO

MICHEL.
HOUSE

V. CALZAIUOLI

PANTE

V. PROCON-

VIA GHIB.

ORSAN-
MICHELE

CONR.

PORTA ROSSA

V. COV. MKT.

TERME

S. MARIA

V. G. VECCHIA

V. ANG.

B. S. APOST.

BORGO GRECI

P. S.
CROCE

L. ACCIAIUOLI

EXIT

PALAZZO
VECCHIO

V. D. NERI

BENCI

S. JAC.

SCI.
MUS.

SANTA
CROCE

GUICC.

UFFIZI
GALLERY

LUNG. DIAZ

ARNO

TINTORI

PONTE
VECCHIO
FINISH

OLTRARNO

DCH

★ PIAZZA DELLA
SIGNORIA

compare medieval and Renaissance statues on the exterior of the Orsanmichele Church. Via Calz connects the cathedral with the central square (Piazza della Signoria), the city palace (Palazzo Vecchio), and the Uffizi Gallery, which contains the greatest collection of Italian Renaissance paintings in captivity. Finally, walk through the Uffizi courtyard—a statuary think tank of Renaissance greats—to the Arno River and Ponte Vecchio.

Sights on a Renaissance Walk through Florence

▲▲▲**Accademia (Galleria dell'Accademia)**—This museum houses Michelangelo's *David* and powerful (unfinished) *Prisoners*. Eavesdrop as tour guides explain these masterpieces. More than with any other work of art, when you look into the eyes of *David*, you're looking into the eyes of Renaissance man. This was a radical break with the past. Hello, humanism. Man was now a confident individual, no longer a plaything of the supernatural. And life was now more than just a preparation for what happened after you died.

The Renaissance was the merging of art, science, and humanism. In a humanist vein, *David* is looking at the crude giant of medieval darkness and thinking, "I can take this guy." (David was an apt mascot for a town surrounded by big bully city-states.) Back on a religious track, notice *David*'s large and overdeveloped right hand. This is symbolic of the hand of God that powered David to slay the giant...and enabled Florence to rise above its crude neighboring city-states.

Beyond the magic marble are two floors of interesting pre-Renaissance and Renaissance paintings, including a couple of lighter-than-air Botticellis.

Cost, Hours, Location: €9.50, plus €3 reservation fee, Tue–Sun 8:15–18:50, closed Mon, last entry 45 min before closing, Via Ricasoli 60, tel. 055-238-8609. To avoid waiting in line, reserve ahead; see page 331 for details. In July and August, the museum may be open and free on Tuesday evenings (19:00–22:00).

Nearby: Piazza Santissima Annunziata, behind the Accademia, displays lovely Renaissance harmony. Facing the square are two fine buildings: the 15th-century Santissima Annunziata church (worth a peek) and Brunelleschi's Hospital of the Innocents (Spedale degli Innocenti, not worth going inside), with terra-cotta medallions by Luca della Robbia. Built in the 1420s, the hospital is considered the first Renaissance building.

▲▲**Duomo**—Florence's Gothic Santa Maria del Fiori cathedral has the third-longest nave in Christendom (free, Mon–Wed and Fri–Sat 10:00–17:00 except 1st Sat of month 10:00–15:30, Thu 10:00–15:30, Sun 13:30–16:45, modest dress code enforced, tel. 055-230-2885). Note: The massive crowds that overwhelm the entrance in the morning usually clear out by afternoon.

The church's noisy neo-Gothic facade from the 1870s is covered with pink, green, and white Tuscan marble. Since nearly all of its great art is stored in the Museo dell'Opera del Duomo (behind the church), the best thing about the interior is the shade. The inside of the dome is decorated by one of the largest paintings of the Renaissance, a huge (and newly restored) *Last Judgment* by Vasari and Zuccari.

Think of the confidence of the age: The Duomo was built with a hole awaiting a dome in its roof. This was before the technology to span it with a dome was available. No matter. They knew that someone soon could handle the challenge...and the local architect Brunelleschi did. The cathedral's claim to artistic fame is Brunelleschi's magnificent dome—the first Renaissance dome and the model for domes to follow.

▲**Climbing the Cathedral's Dome**—For a grand view into the cathedral from the base of the dome, a peek at some of the tools used in the dome's construction, a chance to see Brunelleschi's "dome-within-a-dome" construction, a glorious Florence view from the top, and the equivalent of 463 plunges on a Stairmaster, climb the dome. When planning St. Peter's in Rome, Michelangelo rhymed (not in English), "I can build its sister—bigger, but not more beautiful" than the dome of Florence.

To avoid the long, dreadfully slow-moving line, arrive by 8:30 or drop by very late (€6, Mon–Fri 8:30–19:00, Sat 8:30–17:40 except 1st Sat of month 8:30–16:00, closed Sun, enter from outside church on north side, tel. 055-230-2885).

▲**Giotto's Tower (Campanile)**—The 270-foot bell tower has 50 fewer steps than the Duomo's dome, offers a faster, less crowded climb, and has a view of the Duomo to boot, but the cage-like top isn't great for photo ops (€6, daily 8:30–19:30, last entry 40 min before closing).

▲▲**Duomo Museum (Museo dell'Opera del Duomo)**—The underrated cathedral museum, behind the church, is great if you like sculpture. It has masterpieces by Donatello (a gruesome wood carving of Mary Magdalene clothed in her matted hair, and the *cantoria,* a delightful choir loft bursting with happy children) and by Luca della Robbia (another choir loft, lined with the dreamy faces of musicians praising the Lord). Look for a late Michelangelo *Pietà* (Nicodemus, on top, is a self-portrait), Brunelleschi's models for his dome, and the original restored panels of Ghiberti's doors to the Baptistery. This is one of the few museums in Florence open on Monday (€6, Mon–Sat 9:00–19:30, Sun 9:00–13:40, last entry 40 min before closing, closed on holidays, tel. 055-230-2885).

If you find all this church art intriguing, look through the open doorway of the Duomo art studio, which has been making and restoring church art since the days of Brunelleschi (a block toward the river from the Duomo at 23a Via dello Studio).

▲**Baptistery**—Michelangelo said its bronze doors were fit to be the gates of Paradise. Check out the gleaming copies of Lorenzo Ghiberti's bronze doors facing the Duomo. Making a breakthrough in perspective, Ghiberti used mathematical laws to create the illusion of receding distance on a basically flat surface.

The doors on the north side of the building were designed by Ghiberti when he was young; he'd won the honor and opportunity by beating Brunelleschi in a competition (the rivals' original entries are in the Bargello—see page 342).

Inside, sit and savor the medieval mosaic ceiling where it's always Judgment Day and Jesus is giving the ultimate thumbs up and thumbs down (€3, interior open Mon–Sat 12:00–19:00, Sun 8:30–14:00; bronze doors are on the outside, so always "open"; original panels are in the Duomo Museum).

Orsanmichele Church—In the ninth century, this loggia (a covered courtyard) was a market used for selling grain (stored upstairs). Later, it was closed in to make a church. Outside, check out the dynamic statue-filled niches, some with accompanying symbols from the guilds that sponsored the art. Donatello's *St. Mark* and *St. George* (on the northeast and northwest corners) step out boldly in the new Renaissance style. The interior, viewable only during evening concerts, has a glorious Gothic tabernacle (1359) by Orcagna. The iron bars spanning the vaults were the Italian Gothic answer to the French Gothic external buttresses.

The museum upstairs holds many of the church's precious originals. Someday tourists may be able to enjoy its fine statues by Ghiberti, Donatello, and company. (But don't hold your breath.)

A block away, you'll find the...

▲**Mercato Nuovo (a.k.a. the Straw Market)**—This market *loggia* is how Orsanmichele looked before it became a church. Originally a silk and straw market, Mercato Nuovo still functions as a rustic yet touristy market today (at the intersection of Via Calimala and Via Porta Rossa). Prices are soft, but the San Lorenzo Market is much better for haggling. Notice the circled X in the center, marking the spot where people hit after being hoisted up to the top and dropped as punishment for bankruptcy. You'll also find *Porcellino* (a statue of a wild boar nicknamed "little pig"), which people rub and give coins to in order to ensure their return to Florence. This new copy, while only a few years old, already has a polished snout. Nearby, a wagon sells tripe (cow innards) sandwiches—a local favorite.

▲**Palazzo Vecchio**—With its distinctive castle turret, this fortified palace, once the home of the Medici family, is a Florentine landmark. But if you're visiting only one palace interior in town, the Pitti Palace is better. The Palazzo Vecchio interior is worthwhile only if you're a real fan of Florentine history or of the artist Giorgio Vasari, who wallpapered the place with mediocre magnificence. The museum's most famous statues are Michelangelo's *Victory* and Donatello's bronze statue of *Judith and Holerfernes* (€5.70, €8 combo-ticket with Brancacci Chapel, Fri–Wed 9:00–19:00, Thu 9:00–14:00, ticket office closes one hour earlier, tel. 055-276-8224).

Even if you don't go to the museum, do step into the **free courtyard** (behind the fake *David*) just to feel the essence of the Medicis. Until 1873, Michelangelo's *David* stood at the entrance, where the copy is today. While the huge statues in the square are important only as the whipping boys of art critics and as rest stops for pigeons, the nearby **Loggia dei Lanzi** has several important statues. Look for Cellini's bronze statue of Perseus holding the head of Medusa. The plaque on the pavement in front of the fountain marks the spot where the monk Savonarola was burned in MCDXCVIII, or 1498.

The square fronting the Palazzo Vecchio, Piazza della Signoria, is a tourist's world with pigeons, postcards, horse buggies, and tired hubbies. And, if it would make your tired hubby happy, the ritzy Café Rivoire—with the best view seats in town—is famous for its fancy desserts and hot chocolate (closed Mon).

▲▲▲**Uffizi Gallery**—This greatest collection of Italian paintings anywhere features works by Giotto, Leonardo, Raphael, Caravaggio, Rubens, Titian, and Michelangelo, and a roomful of Botticellis, including his *Birth of Venus*.

The museum is nowhere near as big as it is great. Few tourists spend more than two hours inside. The paintings are displayed on one comfortable U-shaped floor in chronological order, from the 13th through 17th centuries. The left wing—starring the Florentine Middle Ages to the Renaissance—is the best. The connecting corridor contains sculpture, and the right wing focuses on High Renaissance and Baroque.

Essential stops are (in this order): Gothic altarpieces (narrative, pre-Realism, no real concern for believable depth) including Giotto's altarpiece, which progressed beyond "totem-pole angels"; Uccello's *Battle of San Romano,* an early study in perspective (with a few obvious flubs); Fra Filippo Lippi's cuddly Madonnas; the Botticelli room, filled with masterpieces, including a pantheon of classical fleshiness and the small *La Calùnnia,* showing the glasnost of Renaissance free-thinking being clubbed back into the darker age of Savonarola; two minor works by Leonardo; the octagonal classical sculpture room with an early painting of Bob Hope and a copy of Praxiteles' *Venus de' Medici*—considered the epitome of beauty in Elizabethan Europe; a view through the window of the Ponte Vecchio—dreamy at sunset; Michelangelo's only surviving easel painting, the round *Holy Family;* Raphael's noble *Madonna*

Uffizi Gallery Overview

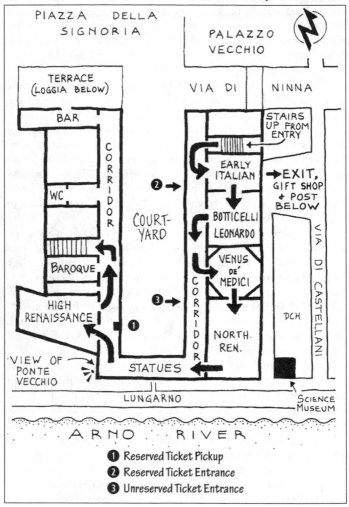

PIAZZA DELLA SIGNORIA

PALAZZO VECCHIO

TERRACE (LOGGIA BELOW)

BAR

CORRIDOR

WC

COURT-YARD

BAROQUE

HIGH RENAISSANCE

VIEW OF PONTE VECCHIO

VIA DI NINNA

STAIRS UP FROM ENTRY

EARLY ITALIAN

→ EXIT, GIFT SHOP & POST BELOW

BOTTICELLI LEONARDO

VENUS DE' MEDICI

CORRIDOR

NORTH. REN.

VIA DI CASTELLANI

PCH

STATUES

LUNGARNO

SCIENCE MUSEUM

ARNO RIVER

❶ Reserved Ticket Pickup
❷ Reserved Ticket Entrance
❸ Unreserved Ticket Entrance

of the Goldfinch; Titian's voluptuous *Venus of Urbino;* and Duomo views from the café terrace (WC near café).

Cost, Hours, Reservations: €9.50, plus €3 for recommended reservation, Tue–Sun 8:15–18:50, closed Mon, last entry 45 min before closing. (After entering, take the elevator or climb four long flights of stairs to reach the art.)

As only 600 are allowed into the museum at a time, there are infamously long lines to get in. Avoid the two-hour peak-season wait by getting a reservation at least a month in advance (see page 331).

After you have your reservation, go to the Uffizi at your

appointed time. Walk briskly past the 200-yard-long line, pondering the collective IQ of this gang, to the special ticket office (across the courtyard from the entry—see map) for those with reservations (labeled in English *Entrance for Reservations Only*), give your number, pay (cash only), and scoot right in.

If you arrive in Florence without a Uffizi booking, there are other ways to get a reservation—sometimes for the same day, depending on luck and availability: try booking directly at the Uffizi (ask the clerk at the reserved-ticket office if you can reserve in person); take a tour of the museum with Walking Tours of Florence (booking required, see "Tours," page 330); or for a fee, you can reserve online through various agencies such as www.weekendafirenze .it or www.florenceart.it. Sometimes, by the end of the day (an hour before closing), there are no lines and you can just walk right in.

In the Uffizi Courtyard: Enjoy the Uffizi's courtyard (free), full of artists and souvenir stalls. The surrounding statues honor earthshaking Florentines: artists (Michelangelo and Leonardo), philosophers (Machiavelli), scientists (Galileo), writers (Dante), and explorers (Amerigo Vespucci), and the great patron of so much Renaissance thinking, Lorenzo "the Magnificent" de' Medici.

▲**Ponte Vecchio**—Florence's most famous bridge is lined with shops that have traditionally sold gold and silver. A statue of Cellini, the master goldsmith of the Renaissance, stands in the center, ignored by the flood of tacky tourism. This is a romantic spot late at night. In fact, hanging over the edge of the bridge (on either side of the Cellini bust) are piles of padlocks. Guys demonstrate the enduring quality of their love by ceremonially taking their girls here, locking a lock, and throwing the key into the Arno. (But what's with the combination lock?)

Notice the "prince's passageway" above the bridge. In less secure times, the city leaders had a fortified passageway connecting the Vecchio Palace and Uffizi with the mighty Pitti Palace, to which they could flee in times of attack. This passageway, called the **Vasari Corridor,** is technically open to the public, but good luck getting an appointment (open "seasonally," try the museum reservation line, tel. 055-294-883).

SIGHTS

Near the Accademia

▲▲**Museum of San Marco (Museo di San Marco)**—One block north of the Accademia, this 15th-century monastery houses the greatest collection anywhere of frescoes and paintings by the early Renaissance master Fra Angelico. The ground floor features the monk's paintings, along with some works by Fra Bartolomeo. Upstairs are 43 cells decorated by Fra Angelico and his assistants.

While the monk/painter was trained in the medieval religious style, he also learned and adopted Renaissance techniques and sensibilities, producing works that blended Christian symbols and Renaissance realism. Don't miss the cell of Savonarola, the charismatic monk who rode in from the Christian right, threw out the Medicis, turned Florence into a theocracy, sponsored "bonfires of the vanities" (burning books, paintings, and so on), and was finally burned himself when Florence decided to change channels (€4, Mon–Fri 8:15–13:50, Sat–Sun 8:15–19:00, but closed 1st, 2nd, and 5th Sun and 2nd and 4th Mon of each month, on Piazza San Marco, tel. 055-238-8608). While you can reserve an entrance time here, it's entirely unnecessary.

Museum of Precious Stones (Museo dell'Opificio delle Pietre Dure)—This unusual gem of a museum features mosaics of inlaid marble and stones. You'll see remnants of the Medici workshop from 1588, including 500 different precious stones, the tools used to cut and inlay them, and room after room of the sumptuous finished product. The fine loaner booklet describes it all in English. Because of staffing problems, the museum is only open during certain windows of time: 9:00–10:00, 10:45–11:45, and 12:30–13:30 (€2, open Mon–Sat, closed Sun, Via degli Alfani 78, around corner from Accademia).

Heart of Florence

▲▲▲**Bargello (Museo Nazionale)**—This under-appreciated sculpture museum is in a former police-station-turned-prison that looks like a mini–Palazzo Vecchio. It has Donatello's painfully beautiful *David* (the very influential 1st male nude to be sculpted in a thousand years), works by Michelangelo, and rooms of Medici treasures cruelly explained in Italian only (politely suggest to the staff that English descriptions would be wonderful). Moody Donatello, who embraced realism with his lifelike statues, set the personal and artistic style for many Renaissance artists to follow. The best works are in the ground-floor room at the foot of the outdoor staircase and in the room directly above (€4, daily 8:15–13:50 but closed 1st, 2nd, and 5th Sun and 2nd and 4th Mon of each month, last entry 40 min before closing, Via del Proconsolo 4, tel. 055-238-8606).

▲▲**Medici Chapels (Cappelle Medicee)**—The chapel, containing Medici tombs, is drenched in lavish High Renaissance architecture and sculpture. The highlight is a chapel with interior decoration by Michelangelo, including the brooding Night, Day, Dawn, and Dusk statues (€6, daily 8:15–16:50 but closed the 2nd and 4th Sun and the 1st, 3rd, and 5th Mon of each month, tel. 055-238-8602).

Nearby: Behind the chapels on Piazza Madonna degli Aldobrandini is a lively market scene that I find just as interesting.

Take a stroll through the huge double-decker Mercato Centrale (central food market) one block north.

▲**Medici-Riccardi Palace (Palazzo Medici-Riccardi)**—Lorenzo the Magnificent's home is worth a look for its art. The tiny Chapel of the Magi contains the colorful Renaissance gem the *Procession of the Magi* frescoes by Benozzo Gozzoli. The former library has a Baroque ceiling fresco by Luca Giordano, a prolific artist from Naples known as Fast Luke *(Luca fa presto)* for his ambidextrous painting abilities. While the Medicis originally occupied this 1444 house, in the 1700s it became home to the Riccardi family, who added the Baroque flourishes. As only eight people are allowed into the Chapel of the Magi every seven minutes, it can be smart to call for an appointment (€4, Thu–Tue 9:00–19:00, closed Wed, Via Cavour 3, kitty-corner from San Lorenzo Church, 1 long block north of Baptistery, tel. 055-276-0340).

▲**Piazza della Repubblica and nearby**—This large square sits on the site of Florence's original Roman Forum. The lone column—nicknamed the belly button of Florence—once marked the intersection of the two main Roman roads. All that survives of Roman Florence is its grid street plan and this column. Look at the map (by the benches—where the old boys hang out to talk sports and politics) to see the ghost of Rome in its streets. Roman Florence was a garrison town—a rectangular fort with this square marking the intersection of the two main roads (Via Corso and Via Roma).

Today's piazza, framed by a triumphal arch, is really a nationalistic statement celebrating the unification of Italy. Florence, the capital of the country (1865–1870) until Rome was liberated, lacked a square worthy of this grand new country. So the neighborhood here was razed to open up an imposing modern forum surrounded by stately circa-1890 buildings.

The fancy La Rinascente department store, facing the Piazza della Repubblica, is one of the city's finest (WC on 4th floor, view terrace in small pricey bar above that).

▲▲**Science Museum (Istituto e Museo di Storia della Scienza)**—When we think of the Florentine Renaissance, we think of visual arts: painting, mosaics, architecture, and sculpture. But when the visual arts declined in the 1600s (abused and co-opted by political powers), music and science flourished in Florence. The first opera was written here. And Florence hosted many breakthroughs in science, as you'll see in this fascinating collection of Renaissance and later clocks, telescopes, maps, and ingenious gadgets. Trace the technical innovations as modern science emerges from 1000 to 1900. One of the most talked-about bottles in Florence is the one here containing Galileo's finger. The first floor features various tools for gauging the world, from a compass and thermometer to Galileo's telescopes. The second floor delves into clocks, pumps, medicine, and chemistry. Loaner English guide-booklets are available. It's friendly, comfortably cool, never crowded, and just a block east of the Uffizi on the Arno River (€6.50, Mon and Wed–Fri 9:30–17:00, Tue and Sat 9:30–13:00, closed Sun, Piazza dei Giudici 1, tel. 055-265-311).

▲▲**Church of Santa Maria Novella**—The 13th-century Dominican church, just south of the train station, is rich in art. Along with crucifixes by Giotto and Brunelleschi, there's every textbook's example of the early Renaissance mastery of perspective: *The Holy Trinity* by Masaccio; it's opposite the side entrance. The exquisite chapels trace art in Florence from medieval times to early Baroque. The outside of the church features a dash of Romanesque (horizontal stripes), Gothic (pointed arches), Renaissance (geometric shapes), and Baroque (scrolls). Step in and look down the 330-foot nave for a 14th-century optical illusion (€2.50, Mon–Thu and Sat 9:30–17:00, Fri and Sun 13:00–17:00). No photos are allowed.

Nearby: Art lovers can seek out the adjacent **cloisters** (separate fee and entry to the left of the church's facade); the Chapel of the Spaniards—currently under restoration—is notable for Bonaiuto's fresco *Allegory of the Dominican Order*. A palatial **perfumery** is around the corner 100 yards down Via della Scala at #16 (free but shopping encouraged, Mon–Sat 9:30–19:30, closed Sun, tel. 055-216-276). Thick with the lingering aroma of centuries of spritzes, it started as the herb garden of the Santa Maria Novella monks. Well-known even today for its top-quality products, it is extremely Florentine. Pick up the history sheet at the desk and wander deep into the shop. From the back room, you can peek at Santa Maria Novella's cloister with its dreamy frescoes and imagine a time before Vespas and tourists.

Dante's House (Casa di Dante)—Dante's house—actually a copy built near his house—is closed indefinitely for restoration. And during this restoration period, an inferno burnt most of the exhibit items in storage, so Dante fans will have to wait even longer to see his digs (Via S. Margherita 1, near the Bargello, tel. 055-219-416).

Santa Croce and Nearby

▲▲**Santa Croce Church**—The 14th-century Franciscan church, decorated with centuries of precious art, holds the tombs of great Florentines (€4, Mon–Sat 9:30–17:30, Sun 13:00–17:30; winter Mon–Sat 9:30–12:30 & 15:00–17:30, Sun 13:00–17:30, modest dress code enforced, tel. 055-246-6105).

The loud 19th-century Victorian Gothic facade faces a huge square ringed with tempting shops and littered with tired tourists. Escape into the church and admire its sheer height and spaciousness. Look for the **tomb of Galileo Galilei** (1564–1642), on your left as you enter. Having defied the Church by saying the earth revolved around the sun, his heretical remains were only allowed in the church long after his death. Directly opposite (on the right side of the nave) is the **tomb of Michelangelo Buonarroti** (1475–1564).

The first chapel to the right of the main altar features the famous fresco by Giotto of the *Death of Saint Francis*. With simple but eloquent gestures, Francis' brothers bid him a sad farewell, one of the first expressions of human emotion in modern painting.

At the end of the right transept, a door leads into the sacristy where you'll find a rumpled bit of St. Francis' tunic *(Parte di Tunica)* and old sheets of music. In the bookshop, notice the photos of the devastating flood of 1966 high on the wall. Beyond that is the "leather school" that's really more of a touristy leather store, but is mildly interesting. Exit between the Rossini and Machiavelli tombs into the cloisters. On the left, enter Brunelleschi's Pazzi Chapel, considered one of the finest pieces of Florentine Renaissance architecture.

▲**Michelangelo's House (Casa Buonarroti)**—Fans enjoy a house standing on property once owned by Michelangelo. His grand-nephew, who built the house, turned it into a little museum honoring his famous relative. You'll see some of Michelangelo's early, much-less-monumental statues and a few sketches. Be warned: Michelangelo's descendants attributed everything they could to their famous relative, but very little here (beyond 2 marble relief panels and a couple of sketches) is actually by Michelangelo (€6.50, Wed–Mon 9:30–14:00, closed Tue, English descriptions, Via Ghibellina 70, tel. 055-241-752).

Leonardo Museum—This small, entrepreneurial venture is overpriced but fun for anyone who wants to actually crank the shaft and spin the ball bearings of Leonardo's genius inventions. While this exhibit has no actual historic artifacts, it shows about 30 of Leonardo's inventions made into models, each described in English. What makes this exhibit special is that you're encouraged to touch and play with the models (€7, daily 10:00–19:00, Via dei Servi 66 red).

South of the Arno River

To locate these sights, see map on page 329.

▲▲**Pitti Palace**—From the Uffizi, follow the course of the elevated passageway (closed to non-Medicis) across the Ponte Vecchio to the gargantuan Pitti Palace, which has several separate museums.

The **Palatine Gallery/Royal Apartments** (Galleria Palatina) is the biggie, featuring palatial room after chandeliered room, its walls sagging with masterpieces by 16th- and 17th-century masters including Rubens, Titian, and Rembrandt. Its Raphael collection is the biggest anywhere (1st floor, €8.50, Tue–Sun 8:15–18:50, closed Mon, buy tickets on right-hand side of courtyard, tel. 055-238-8614).

The **Modern Art Gallery** features Romanticism, neoclassicism, and Impressionism by 19th- and 20th-century Tuscan painters (2nd floor, €5 admission includes mildly interesting Costume Museum, daily 8:15–13:50 but closed 2nd and 4th Sun and 1st, 2nd, and 5th Mon).

The **Grand Ducal Treasures** (Museo degli Argenti) is the Medici treasure chest, with jeweled crucifixes, exotic porcelain, gilded ostrich eggs, and so on, made to entertain fans of applied arts (ground floor, €6, includes Porcelain Museum and Boboli Gardens, same hours as Boboli Gardens).

Behind the palace, the huge landscaped **Boboli Gardens** offer a shady refuge from the city heat (€6, daily 9:00–18:30 fall and spring, 9:00–19:30 June–Aug, 9:00–16:30 winter, but closed 1st and last Mon of month).

▲▲**Brancacci Chapel**—For the best look at Masaccio's works (he's the early Renaissance master who reinvented perspective), see his restored frescoes at the Brancacci (brahn-KAH-chee) Chapel. Instead of medieval religious symbols, Masaccio's paintings feature simple, strong human figures with facial expressions that reflect their emotions. The accompanying works of Masolino and Filippino Lippi provide illuminating contrasts.

Call the chapel for free, mandatory **reservations** in English, often available for the same day (tel. 055-276-8224). Reservation times begin every 15 minutes, with a maximum of 30 visitors per time slot. You have 15 minutes in the actual chapel. Visits on the top of each hour include a free 40-minute video in English; ask about this when booking your visit.

Cost, Hours, Location: €4, free reservations required—it's very easy...just call 055-276-8224, €8 combo-ticket with Palazzo Vecchio, limit of 30 visitors every 15 minutes, Mon and Wed–Sat 10:00–17:00, Sun 13:00–17:00, closed Tue, ticket office closes at 16:30, cross Ponte Vecchio and turn right and hike to Piazza del Carmine.

The neighborhoods around the church are considered the last surviving bits of old Florence.

Santo Spirito Church—This has a classic Brunelleschi interior and a very early crucifix attributed to Michelangelo, painted on carved wood, given by the sculptor to the monastery in appreciation for the opportunity that they gave him to dissect and learn about bodies. Pop in here for a delightful Renaissance space and a chance to marvel at a Michelangelo all alone (free, most days 10:00–12:00 & 16:00–17:30, closed Wed afternoon, Piazza Santo Spirito, tel. 055-210-030).

▲**Piazzale Michelangelo**—Overlooking the city from across the river (look for the huge statue of David), this square is worth the 30-minute hike, drive, or bus ride (either #12 or #13 from the train station) for the view of Florence and the stunning dome of the Duomo. After dark, it's packed with local schoolkids licking ice cream and each other. About 200 yards beyond all the tour groups and teenagers is the stark, beautiful, crowd-free, Romanesque San Miniato Church.

▲**San Miniato Church**—Basilica di San Miniato al Monte was dedicated to a martyred saint who died on this hill. Its green-and-white marble facade is classic Florentine Romanesque. The church has wonderfully 3-D paintings, a plush ceiling of glazed terra-cotta panels by della Robbia, and a sumptuous Renaissance chapel (located front and center). For me, though, the highlight is the brilliantly preserved art in the sacristy (behind altar on right) showing the scenes from the life of St. Benedict (c. 1350) by a follower of Giotto. Pop a euro into the box to light the room (free, daily 9:00–19:00, 200 yards above Piazzale Michelangelo, bus #12 from train station).

EXPERIENCES

Gelato

Gelato is an edible art form. Italy's best ice cream is in Florence—one souvenir that can't break and won't clutter your luggage. But beware of scams at touristy joints on busy streets that turn a simple request for a cone into a €10 "tourist special." A key to gelato appreciation is sampling liberally and choosing flavors that go well together. Ask, as the locals do, for *"Un assaggio, per favore?"* (A taste, please?) and *"Che si sposano bene?"* (What marries well; kay see spoh-ZAH-noh BEN-ay).

Gelateria Carrozze is very good (daily 11:00–24:00, closes at 21:00 in winter; on riverfront 30 yards from Ponte Vecchio toward the Uffizi, Via del Pesce 3, also has decent sandwiches to go).

Gelateria dei Neri is another local favorite worth tracking down (daily in summer 12:00–23:00, closed Wed in winter, 2 blocks east of Palazzo Vecchio at Via dei Neri 20/22 red).

Vivoli's, which serves "only today's production" is the most famous (Tue–Sun 8:00–01:00; closed Mon, the last 3 weeks in Aug, and winter; opposite the Church of Santa Croce, go down Via Torta a block, turn right on Via Stinche). Before ordering, try a free sample of their *riso* flavor—rice.

If you want an excuse to check out the little village-like neighborhood across the river from Santa Croce, enjoy a gelato at the tiny **no-name** *gelateria* at Via San Miniato 5 red (just before Porta San Miniato).

SHOPPING

Florence is a great shopping town. Busy street scenes and markets abound, especially near San Lorenzo, near Santa Croce, on Ponte Vecchio, and at Mercato Nuovo (a covered market square 3 blocks north of Ponte Vecchio, listed on page 338). Leather (often better quality for less than the U.S. price), gold, silver, art prints, and tacky plaster mini-*David*s are most popular. Shops usually have promotional stalls in the market squares. Prices are soft in markets. Many visitors spend entire days shopping.

For ritzy Italian fashions, browse along Via de Tornabuoni, Via della Vigna Nuova, and Via Strozzi. Typical chain department stores are **Coin,** the local "Macy's" (Mon–Sat 9:30–20:00, Sun 11:00–20:00, on Via Calzaiuoli, near Orsanmichele Church); the similar, upscale **La Rinascente** (Mon–Sat 9:00–21:00, Sun 10:30–20:00, on Piazza della Repubblica, expensive café and view terrace on 4th floor); and **Oviesse,** the local "Penney's," a discount clothing chain (Mon–Sat 9:00–19:55, closed Sun; at intersection of Via Panzani and Via del Giglio, near train station).

For shopping ideas, ads, and a list of markets, see the *Florence Concierge Information* magazine described under "Tourist Information," page 323 (free from TI and many hotels).

SLEEPING

For hassle-free efficiency, I favor hotels and restaurants handy to your sightseeing activities. Nearly all of my recommended accommodations are located in Florence's downtown core.

The accommodations scene varies wildly with the season. Spring and fall are very tight and expensive, while mid-July through August is wide open and discounted. November through February is also generally empty. I've listed prices for peak season: April, May, June, September, and October.

With good information and an e-mail or phone call beforehand, you can find a stark, clean, and comfortable double with breakfast and a shower down the hall for about €70 (for the room, not per person). A basic room with a private bath costs around €100 (less at the smaller places, such as the *soggiorni*—inns). You get elegance in peak season for €150. Virtually all of the accommodations are central, within minutes of the great sights. Some places listed are old and rickety, and I've described them as such. I like places that are clean, small, central, relatively quiet at night, traditional, inexpensive, and friendly—and not listed in other guidebooks. (In Florence, 6 out of 8 means it's a keeper.)

Book ahead, especially on weekends and holidays (see page 34). Places will hold a room until early afternoon. If they say

Sleep Code

(€1 = about $1.20, country code: 39)
S = Single, **D** = Double/Twin, **T** = Triple, **Q** = Quad, **b** = bathroom, **s** = shower only. Breakfast is included, credit cards are accepted, and English is spoken unless otherwise noted. Air-conditioning, when available, is usually only turned on in summer.

To help you sort easily through these listings, I've divided the rooms into three categories based on the price for a standard double room with bath:

$$$ **Higher Priced**—Most rooms €160 or more.
$$ **Moderately Priced**—Most rooms between €110–160.
$ **Lower Priced**—Most rooms €110 or less.

they're full, mention that you're using this book. If you're traveling off-season, you can show up without reservations and find huge discounts.

Book direct—not through a tourist agency or Web site. These room-finding services cannot give opinions on quality and they generally take a commission (up to 20 percent) from the hotel. A major advantage of this book is its extensive listing of good-value rooms offered at discounted "net prices." These prices assume (and require) that you book direct so the hotel gets the full room fee, and can pass along their savings to you.

Museum-goers take note: When you book your room, you can usually ask your hotelier to book entry times for you to visit the popular Uffizi Gallery and the Accademia (Michelangelo's *David*). This service is fast, easy, and free for you and the hotel—the only requirement is advance notice. Ask them to make appointments for you any time the day after your arrival for the Uffizi and the Accademia.

Between the Station and Duomo

$$ **Hotel Accademia** is an elegant place with marble stairs, parquet floors, attractive public areas, 21 pleasant but pricey rooms, and a floor plan that defies logic (Db-€140, Tb-€170, prices promised through 2006 with this book, 5 percent additional discount with cash, air-con, tiny courtyard, Via Faenza 7, tel. 055-293-451, fax 055-219-771, www.accademiahotel.net, info@accademiahotel.net).

$$ **Residenza dei Pucci,** a block north of the Duomo, has 12 tastefully decorated rooms—in soothing earth tones—with aristocratic furniture and tweed carpeting. It's fresh and bright (Sb-€130,

Florence Hotels

1. Hotel Aldobrandini
2. Hotel Accademia
3. Florence Dream Domus B&B
4. Residenza dei Pucci
5. Hotel Basilea
6. Casa Rabatti
7. Affitacamere Lucia Freda
8. Soggiorno Magliani
9. Hotel Loggiato dei Servìti
10. Hotel Morandi alla Crocetta
11. Hotel Enza & Locanda Pitti
12. Oblate Sisters of the Assumption
13. Hotel Pendini
14. Palazzo Niccolini al Duomo
15. Pensione Maxim
16. Soggiorno Battistero
17. Albergo Firenze
18. Hotel Torre Guelfa & Hotel Pensione Alessandra
19. In Piazza della Signoria B&B
20. Hotel Davanzati
21. Hotel Pensione Elite
22. Bellevue House
23. Hotel Sole
24. Hotel il Bargellino
25. Residenza il Villino
26. Hotel Dalí
27. Hotel Centrale

Db-€145, Tb-€165, Db suite with grand Duomo view-€207, €233 for 4, claim a 10 percent discount through 2006 with cash and this book, includes breakfast, Via dei Pucci 9, tel. 055-281-886, fax 055-264-314, www.residenzadeipucci.com, residenzadeipucci @residenzadeipucci.com).

Hotel Centrale, with 18 spacious and newly renovated rooms, is indeed central (Db-€134, Tb-€165, 5 percent discount with this book through 2006, air-con, elevator, Via de' Conti 3, tel. 055-215-761, fax 055-215-216, www.hotelcentralefirenze.it, info@hotelcentralefirenze.it).

$ Hotel Aldobrandini, a budget choice in a drab old palazzo, has 15 basic, clean rooms, with the San Lorenzo market at its doorstep and the entrance to the Medici Chapels a few steps away (Ss-€40, Sb-€50, D-€65, Db-€80 with this book in 2006, €75 with cash, lots of night noise but has double-paned windows, fans, hiding behind market stalls and mopeds at Piazza Madonna degli Aldobrandini 8, tel. 055-211-866, fax 055-267-6281, www .hotelaldobrandini.it, info@hotelaldobrandini.it; Ignazio speaks English, though his one-legged mother in a wheelchair, who often greets people, speaks only Italian).

Near the Central Market

$$ Hotel Basilea has predictable three-star, air-conditioned comfort in its 38 modern rooms. This hotel has made an impressive offer for readers of this book in 2006—great double rooms with bath and breakfast for no more than €114 (Sb-€84, Db-€114, Tb-€160, elevator, terrace, Via Guelfa 41, at intersection with Nazionale—a busy street, ask for a room in the back, tel. 055-214-587, fax 055-268-350, www.hotelbasilea.net, basilea@dada.it).

$$ Florence Dream Domus B&B, with six precious little rooms, is well-run and appropriately named—you'll feel like a Medici princess here settling into its doily world of aristocratic pastels (Db-€130, pricier bigger rooms, 2-night minimum, air-con, Via de Ginori 26, tel. 055-295346, fax 055-2675-643, www.florencedream .it, info@florencedream.it).

$ Hotel Enza, which is plain, basic, and hard-working, rents 19 decent rooms (S-€40, Sb-€50, D-€60, Db-€80, 10 percent discount with this book and cash, breakfast-€5, Via San Zanobi 45, tel. 055-490990, fax 055-473-672, www.hotelenza.it, info@hotelenza.it).

$ Casa Rabatti is the ultimate if you always wanted to be a part of a Florentine family. Its four simple, clean rooms are run with motherly warmth by Marcella, who speaks minimal English. Seeing 10 years of my family Christmas cards on their walls, I'm reminded of how long she has been keeping budget travelers happy (D-€50, Db-€60, €25 per bed in shared quad or quint, prices good with this book in 2006, cash only, fans, 5 blocks from station, Via

San Zanobi 48 black, tel. 055-212-393, casarabatti@inwind.it). If booked up, Marcella will put you up in her daughter's place nearby at Via Nazionale 20 (5 big, airy rooms with fans, closer to the station). While daughter Patricia works, her mom runs the B&Bs. Getting bumped to Patricia's gives you slightly more comfort and slightly less personality...certainly not a net negative.

$ **Affitacamere Lucia Freda** is basic, clean, and cheap. Its four ground floor-yet-quiet rooms share two bathrooms, a kitchenette, and a leafy garden terrace (S-€45, D-€50, T-€70, cash only, no breakfast, Via San Zanobi 76, but ring at #31, tel. 055-487-533, luciafreda@libero.it, run by kind Lucia and son Claudio).

$ **Locanda Pitti,** tiny and funky with simple rooms, is run by a young couple (Db-€60 with this book and cash in 2006, air-con-€5 extra, no breakfast, next to Hotel Enza at Via San Zanobi 43, tel. 055-462-7327, mobile 348-597-2670, www.roomsinflorence.it, info@roomsinflorence.it, Isabella and Marco).

$ **Soggiorno Magliani** is central and humble, with seven rooms that feel and smell like a great-grandmother's home (S-€39, D-€49, T-€65, cash only but secure reservation with credit card, no breakfast, a little traffic noise but has double-paned windows, near Via Guelfa at Via Santa Reparata 1, tel. 055-287-378, hotel-magliani @libero.it, run by the friendly duo Vincenza and her English-speaking daughter, Cristina).

East of the Duomo

$$$ **Hotel Loggiato dei Serviti,** at the most prestigious address in Florence on the most Renaissance square in town, gives you Old World romance with hair dryers. Stone stairways lead you under open-beam ceilings through this 16th-century monastery's classy public rooms. The 33 cells—with air-conditioning, TVs, mini-bars, and telephones—wouldn't be recognized by their original inhabitants. The hotel staff is both professional and warm (Sb-€120, Db-€180 promised with this book in 2006, family suites from €263, elevator, Piazza S.S. Annuziata 3, tel. 055-289-592, fax 055-289-595, www.loggiatodeiservitihotel.it, info@loggiatodeiservitihotel .it, Simonetta and Francesca). Ask for a room in the back to avoid piazza noise at night. When full, they rent five spacious and elegant rooms in 17th-century annex a block away. While it lacks the monastic mystique, the rooms are bigger and gorgeous.

$$$ **Hotel Morandi alla Crocetta,** another former convent, envelops you in a 16th-century cocoon. Located on a quiet street, with 10 rooms, period furnishings, parquet floors, and wood-beamed ceilings, it takes you back a few centuries (Sb-€110, Db-€170, breakfast not worth €11, a block off Piazza S.S. Annunziata at Via Laura 50, tel. 055-234-4747, fax 055-248-0954, www .hotelmorandi.it, welcome@hotelmorandi.it). The hotel is well run

by a terrific English-speaking team: Claudio, Maurizio, Rolando, and Paolo.

$$$ Palazzo Niccolini al Duomo is one of five elite Historic Residence Hotels in Florence. The lady of the house, Ginevra Niccolini di Camugliano, actually greets the guests. The lounge is palatial and the 10 rooms big and splendid with original 16th-century frescos. If you have the money and want a Florentine palace to call home, this is a very good bet. Opened in 2003, it's just one block from the Duomo (Db-€280 April, May, June, Sept and Oct, then €250 in off-season, deluxe suites available, see Web for deals, Via dei Servi 2, tel. 055-282-412, fax 055-290-979, www.niccolinidomepalace .com, info@niccolinidomepalace.com).

$$ Residenza il Villino is popular and friendly, with 10 rooms and a pleasant, peaceful little courtyard (Db-€130, 5 percent discount with cash and this book in 2006, Qb apartment-€150, air-con, just north of Via degli Alfani at Via della Pergola 53, tel. 055-200-1116, fax 055-200-1101, www.ilvillino.it, info@ilvillino.it, Sergio).

$ Hotel Dalí (in all the guidebooks) has 10 decent, basic rooms in a nice location for a great price. Rare in this area and price range, the hotel has plenty of free parking (S-€40, D-€60, Db-€75, extra bed-€20, no breakfast, has fans, 2 blocks behind the Duomo at Via dell'Oriuolo 17, tel. and fax 055-234-0706, www.hoteldali.com, hoteldali@tin.it, Marco).

$ Oblate Sisters of the Assumption run an institutional 20-room hotel in a Renaissance building with a dreamy garden, fine (if simple) rooms, and a quiet, prayerful ambience (S-€38, D-€76, T-€114, Q-€152, cash only, only single beds, elevator, Borgo Pinti 15, tel. 055-248-0582, fax 055-234-6291, staff speak no English).

Near Piazza della Repubblica

These are the most central of my accommodations recommendations (and therefore a little overpriced). While worth the extra cost for many, given Florence's walkable core, nearly every hotel can be considered central.

$$ Hotel Pendini, a well-run, venerable three-star hotel with Old World tiles, chandeliers, and 42 rooms, is popular and central, overlooking the grand Piazza della Repubblica (Sb-€110, Db-€150, air-con, elevator, fine lounge and breakfast room, Via Strozzi 2, tel. 055-211-170, fax 055-281-807, www.hotelpendini.net, pendini@florenceitaly.net, Barbara).

$ Pensione Maxim, right on Via dei Calzaiuoli, is a big, institutional-feeling place as close to the sights as possible. Its halls are narrow, but the 29 basic rooms are comfortable and well-maintained (Sb-€68, Db-€93, Tb-€118, Qb-€138, air-con, elevator, Via dei Calzaiuoli 11, tel. 055-217-474, fax 055-283-729, www .hotelmaximfirenze.it, hotmaxim@tin.it, Paolo Maioli and Lorella).

$ Soggiorno Battistero, literally next door to the Baptistery, has seven simple, airy rooms, most with great views, overlooking the Baptistery and square (Sb-€75, Db-€98, Tb-€135, Qb-€145, prices good through 2006 with this book, 5 percent cash discount, breakfast served in room, air-con, double-paned windows, Piazza San Giovanni 1, 3rd floor, no elevator, tel. 055-295-143, fax 055-268-189, www.soggiornobattistero.it, info@soggiornobattistero.it, lovingly run by Italian Luca and his American wife, Kelly).

$ Albergo Firenze, a big, efficient place, offers 58 modern, and basic rooms in a central locale two blocks behind the Duomo (Sb-€75, Db-€95, Tb-€129, Qb-€160, cash only; prepay 1st night with traveler's check, bank draft, or international money order; air-con, elevator, at Piazza Donati 4 across from Via del Corso 8, tel. 055-214-203, fax 055-212-370, www.hotelfirenze-fi.it, firenze.albergo@tiscali.it).

Near Piazza della Signoria and Ponte Vecchio

$$$ Hotel Torre Guelfa is topped by a fun medieval tower with a panoramic rooftop terrace and a huge living room. Its 29 pricey rooms vary wildly in size (Sb-€120, small Db-€160, standard Db-€185, Db junior suite-€230, family deals, 5 percent discount with cash in 2006). Room #15, with a private terrace (€210) is worth reserving several months in advance (air-con, elevator, a couple blocks northwest of Ponte Vecchio, Borgo S.S. Apostoli 8, tel. 055-239-6338, fax 055-239-8577, www.hoteltorreguelfa.com, torre.guelfa@flashnet.it; Sabina, Giancarlo, Carlo, and Sandro).

$$$ In Piazza della Signoria B&B, overlooking Piazza della Signoria, is peaceful, classy, and homey at the same time. It comes with all the special touches and little extras you'd expect in a top-end American B&B (viewless Db-€200, view Db–€260, Tb-€280, family apartments, lavish bathrooms, tiny elevator, air-con, Via dei Magazzini 2, tel. 055-239-9546, mobile 348-321-0565, fax 055-267-6616, www.inpiazzadellasignoria.it, info@inpiazzadellasignoria.it, Sonia and Sylke).

$$ Hotel Pensione Alessandra is 16th-century, tranquil, and sprawling, with 27 big, modern rooms (S-€67, Sb-€113, D-€113, Db-€150, T-€150, Tb-€196, Q-€165, Qb-€217, 5 percent discount with cash, air-con, Borgo S.S. Apostoli 17, tel. 055-283-438, fax 055-210-619, www.hotelalessandra.com, info@hotelalessandra.com, Andrea).

$$ Hotel Davanzati, bright and shiny with artistic touches, has 21 cheery rooms with all the comforts. A family affair, friendly Tomasso and father Fabrizio also book dinners, museums, and excursions (Sb-€95, Db-€150, Tb-€195, prices good in 2006 with this book, 5 percent cash discount, elevator, air-con, Via Porta Rossa 5, tel. 055-286-666, fax 055-265-8252, www.hoteldavanzati.it, info@hoteldavanzati.it).

Near the Train Station

Note: As with any big Italian city, the area around the train station is a magnet for hardworking pickpockets on alert for lost, vulnerable tourists with bulging moneybelts hanging out of their khakis.

$ Hotel Pensione Elite is run with warmth by sunny Nadia. It has 10 comfortable—if plainly furnished—rooms (Ss-€70, Sb-€80, Ds-€75, Db-€90, Tb-€110, Qb-€130, breakfast-€6, air-con, fans, Via della Scala 12, 2nd floor, tel. & fax 055-215-395, hotelelitefi @libero.it).

$ Bellevue House is a fourth-floor oasis (no elevator) with six spacious rooms flanking a long, mellow yellow lobby. It's a peaceful time-warp thoughtfully run by Rosanna and Antonio di Grazia (Db-€95 in April–June, Sept, and Oct, Db-€75 in off-season, prices promised through 2006 with this book, 5 percent cash discount, includes breakfast in a street level bar, Via della Scala 21, tel. 055-260-8932, mobile 333-612-5973, fax 055-265-5315, www .bellevuehouse.it, info@bellevuehouse.it).

$ Hotel Sole, a clean, cozy, non-English-speaking family-run place with eight bright, modern rooms, feels like a mini-hotel (Sb-€50, Db-€80, Tb-€110, 6 percent cash discount, no breakfast, air-con, elevator, 1:00 curfew, a block toward river from Piazza Santa Maria Novella at Via del Sole 8, tel. & fax 055-239-6094, htlsole@tiscali.it).

$ Hotel il Bargellino, run by Bostonian Carmel and her Italian husband Pino, has 10 rooms with a traditional faded-paint charm and funky antique furniture just a few blocks north of the train station. Guests are welcome to relax with Carmel on her big, breezy terrace (S-€43, D-€70, Db-€80, T-€105, no breakfast, Via Guelfa 87, tel. 055-238-2658, www.ilbargellino.com, carmel @ilbargellino.com).

Oltrarno, South of the River

Across the river in the Oltrarno area, between the Pitti Palace and Ponte Vecchio, you'll still find small traditional crafts shops, neighborly piazzas, and family eateries. The following places are an easy walk from the Ponte Vecchio.

$$$ Hotel Silla, a classic three-star hotel with 36 cheery, spacious, pastel, and modern rooms, is a fine value. It faces the river and overlooks a park opposite the Santa Croce Church (Db-€165, Tb-€210, mention this book for a discount, air-con, elevator, Via dei Renai 5, tel. 055-234-2888, fax 055-234-1437, www.hotelsilla.it, hotelsilla@hotelsilla.it, Laura and Stefano).

$$ Hotel la Scaletta, ramshackle and reeking in character, is a dark, cool place with 14 rooms, a labyrinthine floor plan, senseless stairs, lots of Old World lounges, and a romantic, panoramic roof terrace (S-€60, Sb-€90, Db-€140, Tb-€160, Qb-€180, €10

Oltrarno Hotels

① Hotel la Scaletta
② To Hotel Silla
③ Pensione Sorelle Bandini
④ Soggiorno Alessandra
⑤ Istituto Gould
⑥ Ostello Santa Monaca
⑦ Casa Santo Nome di Gesù

with this book in 2006, air-con, elevator, Via Guicciardini 13 black, 150 yards south of Ponte Vecchio, tel. 055-283-028, fax 055-289-562, www.hotellascaletta.it, info@hotellascaletta.it, Giovanna, Paolo, Andrea, and Fabrizio). To fully enjoy their wonderful roof terrace, consider their light "Taste of Tuscany" meal—fine cold cuts, bread, and wine—for €10 per person.

$$ Pensione Sorelle Bandini is a rickety 500-year-old palace on a perfectly Florentine square, with 12 cavernous rooms, museum-warehouse interiors, a musty youthfulness, a balcony lounge-*loggia* with a view, and an ambience that, for romantic bohemians, can be a highlight of Florence. Mimmo or Sr. Romeo will hold a room until 16:00 with a phone call (D-€102, Db-€115, T-€145, Tb-€149, cash only, elevator, Piazza Santo Spirito 9, tel. 055-215-308, fax 055-282-761, pensionebandini@tiscali.it).

$ Istituto Gould is a Protestant Church–run place with 41 clean and spartan rooms with twin beds and modern facilities

(S-€36, Sb-€41, D-€50, Db-€58, Tb-€72, Qb-€84, no breakfast, quieter rooms in back, Via dei Serragli 49, tel. 055-212-576, fax 055-280-274, www.istitutogould.it, gould.reception@dada.it). You must arrive when the office is open (Mon–Fri 9:00–13:00 & 15:00–19:30, Sat 9:00–13:00 & 14:30–18:00, no check-in Sun or holidays).

$ Soggiorno Alessandra is a fine little place with five bright and comfy rooms. With double-paned windows, you'll hardly notice the traffic noise (D-€65, Db-€70, Tb-€90, Qb-€120, air-con-€8 extra, just past the Carraia Bridge at Via Borgo San Frediano 6, tel. 055-290-424, fax 055-218-464, www.soggiornoalessandra.it, info@soggiornoalessandra.it, Alessandra).

$ Casa Santo Nome di Gesù is a grand 29-room convent whose sisters—Franciscan Missionaries of Mary—are thankful to rent rooms to tourists. Staying in this 15th-century palace, you'll be immersed in the tranquil and thoughtful ambience created by a huge peaceful garden, generous prayerful public spaces, and smiling nuns (D-€68, Db-€80, only twin beds, time-warp breakfast room, cheap dinners, Piazza del Carmine 21, tel. 055-2138 56, fax 055-281835, www.fmmfirenze.it, info@fmmfirenze.it).

$ Ostello Santa Monaca, a cheap, well-run hostel, is a long block south of the Brancacci Chapel and attracts a young backpacking crowd (€17 beds with sheets, 4- to 20-bed rooms, 1:00 curfew, Via Santa Monaca 6, tel. 055-268-338, fax 055-280-185, www.ostello.it, info@ostello.it).

Away from the Center

$$ Hotel Ungherese is good for drivers. It's northeast of the city center (near *stadio,* en route to Fiesole), with a nice backyard garden, easy, free street parking and quick bus access (#11 and #17) into central Florence (Sb-€55, Db-€100, extra bed-€20, prices good through 2006 with this book, additional cash discount, air-con, Via G. B. Amici 8, tel. & fax 055-573-474, www.hotelungherese.it, info@hotelungherese.it, Veronica and Diane). Ask for a room on the garden. They can recommend good eateries nearby.

$ Villa Camerata, classy for an IYHF hostel, is in a pretty villa on the outskirts of Florence (€17 per bed with breakfast, 4- to 12-bed rooms, must have hostel membership card, cash only, ride bus #17 to Salviatino stop, Via Righi 2, tel. 055-601-451).

EATING

To save money and time for sights, you can keep lunches fast and simple, eating in one of the countless self-service places and pizzerias or just picnicking (try juice, yogurt, cheese, and a roll for €5). For good sit-down meals, consider the following. Remember, restaurants like to serve what's fresh. If you're into flavor, go for the seasonal best bets—featured in the *Piatti del Giorno* ("special of the day") sections of the menus.

North of the River

Near Santa Maria Novella and the Train Station

Trattoria al Trebbio serves traditional food with simple Florentine elegance at excellent prices in its candle-lit interior. Tables spill out onto a romantic little square—an oasis of Roman Trastevere-like charm (Wed–Mon 12:00–15:00 & 19:00–23:00, Tue 12:00–15:00 only, reserve for outdoor seating, half a block off of Piazza Santa Maria Novella at Via delle Belle Donne 47, tel. 055-287-089).

At **Osteria Belledonne,** you'll feel like you're eating dinner in a crowded terrarium. They serve old-fashioned Tuscan food on tight tables. While the interior has a nearly edible air, a few tables hunker on the street. They take only a few reservations; arrive early or wait (daily 12:00–14:30 & 19:00–22:30, Via delle Belledonne 16 red, tel. 055-238-2609, run by Juliano).

Trattoria Marione serves good home-cooked-style meals to a local crowd in a happy, food-loving, and steamy ambience. Dinners run about €15 plus wine (open daily, Via della Spada 27 red, tel. 055-214-756).

Trattoria Sostanza-Troia, characteristic and well-established, is famous for its beef. Hearty steaks and pastas are splittable. Whirling ceiling fans and walls strewn with old photos create a time warp, while the artichoke pies remind locals of grandma's cooking. The crowded, shared tables with paper tablecloths give the place a bistro feel. They offer two seatings, requiring reservations: one at 19:30 and one at 21:00 (dinners for about €30 plus wine, lunch Mon–Sat 12:00–14:00, closed Sun year-round and Sat in off-season, Via del Porcellana 25 red, tel. 055-212-691).

Trattoria 13 Gobbi (13 Hunchbacks) is a trendy favorite, glowing with a candle-lit atmosphere. It serves beautifully presented, surprisingly reasonable Tuscan food on big, fancy plates to a dressy, local crowd (daily 12:00–15:00 & 19:30–23:00, Via del Porcellana 9 red, tel. 055-284-015).

Near the Central and San Lorenzo Markets

For piles of picnic produce, people-watching, or just a rustic sandwich, try the huge **Central Market** (Mercato Centrale, Mon–Sat 7:00–14:00, closed Sun, a block north of San Lorenzo street market). **Trattoria Nerbone,** actually located within the market, has been serving super-cheap pastas amid a wonderful, bustling scene since 1872. Muscle up to the bar to grab a pasta and then find a spot at the shared tables (lunch only, Mon–Fri).

Each of the following market neighborhood eateries is distinct, but within about a hundred yards of each other.

Scout around at a few of them and then choose your favorite.

Trattoria Za-Za is a fun, old, characteristic high-energy place facing the Central Market. Locals lament the invasion of tourists, but everyone's happy and the food is still great. *Ribollita*, a Tuscan soup, is their specialty. Arrive early or make a reservation, especially for the wonderful outdoor piazza seating. Consider cobbling together a meal of *antipasti* (daily 11:30–23:00, Piazza del Mercato Centrale 26 red, tel. 055-215-411).

Trattoria Mario's, next to Za-Za, has been serving market-goers hearty lunches since 1953. They have a simple formula: bustling service, old-fashioned good value, a lunch-only menu, and shared tables. It's *cucina casalinga*—home cooking. Mario's is extremely popular, so come early. If there's a line, put your name on the list (€4 pastas, €5 *secondi*, Mon–Fri 12:00–15:30, closed Sat–Sun, cash only, Via Rosina 2, tel. 055-218-550).

Trattoria la Burrasca is Flintstone-chic, family-run, and ideal for Tuscan home cooking. It's small—10 tables—and often filled with our readers. Anna and Antonio Genzano have cooked and served here with passion since 1982. If Andy Capp were Italian, he'd eat here for special nights out. Everything is homemade except the desserts. And if you want good wine cheap, this is the place (Fri–Wed 12:00–15:00 & 19:00–22:00, closed Thu, not many veggies, Via Panicale 6 black, at north corner of Central Market, tel. 055-215-827, very little English spoken).

Osteria la Congrega brags it's "a Tuscan wine bar designed to help you lose track of time." In a fresh, romantic two-level setting, chef/owner Mahyar takes pride in his fun, easy menu featuring modern Tuscan cuisine, with top-notch meat and seasonal produce. He offers quality vegetarian dishes, creative salads, and an inexpensive but excellent house wine. With just 10 uncramped tables, reservations are required for dinner (€6 pastas, €12 nightly specials, daily 12:00–15:00 & 19:00–23:00, Via Panicale 43 red, tel. 055-264-5027). Mahyar offers fine wines by the glass (see list on blackboard).

Osteria Vineria i'Brincello is a bright, happy, no-frills diner with lots of spirit, friendly service, and few tourists. Notice the Tuscan daily specials on the blackboard hanging from the ceiling (daily 12:00–15:00 & 18:00–22:30, corner of Via Nazionale and Via Chaira at Via Nazionale 110 red, tel. 055-282-645).

Near the Accademia and Museum of San Marco

Pasticceria Robiglio, a classy little café, opens up its stately dining area for lunch on workdays. They have a small menu of daily specials and seem determined to do things like they did in the elegant pre-tourism days (generous €8 plates, good wines by the glass, smiling service, Mon–Fri 12:00–14:30, longer hours as a café, closed

Florence Restaurants

1. Osteria Belledonne
2. Trattoria al Trebbio
3. Trattoria Marione
4. Trattoria Sostanza-Troia
5. Trattoria 13 Gobbi
6. Trattoria Za-Za & Trattoria Mario's
7. Central Market, Tratt. la Burrasca & Tratt. Nerbone
8. Osteria la Congrega
9. Gran Caffè San Marco
10. Self-Service Rist. Leonardo
11. Antico Ristorante il Sasso di Dante
12. Ristorante il Ritrovo
13. Ristorante il Cavallino
14. Osteria Vini e Vecchi Sapori
15. Cantinetta dei Verrazzano & Ristorante Paoli
16. I Fratellini Wine & Sandwiches
17. Trattoria Icche C'è C'è
18. Osteria del Porcellino
19. Trattoria Nella
20. Gelateria Carrozze
21. Gelateria dei Neri
22. Vivoli's Gelateria
23. Café Rivoire
24. Osteria Vineria i'Brincello
25. Trattoria Buzzino
26. Pasticceria Robiglio
27. Il Centro Supermarcati

Sat–Sun, a block toward the Duomo off Piazza SS Annunziata at Via dei Servi 112 red, tel. 055-212-784).

Gran Caffè San Marco, located on Piazza San Marco across from the entrance of the San Marco Museum, might tempt you with its convenience, but it churns out horrible cafeteria fare to cheap but tired tourists (no cover charge, self-service and restaurant, Piazza San Marco 11, entrance is around the corner on Via Cavour near #50, tel. 055-215-833).

Picnic on the Ultimate Renaissance Square: There's a handy supermarket across from the Accademia *(David)* that happily makes sandwiches to your specs (Il Centro Supermarcati, Mon–Sat 8:00–20:00, Sun 9:00–19:00, Via Ricasoli 109). Choose your fresh bread and tasty meat and cheese (assembled and sold by the weight); embellish with some veggies, milk, yogurt, or juice; and hike around the block to Piazza della S. S. Annunziata, the first Renaissance square in Florence. There's a fountain for washing fruit on the square. Grab a stony seat anywhere you like and savor one of my favorite cheap Florence eating experiences. (Or, drop by Pasticceria Robiglio, half a block from the square—see above—for a sandwich and juice to go.)

Near the Duomo

Self-Service Ristorante Leonardo is fast, cheap, air-conditioned, and handy, just a block from the Duomo, southwest of the Baptistery (€3 pastas, €4 main courses, Sun–Fri 11:45–14:45 & 18:45–21:45, closed Sat, upstairs at Via Pecori 5, tel. 055-284-446). Luciano (like Pavarotti) runs the place with enthusiasm.

Antico Ristorante il Sasso di Dante serves standard Tuscan fare in a surprisingly pleasant indoor/outdoor setting in the shadow of the Duomo (€20 meals, always good vegetarian dishes and special menu of the day, daily 12:00–14:30 & 19:00–22:30, come early to snare front-row seats, Piazza delle Pallottole 6, tel. 055-282-113).

Ristorante il Ritrovo, which may close in 2006, hides down some nondescript stairs off a boring street and offers a bright, dressy setting with a homey welcome. Its meaty Tuscan cuisine, cooked with family pride, is popular for lunch with local office workers (€25 meals, Tue–Sun 12:30–15:00 & 19:00–23:00, closed Mon, 12 tables, air-con, a long block north of the Duomo at Via dei Pucci 4, tel. 055-281-688, Marco speaks English).

Near Palazzo Vecchio

Piazza della Signoria, the square facing Palazzo Vecchio, is ringed by beautifully situated yet touristy eateries. Any will do for a reasonably priced pizza. Perhaps the least of these evils is **Ristorante il Cavallino** with its glum crowd of tourists, a dumbed-down menu, rude waiters, and great outdoor seating in the shadow of the palace (€18 fixed-price dinner *menu,* open daily, tel. 055-215-818). For a fancy dessert and hot chocolate, consider **Café Rivoire** (closed Mon).

Osteria Vini e Vecchi Sapori, half a block north of Palazzo Vecchio, is a colorful hole-in-the-wall serving traditional food, including plates of mixed *crostini* (€1 each—step right up and choose at the bar) and €10 daily specials (Tue–Sun 11:00–22:00, closed Mon, Via dei Magazzini 3 red, facing the bronze equestrian statue in Piazza della Signoria, go behind its tail into the corner and to your left, run by Mario and Thomas).

Cantinetta dei Verrazzano is a long-established bakery/café/wine bar, serving delightful sandwich plates in an elegant old-time setting, and hot focaccia sandwiches to go. Their *Specialità Verrazzano* is a fine plate of four little *crostini* (like mini bruschetta) featuring different local breads, cheeses, and meats (€7). The *Tagliere di Focacce* (confirm the €6 per person price), a sampler plate of mini–focaccia sandwiches, is also fun. Either of these dishes with a glass of Chianti makes a fine light meal. As office workers pop in for a quick bite, it's traditional to share tables at lunchtime (Mon–Sat 8:00–21:00, closed Sun, just off Via Calzaiuoli on a side street across from Orsanmichele Church at Via dei Tavolini 18, tel. 055-268-590).

I Fratellini is a rustic little eatery where the "little brothers" have served peasants 27 different kinds of sandwiches and cheap glasses of Chianti wine (see list on wall) since 1875. Join the local crowd, then sit on a nearby curb or windowsill to munch, placing your glass on the wall rack before you leave (€4 for sandwich and wine, daily 8:00–20:00, 20 yards in front of Orsanmichele Church on Via dei Cimatori). Be adventurous with the menu (easy-order by number). Consider *Finocchiona* (the special local salami), *Lardo di Colonnata* (lard aged in Carrara marble), and *Cinghiale Piccante* (spicey wild boar) sandwiches. Order the most expensive wine they've corked (Brunello for €4). Bottles are labeled.

Ristorante Paoli serves wonderful local cuisine to piles of happy eaters under a richly frescoed Gothic vault. Because of its fame and central location, it's filled mostly with tourists, but for a classy, traditional splurge meal, this is my choice (Wed–Mon 12:00–14:30 & 19:00–22:30, closed Tue, reserve for dinner, €21 tourist menu, à la carte is pricier, midway between Piazza della Signoria and the Duomo at Via de Tavolini 12 red, tel. 055-216-215). Salads are flamboyantly cut and mixed from a trolley right at your table. The walls are sweaty with memories that go back to 1824 and the service is flamboyant and fun-loving—but don't get taken. Confirm prices. Woodrow Wilson slurped spaghetti here (his bust looks down on you as you eat).

Trattoria Icche C'è C'è (ee-kay chay chay; dialect for "whatever is, is") is a small, family-style eatery where fun-loving Gino serves good traditional meals (3-course €11 meals, not too touristy, Tue–Sun 12:30–14:30 & 19:00–24:00, closed Mon, midway between Bargello and river at Via Magalotti 11 red, tel. 055-216-589). If **C'è C'è** is full, the nearby **Trattoria Buzzino** has a similar style and ambience but with fewer smiles and less energy (closed Mon, Via dei Leoni 8 red, tel. 055-239-8013).

Osteria del Porcellino offers a romantic setting and a fresh, seasonal menu. A rare place that serves late, this dark, dense, candlelit place is packed with a mix of locals and tourists and run with style and enthusiasm by friendly chef Enzo. In summer, they also have inviting outdoor seating in a secretive setting out back (€8 pastas, €16 *secondi*, daily 12:00–14:30 & 19:00–1:00, reserve for dinner, Via Val di Lamona 7 red, half a block behind Mercato Nuovo, tel. 055-264-148).

Trattoria Nella serves good, typical Tuscan cuisine at affordable prices. Arrive early or be disappointed—it's understandably popular (€20 meals, Mon–Sat 12:00–14:30 & 19:00–22:00, closed Sun, 3 blocks northwest of Ponte Vecchio, Via delle Terme 19 red, tel. 055-218-925). Twin brothers Federico and Lorenzo speak English and carry on their dad's tradition of keeping their clientele well-fed and happy.

Oltrarno, South of the River

Near Ponte Vecchio

Ristorante Bibo serves *cucina tipica Fiorentina* with a pink-tablecloth-and-black-bowtie dressiness and leafy, candlelit outdoor seating. It's quiet and romantic (good €15 3-course meal, leave this book face up on the edge of the table for a 15 percent discount, daily 12:00–14:30 & 19:00–22:30, Piazza Santa Felicita 6 red, tel. 055-239-8554, enthusiastic Tonino speaks English).

Golden View Open Bar is a lively, trendy place, good for a salad, pizza, or pasta with fine wine and a view of Ponte Vecchio and the Arno River. Reservations for window tables are recommended (reasonable prices, €10 pizzas and huge salads, daily 11:30–24:00, impressive wine bar, 50 yards upstream from Ponte Vecchio at Via dei Bardi 58, tel. 055-214-502, run by Francesco and Tomaso). They have three zones: a river-side pizza place, a classier restaurant, and a jazzy lounge plus a wine bar. The live jazz (Sun, Mon, and Wed at 21:00) makes for a wonderful evening.

Via Santo Spirito and Borgo San Jacopo

Several good and colorful restaurants line this multi-named street a block off the river in Oltrarno. I'd survey the scene before making a choice.

Oltrarno Restaurants

●1 Ristorante Bibo

●2 Golden View Open Bar

●3 Trattoria Cammillo

●4 Trattoria Angiolino

●5 To Trattoria Sabatino & Trattoria da Sergio

●6 Borgo Antico, Osteria Santo Spirito, Ricchi Caffè & Café Cabiria

●7 Trattoria Casalinga

●8 Olio & Convivium Gastronomia Restaurant

Trattoria Cammillo was formerly run by Cammillo, who is now slurping spaghetti in heaven. But his granddaughter Chiara carries on the legacy, mixing traditional Tuscan and creative, modern cuisine. With a charcoal grill and a team of white-aproned waiters cranking out terrific food in a fun, noisy, dressy-but-down-to-earth ambience, this place is a hit (full dinners about €36 plus wine, Thu–Tue 12:00–14:30 & 19:30–22:30, closed Wed, reservations smart, Borgo San Jacopo 57 red, tel. 055-212-427).

Trattoria Angiolino serves good, old-fashioned local cuisine. Sit in the main hall rather than the stuffy side rooms (€20 for dinner plus wine, Tue–Sun 12:00–14:30 & 19:30–22:30, closed Mon, Via di Santo Spirito 36 red, tel. 055-239-8976).

Olio & Convivium Gastronomia Restaurant is an elegant deli with a refined oil-tasting room that has morphed into a romantic aristocratic-feeling restaurant. Their six or eight tables are surrounded by fine hams, cheeses, and other high-end edibles. It's a gentle, friendly place with a quiet atmosphere and fine wines by the glass (€10 pastas, €15 *secondi*, Mon 10:00–15:00, Tue–Sat 10:00–15:00 & 17:30–22:30, Via Santo Spirito 4, tel. 055-265-8198).

Trattoria Sabatino, farthest away and least touristy, is spacious and disturbingly cheap, with family character, red-checkered tablecloths, and a simple menu. A super place to watch locals munch, it's just outside the Porta San Frediano (medieval gate), a 15-minute walk from Ponte Vecchio (Mon–Fri 12:00–14:30 & 19:20–22:00, closed Sat–Sun, Via Pisana 2 red, tel. 055-225-955, little English spoken).

Trattoria da Sergio, a tiny eatery about a block before Porta Dan Frediano, has homey charm and a strong local following. The food is on the gourmet side of home-cooking and therefore a little more expensive but worth the splurge (€9 pastas, €15 *secondi*, Wed–Mon 10:00–14:30 & 19:30–22:30, closed Tue, reservations smart for dinner, Borgo San Frediano 145 red, tel. 055-223-449).

Piazza Santo Spirito

This classic Florentine square (a bit seedy-feeling but favored by locals) has several popular little restaurants and bars that are open nightly. They offer good local cuisine, moderate prices, and impersonal service, with a choice of indoor or romantic on-the-square seating (reservations smart).

Lively **Borgo Antico** is the hit of the square, with enticing pizzas, big deluxe plates of pasta, a delightful setting, and a trendy and boisterous young local crowd (daily 12:00–24:00, reserve for a seat on the square, Piazza Santo Spirito 6 red, tel. 055-210-437). The quieter **Osteria Santo Spirito** has good seating on the square (Piazza Santo Spirito 16 red, tel. 055-238-2383).

Ricchi Caffè, next to Borgo Antico, has fine gelato and shaded outdoor tables. After noting the plain facade of the Brunelleschi church facing the square, step inside the café and pick your favorite of the many ways it might be finished. **Café Cabiria,** on the other side of Borgo Antico, is a trendy local hangout with good, light meals, noisy 21st-century music, and a cozy Florentine-funky room in back.

Trattoria Casalinga, an inexpensive standby, comes with aproned women bustling around the kitchen. It's probably been too popular for too long, as the service has gone a bit surly and it feels like every student group and backpacker ends up here. But people seem to leave full and happy, with euros to spare for gelato (Mon–Sat 12:00–14:30 & 19:00–21:45, after 20:00 reserve or wait, closed Sun and all of Aug, just off Piazza Santo Spirito, near the church at Via dei Michelozzi 9 red, tel. 055-218-624).

TRANSPORTATION CONNECTIONS

From Florence by Train to: Pisa (hrly, 1 hr), **Lucca** (9/day, 1.5 hrs), **Siena** (9/day, 1.75 hrs, more with transfer in Empoli; bus is better), **La Spezia** (for the Cinque Terre, 2/day direct, 2 hrs, or change in Pisa), **Milan** (12/day, 3–5 hrs), **Venice** (7/day, 3 hrs), **Assisi** (3/day, 2 hrs, more frequent with transfers, direction: Foligno), **Orvieto** (6/day, 2 hrs), **Rome** (hrly, 2.5 hrs), **Naples** (10/day, 4 hrs), **Brindisi** (3/day, 11 hrs with change in Bologna), **Frankfurt** (3/day, 12 hrs), **Paris** (1/day, 12 hrs overnight), **Vienna** (4/day, 9–10 hrs).

Buses: The SITA bus station, a block west of the Florence train station, is user-friendly. Schedules are posted everywhere, and TV monitors show looming departures. Bus service drops dramatically on Sunday. You'll find buses to: **San Gimignano** (€6, 2/hr, 1.25–2 hrs, change in Poggibonsi), **Siena** (€6.50, hrly, 75-min *corse rapide* buses are faster than the train, avoid the 2-hr *diretta* slow buses), and the **airport** (€4, buy ticket on bus 2/hr, 20 min). Bus info: tel. 800-373-760 or 055-214-721 9:30–12:30; some schedules are in the *Florence Concierge Information* magazine.

Taxi to Siena: For around €100, you can arrange a ride directly from your Florence hotel to your Siena hotel. For a small group or for people with more money than time, this can be a good value.

Airports

The **Amerigo Vespucci Airport** (www.aeroporto.firenze.it), several miles northwest of Florence, has a TI, cash machines, car-rental agencies, and easy connections by airport shuttle bus with Florence's bus station, a block west of the train station (€4, 2/hr, 30 min, from Florence runs 5:30–23:00, from airport 6:00–23:30). Airport info: 055-306-1300, flight info: 055-306-1700 (domestic), 055-306-1702 (international, automated). Allow about €16–20 for a taxi.

International flights often land at Pisa's **Galileo Galilei Airport** (also has TI and car-rental agencies, www.pisa-airport .com), a little over an hour from Florence by train (2/hr, 70 min). Flight info: 050-849-300.

Fiesole

Perched on a hill overlooking the Arno valley, Fiesole gives weary travelers a break in the action and, during the heat of summer, a breezy location from which to admire the city below. The ancient

Etruscans knew a good spot when they saw one, and chose to settle here, establishing Fiesole about 400 years before the Romans founded Florence. Wealthy Renaissance families in pre-air-conditioning days also chose Fiesole as a preferred vacation spot and built villas in the surrounding hillsides. Later, 19th-century Romantics spent part of the Grand Tour admiring the vistas, much like the hordes of tourists do today. Most come here for the view—the actual sights pale in comparison to those in Florence.

ORIENTATION

Getting to Fiesole: From the Florence train station, take bus #7—enjoying a peek at gardens, vineyards, orchards, and villas—to the last stop, Piazza Mino (€1, 4/hr, fewer after 20:00, 30 min, departs Florence from Piazza Adua at northeast side of train station and also from south side of Piazza San Marco). Taxis from Florence cost about €20 (take taxi to highest point you want to visit—La Reggia Ristorante for view terrace, or Church of San Francesco—then explore downhill).

Tourist Information: To reach the TI from the bus stop, walk toward the bell tower and take the first right. Pick up a free map (Mon–Sat 9:00–18:00, Sun 10:00–13:00 & 14:00–18:00, closes 1 hour earlier in winter, Via Portigiani 3, tel. 055-598-720). Market day is Saturday, when a modest selection of food and household items fills Piazza Mino (8:00–13:00).

SIGHTS

▲▲**Terrace with a View**—Catch the sunset (and your breath) from the view terrace just below La Reggia Ristorante. It's a steep hike from the Fiesole bus stop (face bell tower, take Via San Francesco on left).

Church of San Francesco—For even more hill-climbing, continue up from the view terrace to this charming little church. Several colorful altar paintings and an intimate scale make this church more enjoyable than Fiesole's Duomo (free, Mon–Sat 7:30–12:00 & 15:00–18:00, Sun 13:00–19:00, Via San Francesco 13).

Duomo—While this church has a drab 19th-century exterior, the interior is worth a look, if only for the blue- and white-glazed Giovanni della Robbia statue of St. Romulus over the entry door (free, daily 7:30–12:00 & 15:00–18:00, across Piazza Mino from the bus stop).

Roman Theater and Archaeological Park—Occasionally used today for plays, this well-preserved theater held up to 2,000 people. The site's other ruins are, well, ruined, and lacking in explanation. But the valley view and peaceful setting are lovely (€6.50

combo-ticket includes the Civic and Bandini Museums, daily 9:30–19:00, until 17:00 in winter, from the bus stop, cross Piazza Mino toward the back of the Duomo, entrance is on the right).

Civic Museum (Museo Civico)—As the mandatory exit to the Archaeological Park, the museum might seem like a funnel into the gift shop, but its decent collection of Roman artifacts is fairly interesting. Look for English explanations (€6.50 combo-ticket, daily 9:30–19:00).

Bandini Museum (Museo Bandini)—This teensy museum displays a modest morsel of quality Gothic and Renaissance art (€6.50 combo-ticket, daily 10:00–19:00, behind Duomo, Via Dupre 1).

Private Villas—Although most villas in the area are privately owned, many open their gardens to the public on a seriously limited, reservation-only basis. For the tenacious tourist, the TI can sort out schedules and entries (€4, not practical without a car, reservations and information in Italian, tel. 800-414-240).

SLEEPING

(€1 = about $1.20, country code: 39)
For the "Sleep Code," see page 349.

$ **Hotel Villa Bonelli** has three-stars, 20 rooms, and a view from the breakfast room (Sb-€60, Db-€80-110, Tb-€120, air-con, 250 yards from bus stop up Via Gramsci, right on Via Poeti to #1, tel. 055-59513, fax 055-598-942, www.hotelvillabonelli.com, info@hotelvillabonelli.com).

EATING

The two restaurants are on Piazza Mino, where the bus stops from Florence.

Ristorante Perseus serves authentic Tuscan dishes at a fair price. A local favorite with its rambling interior, the specials are scrawled on a scrap of paper (daily 12:00–15:00 & 19:00–23:30, Piazza Mino 9, tel. 055-59143, friendly Ago speaks English).

Ristorante Aurora is an upscale alternative with a territorial view terrace (daily 12:30–14:30 & 19:30–22:30, next to bus stop on Piazza Mino).

Fiesole is made to order for a scenic and breezy **picnic.** Pick up your goodies at the Co-Op supermarket on Via Gramsci and walk to the panoramic terrace (see "Sights," page 367). Or, for more convenience and less view, picnic at the shaded park on the way to the view terrace (walk up Via San Francesco about halfway to the terrace and climb the stairs to the right).

PISA AND LUCCA

Florence is within easy striking distance of a number of great cities—as their fortifications attest. Along with Siena (which merits solo coverage in another chapter), Pisa and Lucca show that Florence wasn't the only power and cultural star of the late Middle Ages and Renaissance.

Pisa is touristy, but worth visiting for its Field of Miracles (Leaning Tower, Cathedral, and Baptistery). Lucca, contained within its fine Renaissance wall, has a charm that causes many connoisseurs of Italy to claim it as a favorite stop. While Pisa is best as a short stop-over, to really enjoy Lucca it's best to spend the night. Thirty minutes from each other, each is a 90-minute train ride from Florence and well-served by the excellent autostrada.

Pisa

In A.D. 1200, Pisa's power peaked. For nearly three centuries (1000–1300), Pisa rivaled Venice and Genoa as a sea-trading power, exchanging European goods for luxury items in Muslim lands. As a port near the mouth of the Arno River (6 miles from the coast), the city enjoyed easy access to the Mediterranean, plus the protection of sitting a bit upstream. ("Pisa" is an ancient word meaning delta.) The Romans had made it a navy base, and by medieval times, it was a major player.

Pisa's 150-foot galleys cruised the Mediterranean, gaining control of the islands of Corsica, Sardinia, and Sicily, and trading with Europeans, Muslims, and Byzantine Christians as far south as North Africa and as far east as Syria. European Crusaders hired

Pisa and Lucca

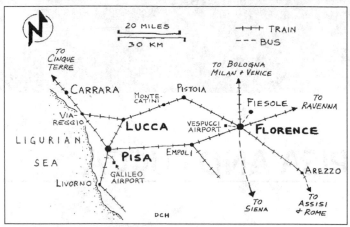

Pisan boats to carry them and their supplies as they headed off to conquer the Muslim-held Holy Land. The Pisan "Republic" prided itself on its independence from both popes and emperors. The city used its sea-trading wealth to build the grand monuments of the Field of Miracles, including the now-famous Tower.

But the Pisa fleet was routed in battle by Genoa (1284, at Meloria, off Livorno), their overseas outposts were taken away, the port silted up, and Pisa was left high and dry, with only its Field of Miracles and its university keeping it on the map.

Pisa's three important sights—the Duomo, Baptistery, and bell tower—float regally on the best lawn in Italy. The style throughout is Pisa's very own "Pisan Romanesque." Even as the church was being built, the Piazza del Duomo was nicknamed the "Campo dei Miracoli," or Field of Miracles, for the grandness of the undertaking.

The Leaning Tower recently reopened after a decade of restoration and topple prevention. To ascend, you'll have to make a reservation when you buy your €15 ticket (for details, see "Climbing the Tower," page 377).

Planning Your Time

Seeing the Tower, visiting the square, and wandering through the church are 90 percent of the Pisan thrill. Pisa is a touristy quickie. By car, it's a headache. By train, it's a joy. Train travelers may need to change trains in Pisa anyway. Hop on the bus and see the Tower (a 15-min ride each way). If you want to climb it, go straight to the ticket booth to snare an appointment—usually for a couple of hours later (or for an extra €2, you can book a time online at www.opapisa.it). Sophisticated sightseers stop more for the Pisano carvings in the Duomo and Baptistery than for a look at the tipsy Tower. There's nothing wrong with Pisa, but I'd stop only to see the Field of Miracles and get out of town. By car, it's a 45-minute detour from the freeway.

If you explore the rest of the city, it stretches southeast of the Field of Miracles, framed by the Arno on the south and bordered on the east and west by two streets, Borgo Stretto and Via Santa Maria.

ORIENTATION

Tourist Information

One TI is about 200 yards from the train station—exit and walk straight up left side of the street to the big, circular Piazza Vittorio Emanuele II. The TI is on the left, around the corner from #16 (Mon–Fri 9:00–19:00, Sat 9:00–13:30, closed Sun, tel. 050-42-291, www.pisa.turismo.toscana.it). The other, less-enthusiastic TI is behind the Leaning Tower, next to the ticket office (summer daily 8:00–20:00, winter Mon–Fri 9:00–18:00, Sat–Sun 10:30–16:30, tel. 050-560-464). There's also one at the airport (daily 10:30–16:30 & 18:00–22:00, tel. 050-503-700).

Arrival in Pisa

By Train: If you want to check your baggage upon arrival, look for *deposito bagagli;* if you're facing the tracks, it's to the left at the far end of platform #1, past the police office (€3/bag per 12 hrs, daily 6:00–21:00, they photocopy your passport to check ID, ignore nonfunctional lockers).

To get to the Field of Miracles from the station, you can **walk** (45 min, get free map from TI and they'll mark the best route or follow the walk below), take a **taxi** (€6, at taxi stand at station or tel. 050-541-600; when you're returning, you'll find a taxi stand 30 yards from the Leaning Tower, just in front of the Bar Duomo), or catch a **bus** (10-min ride to the Tower). To go by city bus, take bus #3 (3/hr) or *navetta* shuttle bus #A (4/hr)—both stop across the street from the train station, in front of Jolly Hotel Cavaliere. Buy an €0.80 bus ticket from the *tabacchi*/magazine kiosk in the station's main hall or at any *tabacchi* shop (good for 1 hour, round-trip permitted). Before getting on the bus, confirm that your bus is indeed going to "Campo dei Miracoli" (ask the driver, a local, or TI) or risk taking a long tour of Pisa's suburbs. The right buses let you off at Piazza Manin, in front of the gate to the Field of Miracles; drivers make sure tourists don't miss it. To return to the train station from the Tower, catch the bus across the street from where you got off (again, confirm the stop with a local or at the TI). You can buy the ticket from the driver for a small extra fee.

By Car: To get to the Leaning Tower, follow signs to the *Duomo* or *Campo dei Miracoli*, located on the north edge of town. If you're coming from the Pisa Nord autostrada exit, you won't have to mess with the city center, but you will likely have to endure some terrible traffic. There's no better option than the €1/hour pay lot just outside the town wall a block from the Tower.

By Plane: From Pisa's airport, take bus #3 (€0.80, 3/hr, 15 min) or a taxi (€6) into town.

Helpful Hints

Markets: An open-air produce market attracts picnickers to Piazza della Vettovaglie, one block north of the Arno River near Ponte di Mezzo (Mon–Sat 7:00–18:00, closed Sun). A street market bustles on Wednesday and Saturday mornings between Via del Brennero and Via Paparrelle (just outside of wall, about 6 blocks east of the Tower).

Festivals: The month of June has many events, culminating in a celebration for Pisa's patron saint Ranieri (June 16–17).

SELF-GUIDED WALK

Welcome to Pisa:
From the Train Station to the Tower

A leisurely 45-minute stroll from the station to the Tower is a good way to get acquainted with the more subtle virtues of this Renaissance city. It's also a more pleasant alternative to the tourist-mobbed buses. You'll find Pisa to be a student-filled, classy, Old World town with an Arno-scape much like its rival upstream.

Exit straight out of the station, walking north up Viale Gramsci to the circular Piazza Vittorio Emanuele II (where the TI is). Continue straight north, up the pedestrian-only shopping street Corso Italia, and cross the Arno River over Ponte di Mezzo. This modern bridge, constructed on the same site where the Romans built theirs, is the center of Pisa and the heart of local festivals. Cross and continue north up the elegantly arcaded Borgo Stretto, Pisa's main shopping street.

The first left, Via delle Colonne, is a worthwhile one-block detour, leading to Piazza Vettovaglie, some atmospheric restaurants, and the small but lively open-air produce market just beyond (Mon–Sat 7:00–18:00, closed Sun).

Continue north on Borgo Stretto another 100 yards or so. Take the second left on nondescript Via Ulisse Dini (it's not obvious—turn left immediately after the arcade's end). From here, angle northwest to the Tower. Along the way, you pass through Pisa's historic core, including Piazza dei Cavalieri, with its colorfully decorated palace and statue of Cosimo I de' Medici (the Florentine

Pisa

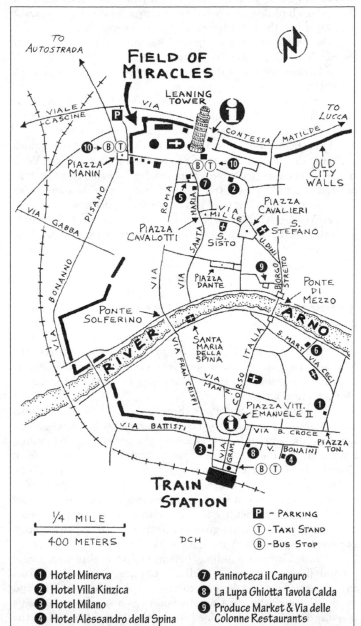

TO AUTOSTRADA

FIELD OF MIRACLES

LEANING TOWER

TO LUCCA

VIA CONTESSA MATILDE

OLD CITY WALLS

VIALE CASCINE

P

PIAZZA MANIN

VIA PISANO

VIA GABBA

VIA BONANNO PISANO

VIA ROMA

SANTA MARIA

PIAZZA CAVALOTTI

VIA MILLE

PIAZZA CAVALIERI

S. STEFANO

S. SISTO

VIA ULDINI

VIA

VIA

PIAZZA DANTE

BORGO STRETTO

PONTE DI MEZZO

PONTE SOLFERINO

RIVER ARNO

SANTA MARIA DELLA SPINA

VIA FRAN CRISPI

VIA ITALIA

S. MART.

VIA CECI

VIA MANZ.

CORSO ITALIA

PIAZZA VITT. EMANUELE II

VIA B. CROCE

PIAZZA TON.

VIA BATTISTI

VIA GRAM.

V. BONAINI

B T

TRAIN STATION

¼ MILE

400 METERS

DCH

P – PARKING
T – TAXI STAND
B – BUS STOP

1. Hotel Minerva
2. Hotel Villa Kinzica
3. Hotel Milano
4. Hotel Alessandro della Spina
5. Pizzeria/Trattoria La Buca
6. Ristorante Galileo
7. Paninoteca il Canguro
8. La Lupa Ghiotta Tavola Calda
9. Produce Market & Via delle Colonne Restaurants
10. Bus To/From Train Station (2)

who ruled Pisa in the 16th century). The frescoes on the exterior of the square's buildings, though damaged by salty sea air and years of neglect, reflect the fading glory of Pisa under the Medicis.

The palace and the compound behind the gates to the left (Scuola Normale) house Pisa's famous university. The university is one of Europe's oldest, with roots in a law school dating as far back as the 11th century.

In the mid-16th century, it was a hotbed of controversy, as spacey professors like Galileo Galilei studied the solar system—with results that challenged the church's powerful doctrine.

From here, continue straight on to Via Corsica. Take a quick peek into the humble church of San Sisto, ahead on the left. With simple bricks, assorted reused columns, heavy walls, and few windows, this is the typical "Romanesque" style before the more lavish "Pisan Romanesque" of the Field of Miracle structures.

Follow Via Corsica to Via Santa Maria, where a right turn leads you north, through increasingly touristy claptrap, directly to the Tower.

SIGHTS

▲▲**Field of Miracles (Campo dei Miracoli)**—Scattered across a golf-course-green lawn are four large white buildings that make up Pisa's religious center—the cathedral (or Duomo), its bell tower (the Leaning Tower), Baptistery, and Camposanto Cemetery. The four buildings share similar building materials, similar decoration, and a tendency toward circular designs—giving the Campo a pleasant visual unity.

The style is dubbed Pisan Romanesque. Where traditional Romanesque has a heavy fortress feel—thick walls, barrel arches, few windows—Pisan Romanesque is light and elegant. At ground level, most of the structures have a solid Romanesque base of simple pilasters and blind arches (columns and arches in relief). On the upper levels, you'll see a little of everything—tight rows of thin columns borrowed from the Lombards (barbarians); pointed Gothic gables and prickly spires; Byzantine mosaics and horseshoe arches; and geometric designs (such as diamonds) and striped colored marbles inspired by mosques in Muslim lands.

All the Campo's buildings have bright white marble, a simple ground floor, and rows of delicate columns and arches forming open-air arcades. Architecturally, the Campo is unique and exotic. Theologically, the Campo's buildings mark the main events of every Pisan's life: christened in the Baptistery, married in the Duomo, honored in ceremonies at the Tower, and buried in the Camposanto.

Lining this field of artistic pearls is a gauntlet of Europe's

Pisa's Field of Miracles

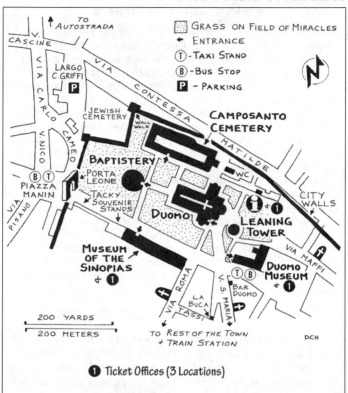

GRASS ON FIELD OF MIRACLES
← ENTRANCE
(T) - TAXI STAND
(B) - BUS STOP
(P) - PARKING

TO AUTOSTRADA
V. CASCINE
VIA CARLO CAMEO
VIA CONTESSA MATILDE
LARGO C. GRIFFI
V. NICO
JEWISH CEMETERY
WALL WALK
CAMPOSANTO CEMETERY
BAPTISTERY
PORTA LEONE
PIAZZA MANIN
VIA PISANO
TACKY SOUVENIR STANDS
DUOMO
WC
LEANING TOWER
CITY WALLS
VIA MAFFI
MUSEUM OF THE SINOPIAS
VIA ROMA
V. S. MARIA
LA BUCA TASSI
BAR DUOMO
DUOMO MUSEUM
200 YARDS
200 METERS
TO REST OF THE TOWN + TRAIN STATION
DCH

❶ Ticket Offices (3 Locations)

tackiest souvenir stands, as well as dozens of amateur mimes "propping up" the Leaning Tower while tourists take photos.

▲▲**Leaning Tower**—The Tower is nearly 200 feet tall and 55 feet wide, weighing 14,000 tons and leaning at an 85-degree angle (15 feet off the vertical axis). It started to lean almost immediately after construction began. There are eight stories—a simple base, plus six stories of columns (forming arcades), and a belfry on top. The inner, structural core is a hollow cylinder built of limestone bricks, faced with white marble barged here from San Giuluano, northeast of the city. The thin columns of the open-air arcades make the heavy Tower seem light and graceful.

The Tower was built over two centuries by at least three different architects. You can see how each successive architect tried to "correct" the problem of leaning—once halfway up (after the 4th story), once at the belfry on the top.

The first stones were laid in 1173, probably under the architect Bonanno Pisano (who also designed the Duomo's bronze back door). Five years later, just as they'd finished the base and the first

Field of Miracles Tickets

Pisa has a scheme to get you into its neglected secondary sights: the Baptistery, the Duomo Museum, Camposanto Cemetery, and the Museum of the Sinopias (fresco pattern museum). Since you may be visiting these lesser sights anyway, I give more sightseeing information on these than they may deserve.

For any one monument, you'll pay €5; for two monuments the cost is €6; for four monuments minus the Duomo it's €8.50; and for the works (including the Duomo) you'll pay €10.50 (cash only). By comparison, the Duomo alone is a bargain (€2).

You can buy any of these tickets at one of the three ticket offices: behind the Leaning Tower, at the Duomo Museum, or at the Museum of the Sinopias (near the Baptistery, almost suffocated by souvenir stands). All three offices are have big, yellow "i" triangle-shaped signs. Note that you can buy a ticket just for, say, the Duomo at any of these points.

No matter what ticket you get, you'll have to pay another €15 to climb the Leaning Tower. Tickets for the ascent are sold at the three ticket offices (listed above) or online at www .opapisa.it.

arcade, someone said, "Is it just me, or does that look crooked?" The heavy Tower—resting on a very shallow 13-foot foundation—was obviously sinking on the south side into the marshy, multilayered, unstable soil. (Actually, all the Campo's buildings tilt somewhat.) They carried on anyway, until they'd finished four stories (the base plus 3 arcade floors). Then, construction was suddenly halted—no one knows why—and for a century the Tower sat half-finished and visibly leaning.

Around 1272, the next architect continued, trying to correct the problem by angling the next three stories backward, in the opposite direction of the lean. The project then sat (mysteriously) idle for nearly another century. Finally, Tommaso Pisano put the belfry on the top (c. 1350–1372), also kinking it backward.

Man versus Gravity: After the Tower's completion, several attempts were made to stop its slow-motion fall. The architect/artist/writer Giorgio Vasari reinforced the base (1550), and it actually worked. But in 1838, well-intentioned engineers pumped out ground water, destabilizing the Tower, causing it to fall at a rate of a millimeter a year.

It got so bad that, in 1990, it was closed for repairs. Thirty million dollars were spent to stabilize the Tower. Engineers dried the soil with steam pipes, anchored the Tower to the ground with steel cables, and buried 600 tons of lead on the north side as a counterweight (not visible)—all with little success. The break-through came when they drilled 15-foot holes in the ground on the north side and sucked out sixty tons of soil, allowing the Tower to sink on the north side. The Tower has actually been straightened by about six inches, turning the clock back 200 years on the still-leaning (and probably still falling) Tower.

As well as gravity, erosion threatens the Tower. Since its construction, 135 of the Tower's 180 marble columns have had to be replaced. Stone decay, deposits of lime and calcium phosphate, accumulations of dirt and moss, cracking from the stress of the lean—all of these are factors in its decline.

Thanks to the Tower's lean, there are special trouble spots. The lower south side (which is protected from cleansing rain and wind) is black from dirty airborne particles, while the upper areas, though clean, have more stone decay (from eroding rain and wind).

The Tower, now stabilized, is getting cleaned. Cracks are filled, and accumulations removed, using atomized water sprays and poultices of various solvents.

Climbing the Tower: Thirty people every 30 to 40 minutes can clamber up the 294 tilting stairs to the top for €15 (daily 8:30–20:30, off-season 9:00–17:00, ticket office opens 30 min early).

If you want to make the necessary reservation in person (rather than online), go straight to the ticket office behind the Tower. You choose a (30–40 min) time slot for your visit at the time of purchase. During the tourist season it will likely be a couple of hours before you're able to go up (you could see the rest of the monuments and grab lunch while waiting), but the wait will probably be much shorter if you arrive at the beginning or end of the day. For an extra €2, you can book a time at www.opapisa.it. Online bookings are accepted no more than 45 days—and no fewer than 14 days—in advance.

You can pick up your tickets any time, but do so at least an hour before your time slot in case there's a line. You must show up 10 minutes early for your appointment. You can't take any bags up the Tower, but daybag-sized lockers are available at the TI behind the Tower (a guard opens the room every half-hour; you must leave your passport with your bag for security). Even though the ticket-office sign says the visit is guided, that only means you'll be accompanied by a museum guard to make sure you don't stay up past your scheduled appointment time. Not including the climb, you'll have about 15 minutes for vertigo on top.

Caution: There are no railings, the steps are slanted, and rain makes the marble slippery. Anyone with balance issues of any sort should think twice before ascending.

▲▲**Duomo (Cathedral)**—The gargantuan Pisan Romanesque church has a Pisano pulpit and is artistically more important than its more famous bell tower (€2, free Nov–March; summer Mon–Sat 10:00–19:45, Sun 13:00–19:45; spring and fall Mon–Sat 10:00–17:30, Sun 13:00–17:45; winter Mon–Sat 10:00–12:30 & 15:00–16:30, Sun 15:00–16:30). Shorts are OK as long as they're not short shorts, but shoulders should be covered (although it's not really enforced). Big backpacks are not allowed, nor is storage provided, but if you're climbing the Tower you can leave your daybag in its locker room (see above, must leave passport with left luggage); technically, these small lockers are for Tower climbers, but they could work for clever cathedral visitors.

Begun in 1063, the Duomo is the centerpiece of the Field of Miracles' complex of religious buildings. The architect Buschetto created the style of Pisan Romanesque that set the tone for the Baptistery and Tower.

The **bronze back door** (the one at the Tower end), designed by Bonnano Pisano (c. 1186), has 24 different panels that show Christ's story using the same simple, skinny figures found in Byzantine icons. Cast using the lost-wax technique, this door was an inspiration for Lorenzo Ghiberti's bronze doors in Florence.

Go inside. The 320-foot nave was the longest in Christendom when it was built. The striped marble and arches-on-columns give it an exotic, almost mosque-like feel. Dim light filters in from the small upper windows of the galleries, where the women worshipped. The gilded coffered ceiling has shields of Florence's Medicis, including the round symbols ("pills"). This powerful family—who began as medics, later became cloth merchants, and finally bankers—took over Pisa after its glory days.

The 15-foot-tall, octagonal **pulpit** by Giovanni Pisano is the last, biggest, and most complex of the four pulpits by the Pisano father-and-son team (which also include the Baptistery and Siena's Duomo). Christ's life unfolds in a series of panels crammed with figures. Giovanni left no stone uncarved in his pursuit of beauty. Originally, this and the other pulpits were frosted with paint, gilding, and colored pastes.

The bronze **incense burner** that hangs from the ceiling (near the pulpit) is a replica of the one that supposedly caught teenage Galileo's attention when a gust of wind set the lamp swinging. He timed the swings, and realized that the burner swung back and forth in the same amount of time regardless of how wide the arc. It's thought the Pisa-born Galileo also threw objects off the Tower to time their fall.

Pause at the **tomb of Holy Roman Emperor Henry VII,** the German king (c. 1275–1313) who invaded Italy and was welcomed by Pisans as a leader of unity and peace. Unfortunately, Henry took ill and died young, leaving Ghibelline Pisa at the mercy of its Guelph rivals. Pisa never recovered.

▲**Baptistery**—The Baptistery, the biggest in Italy, is interesting for its great acoustics (summer daily 8:00–20:00, spring and fall 9:00–17:30, winter 9:00–16:30, located in front of the Duomo).

The building is 180 feet tall—John the Baptist on top looks eye-to-eye with the tourists atop the nearly 200-foot Leaning Tower. Notice that the Baptistery leans nearly six feet to the north (the Tower leans 15 to the south). The building (begun 1153) is modeled on the circular, domed church of the Holy Sepulchre in Jerusalem, seen by Pisan Crusaders who occupied Jerusalem in 1099.

Inside, it's simple, spacious, and baptized with light. Tall arches encircle just a few pieces of religious furniture. In the center sits the **octagonal font** (1246, topped with a statue of the first baptist...John), which contains plenty of space for baptizing adults by immersion (the medieval custom), plus four wells for dunking babies.

Nicola Pisano's **pulpit** is arguably the world's first Renaissance sculpture. (It's the first signed work by the "Giotto of sculpture," working in what came to be called the "Renaissance" style.) The pulpit is a freestanding sculpture with classical columns, realistic people and animals, and 3-D effects in the carved panels. The speaker's platform stands on columns that rest on the backs of animals, representing Christianity's triumph over paganism. The relief panels, with scenes from the life of Christ, are more readable than the Duomo pulpit. Read left to right, starting from the back: Nativity, adoration of the Magi, presentation in the temple, Crucifixion, Last Judgment.

The remarkable **acoustics** of the building are due to the 250-foot-wide dome. Recent computer analysis suggests that the 15th-century architects who built the dome intended this building to be not just a Baptistery but also a musical instrument. If you ask nicely (*Mi scusi...Cante, per favore?*; pronounced mee SKOO-zee KAHN-tay pehr fah-VOH-ray) and leave a tip (a couple of euros), the ticket-taker uses the place's echo power to sing haunting harmonies with himself.

Camposanto Cemetery—This site, bordering the cathedral square on the north, has been a cemetery since ancient times. Lined with faint frescoes, the ancient cemetery is famous for its "Holy Land" dirt, said to reduce a body into a skeleton within a day (same hours as Baptistery, on north side of Field of Miracles).

Highlights are the building's cloistered interior courtyard (with intricately-carved arches surrounding grass growing in Holy Dirt); some ancient Roman and Greek sarcophagi; and the 1,000-square-foot, 14th-century fresco, *The Triumph of Death*. The fresco captures Pisa's mood in the wake of the bubonic plague (1348), which killed one in three Pisans.

Museum of the Sinopias (Museo delle Sinopie)—Housed in a 13th-century hospital, the museum displays some of the original sketches used to make the frescoes in the Camposanto Cemetery. If you loved the *Triumph of Death* and others in the Camposanto Cemetery, or if you're interested in fresco technique, this museum is worthwhile (same hours as Baptistery, entrance smothered by souvenir stands, across from Baptistery).

Sinopias are sketches in red paint painted directly on the wall just before the final colored version. The master always did the sinopia himself; if he liked the results, his assistants copied or traced the sinopia onto paper, called a cartoon. Then the wall was covered with plaster (completely covering up the sinopia), and the assistants retraced the outlines, using the cartoon as a guide. While the plaster was still wet, the master quickly filled in the color and details, producing the final frescoes. These sinopias—never meant to be seen—were uncovered by the bombing and restoration of the Camposanto.

Duomo Museum (Museo dell' Opera del Duomo)—The museum is big on Pisan art, displaying treasures of the cathedral, sculptures (12th–14th century), paintings, and silverware, as well as ancient Egyptian, Etruscan, and Roman artifacts. It houses many of the original statues that once adorned the Campo's buildings (where copies stand today), notably the statues by Nicola and Giovanni Pisano. You can stand face-to-face with the Pisanos' very human busts that ring the outside of the Baptistery. You'll see a mythical sculpted hippogriff (a medieval jackalope) and other oddities brought back from the Holy Land by Pisan Crusaders. The museum also has several large-scale wooden models of the Duomo and Baptistery (same hours as Baptistery, behind Leaning Tower, Piazza Arcivescovado 18).

Panoramic Walk on the Wall—This much-advertised walk, which includes just a small section of the 12th-century wall, isn't worth your time or €2 (March–Dec daily 10:00–18:00, entrance near Baptistery, at Porta Leone).

Museo Nazionale di San Matteo—On the river and in a former convent, this art museum displays 12th- to 15th-century sculptures, illuminated manuscripts, and paintings by Martini, Ghirlandaio, Masaccio, and others (€4, Tue–Sat 8:30–19:00, Sun 8:30–13:00, closed Mon, near Piazza Mazzini at Lungarno Mediceo, tel. 050-541-865).

SLEEPING

$$$ **Hotel Alessandro della Spina,** located in a nondescript neighborhood near the train station, has 16 elegant and colorful rooms, each named after a flower (Sb-€105, Db-€125, air-con, free

---

Sleep Code

(€1 = about $1.20, country code: 39)
S = Single, **D** = Double/Twin, **T** = Triple, **Q** = Quad, **b** = bathroom, **s** = shower only. Unless otherwise noted, credit cards are accepted and breakfast is included (but usually optional). English is generally spoken.

To help you sort easily through these listings, I've divided the rooms into three categories based on the price for a standard double room with bath:

$$$ **Higher Priced**—Most rooms €120 or more.
$$ **Moderately Priced**—Most rooms between
€80–120.
$ **Lower Priced**—Most rooms €80 or less.

---

parking, Via Alessandro della Spina 7; head straight out of train station, turn right onto Viale F. Bonaini, take 3rd right onto Via Alessandro della Spina and follow signs; tel. 050-502-777, fax 050-20583, www.hoteldellaspina.it, info@hoteldellaspina.it).

$$ Hotel Minerva, a seven-minute walk from the train station, is a classy, peaceful place with all the comforts (Sb-€85, Db-€110, Tb-€128, air-con, garden terrace, Piazza Toniolo 20; head straight out of station to Piazza Vittorio Emanuele, turn right onto Viale B. Croce, at next square—Piazza Toniolo—turn left; tel. 050-501-081, fax 050-501-559, hotelminerva@pisaonline.it).

$$ Hotel Villa Kinzica, with 33 decent rooms, is just steps away from the Field of Miracles—ask for a room with a view of the Tower (Sb-€78, Db-€108, Tb-€124, Qb-€135, elevator, air-con, attached restaurant, Piazza Arcivescovado 2, tel. 050-560-419, fax 050-551-204, www.hotelvillakinzica.it, info@hotelvillakinzica.it).

$ Hotel Milano, near the station, offers 10 spacious, tidy rooms handy for train travelers (D-€53, Db-€73, breakfast-€3, air-con, Via Mascagni 14, tel. 050-23162, fax 050-44237, hotelmilano@pisaonline.it).

EATING

For a quick lunch or dinner, the pizzeria/trattoria **La Buca,** just a block from the Leaning Tower, is adequate and convenient (Sat–Thu 12:00–15:30 & 19:00–22:30, closed Fri, at Via Santa Maria 171 and Via A. G. Tassi, tel. 050-560-660).

Ristorante Galileo, south of the Arno, has excellent pizza and pasta (€4.50–8, Wed–Mon 12:00–15:00 & 19:30–22:00, closed Tue, Via Silvestri 12, tel. 050-28-287).

Paninoteca il Canguro makes warm, hearty sandwiches to order. Try their popular primavera sandwich (Mon–Fri 11:00–22:00, Sat 11:00–15:00, closed Sat night and Sun, Via Santa Maria 151, tel. 050-561-942).

For a cheap, fast, and tasty meal a few steps from the train station, drop by cheery **La Lupa Ghiotta Tavola Calda.** It's got everything you'd want from a *ristorante* at half the price with faster service (build your own salad—5 ingredients for €4.50; Mon and Wed–Fri 12:15–15:30 & 19:15–24:00, Sat-Sun 19:15–24:00 only, closed Tue, Viale F. Bonaini 113, tel. 050-21018).

The street that houses the daily market, **Via delle Colonne** (a block north of the Arno, west of Borgo Stretto), has a few atmospheric, mid-priced restaurants and several fun, greasy, take-out options.

TRANSPORTATION CONNECTIONS

From Pisa by Train to: Florence (hrly, 1 hr, €5), **Rome** (about hrly, 4 hrs), **La Spezia,** gateway to Cinque Terre (hrly, 1 hr), **Siena** (change at Empoli: Pisa–Empoli, hrly, 45 min; Empoli–Siena, hrly, 1 hr), **Lucca** (hrly, 2/day Sun, 30 min). Even the fastest trains stop in Pisa, and you might be changing trains here whether you plan to stop or not.

By Car: The drive between Pisa and Florence is that rare case where the non-autostrada highway (free, more direct, and at least as fast) is a better deal than the *autostrada*.

Lucca

Surrounded by well-preserved ramparts, layered with history, alternately quaint and urbane, Lucca charms its visitors. Romanesque churches seem to be around every corner, as do fun-loving and shady piazzas filled with soccer-playing children. Despite Lucca's appeal, few tourists seem to put it on their maps, and it remains a city for the Lucchesi (loo-KAY-zee).

ORIENTATION

Tourist Information

The TI is just inside the Porta Santa Maria gate, on Piazza Santa Maria (daily April–Oct 9:00–20:00, Nov–March 9:00–13:00 & 15:00–18:00, Internet access, Piazza Santa Maria 35, tel. 0583-919-931, fax 0583-469-964, www.luccatourist.it, info@luccaturismo.it).

A glossy, privately owned information office on Piazzale Verdi (marked with an *i*) offers information and a room-booking service (daily 9:00–19:00, off-season 9:00–17:30, bike rental, 80-min city-walk audioguide-€9, €6 more for each additional audioguide, futuristic WC, tel. 0583-583-150).

Arrival in Lucca

To reach the city center from the train station, walk toward the walls and head left, to the entry at Porta San Pietro. Taxis are sparse at midday, but try calling 0583-333-434 or 0583-955-200. There is no baggage check at the train station, but you can leave bags at the TI on Piazzale Verdi (price per bag: €2/hr, or €5 for up to 5 hours, they need to photocopy your passport).

Helpful Hints

Combo-Tickets: A €6 combo-ticket includes visits to the Ilaria del Carretto tomb in San Martino Cathedral (€2), the Cathedral Museum (€4), and San Giovanni Church (€2.50). A different €6 ticket combines the Guinigi Tower (€4) and the Clock Tower (€3.50). Yet another combo-ticket covers Palazzo Mansi and Villa Guinigi for €6.50 (€4 each if purchased separately).

Shops and Museums Alert: Shops close most of Sunday and Monday mornings. Many museums are closed on Monday as well.

Markets: Lucca's atmospheric markets are worth visiting. Every third Saturday and Sunday of the month, one of the largest **antiques market** in Italy unfurls in the blocks around Piazza Antelminelli (8:00–15:00). The last weekend of the month, local artisans sell **arts and crafts** throughout the town (also 8:00–15:00). At the **general market,** held Wednesdays and Saturdays, you'll find produce and household goods (8:00–13:00, outside of the walls, a few blocks north of Porta Elisa around the stadium).

Concerts: San Giovanni Church hosts several musical concerts each week throughout the year, featuring highlights from hometown composer Giacomo Puccini (get schedule at church or TI, or check www.puccinielasualucca.com).

Festival: On September 13 and 14, the city celebrates Volto Santo ("Holy Face"), with a procession of the treasured local crucifix and a fair in Piazza Antelminelli.

Internet Access: Each of the TIs has an Internet point (see "Tourist Information," above). Mondo Chiocciola has several terminals (Mon–Sat 9:30–13:00 & 15:30–20:00, closed Sun, conveniently located across from launderette at Via del Gonfalone 12, tel. 0583-440-510).

Laundry: Lavanderia Self-Service Niagara is just off Piazza Santa Maria at Via Rosi 26 (daily 8:00–22:00).

Bike Rental: Several places with identical prices cluster around Piazza Santa Maria (€2.10/hr, €10/day, tandem bikes

The History of Lucca

Lucca began as a Roman settlement. In fact, the grid layout of the streets (and the shadow of an amphitheater) survives from Roman times. Trace the rectangular Roman wall—indicated by today's streets—on the map. As in typical Roman towns, two main roads quartered the fortified town, crossing at what was the forum (main market and religious/political center)—today's Piazza San Michele.

Christianity came early here; it's said that the first bishop of Lucca was a disciple of St. Peter. While churches were built here as early as the fourth century, the majority of Lucca's elegant Romanesque churches date from around the 12th century.

Feisty Lucca, though never a real power, enjoyed a long period of independence (maintained by clever diplomacy). Aside from 30 years of being ruled from Pisa in the 14th century, Lucca was basically an independent city-state (until Napoleon came to town).

In the Middle Ages, wealthy Lucca's economy was built on the silk industry, dominated by the Guinigi (gwee-NEE-gee) family. Without silk, Lucca would have been just another sleepy Italian town. In 1500, the town had 3,000 silk looms employing 25,000 workers. Banking was also big. Many pilgrims stopped here on their way to the Holy Land, deposited their money for safety...and never returned to pick it up.

In its heyday, Lucca packed 160 towers—one on nearly every corner—and 70 churches within its walls. Each tower was the home of a wealthy merchant family. Towers were many stories tall, with single rooms stacked atop each other: ground-floor shop, upstairs living room, and top-floor fire-safe kitchen, all connected by exterior wooden staircases. The rooftop was generally a vegetable garden with trees providing shade. Later, the wealthy city folk moved into the countryside, trading away life in their city palazzos to establish farm estates complete with fancy villas. (You can visit some of these villas today—the TI has a brochure—but they're convenient only for drivers and are generally not worth the cost of admission.)

In 1799, Napoleon stormed into Italy and took a liking to Lucca. He liked it so much, he gave it to his sister as a gift. It was later passed on to Napoleon's widow, Marie Louise. With a feminine sensitivity, Marie Louise was partially responsible for turning the city's imposing (but no longer particularly useful) fortified wall into a fine city park much enjoyed today.

available, open daily, last rental around 19:00). **Antonio Poli** (Piazza Santa Maria 42, tel. & fax 0583-493-787, enthusiastic Cristiana speaks English) and **Cicli Bizzarri** (Piazza Santa Maria 32, tel. 0583-496-031) are both easygoing and rent good bikes. A one-hour rental gives you two leisurely loops around the ramparts.

SIGHTS AND ACTIVITIES

▲▲**Bike the Ramparts**—Lucca's most remarkable feature, its Renaissance wall, is also its most enjoyable attraction—especially when circled on a rental bike. Stretching for 2.5 miles, this is an ideal place to come for an overview of the city by foot or bike.

Lucca has had a protective wall for 2,000 years. You can read three walls into today's map: the first rectangular Roman wall, the later medieval wall (nearly the size of today's), and the 16th-century Renaissance wall.

With the advent of cannons, thin medieval walls were suddenly vulnerable. A new design—the same one that stands today—was state-of-the-art when it was built (1550–1650). Much of the old medieval wall (look for the old stones) was incorporated into the Renaissance wall (with uniform bricks). The new wall was squat: a 100-foot-wide mound of dirt faced with bricks, engineered to absorb a cannonball pummeling. The townspeople cleared a wide no-man's-land around the town, exposing any attackers from a distance. Ten heart-shaped bastions (inviting picnic areas today) were designed to minimize exposure to cannonballs and maximize defense capabilities. The ramparts were armed with 130 cannons.

The town invested a third of its income for over a century to construct the wall, and—since it kept away the Florentines and nasty Pisans—it was considered a fine investment. In fact, nobody ever bothered to try to attack the wall. Locals say the only time it actually defended the city was during an 1812 flood, when the gates were sandbagged and its ramparts kept the high water out.

Today the ramparts seem made-to-order for a leisurely bike ride (20-min pedal, wonderfully smooth). You can rent bikes cheap and easy from one of several bike-rental places in town (see "Helpful Hints," above).

Roman Amphitheater—Just off the main shopping street, the architectural ghost of a Roman amphitheater can be felt in the delightful Piazza Anfiteatro. With the fall of Rome, the theater (which seated 10,000) was gradually cannibalized for its stones and inhabited by a mish-mash of huts. The huts were cleared away at the end of the 19th century to better appreciate the town's illustrious past. Today the square is a circle of touristy shops and mediocre restaurants that becomes a lively bar-and-café scene after dark.

Lucca

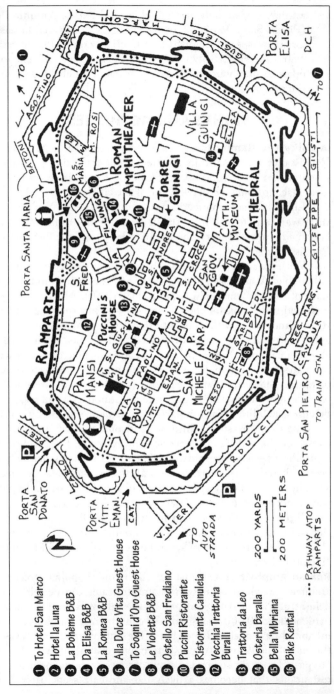

1 To Hotel San Marco
2 Hotel la Luna
3 La Bohème B&B
4 Da Elisa B&B
5 La Romea B&B
6 Alla Dolce Vita Guest House
7 To Sogni d'Oro Guest House
8 Le Violette B&B
9 Ostello San Frediano
10 Puccini Ristorante
11 Ristorante Canuleia
12 Vecchia Trattoria Buralli
13 Trattoria da Leo
14 Osteria Baralla
15 Bella 'Mbriana
16 Bike Rental

Today's street level is nine feet above the original arena floor. The only bits of surviving Roman stonework are a few arches on the northwest exterior (#42).

Via Fillungo—This main pedestrian drag, *the* street to stroll, takes you from the amphitheater almost all the way to the cathedral. Along the way you'll get a taste of Lucca's rich past, including several elegant, century-old storefronts. Many of the original storefront paintings, reliefs, or mosaics survive—even if today's occupant of that shop sells something entirely different.

At #97 is a classic old **jewelry store** with a rare storefront that has kept its T-shaped arrangement (when closed, you see a wooden T, and during open hours, it unfolds with a fine old-time display). This design dates from a time when the merchant sold his goods in front, did his work in the back, and lived upstairs.

Di Simo Caffè at #58 has long been the hangout of Lucca's artistic and intellectual elite. Composer and hometown boy Giacomo Puccini tapped his foot while sipping coffee here. Pop in to check out the 1880s ambience.

A surviving five-story **tower house** is at #67. Remember, there was a time when each corner sported its own tower. The stubby stones that still stick out once supported wooden staircases (there were no interior connections up or down). So many towers cast shadows over this part of town that the next street is called Via Buia (literally, "Dark Street").

At #45 and #43, you'll see two more good examples of tower houses. Across the street, the **Clock Tower** (Torre delle Ore) has a hand-wound Swiss clock that has clanged four times an hour since 1754 (€3.50 to climb up and see the mechanism flip into action on the quarter hour, covered by €6 combo-ticket with Guinigi Tower, daily 10:00–19:00).

The intersection of Via Fillungo and Via Roma/Via Santa Croce marks the center of town (where the two original Roman roads crossed). As you go down Via Santa Croce, you'll pass a Leonardo exhibit (€5 to see a room full of "don't touch" modern models of his sketches...not worth the money, open daily 9:30–19:30) before reaching **Piazza San Michele** (once the Roman Forum). Towering above the church's fancy Pisan Romanesque facade, the archangel Michael stands ready to flap his wings—which he actually did on special occasions. (See the stairs behind the facade, which church officials would climb to pull some strings and wow their gullible flock.) Piazza San Michele is as fun a people center today as it has been since Roman times.

▲**San Martino Cathedral**—This church, begun in the 11th century, is an entertaining mix of architectural and artistic styles. Its elaborate Pisan-Romanesque **facade**—featuring Bible scenes, animals, and candy-cane-striped columns—dominates the piazza. The central figure of the facade is St. Martin, a Roman military officer from Hungary who, by offering his cloak to a beggar, more fully understood the beauty of Christian compassion. (The impressive original, a fine example of Romanesque sculpture, is just inside, hiding from the pollution.) Each of the columns on the facade is unique. Notice how the facade is asymmetrical: The clock tower was already in place when the cathedral was built, so the builders cheated the right side to make it fit the space. On the lower right, the architect Guideo from Como holds a document declaring he finished the facade in 1204. On the right (at eye level), a labyrinth set into the wall relates the struggle and challenge our souls face in finding salvation. The Latin plaque just left of the main door is where moneychangers and spice traders met to seal deals (on the doorstep of the church—to underscore the reliability of their promises). Notice the date: An Dni MCXI (A.D. 1111).

The **interior** features Gothic arches, Renaissance paintings, and stained glass from the 19th century. On the left side of the nave, a small, elaborate temple displays the wooden crucifix called Volto Santo. It's said to have been sculpted by Nicodemus in Jerusalem and set afloat in an unmanned boat that landed on the coast of Tuscany, from where wild oxen miraculously carried it to Lucca in 782. The sculpture (which is actually 12th-century Byzantine-style) has quite a jewelry collection, which you can see in the Cathedral Museum (see below).

On the right side of the nave, the sacristy houses the enchantingly beautiful **memorial tomb of Ilaria del Carretto** by Jacopo della Quercia (1407). This young bride of silk baron Paolo Guinigi is decked out in the latest, most expensive fashions, with the requisite little dog curled up at her feet in eternal sleep. She's so realistic that the statue was nicknamed "sleeping beauty." Her nose is partially worn off because of a long-standing tradition of lonely young ladies rubbing it for luck in finding a boyfriend (cathedral entry is free, Ilaria tomb-€2, included in €6 combo-ticket with Cathedral Museum and San Giovanni Church, Mon–Fri 9:30–17:45, Sat 9:30–18:45; Sun open sporadically between Masses: 9:00–9:50, 11:20–11:30 & 13:00–17:45; Piazza San Martino).

Cathedral Museum (Museo della Cattedrale)—This beautifully presented museum houses original paintings, sculptures, and vestments from the cathedral and other Lucca churches. The first room displays jewelry made to dress up the Volto Santo crucifix, including gigantic gold shoes. Upstairs, notice the fine red brocaded silk—a reminder that this precious fabric is what brought riches and power to the city. The exhibits in this museum take on meaning only with the €1 audioguide—if you're not in the mood to listen to this, I'd skip the place altogether (€4; included in €6 combo-ticket with Ilaria tomb and San Giovanni Church; peak season daily 10:00–18:00; off-season Mon–Fri 10:00–14:00, Sat–Sun 10:00–17:00; next to cathedral on Piazza Antelminelli).

San Giovanni Church—This first cathedral of Lucca is interesting only for its archaeological finds. The entire floor of the 12th-century church has been excavated (1969–1992), revealing layers of Roman houses, early churches, and ancient hot tubs dating back to the time of Christ. Eager students can request an English translation of the floor plans from the ticket office to know what's what. As you climb under the church's present-day floor and wander the lanes of Roman Lucca, remember that the entire city sits on similar ruins (€2.50, included in €6 combo-ticket with Ilaria tomb and Cathedral Museum; peak season daily 10:00–18:00; off-season Sat–Sun 10:00–17:00, closed Mon–Fri; kitty-corner from cathedral at Piazza San Giovanni).

Puccini's House—Opera enthusiasts (but nobody else) will want to visit the home where Giacomo Puccini (1858–1924) grew up. The museum has the great composer's piano and a small collection of his personal belongings (€3; June–Sept daily 10:00–18:00; Oct–May Tue–Sun 10:00–13:00 & 15:00–18:00, closed Mon; closed for renovation through February 2006, Corte San Lorenzo 9, tel. 0583-584-028).

Guinigi Tower (Torre Guinigi)—Many Tuscan towns have towers, but none quite like the Guinigi family's. Up 227 steps is a small garden with fragrant trees surrounded by fantastic views (€4, mid-May–mid-Sept daily 9:30–24:00, March–mid-May and late Sept daily 9:30–18:00, Oct–Feb Sat–Sun only 10:00–17:00, Via S. Andrea, tel. 336-203-221). Tower-climbers can also purchase a combo-ticket (€6) that covers both the Guinigi Tower and the medieval **Clock Tower** (Torre delle Ore—described under "Via Fillungo," above; €3.50 for Clock Tower alone, daily 10:00–19:00, corner of Via Fillungo and Via del'Arancio).

Palazzo Mansi—Minor paintings by Tintoretto, Pontormo, Veronese, and others vie for attention, but the palazzo itself, a furnished and decorated 17th-century confection, steals the show. This is your chance to appreciate the wealth of Lucca's silk merchants (€4, €6.50 combo-ticket includes Villa Guinigi, Tue–Sat 8:30–19:30, Sun 8:30–13:30, closed Mon, last entry 30 min before closing, no photos, no English descriptions—politely suggest they make some for future visitors; Via Galli Tassi 43, tel. 0583-55-570). All visitors must be accompanied by a museum custodian, so there may be a bit of a wait during high season.

Villa Guinigi—Built by Paolo Guinigi in 1418, the family villa is now a stark museum displaying artifacts, sculptures, and paintings. Monumental paintings by multitalented Giorgio Vasari are the best reason to visit (€4, €6.50 combo-ticket includes Palazzo Mansi, Mon–Sat 8:30–19:30, Sun 8:30–13:30, last entry 30 min before closing, may have to wait in high season for a museum custodian to accompany you, Via della Quarquonia, tel. 0583-496-033).

SLEEPING

(€1=about $1.20, country code: 39)

$$$ La Romea B&B, in an air-conditioned, restored 14th-century palazzo near Guinigi Tower, feels like a royal splurge. Its four posh rooms and one suite are lavishly decorated in handsome colors, with stately parquet floors (Db-€130–140, Qb suite-€160, 3 percent cheaper with cash; from Via Fillungo, take Via Sant'Andrea to the Church of Sant'Andrea and turn right on Vicolo delle Ventaglie to #2; tel. 0583-464-175, fax 0583-471-280, www.laromea.com, info@laromea.com, Giulio and his wife Gaia).

$$$ Hotel San Marco, a seven-minute walk outside the Porta Santa Maria, is a postmodern place decorated à la Stanley Kubrick. Its 42 rooms are sleek, with all the comforts (Sb-€87, Db-€126, includes nice breakfast spread, air-con, elevator, pool, free parking, taxi from station-€6, Via San Marco 368, tel. 0583-495-010, fax 0583-490-513, www.hotelsanmarcolucca.it, info @hotelsanmarcolucca.it).

$$ Albergo la Luna has 29 professional, spotless rooms in the heart of the city. Updated rooms are split between two adjacent buildings right off of the main shopping street. Frescoed top-floor suites are a palatial, romantic splurge (Sb-€80, Db-€95–110, suite-€175, overpriced breakfast-€11, air-con, free Internet in lobby, elevator, parking-€11/day, Via Fillungo Corte Compagni 12, tel. 0583-493-634, fax 0583-490-021, www.hotellaluna.com, info@hotellaluna.com, Barbieri family).

$$ La Bohème B&B has a cozy yet elegant ambience, offering five spacious, charming, chandeliered rooms, each painted with a different rich color scheme (Db-€110, less off-season, 5 percent discount with cash and this book in 2006, air-con, Via del Moro 2, tel. & fax 0583-462-404, www.boheme.it, info@boheme.it, run by gracious Ranieri).

$ Alla Dolce Vita Guest House is a good value, with four clean, comfortable, and spacious rooms in a handy location right next to the medieval gate at the end of Via Fillungo (Db-€67, Tb-€77, communal kitchen; follow Via Fillungo to the end, turn left at the medieval gate, and follow the rounded tower around to the right to #232—right of the bar; Via Fillungo 232, tel. 0583-467-768, mobile 329-582-5062, www.luccabed.com, info@luccabed .com, helpful Davide).

$ At Le Violette B&B, kindly Anna (still learning English, her granddaughter Sara speaks English) will settle you into one of her six homey, tidy, quiet rooms just a couple of blocks away from the station inside Porta San Pietro (D-€55, Db-€65, extra bed-€15, communal kitchen, €5 to use washer and dryer—but only if staying several days; once inside Porta San Pietro, head inward on Via G. Saladini and turn left onto Via F. Carrara, then right onto Via Girolamo, then left onto Via della Polveriera to #6; tel. 0583-493-594, mobile 349-823-4645, fax 0583-980-064, www.leviolette.it, leviolette@virgilio.it).

$ Da Elisa B&B is cheap and cheery, with six simple, old-fashioned rooms sharing three worn-but-clean bathrooms (S-€47, D-€52, T-€67, Q-€80, breakfast-€7, ask for a room off the street for more tranquility, shared kitchen, Via Elisa 25, tel. 0583-494-539, fax 0583-471-609, www.daelisa.com, info@daelisa.com).

$ Sogni d'Oro Guest House, run by Davide from Alla Dolce Vita (listed above), is a handy budget option for drivers, with five neat, basic rooms, cheery floor tiles, and a communal kitchen (convenient grocery store next door). It's a 10-minute walk from the station, and a five-minute walk from the city walls (D-€60, Db-€65; from the station, head straight out to main boulevard Viale Regina Margherita and turn right, following the street as it turns into Viale della Curtatone, then taking a right onto Via A. Cantore to #169l; mobile 333-498-3045, tel. 0583-467-768, www.bbsognidoro.com, info@bbsognidoro.com).

$ Ostello San Frediano, in a central palazzo with a peaceful garden, is a cut above the average hostel. The rooms are bright and modern, and some have fun lofts (Db-€43, Qb-€86, €18 beds in 6- to 8-person dorms, €3 extra for non-members, cash only, lockout 10:00–15:30, curfew-1:00 in the morning, Internet access, cheap restaurant, free parking, Via della Cavallerizza 12, tel. 0583-469-957, fax 0583-461-007, www.ostellolucca.it, info@ostellolucca.it).

EATING

Puccini Ristorante is *the* place for a fancy €50 dinner. Fish and meat are featured here, as well as homemade bread, pasta, and desserts, with gourmet preparations and elegant presentation. Skip the basic sidewalk seats for the classy, modern art–strewn dining room (€40–45 tasting *menu*s, daily 12:30–14:30 & 19:30–22:30, closed Tue and midday in winter, reserve on weekends, across the street from Puccini's House, Corte San Lorenzo 1, tel. 0583-316-116).

Ristorante Canuleia makes everything fresh in their small kitchen. While the portions aren't huge, the food is great. You can eat in their tiny dining room or garden courtyard (€12–15 tourist lunch *menu*s, daily 12:30–14:00 & 19:30–21:30, dinner reservations recommended, Via Canuleia 14, tel. 0583-467-470).

Vecchia Trattoria Buralli, on quiet Piazza San Agostino, is a good bet for traditional cooking, with fine indoor and piazza seating. Service can be uneven (€20–40 dinner, Thu–Tue 12:00–14:45 & 19:15–22:30, closed Wed, Piazza San Agostino 10, tel. 0583-950-611).

Trattoria da Leo, a cousin of Trattoria Buralli above, packs in chatty locals for typical, low-priced home-cooking. Arrive early or reserve a spot (daily 12:00–14:30 & 19:30–22:30, cash only, Via Tegrimi 1 just off Piazza San Salvatore, tel. 0583-492-236).

Osteria Baralla, a few steps from the Roman Amphitheater, is popular with locals for its quality meals. They have a breezy, spacious dining room under medieval vaults or a few quiet tables on the pedestrian street (Mon–Sat 12:30–15:00 & 19:30–22:00, closed Sun, reservations wise, Via Anfiteatro 7/9, tel. 0583-440-240).

Bella 'Mbriana focuses on doing one thing very well: turning out piping hot, wood-fired pizzas to happy locals in a cheery wood-paneled dining room. Order at the counter, and they bring your pizza to you on a cutting board. Prices range from €3.50 for your basic *Napolitano* to €12 for their specialty, with buffalo mozzarella and other gourmet ingredients (Wed–Mon 12:30–14:30 & 18:30–23:30, closed Tue, Via della Cavalerizza 29, to the right as you face San Frediano Church, tel. 0583-495-565).

TRANSPORTATION CONNECTIONS

From Lucca by Train to: Florence (9/day, 90 min), **Pisa** (hrly, 2/day Sun, 30 min), **Milan** (nearly hrly except Sun, 4–5 hrs, transfer in Florence or Prato), **Rome** (hrly except Sun, 3 hrs, change in Florence or Pisa).

Drivers: Lucca has a serious lack of public parking places. Try parking lots at Porta Santa Maria and Porta Sant'Anna, or consider parking outside of the gates near the train station or on the boulevard surrounding the city.

SIENA

Siena was medieval Florence's archrival. And while Florence ultimately won the battle for political and economic superiority, Siena still competes for the tourists. Sure, Florence has the heavyweight sights. But Siena seems to be every Italy connoisseur's favorite pet town. In my office, whenever Siena is mentioned, someone moans, "Siena? I looove Siena!"

Seven hundred years ago (from about 1260–1348), Siena was a major banking and trade center, and a military power in a class with Florence, Venice, and Genoa. With a population of 60,000, it was even bigger than Paris. Situated on the north-south road to Rome (the Via Francigena), Siena traded with all Europe. Then, in 1348, the Black Death (bubonic plague) that swept through Europe hit Siena and cut the population by more than a third. Siena never recovered. In the 1550s, Florence, with the help of Philip II's Spanish army, conquered the flailing city-state, forever rendering Siena a nonthreatening backwater. Siena's loss became our sight-seeing gain, as its political and economic irrelevance pickled the city in a purely medieval brine. Today, Siena's population is still 60,000, compared to Florence's 420,000.

Siena's thriving historic center, with redbrick lanes cascading every which way, offers Italy's best medieval city experience. Most people do Siena, just 35 miles south of Florence, as a day trip, but it's best experienced at twilight. While Florence has the block-buster museums, Siena has an easy-to-enjoy soul: Courtyards sport flower-decked wells, alleys dead-end at rooftop views, and the sky is a rich blue dome.

For those who dream of a Fiat-free Italy, pedestrians rule in the old center of Siena. Sit at a café on the redbrick main square.

Wander narrow streets lined with colorful flags and iron rings to tether horses. Take time to savor the first European city to eliminate automobile traffic from its main square (1966) and then, just to be silly, wonder what would happen if they did it in your home town.

Planning Your Time

On a quick trip, consider spending two nights in Siena (or 3 nights with a whole-day side trip into Florence). Whatever you do, enjoy a sleepy medieval evening in Siena. The next morning, you can see the city's major sights in half a day.

ORIENTATION

Siena lounges atop a hill, stretching its three legs out from Il Campo. This main square, the historic meeting point of Siena's neighborhoods, is pedestrian-only. And most of those pedestrians are students from the local university.

Everything I mention is within a 15-minute walk of the square. Navigate by three major landmarks (Il Campo, Duomo, and Church of San Domenico), following the excellent system of street-corner signs. The typical visitor sticks to the San Domenico–Il Campo axis. Make a point to stray from the current of this main artery.

Siena itself is one big sight. Its individual sights come in two little clusters: the square (Civic Museum and City Tower) and the cathedral (Baptistery and Duomo Museum with its surprise view-point). Check these sights off, and you're free to wander.

Tourist Information

This office is an exasperating place. TI employees claim that transit officials and museum officials don't want them to know anything about the town's buses or sights. They do offer a decent free map (daily 9:00–19:00, #56 on Il Campo, tel. 0577-280-551, www.terresiena .it, infoaptsiena@terresiena.it). The helpful booklet *Terre di Siena* lists current hours and prices for sights in Siena and outlying towns. The little TI at San Domenico, while primarily for hotel promotion, sells a €0.50 Siena map and organizes daily walking tours of the old town and San Gimignano (across street from church).

Arrival in Siena

By Train: The small train station, located on the edge of town, has a bar and bus office (no baggage check or lockers). To get from the station to the city center, hike about 20 minutes uphill or catch a city bus or taxi. The **taxi stand** is to your far right as you exit the station (about €8 to Il Campo, taxi tel. 0577-49222).

To get from the station into town by **city bus,** buy a €1 ticket from the newsstand in the station lobby (daily 6:00–20:00), or from the blue machine in the lobby (touch screen for English and select "urban" for type of ticket). Then walk to the bus stop—a covered shelter a hundred yards away—by crossing the parking lot and the wide roundabout in front of the station. Buses only drop off passengers at the station; they pick up travelers at this covered stop. Buses run about every 15 minutes (fewer on Sun and after 21:00).

Every orange bus goes from here to the center. (Caution: Blue ones go to other cities.) Confirm by asking *"Centro?,"* punch your ticket in the machine on the bus to validate it, and ride to the last stop. (Buses go to Piazza Gramsci/Lizza, Piazza Sale, or Via della Stufasecca—all within several blocks of each other. If you don't get dropped off in Piazza Gramsci, head uphill on the main street until you get to Piazza Gramsci.)

When leaving Siena, you can catch the city bus to the train station from Piazza Gramsci, Piazza del Sale, or Via della Stufasecca (bus stops are marked with a posted schedule and sometimes with yellow lines painted on the pavement, showing a bus-sized rectangle and the word "bus"). Confirm with the driver that the bus is going to the *stazione* (stat-zee-OH-nay). Remember to purchase your ticket in advance from a *tabacchi* shop.

By Intercity Bus: Some buses arrive in Siena at the train station (see "By Train," above), others at Piazza Gramsci (a few blocks from city center), and some stop at both. The main bus companies are Sena and the confusingly named Tra-In (TRAH-in). You can store baggage underneath Piazza Gramsci in Sottopassaggio la Lizza (€3.50, daily 7:00–19:45, no overnight).

By Car: Drivers coming from the autostrada take the Siena Ovest exit and follow signs for *Centro,* then *Stadio* (stadium, soccer ball). The soccer-ball signs take you to the stadium lot (Parcheggio Stadio, €1.60/hr, pay for number of hours parked when you leave) at the huge, bare-brick Church of San Domenico. The Fortezza lot nearby charges the same amount. Another option is to park in the lot under the train station. Technically, hotel customers are allowed to drop bags at their hotel, but I wouldn't bother. You can park free in the lot west of the Fortezza, in white-striped spots behind Hotel Villa Liberty, behind the Fortezza, and overnight in most city lots from 20:00–8:00. (The signs showing a street cleaner and a day of the week indicate which day the street is cleaned; there's a €100 tow-fee incentive to learn the days of the week in Italian.)

Helpful Hints

Combo-Tickets: A deranged person cobbled together a pile of illogically paired combo-tickets to give some travelers a small savings. Nothing covers everything and most are conflicting.

You can buy a combo-ticket *(biglietto cumulativo)* that gets you into the Duomo, Baptistery, and Duomo Museum (€10, saves €5, doesn't cover the Duomo when the lovely floors are uncovered mid-Aug–Oct). Another combo-ticket, sold at the City Tower, includes the tower and Civic Museum (€10, saves €3). Yet another is for the Civic Museum and Santa Maria della Scala (€10, saves €3). There's also a big €13 combo-ticket *(Itinerari d'Arte)* that doesn't include entry to the Duomo or the City Tower but saves you €12 if you visit the Duomo Museum, Santa Maria della Scala, Civic Museum, and the Baptistery (costs €16 Nov–March, so only €9 savings in winter, both versions valid 7 days).

Museums Open Late on Weekends: Museums are often open late on summer Fridays and Saturdays (check with the TI for current hours).

Wednesday Morning Market: The weekly market, consisting mainly of clothes, knickknacks, and food, sprawls between the Fortress and Piazza Gramsci along Viale Cesare Maccari and the adjacent Viale XXV Aprile.

Internet Access: In this university town, there are lots of places to get plugged in. **Internet Point** is just off Piazza Matteotti, at Via Paradiso #10 (across street and a few steps downhill from McDonald's, Mon–Fri 9:00–13:00 & 15:00–20:00, closed Sat–Sun) and **Internet Train** is near Il Campo, at Via di Città 121 (Mon–Sat 10:00–20:00, Sun 12:00–20:00, tel. 0577-226-366).

Laundry: Two modern, self-service launderettes are **Lavarapido Wash and Dry** (Via di Pantaneto 38, near Logge del Papa) and **Onda Blu** (Via del Casato di Sotto 17, 50 yards from Il Campo); both are open daily 8:00–22:00, last loads at 21:00.

Travel Agency: Palio Viaggi on Piazza Gramsci sells train and plane tickets but no bus tickets (Mon–Fri 9:00–13:00 & 15:00–19:00, Sat 9:00–13:00, closed Sun, La Lizza 12, tel. 0577-280-828, info@palioviaggi.it).

Local Guides: Roberto Bechi, a hardworking Sienese guide, specializes in off-the-beaten-path tours of the surrounding countryside by minibus (up to 6 passengers, convenient pick-up at hotel). Married to an American (Patti) and having run restaurants in Siena and the U.S., Roberto communicates well with Americans. His passions are Sienese culture, Tuscan history, and local cuisine. Ideally, book well in advance but you may be able to schedule a visit if you call no later than the day before (full-day tours from €70–100 per person, half-day tours from €30–70 per person, mobile 328-727-3186 or 328-425-5648, www.toursbyroberto.com, tourrob@tin.it). If he's booked, Roberto can recommend other good guides.

Siena at a Glance

▲▲▲**Il Campo** Best square in Italy. **Hours:** Always open.

▲▲▲**Duomo** Art-packed cathedral with mosaic floors and statues by Michelangelo and Bernini. **Hours:** Mid-March–Oct Mon–Sat 10:30–19:30, Sun 13:30–17:30, Nov–mid-March Mon–Sat 10:30–18:30, Sun 13:30–16:30.

▲▲**Duomo Museum** Displays cathedral art (including Duccio's *Maestà*) and offers sweeping Tuscan view. **Hours:** Daily March–Oct 9:00–19:00, Nov–Feb 10:30–17:00.

▲**Baptistery** Cave-like building has baptismal font decorated by Ghiberti and Donatello. **Hours:** Daily mid-March–Sept 9:30–19:30, Oct 9:30–18:00, Nov–mid-March 10:00–13:00 & 14:00–17:00.

▲**Civic Museum** City museum in City Hall with Sienese frescoes of Good and Bad Government. **Hours:** Daily March–Oct 10:00–19:00, Nov–Feb 10:00–16:00. May be open summer eves.

▲**City Tower** (Torre del Mangia) 330-foot tower climb. **Hours:** Same as Civic Museum.

▲**Pinacoteca** Fine Sienese paintings. **Hours:** Sun–Mon 8:30–13:15, Tue–Sat 8:15–19:15.

▲**Santa Maria della Scala** Museum with vibrant ceiling and wall frescoes depicting day-to-day life in a medieval hospital, much of the original *Fountain of Joy*, and an Etruscan artifact exhibit. **Hours:** Daily 10:30–18:30, Nov–mid-March 10:30–16:30.

Church of San Domenico Huge brick church with St. Catherine's head and thumb. **Hours:** Daily March–Oct 7:00–18:30, Nov–Feb 9:00–18:00.

Sanctuary of Saint Catherine Home of St. Catherine. **Hours:** Daily 9:00–12:30 & 15:00–17:00.

Il Casato Viaggi runs half-day bus tours from Siena into the Tuscan countryside. They offer two different itineraries, both including a winery tour and wine-tasting: the Chianti area (€28, Wed and Fri, includes visits to 2 medieval villages) and Brunello and the Crete Senesi hills (€35, Sun). Full-day wine-tasting tours in the countryside are also available (€150/person for 2 people, €105/person for 4 people, 10 percent discount with this book; includes 3 tastings, lunch, minivan, and guide; Via Il Casato di Sotto 12 in Siena, tel. 057-746-091, fax 057-727-9863, www.sienaholiday.com).

SIGHTS

Siena's Main Square

▲▲▲**Il Campo**—This is the heart—geographically and meta-phorically—of Siena. Seen from the top of the City Tower, this "heart" appears to pump people through the busy city's veins. The square fans out from the City Hall (Palazzo Pubblico) to create an amphitheater, where the citizens are the stars.

Originally, this area was just a "field" *(campo)* located outside the former city walls. You can still see some of the old tufa-stone blocks incorporated into today's redbrick Caffè Fonte Gaia, along the right side of the square (to your right as you face City Hall).

As the city expanded, Il Campo eventually became the historic junction of Siena's various competing districts, or *contrade*, on the old marketplace. The brick surface is divided into nine sections, representing the council of nine merchants and city bigwigs who ruled medieval Siena. The square and its buildings are the color of the soil upon which they stand...a color known to artists and Crayola-users as "Burnt Sienna."

City Hall and its 330-foot tower dominate the square. In medieval Siena, this secular building was the center of the city, and the whole focus of the Campo flows down to it.

The City Hall's 330-foot-tall **City Tower** (Torre del Mangia), Italy's tallest secular tower, was named after a hedonistic watchman who consumed his earnings like a glutton consumes food—his chewed-up statue is in the courtyard, to the left as you enter. (Tower admission details below.)

The chapel located at the base of the tower was built in 1348 as thanks to God for ending the Black Death (after it killed more than a third of the population). It should also be used to thank God that the tower—just plunked onto the building with no extra foundation—still stands. These days, the chapel is used only to bless the Palio contestants and the tower's bell only rings for the race.

The *Fountain of Joy (Fonte Gaia)* by Jacopo della Quercia marks the square's high point. Find the snake-handler woman, the two naked guys about to be tossed in, and the pigeons politely wait-ing their turn to gingerly tightrope down slippery spouts to slurp a drink from wolves' snouts. The relief panel on the left (as you face the fountain) shows God creating Adam by helping him to his feet. It's said that this reclining Adam influenced Michelangelo when he painted his Sistine Ceiling. This fountain is a copy. You can see parts of the original fountain in an interesting exhibit at Siena's Santa Maria della Scala, described on page 405.

To say Siena and Florence have always been competitive is an understatement. In medieval times, a statue of Venus stood on Il Campo. After the plague hit Siena, the monks blamed the pagan statue. The people cut it to pieces and buried it along the walls of Florence.

The "heart" of Siena beats fastest at Palio time. Picture the Campo when the famous horse races are held (July 2 and Aug 16). Ten snorting horses and their nervous riders (selected from 17 *con-trade*, or neighborhoods) line up near the "Antica Siena" shop (right side of square) to await the starting signal. Then they race like crazy three times around the perimeter (the gray pavement), which is covered with dirt. Mattresses pad the sharpest turns. Spectators waving the banners of their neighborhoods cram (for free) into the center of the square or watch from temporary bleachers or, if they have the money, from the balconies. The winner crosses the line, and 1/17th of Siena goes berserk for the next 365 days.

▲**Civic Museum (Museo Civico)**—At the base of the City Tower is Siena's City Hall (Palazzo Pubblico), the spot where secular gov-ernment got its start in early Renaissance Europe. There, you'll find city government still at work, along with a sampling of local art.

In the following order, you'll see: the Sala Risorgimento, with dramatic scenes of Victor Emmanuel's unification of Italy (surrounded by statues that don't seem to care); the chapel, with impressive inlaid wood chairs in the choir; and the Sala del Mappamondo, with Siena's first fresco, Simone Martini's *Maestà* (*Enthroned Virgin*—a groundbreaking, down-to-earth Madonna), facing the faded *Guidoriccio da Folignano* (a mercenary providing a more concrete form of protection).

Next is the Sala della Pace—where the city's fat cats met. Looking down on the oligarchy during their meetings were two interesting frescoes, *Effects of Good and Bad Government*. Notice the whistle-while-you-work happiness of the utopian community ruled by the utopian government (in the better-preserved fresco) and the fate of a community ruled by politicians with more typical values (in a terrible state of repair). The message: Without justice, there can be no prosperity.

Take a moment to savor one of those to-sigh-for rural panora-mas out the window of the Sala della Pace. The view out the window

Siena's Palio

In the Palio, the feisty spirit of Siena's 17 *contrade* (neighborhoods) lives on. These neighborhoods celebrate, worship, and compete together. Each has its own parish church, well or fountain, and even its own historical museum. *Contrada* pride is evident any time of year in the parades and colorful neighborhood banners, lamps, and wall plaques. (If you hear distant drumming, run to it for some medieval action, often featuring flag-throwers.) But *contrada* passion is most visible twice a year—on July 2 and August 16—when they have their world-famous horse race, the Palio di Siena.

Ten of the 17 neighborhoods compete (chosen by rotation and lot), hurling themselves with medieval abandon into several days of trial races and traditional revelry. Jockeys are considered hired guns...paid mercenaries. But on the big day, the horses are taken into their *contrada*'s church to be blessed. ("Go and win," says the priest.) It's considered a sign of luck if a horse leaves droppings in the church.

On the evening of the big day, Il Campo is stuffed to the brim with locals and tourists, as the horses charge wildly around the square in this literally no-holds-barred race. A horse can win even if its rider has fallen off. Of course, the winning neighborhood is the scene of grand celebrations afterward. Winners receive a *palio* (banner), typically painted by a local artist and always featuring the Virgin Mary. But the true prize is simply proving your *contrada* is *numero uno*. All over town, sketches and posters depict the Palio. This is not some folkloristic event. It's a real medieval moment. If you're packed onto the square with 15,000 people, all hungry for victory, you won't see much, but you'll feel it. While the actual Palio packs the city, you could side-trip in from Florence to see horse-race trials each of the three days before the main event (usually at 9:00 and around 19:30). For more information, visit www.ilpalio.org.

▲**Palio al Cinema**—This 20-minute film, *Siena, the Palio, and its History,* helps recreate the craziness. See it at the air-conditioned Cinema Moderno in Piazza Tolomei, two blocks from Il Campo (€5.25, with this book pay €4.25/person or €8/2, get the DVD for €10, film shows May–Oct only; May–mid-June and mid-Sept–Oct Mon–Sat 9:30–15:30, from mid-June–mid-Sept Mon–Sat 9:30–17:30, closed Sun; English showings generally hourly at half past the hour—schedule posted on door, tel. 0577-289-201). Call or drop by to confirm when the next English showing is scheduled—there are usually nine a day.

is essentially the same as that from the top of the big stairs (€7, €10 combo-ticket includes tower—sold only at tower, daily March–Oct 10:00–19:00, Nov–Feb 10:00–16:00, may be open later on summer evenings, last entry 45 min before closing, ask if audioguides are available, tel. 0577-292-232).

▲**City Tower (Torre del Mangia)**—Siena gathers around its City Hall, not its church. Medieval Siena was a proud republic, and this tall tower is the exclamation point of its "declaration of independence." Its 300 steps get pretty skinny at the top, but the reward is one of Italy's best views (€6, €10 combo-ticket with Civic Museum only sold here, daily March–Oct 10:00–19:00, Nov–Feb 10:00–16:00, closed in rain, sometimes long lines, avoid midday crowd, limit of 30 tourists at a time, often sold out, mandatory and free bag check).

▲**Pinacoteca**—Siena was a power in Gothic art. But the average tourist, wrapped up in a love affair with the Renaissance, hardly notices. This museum takes you on a walk through Siena's art, chronologically from the 12th through the 15th centuries. For the casual sightseer, the Sienese art in the Civic and Duomo Museums is adequate. But art fans enjoy this opportunity to trace the evolution of Siena's delicate and elegant works, from stiff, gold-backed icon-like Madonnas to curvy, graceful Madonnas to Italian Renaissance. Concentrate on pieces by Duccio (artist of the *Maestà* in the Duomo Museum), Simone Martini (who did the *Maestà* in the Civic Museum), the brothers Ambrogio and Pietro Lorenzetti (Ambrogio did the *Effects of Good and Bad Government* in the Civic Museum), Pinturicchio (who did the Piccolomini Library in the Duomo), and Domenico Beccafumi (who inlaid pavement in the Duomo). To reach the museum from Il Campo, walk out Via di Città and go left on Via San Pietro (€4, Sun–Mon 8:30–13:15, Tue–Sat 8:15–19:15, last entry 30 min before closing, audioguide-€4, free and mandatory bag check, tel. 0577-281-161).

Siena's Cathedral Area

▲▲▲**Duomo**—If the Campo is the heart of Siena, the Duomo (or cathedral) is its soul. The white and dark-green striped church, sitting on an artificial platform atop Siena's highest point, is visible for miles around. The current structure dates from 1215, with the major decoration done during Siena's heyday from 1250–1350. This ornate but surprisingly secular shrine to the Virgin Mary is stacked with colorful art inside and out, from the inlaid-marble floors to the stained glass windows. Along with sculptures by Bernini and Michelangelo, the church features the Piccolomini Library. The Library holds a series of captivating Pinturicchio frescoes telling the story of Aeneas Piccolomini, Siena's consummate Renaissance man who later became Pope Pius II.

Siena

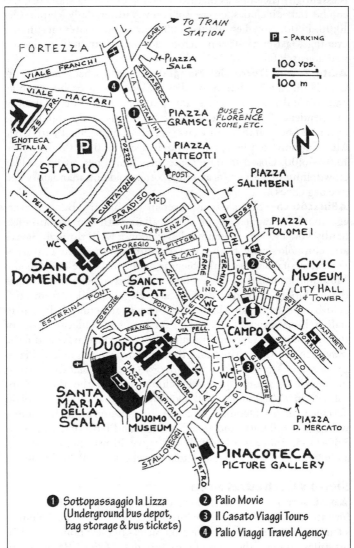

- ❶ Sottopassaggio la Lizza (Underground bus depot, bag storage & bus tickets)
- ❷ Palio Movie
- ❸ Il Casato Viaggi Tours
- ❹ Palio Viaggi Travel Agency

Cost and Hours: €3 includes cathedral and Piccolomini Library, covered by €10 *biglietto cumulativo* combo-ticket except mid-Aug-Oct when all of the church's intricate inlaid pavements are uncovered and entry costs €6. Duomo and Library are both open mid-March–Oct Mon–Sat 10:30–19:30, Sun 13:30–17:30, Nov–mid-March Mon–Sat 10:30–18:30, Sun 13:30–16:30, last entry 30 minutes before closing, opening hours can vary—confirm with TI. Modest dress is required to enter, but paper ponchos are provided if needed.

Audioguides: Audioguide for church and library-€3.50, ID required for deposit, add the Duomo Museum-€4.50. Two headphones are available at a price break. Modest dress is required. Tel. 0577-283-048.

Self-Guided Tour: In the **nave,** the heads of 172 popes peer down from above, looking over the fine inlaid art on the floor. With a forest of striped columns, a coffered dome, a large stained-glass window at the far end, and a museum's worth of early Renaissance art, this is one busy interior. Looking closer at the popes, you see the same four faces repeated over and over.

For almost two centuries (1373–1547), 40 artists paved the marble floor with scenes from the Old Testament, allegories, and intricate patterns. The earliest are simple black-and-white, with engraved details, but the later ones use inlay technique with many colored marbles. The series starts with historical allegories near the entrance. The larger, more elaborate scenes surrounding the altar are mostly stories from the Old Testament. Many of the floor panels may be protected with sheet flooring when you visit.

Grab a seat under the **dome**. It sits on a 12-sided base but its "coffered" ceiling is actually a painted illusion. Get oriented to the vast church's array of sights by thinking of the floor as a big 12-hour clock. You're the middle, and the altar is high noon: You'll find the *Slaughter of the Innocents* pavement panel roped off on the floor at 10:00, Pisano's pulpit between two pillars at 11:00, Duccio's round stained glass window at high noon, Bernini's chapel at 3:00, the Piccolomini Altar with a Michelangelo statue (next to doorway leading to a shop, snacks, and WC) at 7:00, the Piccolomini Library at 8:00, and a Donatello statue at 9:00.

Look for the *Slaughter of the Innocents* inlaid pavement panel. Herod (left), standing amid Renaissance arches, orders the massacre of all babies to prevent the coming of the promised Messiah. It's a chaotic scene of angry soldiers, grieving mothers, and dead babies, reminding locals that a republic ruled by a tyrant will experience misery.

Nicola Pisano's octagonal Carrara marble **pulpit** (1268) rests on the backs of lions—symbols of Christianity triumphant. Like the lions, the Church eats its catch (devouring paganism) and nurses its cubs. The seven relief panels tell the life of Christ in rich detail. (Buy light from a coin-op machine.)

To understand why Bernini is considered the greatest Baroque sculptor, step into his sumptuous chapel, *Cappella della Madonna del Voto*. This last work in the cathedral, from 1659, is enough to make even a Lutheran light a candle. Move up to the altar and look back at the two Bernini statues: Mary Magdalene in a state of spiritual ecstasy and St. Jerome playing the crucifix like a violinist lost in beautiful music.

Over the chapel's altar is the *Madonna del Voto*, a Madonna and Child painted by Duccio and adorned with a real crown of gold and jewels. Tilting her head, she looks out sympathetically. This is the Mary that the Palio is dedicated to, special in the hearts of the Sienese. The faithful's prayers to Mary are accompanied by offerings, found outside the chapel, hanging on the wall to the left, as you exit.

The **Piccolomini Altar** (left wall, marble altarpiece decorated with statues), designed for the tomb of the Sienese-born Pope Pius III, is most interesting for Michelangelo's statue of Paul (lower right, who is clearly more interesting than the bland, bored popes above him). Paul has the look of Michelangelo's *Moses*, the broken-nosed self-portrait of the sculptor himself, and the dangling hand of his *David*. It was the chance to sculpt *David* in Florence that enticed Michelangelo to abandon the Siena project.

The brilliantly-frescoed **Piccolomini Library** captures the exuberant, optimistic spirit of the 1400s, when humanism and the Renaissance were born. The painter Pinturicchio (c. 1454–1513) was hired to celebrate the life of one of Siena's hometown boys. Start from the window and work clockwise, following 10 scenes in the life of the man many call "the first humanist," Aeneas Piccolomini (1405–1464), who became Pope Pius II. The library also contains intricately decorated, illuminated music scores, and a statue (a Roman copy of a Greek original) of the Three Graces.

Donatello's rugged *St. John the Baptist* (1457), wearing his famous rags, stands in a chapel to the right of the library.

Exit the Duomo, and make a U-turn to the left, walking alongside the church to Piazza Jacopo della Quercia. In a grand plan that fizzled, the nave of the Duomo was supposed to be where the piazza is today. When rival republic Florence began its grand cathedral, proud Siena decided to build the biggest church in all Christendom. The existing cathedral would be used as a transept. Some of the nave's green-and-white-striped columns were built, but are now filled in with a brick wall. The wall, connecting the Duomo with the museum of the cathedral, was as far as Siena got before a plague killed the city's ability to finish the project. Round white stones in the pavement mark the place where columns would have stood. Look through the unfinished entrance facade, seeing blue sky where the stained glass windows might have been, and ponder the struggles, triumphs, and failures of the human spirit... or humanism.

▲▲**Duomo Museum (Museo dell'Opera e Panorama)**—Siena's most enjoyable museum, on the Campo side of the church (look for the yellow signs), was built to house the cathedral's art. The ground floor is filled with the cathedral's original Gothic sculpture by Giovanni Pisano (who spent 10 years in the late 1200s carving and orchestrating the decoration of the cathedral) and a fine Donatello *Madonna and Child*. A slender, tender Mary gazes down at her chubby-cheeked baby, and her sad eyes say she knows the eventual fate of her son.

Upstairs to the left awaits a private audience with Duccio's *Maestà* (*Enthroned Virgin*, 1311). Pull up a chair and study one of the great pieces of medieval art. The flip side of the *Maestà* (displayed on the opposite wall), with 26 panels—the medieval equivalent of pages—shows scenes from the Passion of Christ.

Climb onto the "Panorama del Facciatone." For a surprise view of Siena, leave the landing on the top floor and walk to the end of the room on the right—the entrance is through the small doorway. Climb down the steps and then up the claustrophobic spiral staircase to the viewpoint. Look back over the Duomo and consider this: If the grandiose plan for the church had been completed, you'd be looking straight down the nave.

Cost and Hours: €6, €10 *biglietto cumulativo* combo-ticket with Baptistery and Duomo except mid-Aug–Oct, when Duomo floors are uncovered, worthwhile 40-min audioguide-€3, ID required for deposit, daily March–Oct 9:00–19:00, Nov–Feb 10:30–17:00, confirm hours with TI or call tel. 0577-283-048.

▲**Baptistery**—Siena is so hilly that there wasn't enough flat ground on which to build a big church. What to do? Build a big church and prop up the overhanging edge with the Baptistery. This dark and quietly tucked-away cave of art is worth a look (and €3, covered by €10 *biglietto cumulativo* or more expensive *Itinerari d'Arte* combo-tickets) for its cool tranquility and the bronze panels and angels—by Ghiberti, Donatello, and others—adorning the pedestal of the baptismal font (daily mid-March–Sept 9:30–19:30, Oct 9:30–18:00, Nov–mid-March 10:00–13:00 & 14:00–17:00, confirm with TI). Note: The "crypt" of the cathedral (entrance above the baptistery, separate €6 entry fee but covered by €10 *biglietto cumulativo* combo-ticket) is important archaeologically, but of little interest to the average tourist. I'd skip it.

▲**Santa Maria della Scala**—This museum (opposite the Duomo entrance) was used as a hospital until the 1980s. Its labyrinthine 12th-century cellars—carved out of tufa and finished with brick—go down several floors. They once stored supplies for the medieval hospital upstairs. Today the hospital and its cellars are filled with museum exhibits, including these main attractions: the fancy frescoed hall (Pellegrinaio Hall, ground floor), much of the original *Fountain of Joy* (from which the replica in Il Campo was modeled), St. Catherine's Oratory chapel (first basement), and the Etruscan collection in the Archaeological Museum (second basement).

Cost and Hours: €6, €10 combo-ticket with Civic Museum, daily mid-March–Oct 10:30–18:30, Nov–mid-March 10:30–16:30, last entry 45 minutes before closing. The chapel just inside the door to your left is free (English description inside chapel entrance).

Pellegrinaio Hall: Sumptuously frescoed, this hall shows medieval Siena's innovative health care and social welfare system in action (c. 1442, wonderfully described in English). Starting in the 11th century, the hospital nursed the sick and cared for abandoned children, as is vividly portrayed in these frescoes. The good works paid off, as bequests and donations poured in, creating the wealth that's evident throughout this building.

***Fountain of Joy* Exhibit:** Downstairs you'll find an engaging exhibit on Jacopo della Quercia's early 15th-century *Fountain of Joy (Fonte Gaia)*—and the disassembled pieces of the original fountain itself. In the 19th century, after serious deterioration, the ornate fountain was dismantled and plaster casts were made. (From these casts, they made the replica that graces Il Campo today.) Here you'll see the eroded original panels paired with their restored casts, along with the original statues that used to stand on the edges of the fountain.

On the same floor, pop into the small chapel or oratory where St. Catherine prayed and received visions. A holy nail thought to be from Jesus' cross is on the altar.

Archaeological Museum: Descend into the cavernous second basement under fat groin vaults to be alone with piles of ancient Etruscan stuff excavated from tombs centuries before Christ (displayed in a labyrinthine exhibit). Remember, the Etruscans dominated this part of Italy before the Roman Empire swept through—Rome originated as an Etruscan town.

Siena's San Domenico Area

Church of San Domenico—This huge brick church is worth a quick look. The spacious, plain interior (except for the colorful flags of the city's 17 *contrade* or neighborhoods) fits the austere philosophy of the Dominicans and invites meditation on the thoughts and deeds of St. Catherine. Walk up the steps in the rear for paintings from the life of St. Catherine, patron saint of Siena. Halfway up the church on the right, find a metal bust of St. Catherine and a small case containing her thumb (sometimes loaned out to other

St. Catherine of Siena
(1347–1380)

The youngest of 25 children born to a Sienese cloth dyer, Catherine began experiencing heavenly visions even in child- hood. At 16, she became a Dominican nun, locking herself away for three years in a room in her family's house. She lived the life of an ascetic, which culminated in a vision wherein she married Christ. Catherine emerged from solitude to join her Dominican sisters, sharing her experiences, caring for the sick, and gathering both disciples and enemies. At age 23, she lapsed into a spiritual coma, waking with the heavenly com- mand to spread her message to the world. She wrote essays and letters to kings, dukes, bishops, and popes, imploring them to find peace for a war-ravaged Italy. While visiting Pisa during Lent of 1375, she had a vision in which she received the stigmata, the wounds of Christ.

Still in her twenties, Catherine was invited to Avignon, France, where the pope had taken up residence. With her charm, sincerity, and reputation for holiness, she helped convince Pope Gregory XI to return the papacy to the city of Rome. Catherine also went to Rome, where she died young. She was canonized in the next generation (by a Sienese pope) and her relics were distributed to churches around Italy.

churches) and a small reliquarium on the lowest shelf contain- ing the chain she used to scourge herself. In the chapel (15 feet to the left) surrounded with candles, you'll see Catherine's actual head atop the altar (free, daily March–Oct 7:00–18:30, Nov–Feb 9:00–18:00; WC for €0.50 at far end of parking lot—facing church entrance, it's to your right).

Sanctuary of St. Catherine—Step into Catherine's cool and peaceful home. Siena remembers its favorite hometown gal, a sim- ple, unschooled, but mystically devout soul who, in the mid-1300s, helped convince the pope to return from France to Rome. This schism split the Continent in the 14th century, but because of her intervention, Catherine is honored today as Europe's patron saint. Pilgrims have come to her home since 1464. Since then, architects and artists have greatly embellished what was probably a humble home (her family worked as wool-dyers). Enter through the court- yard and walk to the far end. The chapel on your right contains the wooden crucifix upon which Catherine was meditating when she received the stigmata. The chapel on your left used to be the kitchen. Go down the stairs to the left of the chapel/kitchen to reach the saint's room. Catherine's bare cell is behind see-through doors. Much of the art throughout the sanctuary depicts scenes from her life (free, daily 9:00–12:30 & 15:00–17:00, Via Tiratoio). It's a few downhill blocks toward the center from San Domenico (follow signs to *Santuario di Santa Caterina*).

SHOPPING

The main drag, Via Banchi di Sopra, is a can-can of fancy shops. The big local department store is **Upim** (Mon–Sat 8:30–20:00, Sun 9:00–20:00, Piazza Matteotti). The **Feltrinelli** bookstore closest to the Campo sells books and magazines in English (Mon–Sat 9:00–19:30, Sun 11:00–13:30 & 15:30–19:30, Banchi di Sopra 52). The large, colorful scarves/flags, each depicting the symbol of one of Siena's 17 different neighborhoods (such as the wolf, the turtle, and the snail), are easy-to-pack souvenirs, fun for decorating your home (€7 apiece for large size, sold at souvenir stands).

Local Sweets: All over town, Prodotti Tipici shops sell Sienese specialties. Siena's claim to caloric fame is its *panforte,* a rich, chewy concoction of nuts, honey, and candied fruits that impresses even fruitcake-haters. There are a few varieties to try: *margherita,* dusted in powdered sugar, is more fruity; *panpepato* has a spicy, peppery crust. Locals prefer a chewy white macaroon-and-almond cookie called *ricciarelli.*

NIGHTLIFE

Join the evening *passeggiata* (peak strolling time is 19:00) along Via Banchi di Sopra with gelato in hand.

The **Enoteca Italiana** is a good wine bar in a cellar in the Fortezza (sample glasses in 3 different price ranges: €2, €3, €5.50; Mon 12:00–20:00, Tue–Sat 12:00–24:00, closed Sun; bottles and snacks available; cross bridge and enter fortress, go left down ramp, not to be confused with Enoteca Toscana—same location but not as nice, tel. 0577-288-497).

SLEEPING

Finding a room in Siena is tough during Easter (April 16 in 2006) or the Palio (July 2 and Aug 16). Call ahead any time of year, as all the guidebooks list Siena's few budget places. While day-tripping tour groups turn the town into a Gothic amusement park in mid-summer, Siena is basically yours in the evenings and off-season.

Most of the listed hotels lie between Il Campo and the Church of San Domenico. Part of Siena's charm is its lively, festive character—this means that all hotels can be plagued with noise, even (and sometimes especially) the hotels in the pedestrian-only zone. If tranquility is important for your sanity, ask for a room that's off the street

Sleep Code

(€1 = about $1.20, country code: 39)
S = Single, **D** = Double/Twin, **T** = Triple, **Q** = Quad, **b** = bathroom, **s** = shower only.

Breakfast is generally not included. Have breakfast on Il Campo or in a nearby bar. You can assume a hotel takes credit cards unless you see "cash only" in the listing. (If not, there are ATMs all over town.) The hotel staff speaks basic English unless otherwise noted.

To help you sort easily through these listings, I've divided the rooms into three categories based on the price for a standard double room with bath:

$$$ **Higher Priced**—Most rooms €120 or more.
$$ **Moderately Priced**—Most rooms between €90–120.
$ **Lower Priced**—Most rooms €90 or less.

or consider staying at the recommended places outside the center.

Near Il Campo

Each of these listings is forgettable but inexpensive, and just a horse wreck away from one of Italy's most wonderful civic spaces.

$ Albergo Tre Donzelle is a fine budget value with 28 plain, institutional rooms. Don't hang out here...think of Il Campo, a block away, as your terrace (S-€33, D-€46, Db-€60, T-€65, Tb-€82; with your back to the tower, leave Il Campo to the right at 2:00, Via Donzelle 5; tel. 0577-280-358, fax 0577-223-933, Signora Valentina).

$ Piccolo Hotel Etruria, has 20 decent air-conditioned rooms but not much soul. The hotel is a bit overpriced though well-located and sleepable (S-€45, Sb-€50, Db-€80, Tb-€105, Qb-€130, optional breakfast-€5, curfew at 1:00, next to Albergo Tre Donzelle at Via Donzelle 1-3, tel. 0577-288-088, fax 0577-288-461, www.hoteletruria .com, info@hoteletruria.com, Fattorini family).

$ Locanda Garibaldi is a modest, very Sienese restaurant/ *albergo* (hotel). Gentle Marcello wears two hats, running a busy restaurant downstairs and renting seven pleasant rooms up a funky, artsy staircase (Db-€75, Tb-€95, family deals, cash only, takes reservations only a week in advance, half a block downhill off the square at Via Giovanni Dupre 18, tel. 0577-284-204, Marcello doesn't speak English).

$ Palazzo Bruchi B&B offers nine tranquil rooms situated in a 17th-century palazzo overlooking the Tuscan countryside. Two spacious *luxe* rooms feature Old World-heavy walnut furnishings and period paintings, while seven smaller rooms named for flowers have bright, cheery decor and overlook a quiet interior courtyard. Mariacristina and her daughter Camilla take good care of their guests (Sb-€60, Db-€80, Tb-€120, elevator, Via Pantaneto 105, take Banchi di Sotto until it turns into Via Pantaneto, located on the left, just before the Church of San Giorgio, tel. & fax 0577-287-342, www.palazzobruchi.it, masignani@hotmail.com.

$ **Hotel Cannon d'Oro,** a few blocks up Via Banchi di Sopra, is spacious and comfortable, if a bit noisy and group-friendly (Sb-€71, Db-€90, Tb-€115, Qb-€136, these discounted prices promised through 2006 with this book, family deals, 30 rooms, includes breakfast, Via Montanini 28, tel. 0577-44321, fax 0577-280-868, www.cannondoro.com, cannondoro@libero.it, Maurizio and Debora). This is just a couple blocks from the bus station.

$ **Casa di Antonella B&B,** in the heart of town, is neat-as-a-pin, relaxing, and a decent value. Antonella's five rooms have views of the Duomo, San Domenico, or the rooftops of Siena, and share a communal kitchen and dining room. Four rooms share two baths, and only one room has its own bathroom (D-€65, includes buffet breakfast, no elevator, 3 floors up, located between Piazza Matteotti and Piazza Indipendenza on Via delle Terme 72, tel. & fax 0577-48436, mobile 330-180-5557, anto.landi@libero.it).

Sleeping Fancy, Southwest of Il Campo

These two classy and well-run places are a 10-minute walk from Il Campo.

$$$ **Hotel Duomo,** with 23 spacious rooms and a bizarre floor plan, is a great value (Sb-€104, Db-€130, Tb-€171, Qb-€186, includes breakfast, air-con, elevator, picnic-friendly roof terrace, free parking; follow Via di Città, which becomes Via Stalloreggi, to Via Stalloreggi 38; tel. 0577-289-088, fax 0577-43043, www.hotelduomo.it, booking@hotelduomo.it, Alessandra and Stefania). If you arrive by train, take a taxi (€8) or bus #3 to the Due Porte stop just a few steps from the hotel; if you drive, go to Porta San Marco, turn right and follow the signs to the hotel, drop off your bags, and then park in nearby "Il Campo" lot.

$$$ **Pensione Palazzo Ravizza,** elegant and friendly, with an aristocratic feel and a peaceful garden, is a worthwhile splurge (Sb-€130, small loft Db-€120, standard Db-€160, superior Db-€180—see Web site for room differences, Tb-€220–310, suites available, cheaper mid-Nov–Feb, includes breakfast, back rooms face open country, air-con, free Internet in 2006, elevator, good restaurant, free parking, Via Piano dei Mantellini 34, tel. 0577-280-462, fax 0577-221-597, www.palazzoravizza.it, bureau@palazzoravizza.it).

Siena Hotels and Restaurants

1 Piccolo Hotel Etruria
2 Albergo Tre Donzelle
3 Locanda Garibaldi & Rist. Guidoriccio
4 Hotel Cannon d'Oro
5 To Hotel Duomo, Pen. Pal. Ravizza & Ost. Nonna Gina
6 To Hotel Villa Liberty
7 Hotel Chiusarelli
8 Alma Domus
9 Albergo Bernini & Ost. la Chiacchera

10 Casa di Antonella B&B
11 To Hotel Sta. Caterina, Palazzo Bruchi B&B & Res. d'Epoca Borgognini
12 To Hostel
13 Antica Ost. Da Divo
14 To Taverna S. Giuseppe
15 Osteria il Tamburino
16 Le Campane Rest.
17 Nello la Taverna
18 Pizzeria Spadaforte
19 Gelateria la Costarella

20 Ciao Cafeteria, Spizzico Pizza & Key Largo Bar
21 Bar Paninoteca San Paolo
22 Consorzio Agrario Siena Grocery
23 Lavarapido Launderette
24 Onda Blu Launderette

Near San Domenico Church

These hotels are within a 10-minute walk northeast of Il Campo. Albergo Bernini and Alma Domus, which enjoy views of the old town and cathedral, are about the best values in town.

$$$ Hotel Chiusarelli is a proper hotel with 49 rooms in a beautiful building with a handy location. Comes with traffic noise at night—ask for a quieter room in the back (S-€64, Sb-€82, Db-€121, Tb-€164, suites available, ask for Rick Steves discount when you book, includes buffet breakfast, reasonable dinner menu, air-con, Internet in lobby, pleasant garden terrace, rental bikes-€4/half day, across from San Domenico at Viale Curtatone 15, tel. 0577-280-562, fax 0577-271-177, www.chiusarelli.com, info@chiusarelli.com, Barbara).

$$ Hotel Villa Liberty, a bit farther out, has 18 big, bright, comfortable rooms and lots of street noise (S-€65, Db-€100, can be pricier during high season, includes breakfast, only 2 rooms with twin beds, air-con, elevator, bar, courtyard, free and easy street parking, facing fortress at Viale V. Veneto 11, tel. 0577-44966, fax 0577-44770, www.villaliberty.it, info@villaliberty.it).

$ Alma Domus is ideal—unless nuns make you nervous, you need a double bed, or you plan on staying out past the 23:30 curfew (no mercy given). This quasi-hotel (not a convent) is run with firm but angelic smiles by non-English-speaking sisters who offer 43 clean and quiet rooms for a steal and save the best views for foreigners. Bright lamps, quaint balconies, fine views, grand public rooms, top security, and a friendly atmosphere make this a great value. The checkout time is strictly 10:00, but they will store your luggage in their secure courtyard (Db-€60, Tb-€75, Qb-€90, cash only, ask for view room—*con vista*, air-con, elevator; from San Domenico walk downhill with the church on your right toward the view, turn left down Via Camporegio, make a U-turn at the little chapel down the brick steps to Via Camporegio 37; tel. 0577-44177, fax 0577-47601).

$ Albergo Bernini makes you part of a Sienese family in a modest, clean home with nine fine rooms. Friendly Nadia, Mauro, and son Alessandro (who speaks English) welcome you to their spectacular view terrace for breakfast and picnic lunches and dinners. Aside from breakfast and checkout time, Mauro, an accomplished accordionist, might play a song for you if you ask (Sb-€78, D-€62, Db-€82, less in winter, breakfast-€7, cash only, non-smoking, midnight curfew, on the main San Domenico–Il Campo drag at Via Sapienza 15, tel. & fax 0577-289-047, www.albergobernini.com, hbernin@tin.it). When full, they recommend their charming, bigger, but more expensive apartments (Db-€100, non-smoking, no curfew, located just a few steps downhill from the albergo).

Southeast of Il Campo, farther from the Center

The first two places are near each other, in the direction of Porta Romana city gate. The last two are well-served by city buses, but are less convenient.

$$$ Hotel Santa Caterina is a three-star, 18th-century place, great for drivers who need air-conditioning. Professionally run with real attention to quality, most of the hotel's 22 comfortable rooms are newly renovated, and there's a delightful garden outside (Sb-€105, small Db-€105, Db-€145, Tb-€195, prices promised through 2006 with this book, includes buffet breakfast, fridge in room, elevator; garden side is quieter, but street side—with multi-paned windows—isn't bad; parking-€15/day—request when you reserve, 100 yards outside Porta Romana at Via E.S. Piccolomini 7, tel. 0577-221-105, fax 0577-271-087, www.hscsiena.it, info@hscsiena.it, Lorenza). A city shuttle bus runs frequently (4/hr) to the town center.

$$$ Frances' Lodge is a small farmhouse B&B a mile out of Siena. Franca and Franco rent four modern rooms and two apartment-suites in a rustic yet elegant old place with a swimming pool, peaceful garden, eight acres of olive trees and vineyards, and great Siena views (Db-€160–190 depending upon room size, Tb-€210-220, Db suite-€220, Tb suite-€240, Qb suite-€260, these prices promised to our readers through 2006 so let them know when you book, includes great breakfast, easy parking, near shuttle bus "B" into town, Strada di Valdipugna 2, tel. 0577-281-061, fax 0577-222-224, www.franceslodge.it, info@franceslodge.it).

$$ Residenza d'Epoca Borgognini is a grand old palazzo with seven cool, solid, and tastefully decorated rooms. You'll find high ceilings, lots of stairs, and a warm welcome from Maria Antonietta (D-normally €80 but €120 in July–Aug, Db-normally €90 but €130 in July–Aug, Tb-€120–150, 10 percent discount with this book in 2006, includes breakfast at nearby bar, Via Pantaneto 160, tel. & fax 0577-44055, mobile 338-7640933, www.hotelborgognini.it, hotelborgognini@yahoo.it).

$ Siena's Guidoriccio Youth Hostel has 100 cheap beds, but is outside the center. Given the hassle of the bus ride and the charm of downtown Siena at night, I'd skip it (€14 beds in doubles, triples, and dorms with sheets, cash only, cheap breakfast, lock-out 9:30–13:30, bus #10 from train station or bus #10 or #15 from Piazza Gramsci—about 20 min, Via Fiorentina 89 in Stellino neighborhood, tel. 0577-52212, fax 0577-50277).

Outside of Siena

The following accommodations, best for dirivers, are in the lush, peaceful countryside surrounding Siena.

$$$ Borgo Argenina is a well-maintained, pricey splurge of a B&B, located a 20-minute drive north of Siena in the Chianti region. It's run by helpful Elena Nappa (Db-€150, Db suite-€180, beautiful gardens, tel. 0577-747-117, fax 0577-747-228, www.borgoargenina.it, borgoargenina@libero.it).

$$ Agriturismo Poggio Salvi, has three inviting, spacious apartments—rentable only by the week—set in a grassy field near the tiny burg of Poggio Salvi, 15 minutes southwest of Siena. Dwellings are separate with modern conveniences (rentals from Sat–Sat, €800/2 people and €1250/4 people during high season, e-mail Massimo and ask for Rick Steves discount, Loc. Poggio Salvi 249/A, 53010 San Rocco a Pilli, tel. 0577-349-443, mobile 333-290-7890, fax 0577-347-686, www.poggiosalvi.net, info@poggiosalvi.net).

$ Agriturismo le Trappoline, 12 miles northeast of Siena in the Chianti region, is a renovated farmhouse—in peak season rentable only by the week—with panoramic vistas and ample grounds for country walks (rentals from Sat–Sat, mid-June–mid-Sept) and for a minimum of three nights otherwise (4-person apartments-€100, discounts off-season, pool with terrace, on I Sodi Farm, Località Monti Gaiole in Chianti, tel. 0577-747-012, www.letrappoline.it, info@letrappoline.it, Danilo and Gabriella Casini).

$ Parri Nada Farmhouse, a good choice for families, is tucked away in the vineyards in the hills of Chianti 12 miles northeast of Siena. Luca and Elena Masti rent two rooms in their comfortable home (D-€75, T-€90, Q-whole apartment-€110, 1-night rentals OK, kitchen, pool, private yard, Località Santa Chiara 4, tel. & fax 0577-359-072, mobile 333-840-8448, www.farm-house.it, info@farm-house.it).

EATING

Sienese restaurants are reasonable by Florentine and Venetian standards. Enjoy ordering high on the menu here without going broke.

Antica Osteria Da Divo is *the* place for a fine €40 meal. The kitchen is creative, the ambience is candlelit, and the food is fresh and top-notch. The lamb goes *baaa* in your mouth. They offer a basket of fresh exotic breads and excellent seasonal dishes. And the chef is understandably proud of his desserts (Wed–Mon 12:00–14:30 & 19:00–22:00, closed Tue, reserve for summer eves; Via Franciosa 29; facing baptistery door, take the far right and walk one long curving block; tel. 0577-286-054). Readers of this book finish their meal with a complimentary biscotti and *vin santo* or coffee.

Ristorante Guidoriccio, just a few steps below Il Campo, feels warm, classy, and delightful, with smiling service by Ercole and Elisabetta and prices good for the locale (pastas-€7, *secondi*-€13, Mon–Sat 12:30–14:30 & 19:00–22:30, closed Sun, air-con, Via G. Dupre 2, tel. 0577-44350).

Taverna San Giuseppe, a local favorite, offers modern Tuscan cuisine in a dressy grotto atmosphere. Check the posters tacked around the entry for daily specials. Reserve or arrive early to get a table (Mon–Sat 12:00–14:30 & 19:00–22:00, closed Sun, 7-min walk up street to the right of the City Hall, Via Giovanni Dupre 132, tel. 0577-42286).

Osteria il Tamburino is friendly, popular, and serves up tasty, inexpensive meals in a narrow dining room (Mon–Sat 12:00–15:00 & 19:00–21:30, closed Sun; follow Via di Città off Il Campo, becomes Stalloreggi, Via Stalloreggi 11; tel. 0577-280-306).

Le Campane, two blocks off Il Campo, is more formal. It features modern Tuscan fare with an elegant interior and outdoor tables on a quiet square (pastas-€9, *secondi*-€14, daily 12:15–14:30 & 19:30–22:00, closed Mon in winter, reservations smart, indoor/outdoor seating, a few steps off Via di Città at Via delle Campane 6, tel. 0577-284-035).

Osteria Nonna Gina wins praise from locals for its good quality and prices (Tue–Sun 12:30–14:30 & 19:30–22:30, closed Mon, 10-min walk from Il Campo, 2 blocks beyond Hotel Duomo, Piano dei Mantellini 2, tel. 0577-287-247).

Osteria la Chiacchera is a youthful hole-in-the-brick-wall playing hip music and serving "peasant food" at peasant prices on rustic tables and paper place mats (pastas-€4, *secondi*-€5–6, daily 12:00–15:30 & 19:00–24:00, reservations wise, understandably proud of their cakes, skip the *trippa*—tripe, 2 rooms, below Pension Bernini at Costa di San Antonio 4, tel. 0577-280-631). Their outside tables cling to a steep lane.

Nello la Taverna, an artsy trattoria with a minimalist dining room, is run by English-speaking Mauro and Simonetta with stylish flair. Their menu features whatever's in season paired with homemade pasta, lots of creative vegetarian options, and well-presented hot desserts (Mon–Sat 12:00–15:00 & 19:00–22:30, closed Sun, a few steps off Il Campo on Via Porrione 38, to the left of City Tower as you're facing it, tel. 0577-289-043).

Locanda Garibaldi offers authentic Sienese dining at a fair price (pastas-€6, *secondi*-€9, €20 menu, Sun–Fri 12:00–14:00 & 19:00–21:00, closed Sat, arrive early to get a table, within a block of Il Campo down Via Giovanni Dupre at #18, tel. 0187-284-4204). Marcello does a little *piatto misto dolce* (sweet mixed plate) for €4, featuring several local desserts with sweet wine.

Even with higher prices, lousy service, and lower-quality food, consider eating on Il Campo—a classic European experience. Given the real estate, the prices (if you order carefully and are treated fairly) are actually pretty good. Wander across the square and sit wherever your stomach and heart tell you to. **Pizzeria Spadaforte,** at the edge of Il Campo, has a fine perch, decent food, and slanted tables (€7 pizzas and pastas, daily 12:00–16:00 & 19:30–22:30, to far right of City Tower as you face it, tel. 0577-281-123).

Drinks or Snacks Overlooking Il Campo

Three places have skinny balconies with benches overlooking the main square for their customers. Sipping a coffee or nibbling a pastry here while marveling at the Il Campo scene is one of my favorite things to do in Europe. And it's very cheap. Survey these three places from Il Campo (from the base of the tower, using an imaginary 12-hour clock, they are at 10 o'clock, high noon, and 3 o'clock, respectively).

Gelateria la Costarella has good ice cream, drinks, and light snacks (Mon–Wed & Fri–Sun 8:00–late, closes 22:00 off-season, closed Thu, off Via di Città). **Bar Paninoteca San Paolo,** with a youthful pub ambience, has a row of stools overlooking the square and serves 50 kinds of sandwiches (hot and cold, €3 each, €0.50 extra if you sit outside, food served daily 11:30–2:00, on Vicolo di S. Paolo on the stairs leading down to the top of Il Campo). **Key Largo Bar** has two benches in the corner offering a great secret perch (daily 7:00–22:00 or until midnight, closed Sun in winter, on Via Rinaldini). Buy your drink or snack at the bar (no extra charge to sit), climb upstairs, and slide the ancient bar to open the door. Suddenly you're imagining Palio ponies zipping wildly around your corner.

Eating Cheaply in the Center

At the bottom of Il Campo, a **Ciao** cafeteria offers easy self-service meals, no ambience, and no views (daily 12:00–15:00 & 19:00–21:30). The crowded **Spizzico,** a pizza counter in the front half of Ciao, serves huge, inexpensive quarter-pizzas; on sunny days, people take the pizza—trays and all—out on Il Campo for a picnic (daily 11:00–22:00, to left of City Tower as you face it).

Budget eaters look for *pizza al taglio* shops, scattered throughout Siena, selling pizza by the slice. Of all the grocery shops, the biggest is **Consorzio Agrario Siena** (Mon–Sat 8:00–19:30, closed Sun.

TRANSPORTATION CONNECTIONS

Siena has sparse train connections, but is a great hub for buses to the hill towns.

From Siena by Train to: Florence (9/day, 1.75 hrs, more with transfer in Empoli), **Pisa** (hrly, 2 hrs, transfer in Empoli), **Rome**

(every 2 hrs, 2.75–4 hrs, transfer in Florence or Chiusi).

From Siena by Bus to: Florence (€6.50, hrly, 1.75 hrs, by Tra-In bus, last bus at 20:45, can buy tickets at *tabacchi* shops if bus ticket office is closed), **San Gimignano** (€5.20, 6/day, 75 min, by Tra-In bus, more frequent with transfer in Poggibonsi, tickets also available at *tabacchi* shops), **Assisi** (2/day, 2 hrs, €10, by Sena bus; the morning bus goes direct to Assisi though the afternoon bus might terminate at Santa Maria degli Angeli—from here catch a local bus to Assisi, 2/hr, 20 min), **Rome** (€17.50, 8/day, 3 hrs, by Sena bus, arrives at Rome's Tiburtina station), **Milan** (€25, 4/day, 4.5 hrs). Schedules get sparse on Sundays and holidays.

Buses depart Siena from Piazza Gramsci, the train station, or both; confirm when you purchase your ticket. You can get tickets for Tra-In buses or Sena buses at the train station: Tra-In at the newsstand (Mon–Sat 6:00–20:00, Sun 6:00–16:00), Sena at the window to the left of the train ticket office (Mon–Sat 7:40–12:40 & 14:30–18:30, closed Sun). You can also get tickets under Piazza Gramsci at **Sottopassaggio la Lizza**—look for stairwells to this underground passageway on sidewalks surrounding Piazza la Lizza (Tra-In bus office: Mon–Sat 5:50–20:00, Sun 6:00–19:30, tel. 0577-204-246, toll-free tel. 800-570-530, www.trainspa.it; Sena bus office: Mon–Sat 7:45–19:45, closed Sun, if Sena bus ticket office is closed, buy Sena tickets next door at Tra-In office, tel. 800-930-960, www.senabus.it).

Sottopassaggio la Lizza, the passageway under Piazza Gramsci, also has a cash machine (neither bus office accepts credit cards), luggage storage (€3.50/day, daily 7:00–19:45, no overnight storage), posted bus schedules, TV monitors (listing imminent departures for all three companies), an elevator, and expensive WCs (€0.55). Those departing Siena after the bus offices close can buy the ticket from *tabacchi* shops (only for buses staying within Tuscany). Longer distance buses all depart before the bus ticket offices close. On schedules, the fastest buses are marked *corse rapide*. I'd stick with these. Note that if a schedule lists your departure point as Via Tozzi or La Lizza, you catch the bus at Piazza Gramsci (Via Tozzi is the street that runs alongside Piazza Gramsci and Piazza la Lizza is the name of the bus hub square).

ASSISI

Assisi is famous for its hometown boy, St. Francis, who made very good. While Francis the saint is interesting, Francesco Bernardone the man is even more so, and mementos of his days in Assisi are everywhere—where he was baptized, a shirt he wore, a hill he prayed on, and a church where he saw a life-changing vision.

Around the year 1200, this simple friar from Assisi countered the decadence of Church government and society in general with a powerful message of non-materialism and a "slow down and smell God's roses" lifestyle. Like Jesus, Francis taught by example, living without worldly goods and aiming to love all creation. A huge monastic order grew out of his teachings, which were gradually embraced (some would say co-opted) by the Church. Christianity's most popular saint and purest example of simplicity is now glorified in beautiful churches, along with his female counterpart, St. Clare. In 1939, Italy made Francis and Clare its patron saints.

Francis' message of love, simplicity, and sensitivity to the environment has a broad and timeless appeal. But every pilgrimage site inevitably gets commercialized, and Francis' legacy is now Assisi's basic industry. In summer, this Umbrian town bursts with flash-in-the-pan Francis fans and Franciscan knickknacks. Those able to see past the glow-in-the-dark rosaries and bobble-head friars can actually have a "travel on purpose" experience.

Planning Your Time

Assisi is worth a day and a night. Its old town has a half day of sightseeing and another half day of wonder. The essential sight is the Basilica of St. Francis. For a good visit, take my self-guided "Welcome to

Assisi Area

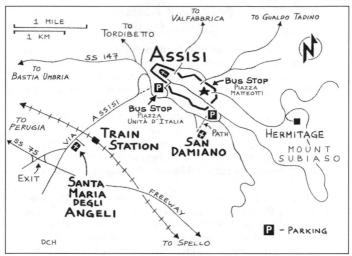

Assisi" walk (below), ending at the Basilica of St. Francis. Schedule time to linger on the main square, Piazza del Comune.

Most visitors are day-trippers. While the town's a zoo by day, it's a delight at night. Assisi after dark is closer to a place Francis could call home.

ORIENTATION

Crowned by a ruined castle, Assisi spills downhill to its famous Basilica of St. Francis. The town is beautifully preserved and rich in history. A 5.5-magnitude earthquake in 1997 did more damage to the tourist industry than to the local buildings. Fortunately, tourists—whether art-lovers, pilgrims, or both—have returned, drawn by Assisi's special allure.

The city sprawls across a ridge that rises from a flat plain. The Basilica of St. Francis sits at the low end of town, Piazza Matteotti is at the high end (bus station and car parking), and the main square, Piazza del Comune, lies in between. Via San Francesco runs from Piazza del Comune to the basilica. Capping the hill above the town is a ruined castle called the Rocca Maggiore, and rising above that is Mt. Subasio. The town is small, but it slopes uphill from west to east. Walking from the basilica to Piazza Matteotti (uphill) takes 45 minutes, while the downhill journey is quicker. Some Francis sights lie outside the city walls, both in the valley beneath the ridge, and in the hills above.

Francis of Assisi
(1181/82–1226)

In 1202, young Francesco Bernardone (the future St. Francis) donned armor and rode out to battle the Perugians. The battle went badly, and 20-year-old Francis was captured and imprisoned for a year. He returned a changed man. He avoided friends and his father's lucrative business and spent more and more time outside the city walls fasting, praying, and searching for something. In 1206, a vision changed his life, culminating in a dramatic confrontation. He stripped naked before the town leaders, threw his clothes at his father—turning his back on the comfortable material life—and declared his loyalty to God alone.

Idealistic young men flocked to Francis, and they wandered Italy like troubadours, spreading the joy of the Gospel to rich and poor. Francis became a cult figure, attracting huge crowds. They'd never seen anything like it—sermons preached outdoors, in the local language (not Church Latin), making God accessible to all. Francis' new order of monks was radically anti-materialist, but it eventually gained the Pope's own approval and spread through the world. Francis, who died in Assisi at the age of 45, left a legacy of humanism, equality, and love of nature that would eventually flower in the Renaissance.

In Francis' Sandal-Steps
1. Baptized in Assisi'a **Church of San Rufino** (then called St. George's).
2. Raised in the family home just off Piazza del Comune (now the **Chiesa Nuova**).
3. Heard call to "rebuild church" in **San Damiano.** (The crucifix of the church is now in the **Basilica of St. Clare.**)
4. Settles and establishes his order of monks at the **Porziuncola Chapel** (today's **Santa Maria degli Angeli**).
5. Meets Clare. (Her tomb and possessions are at the **Basilica of St. Clare.**)
6. Gets the pope's blessing for his order (1223 document in the **Basilica of St. Francis' relic chapel**).
7. Has many visions and is associated with miracles during his life (depicted in **Giotto's frescoes** in the Basilica of St. Francis' upper level).
8. Dies at the **Porziuncola.** His body is later interred beneath the **Basilica of St. Francis.**

Tourist Information

The TI is in the center of town on Piazza del Comune (Mon–Sat 8:00–14:00 & 15:00–18:00, Sun 10:00–13:00; tel. 075-812-534).

A combo-ticket (*biglietto cumulativo*, €4.50/1 day, includes audioguide) covers three sights: Rocca Maggiore (castle), Pinacoteca (paintings), and the Roman Forum. You'd need to see all three to save money.

A Saturday morning market fills Piazza Matteotti (which has a good parking garage). Your hotel may give you an Assisi Card, which offers discounts on parking and some affiliated restaurants and shops.

Arrival in Assisi

By Train and Bus: City buses connect Assisi's train station with the old town of Assisi on the hilltop (€0.80, 2/hr, about 15–20 min), stopping at Piazza Unità d'Italia (near Basilica of St. Francis), then Largo Properzio (near Basilica of St. Clare), and finally Piazza Matteotti (top of old town). Going to the old town, buses usually leave from the train station at :16 and :46 past the hour. Going to the train station from the old town, buses usually run from Piazza Matteotti at :10 and :40 past the hour, and from Piazza Unità d'Italia at :17 and :47 past the hour. At Piazza Unità d'Italia, there are two bus stops (*fermata bus):* one sign reads *per f.s. S.M. Angeli* (to the train station), and the other reads *per P. Matteotti* (to the top of the old town).

Taxis from the train station to the old town run about €10. There are legitimate extra charges for luggage, night service, and for each person above four passengers, but beware: Many taxis rip off tourists by using tariff #2 (Sunday and holiday fare); the meter should be set on tariff #1 (€2.85 drop). You can check bags at the train station (€2.60/12 hrs, daily 6:30–19:30), but not in the old town. When departing the old town of Assisi, you'll find taxi stands at Piazza Unità d'Italia, the Basilica of St. Clare, and Piazza del Comune (or have your hotel call for you, tel. 075-813-100).

By Car: Drivers just coming in for the day should follow the signs to Piazza Matteotti's wonderful underground parking garage at the top of the town (which comes with bits of ancient Rome in the walls; €1/hr, daily 7:00–21:00, until 23:00 in summer).

Helpful Hints

New Minibuses in Old Town: Two routes make this hilly town easy to manage. Minibus #B runs between the Basilica of St. Francis (get on at Piazza San Pietro) up to Assisi's main square, Piazza del Comune (other stops are the hospital and Largo Properzio, near Porta Nuova gate). Minibus #A runs between Piazza del Comune up to Piazza Matteotti, with

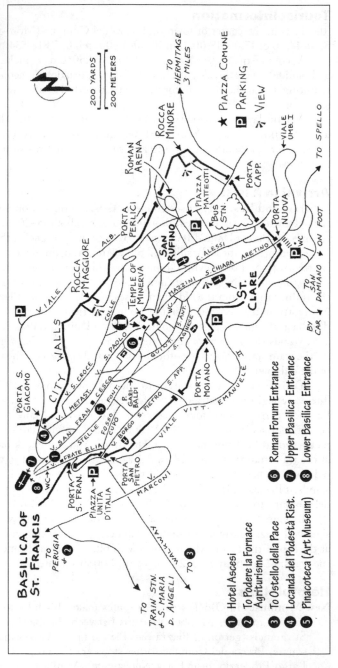

Assisi

200 YARDS
200 METERS

★ PIAZZA COMUNE
P PARKING
🏃 VIEW

TO HERMITAGE 3 MILES

Rocca Minore

Roman Arena

PORTA PERLICI

PIAZZA MATTEOTTI

Bus Stn.

PORTA CAPP.

PORTA NUOVA

SAN RUFINO

C. ALESSI

ARETINO

S. CHIARA

ST. CLARE

Rocca Maggiore

ALB.

Temple of Minerva

MAZZINI

WC

TO SAN DAMIANO

BY CAR   ON FOOT

VIALE

COLLE

V. S. CROCE

S. PAOLO

V. METAST.

C. ESCO

V. SAN FRAN.

STELLE

FOSSO

FONT.

V. BORGO S. PIETRO

S. ANT.

S. AGNESE

QUOT.

PORTA MOIANO

PORTA S. GIACOMO

CITY WALLS

FRATE ELIA

WC

PORTA S. FRAN.

PIAZZA UNITÀ D'ITALIA

PORTA SAN PIETRO

V. MARCONI

P. GARI-BALDI

VIALE VITT. EMANUELE II

S. APP.

BASILICA OF ST. FRANCIS

TO PERUGIA

TO TRAIN STN. & S. MARIA D. ANGELI

WALKWAY

TO 3

TO SPELLO

VIALE UMB. I

1 Hotel Ascesi
2 To Podere la Fornace Agriturismo
3 To Ostello della Pace
4 Locanda del Podestà Rist.
5 Pinacoteca (Art Museum)
6 Roman Forum Entrance
7 Upper Basilica Entrance
8 Lower Basilica Entrance

stops at the cemetery and a newer part of Assisi. You can buy a bus ticket (good on any city bus) at a newsstand or kiosk for €0.80, or get a ticket from the driver and pay €1 (valid for 1 hour, can't transfer between routes).

Travel Agency: You can get train tickets and most bus tickets (but not for Siena) at Agenzia Viaggi Stoppini, between Piazza del Comune and the Basilica of St. Clare (Mon–Fri 9:00–12:00 & 15:30–19:00, Sat 9:00–12:00, closed Sun, Corso Mazzini 31, tel. 075-812-597). For Siena, you can buy tickets at Agenzia Viaggi Maritur (Via Frate Elia 1b, near Basilica of St. Francis, or pay more to purchase tickets on the bus; see "Transportation Connections," page 445).

Local Guide: Anne Robichaud, an American who has lived here since 1975, gives informative tours of Assisi and the country-side with the aim of connecting tourists to locals and their customs and culture. Set your own itinerary or use one of her suggestions, such as day trips to neighboring hill towns and local festivals (half-day from €55 per person, full day from €99, cooking lessons, can combine small groups for price reduction, tel. 075-802-334, mobile 333-923-8448, www.annesitaly.com). Thanks to Anne for her help with the following walk.

SELF-GUIDED WALK

Welcome to Assisi

There's much more to Assisi than St. Francis and what the blitz tour groups see.

This walk, rated ▲▲, covers the town from Piazza Matteotti at the top, down to the Basilica of St. Francis at the bottom. To get to Piazza Matteotti, ride the bus from the train station (or from Piazza Unità d'Italia) to the last stop; take Minibus #A from Piazza del Comune; or drive there (underground parking with Roman ruins).

• Start 50 yards beyond Piazza Matteotti (at intersection at far end of parking lot, away from city center—see map).

The Roman Arena: A lane named Via Anfiteatro Romano leads to a cozy circular neighborhood built around a Roman arena, when Assisi was an important Roman town. Circle the arena counterclockwise (the chain keeps cars out but pedestrians are welcome). Imagine how colorful the town laundry must have been in the last generation when the women of Assisi gathered here to do their wash. Adjacent to the laundry is a small rectangular pool filled with water; above it are the coats of arms of Assisi's leading families. A few steps farther, hike up the stairs to the top of the hill for an aerial view of the oval arena. The Roman stones have long been absorbed into the medieval architecture. It was Roman tradition to locate the arena outside of town...which this was.

• *Continue on. The lane leads down to a city gate and an...*

Umbrian View: Step outside of Assisi at the Porta Perlici for a commanding view. Umbria, called the "green heart of Italy," is the country's geographical center and only landlocked state. Enjoy the greens: silver green on the valley floor (olives), emerald green 10 yards below you (grapevines), and deep green on the hillsides (evergreen oak trees). Also notice Rocca Maggiore ("big fortress"), which provided townsfolk a refuge in times of attack, and, behind you atop the hill, Rocca Minore (little fortress). Now return to Piazza Matteotti. Go to the opposite end of this square, to the corner with the blobby stone tower. As you walk down the lane next to this tower, you'll see the big dome of the Church of San Rufino.

• *Walk to the courtyard of the church; its big bell tower is on your left.*

Church of San Rufino: While Francis is Italy's patron saint, Rufino (the town's first bishop, martyred and buried here in the 3rd century) is Assisi's. The church is 12th-century Romanesque with a neoclassical interior. Enter the church (daily 8:00–13:00 & 15:00–19:00). To your right (in the back corner of the church with the black iron grate) is an old baptism font. Around the year 1182, a baby boy was baptized in this font. His parents were upwardly-mobile Francophiles who called him Francesco ("Frenchy"). In 1194, a nobleman baptized his daughter Clare here. Eighteen years later, Clare's and Francis' paths crossed in this same church, when Clare attended a class and became mesmerized by the teacher—Francis. Traditionally, the children of Assisi are still baptized here.

The striking glass panels in the church floor reveal foundations preserved from the ninth-century church that once stood here. You're walking on history. After the 1997 earthquake, the church was checked from ceiling to floor by structural inspectors. When they looked under the paving stones, they discovered graves (it used to be a common practice to bury people in church, until Napoleon decreed otherwise), and underneath, Roman foundations and some animal bones (suggesting the possibility of animal sacrifice). There might have been a Roman temple here; churches were often built upon temple ruins. Standing at the back of the church (facing the altar), look left to the Roman cistern (inside the great stone archway). In the Middle Ages, this was the town's emergency water source when under attack.

Underneath the church, incorporated into the Roman ruins, are the foundations of an earlier Church of San Rufino, now the crypt. When it's open, you can go below to see the saint's sarcophagus (€3, mid-March–mid-Oct daily 10:00–13:00 & 15:00–18:00, in winter closes 17:30 and all day Wed). With your back to the crypt entrance, you'll see the door to the museum of the church (entry included with crypt ticket, same hours as above except 10:00–18:00 in Aug).

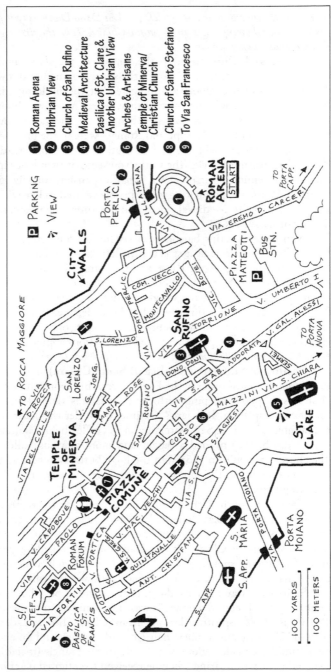

"Welcome to Assisi" Walk

1. Roman Arena
2. Umbrian View
3. Church of San Rufino
4. Medieval Architecture
5. Basilica of St. Clare & Another Umbrian View
6. Arches & Artisans
7. Temple of Minerva/ Christian Church
8. Church of Santo Stefano
9. To Via San Francesco

P PARKING
VIEW

CITY WALLS

• *Leaving the church, take a sharp left (on Via Dono Doni—say it fast three times), following the sign to Santa Chiara. Take the first right, down the stairway to see some...*

Medieval Architecture: At the bottom of the stairs, notice the pink limestone pavement, part of the surviving medieval town. The arches built over doorways indicate that the buildings date from the 12th through the 14th century, when Assisi was booming. Italian cities such as Assisi—thriving on the north-south trade between northern Europe and Rome—were in the process of inventing capitalism, dabbling in democratic self-rule, and creating the modern urban lifestyle. The vaults you see that turn lanes into tunnels are reminders of medieval urban expansion (mostly 15th century). While the population grew, people wanted to live within its protective walls. Medieval Assisi had five times the population density of today's Assisi.

Notice the flowering balconies; Assisi holds a competition each June. When you arrive at a street, turn left, going slightly uphill for a block, then jog right. Pause at Via Sermei 6b (on your left) to check out Signore Silvano Giombolini's display of mechanized figures petting sheep, sawing wood, and drawing well water. Look for the nativity scene, featuring an adored baby Jesus captioned with scriptures and Franciscan-style admonitions to love one another and appreciate life's simple pleasures (free but donations appreciated).

• *Continue ahead, following the* S. Chiara *sign down to the...*

Basilica of St. Clare (Basilica di Santa Chiara): Dedicated to the founder of the order of the Poor Clares, this Umbrian Gothic church is simple, in keeping with the Poor Clares' dedication to a life of contemplation. In Clare's lifetime, the order was located in the humble Church of San Damiano, in the valley below, but after Clare's death, they needed a bigger and more glorious building. The church was built in 1265, and the huge buttresses were added in the next century. The interior's fine frescoes were whitewashed in Baroque times.

The Chapel of the Crucifix of San Damiano, on the right, has the wooden crucifix that changed Francis' life. In 1206, an emaciated, soul-searching, stark-raving Francis knelt before this crucifix (then located in the Church of San Damiano) and asked for guidance. The crucifix spoke: "Go and rebuild my Church, which you can see has fallen into ruin." And Francis followed the call.

Stairs lead from the nave down to the tomb of St. Clare. Her tomb is at the far end (the image is wax, her bones lie underneath). The walls depict spiritual lessons from Clare's life and death (1194–1253). The saint's robes, hair (in a silver box), and an enormous tunic she made—along with relics of St. Francis (including a shoe that he was wearing when he received the stigmata) are in a large case, in the back between the stairs. The attached cloistered

St. Clare
(1194–1253)

The 18-year-old rich girl of Assisi fell in love with 30-year-old Francis' message, and made secret arrangements to meet him. The night of Palm Sunday, 1212, she slipped out of her father's mansion in town and escaped to the valley below. A procession of friars with torches met her and took her to (today's) Santa Maria degli Angeli. There, Francis cut her hair, clothed her in a simple brown tunic, and welcomed her into a life of voluntary poverty. Clare's father begged, ordered, and physically threatened her to return, but she would not budge.

Clare was joined by other women who banded together as the Poor Clares. She spent the next 40 years of her life within the confines of the convent of San Damiano, barefoot, vegetarian, and largely silent. Her regimen of prayer, meditation, and simple manual labor—especially knitting—impressed commoners and popes, leading to her canonization almost immediately after her death. St. Clare is often depicted carrying a monstrance (a little temple holding the Eucharist wafer), because according to legend, she saved the convent from attack by holding up a monstrance.

community of the Poor Clares has flourished for 700 years (church open daily 6:30–12:00 & 14:00–19:00, until 18:00 in winter).

• *Belly up to the viewpoint in front of the basilica for...*

Another Umbrian View: On the left is the convent of St. Clare; below you, the olive grove of the Poor Clares since the 13th century; and, in the distance, a grand Umbrian view. Assisi overlooks the richest and biggest valley in otherwise hilly and mountainous Umbria. The municipality of Assisi has a population of 29,000, but only 1,000 people live in the old town. The lower town grew up with the coming of the railway in the 19th century. In the haze, the blue-domed church is St. Mary of the Angels (Santa Maria degli Angeli, see page 439), the cradle of the Franciscan order, marking the place St. Francis lived and worked and a popular pilgrimage sight today. Franciscans settled in California, naming Los Angeles after this church, San Francisco after St. Francis, and Santa Clara after St. Clare.

• *From Via Santa Chiara, you can see two arches over the street.*

Arches and Artisans: The arch at the back of the church dates from 1265. (Beyond it but out of view, the 1316 Porta Nuova marks the final expansion of Assisi.) Toward the city center (on Via Santa Chiara, the high road), an arch marks the site of the Roman wall.

About 40 yards before this arch, pop into the souvenir shop at #1b. The plaque over the door explains that the old printing press (a national monument now, just inside the door) was used to make fake documents for Jews escaping the Nazis in 1943 and 1944. The shop is run by a couple of artisans: The man makes frames out of medieval Assisi timbers; the woman cross-stitches the traditional Assisi, or Franciscan, embroidery.

Just past the gate and on your left is the La Pasteria natural products shop (Corso Mazzini 18b, across from entrance of Hotel Sole). Cooks love to peruse Umbrian wines, herbs, pâtés, and truffles, and to sample an aromatic "fruit infusion." The Lisa Assisi clothing shop (Corso Mazzini 25b, across the street and to your right) has a delightful basement, with surviving bits of a 2,000-year-old mortar-less Roman wall. Ahead at Corso Mazzini 14d, the small shop (Poiesis) sells olive-wood carvings. Drop in. It's said that St. Francis made the first nativity scene to help humanize and, therefore, teach the Christmas message. That's why you'll see so many crèches in Assisi. Even today, nearby villages are enthusiastic about their "living" manger scenes, and Italians everywhere enjoy setting up elaborate crèches in churches for Christmas.

Ahead of you, the six fluted Corinthian columns of the Temple of Minerva mark the Piazza del Comune. Sit at the fountain on the Piazza for a few minutes of people-watching—don't you love Italy? Within 200 yards of this square, on either side, were the medieval walls. Imagine a commotion of 5,000 people confined within these walls. No wonder St. Francis needed an escape for some peace and quiet.

• *Now, let's head over at the temple on the square.*

Temple of Minerva/Christian Church: Assisi has always been a spiritual center. The Romans went to great lengths to make this first-century B.C. Temple of Minerva (or maybe of Hercules) a centerpiece of their city. Notice the columns cutting into the stairway. It was a tight fit here on the hilltop. The stairs probably went down triple the distance you see today. The Church of Santa Maria sopra (over) Minerva was added in the ninth century. The bell tower is 13th-century. Pop inside the temple/church (Mon–Sat 7:15–19:00, Sun 8:15–19:00, closes at sunset and midday in winter). Today's interior is 17th-century Baroque. Flanking the altar are the original Roman temple floor stones. You can even see the drains for the bloody sacrifices that took place here. Behind the statues of Peter and Paul the original Roman embankment peeks through.

Across the square at #11, step into the 16th-century frescoed vaults from the old fish market. Notice the Italian flair for design. Even this smelly fish market was once finely decorated. The art style was "grotesque"—literally, a painting in a grotto. This was painted in the early 1500s, a few years after Columbus brought turkeys back from the New World. The turkeys painted here may have been that bird's European debut.

• *From the main square, hike past the temple up the high road, Via San Paolo. After 200 yards, a sign directs you down a lane to the...*

Church of Santo Stefano: Surrounded by cypress, fig, and walnut trees, Santo Stefano—which used to be outside the town walls in the days of St. Francis—is a delightful bit of offbeat Assisi. Legend has it that Santo Stefano's bells miraculously rang on October 3, 1226, the day St. Francis died. Step inside. This is the typical rural Italian Romanesque church—no architect, just built by simple stonemasons who put together the most basic design (daily 8:30–21:30, closes 17:30 in winter).

• *The lane zigzags down to Via San Francesco. Turn right and walk under the arch toward the Basilica of St. Francis.*

Via San Francesco: This was the main drag leading from the town to the basilica holding the body of St. Francis. Francis was a big deal even in his own day. He died in 1226 and was made a saint in 1228—the same year the basilica's foundations were laid—and his body was moved in by 1230. Assisi was a big-time pilgrimage center, and this street was its booming main drag. Notice the fine medieval balcony just below the arch. A few yards farther down (on the left), cool yourself at the fountain. The hospice next door was built in 1237 to house pilgrims. Notice the three surviving faces of its fresco: Jesus, Francis, and Clare. Continuing on, you'll eventually reach Assisi's main sight, the Basilica of St. Francis.

SIGHTS

Basilica of St. Francis

A ▲▲▲ sight, the Basilica di San Francesco is one of the artistic and religious highlights of Europe. In 1226, St. Francis was buried (with the outcasts he had stood by) outside of his town on the "Hill of the Damned"—now called the "Hill of Paradise." The basilica is frescoed from top to bottom by the leading artists of the day: Cimabue, Giotto, Simone Martini, and Pietro Lorenzetti. A 13th-century historian wrote, "No more exquisite monument to the Lord has been built."

From a distance, you see the huge arcades "supporting" the basilica. These were 15th-century quarters for the monks. The arcades lining the square leading to the church housed medieval pilgrims.

Orientation: There are three parts to the church: the upper basilica, the lower basilica, and the saint's tomb (below the lower basilica). In the 1997 earthquake, the lower basilica—with walls nearly nine feet thick—was unscathed. The upper basilica, with bigger windows and walls only three feet thick, was damaged. After restoration was completed, the entire church was reopened to visitors in late 1999.

The Message

Francis' message caused a stir. Not only did he follow Christ's teachings, he adopted his lifestyle, living as a poor, wandering preacher. He traded a life of power and riches for one of obedience, poverty, and chastity. He was never ordained a priest, but his influence on Christianity was monumental.

The Franciscan existence (Brother Sun, Sister Moon, and so on) is a space where God, man, and the natural world frolic harmoniously. Francis treated every creature—animal, peasant, pope—with equal respect. He and his "brothers" (friars, *fratelli*) slept in fields, begged for food, and exuded the joy of non-materialism. Franciscan friars were known as the "Jugglers of God," modeling themselves on French troubadours (*jongleurs*, jugglers) who roved the countryside singing, telling stories, and cracking jokes.

In an Italy torn by conflict between towns and families, Francis promoted peace and the restoration of order. (He set an example by reconstructing the crumbled San Damiano chapel.) While the Church was waging bloody Crusades, Francis pushed ecumenism and understanding. Even today the leaders of the world's great religions meet here for summits.

This richly decorated basilica seems to contradict the teachings of the poor monk it honors, but it was built as an act of religious and civic pride to remember the hometown saint. It was also designed, and still functions, as a pilgrimage center and a splendid classroom. Monks in robes are not my idea of easy-to-approach people, but the Franciscans of today are still God's jugglers (and most of them speak English).

Here is Francis' message, in his own words:

The Canticle of the Sun

Good Lord, all your creations bring praise to you!

Praise for Brother Sun, who brings the day. His radiance reminds us of you!

Praise for Sister Moon and the stars, precious and beautiful.

Praise for Brother Wind, and for clouds and storms and rain that sustain us.

Praise for Sister Water. She is useful and humble, precious and pure.

Praise for Brother Fire who cheers us at night.

Praise for our sister, Mother Earth, who feeds us and rules us.

Praise for all those who forgive because you have forgiven them.

Praise for our sister, Bodily Death, from whose embrace none can escape.

Praise and bless the Lord, and give thanks, and, with humility, serve him.

To get oriented, stand at the lower entrance in the courtyard. Opposite the entry to the lower basilica is the information center. You'll find two different WCs within a half-block (up the road in a squat building and halfway down the big piazza on the left).

Cost, Hours, Information: Free entry, lower basilica daily 6:30–18:50, relic chapel in lower basilica supposedly 9:00–18:00 but often closed, upper basilica daily 8:30–18:50 (tel. 075-819-100, www.sanfrancescoassisi.org). Modest dress is required to enter the church—no sleeveless tops or shorts for men, women, or children. The info center sells an excellent guidebook, *The Basilica of Saint Francis—A Spiritual Pilgrimage* (€2.50, by Goulet, McInally, and Wood), which I used as a source for my self-guided tour (see below). To worship in the basilica, consider joining the Franciscan brothers in the lower basilica in the early morning (sung morning prayers at 6:25, Mass at 7:00).

Tours: At the info center, ask about tours in English—or better yet, call or e-mail in advance (tours Mon–Sat 9:00–12:30 & 14:30–17:30, no tours Sun, tel. 075-819-0084, sacroconvento @sanfrancescoassisi.org). Tours are free, but a €25 donation per group is appropriate. A 75-minute audioguide may be available (€4/person).

➜ **Self-Guided Tour:** The Basilica of St. Francis, a theological work of genius, can be difficult for the 21st-century tourist/pilgrim to appreciate. Since the basilica is the reason most people visit Assisi, and the message of St. Francis has even the least devout blessing the town Vespas, I've designed this self-guided tour with an emphasis on the place's theology (rather than art history).

Enter through the grand doorway of the lower basilica. Just inside, decorating the top of the first arch, look up and see St. Francis, who greets you with a Latin inscription. Sounding a bit like John Wayne, he says the equivalent of "Slow down and be joyful, pilgrim. You've reached the Hill of Paradise, and this church will knock your spiritual socks off."

• *Start with the tomb (turn left into the nave; midway down the nave to your right, follow signs and go downstairs to the tomb).*

The Tomb: The saint's remains are above the altar in the stone box with the iron ties. In medieval times pilgrims came to Assisi because St. Francis was buried here. Holy relics were the "ruby slippers" of medieval Europe. Relics gave you power—they answered your prayers and won your wars—and ultimately helped you get back to your eternal Kansas. Assisi made no bones about promoting the saint's relics, but hid his tomb for obvious reasons of security. His body was buried secretly while the basilica was under construction, and over the next 600 years, the exact location was forgotten. When the tomb was to be opened to the public in 1818, it took a month and a half to find it.

Francis' four closest friends and first followers are buried in the corners of the room. Opposite the altar, up four steps in between the entrance and exit, notice the small gold box behind the metal grill. This contains the remains of Francis' rich Roman patron, Jacopa dei Settesoli. She traveled to see him on his deathbed, but was turned away because she was female. Francis waived the rule and welcomed "Brother Jacopa" to his side.

• *Climb back to the lower nave.*

Nave of Lower Basilica: Appropriately Franciscan, subdued and Romanesque, its nave was frescoed with parallel scenes from the lives of Christ and Francis, connected by a ceiling of stars. Unfortunately, after the church was built and decorated, the popularity of the Franciscans meant side chapels needed to be built. Huge arches were cut out of some scenes, but others survive. In the fresco directly above the entry to the tomb, Christ is being taken down from the cross (just the bottom half of his body can be seen, to the left), and it looks like the story is over. Defeat. But in the opposite fresco (above the tomb's exit), we see Francis preaching to the birds, reminding the faithful that the message of the Gospel survives.

These stories directed the attention of the medieval pilgrim to the altar, where he could meet God through the sacraments. The church was thought of as a community of believers sailing toward God. The prayers coming out of the nave (*navis,* or ship) fill the triangular sections of the ceiling—called *vele,* or sails—with spiritual wind. With a priest for a navigator and the altar for a helm, faith propels the ship.

Stand behind the altar (toes to the bottom step) and look up. The three scenes in front of you are, to the right, *Obedience* (Francis wearing a rope harness); to the left, *Chastity* (in a tower of purity held up by two angels); and straight ahead, *Poverty*. Here Jesus blesses the marriage as Francis slips a ring on Lady Poverty. In the foreground, two "self-sufficient" merchants (the new rich of a thriving North Italy) are throwing sticks and stones at the bride. But Poverty, in her patched wedding dress, is fertile and strong, and even those brambles blossom into a rosebush crown.

Putting your heels to the altar and bending back like a drum major, look up at Francis on a heavenly throne, who traded a life of earthly simplicity for glory in heaven.

• *Now, turn to the right and march to the corner, where steps lead down into the...*

Relic Chapel: This chapel is filled with fascinating relics (which a €0.50 flier explains in detail). Step in and circle the room clockwise. You'll see the silver chalice and plate that Francis used for the bread and wine of the Eucharist (in small, dark, windowed case set into wall, marked *Calice con Patena*). Francis believed that his personal possessions should be simple, but the items used for

Basilica of St. Francis—Lower Level

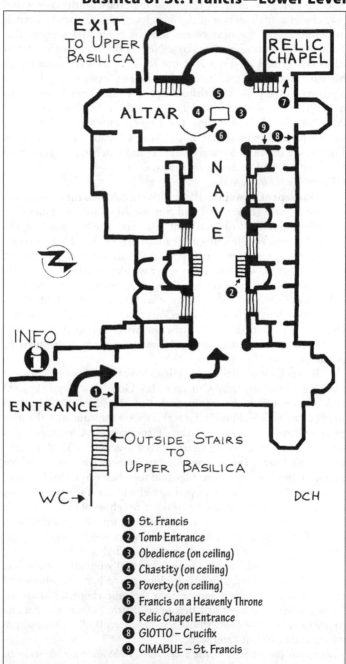

EXIT
TO UPPER
BASILICA

RELIC
CHAPEL

ALTAR

NAVE

INFO

ENTRANCE

OUTSIDE STAIRS
TO
UPPER BASILICA

WC→

DCH

❶ St. Francis
❷ Tomb Entrance
❸ Obedience (on ceiling)
❹ Chastity (on ceiling)
❺ Poverty (on ceiling)
❻ Francis on a Heavenly Throne
❼ Relic Chapel Entrance
❽ GIOTTO – Crucifix
❾ CIMABUE – St. Francis

worship should be made of the finest materials. In the corner display case is a small section of the haircloth *(cilizio)* worn by Francis as penitence. In the next corner are the tunic and slippers that Francis wore during his last days. Next, find a prayer (in a fancy silver stand) that St. Francis wrote for Brother Leo, signed with his tau cross. Tav ("tau" in Greek), the last letter in the Hebrew alphabet, is symbolic of faithfulness to the end. Francis signed his name with this simple capital-T shaped character. Next is a papal document (1223) legitimizing the Franciscan order and assuring his followers that they were not risking a (deadly) heresy charge. Finally, see the tunic lovingly patched and stitched by followers of the five-foot, four-inch-tall St. Francis.

• *Return up the stairs to the...*

Transept of Lower Basilica: This church brought together the greatest Sienese (Lorenzetti and Simone Martini) and Florentine (Cimabue and Giotto) artists of the day. Look around at the painted scenes. In 1300, this was radical art—believable homespun scenes, landscapes, trees, real people. Study Giotto's painting of the Crucifixion, with the eight sparrow-like angels. For the first time, holy people are expressing emotion: One angel turns her head sadly at the sight of Jesus, and another scratches her hands down her cheeks, drawing blood. Mary (lower left), previously in control, has fainted in despair. The Franciscans, with their goal of bringing God to the people, found a natural partner in Europe's first modern painter, Giotto.

To see Giotto's Renaissance leap, compare his work with the painting to the right, by Cimabue. It's Gothic, without the 3-D architecture, natural backdrop, and slice-of-life reality of Giotto's work. Cimabue's St. Francis (far right) shows the saint with the stigmata—Christ's marks of the Crucifixion. Contemporaries described Francis as being short, with a graceful build, dark hair, and sparse beard. The sunroof haircut (tonsure) was standard for monks of the day. The brown robe and rope belt was an invention of necessity. When Francis stripped naked and ran away from Assisi, he grabbed the first clothes he could, a rough wool peasant's tunic and piece of rope, which became the uniform of the Franciscan order. To the left, at eye level (under the sparrow-like angels), enjoy Simone Martini's saints and their exquisite halos.

Francis' friend, "Sister Death," was really not all that terrible. In fact, Francis would like to introduce you to her now (above and to the right of the door leading into the relic chapel). Go ahead, block the light and meet her. Before his death, Francis added a line to *The Canticle of the Sun*: "Praise for our sister, Bodily Death, from whose embrace none can escape."

• *Now cross the transept to the other side of the altar for the staircase going up.*

Courtyard: The treasury to the left of the bookstore is free (donation requested) and features ornately-decorated chalices, reliquaries, vestments, and altarpieces. There's a clean WC two-thirds of the way down the great hall on your right.

• *From the courtyard, climb the stairs (next to the bookshop) to the...*

Upper Basilica: Built later than the lower, the upper basilica is brighter, Gothic (the first Gothic church in Italy, 1228), and practically wallpapered by Giotto and his assistants around 1297–1300 (or perhaps by other artists—scholars debate it). For more on Giotto, see page 123 of Near Venice chapter. The gallery of frescoes shows 28 scenes from the life of St. Francis. The events are a mix of documented history and folk legend.

• *Get oriented by facing the basilica's main altar. Start on the right-hand (north) wall and work clockwise.*

❶ **A common man spreads his cape before Francis** in front of the Temple of Minerva on Piazza del Comune. Before his conversion, young Francis was the model of Assisian manhood—handsome, intelligent, and well-dressed, being the son of a wealthy cloth dealer. Above all, he was liked by everyone, a natural charmer who led his fellow teens in nights of wine, women, and song. Medieval pilgrims understood a deeper meaning in this scene: The "eye" of God (symbolized by the rose window in the Temple of Minerva) looks over 20-year-old Francis, a dandy "imprisoned" in his own selfishness (the Temple was once a prison).

❷ **Francis offers his cape to a needy stranger** (next panel). Francis was always generous of spirit. He became more so after he'd been captured in battle, held for a year as a prisoner of war, and suffered illness. That's Assisi in the distance.

❸ **Francis is visited by the Lord in a dream**. Still unsure of his calling, Francis rode off to the Crusades. One night, he dreams of a palace filled with armor marked with crosses. Christ tells him to leave the army and go home to wait for a nonmilitary assignment in a new kind of knighthood. He returned to Assisi and was reviled as a coward.

❹ **Francis prays to the crucifix** in the Church of San Damiano. After months of living in a cave, fasting, and meditating, Francis kneels in the rundown church and prays. The crucifix speaks, telling him: "Go and rebuild my Church, which you can see has fallen into ruin." Francis hurried home and sold his father's cloth to pay for God's work. His furious father dragged him before the bishop.

❺ **Francis relinquishes his possessions.** In front of the bishop and the whole town, Francis strips naked, gives his dad his clothes, credit cards, and time-share on Capri. Francis raises his hand and says, "Until now, I called you father. From now on, my only father is my Father in Heaven." He then ran off into the hills,

Basilica of St. Francis—Upper Level

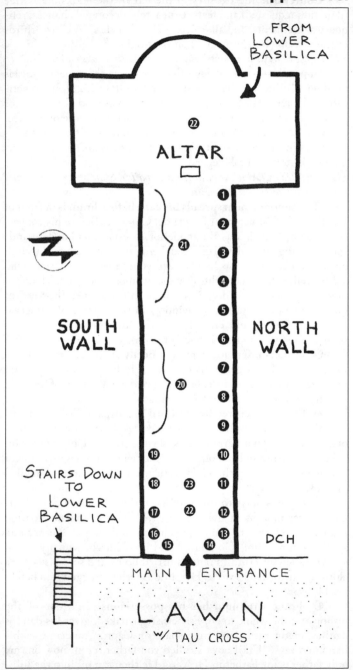

FROM LOWER BASILICA

㉒

ALTAR

① ② ③ ④ ⑤ ⑥ ⑦ ⑧ ⑨ ⑩ ⑪ ⑫ ⑬ ⑭

㉑

⑳

SOUTH WALL

NORTH WALL

⑲ ⑱ ㉓ ⑰ ㉒ ⑯ ⑮ ⑭ ⑬ ⑫ ⑪ ⑩

DCH

STAIRS DOWN TO LOWER BASILICA

MAIN ↑ ENTRANCE

LAWN
w/ TAU CROSS

❶ A Common Man Spreads his Cape Before Francis

❷ Francis Offers his Cape to a Needy Stranger

❸ Francis is Visited by the Lord in a Dream

❹ Francis Prays to the Crucifix

❺ Francis Relinquishes his Possessions

❻ The Pope has a Vision

❼ The Pope Confirms the Franciscan Order

❽ A Vision of the Flaming Chariot

❾ A Vision of Thrones

❿ Exorcism of Demons

⓫ St. Francis Before the Sultan

⓬ Ecstasy of St. Francis

⓭ The Crèche at Greccio

⓮ Miracle of the Spring

⓯ Sermon to the Birds

⓰ The Knight of Celano at his Death

⓱ Preaching for Pope Honorius III

⓲ The Apparition at Arles

⓳ Francis Receives the Stigmata

⓴ Francis' Death, Funeral, Burial, and Canonization

㉑ Miracles Associated with St. Francis

㉒ Large Tan Patches on Ceiling (1997 Earthquake Damage)

㉓ Tau Sculpture

naked and singing. In this version, Francis is covered by the bishop, symbolizing his transition from a man of the world to a man of the Church. Notice the disbelief and concern on the bishop's advisors' faces; subtle expressions like these wouldn't have made it into other medieval frescoes of the day. Three panels later...

❻ **The pope has a vision.** Francis headed to Rome, seeking the pope's blessing on his fledgling movement. Initially rebuffing Francis, the pope then dreams of a simple man propping up his teetering Church, and then...

❼ **The pope confirms the Franciscan order,** handing Francis the document now displayed in the relic chapel.

Francis' life was surrounded by miracles, shown in three panels in a row: (❽) **A vision of the flaming chariot,** (❾) **A vision of thrones,** and (❿) **Exorcism of demons.** Next see...

⓫ **St. Francis before the sultan.** Francis' wandering ministry took him to Egypt during the Crusades (1219). He walked unarmed into the Muslim army camp. They captured him, but the sultan was impressed with Francis' manner and let him go. Here, the sultan on his throne gestures and reportedly whispered, "I'd convert to your faith, but they'd kill us both."

⓬ **Ecstasy of St. Francis.** This oft-painted scene shows the mystic communing with God.

⓭ **The Crèche at Greccio.** Francis invents the tradition of manger scenes in 1223.

• *Continue clockwise to the main entrance (east wall) for the next two panels.*

⓮ **Miracle of the Spring.** Francis felt closest to God when in the hills around Assisi, seeing the Creator in the creation.

⓯ **Sermon to the Birds.** The most well-known instance is when Francis was surrounded by birds who listened to him preach until he dismissed them. The birds, of different species, represent the diverse flock of humanity and nature, all created and beloved by God and worthy of each other's love.

• *Continue to the south wall for the rest of the panels.*

Despite the hierarchical society of his day, Francis was welcomed by all classes, shown in these three panels: (⓰) **The knight of Celano at his death, (⓱) Preaching for Pope Honorius III,** and (⓲) **The apparition at Arles.** Next see...

⓳ **Francis receives the stigmata.** It's September 17, 1224, and Francis is fasting and praying on nearby Mt. Alverna when a six-winged angel appears. For the strength of his faith in the new knighthood, Francis is given the marks of his master, the "battle scars of love"...the stigmata. These five wounds Christ suffered during crucifixion (nails in palms and feet, lance in side) marked Francis' body for the rest of his life.

The next four panels (⓴)deal with **Francis' death, funeral, burial, and canonization.** The last panels (㉑) show **miracles** associated with the man-saint.

Before you leave, look up at the ceiling above the front entrance (and above the altar) to see large **tan patches** (㉒). In 1997, when a 5.5-magnitude quake hit Assisi, it shattered the upper basilica's frescoes into 300,000 fragments that had to be meticulously picked up and pieced back together. Shortly after the quake, two monks and two art scholars were standing here when an aftershock shook the ceiling frescoes down, killing them.

The graceful new **Tau sculpture** (㉓), by Guido Dettoni della Grazia, is a cross between a crucifix and the Tau symbol. The cross-shaped Greek letter "Tau" became the Franciscan logo, symbolizing how the world was redeemed by Christ's Crucifixion. Francis had first come across the symbol used by those who cared for lepers to magically keep away infection. For Francis, it was a promise to serve even the lowest on society's ladder. He quickly recognized that the Franciscan robe—with arms outstretched—formed a tau cross. Bible scholars today speculate that Jesus may have been crucified on a tau-shaped cross, rather than on the commonly depicted Latin cross.

Outside, on the lawn, are the Latin pax (peace) and the Franciscan tau cross. Tau and pax. For more pax, take the high lane back to town, up to the castle, or into the countryside.

More Sights

Roman Forum (Foro Romano)—For a look at Assisi's Roman roots, tour the Roman Forum, which is actually under Piazza del Comune. The floor plan is sparse, and there are odd bits and obscure pieces, but it's well-explained in English (a 10-page booklet is loaned to you when you enter). During your visit you will actually walk on an ancient Roman road. For a better understanding of the original setting of the Forum and temple, check out the poster for sale at the entry (€3.50 entry, or included in €5.25 combo-ticket, daily 10:00–13:00 & 14:30–18:00, closes at 17:00 in winter; from Piazza del Comune, go one-half block down Via San Francesco—it's on your right; tel. 075-813-053).

Pinacoteca—This small museum attractively displays its 13th- to 17th-century art (mainly frescoes), with general English information in nearly every room. There's a damaged Giotto Madonna and a rare secular fresco (to the right of Giotto art), but it's mainly a peaceful walk through a pastel world—best for art-lovers (€3.50, or included in €5.25 combo-ticket, daily 10:00–13:00 & 14:30–18:00, Via San Francesco, no building number, look for banner above entryway, on main drag between Piazza del Comune and Basilica of St. Francis, tel. 075-812-033).

▲**Rocca Maggiore**—The "big castle" offers a good look at a 14th-century fortification and a fine view of Assisi and the Umbrian countryside (€2, or included in €4.50 combo-ticket, daily from 10:00 until an hour before sunset). If you're pinching your euros, the view is just as good from outside the castle, and the interior is pretty bare.

Commune with Nature—For a picnic with the same birdsong and views that inspired St. Francis, leave the tourists behind and hike to the Rocca Minore (small private castle, not tourable) above Piazza Matteotti.

Santa Maria degli Angeli

This modern part of Assisi, in the flat valley below the hill town, has two sights: The basilica that marks the spot where Francis lived, worked, and died; as well as the church where the crucifix spoke to him.

▲▲**St. Mary of the Angels (Basilica di Santa Maria degli Angeli)**—This huge basilica, towering above the buildings below Assisi, was built in the 18th century around the tiny but historic Porziuncola Chapel (now directly under the dome). After Francis' conversion, some local monks gave him this *porziuncola*, or "small portion"—a little land with a fixer-upper chapel. Francis lived here after he founded the Franciscan Order in 1208, and this was where he consecrated St. Clare as a Bride of Christ. What would humble Francis think of the huge church—Christianity's seventh largest—that was built over his tiny chapel?

Follow signs to the Roseta or Rose Garden (to the right of the Porziuncola Chapel). Francis, fighting a temptation that he never named, threw himself onto roses. As the story goes, the thorns immediately dropped off. Ever since, thornless roses have grown here. Look through the window at the rose garden (to the right of the statue of Francis petting a sheep). The Rose Chapel (Cappella delle Rose) is built over the place where Francis lived.

Continue on to the Cappella del Transito where a low window marks the site of Francis' death. Francis died as he'd lived—simply, in a small hut located here. On his last night on earth, he invited some friars to join him in a Last Supper-style breaking of bread. Then he undressed, lay down on the bare ground, and began to recite Psalm 141, "Lord, I cry unto thee." He spoke the last line, "Let the wicked fall into their own traps, while I escape"...and he passed on (Oct 3, 1226).

In the autumn, a room in the next hallway displays a giant, animated nativity scene. The bookshop has some books in English and the free *museo* has a few monastic cells interesting to pilgrims (donation requested, museum open Mon–Fri 9:00–12:30 & 15:00–18:30).

Hours: The basilica is open daily 7:00–19:00. There's a little TI across the street in the arcaded building (April–Oct daily 10:00–12:30 & 16:30–19:00, closed in winter, tel. 075-804-4554). A WC is in front of the church on the left, behind the hedge.

Getting There: To get to Basilica di Santa Maria degli Angeli from Assisi's train station, it's a five-minute walk (exit station left, take first left at McDonald's—you'll see the dome in the distance). When you leave the basilica, you can catch a bus directly to the station and on to Assisi's old town (leaving church, stop is on your right). The orange city buses run twice hourly (buses to the old town depart the basilica at :10 and :40 after the hour; tickets cost €0.80 if you buy at *tabacchi* or newsstand, €1.50 if you buy from driver; 20-min ride up to old town).

It's efficient to visit this basilica either on your way to the old town of Assisi or when you leave. You can easily walk to the basilica from the station (baggage check available, €2.60/12 hrs, see "Arrival in Assisi," page 421).

Church of San Damiano—Located in the valley beneath the Basilica of St. Clare, this church and convent was where Francis received his call and where Clare spent her days as Mother Superior of the Poor Clares. Today, there's not much to see, but it's a peaceful escape from touristy Assisi. Drivers can zip right there, while walkers descend pleasantly from Assisi for 15 minutes through an olive grove (start at Porta Nuova parking lot at the south end of town; see "Assisi" map on page 422).

In 1206, Francis was inside the church when he heard the wooden crucifix order him to rebuild the church. (The crucifix in San Damiano is a copy; the original is now displayed in the Basilica of St. Clare.) Francis initially interpreted these miraculous words as a call to rebuild crumbling San Damiano. He sold his father's cloth for stones and physically rebuilt it himself. (The church we see today, however, was rebuilt later by others.) Eventually, Francis realized the call was to revitalize the Christian Church at large.

Approaching the end of his life, Francis came to San Damiano to visit his old friend Clare. She set him up in a simple reed hut in the olive grove where, in September, 1225, he was inspired to write his poem, *The Canticle of the Sun* (see page 430).

Outside of Assisi

Hermitage (Eremo delle Carcere)—If you want to follow further in St. Francis' footsteps, take a trip up the rugged slopes of nearby Mt. Subiaso to the humble hermitage Francis and his followers retreated to for solitude. The highlight is a look at the tiny dank cave he retired to for prayer (daily 6:30–19:30, until 17:30 off-season, tel. 075-812-301). There is no public transportation; either take a taxi or walk up. Starting from Assisi's Porta Cappuccini gate, it's a stiff three-mile, 90-minute hike with an elevation gain of 800 feet. Wear sturdy shoes and bring water.

SLEEPING

The town accommodates large numbers of pilgrims on religious holidays. Finding a room at any other time should be easy. See the map on page 443 for hotel locations.

$$$ Hotel Umbra, a quiet villa in the middle of town, has 25 rooms with great views and fine accommodations (Sb-€75, Db-€98–113, Tb-€155, 10 percent cash discount with this book in 2006, includes breakfast, air-con, peaceful garden and view sun terrace, most rooms have views, good restaurant, dinner only, closed Nov–mid-March, just off Piazza del Comune under the arch at Via degli Archi 6, tel. 075-812-240, fax 075-813-653, www.hotelumbra .it, info@hotelumbra.it, family Laudenzi).

$$ Hotel Ideale, on the top edge of town overlooking the valley, offers 12 bright, modern rooms (all with view, 10 with balconies), a tranquil garden setting, free parking, and a warm welcome (Sb-€50, Db-€85, includes breakfast, air-con-€5/day, confirm your arrival time especially if arriving after 17:00, Piazza Matteotti 1, tel. 075-813-570, fax 075-813-020, www.hotelideale .it, info@hotelideale.it, sisters Lara and Ilaria). This hotel, close to the bus stop (and parking lot) at Piazza Matteotti at the top end of town, is easy to reach by public transportation.

$$ Hotel Sole is well-located, with 35 decent rooms in a 15th-century building (Sb-€42, Db-€64, Tb-€85, breakfast-€6, half its rooms are in a newer annex across the street, elevator in annex, easy parking, Corso Mazzini 35, 100 yards before Basilica of St. Clare, tel. 075-812-373, fax 075-813-706,

Sleep Code

(€1 = about $1.20, country code: 39)
S = Single, **D** = Double/Twin, **T** = Triple, **Q** = Quad, **b** = bathroom, **s** = shower only. Unless otherwise noted, credit cards are accepted, English is spoken, and breakfast is included.

To help you sort easily through these listings, I've divided the rooms into three categories based on the price for a standard double room with bath:

$$$ **Higher Priced**—Most rooms €90 or more.
$$ **Moderately Priced**—Most rooms between €55–90.
$ **Lower Priced**—Most rooms €55 or less.

www.assisihotelsole.com, info@assisihotelsole.com).

$$ Hotel Belvedere is a modern building with big, spacious rooms—nine out of 16 come with sweeping views (Sb-€45, Db-€65, breakfast-€5, elevator, large communal view terrace, 2 blocks past Basilica of St. Clare at Via Borgo Aretino 13, tel. 075-812-460, fax 075-816-812, www.assisihotelbelvedere.it, info @assisihotelbelvedere.it).

$ Hotel Ascesi has an inviting little lobby, nine pleasant rooms, and a tiny terrace, all within a block of the Basilica of St. Francis (Sb-€40, Db-€55, breakfast-€5, air-con, Via Frate Elia 5; walk up from Piazza Unità d'Italia, turn left at Piazzetta Ruggero Bonghi, see sign on right; tel. & fax 075-812-420, hotelascesi@libero.it). This hotel is near the bus stop and parking lot at the bottom of town (Piazza Unità d'Italia), handy if you're packing lots of luggage.

$ Albergo Il Duomo is tidy and *tranquillo,* with nine rooms on a stair-step lane one block up from San Rufino. Check in at Hotel Rufino, just before you head up the lane (Sb-€33, Db-€44, breakfast-€5, Vicolo S. Lorenzo 2; from Church of San Rufino follow sign, then turn left on stair-stepped alley; tel. & fax 075-812-742, www.hotelsanrufino.it, info@hotelsanrufino.it).

$ Camere Annalisa Martini is a cheery home swimming in vines, roses, and cats in the town's medieval core. Annalisa speaks English and enthusiastically accommodates her guests with a picnic garden, a washing machine (€7 per small load, including drying and ironing), a communal refrigerator, and six homey rooms (S-€25, Sb-€26, D-€35, Db-€38, Tb-€55, Qb-€65, cash only, 3 rooms share 2 bathrooms, no breakfast, 1 block from Piazza del Comune, go downhill toward basilica, turn left on Via S. Gregorio to #6; tel. & fax 075-813-536, cameremartini@libero.it).

Central Assisi Hotels and Restaurants

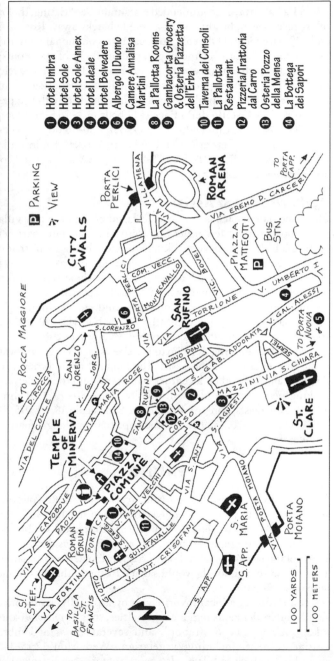

1 Hotel Umbra
2 Hotel Sole
3 Hotel Sole Annex
4 Hotel Ideale
5 Hotel Belvedere
6 Albergo Il Duomo
7 Camere Annalisa Martini
8 La Pallotta Rooms
9 Gambacorta Grocery & Osteria Piazzetta dell'Erba
10 Taverna dei Consoli
11 La Pallotta Restaurant
12 Pizzeria/Trattoria dal Carro
13 Osteria Pozzo della Mensa
14 La Bottega dei Sapori

$ La Pallotta, a recommended restaurant (see "Eating," below), offers seven clean, bright rooms a couple blocks away. Rooms #12 and #18 have views (Db-€55, no breakfast, communal view room on top floor, Via San Rufino 6, go up short flight of stairs outside building to reach entrance, a block off Piazza del Comune, tel. & fax 075-812-307, www.pallottaassisi.it, pallotta@pallottaassisi.it).

$ *Hostel:* Francis probably would have bunked with the peasants in Assisi's **Ostello della Pace** (€14 beds in 4- to 8-bed rooms, includes breakfast, dinner-€8.50, lock-out 9:30–16:00, 23:30 curfew; get off bus at Piazza Unità d'Italia, then take 10-min walk to Via di Valecchie 177; tel. & fax 075-816-767, www.assisihostel.com, assisi.hostel@tiscalinet.it).

Agriturismi near Assisi

$$ Podere la Fornace is a renovated farmhouse in the tiny village of Tordibetto, just a few miles outside Assisi. The four apartments (with 1–3 bedrooms) have full kitchens and a living room that can sleep an extra person. Local wine, olive oil, and pasta are available on site; if you stay for a week, they'll include your breakfast ingredients (Db-€60, apartment-€70–130 depending on size and season, 2-night minimum, games for children, swimming pool, bikes, Via Ombrosa 3, tel. 075-801-9537, mobile 338-990-2903, fax 075-801-9630, www.lafornace.com, info@lafornace.com).

$$ Alla Madonna del Piatto is a six-room *agriturismo* located about five miles outside of Assisi. The Dutch-Italian owners speak English, and have taken a centuries-old farm into the modern age, making pesticide-free olive oil on site (Db-€80–90, €20-dinner available for guests, non-smoking, Pieve San Nicolo' 18, tel. 075-819-9050, mobile 328-702-5297, www.incampagna.com, letizia.mattiacci @libero.it).

EATING

I've listed decent, central, good-value restaurants. But if you want a memorable meal splurge, get advice from your hotelier—ask about Ristorante Medioevo (just downhill from Piazza del Comune) or anything in that range. To bump up any meal, consider a glass or bottle of the favorite local red wine, Sagrantino, Umbria's answer to Brunello (although locals would say it's Brunello that has to measure up to Sagrantino).

La Pallotta, a local favorite run by a friendly, hardworking family, offers delicious regional specialties, such as *piccione* (squab, a.k.a. pigeon), *coniglio* (rabbit), and several *menus* of Umbrian cuisine (€15–25, including vegetarian, Wed–Mon 12:15–14:30 & 19:15–21:30, closed Tue, also rents rooms—see listing above, a few steps off Piazza del Comune, through gate across from temple/church, Vicolo della Volta Pinta 2, tel. 075-812-649).

At **Locanda del Podestà,** chef Selvio serves up tasty grilled Umbrian sausages, *gnocchi alla sacrantina* (cooked in local wine), and all manner of truffles while English-speaking Romina graciously serves happy diners. Try the tasty *scottaditto* ("scorch your fingers") lamb chops (Thu–Tue 12:00–15:00 & 19:00–22:00, closed Wed and Jan, 5-min walk uphill from basilica, San Giacomo 6c, tel. 075-813-034).

For a fine Assisian perch, snappy service, and a sampling of regional cooking, relax on a terrace overlooking Piazza del Comune at the third-generation **Taverna dei Consoli** (Thu–Tue 12:00–14:30 & 19:00–21:30, closed Wed and Jan, tel. 075-812-516). Friendly owner Moreno, who speaks a leetle English, recommends the bruschetta, *filet al tartufo, cinghiale* (boar), and *stringozzi* (noodles named for the cords that poor people used to strangle priests who extorted sky-high tithes).

Osteria Piazzetta dell'Erba is a block above Piazza del Comune, serving good, creative Umbrian specialties next to the Gambacorta grocery (Tue–Sun 12:30–14:00 & 19:00–21:45, closed Mon, Via San Gabriele 15b, tel. 075-815-352).

Pizzeria/Trattoria dal Carro lacks any romantic atmosphere, but is popular, friendly, and affordable. Watch them grill up your steak or Umbrian sausages over the fire in their open kitchen (good €5 pizzas and €13 *menu*, Thu–Tue 12:00–15:00 & 19:00–22:00, closed Wed, Vicolo di Nepis 2b; leave Piazza del Comune on Via San Gabriele, then take first right—down a stepped lane; tel. 075-815-249).

Osteria Pozzo della Mensa offers up organic salads and other typical Umbrian vegetarian choices, as well as locally-produced *salumi* and cheeses. Ask Paolo to explain how these light, modern meals have a medieval inspiration (Thu–Tue 12:00–15:00 & 19:00–22:30, closed Wed, Via del Pozzo della Mensa 11b; head up Via San Rufino from Piazza del Comune and take first right, then straight ahead 50 yards; tel. 347-344-0644).

For a picnic of Umbrian treats, try **La Bottega dei Sapori** for its good prosciutto sandwiches and specialty items, including truffle paste and olive oil. Friendly Fabrizio may give you a taste (daily 9:00–20:00, closed Tue in winter, Piazza del Comune 34, tel. 075-812-294). The **Gambacorta** store also sells tasty picnic supplies; the owner carves prosciutto like he's playing a violin (closed Thu, San Gabriele 17).

TRANSPORTATION CONNECTIONS

From Assisi by Train to: Rome (5/day, 2–3 hrs), **Florence** (5/day, 2–2.75 hrs, more with transfers at Terontola and Cortona), **Orvieto** (7/day, 2.5 hrs, transfer in Terontola), **Siena** (6/day, 3.25 hrs, transfers in Chiusi and Terontola; bus is more efficient). Train station: tel. 075-804-0272.

From Assisi by Bus: Several different bus companies offer service to: **Rome** (3/day, 3 hrs, €16.50, pay driver, departs Assisi's Piazza Unità d'Italia, arrives at Rome's Tiburtina station), **Siena** (€13 if you buy from driver, sold for €10 at Assisi's Agenzia Viaggi Maritur at Via Frate Elia 1b, 2/day at around 7:00 and 16:00, 2 hrs, departs from Porta S. Pietro below the basilica). Don't take the bus to **Florence;** the train is better (see previous page). From mid-June to mid-October, buses make day-trip runs to the nearby hill towns of **Gubbio, Spello, Perugia, Todi, Lake Trasimeno**, and more. Pick up a schedule from the TI or call 075-812-534.

HILL TOWNS
of CENTRAL ITALY

The sun-soaked hill towns of central Italy offer what to many is the quintessential Italian experience: sun-dried tomatoes, homemade pasta, wispy cypress-lined driveways following desolate ridges to fortified 16th-century farmhouses, and dusty old-timers warming the same bench day after day while soccer balls buzz around them like innocuous flies.

Italy's hill towns retain their medieval charm, and are best enjoyed by adapting to the pace of the countryside. So...slow... down...and enjoy the delights that these villages offer. Spend the night if you can, as many hill towns are mobbed by day-trippers.

Planning Your Time

How in Dante's name does a traveler choose from Italy's hundreds of hill towns? I cover some of the best towns in this chapter (listed roughly from north to south). The one(s) you visit will depend on your time, interests, and mode of transportation. There's no hard-and-fast best plan. Go where you want and stay as long as you want.

Multi-towered San Gimignano is a classic, but peak-season crowds can overwhelm the town's charms. I prefer Volterra; it's like San Gimignano—but without the tourist mob scene. Chiusi rates highly on the Etruscan trail. Wine aficionados won't want to miss Montalcino or Montepulciano. Fans of architecture and urban design will appreciate Pienza's well-planned streets and squares. Art-lovers and those eager to trace Frances Mayes' footsteps under the Tuscan sun will make the pilgrimage to Cortona. The grand, classic town of Orvieto is famous for its wine, ceramics, and colorful cathedral. But my longtime favorite is the tiny, obscure, and (to be honest) dying hill town of Civita.

Hill Towns of Central Italy

For a relaxing break from big-city Italy, settle down in an *agriturismo*—a farmhouse that rents out rooms to travelers (usually for a minimum of a week in high season). These rural B&Bs—almost by definition in the middle of nowhere—provide a good home base from which to find the magic of Italy's hill towns. I've listed several good options throughout this chapter (for more information, see "Agritourism" in the Introduction, page 33).

Getting Around the Hill Towns

Bigger destinations (such as Cortona, Orvieto, and Civita) are doable by public transportation. Smaller hill towns are easier to visit by car.

By Bus or Train: Traveling by public transportation is cheap and connects you with the locals. While trains link some of the towns, hill towns—being on hills—don't quite fit the railroad plan. Stations are likely to be in the valley a couple miles from the town center, usually connected by a local bus.

Buses are most often the better, if not the only, choice to get between destinations. Siena is a great hub of local bus lines. Find

Hill Towns: Public Transportation

TO GENOA
TO MILAN
TO VENICE
CINQUE-TERRE
FERRARA
LA SPEZIA
LUCCA
BOLOGNA
CARRARA
FLORENCE
EMPOLI
AIRPORT
FIESOLE
PISA
RAVENNA
AIRPORT
A B
POGG.
CORTONA
(TERENTOLA)
RIMINI
LIVORNO
SIENA
URBINO
PESARO
CECINA
PERUGIA
FALCO-NARA
C D E
ASSISI
CHIUSI
SPELLO
CIVITA
TODI
FOLIGNO
SPOLETO
VITERBO
ORVIETO
ANCONA
TARQUINIA
CIVITAVECCHIA
ORTE
CERVETERI
TO BARI & BRINDISI
N
ROME
AIRPORT
TO NAPLES
DCH

A - VOLTERRA
B - SAN GIMIGNANO
C - MONTALCINO
D - PIENZA
E - MONTEPULCIANO

--- BUS
— RAIL

NOT TO SCALE

schedules at local TIs and buy tickets at newsstands or *tabacchi* shops (with the big T signs). Confirm the departure point *(Dov'è la fermata?)*—some piazzas have more than one bus stop, so double-check that the posted schedule lists your destination and departure time. In general, orange buses are local city buses and blue buses are for long distances.

Once the bus arrives, confirm the destination with the driver. You are expected to stow big backpacks underneath the bus (open the luggage compartment if it's closed).

Sundays and holidays are problematic; even from large cities like Siena, schedules are sparse, departing buses are jam-packed, and ticket offices are often closed. Plan ahead and buy your ticket in advance. Most agencies book bus and train tickets with little or no commission.

By Car: Exploring small-town Tuscany by car is a great experience. But since a car is an expensive, worthless headache in big cities (such as Florence and Siena), wait to pick up your car until the last big city you visit. Then use it for lacing together the hill towns and exploring the countryside. Buy a big, detailed Tuscany road map at a newsstand. Although roads are numbered on maps, actual road signs don't list any route numbers. Instead, roads are indicated by blue signs with a city name on them (e.g., if you want to take the road heading west out of Montepulciano—marked route #146 on your map—you'd follow signs to Pienza, the next town along this route). The signs are inconsistent—they may direct you to the nearest big city or simply the next town along the route. For two particularly scenic drives, from Siena to Montalcino, and from Montalcino to Montepulciano, see the Crete Senese Drives suggested below, under "More Hill Towns," page 507.

If you are staying overnight, ask your hotelier for parking suggestions. Keep valuables out of sight and locked in the trunk of the car.

By Tour: Il Casato Viaggi runs bus tours from Siena to the Tuscan countryside, with plenty of wine-tasting opportunities (see "Helpful Hints" on page 398, Via Il Casato di Sotto 12 in Siena, tel. 057-746-091, fax 057-727-9863, www.sienaholiday.com).

San Gimignano

The epitome of a Tuscan hill town, with 14 medieval towers still standing (out of an original 60), San Gimignano is a perfectly preserved tourist trap. The locals seem corrupted by the easy money of tourism, and most of the rusticity is faux. But San Gimignano is so easy to visit and visually so beautiful that it remains a good stop.

In the 13th century, back in the days of Romeo and Juliet, feuding noble families ran the towns. They'd periodically battle things out from the protection of their respective family towers. Pointy skylines, like San Gimignano's, were the norm in medieval Tuscany.

While the basic ▲▲▲ sight here is the town of San Gimignano itself, there are a few worthwhile stops. From the town gate, head straight up the traffic-free town's cobbled main drag to Piazza della Cisterna (with its 13th-century well). The town sights cluster around the adjoining Piazza del Duomo.

Tourist Information: The helpful TI is in the old center on Piazza del Duomo (daily March–Oct 9:00–13:00 & 15:00–19:00, Nov–Feb 9:00–13:00 & 14:00–18:00, free maps, sells bus tickets, books rooms, tel. 0577-940-008, www.sangimignano.com, prolocsg@tin.it). You can drop your bag at the TI. The TI rents **audioguides** (€5 for 2-hr tour, only exteriors).

The town offers a two-hour **guided walk** in English and Italian at 15:00 daily except Sunday (€15, pay and meet at small

TI—actually a hotel booking office—at Porta San Giovanni, runs March–Oct).

Helpful Hints: Market day is Thursday on Piazza del Duomo, but for local merchants, every day is a sales frenzy. A public **WC** is just off Piazza della Cisterna (€0.50). A little electric **shuttle bus** does its laps all day from Porta San Giovanni to Piazza della Cisterna to Porta San Matteo (€0.50, 2/hr, buy ticket from TI or *tabacchi* shop).

SELF-GUIDED WALK

Welcome to San Gimignano

This quick walking tour will take you from the bus stop at Porta San Giovanni through the town's main squares to the Duomo and Sant'Agostino Church.

• *Start, as most tourists do, at the Porta San Giovanni gate at the bottom end of town.*

Porta San Giovanni: San Gimignano lies about 25 miles from both Siena and Florence, a good stop for pilgrims en route to those cities, and on a naturally-fortified hilltop that encouraged settlement. The town's walls were built in the 13th century, with gates that helped regulate who came and went. Today, modern posts keep out all but service and emergency vehicles. The small square just outside the gate features a memorial to the town's WWII dead. Follow the pilgrims' route (and flood of modern tourists) through the gate and up the main drag.

About 100 yards up, on the right, is a pilgrims' shelter (12th-century, Pisan Romanesque). The Maltese cross indicates this was built by the Knights of Malta. It was one of 11 such shelters in town. Today, only this shelter's wall remains.

• *Carry on, up to the town's central Piazza della Cisterna. Sit on the steps of the well.*

Piazza della Cisterna is named for the cistern that is served by the old well standing in the center of this square. A clever system of pipes drained rainwater from the nearby rooftops into the underground cistern. This square has been the center of the town since the ninth century. Each Thursday, it fills with a weekly market—as it has for over a thousand years.

• *Notice San Gimignano's famous towers.*

The Towers: Of the original 60 towers, only 14 survive. Before effective walls were developed, rich people fortified their own homes with these towers: They provided a handy refuge when ruffians and rival city-states were sacking the town. These towers became a standard part of medieval skylines. Even after town walls were built, the towers continued to rise—now to fortify noble families feuding within a town (Montague and Capulet style).

San Gimignano

TO CERTALDO & S-429

SANT' AGOSTINO

PORTA SAN JACOPO

PORTA SAN MATTEO

VIA FOLGORE DI SAN GIM.

PORTA DELLE FONTI

PIAZZA DEL DUOMO

COLLEGIATA

ROCCA

PRUN.

QUERCECCHIO

WC

PORTA QUER- CECCHIO

PIAZZA DELLA CISTERNA

Post

CIVIC MUSEUM, TORRE GROSSA

DCH

Bus Stop -Depart-

TO VOLTERRA, POGGIBONSI, SIENA

VIA ROMA

Bus Stop -Arrival-

PORTA SAN GIOVANNI

300 YARDS

300 METERS

⇩ Stepped Streets

P -Parking

TO ❶

① To Ponte a Nappo Rooms
② Hotel la Cisterna
③ Arco di Goro Rooms
④ Santa Fina Rooms
⑤ Tortoli Rooms
⑥ Palazzo al Torrione
⑦ Trattoria Chiribiri
⑧ La Grotta Ghiotta
⑨ Locanda il Pino & Rist. il Pino
⑩ La Mangiatoia
⑪ Locanda di Sant'Agostino
⑫ Co-op Supermarket

In the 14th century, San Gimignano's good times turned very bad. In the year 1300, about 13,000 lived within the walls. Then in 1348, a six-month plague decimated the population, leaving the once mighty town with barely 4,000 alive. Once fiercely independent, a now crushed and demoralized San Gimignano came under Florence's control, and was forced to tear down its towers. (The Banca Toscana building is the remains of one such topped tower.) And, to add injury to injury, Florence redirected the vital trade route away from San Gimignano. The town never recovered, and poverty left it in a 14th-century architectural time-warp. That well-preserved cityscape, ironically, explains the town's prosperity today.

• *From the well, walk 30 yards uphill to the adjoining square with the cathedral.*

Piazza del Duomo faces the former cathedral. The twin towers to the right are 10th-century, among the first in town. The stubby tower opposite the church is typical of a merchant's tower: main door on ground floor, warehouse upstairs, holes to hold beams that once supported woody balconies and exterior staircases, heavy stone on the first floor, cheaper and lighter brick for upper stories.

• *On the piazza are the Civic Museum and Torre Grossa, worth checking out (see "Sights," below). You'll also see the...*

Duomo (or Collegiata): Walk inside San Gimignano's Romanesque cathedral. Inside, Sienese Gothic art (14th-century) lines the nave with parallel themes, Old Testament on the left and New Testament on the right. (For example: the suffering of Job opposite the suffering of Jesus; Creation facing the Annunciation; and the birth of Adam facing the Nativity.) This is a classic use of art to teach. Study the fine Creation series (top left). Many scenes are portrayed with a local 14th-century "slice of life" setting, to help lay townspeople relate to Jesus—in the same way that many white Christians are more comfortable thinking of Jesus as white (€3.50, €5.50 combo-ticket includes mediocre Religious Art Museum, Mon–Fri 9:30–19:30, Sat 9:30–17:00, Sun 12:30–17:30).

From the church, hike uphill (passing the church on your left) following signs to *Rocca e Parco di Montestaffoli*. You'll enter a peaceful hilltop park and olive grove within the shell of a 14th-century fortress. A few steps takes you to the top of a little tower (free) for the best views of San Gimignano's skyline; the far end of town and the Church of Sant'Agostino (where this walk ends); and a commanding 360-degree view of the Tuscan countryside. San Gimignano is surrounded by olives, grapes, cypress trees and—in the Middle Ages—lots of wild dangers. Back then, farmers lived inside the walls and were thankful for the protection.

• *Return to the bottom of Piazza del Duomo, turn left, and continue your walk across town, cutting under the double arch (from the town's first wall) and into the new section where a line of fine noble palaces—now a happy can-can of wine cantinas and galleries—cheers you down Via San Matteo to...*

Sant'Agostino Church: This tranquil church, at the opposite end of town, has fewer crowds and more soul. Behind the altar, a lovely fresco cycle by Benozzo Gozzoli (who painted the exquisite Chapel of the Magi in the Medici-Riccardi Palace in Florence—see page 343) tells of the life of St. Augustine, a North African monk who preached simplicity. The kind, English-speaking friars (from England and the U.S.) are happy to tell you about their church and way of life, and also have Mass in English on Sundays at 11:00. Pace the tranquil cloister before heading back into the tourist mobs (free, but €0.50 lights the frescoes, daily 7:00–12:00 & 15:00–19:00).

SIGHTS

Civic Museum (Museo Civico)—This small, fun museum is inside city hall (Palazzo Comunale). Enter the room called Sala di Consiglio (a.k.a. Danti Hall). It's *molto* medieval and covered in festive frescoes, including the *Maestà* by Lippo Memmi. This virtual copy of Simone Martini's *Maestà* in Siena proves that Memmi doesn't have quite the same talent as his famous brother-in-law. Upstairs, the Pinacoteca displays a classy little painting collection, with a 1422 altarpiece by Taddeo di Bartolo honoring St. Gimignano. You can see the saint, with the town in his hands, surrounded by events from his life. As you exit, be sure to stop by the Camera del Podesta to check out the medieval dating scene (€5, includes Torre Grossa, audioguide-€2, daily 9:30–19:00, Nov–Feb 10:00–17:00, Piazza del Duomo).

Torre Grossa—The city's tallest tower, at 200 feet, can be scaled (€5, includes Civic Museum, same hours as museum, Piazza del Duomo).

SLEEPING

Although a zoo during the daytime, when evening comes, locals outnumber tourists and San Gimignano becomes peaceful and enjoyable.

$$ Hotel la Cisterna, right on Piazza della Cisterna, offers 49 overpriced, predictable rooms, some with panoramic view terraces (Sb-€70, Db-€95, Db with view-€115, Db with terrace-€122, buffet breakfast, elevator, good restaurant with great view, discounts off-season, closed Jan–Feb, Piazza della Cisterna 24, tel. 0577-940-328, fax 0577-942-080, www.hotelcisterna.it, info@hotelcisterna.it, Alessio).

Sleep Code

(€1 = about $1.20, country code: 39)
S = Single, **D** = Double/Twin, **T** = Triple, **Q** = Quad, **b** = bathroom, **s** = shower only. Unless otherwise noted, credit cards are accepted and breakfast is included (but usually optional). English is generally spoken, but I've noted exceptions.

To help you sort easily through these listings, I've divided the rooms into three categories based on the price for a standard double room with bath:

$$$ **Higher Priced**—Most rooms €100 or more.
 $$ **Moderately Priced**—Most rooms between
€70–100.
  $ **Lower Priced**—Most rooms €70 or less.

$$ Ponte a Nappo, run by enterprising Carla Rossi (who doesn't speak English) and her son Francisco (who does), has comfortable rooms and apartments in a farm just outside San Gimignano (Db-€70, apartment Tb-€100, apartment Qb-€120, 15-min walk or 5-min drive from Porta San Giovanni, air-con, parking, tel. & fax 0577-955-041, mobile 349-882-1565, www.rossicarla .it, info@rossicarla.it). A picnic dinner—lounging on their comfy garden furniture as the sun sets—is good Tuscan living. About 100 yards below the monument square at Porta San Giovanni, find Via Vecchia (not left or right, but down a tiny road toward several listed accommodations).

$ In-town Rossi Apartments, owned by the same family, are in the town center (Arco di Goro, Santa Fina, and Tortoli, Db-€55 with book, fancy Db overlooking square-€85, same contact info as Ponte a Nappo farm, above). See their Web site for details on their confusing array of rooms for rent.

$ Palazzo al Torrione, just inside Porta San Giovanni, is quiet and handy. They generally offer better rooms than hotels at two-thirds the price, but don't have a full-time reception (10 modern rooms-€70, family suites, cheap parking, inside and left of gate at Via Berignano 76, run from *tabacchi* shop 2 blocks away, just inside the gate on the main drag at Via San Giovanni 59, tel. 0577-940-480, www.palazzoaltorrione.com, palazzoaltorrione@palazzoaltorrione .com, Francesco).

$ Locanda Il Pino is tiny (5 rooms), super-clean, and quiet, run by a family above their elegant restaurant just inside Porta San Matteo (Db-€55, no breakfast, easy parking just outside the gate, Via Cellolese 4, tel. 0577-940415, laurabeconcini@supereva.it). While far from the bus stop, this is a great value for those with a car.

EATING

Trattoria Chiribiri, just inside Porta San Giovanni, serves home-made pastas and desserts at a remarkably fair price (daily 11:00–23:00, Piazza della Madonna 1, tel. 0577-941-948).

La Mangiatoia is a good local splurge, especially if you like wild game and candlelight (pastas-€10, *secondi*-€15, Wed–Mon 12:30–14:45 & 19:30–22:00, closed Tue, good outdoor seating, near Porta San Matteo at Via Mainardi 5, tel. 0577-941-528).

Ristorante Il Pino, run by the same family since 1929, is subdued, pricey, and dressy. It's *the* place for "dainty game" on pink tablecloths under medieval arches (closed Thu, seafood as well as game, Via Cellolese 8, tel. 0577-940-415).

La Grotta Ghiotta makes good soup and sandwiches that can be packed up *portare via*—to go (daily 12:00–20:00, Via Santo Stefano 10, tel. 0577-942-074).

Locanda di Sant'Agostino spills out onto the peaceful square, facing Sant'Agostino Church. It's cheap and cheery, serving lunch and dinner daily. Dripping with onions and atmosphere on the inside, there's shady on-the-square seating outside (tel. 0577-943-141).

Picnics: The big, modern **Co-Op supermarket** sells all you need for a nice spread (Mon–Sat 8:30–20:00, closed Sun, at parking lot below Porta San Giovanni). Or browse the little shops guarded by wild boar heads within the town walls; they sell boar meat (*cinghiale;* cheeng-gee-AH-lay). Pick up 100 grams (about a quarter pound) of boar, cheese, bread, and wine and enjoy a picnic in the garden at the Rocca or the park outside Porta San Giovanni.

TRANSPORTATION CONNECTIONS

From San Gimignano by Bus to: Florence (hrly, 75 min, change in Poggibonsi), **Siena** (5/day, 1.25 hrs, more with change in Poggibonsi), **Volterra** (4/day, 2 hrs, change in Colle di Val d'Elsa). Sunday buses are few, far between, and crowded. In San Gimignano, bus tickets are sold at the bar just inside the town gate or at the TI. While the town has no formal baggage-check service, the TI will let you park your bags there for free.

Drivers: You can't drive within the walled town of San Gimignano, but a parking lot waits just a few steps outside the town. San Gimignano is an easy 45–minute drive from Florence (exit Florence via Porta Romana, follow blue signs to Siena, Route SS2; exit the freeway at Poggibonsi). San Gimignano has three pay lots a short walk outside the walls and free places farther away. The handiest lot (Parcheggio Montemaggio, just outside Porta San Giovanni) fills up early, but those arriving from the north can wait for a spot—as one car leaves, the gate allows another to enter (€2/hr).

Volterra

Encircled by impressive walls and topped with a grand fortress, Volterra sits high above the rich farmland. More than 2,000 years ago, Volterra was one of the most important Etruscan cities, much, much larger than the town we see today. Greek-trained Etruscan artists worked here, leaving a significant stash of art, particularly funerary urns. Eventually absorbed into the Roman Empire, the city bitterly fought against the Florentines in the Middle Ages, but like many Tuscan towns, it lost in the end and was given a fortress atop the city to "protect" its citizens.

Compact and walkable, the city stretches out from the pleasant Piazza dei Priori to the old city gates. Unlike other famous towns in Tuscany, Volterra feels not cutesy or touristy...but real, vibrant, and almost oblivious to the allure of the tourist dollar. A refreshing break from its more commercial neighbors, it's my favorite small town in Tuscany. **Market day** is on Saturday.

Local Guide: American Annie Adair married into the local community and is an excellent guide (€100/half-day, €200/day, mobile 347-1435004, tel. & fax 0588-87774, www.tuscantour.com, info@tuscantour.com).

SIGHTS

▲**Porta all'Arco**—Volterra's most famous sight is its Etruscan Gate, built of massive tufa stones in the fourth century B.C. Volterra's original wall was four miles around—twice the size of the wall that circles it today. With 25,000 people, Volterra was a key Etruscan trade center—one of 12 leading towns that made up the Etruscan Dodecapolis (a league of Etruscan cities). The three seriously eroded heads, dating from the first century B.C., show what happens when you leave something outside for 2,000 years. The newer stones are part of the 13th-century city wall, which incorporated parts of the much older Etruscan wall.

A plaque just outside remembers June 30, 1944. Near that time, Nazi forces were planning to blow up the arch to slow the Allied advance. To save their treasured landmark, Volterrans ripped up the stones that pave Via Porta all'Arco and plugged the gate, managing to convince the Nazi commander that there was no need to blow up the arch. Today, all the stones are back in their places, and, like silent heroes, they welcome you through the oldest standing Etruscan gate into Volterra.

Pass through the arch. Wander up Via Porta all'Arco 50 yards, then climb left up Via Laberinti to a viewpoint. (On a clear day you can see the Mediterranean and the mountains of Corsica.)

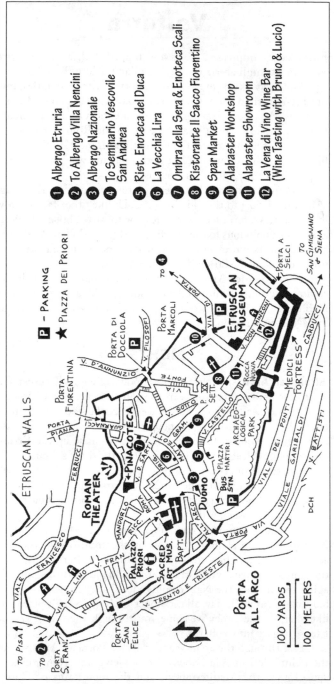

Volterra

1 Albergo Etruria
2 To Albergo Villa Nencini
3 Albergo Nazionale
4 To Seminario Vescovile San Andrea
5 Rist. Enoteca del Duca
6 La Vecchia Lira
7 Ombra della Sera & Enoteca Scali
8 Ristorante Il Sacco Fiorentino
9 Spar Market
10 Alabaster Workshop
11 Alabaster Showroom
12 La Vena di Vino Wine Bar (Wine Tasting with Bruno & Lucio)

Continue uphill, pondering the town's nickname, "The City of Wind and Rock," until Vicolo degli Abbandonati deposits you on Piazza San Giovanni, where you face the cathedral.

Duomo—A common arrangement in the Middle Ages was for the church to face the Baptistery (people were baptized in a building separate from the church because copious amounts of water were needed for immersion)...and for the hospital to face the cemetery. All of these overlooked the same square. That's how it is in Pisa, as it is here.

This 12th-century church is not as elaborate as its cousin in Pisa, but the simple facade and central nave flanked by monolithic stone columns are beautiful examples of the Pisan Romanesque style. The chapel to the left of the entry has unusual, large dioramas with painted terra-cotta figures. The interior was decorated mostly in the late 16th century, during Florentine rule under the Medici family (and much restored in the 19th century). You'll see a lot of the Medici coat of arms (with the 6 pills representing the family's first trade—doctors or *medici*). The 12th-century pulpit is beautifully carved. All the apostles are together except Judas, who's under the table with the evil dragon (his name is the only one not carved onto the relief). The dreamy painted-and-gilded-wood Deposition (Jesus being taken down from the cross, 13th-century) is restored true to its original form, showing emotion and motion way ahead of its time. Recorded Gregorian chants add to the church's wonderful ambience (free, daily 8:00–12:30 & 15:00–17:00).

Sacred Art Museum—This humble three-room museum collects sacred art from deconsecrated churches and small, unguarded churches from nearby villages (daily 9:00–13:00 & 15:00–18:00, morning only in winter, well-explained in English, next to the Duomo at Via Roma 1).

▲Etruscan Museum (Museo Etrusco Guarnacci)—Filled top to bottom with rare Etruscan artifacts, this museum—even with few English explanations—makes it easy to appreciate how advanced this pre-Roman culture was. (For information on the Etruscans, see page 694.) The exhibit—considered the third best Etruscan museum anywhere, after the Vatican and the British Museum—starts with the pre-Etruscan Villanovian artifacts (c. 1500 B.C.). The seemingly endless collection of sarcophagi—all with the subject lounging, as if kicking back with the gods at some heavenly banquet, popping grapes and just enjoying the moment—is a reminder that the Etruscans believed you'd have fun in the afterlife. Artifacts such as mirrors, coins, and jewelry offer a peek into this fascinating culture. Giacometti fans will be amazed at how *The Shadow of Night (L'ombra della sera)* looks just like the modern Swiss sculptor's work—only 2,500 years older (€8, includes—like it or not—the Pinacoteca and Sacred Art Museum, daily 9:00–18:45, Nov–March closes at 13:45, mildly interesting English pamphlet available, audioguide-€3, Via Don Minzoni 15, tel. 0588-86-347). An alabaster workshop and a wine bar are across the street; see listings below.

Pinacoteca—This museum fills a 14th-century palace with fine paintings that feel more Florentine than Sienese—a reminder of whose domain this town was in. Its highlights are Luca Signorelli's beautifully-lit *Annunciation*, an example of classic High Renaissance (from the town cathedral); and (to the right) the *Deposition from the Cross*, the ground-breaking Mannerist work by Rosso Fiorentino (note the elongated bodies and harsh emotional lighting and colors). Notice also Ghirlandaio's *Christ in Glory*. The two devout-looking, kneeling women are actually pagan, pre-Christian Etruscan demi-goddesses, Attinea and Greciniana, but the church identified them as obscure saints to make the painting acceptable (€8 combo-ticket, includes Etruscan and Sacred Art museums, daily 9:00–18:45, Nov–March closes at 13:45, Via dei Sarti 1, tel. 0588-87580).

Roman Theater—Built in about 10 B.C., this well-preserved the-ater is considered to have some of the best acoustics of any of its kind. Because of the fine aerial view you get from the city wall promenade, you may find it unnecessary to pay admission to enter. Belly up to the 13th-century wall and look down. The wall you're standing on divided the theater from the town center...so, natu-rally, the theater became the town dump. Over time, the theater was forgotten—covered in the garbage of Volterra. Luckily, it was rediscovered in the 1950s.

The stage wall was standard Roman design—with three levels from which actors would appear: one for humans, one for heroes, and the top one for gods. Parts of two levels still stand. Gods leaped out onto the third level for the last time in the fourth century A.D., when the town decided to abandon the theater and use its stones to build fancy baths instead. You can see the remains of the baths behind the theater, including the round sauna with brick supports to raise the heated floor (€2, but you can view the theater free from Via Lungo le Mure, daily 10:30–17:30, Nov–March Sat–Sun only 10:00–16:00).

From the vantage point on the city wall promenade, you can trace Volterra's vast Etruscan wall. Find the church in the distance, on the left, and notice the stones just below. They are from the Etruscan wall that followed the ridge into the valley and defined Volterra five centuries before Christ.

Palazzo dei Priori—Volterra's city hall (c. 1209) claims to be the oldest of any Tuscan city-state. It clearly inspired the more famous Palazzo Vecchio in Florence. Town halls like this were emblem-atic of an era when city-states were powerful. They were architec-tural exclamation points declaring that, around here, no pope or emperor called the shots. Towns such as Volterra were truly city-states—proudly independent and relatively democratic. They had their own armies, taxes, and even weights and measures. Notice the horizontal "cane" cut into the city hall wall. For a thousand years, this square hosted a market and the "cane" was the local yardstick. When not in use for meetings, the city council chambers—lavishly painted and lit with fun dragon lamps—are open to visitors (€1, may be possible to scale tower, April–Oct daily 10:30–17:30, Nov–March Sat–Sun only 10:00–17:00).

▲**Via Matteotti**—The town's main drag, named after the popular socialist leader killed by the Fascists in 1924, provides a good cultural scavenger hunt and guided walk. Start your walk just 30 yards from the city hall (Palazzo dei Priori) at the start of Via Matteotti. At #1 there's a typical Italian bank security door. (Step in and say, "Beam me up Scotty.") Look up and all around. Find the medieval griffin torch holder—symbol of Volterra. Imagine the town torch lit. The pharmacy sports the symbol of its medieval guild. As you head down Via Matteotti, notice how the doors show centuries of refitting work. Be careful. There's a wild boar at #10. This is a local delicacy—walk in to pet a hairy wild boar hamhock.

At #12, notice how the typical palace, once the home of a single rich family, is now occupied by many middle-class families (judging from the line of doorbells). After the social revolution (18th century) and the rise of the middle class, former palaces were condominiumized. Even so (like in Dr. Zhivago), the original family still lives here. Apartment #1 is the home of Count Guidi.

At #19, La Vecchia Lira is a lively cafeteria (see below). The Bar L'Incontro is a favorite for homemade gelato and pastries. At #20 you'll see a plaque marking the local communist party headquarters. Americans get all Khrushchev-nervous when confronted with euro-communism, but in Western Europe it's actually a mild form of socialism that remains pretty strong today. Bologna is famously red, as is Tuscany in general. In the 1970s, 60 percent of Tuscany voted communist. The strength of the local communist party has its roots in WWII anti-fascism.

Across the street, up Vicolo delle Prigioni, is a fun bakery. They're happy to sell small quantities if you want to try the local *cantuccini* (almond biscotti) or munch a cannoli.

At #27, look up and imagine heavy beams cantilevered out, supporting extra wooden rooms, and balconies crowding out over the street. Throughout Tuscany, today's stark and stony old building fronts once supported a tangle of wooden extensions. Doors that once led to these extra rooms are now half-bricked up to make windows. Imagine the density in the 14th century, before the plague thinned out the population.

At #48, pop into the showroom of a fine alabaster artist. Alabaster, quarried nearby, has long been a big industry here. Volterra alabaster—softer and more porous than marble—was sliced thin to serve as windows for Italy's medieval churches. At #51, a bit of Etruscan wall is artfully used to display more alabaster art. And #56 is the surreal alabaster art gallery of Paolo Sabatini.

Locals gather early each evening at #57 for the best cocktails in town—aperitivos served with free munchies. The cinema is across the street. Movies in Italy are rarely in *versione originale*. Italians are used to getting their movies dubbed into Italian.

At #66, the end of the street is marked by another Tuscan tower. This noble house has a ground floor with no interior access to the safe upper floors. Rope ladders were used to get upstairs. The tiny door was wide enough to let in your skinny friends...but definitely no one wearing armor and carrying big weapons.

Alabaster Workshop—Alab'Arte offers a fun peek into the art of alabaster. Their showroom is across from the Etruscan Museum. A block downhill is their powdery workshop, where you can watch Roberto Chiti and Giorgio Finazzo at work. Lighting shows off the translucent quality of the stone and the expertise of these artists (Mon–Sat 9:00–13:00 & 15:00–19:00, closed Sun, showroom at Via Don Minzoni 18, workshop at Via Orti S. Agostino 28, tel. 0588-85506). If you want to see more artisans in action, ask the TI for their list of the town's many workshops open to the public.

Wine Tasting with Bruno and Lucio—La Vena di Vino, also just across from the Etruscan Museum, is a fun *enoteca* wine bar where two guys have devoted themselves to the wonders of wine and share it with a fun-loving passion. Each day Bruno and Lucio open six or eight bottles, serve your choice by the glass, pair it with characteristic food, and offer fine music (guitars available for patrons). Here is your chance to try the latest phenom in the wine world, the Super Tuscan—a creative mix of non-native grapes grown in Tuscany, aged in small oak barrels for only two years. According to Bruno, "While the Brunello (€6 a glass) is just right for wild boar, the Super Tuscan (€5) is just right for meditation" (Wed–Mon 12:00–24:00, closed Tue, Via Don Minzoni 30, tel. 0588-81491).

Medici Fortress and Archaeological Park—The Parco Archeologico marks what was the acropolis of Volterra from 1500 b.c. until a.d. 1472, when Florence conquered the pesky city and burned its political and historic center, turning it into a grassy commons (today's park) and building the adjacent Medici Fortress. The old fortress—a symbol of Florentine dominance—now keeps people in rather than out. It's a maximum-security prison housing only 60 or so special prisoners. (Note that when you're driving from San Gimignano to Volterra, you pass another big modern prison—almost surreal in the midst of all the Tuscan wonder.) Authorities prefer to keep organized crime figures locked up far away from their family ties in Sicily.

SLEEPING

(€1 = about $1.20, country code: 39)

$$ Albergo Etruria, on Volterra's main drag, rents 20 fresh, modern, and spacious rooms within an ancient stony structure. They have a welcoming TV lounge and a great roof garden (Sb-€60, Db-€80, 10 percent discount with cash and this book in 2006, includes breakfast, Via Matteotti 32, tel. 0588-87377, fax 0588-92784, www.albergoetruria.it, info@albergoetruria.it, Lisa and Giuseppina).

$$ Albergo Villa Nencini, just outside of town, is big, modern, and professional, with 36 fine rooms, a large pool, and free parking (Sb-€62, Db-€83, Tb-€112, 10 percent discount with cash and this book in 2006, includes breakfast, Borgo San Stefano 55, a 10-minute walk to main square, tel. 0588-86386, www.villanencini.it, villanencini@sirt.pisa.it, run by Nencini family).

$ Albergo Nazionale, with 35 big rooms, is clean, simple, and steps from the bus stop (Sb-€50, Db-€69, Tb-€80, less off-season, breakfast-€6, Via dei Marchesi 11, tel. 058-886-284, fax 058-884-097, nazionalevolterra@tiscali.it).

$ Seminario Vescovile San Andrea has been training priests for 500 years. Today, the remaining eight priests still train students, and the rooms—separated by vast and holy halls—are rented very cheap to travelers (30 rooms, S-€14, Sb-€18, D-€28, Db-€36, T-€42, Tb-€54, breakfast-€3, closed at 24:00, groups welcome, Viale Vittorio Veneto 2, tel. 0588-860-28, semvescovile@diocesivolterra.it).

EATING

Ristorante Enoteca del Duca, with a locally-respected chef, serves refined Tuscan cuisine. You can dine under a medieval arch, with walls lined with wine bottles, or on a nice little patio out back (food-sampler menu-€40, pastas-€8, *secondi*-€15, a good place for truffles, fine wine list, closed Tue, near city hall at Via di Castello 2, tel. 0588-81510).

La Vecchia Lira is a classy self-serve eatery that's a hit with locals as a quick and cheap lunch spot by day, and a fancier fish restaurant at night (Fri–Wed 11:45–15:00 & 19:30–22:00, closed Thu, Via Matteotti 19, tel. 0588-86180).

Ombra della Sera serves the best pizza in town and more (closed Mon, Via Guarnacci 16, tel. 0588-85274).

Ristorante Il Sacco Fiorentino is a local favorite for traditional cuisine (closed Wed, Piazza XX Settembre 18, tel. 0588-88537).

For fresh sandwiches and wine, try friendly **Enoteca Scali** (daily 9:00–21:00, Via Guarnacci 13, tel. 058-881-170).

You can assemble a picnic at the few *alimentari* around town (try Spar Market at Via Gramsci 12) and eat in the breezy Parco Archeologico.

TRANSPORTATION CONNECTIONS

From Volterra by Bus to: Florence (4/day, 2 hrs, change in Colle Val d'Elsa), **Siena** (4/day, 2 hrs, change in Colle Val d'Elsa), **San Gimignano** (4/day, 2 hrs, change in Colle Val d'Elsa), **Pisa** (9/day, 2 hrs, change in Pontedera). Buses come and go from Volterra's Piazzi Martiri della Libertà (buy tickets at any *tabacchi* shop). For Siena, Florence, and San Gimignano, Tra-In bus tickets only get you as far as Colle Val d'Elsa; you must buy another ticket (from another bus company) at the newsstand near the bus stop. There is virtually no bus service in or out of Volterra on Sundays or holidays.

Drivers: The town is ringed with easy and free parking lots. The most central and only underground lot is a pay lot at Piazza Martiri della Libertà (La Dobana, €1.40/hr or €10/24 hrs).

Montalcino

On a hill overlooking vineyards and valleys below, Montalcino—famous for its delicious and pricey Brunello di Montalcino red wines—is a must-sip for wine lovers.

In the Middle Ages, Montalcino (mohn-tahl-CHEE-noh) was considered Siena's biggest ally. Originally allied with Florence, the town switched sides after the Sienese beat up Florence in the battle of Monteaperti in 1260. The Sienese persuaded the Montalcini to join their side by forcing them to sleep one night in the bloody Florentine-strewn battlefield.

Montalcino prospered under Siena, but like its ally, it waned after the Medici family took control of the region. The village regained fame when, in the late 19th century, the Biondi Santi family created a fine, dark red wine, calling it "the brunette."

Non-wine-lovers may find Montalcino a bit too focused on *vino*, but one sip of Brunello makes even wine skeptics believe that Bacchus was on to something. Note that Rosso di Montalcino (a younger version of Brunello) is also very good, at half the price. Those with sweet tooths will enjoy munching Ossi di Morta ("Bones of the Dead"), a crunchy cookie with almonds.

Day-trippers be warned: Montalcino has no baggage-check service. In a jam, try the TI.

Tourist Information: The TI, just off Piazza Garibaldi in the city hall, can find you a room (Db-€50–60) for no fee (daily 10:00–13:00 & 14:00–17:50, closed Mon in winter, tel. & fax

Montalcino

P –PARKING

100 YARDS

100 METERS

TO
SANT'ANTIMO
& ⑤

TO
VIA CASSIA,
SIENA, PIENZA &
MONTEPULCIANO

DCH

① Palazzina Cesira B&B
② Hotel il Giglio
③ Ristorante il Moro Rooms
④ Affittacamere Mariuccia
⑤ To La Crociona Agriturismo
⑥ Taverna il Grappolo Blu
⑦ Trattoria Sciame
⑧ Osteria al Giardino
⑨ Café Fiaschetteria Italiana

0577-849-331, www.prolocomontalcino.it). **Market day** is Friday (7:00–13:00) on Viale della Libertà.

SIGHTS

Fortezza—This 14th-century fort, built under the rule of Siena, is now little more than an empty shell. People visit for its *enoteca,* or wine bar (see below). Climb the ramparts to enjoy a panoramic view of the Asso and Orcia valleys, or enjoy a picnic in the park surrounding the fort (€3.50 for rampart walk, €6 combo-ticket includes Civic Museum, daily 9:00–20:00, closed Mon off-season).

Civic Museum (Museo Civico)—Gothic art is the star of this museum, with works from Montalcino's heyday, the 13th to 16th centuries. Wooden sculptures and religious objects round out the collection (€4.50, €6 combo-ticket includes Fortezza, Tue–Sun 10:00–13:00 & 14:00–17:50, closed Mon, Via Ricasoli, tel. 0577-846-014).

Wineries—While there are plenty of *enoteche,* there are no real wineries inside the city. The nearby countryside, however, is littered with them, and most wineries will give tastings. While some require an appointment, many also are happy to serve a potential buyer a glass and show them around. Banfi, the most touristy, produces well-respected wines (daily 10:00–17:00, tours Mon–Fri at 16:00, reserve in advance, 10-min drive south of Montalcino in Sant'Angelo Scalo, tel. 0577-840-111, www.castellobanfi.com, reservations@banfi.it).

The Montalcino TI can give you the list of more than 150 regional wineries. Or check with the vintners' consortium (tel. 0577-848-246, www.consorziobrunellodimontalcino.it, consbrun@tin.it).

SLEEPING

(€1 = about $1.20, country code: 39)
$$ Palazzina Cesira, right in the heart of the old town, rents five spacious and thoughtfully appointed rooms in a fine 13th-century residence with a palatial lounge. You'll enjoy a refined and tranquil ambience and the chance to get to know Lucilla and her American husband Roberto (Db-€80, suites-€95–105, cash only, Via Soccorso Saloni 2, tel. & fax 0577-846-055, www.montalcinoitaly.com, cesira@montalcinoitaly.com).

$$ Hotel il Giglio, although lacking in warmth, has 12 comfortable rooms, some with vaulted ceilings. Ask for a room with a view (Sb-€58, Db-€85, Tb-€95, 10 percent discount with this book and cash in 2006, breakfast-€6.50, Via Saloni 5, tel. & fax 0577-848-167, www.gigliohotel.com, hotelgiglio@tin.it).

$ Ristorante il Moro rents four pleasant, modern rooms

around the corner from their restaurant. The two upper rooms have views, the lower rooms have terraces, and they all share a cozy common room with a kitchen (Db-€50, no breakfast, 100 yards from bus station at Via Mazzini 44, tel. 0577-849-384, Alessandro and Julia).

$ Affittacamere Mariuccia is basic and drab, but central and cheap (3 rooms, Sb-€35, Db-€46, no breakfast, check-in at Enoteca Pierangioli, Piazza del Popolo 16, rooms across the street at #28, tel. & fax 0577-849-113, www.enotecapierangioli.com, enotecapierangioli @hotmail.com, Stefania doesn't speak English).

Near Montalcino: **$La Crociona,** an *agriturismo* farm and working vineyard, rents seven fully-equipped apartments. Fiorella Vannoni and Roberto and Barbara Nannetti offer cooking classes and tastes of the Brunello wine grown and bottled on the premises (Db-€95 but €65 in Oct–mid-May, Qb-€130 but €95 in Oct–mid-May, lower weekly rates, pool, La Croce 15, tel. 0577-847-133, tel. & fax 0577-848-007, www.lacrociona.com, crociona@tin.it). The farm is nearly two miles south of Montalcino on the road to the Sant'Antimo Monastery (look for the big yellow *Piombaia La Crociona* sign on the left and then follow directions to Tenuta Crocedimezzo e Crociona). There's a good restaurant next door.

EATING

Taverna il Grappolo Blu is dressy yet friendly, serving local specialties and vegetarian options to an enthusiastic crowd (pastas-€6, *secondi*-€11, Sat–Thu 12:00–15:30 & 19:00–22:00, closed Fri, near the main square, a few steps off Via Mazzini at Scale di Via Moglio 1, tel. 0577-847-150).

Trattoria Sciame, a family-run hole-in-the-wall, has nine small tables and homemade desserts (pastas-€7, meat-€8, Wed–Mon 12:00–14:30 & 19:00–21:30, closed Tue, Via Ricasoli 9, tel. 0577-848-017).

Osteria al Giardino serves near-gourmet local cuisine at the bus station end of town (pastas-€7, *secondi*-€12, closed Wed, Piazza Cavour 1, tel. 0577-849-076).

Gather ingredients for a picnic at the **Co-Op supermarket** on Via Ricasoli, then enjoy your feast in front of the Fortezza.

Wine Tasting

While wine snobs turn up their noses, the medieval setting inside Montalcino's fort at **Enoteca la Fortezza** is a hit for most visitors. Spoil yourself with Brunello in the cozy *enoteca* or at outdoor tables (3 tastes for €12, snacks for 2 people-€9, daily 9:00–20:00, closes at 18:00 and on Mon in off-season, inside the Fortezza, tel. 0577-849-211, www.enotecalafortezza.it).

Café Fiaschetteria Italiana was founded by Ferruccio Biondi-Santi who created the famous Brunello wine. The wine library in the back of the café boasts many local wine choices, including a prized bottle from 1955, a vintage year. A meeting place since 1888, this grand café also serves light lunches and espresso to tourists and locals alike (€15 for a glass of Brunello and plate of snacks, daily 7:30–23:00, Piazza del Popolo 6, tel. 0577-849-043).

TRANSPORTATION CONNECTIONS

From Montalcino by Bus to: Siena (€3, 8/day, 90 min), **Montepulciano/Pienza** (10/day, change to line #114 in Torrenieri, 60 min plus changing time). Anyone going to Rome or Florence changes in Siena. The town bus station is on Piazza Cavour. Bus tickets are sold at *tabacchi* shops or the bar on Piazza Cavour—not on board. Check schedules at the TI or the bus station on Piazza Cavour.

Drivers coming in for a short visit should drive right through the old gate under the fortress (it looks almost forbidden) and grab a spot in the pay lot at the fortress. Otherwise, there is free parking a short walk away.

Montepulciano

Curving its way along a ridge, Montepulciano (mohn-tay-pull-chee-AH-noh) delights visitors with *vino* and views. Alternately under Sienese and Florentine rule, the city still retains its medieval *contrade* districts, each with a mascot and flag. The neighborhoods compete the last Sunday of August in the *Bravio delle Botti*, where teams of men push large wine casks uphill from Piazza Marzocco to Piazza Grande, all hoping to win a banner and bragging rights.

The city is a collage of architectural styles, but the elegant San Biagio Church, at the base of the hill, is its most impressive Renaissance building. Most ignore the architecture and focus more on the city's other creative accomplishment, the tasty Vino Nobile di Montepulciano red wine.

The action in Montepulciano centers on two streets, the steep Via di Gracciano nel Corso and Via Ricci, but the quiet back streets are well worth a visit.

Tourist Information: The TI is on Piazza Don Minzoni (daily 9:30–12:30, 15:00–18:30, tel. 0578-757-341, www.comune .montepulciano.si.it, prolocomp@bccmp.com).

Helpful Hints: Market day is Thursday. Public **WCs** are located next to Palazzo del Comune and the Church of St. Augustine.

Montepulciano

❶ Mueble il Riccio Rooms
❷ Camere Bellavista Rooms
❸ Ai Quattro Venti
❹ Osteria dell'Aquacheta

TO SIENA &
A-1 AUTOSTRADA
FREEWAY

SANT'
AGNESE

VIA E. BERNABEI

PIAZZA
MARZOCCO

PIAZZA
DON
MINZONI

V. CAL.

POGGIO-
FANTI
GARDENS

P

WC

SANG.

PORTA AL
PRATO

VIALE I. MAGGIO

VIA DELLE LETTERE

P

BUS
STATION

PALAZZO
BUCELLI

WC

CORSO

ST.
AUGUSTINE

S.
LUCIA

NEL

Post

PIANA

ARCHI

POGGIOLO

VIA GRACCIANO

SAN
FRAN.

VIA DI ORIOLO

★ PIAZZA GRANDE

TO
SAN
BIAGIO

VIA DI SAN BIAGIO

VIA RICCI

CIVIC
MUSEUM

VIA VOLT.

GESU

P -PARKING

CONTUCCI
CANTINA

PALAZZO
COMUNALE

WC

CIALOSA

DUOMO

FIOR. VECCHIA

VIA DELL'OPIO CORSO

TEATRO

VIA SAN PIETRO

P

VIA CIRCONVALLAZIONE

VIA COLLAZZI

DONATO

FORTEZZA

VIA DI

PORTA DI FARINE

BUS
STOP

V. POLIZIANO

S. MARIA

FILOSOFI

100 YARDS

100 METERS

TO PIENZA

SIGHTS

Piazza Grande—This pleasant, lively piazza is surrounded by a grab bag of architectural sights. The medieval Palazzo Comunale may remind you of Palazzo Vecchio in Florence—that's because Florence dominated this town in the 15th and 16th centuries. The crenellations along the roof were never intended to hide soldiers—they're there just to symbolize power. Climbing the **clock tower** rewards you with a windy, panoramic view (€1.50, daily 10:00–18:00). The Palazzo de' Nobili-Tarugi is a Renaissance arcaded confection; meanwhile, the unfinished Duomo looks glumly on, wishing the city hadn't run out of money for its facade. Many such churches were built until they had a functional interior, and then, for various practical reasons, the facades were left unfinished. You can see the rough stone-work just waiting for the final marble veneer. The Contucci Palace (left of the church) is lucky enough to have a 16th-century Renaissance facade. The Contucci family still lives in their palace, producing and selling their own wine. The town is fortunate to be graced with so many bold and noble palazzos—Florentine nobility favored Montepulciano as a breezy and relaxed place for a summer or secondary residence.

▲▲**Contucci Cantina**—Montepulciano's most popular attraction isn't made of stone...it's the famous wine, Vino Nobile. This robust red can be tasted in any of the cantinas lining Via Ricci and Via di Gracciano nel Corso, but the cantina in the basement of Palazzo Contucci is the most famous...and fun. While the palace has a formal wine tasting showroom facing the square, head down the lane on the right to the actual cellars where you'll meet lively Adamo, who has been making wine since 1953 and welcomes tourists into his cellar. Adamo usually has a dozen bottles open (tasting is free, no food, daily 9:00–12:30 & 14:30–18:30, Piazza Grande 7, tel. 0578-757-006). Groups are welcome with a reservation.

After sipping a little wine with Adamo, explore the 13th-century vaults of the palace basement, now filled with huge barrels of wine. These include an evocative former prison, holding not criminals but...more good red wine. Countless barrels of Croatian, Italian, and French oak (1,000–2,500 liters each) cradle the wine through a two year in-the-barrel aging process, while the wine picks up the personality of the wood. After about 35 years, an exhausted barrel has nothing left to offer its wine, and it's retired. Adam explains that the French oak gives the wine "pure elegance," the Croatian is more masculine, and the Italian oak is a marriage of the two. Each barrel is labeled with the size in liters, the year the wine was barreled, and the percentage of alcohol (determined by how much sun shone in that year). "Nobile" grade wine needs a minimum of 13 percent alcohol.

The information office for the "Strada del Vino" (Wine Road) organizes **wine tours** in the city and minibus winery tours farther afield (Piazza Grande, tel. 0578-717-484, www.stradavinonobile.it, info@stradavinonobile.it).

Civic Museum (Museo Civico)—Small and eclectic, the highlight of this well-presented museum is its colorful della Robbia ceramic altarpieces (€4, Tue–Sat 10:00–13:00 & 15:00–18:00, Sun 10:00–18:00, closed Mon, Via Ricci 10, tel. 0578-717-300).

San Biagio Church—Down a picturesque driveway lined with cypress, this church—designed by Antonio da Sangallo—is Renaissance perfection. The proportions of the Greek cross plan give the building a pleasing rhythmic quality. The lone tower was supposed to have a twin, but it was never built. The soaring interior, with a high dome and lantern, creates a fine Renaissance space (daily 9:00–13:00 & 15:00–19:00). The street Via di San Biagio, leading from the church up into town, makes for an enjoyable, if challenging, walk.

SLEEPING

(€1 = about $1.20, country code: 39)

$$ Mueble il Riccio (literally, "hedgehog") is medieval-elegant, with six modern rooms, an awesome roof terrace, and friendly owners. When Gio isn't manning the desk, he's out giving country tours in one of his classic Italian cars; for tour details, see their Web site (Sb-€75, Db-€85, Tb-€101, breakfast-€8, air-con, a block below the main square at Via Talosa 21, tel. & fax 0578-757-713, www .ilriccio.net, info@ilriccio.net, Gio and Ivana speak English).

$ Camere Bellavista has simple rooms with views, and nicer rooms without. (Db-€55, nicer Db-€65, cash only, no breakfast, no elevator, Via Ricci 25, mobile 347-823-2314, bellavista@bccmp.com, no English spoken).

EATING

Ai Quattro Venti is fresh, flavorful, fun, and right on Piazza Grande, offering good indoor and outdoor seating (pastas-€7, Fri–Wed 12:00–14:00 & 19:30–22:00, closed Thu, next to city hall on Piazza Grande, tel. 0578-717-231).

Osteria dell'Aquacheta serves pastas and salads at reasonable prices, with a mix of locals and tourists (€5 pastas and salads, Wed–Mon 12:30–15:00 & 19:30–22:30, closed Tue, Via del Teatro 22, tel. 0578-717-086).

TRANSPORTATION CONNECTIONS

From Montepulciano by Bus to: Siena (8/day, 1.25 hrs, few in afternoon, none on Sun), **Pienza** (8/day, 30 min). All buses leave from Piazza Pietro Nenni.

Drivers: Route #146 to Montalcino is particularly scenic (see "Crete Senese Drives," page 509). It isn't wise to tackle the tiny roads inside the city, so park outside the walls, either at the bus station or the numerous lots on the edge of town.

Pienza

Set on a crest, surrounded by green, rolling hills, the small town of Pienza packs a lot of Renaissance punch. In the 1400s, locally born Pope Pius II of the Piccolomini family (see page 404) decided to remodel his birthplace in the style that was all the rage—Renaissance. Propelled by papal clout, the town of Corsignano was transformed—in only five years' time—into a jewel of Renaissance architecture. It was renamed Pienza, after Pope Pius. The plan was to remodel the entire town, but work ended in 1564 when both the pope and his architect, Bernardo Rossellino, died. The architectural focal point is the square Piazza Pio II, surrounded by the Duomo and the pope's family residence, Palazzo Piccolomini. While the Piazza Pio II is Pienza's pride and joy, the entire town—a mix of old stone-work, potted plants, and grand views—is fun to explore, especially with a camera or sketchpad in hand. You can walk each lane in the tiny town in a few minutes. Nearly every shop sells the town's specialty—pecorino cheese—a pungent sheep's cheese available fresh *(fresco)* or aged *(secco)*.

Tourist Information: The TI is on Piazza Pio II, across from the Duomo (Mon–Sat 10:00–13:00 & 15:00–19:00, closed Sun, tel. & fax 0578-749-071). They rent audioguides for self-guided hour-long town walks (€5). The TI will let you leave your bags there. **Market day** is Friday.

SIGHTS

▲**Piazza Pio II**—One of Italy's classic piazzas, this square is famous for its elegance and artistic unity. The square and the surrounding buildings were all designed by Rossellino to form an "outdoor room." Spinning around, you'll see the city hall (13th-century bell tower with a Renaissance facade and a fine loggia), the Bishop's Palace (now an art museum), the Piccolomini family palace (well worth touring—see below), and the Duomo. Just to the left of the church, a lane leads to the best viewpoint in town.

Duomo—Its classic, symmetrical Renaissance facade—with the Piccolomini family coat of arms (modestly) front and center—dominates Piazza Pio. The interior is charming, with several Gothic altarpieces and painted arches. Windows feature the crest of Pius II, with five half-moons advertising the number of crusades that his family funded.

▲▲Palazzo Piccolomini—The home of Pius II and the Piccolomini family until 1962 can be visited with a guided tour. While the 30-minute tour (in English and Italian) visits only six rooms and the loggia, it offers a fascinating slice of 15th-century aristocratic life and is the sightseeing highlight of the town. In fact, it's the most impressive small-town palace experience I've found in Tuscany. Don't miss this one. Check out the well-preserved painted courtyard for free. In Renaissance times, most buildings were covered with elaborate paintings like these (€3.50, Tue–Sun 10:00–12:30 & 15:00–18:00, closed Mon and in winter, tel. 0578-749-071).

Museo Diocesano—This collection of religious paintings from local churches fills the cardinal's Renaissance palace. The art is provincial Sienese, displayed in chronological order from 12th through 17th centuries, conveniently all on one floor (€4.10, Wed–Mon 10:00–13:00 & 15:00–19:00, closed Tue, in winter open Sat–Sun only, Corso il Rossellino 30).

View Terrace—Facing the church, a lane leads left to the panoramic promenade. Views from the terrace include the Tuscan countryside and 5,700-foot Monte Amiata, the tallest mountain in southern Tuscany, in the distance.

SLEEPING

(€1 = about $1.20, country code: 39)
$$ Agriturismo Terrapille sits just below Pienza, on a little grassy bluff surrounded by 360 degrees of dreamy Tuscan scenery. It's private and rustic yet cozy and romantic. Four country rooms and two apartments come with modern comforts (Db-€95, Qb-€160, breakfast-€7.50, dinner available on request for €25, pool, about a mile out of town, take road #18 in direction of Monticchiello, tel. & fax 0578-749-146 at farm, www.terrapille.it, terrapille@bccmp .com). Lucia, who runs the place, lives in Pienza (home tel. 0578-748434, mobile 338-920-4470).

$ Oliviera Camere, which has six simple rooms in the town center, is run by soft-spoken Nello, who doesn't speak English (Db-€50, breakfast in room, cash only, Via Condotti 4, tel. 0578-748-205, mobile 338-952-0459).

$ Il Giardino Segreto Camere rents six humble rooms with a lush, peaceful garden (Db-€62, apartment Db-€67, Via Condotti

13, tel. 0578-748-539, mobile 338-899-5879, www.ilgiardinosegreto
.toscana.nu, muccirossi@bcc.tin.it).

EATING

Latte di Luna, lively with great indoor and outdoor seating, is a
good, quality choice (Wed–Mon 12:30–14:30 & 19:30–21:30, closed
Tue, at Porta al Giglio, Via San Carlo 2, tel. 0578-748-606).

La Taverna di Re Artu serves bruschetta and a variety of
wines (daily 10:30–20:30, Via della Rosa 4).

Ristorante dal Falco, a modern place just outside the town
wall, is out of the tourist zone and therefore forced to offer a fine
value to survive. Its comfortable indoor and outdoor seating and lack
of tourists makes it a favorite with tour guides (pastas-€6, *secondi*-
€11, closed Fri, Piazza Dante Alighieri 3, tel. 0578-749-856).

Assemble a **picnic** at any of the numerous cheese and wine
shops, and dine with a fantastic view along the walls of the view
terrace.

TRANSPORTATION CONNECTIONS

Bus tickets are sold at the bar just inside Pienza's town gate.

From Pienza by Bus to: Siena (6/day, 90 min), **Montepulciano**
(8/day, 30 min).

Cortona

Cortona blankets a 1,700-foot hill surrounded by dramatic Tuscan
and Umbrian views. Frances Mayes' books, such as *Under the Tuscan
Sun,* have placed this town in the touristic limelight, just as Peter
Mayle's books popularized the Luberon region in France. But long
before Mayes ever published a book, Cortona was popular with
Romantics and considered one of the classic Tuscan hill towns.
Unlike San Gimignano, Cortona maintains a rustic and gritty personality—even with its long history of foreigners who, enamored
with its Tuscan charm, made this their adopted home.

The city began as one of the largest Etruscan settlements, the
remains of which can be seen at the base of the city walls, as well
as in the nearby tombs. It grew to its present size in the 13th to
16th centuries, when it was a colorful and crowded city, eventually allied with Florence. The farmland that fills almost every view
from the city was marshy and uninhabitable until about 200 years
ago, when it was drained and turned into some of Tuscany's most
fertile land.

Art-lovers know Cortona as the home of Renaissance painter Luca Signorelli, Baroque master Pietro da Cortona (Berretini), and the 20th-century Futurist artist Gino Severini. The city's museums and churches reveal many of the works of these native sons.

ORIENTATION

Most of the main sights, shops, and restaurants cluster around the level streets on the Piazza Garibaldi–Piazza del Duomo axis, but Cortona will have you huffing and puffing up some steep hills.

Tourist Information

The helpful TI is on the main drag at Via Nazionale 42 (daily March–Oct 9:00–13:00 & 15:00–19:00, sells train and bus tickets, tel. 0575-630-352, www.cortonaweb.net, www.cortona-musei.it for museums, infocortona@apt.arezzo.it). **Market day** is Saturday on Piazza Signorelli (early–14:00).

Private Guide: Giovanni Adreani exudes energy and a love of his city and Tuscan high culture. He is great at bringing the fine points of the city to life and can take visitors around in his car for no extra price. As this region is speckled with under-appreciated charms, having Giovanni for a day as your driver/guide promises to be a fascinating experience (€100/half-day, €180/day, tel. 0575-630-665, mobile 347-176-2830, www.adreanigiovanni .com, adreanigiovanni@libero.it).

Arrival in Cortona

Buses stop at Piazza Garibaldi. From here, it's a level five-minute walk down bustling shop-lined Via Nazionale (stop by the TI) to Piazza della Repubblica, the heart of the town, dominated by city hall (Palazzo della Comune). From this square, it's a two-minute stroll past the interesting Etruscan Museum and theater to Piazza Duomo, where you'll find the recommended Diocesan Museum. Steep streets, many of them stepped, lead from Piazza della Repubblica up to the San Niccolo and Santa Margherita churches and the Medici Fortress (a 30-min climb from Piazza della Repubblica).

SELF-GUIDED WALK

Welcome to Cortona

This introductory walking tour will take you from the Piazza Garibaldi, up the main strip, to the town center, its piazzas, and the Duomo.

• *Start at the bus stop in...*

Piazza Garibaldi: Many visits start and finish in this square, thanks to its bus stop. While the piazza, bulging like a big turret out from the town fortifications, looks like part of an old rampart, it's really a souvenir of those early French and English Romantics—they are the ones who first created the notion of a dreamy, idyllic Tuscany. During the Napoleonic age, the French built this balcony (and the scenic little park behind the adjacent San Domenico church) simply to enjoy a commanding view of the Tuscan countryside.

With Umbria about a mile away, Cortona marks the end of Tuscany. This is a major cultural divide, as Cortona was the last town in Charlemagne's empire and the last under Medici rule. Umbria, just to the south, was papal territory for centuries. These deep-seated cultural disparities were a great challenge for the visionaries who unified the fractured region to create the modern nation of Italy during the 1860s. A statue in the center of this square honors one of the heroes of the struggle for Italian unification—the brilliant revolutionary general, Giuseppe Garibaldi.

Enjoy the commanding view from here. Assisi is just over the ridge on the left. Lake Trasimeno peeks from behind the hill, looking quite placid today. But, according to legend, it was blood-red after Hannibal defeated the Romans here in 217 B.C. and 15,000 died in the battle. The only sizable town you can see, on the right, is Montepulciano. Cortona is still defined by its Etruscan walls. Remnants of these walls, with stones laid 2,500 years ago, stretch from here in both directions.

Frances Mayes put Cortona on the map for many Americans with her book and the movie, *Under the Tuscan Sun*. Her book describes her real-life experience buying, fixing up, and living in a villa in Cortona with her husband Ed. The movie romanticized the story, turning Frances into a single, recently-divorced writer who restores the villa and her peace of mind. Frances' villa isn't "under the Tuscan sun" very often; it's named Bramasole—literally, "craving sun." On the wrong side of the hill, it's in the shade after 15:00. She and her husband still live there part of each year and are respected members of their adopted community. The house is outside the walls, behind the hill on the left.

• *From this square, head into town along...*

Via Nazionale: The only level road in town, locals have nicknamed Via Nationale the *ruga piana* (flat wrinkle). This is the main commercial street in this town of 2,500, and it's been that way for a long time. Every shop seems to have a medieval cellar or an Etruscan well. Notice the crumbling sandstone door frames. The entire town is constructed out of this grainy, eroding rock.

• *Via Nazionale leads to...*

Piazza della Repubblica: The city hall faces Cortona's main square, where three flags fly: Europe, Italy, and peace (Tuscany is

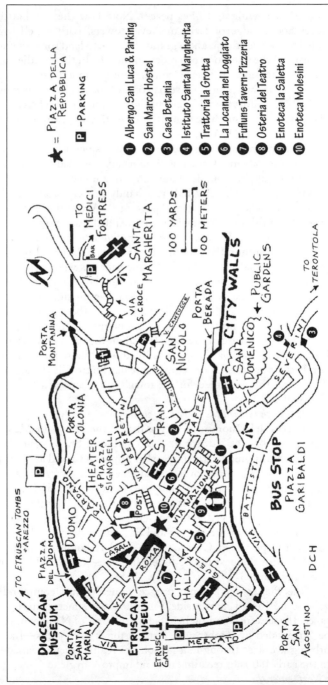

Cortona

★ = PIAZZA DELLA REPUBBLICA

P = PARKING

1 Albergo San Luca & Parking
2 San Marco Hostel
3 Casa Betania
4 Istituto Santa Margherita
5 Trattoria la Grotta
6 La Locanda nel Loggiato
7 Fufluns Tavern-Pizzeria
8 Osteria del Teatro
9 Enoteca la Saletta
10 Enoteca Molesini

famously left-wing and likes peace). Note how the city hall is a clever hodgepodge of twin medieval towers, with a bell tower added to connect them, and a grand staircase to lend some gravitas. Notice also the fine wood balconies on the left. In the Middle Ages, wooden extensions such as balconies were common features on the region's stone buildings. These balconies (not original, but rebuilt in the 19th century) would have fit right in the medieval cityscape. These days, you usually see only the holes that once supported the long-gone wooden beams.

This square has been the town center since Etruscan times. Four centuries before Christ, an important street led from here up to the hill-capping temple. Later, the square became the Roman forum. Opposite the city hall is a handy grocery store for good cheap sandwiches (see "Eating," page 482). Above that is the loggia—once a fish market, now a recommended restaurant.

• *The second half of the square, to the right of the city hall, is...*

Piazza Signorelli: Dominated by Casali Palace, this square was the headquarters of the Florentine captains who used to control control the city. Every six months, Florence would send a new captain to Cortona, who would help establish his rule by inserting his family coat of arms into the palace's wall. These date from the 15th to the 17th century, and were once painted with bright colors. Cortona's fine Etruscan Museum (listed in "Sights," below) is in the Casali Palace courtyard, which is lined with many more of these family coats of arms. The inviting Café del Teatro fills the loggia of the theater that is named for the town's most famous artist, Luca Signorelli.

• *Head a block toward the cathedral, which is on the...*

Piazza del Duomo: Here you'll find the Diocesan Museum (see Sights, below), cathedral, and a statue of St. Margherita. If the cathedral seems a little underwhelming and tucked away, that's because it is. Cortona loves its favorite saint, Margherita, and put the energy it would normally invest in its cathedral into the Santa Margherita Basilica at the top of the hill. Margherita was a 13th-century rich girl who took good care of the poor and was an early follower of St. Francis and St. Clare. Many locals believe Margherita protected Cortona from WWII bombs. (Many also thank her for the best public toilets in town—clean and free, just under her statue.)

The Piazza del Duomo terrace comes with a commanding view of the Tuscan countryside. Find the town cemetery in the distance. If you were standing here before the time of Napoleon, you'd be surrounded by tombstones. But Cortona's graveyards—like all urban graveyards throughout Napoleon's realm—were cleaned out in the early 1800s to reclaim land and improve hygiene.

• *Next, enter the...*

Duomo: The Cortona cathedral is not—strictly speaking—a cathedral, because it no longer has a bishop. The white-and-gray Florentine Renaissance-style interior is mucked up with lots of Baroque chapels filling once spacious side niches. In the rear (on the right) is an altar cluttered with relics. Technically any Catholic altar, in order to be consecrated, needs a relic embedded in it. Go ahead—gently lift up the tablecloth. The priest here doesn't mind. You'll see a little marble patch that holds a bit of a saint.

• *From here, you can visit the nearby Diocesan Museum or head back to the Piazza della Repubblica to visit the Etruscan Museum (see "Sights," below, for both), or to get a bite to eat (see "Eating," page 482).*

SIGHTS

▲**Etruscan Museum (Museo dell'Accademia Etrusca)**— Established in 1727, this was one of the first galleries dedicated to artifacts from the Etruscan civilization (for more on the Etruscans, see page 694). Along with lots of gold and jewelry, you'll find a seventh-century B.C. grater (for some really old Parmesan cheese) and a magnificent fourth-century B.C. bronze oil lamp with 16 spouts, set in a small, four-pillared temple. Don't miss the library of the Etruscan Academy upstairs. The academy was founded in 1727 to promote an understanding of the city through the study of archaeology. This eclectic museum, newly expanded for 2006, also has an Egyptian section, fine Roman mosaics, and a room dedicated to modern works by Severini (€5, daily 10:00–19:00, closed Mon off-season, Palazzo Casali on Piazza Signorelli, tel. 0575-637-235).

▲**Diocesan Museum (Museo Diocesano)**—This collection of the art from the town's many churches has works by Fra Angelico and Pietro Lorenzetti and masterpieces by hometown hero and Renaissance master, Luca Signorelli.

Don't miss Fra Angelico's sumptuous *Annunciation*. In this scene, Mary says "Yes," consenting to bear God's son. Notice how the house sits on a pillow of flowers...the new Eden. The old Eden, featuring the expulsion of Adam and Eve from Paradise, is in the upper left. The painting comes with comic-strip–like narration: the angel's lines are top and bottom, Mary's answer is upside down (logically, since it's directed to God and would be read from heaven).

Another highlight is Luca Signorelli's *Mourning of the Dead Christ (Compianto sul Cristo Morto)*. Signorelli was a generation ahead of Michelangelo and, with his passion for painting ideas, was an inspiration for the young artist. Everything in his painting has a meaning: The skull of Adam sits under the sacrifice of Jesus; the hammer represents the Passion (the Crucifixion leading to the

Resurrection); the lake is blood; and so on. I don't understand all of the medieval symbolism, but it's intense (€5, helpful audioguide-€3, daily April–Oct 10:00–19:00, Nov–March Tue–Sun 10:00–17:00, closed Mon, Piazza del Duomo 1, tel. 0575-62830). For more on Signorelli, see page 494.

Church of St. Francis—Established by St. Francis' best friend, Brother Elias, this church dates from the 13th century. Francis fans visit for its precious Franciscan relics. In the sacristy you'll find his tunic, the little Gospel that he always carried, and his pillow. If the church is closed, you can ring the bell from the cloister of the adjacent Franciscan Monastery and ask to be let in.

San Niccolo Church—Signorelli enthusiasts will want to make the pilgrimage up to this tiny church. Ring the bell and the care-taker will give you a short tour in Italian (generally closed during lunch—13:00–15:00). The highlight of this humble church is an altarpiece painted on both sides by Signorelli. The caretaker acti-vates a tricky arm mechanism that moves the picture away from the wall to reveal the painting behind it. There's no admission fee, but you should tip the caretaker a euro or two.

Santa Margherita Basilica—From San Niccolo Church, a steep path leads uphill 10 minutes to this basilica, which houses the remains of the town's favorite saint. St. Margherita, an unwed mother from Montepulciano, found her calling with the Franciscans in Cortona, tending to the sick and poor. Her son eventually became a Franciscan monk.

Still need more altitude? Head uphill five more minutes, to the Medici Fortress. It's usually open and the views are stunning, stretching all the way to distant Lake Trasimeno.

Etruscan Tombs near Cortona—Guided tours to nearby "Il Sodo" tombs (called *melone*, for their melon-like shape) are complicated to arrange. But the excavation site and bits of the ruins are easy to visit and can be seen from outside the fence in the morning. It's just a couple miles out of Cortona on the Arezzo road (#71), at the edge of Camucia at the foot of the Cortona hill; ask anyone for "Il Sodo."

SLEEPING

(€1 = about $1.20, country code: 39)

In Cortona

$$$ Albergo San Luca, perched on a cliff side, has 54 modern, business-class, impersonal rooms, half with stunning views of Lago Trasimeno. It's friendly, well-run, and conveniently located right at the bus stop (Sb-€70, Db-€100, request a view room when you reserve, popular with Americans and groups, Piazza Garibaldi 1, tel. 0575-630-460, fax 0575-630-105, www.sanlucacortona.com, info@sanlucacortona.com). If driving, there's a small public parking lot at the hotel where you might find a spot (cheap and easy meters).

$ Casa Betania, a big wistful convent with a large inviting view terrace, rents 35 fine rooms (only twin beds) for the best price in town. While it's primarily for "thoughtful travelers," anyone looking for a peaceful place to call home will feel welcome in this pilgrims' resort (S-€26, Sb-€31, D-€37, Db-€42, breakfast-€3, about a third of a mile out of town, a few minutes' walk below Piazza Garibaldi at Via Gino Severini 50, tel. 0575-62829, fax 0575-604-299, casabetaniacortona@interfree.it).

$ Istituto Santa Margherita, run by the Suore Serve di Maria Riparatrici sisters, rents 25 cheap and simple beds in a smaller and more institutional-feeling convent across the street (Sb-€32, Db-€46, breakfast-€3, Viale Cesare Battisti 15, tel. 0575-630-336, fax 0575-630-549, comunitacortona@smr.it).

$ San Marco Hostel, at the top of town, housed in a remodeled 13th-century palace, is one of Italy's best hostels (€12/bed in rooms with 2, 4, or 8 beds, lockout 11:00–17:00, Via Maffei 57, tel. 0575-601-392, English spoken).

Near Cortona

$$$ Casa San Martino, 12 miles east of Cortona near the isolated village of Lisciano Niccone, is a 250-year-old countryside farmhouse run as a B&B by American Italophile Lois Martin. While Lois reserves the summer (June–Aug) for one-week stays, she'll take guests staying a minimum of three nights for the rest of the year (Db-€140, 10 percent discount for my readers in 2006—mention this book when you reserve, includes breakfast, pool, washer/dryer, house rental available, Casa San Martino 19, Lisciano Niccone, tel. 075-844-288, fax 075-844-422, csm@tuscanyvacation.com). Lois' neighbors, Ernestine and Gisbert Schwanke, run the tidy, **La Villetta di San Martino B&B** (Db-€100, 2-night minimum, cash only, common kitchen and sitting room, San Martino 36, tel. & fax 075-844-309, www.tuscanyvacation.com, erni@netemedia.net).

$$ Castello di Montegualandro is a well-preserved castle on a hill opposite Cortona, overlooking the lake and countryside. The Marti family rent four charming medieval apartments, formerly peasant's quarters, inside the peaceful castle walls. Each one is unique and named for its former use—the Fornacci's sunken living room used to be a kiln. The castle's chapel is a popular spot for weddings (3- or 4-person apartment starts at €120, 3-night minimum, mention this book for a 7 percent discount in 2006, discounts for longer stays, cash only, 10 min southeast of Cortona, Tuoro sul Trasimeno, tel. & fax 075-8230-267, www.montegualandro .com, info@montegualandro.com).

EATING

Trattoria la Grotta, just off Piazza Repubblica, is a traditional, cave-like place with daily specials and an enthusiastic following (pastas–€7, meat–€8, Wed–Mon 12:00–15:00 & 19:00–22:00, closed Tue, Piazza Baldelli 3, tel. 0575-630-271).

La Locanda nel Loggiato serves up big portions of Tuscan cuisine on the loggia overlooking Piazza Repubblica. While they have fine indoor seating, I'd eat here only for the chance to gaze at the square over a meal (pastas–€7, meat–€7–15, Thu–Tue 12:00–15:00 & 19:00–23:00, closed Wed, Piazza Pescheria 3, tel. 0575-630-575).

Fufluns Tavern Pizzeria (that's the Etruscan name for Dionysus) is easy-going, friendly, and remarkably unpretentious for its location in the town center. It's popular with locals for its good, inexpensive Tuscan cooking and friendly staff (cheap, lots of pizzas but plenty more, good house wine, a block below Piazza Repubblica at Via Ghibellina 3, tel. 057-560-4140, run by Alessio and Simona).

Osteria del Teatro tries very hard to create an Old World atmosphere and does well. It serves nicely-presented and tasty Tuscan standards amid feminine, nostalgic elegance (closed Wed, 2 blocks uphill from the main square at Via Maffei 2, tel. 0575-630-556).

Enoteca la Saletta, dark and classy, is good for some fine wine and a light meal. You can sit inside surrounded by wine bottles or outside to people-watch on the town's main drag (daily 7:30–24:00, Via Nazionale 26, tel. 057-560-3366).

For a Picnic: On the main square, the chic little grocery store, **Enoteca Molesini,** makes tasty sandwiches (see list on counter and order by number) and sells whatever you might want for a picnic (daily including Sun morning, Piazza della Repubblica 23). Munch your picnic across the square on the steps of city hall, or just past Piazza Garibaldi in the public gardens behind San Domenico Church.

TRANSPORTATION CONNECTIONS

You'll connect Cortona with the rest of Italy by train. To get from Cortona down to the town's train station, at the foot of the hill, take a taxi or bus (€1.60, 2/hr between Piazza Garibaldi and station, buy tickets at newsstand or *tabacchi* shop).

From Cortona by Train to: Rome (10/day, 2.25 hrs), **Florence** (hrly, 1.5 hrs), **Assisi** (4/day, 1 hr), **Montepulciano** (8/day, 1.25 hrs, change in Chiusi). Most trains stop at Cortona's Camucia train station (tel. 0575-603-018), but fast trains from Rome and Florence stop at Terontola, 10 miles away (tel. 0575-670-034).

Drivers: Some free parking is available inside the town walls, if you can find it (best bets: Piazzale del Mercato and Piazzale di Santa Margherita). But I'd just grab a spot in one of several free lots right outside the walls. Piazza Garibaldi is perfectly central (where the buses stop, 2 minutes' walk from Piazza della Repubblica) and has a handful of pay spots (blue lines, plug the meter, cheap, free from 20:00–8:00). The small town is actually very long and it can be smart to drive to the top for sightseeing there (parking at Santa Margherita Basilica).

Urbino

Urbino is famous as the hometown of the artist Raphael and architect Bramante, yet the town owes much of its fame to the Duke of Montefeltro. This mercenary general turned Urbino into an important Renaissance center, attracting artists such as Piero della Francesca, Paolo Uccello, and Raphael's papa, Giovanni Santi.

Today, Urbino is a small town of 24,000—the majority of whom are students studying at the local university. Its primary economy is in serving the students, rather than tourists, and in spite of its historic and artistic importance, it feels far from the Italian mainstream. Since this was Vatican territory for over 200 years, you'll see lots of churches.

A classic hill town (550 yards above sea level), Urbino's medieval wall has four gates. Two main roads crisscross at the town's main square, Piazza della Repubblica. Called simply "the Piazza," this is café central—a great place to nurse an *aperitivo* or coffee and feel the town's pulse. There's barely a level road, with ridged lanes fading into steep stairways, giving hardy locals traction as they clamber about the village. While everything's a steep hike, it's a small town and the climbs are short.

ORIENTATION

Apart from the ambience, Urbino can be "seen" in half a day. Ninety percent of the tourist thrills are in the Ducal Palace. The only other must-sees are the Oratory of St. John and the town view from the fortress.

Tourist Information: The tiny TI is just across from the Ducal Palace (Tue–Fri 9:00–13:00 & 15:00–18:00, Mon and Sat 9:00–13:00 only, closed Sun, Piazza Duca Federico 35, tel. 0722-2613).

Arrival in Urbino: The big entry square (Borgo Mercatale) holds an underground garage where buses stop and cars park (€1/hr). While it's a short hike through the old gate up Via Mazzini to the town center, an elevator (€0.50) lifts you up fast and easy.

Federico da Montefeltro
(1422–1482)

The Duke of Montefeltro is *the* man in Urbino history. The bastard son of a small-town noble, he became Duke by killing the rightful heir, his half-brother. Federico went on to get rich as a soldier-for-hire with his own private army, fighting other peoples' wars—e.g., fighting for Florence against the pope, then the pope against Florence. In the process, the Duke lost an eye and a hunk of his nose in action, and consequently is portrayed only in profile—with his...relatively...good side showing. He expanded his Duchy into an Italian power, amassed a fortune, then settled down to life as a scholar and gentleman. He studied Latin, collected manuscripts, and renovated the palace. Portraits of the Duke often show his dual personality—holding the helmet of a warrior while reading a manuscript like a scholar. Federico aimed to make the Ducal Palace the "dwelling place of the Muses," attracting the big names of his day to this remote cradle of humanism high on a hill in the Marche region. One visitor, Baladassare Castiglione, wrote a book about life here under Federico's son that became a classic profile of the enlightened Renaissance ruler—*The Courtier*.

Helpful Hints

Internet Access: You can get online at Via Mazzini 17, just off Piazza della Repubblica (daily 10:00–24:00).

Public WC: It's just below the main square on Via Mazzini.

Laundry: A self-service launderette is on Via C. Battisti.

Local Guide: Claudia Taglianetti is a good private guide (€80/3 hrs for 1–5 people, €105/3 hrs for 6 or more people, tel. 0722-350-070, claudiataglianetti@libero.it).

Best Gelato: There are two places—each a few steps off the Piazza della Repubblica—where gelato is made on the premises: One is on Via Vittorio Veneto and the other is across from the Church of St. Francis.

SIGHTS

▲▲**Ducal Palace (Palazzo Ducale)**—Built in the mid-1400s, the Ducal Palace is a sprawling and fascinating place. While the rooms are fairly bare, the palace holds a few very special paintings, as well as exquisite inlaid wood decorations. It's a monument to how one man—the Duke of Montefeltro—motored the Renaissance in his small town, about 50 years after it started in Florence (€4, Tue–Sun 8:30–19:15, Mon 8:30–14:00, last entry 1 hour before closing, tel. 0722-377-483).

Urbino

P – Parking

100 YARDS
100 METERS

FORTRESS

PIAZZALE ROMA

PORTA S. LUCIA

V. MINZONI

V. BUOZZI

MACERI

RAFFAELLO

BRAMANTE

RAPHAEL'S HOUSE

ORATORY OF ST. JOHN

PORTA VALBONA

S. MARG.

POST

VIA

ST. FRANCIS

BAROCCI

BUS STATION

VIA MAZZINI

VIA BATTISTI

TO UNIV.

VIA NAZ. 73

CORSO GARIBALDI

S. FIL. NUOVA

VENETO

TO SAN MARINO

VIALE DI VITTORIO

VIA D. MORTI

ENTRY SQUARE

ELEVATOR

CATHEDRAL

VALERIO

BUDASSI

PIAZZA RIN.

DUCAL PALACE

VIA SAFFI

VIA MATTEOTTI

D. MURA

VIA TRAPARIA

BOCCA

73 BIS

TO TRAIN STATION & ASSISI

VA NAZIONALE DI

★ = PIAZZA DELLA REPUBBLICA

❶ Albergo Italia
❷ Albergo San Domenico
❸ Hotel Raffaello
❹ Taverna degli Artisti
❺ Il Coppiere Ristorante
❻ Ristorante/Pizzeria Tre Piante
❼ Enoteca (Wine Bar)
❽ Internet Café

Your visit is simple: the library and basement (off the main courtyard) and the first floor. The second floor was added a century after the rest of the building; it's filled with porcelain and Mannerist paintings—you can skip it. Precious little is explained in English. Buy a book or follow this basic self-guided tour:

Courtyard: Just past the ticket desk, you'll enter the courtyard, exuberantly Renaissance in its flavor. Architect Luciano Laurana patterned it after the trend-setting Medici palace in Florence, with the same graceful arches atop Corinthian columns. Their light color contrasts pleasantly with the darker colored brick. In the upper story (added later), windows and half-columns match perfectly with the arches and columns beneath them. Notice how the courtyard bows up in good Renaissance style—it collected rainwater, helping power the palace's fancy plumbing system.

Library (Biblioteca del Duca): When the Pope took over Urbino in 1657, he also removed the duke's collection of over 2,000 manuscripts—Duke Federico had preferred manuscripts to newfangled books—transporting them back to the Vatican. Today the library displays the travertine (soft marble) reliefs that used to decorate the palace exterior with scenes of work and war. The duke's eagle-in-the-sun emblem on the ceiling symbolizes how he brought enlightenment to his realm.

Basement (Sotterranei): Wandering through the basement, look for bits of exposed plumbing, a huge cistern-like refrigerator (where snow was packed each winter), and a giant stable with a clever horse-pie disposal system. The palace is so big—with five levels and several hundred rooms—it was called "a city in the shape of a palace."

First Floor: Your route is a one-way system with numbered rooms and meager English descriptions. The first section—the guest rooms—is now filled with the Galleria Nazionale delle Marche, the most important collection of paintings in the Marche region. At one time, this palace held many of the highlights of Florence's Uffizi collection (such as Titian's *Venus of Urbino*). As the Vatican army was about to take the city, the last duchess fled to Florence and later married a Medici. She took with her as many of her family's art treasures as possible—quite a dowry.

Room 1: The fireplace—with an orgy of Greek-style decoration—is typical of the Renaissance, celebrating the rebirth of the cultural greatness that Europe hadn't seen since the glory days of ancient Greece and Rome. Piero della Francesca's *Flagellation* is worth a close look. Pilate, dressed as a Turk, watches Jesus being whipped—an allegory of the Turks threatening Christendom. The three men on the right seem to discuss how Europe will handle this threat from the east. Notice how, in true Renaissance fashion, Jesus stands under a column capped with a classical statue. Together, Jesus and the pre-Christian god seem to illuminate the ceiling. To a Renaissance thinker, there was no contradiction in celebrating Christian and pre-Christian ideals simultaneously.

The Duke's Study: The duke's richly-paneled study is the highlight of the palace. Take time to really look at the exquisite inlaid images. Note the mastery of perspective (for example, the latticed cupboard doors appear perfectly open). Let the duke share his passions: art, culture, religion, war, love, music, and caged birds. The period instruments include a delightful lute with a broken string. The duke considered himself an intellectual, inspired by the many great scholars he portrayed on the walls higher up.

Room 20: In the duke's bedroom, the inlaid door shows a medieval fortress facing a Renaissance palazzo—a clear allegory of how war brings darkness, while the new enlightened thought leads to a wide-open sea (in the background), a symbol of good and cultured living. The mercenary warlord put his initials—FEDVX (Federico Duke)—over the palazzo rather than the old-school fortress.

Room 21: This is called the "Angels' Room" for the fun-loving angels—with golden penises—decorating the fireplace mantle. The whole idea in these humanistic times was that life is good—angels can party, and people are invited, too. It's *dolce vita* time! Note the painting of the ideal city by Luciano Laurana—the primary architect of this complex and marvelous palace.

While Laurana's city was never built, it shows the "divine proportions" of the day—balance, harmony, and light. The church is round, like a classical temple. Uninhabited, with black windows, it has a metaphysical feeling. A utopian city...is it possible? The only hint of real life: two tiny birds.

Nearby, the long, skinny panel by Uccello tells the sad story of a Christian woman who pawns some communion bread to a Jewish moneylender. He toasts it and it overflows with blood. She is executed and so is the Jew (with his entire family—children and all, burned at the stake). Because she asked for forgiveness, angels at the woman's deathbed wait to catch her soul the moment it vacates the body (normal exit path: through the mouth). The devils at her feet don't stand a chance.

Room 23: This room features the early-Renaissance paintings of Giovanni Santi, Raphael's father.

Room 25: You'll find the actual Raphaels here. The prize of the collection is Raphael's *Portrait of a Gentlewoman* (a.k.a. *La Muta*), a divinely beautiful portrait of a young woman. (Some think this artwork is a hidden self-portrait of Raphael.) Her hands are perfectly realistic. One possible interpretation of the scene is that the woman has accepted an offer of marriage: Her necklace is knotted (her heart is tied up); she holds a letter (which told of the offer); and the portrait was sent to the nobleman who asked for her hand. Her melancholy but determined face seems to say, "This is a serious commitment that I am ready to undertake." Raphael painted this (as Leonardo painted the *Mona Lisa*) with oil on wood. Mussolini, thinking it only right that at least one great Raphael should reside in the hometown of the master, had this piece moved from Florence to Urbino. The tiny altar wing (to the right) was purchased from the Marcos estate in the Philippines.

Room 28: Look out the window for a good view of the lower town—the palace is built right on the edge of a cliff. The cluster of houses below you was the Jewish ghetto (synagogue on lower left, with the two semi-circular windows). The fortress on the hilltop guarded the town. Today it offers a postcard view of Urbino—worth the climb (see "Fortress View," below).

Leaving the Palace: Locals consider the adjacent cathedral an eyesore for its towering neoclassical facade. In a town of fine Renaissance facades, this church (built after an earthquake destroyed the original around 1800) sticks out like a dog's balls. Next to the cathedral is the bishop's residence and across the street from that is the City Hall with its three flags: Europe, Italy, and UNESCO (the town is proud of its special World Heritage status).

▲**Oratory of St. John**—The Oratory of St. John (San Giovanni), the only other important interior in town, is worth a look for its remarkable frescoes. This was built by a brotherhood dedicated to St. John the Baptist. They were committed to performing random acts of kindness while wearing masks, in order to be humble about their Christian charity. The interior tells the story of the life of St. John the Baptist, from the events leading up to his birth to his beheading at the request of Herod's dancing daughter Salomé (the actual scene where Herod presents his head to the *femme fatale* is missing).

Study the exuberant scene engulfing the Crucifixion. The two thieves crucified alongside Jesus meet their eternal fates—the soul of the man who repented is grabbed by an angel, the other by the devil. The mischievous devil was given mirrors for eyes—sure to freak out the faithful 600 years ago. Above it all, a pelican pecks flesh from its own breast to feed its children—symbolic of the amazing power of Christian love.

This fresco was painted in 1400, before the Renaissance arrived in Urbino. It's a good example of the last stage of Gothic—called "International Gothic"—characterized by lots of color, jam-packed with detail and decor, and featuring a post-plague "we survived, let's enjoy life" outlook. Take a peek at Urbino circa 1400 in the people and slice-of-life corners of this art.

Before you leave, check out the view of the Duke's Palace and the ghetto from the little room adjacent the chapel (€2, Mon–Sat 10:00–12:30 & 15:00–17:30, Sun 10:00–12:30, 5-min walk from main square—follow signs, Piazza Baricci 31; if no one's there, find attendant at church a few steps away).

Fortress View—For the ultimate Urbino view, complete with its hilly countryside, climb up to the fortress (closed but surrounded by a grassy park). The Franciscan church spire, on the left, marks the main square. The hill behind that is the site of a huge kite festival (first Sun of each Sept). In the distance, on a ridge to the right, is the duke's mausoleum, with the cypress trees next to it marking the community cemetery. The city gathers around the immense Ducal Palace. To the right of the palace, you can see today's parking lot, once the parade ground for the duke's army. The long front of its once-immense horse stables leads to a round tower, which provided a spiral ramp for horses to romp right up to the palace. While the fortress behind you is empty, the nearby bar is inviting.

SLEEPING

(€1 = about $1.20, country code: 39)

In Urbino

The TI has a line on lots of local families renting rooms. Otherwise, Urbino's accommodations scene is limited to a few comfortable, expensive hotels.

$$$ Albergo San Domenico is a four-star place across from the Ducal Palace, with 31 spacious, air-conditioned rooms. It offers all of the modern comforts and none of the traditional character (Db-€107-185, breakfast-€11, convenient parking-€8/day, Piazza Rinascimento 3, tel. 0722-2626, fax 0722-2727, www.viphotels.it, sandomenico@viphotels.it).

$$$ Hotel Raffaello is a more humble place buried in the back streets, a two-minute walk from the main square (14 newly renovated rooms, Db-€118 with breakfast, air-con, Vicolino S. Margherita 40, tel. 0722-4784, fax 0722-328-540, www.albergoraffaello.com, info@albergoraffaello.com).

$$ Albergo Italia has 43 modern, business-class rooms in the old town (Db-€90, air-con, ride elevator from town entry and walk 100 yards down Corso Garibaldi arcade to Corso Garibaldi 38, tel. 0722-2701, fax 0722-322-664, www.albergo-italia-urbino.it, info@albergo-italia-urbino.it).

Near Urbino

$$ *Agriturismo:* At **Locanda della Valle Nuova,** a 185-acre organic farm eight miles outside Urbino, they raise cattle, pigs, and poultry; grow grapes for their wine; and harvest wheat for their homemade bread and pasta. The six rooms are tranquil and cozy (Db-€96, includes buffet breakfast, Db-€144 also includes 5-course evening meal, cash only, closed early Nov–mid June, 3-night minimum, reserve 1 day in advance, swimming pool, horseback riding, 2 miles south of Fermingnano at La Cappella 14, Sagrata di Fermingnano, tel. & fax 0722-330-303, www.vallenuova.it, info@vallenuova.it).

EATING

Taverna degli Artisti is a friendly place with a breezy terrace and good traditional cuisine (daily 12:30–14:30 & 19:30–22:30, sometimes closed Tue, great pizzas, Via Bramante 52, tel. 0722-2676).

At **Il Coppiere,** your entire meal, including the post-dinner *grappa*, can involve truffles (daily 12:00–14:00 & 19:00–22:30, Via Santa Margherita 1, tel. 0722-322-326).

Ristorante/Pizzeria Tre Piante serves great food with a smile on a delightful terrace overlooking the Marche hills (Tue–Sun

12:00–15:00 & 19:30–22:30, closed Mon, Via Voltaccia della Vecchia 1, tel. 0722-4863). The *enoteca* at the top of Via Raphael (at #54)—which sells good locals wines by the glass—is a fun place to drop by.

TRANSPORTATION CONNECTIONS

Buses connect Urbino with Pesaro, on the Ravenna-Pescara train line (buses run hrly, 60-min trip). The Pesaro bus stop is 100 yards from its train station. In Urbino, buses come and go from the Borgo Mercatale parking lot below the town, where an elevator lifts you up to the base of the Ducal Palace (or take a 5-min steep walk up Via Mazzini to Piazza della Repubblica).

Orvieto

Just off the freeway, Umbria's grand hill town is no secret, but it's worth a visit. The town sits majestically a thousand feet above the valley floor on a big chunk of tufa, a very soft and easy-to-dig volcanic stone from Lake Bolsena. Since the Etruscan era, city dwellers have created a honeycomb of tunnels and catacombs underneath its streets.

Orvieto, which has three popular claims to fame (cathedral, Classico wine, and ceramics), is loaded with tourists by day and quiet by night. Drinking a shot of wine in a ceramic cup as you gaze up at the cathedral lets you experience Orvieto all at once. (What I like best about Orvieto is its easy bus connection with my favorite hill town, Civita—covered on page 501.)

Piazza Cahen is a key transportation hub at the entry to the hilltop town. As you exit the funicular, the town center and cathedral are straight ahead.

ORIENTATION

Tourist Information

The TI is at Piazza Duomo 24 on the cathedral square (Mon–Fri 8:15–13:50 & 16:00–19:00, Sat–Sun 10:00–13:00 & 15:00–18:00, tel. 0763-341-772). Pick up the free city map and ask about train and bus schedules. The TI sells a €3 admission ticket for the Chapel of St. Brizio (the highlight of your cathedral visit and not sold there).

For a longer visit, consider buying the €12.50 Carta Unica **combo-ticket.** It covers entry to the chapel, the Archaeological Museum (Museo Claudio Faina e Museo Civico), Underground Orvieto Tours, and Torre del Moro (tower), plus either five hours of parking (at *parcheggio* Campo della Fiera) or a full day of public transportation (bus and funicular).

Arrival in Orvieto

By Train: A handy funicular/bus shuttle will take you quickly from the train station (no baggage storage) and parking lot to the top of the town. Buy your ticket at the entrance to the *funiculare;* look for the *biglietteria* sign. The €0.90 ticket includes the funicular plus the minibus from Piazza Cahen to Piazza Duomo—where you'll find most everything that matters. (Or you can pay €0.65 for the funicular only—the best choice if you're staying at the recommended Hotel Corso.) The funicular runs every 10 minutes (Mon–Sat 7:20–20:30, Sun 8:00–20:30).

As you exit the funicular at the top, you're in Piazza Cahen. To your left is a ruined fortress with a garden, WC, and a commanding view, and to your right are St. Patrick's Well (described below), Etruscan ruins, and another sweeping view. Just in front of you is an orange bus waiting to shuttle you to the town center. It'll drop you off at the TI (last stop, in front of cathedral).

If you forgot to check at the station for the train schedule to your next destination (and now the station is far, far below), Orvieto is ready for you. The train schedule is posted at the top of the funicular and is also available at the TI.

By Car: Drivers park at the base of the hill at the huge, free lot behind the Orvieto train station (follow the *P funiculare* signs), or also for free in Piazza Cahen or on Via Roma; otherwise go to the pay lot to the right of Orvieto's cathedral (€0.80 for first hour, €0.60/hr thereafter).

By Taxi: Taxis from the station to the cathedral cost around €11. You might find a taxi at the station, but it's more likely that you'll need to call (Giuliotaxi tel. 360-433-057). Enthusiastic Giulio and his sister Maria Serena also do tours of the countryside, and can provide easy (but not cheap) transportation to Bagnoregio.

Helpful Hints

Market Days: On Tuesday and Saturday mornings, Piazza del Popolo becomes a busy farmers market.

Day-Trippers: Be warned—there's likely no place to check your bag at the station.

SIGHTS

Piazza Duomo

▲▲**Duomo**—The cathedral has Italy's liveliest facade (from 1330, by Lorenzo Maitani and others). This colorful, prickly face, divided by four pillars, has been compared to a medieval altarpiece. Grab a gelato (buy it to the left of the church) and study this gleaming mass of mosaics, stained glass, and sculpture.

At the base of the cathedral, the broad marble pillars carved

Orvieto

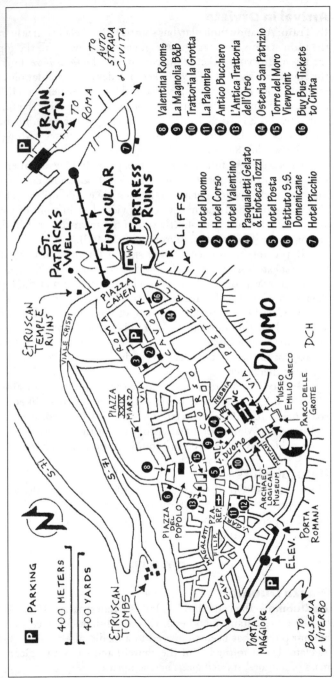

1. Hotel Duomo
2. Hotel Corso
3. Hotel Valentino
4. Pasqualetti Gelato & Enoteca Tozzi
5. Hotel Posta
6. Istituto S.S. Domenicane
7. Hotel Picchio
8. Valentina Rooms
9. La Magnolia B&B
10. Trattoria la Grotta
11. La Palomba
12. Antico Bucchero
13. L'Antica Trattoria dell'Orso
14. Osteria San Patrizio
15. Torre del Moro Viewpoint
16. Buy Bus Tickets to Civita

with biblical scenes tell the story of the world from left to right. The relief on the far left shows the Creation (see the snake and Eve), next is the Tree of Jesse (father of King David), then the New Testament (look for Mary and a manger, etc.), and on the far right, the Last Judgment (with hell, of course, at the bottom).

Each pillar is topped by a bronze symbol of one of the evangelists: angel (Matthew), lion (Mark), eagle (John), and bull (Luke). The bronze doors are modern, by the Sicilian sculptor Emilio Greco. (A museum devoted to Greco's work is to the right of the church; it's labeled simply *Museo*.) In the mosaic below the rose window, Mary is transported to heaven. In the uppermost mosaic, Mary is crowned.

Inside, the nave is spacious and well-lit, highlighting the black-and-white striped stonework. Why such a big and impressive church in such a little town? Well, first of all, it's not as big as it looks. The architect created an illusion—the nave is wider at the back and narrower at the altar so that from the back it looks like a longer distance to the front. Even so, it's a big and rich church. That's because of a blood-stained cloth, kept in a silver-gilt reliquary in the Chapel of the Corporal *(Capella del Corporale)*, found in the north transept, to the left of the altar.

Chapel of the Corporal: In 1263, a puzzled priest named Peter of Prague passed through Bolsena (a few miles from Orvieto) while on a pilgrimage to Rome. He had doubts that the bread used in Communion could really be transformed into the body of Christ. But during Mass, as he held the host aloft and blessed it, the bread began to bleed, running down his arms and dripping onto a linen cloth (a "corporal") on the altar. The bloody cloth was brought to Orvieto, where Pope Urban IV happened to be visiting. The amazed pope proclaimed a new holiday, Corpus Christi ("Body of Christ"), and the Orvieto cathedral was built (begun 1290) to display the miraculous relic. You can see the Miracle of Bolsena depicted in the faded fresco on the chapel's right wall.

The new cathedral put Orvieto (then known as "Urbs Vetus") on the map, and with lots of pilgrims came lots of wealth. Two future popes used the town as a refuge when their enemies forced them to flee Rome.

Chapel of St. Brizio: This chapel, to the right of the altar, is Orvieto's one must-see artistic sight. It features Luca Signorelli's brilliantly lit frescoes of the apocalypse (1499–1502). Step into the chapel and you're surrounded by vivid scenes crammed with figures. The frescoes depict events at the end of the world, but they also reflect the turbulent political and religious atmosphere of late-15th-century Italy.

In the *Sermon of the Antichrist* (left wall), a crowd gathers around a man preaching from a pedestal. It's the Antichrist, who comes posing as Jesus to mislead the faithful. This befuddled Antichrist forgets his lines mid-speech, but the Devil is on hand to whisper what to say next. His words sow wickedness through the world, including mass executions (left side). The worried woman in red and white (foreground, left of pedestal) receives money from a man for something she's not proud of.

Most likely, the Antichrist himself is a veiled reference to Savonarola (1452–1498), the charismatic Florentine monk who defied the pope, drove the Medici from power, and riled the populace with apocalyptic sermons. Many Italians—including the painter Signorelli—viewed Savonarola as a tyrant and heretic, the Antichrist who was ushering in the Last Days.

In the bottom left corner of the scene is a self-portrait of Luca Signorelli (c. 1450–1523), well-dressed in black with long golden hair. Signorelli, from nearby Cortona, was at the peak of his powers, and this chapel was his masterwork. He looks out proudly as if to say, "I did all this in just three years, on time and on budget," confirming his reputation as a speedy, businesslike painter. Next to him is the artist Fra Angelico, who started the chapel decoration five decades earlier, but completed only two of the ceiling frescoes.

On the right wall (opposite the Antichrist) is the *Resurrection of the Bodies*. Trumpeting angels blow a wake-up call, and the dead climb dreamily out of the earth to be clothed with new bodies. On the same wall is a gripping *pietà*.

The altar wall (with the windows) features the Last Judgment. To the left of the altar (and continuing on the left wall) are the *Elect in Heaven*. They spend eternity posing like body-builders while listening to celestial Muzak. To the right (and continuing on the right wall) are the *Damned in Hell*, the scariest mosh pit ever. Devils torment sinners in graphic detail, while winged demons control the airspace overhead. In the center, one lusty demon turns to tell the frightened woman on his back exactly what he's got planned for their date. Signorelli's ability to tell a story through human actions and gestures, rather than symbols, inspired his younger contemporary, Michelangelo, who meticulously studied the elder artist's nudes.

After leaving the cathedral, if you want a break at a viewpoint park, exit left and pass the small parking lot. The nearest WCs are in the opposite direction, down the stairs from the left transept.

Hours of the Duomo: April–Sept daily 7:30–12:45 & 14:30–19:15, March and Oct closes at 18:15, Nov–Feb at 17:15. Admission is free, but there is a charge for the Chapel of St. Brizio.

Cost and Hours of Chapel: Visitors' hours are Mon–Sat 8:00–12:45 & 14:30–19:15, Sun 14:30–17:45 (closes 1 hour earlier in winter). Buy the €3 ticket at the TI or the shop across the square from the facade of the church; it's included in the €12.50 Carta Unica combo-ticket. Only 25 people are allowed in the chapel at a time.

Archaeological Museum (Museo Claudio Faina e Museo Civico)—Across from the entrance to the cathedral is a fine Etruscan art museum (two upper floors; for background on the Etruscans, see page 694). On the ground floor, there's also a miniscule city-history museum that features a sarcophagus and temple bits. The collection consists largely of Etruscan vases, plates, and coins, with some jewelry and bronze dishes. Many of the vases came from the Etruscan necropolis (Crocifisso del Tufo) just outside Orvieto (€4.50, included in €12.50 Carta Unica combo-ticket, April–Sept Tue–Sun 9:30–18:00, Oct–March Tue–Sun 10:00–17:00, closed Mon, audioguide available, WC after ticket desk and on top floor, tel. 0763-341-511). Look out the windows at the cathedral's glittering facade.

▲**Museo Emilio Greco**—This museum displays the work of Emilio Greco (1913–1995), the Sicilian artist who designed the modern doors of Orvieto's cathedral. His sketches and bronze statues show his absorption with gently twisting and turning nudes. In the back left corner of the museum, look for the sketchy outlines of women—simply beautiful. The artful installation of his work in this palazzo, with walkways and even a spiral staircase up to the ceiling, allows you to view his sculptures from different directions (€2.50, €5.50 includes St. Patrick's Well, April–Sept daily 10:30–13:00 & 14:30–18:00, Oct–March closes 1 hour earlier, next to cathedral, marked *Museo*, tel. 0763-344-605).

Underground Orvieto Tours (Parco delle Grotte)—Guides weave a good archaeological history into an hour-long look at about 100 yards of caves (€5.50, included in €12.50 Carta Unica combo-ticket; 1-hr English tours depart daily from TI at 11:15, 12:30, 16:15, and 17:30; confirm times by calling 0763-340-688, 335-733-2764, or checking with TI). Orvieto is honeycombed with Etruscan and medieval caves. You'll see the remains of an old olive press, two impressive 130-foot-deep Etruscan well shafts, and the remains of a primitive cement quarry. If you want underground Orvieto, this is the place to get it.

In Orvieto

Torre del Moro—For yet another viewpoint, this distinctive square tower comes with 250 steps and an elevator. The elevator goes only partway to the top, leaving you with a mere 173 steps to scurry up (€2.80, included in €12.50 Carta Unica combo-ticket, daily March–Oct 10:00–19:00, May–Aug until 20:00, Nov–Feb 10:30–13:00 & 14:30–17:00, terrace on top, at intersection of Corso Cavour and Via Duomo).

St. Patrick's Well (Pozzo di S. Patrizio)—Engineers are impressed by this deep well—175 feet deep and 45 feet wide—designed in the 16th century with a double-helix pattern. The two spiral stairways allow an efficient one-way traffic flow; intriguing now, but critical then. Imagine if donkeys and people, balancing jugs of water, had to go up and down the same stairway. At the bottom is a bridge that people could walk on to scoop up water.

The well was built because a pope got nervous. After Rome was sacked in 1527 by renegade troops of the Holy Roman Empire, the pope fled to Orvieto. He feared that even this little town (with no water source on top) would be besieged. He commissioned a well, which was started in 1527 and finished 10 years later. It was a huge project. Even today, when a local is faced with a difficult task, people say, "It's like digging St. Patrick's Well." The unusual name came from the well's supposed resemblance to the Irish saint's cave. It's not worth climbing up and down a total of 495 steps; a quick look is painless but pricey (€4.50, €5.50 includes Museo Emilio Greco, daily April–Sept 10:00–18:45, Oct–March 10:00–17:45, the well is to your right as you exit *funiculare*). Bring a sweater if you descend to the chilly depths.

View Walks—For short, pleasant walks, climb the medieval wall (access at western end of town, between Piazza S. Gionvenale and Via Garibaldi) or stroll the promenade park on the northern edge of town (along Viale Carducci, which becomes Gonfaloniera). There is a fine cliffside promenade that runs along much of the town. And after dark, head deep into Orvieto's masculine back streets.

Near Orvieto

Wine Tasting—Orvieto Classico white wine is justly famous. For a short tour of a local winery with Etruscan cellars, visit Tenuta Le Velette, where English-speaking Corrado and Cecilia (cheh-CHEEL-yah) Bottai will welcome you—if you've called ahead to set up an appointment (€8 for tour and tasting, Mon–Fri 8:30–12:00 & 14:00–17:00, Sat 8:30–12:00, closed Sun, mobile 348-300-2002, fax 0763-29114). From their sign (5 min past Orvieto at top of switchbacks just before Canale, on Bagnoregio road), cruise down a long, tree-lined drive, then park at the striped gate (must call ahead; no drop-ins).

SLEEPING

(€1 = about $1.20, country code: 39)

In Orvieto

All of the recommended hotels are in the old town except Hotel Picchio, which is in a more modern neighborhood near the station.

$$$ Hotel Duomo, centrally located, is modern, with splashy art and 17 sleek rooms named after artists who worked on the

Duomo (Sb-€70, Db-€105, Db suite-€120, Tb-€130, 5 percent cash discount with this 2006 book, includes buffet breakfast, elevator, air-con, Internet in lobby, sunny terrace out front; a block from Duomo, church bells ring every quarter-hour through the night, behind *gelateria* at Via di Maurizio 7; tel. 0763-341-887, fax 0763-394-973, www.orvietohotelduomo.com, hotelduomo@tiscalinet.it, Massaccesi family).

$$ Hotel Corso is friendly and clean, with 18 comfy, modern rooms. While some rooms come with balconies and views, everyone can enjoy their sunny little terrace (Sb-€60, Db-€82, 10 percent discount with this 2006 book, buffet breakfast-€6.50, elevator, air-con, garage or free parking nearby, on main street up from funicular toward Duomo at Via Cavour 339, tel. & fax 0763-342-020, www.argoweb.it/hotel_corso or www.hotelcorso.net, info@hotelcorso.net, Carla).

$$ Hotel Valentino offers 19 simple, quiet, overpriced rooms in a modern hotel 200 yards off Corso Cavour. I'd consider it a last resort (Db-€80, price promised with this 2006 book, includes breakfast, elevator, air-con, Via Angelo da Orvieto 30/32, tel. & fax 0763-342-464, hotelvalentino@libero.it).

$ Hotel Posta is a five-minute walk from the cathedral into the medieval core. It's a big, old, formerly elegant but well-cared-for-in-its-decline palazzo with a breezy garden, an elevator, and a grand old lobby. Its 20 spacious, clean, plain rooms hold vintage rickety furniture and good mattresses (S-€31, Sb-€37, D-€43, Db-€56, breakfast-€6, cash only, Via Luca Signorelli 18, tel. & fax 0763-341-909, hotelposta@orvietohotels.it, no English spoken).

$ The sisters of the **Istituto S.S. Domenicane** rent 15 spotless twin rooms in their heavenly convent with a peaceful terrace (Db-€55, cash only, elevator, parking, just off Piazza del Popolo at Via del Popolo 1, tel. & fax 0763-342-910, www.argoweb.it/istituto_sansalvatore/istituto.it.html, institutosansalvatore@tiscalinet.it, no English spoken).

$ Hotel Picchio, with 27 newly remodeled rooms, is a wood-and-marble place, more comfortable but with less character than others in the area. It's in the lower, plainer part of town, 300 yards from the train station (Sb-€37, Db-€53, Tb-€63, ask for the Rick Steves 5 percent discount, rooms with air-con cost extra, Via G. Salvatori 17, tel. & fax 0763-301-144, hotelpicchio@tin.it, family-run by Alessandra and Picchio). A trail leads from here up to the old town.

$ Valentina rents six clean, airy, well-appointed rooms and a studio apartment (all with air-con). Her place is located in the heart of Orvieto, behind the grand staircase in Piazza del Popolo (Db-€57, Tb-€71, these special prices with this book in 2006, cash only, includes breakfast, also rents studio with kitchen-€80 and apartment for up to 5-€150, Via Vivaria 7, tel. 0763-341-607, mobile 335-654-9081, valentina.z@tiscalinet.it).

$ La Magnolia, an Italian B&B, has lots of fancy terracotta tiles and welcoming touches. Its seven rooms, some like mini-apartments with kitchens, are *tranquillo* despite being on the town's main drag (Sb-€30–35, Db-€60, Db apartment-€65, extra person-€30, includes breakfast, cash only, no elevator, Via Duomo 29, tel. 0763-342-808, www.bblamagnolia.it, info@bblamagnolia .it, Serena).

Near Orvieto

$$$ Agriturismo le Casette, outside the village of Baschi and seven miles southeast of Orvieto, is outstanding, with rooms in several restored stone farmhouses clustered around a grassy lawn and a swimming pool with a fabulous view of the green Umbrian landscape (Db-€100–120, includes breakfast and half-pension, tel. 0744-957-645, fax 0744-950-500, www.pomurlovecchio-lecasette .it, pomurlovecchio@tiscalinet.it, run by charming Minghelli family, including Daniela). The same family also owns **$ Pomurlo Vecchio,** a 12th-century tower house with three rooms a few miles away (Db-€65–75, includes breakfast, half-pension not required, tel. 0744-950-190, fax 0744-950-500).

$$$ Agriturismo Fattoria di Vibio produces olive oil and honey, selling organic products and offering cooking courses. In August, its 26 rooms rent at peak prices, and you're required to stay a week, arriving and departing on a Saturday (Db-€80-105, includes breakfast and dinner; Db-€595-735 for weekly rental in August, otherwise €455-665; located about 20 miles northeast of Orvieto, tel. 075-874-9607, fax 075-878-0014, www.fattoriadivibio .com, info@fattoriadivibio.com).

$$ Agriturismo La Rocca Orvieto, run by Emiliano and Sabrina, is a fancy, spa-type place located a 15-minute drive north of Orvieto. La Rocca has 10 double rooms and three apartments— all with air conditioning (Db-€84-114, half-board-€130–160, pool, "wellness center" with Jacuzzi and steam room, gym, hiking paths, tel. 0763-344-210, mobile 348-640-0845, fax 0763-395-155, www. laroccaorvieto.com, info@laroccaorvieto.com).

$ Agriturismo Pomonte Umbria, seven miles east of Orvieto, offers home-cooked meals, lovely vistas, and seven comfortable rooms in a recently built guest house (€27 per person, includes breakfast, €43-half-pension, €53-full pension, Loc. Canino di Orvieto 1, Corbara, tel. 076-330-4041, fax 076-330-4080, www .pomonte.it, info@pomonte.it).

EATING

La Palomba features game meats, steak, and truffle specialties in a wood-paneled dining room (Thu–Tue 12:30–14:15 & 19:30–22:00, closed Wed, reservations smart, Via Cipriano Manente 16, just off Piazza della Repubblica, tel. 0763-343-395).

Antico Bucchero makes a nice splurge for its classy candlelit ambience and good food (€8 pastas, €10 *secondi*, daily 12:00–15:00 & 19:00–24:00, indoor/outdoor seating; a half-block south of Corso Cavour, between Torre del Moro and Piazza della Repubblica at Via de Cartari 4; tel. 0763-341-725).

L'Antica Trattoria dell'Orso offers well-prepared Umbrian cuisine paired with fine wines in a homey and peaceful atmosphere. Ciro and chef Gabriele will steer you toward the freshest seasonal plates (Wed–Sun 12:30–14:00 & 19:30–22:00, closed Mon–Tue, just off Piazza della Repubblica, Via della Misericordia 18/20, tel. 0763-341-642).

Osteria San Patrizio, near the funicular, creatively presents traditional Umbrian specialties (Tue–Sat 12:00–15:00 & 19:00–23:00, Sun 12:00–15:00, closed Mon, Corso Cavour 312, tel. 0763-341-245).

Trattoria la Grotta, a cut above the rest in price and elegance, prides itself on serving only the freshest ingredients and good wine. The decor is Signorelli mod, and the ambience is quiet and classy, with attentive service. The owner/chef Franco—who's been at it for 40 years—promises diners a free coffee, grappa, *limoncello*, or *vin santo* with this 2006 book (closed Tue, Via Luca Signorelli 5, tel. 0763-341-348).

For dessert, try the deservedly popular *gelateria* **Pasqualetti** (daily 12:30–24:00, closed in winter, next to left transept of church, Piazza Duomo 14, another branch is at Corso Cavour 56, open until 20:30 during winter).

Enoteca Tozzi, to the left of the Duomo, serves up rustic *panini*—try the roast suckling pig (*porchetta*, por-KET-tah) if it's available (daily 8:30–21:00, 9:00–20:00 in winter, Piazza Duomo 13, tel. 0763-344-393).

TRANSPORTATION CONNECTIONS

From Orvieto by Train to: Rome (19/day, 75 min, consider leaving your car at the large parking lot behind Orvieto station), **Florence** (14/day, 2.25 hrs), **Siena** (8/day, 2–3 hrs, change in Chiusi, all Florence-bound trains stop in Chiusi). The train station's Buffet della Stazione is surprisingly good if you need a quick focaccia sandwich or pizza picnic for the train ride.

Orvieto and Civita Area

By Bus to Bagnoregio (near Civita): It's a one-hour trip (€2 round-trip). Departures in 2005 from Orvieto's Piazza Cahen on the blue Cotral bus, daily except Sunday: 6:20, 9:10, 12:40, 15:45, and 18:20 (buses stop at Orvieto's train station 5 min later). During the school year (roughly Sept–June), there are additional departures at 7:20, 7:50, and 13:55. Confirm the schedule and buy your round-trip ticket at the train-station bar or at the *tabacchi* stop on Corso Cavour, a block up from the *funiculare*. To find the bus stop, face the *funiculare*. The bus stop is at the far left end of Piazza Cahen where the blue buses are parked (no schedule posted; confirm departure and return times with driver). If you catch the bus down below at Orvieto's train station, wait at the left of the base of the funicular station (as you're facing it). Once you're in Bagnoregio, you'll find the Bagnoregio–Orvieto bus schedule posted at the bus stop.

Tip for Drivers: If you're thinking of driving to Rome, consider stashing your car here instead. You can easily park the car, safe and free, behind the Orvieto train station, and zip effortlessly into Rome by train (75 min).

Civita di Bagnoregio

Perched on a pinnacle in a grand canyon, the traffic-free village of Civita is Italy's ultimate hill town. Curl your toes around its Etruscan roots.

Civita (chee-VEE-tah) is terminally ill. Only 14 residents—mostly in their 80s—remain as, bit by bit, the town is being purchased by rich big-city Italians who come here to escape on vacation. Civita is connected to the world and the town of Bagnoregio by a long pedestrian bridge—and a Web site (www.civitadibagnoregio.it).

Civita's history goes back to Etruscan and ancient Roman times. In the early Middle Ages, Bagnoregio was a suburb of Civita, which had a population of around 4,000. Later, Bagnoregio surpassed Civita in size. (You'll notice Bagnoregio is dominated by Renaissance-style buildings while, architecturally, Civita remains stuck in the medieval era.)

While Bagnoregio lacks the pinnacle-town romance of Civita, it's actually a healthy, vibrant community (unlike Civita, the suburb now nicknamed "the dead city"). In Bagnoregio, get a haircut, sip a coffee on the square, and walk down to the old laundry (ask, *"Dov'è la lavanderia vecchia?"*). A Spesa supermarket is 300 yards from the bus stop (Mon–Sat 8:30–13:00 & 17:00–20:00, closed Sun, take main drag from town gate away from Civita and angle right at pyramid monument). A lively market fills the bus parking lot each Monday.

Off-season, Civita and Bagnoregio are deadly quiet—and cold. I'd side-trip in quickly from Orvieto or skip the area altogether.

ORIENTATION

Arrival in Bagnoregio, near Civita

If you're arriving by bus from Orvieto, you'll get off at the bus stop in Bagnoregio. Look at the posted bus schedule and write down the return times to Orvieto. (Drivers, see "Transportation Connections" at the end of this chapter.)

Baggage Check: While there's no official baggage-check service in Bagnoregio, I've arranged with Mauro Laurenti, who runs the Bar/Enoteca/Caffè Gianfu, to let you leave your bags there (€1/bag, daily 7:00–13:00 & 13:30–24:00, closed Thu Oct–March; to get to café from Orvieto bus stop where you got off, go back in the direction that the Orvieto bus just came from and go right around corner).

From Bagnoregio to Civita: Civita sits at the opposite end of Bagnoregio, about a mile away. From Bagnoregio, you can walk (20 min) or take a little orange shuttle bus to the base of the bridge to

Civita. From here, you have to walk the rest of the way. It's a 10-minute hike up a pedestrian bridge that gets steeper near the end.

The little shuttle **bus** runs from Bagnoregio (catch bus across from gas station) to the base of the bridge (€1, pay driver, 10-min ride, first bus at 7:39, last at 18:20, 1–2/hr except during 13:00–15:30 siesta, spotty service off-season). If you'll want to return to Bagnoregio by bus, check the schedule posted near the bridge (at edge of parking lot, where bus let you off) before you head up to Civita.

To **walk** from Bagnoregio to the base of Civita's bridge (about 20 min, fairly level), take the road going uphill (overlooking the big parking lot). Once on the road, take the first right and an immediate left onto the main drag, Via Roma. Follow this straight out to the belvedere for a superb viewpoint. From the viewpoint, backtrack a few steps (staircase at end of viewpoint is a dead end) and take the stairs down to the road leading to the bridge.

SELF-GUIDED WALK

Welcome to Civita

Civita was once connected to Bagnoregio. The saddle between the separate towns eroded away. Photographs around town show the old donkey path, the original bridge. It was bombed in World War II and replaced in 1965 with the new **bridge** you're climbing today. The town's hearty old folks hang on to the bridge's hand railing when fierce winter weather rolls through.

Entering the town, you'll pass through a cut in the rock (made by Etruscans 2,500 years ago) and under a 12th-century Romanesque **arch.** This was the main Etruscan road leading to the Tiber Valley and Rome.

Inside the town gate, on your left (in front of the WC) is the old **laundry**—once a lively village gossip center. On your right, a fancy wooden door and windows (above the door) lead to thin air. This was the facade of a Renaissance palace—one of five that once graced Civita. It fell into the valley riding a chunk of the ever-eroding rock pinnacle. Today, the door leads to a remaining section of the palace—complete with Civita's first hot tub—owned by the "Marchesa," a countess who married into Italy's biggest industrialist family.

Peek into the small Pina's Pizzeria to see some historic photographs of Civita. Pina welcomes visitors to just enjoy the museum-like photos without having to buy anything (although her homemade cookies—*Biscotti de Civita*—are hard to resist). Check out the canyon **viewpoint** a few steps away. Just beyond that is the site of the long-gone home of Civita's one famous son, St. Bonaventure, known as the "second founder of the Franciscans."

Now wander to the **town square** in front of the church, where

Civita di Bagnoregio

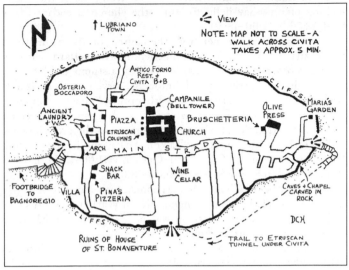

↑ LUBRIANO
TOWN

← VIEW

NOTE: MAP NOT TO SCALE - A
WALK ACROSS CIVITA
TAKES APPROX. 5 MIN.

CLIFFS

ANTICO FORNO
REST. +
CIVITA B+B

OSTERIA
BOCCADORO

CLIFFS

MARIA'S
GARDEN

ANCIENT
LAUNDRY
+ W.C.

CAMPANILE
(BELL TOWER)

OLIVE
PRESS

PIAZZA

BRUSCHETTERIA

ETRUSCAN
COLUMNS

CHURCH

ARCH   MAIN   STRADA

SNACK
BAR

WINE
CELLAR

CAVES + CHAPEL
CARVED IN
ROCK

FOOTBRIDGE
TO
BAGNOREGIO

VILLA

PINA'S
PIZZERIA

DCH

CLIFFS

RUINS OF HOUSE
OF ST. BONAVENTURE

TRAIL TO ETRUSCAN
TUNNEL UNDER CIVITA

you'll find Civita's only public phone, bar, and restaurant—and a wild donkey race on the first Sunday of June and the second Sunday of September. The church marks the spot where an Etruscan temple, and then a Roman temple, once stood. The pillars that stand like giants' bar stools are ancient—Etruscan.

Go into the **church.** It was a cathedral until 1699, with records of about 60 bishops that date back to the seventh century. You'll see frescoes and statues from "the school of Donatello." The central altar is built upon the relics of the Roman martyr St. Victoria, who once was the patron saint of the town. St. Ildebrando served as a bishop here in the ninth century; an altar dedicated to him is on the right.

The fine crucifix, carved out of peach wood in the 15th century, is from the school of Donatello. It's remarkably expressive and greatly venerated by locals. Jesus' gaze is almost haunting. Some say his appearance changes based on what angle you view him from: looking alive from the front, in agony from the left, and dead from the right. Regardless, his eyes follow you from side to side. On Good Friday, this crucifix is the focus of the midnight procession.

On the left side of the nave is the intimate fresco of the *Madonna of the Earthquake,* given this name because—in the shake of 1695—the whitewash fell off and revealed this tender fresco of Mary and her child. (During the Baroque era, a white-and-bright interior was in vogue; churches such as these—which were covered with precious and historic frescoes—were simply whitewashed over.) On the same wall—toward the front—find a faded portrait of Santa Lucia, the patron saint of your teeth; notice the scary-looking pincers. Say hello to Aura, the church attendant (daily 9:30–12:30 & 15:00–18:30).

Just around the corner from the church, on the main street, is Rossana and Antonio's cool and friendly **wine cellar** (their sign reads *bruschette con prodotti locali*). Pull up a stump and let them or their children, Arianna and Antonella, serve you *panini* (sandwiches), *bruschetta* (garlic toast with optional tomato topping), wine, and a local cake called *ciambella*. Climb down into the cellar and note the traditional wine-making gear and the provisions for rolling huge kegs up the stairs. Tap on the kegs in the cool bottom level to see which are full (April–Oct daily 11:00–17:00, later in Aug, Nov–March only Sat–Sun 10:00–18:00).

The rock below Civita is honeycombed with ancient cellars (for keeping wine at the same temperature all year) and cisterns (for collecting rainwater, since there was no well in town). Many of these date from Etruscan times.

Explore farther down the street, until you come to Vittoria's **mill** *(mulino)*, an atmospheric collection of old olive presses, and a quaint little eatery. The huge press in the entry is about 1,500 years old. Until the 1960s, blindfolded donkeys trudged in the circle here, crushing olives, and creating paste that filled the circular filters and was put into a second press. Notice the 2,500-year-old sarcophagus niche. The hole in the floor (with the glass top) was a garbage hole. In ancient times, residents would toss their jewels down when under attack; excavations uncovered a windfall of treasures (donation requested, give about €1).

Antico Frantoio Bruschetteria is a rustic place for a bite to eat. Vittoria's sons, Sandro, Maurizio, and Felice, and her grandson Fabrizio (with his American wife, Heather) run the local equivalent of a lemonade stand, toasting delicious *bruschetta* (roughly 10:00–20:00 in summer, winter Sat–Sun only, tel. 0176-948-429). Peruse the menu, choose your topping (chopped tomato is super), and get a glass of wine for a fun, affordable snack.

Twenty yards farther down (on the left), Maria is waiting to show you through her **garden** with a grand view (Maria's Giardino, €1 donation) and share historical misinformation (she says Civita and Lubriano were once connected). Maria's husband, Peppone, used to carry goods on a donkey back and forth 40 times a day on the path between the old town and Bagnoregio. As you view the canyon in which Civita is stranded, imagine the work the two rivers did—in the same style as the Colorado River—to carve all this. Listen to the roosters and voices from distant farms.

At the end of town, the main drag winds downhill past small **Etruscan caves** to your right. The first two were used as stables until a few years ago. The third cave is an unusual chapel, cut deep into the rock, with a barred door; this is the **Chapel of the Incarcerated** (Cappella del Carcere). In Etruscan times, the chapel—with a painted tile depicting the Madonna and child—may have originally been a tomb, and in medieval times, it was used as a jail. When Civita's few residents have a religious procession, they come here in honor of the Madonna of the Incarcerated.

After the chapel, the paving-stone path peters out into a dirt trail leading down and around to the right to a **tunnel.** Dating from the Etruscan era, the tunnel—tall enough for a woman with a jug on her head to pass through—may have served as a shortcut to the river below. It was widened in the 1930s so farmers could get between their scattered fields more easily. Think of the scared villagers who huddled here for refuge during WWII bombing raids. Backtrack to the town square.

Evenings on the town square are a bite of Italy. The same people sit on the same church steps under the same moon, night after night, year after year. I love my cool, late evenings in Civita. If you visit in the morning, have cappuccino and rolls at the small café on the town square.

Whenever you visit, stop halfway up the donkey path and listen to the sounds of rural Italy. Reach out and touch one of the Monopoly houses. If you know how to turn the volume up on the crickets, do so.

SLEEPING

(€1 = about $1.20, country code: 39)
The Romantica Pucci B&B is decidedly the best option.

In Civita
$ Civita B&B, run by Franco Sala (who also owns Trattoria Antico Forno), has three basic rooms overlooking Civita's main square (D-€62, Db-€68, T-€78, includes miniscule breakfast, €15 more per person for optional half-pension, Piazza del Duomo Vecchio, tel. 0761-760-016, mobile 347-611-5426, www.civitadibagnoregio.it, fsala@pelagus.it).

In Bagnoregio
$$ Hotel Fidanza, near the bus stop in Bagnoregio, is tired but sleepable. Of its 25 rooms, #206 and #207 have views of Civita (Sb-€45, Db-€72, price promised with this book in 2006, includes breakfast, cash only, attached restaurant, Via Fidanza 25, Bagnoregio/Viterbo, tel. & fax 0761-793-444).

$ Romantica Pucci B&B is a haven for city-weary travelers. Its five spacious rooms are indeed romantic, with canopied beds and flowing veils. Both homey and elegant, it's like sleeping at Katharine Hepburn's place. Pucci and Lamberto take special care of their guests (Db-€70, includes breakfast, attached restaurant is popular with guests—go for the "Trust Pucci" €15 special family-style dinner, Piazza Cavour 1, tel. 0761-792-121, www .hotelromanticapucci.it, hotelromanticapucci@libero.it). It's just above the parking lot you see when you arrive in Bagnoregio—look for a sign marking its private parking place—and it's half a block before the town's main square, facing the main drag.

EATING

In and near Civita

While the food's nothing special in Civita, the ambience is hard to beat. **Trattoria Antico Forno** serves up pasta at affordable prices (daily for lunch 12:30–15:30 and sporadically for dinner 19:30–22:00, on main square, also rents rooms—see Civita B&B listing above, tel. 0761-760-016). **Osteria Boccadoro** serves visitors on its cute covered patio just off the main square (tel. 0761-780-775). At **Da Peppone,** the small café/bar on the square, you can get simple treats and Civita souvenirs (daily 9:30–12:30 & 14:00–19:00, closed 17:00 and Mon or Tue in winter, tel. 0761-79320). **Pina's Pizzeria** cooks up good pizza and homemade sweets to eat there or to go (daily 12:00–22:00, near entry into town).

Hostaria del Ponte is *the* place for serious cooking. It offers light, creative, and traditional cuisine with a great view terrace at the parking lot at the base of the bridge to Civita. Big space-heaters make it comfortable to enjoy the wonderful view as you dine from their rooftop terrace even in spring and fall (€5 pastas, €10 *secondi*, Tue–Sun 12:30–14:30 & 19:30–21:30, closed Mon, Nov–April closed Sun, tel. 0761-793-565, Lorena).

If in Bagnoregio, check out **Il Fumatore di Pizzo Ornelio** for Italian cuisine (Fri–Wed 12:30–15:00 & 19:00–22:00, closed Thu, on Piazza Marconi 5, 0761-792-642).

TRANSPORTATION CONNECTIONS

From Bagnoregio to Orvieto: Public buses (6/day, 1 hr, €2 round-trip) connect Bagnoregio to the rest of the world via Orvieto. Departures in 2005 from Bagnoregio, daily except Sunday: 5:30, 9:55, 10:10, 13:00, 14:25, and 17:25. During the school year (roughly Sept–June), buses also run at 6:35, 6:50, 13:35, and 16:40 (for info on coming from Orvieto, see "Transportation Connections" for Orvieto, page 499).

Driving from Orvieto to Bagnoregio: Orvieto overlooks the autostrada (and has its own exit). The shortest way to Civita from the freeway exit is to turn left (below Orvieto) and then simply follow the signs to Lubriano and Bagnoregio.

The more winding and scenic route takes 20 minutes longer: From the freeway, pass under hill-capping Orvieto (on your right, signs to Lago di Bolsena, on Viale I Maggio), then take the first left (direction: Bagnoregio), winding up past great Orvieto views through Canale, and through farms and fields of giant shredded wheat to Bagnoregio.

Either way, just before Bagnoregio, follow the signs left to Lubriano and pull into the first little square by the church on your right for a breathtaking view of Civita. Then return to the Bagnoregio road.

You have two choices for parking your car when you get to the brink of Civita. You can leave your car at the bus lot on the edge of town or drive through Bagnoregio (following yellow *Civita* signs) to the lot at the base of the steep pedestrian bridge (€1/hr—pay at shop or in restaurant, probably free weekdays and off-season when no attendant is around). The bridge at this parking lot leads up to the traffic-free, 2,500-year-old, canyon-swamped pinnacle town of Civita di Bagnoregio.

MORE HILL TOWNS

If you haven't gotten your fill of hill towns, here are more to check out. I've also listed some worthwhile sights, plus a couple of recommended driving routes to connect the dots.

Hill Towns

▲**Gubbio**—This handsome town climbs Monte Ingino in northeast Umbria. Tuesday is market day, when Piazza 40 Martiri (named for 40 local martyrs shot by the Nazis) bustles. Nearby, the ruins of the Roman amphitheater are perfect for a picnic. Head up Via della Repubblica to the main square with the imposing Palazzo dei Consoli. Farther up, Via San Gerolamo leads to the funky lift that will carry you up the hill in two-person "baskets" for a stunning view from the top, where the basilica of St. Ubaldo is worth a look. The **TI** is at Piazza Oderisi 6 (Mon–Fri 8:00–14:00 & 15:30–18:30, Sat 9:00–13:00 & 15:30–18:30, Sun 9:30–12:00 & 15:30–18:30, tel. 075-922-0693).

Buses run to Perugia, Rome, and Florence.

▲**Bevagna**—This sleeper of a town south of Assisi has Roman ruins, interesting churches, and more. Locals offer their guiding services for free (usually Italian-speaking only) and are excited to show visitors their town. Get a map at the **TI** on Piazza Silvestri (daily 9:30–12:30 & 15:00–19:00, tel. 0742-361-667) and wander. Highlights are the Roman mosaics, remains of the arena that now houses a paper-making workshop, the Romanesque church of San Silvestro, and a gem of a 19th-century theater. Bevagna has all the elements of a hill town except one—a hill. You can see the main sights easily in a couple of hours. For an overnight stay, consider the fancy Hotel Palazzo Brunamonti (Db-€75–86, more for *superiore* room, air-con, Corso Matteotti 79, tel. 0742-361-932, fax 0742-361-948, www.brunamonti.com, hotel@brunamonti.com).

Buses connect Bevagna with Foligno (except on Sun).

▲**Spello**—Umbrian hill town aficionados always include Spello on their list. Just six miles south of Assisi, this town is much less touristy than its neighbor to the north. Spello will give your legs a workout. Via Consolare goes up, up, up to the top of town. Views from the terrace of the restaurant Il Trombone will have you singing a tune. The **TI** is on Piazza Matteotti 3 (daily 9:30–12:30 & 15:30–19:30, tel. 0742-301-009).

Spello is on the Perugia–Assisi–Foligno train line. Buses run to Assisi.

▲**Chiusi**—This small hill town (rated ▲▲ for Etruscan fans), once one of the most important Etruscan cities, is now a key train junction on the Florence–Rome line. The region's trains (to Siena, Orvieto, and Assisi) go through or change at this hub.

Highlights include the Archaeological Museum and the Etruscan tombs located just outside of town near Lago di Chiusi (€4, daily 9:00–20:00, Via Porsenna 93, tel. 0578-20177). One of the tombs is multichambered, with several sarcophagi. Another, the Tomba della Scimmia (Tomb of the Monkey), has some well-preserved frescoes. Visiting the tombs requires a guide, arranged through the TI or the Archaeological Museum (5 people allowed to view at a time).

Troglodyte alert! The Cathedral Museum on the main square has a dark, underground labyrinth of Etruscan tunnels (bring a flashlight). The mandatory guided tour of the tunnels ends in a large Roman cistern from which you can climb the church bell tower for an expansive view of the countryside (museum-€2, labyrinth-€3, combo-ticket-€4, daily 9:30–12:45 & 16:00–19:00, tunnel tours at 11:00 and 16:00, Piazza Duomo 1, tel. 0578-226-490). To read up on the Etruscans, see page 694.

The **TI** is on the main square (Mon–Fri 10:00–13:00, maybe afternoons in summer, closed Sat-Sun, tel. 0578-227-667, prolocochiusi@bcc.tin.it). Trains connect Chiusi with Rome, Florence, Siena, and more. Buses link the train station with the town center two miles away.

Sights

▲**U.S. Cemetery**—The compelling sight of endless rows of white marble crosses and Stars of David recalls the heroism of the young

Americans who fought so valiantly to free Italy (and ultimately Europe) from the grips of fascism. This particular cemetery is the final resting place of more than 4,000 Americans who died in the liberation of Italy during World War II. Climb the hill past the perfectly-manicured lawn, lined with grave markers, to the memorial, where maps and a history of the Italian campaign detail the Allied advance (daily mid-April–Sept 9:00–18:00, Oct–mid-April 9:00–17:00, 7 miles south of Florence, off Via Cassia that parallels the *superstrada* between Florence and Siena, 2 miles south of Florence Certosa exit on A-1 autostrada). Buses from Florence stop just outside the cemetery.

San Galgano Monastery—Of southern Tuscany's several evocative monasteries, San Galgano is the best. Set in a forested area called the *Montagnolo* (medium-sized mountains), the isolated abbey and chapel are postcard-perfect. San Galgano was a 12th-century saint who renounced his past as a knight to become a hermit. Lacking a cross to display, he created his own by miraculously burying his sword up to its hilt into a stone, à la King Arthur, but in reverse. After his death, a large Cistercian monastery complex grew. Today all you'll see is the roofless, ruined abbey and, on a nearby hill, the Chapel of San Galgano with its fascinating dome and sword in the stone. The adjacent gift shop sells a little bit of everything, from wine to postcards to herbs, some of it monk-made (free, daily 8:00–sunset). For a quick snack, a small, touristy bar at the end of the driveway is your only option. Other more accessible Tuscan monasteries worth visiting include Sant'Antimo (6 miles south of Montalcino) and Monte Oliveto Maggiore (15 miles south of Siena, mentioned in "Crete Senese Drives" below).

Although a bus reportedly comes here from Siena, this sight is realistically accessible only for drivers. It's just outside of Monticiano (not Montalcino), about an hour south of Siena. A warning to the queasy: These roads are curvy.

▲▲Crete Senese Drives—South of Siena, the hilly area known as the "Sienese Crests" is full of colorful fields and curvy, scenic roads. You'll see an endless parade of classic Tuscan scenes, rolling hills topped with medieval towns, olive groves, rustic stone farmhouses, and a skyline punctuated with cypress trees. You won't find many wineries here, since the clay soil is better for wheat and sunflowers, but you will find the pristine, panoramic Tuscan countryside that you find on calendars and postcards.

During the spring, the fields are painted in yellow and green with fava beans and broom, dotted by red poppies on the fringes. Sunflowers decorate the area during July and August, and expanses of wind-blown grass fill the landscape almost all year.

Most roads to the southeast of Siena will give you a taste, but one of the most scenic stretches is the Laurentina road

(Siena-Asciano-San Giovanni D'Asso, #438 on road maps, can easily continue to Montalcino). There are plenty of turnouts on this road for panoramic photo opportunities, and a few roadside picnic areas.

For a break from the winding road, about 15 miles from Siena, you'll find the quaint and non-touristy village of **Asciano.** With a medieval town center and several interesting churches and museums, this is a great place for lunch (**TI** at Corso Matteotti 18, tel. 0577-719-510). If you're in town on Saturday, gather a picnic at the outdoor market (Via Amendola, 8:00–14:00).

Five miles south of Asciano, the **Abbey of Monte Oliveto Maggiore** houses a famous fresco cycle of the life of St. Benedict, painted by Renaissance masters Sodoma and Luca Signorelli (free, daily April–Oct 9:15–12:00 & 15:15–18:00, Nov–March closes at 17:00, Gregorian chanting Sun at 11:00 and Mon–Fri at 18:15, call to confirm, tel. 0577-707-611). Once you reach the town of **San Giovanni d'Asso,** it's only another 12 miles southwest to Montalcino.

Another scenic drive is the lovely stretch between Montalcino and Montepulciano (#146 on road maps). This route alternates between the grassy hills of the Crete Senese and sun-bathed vineyards of the Orcia River valley. Stop by Pienza en route.

Sleeping in the Crete Senese: **Agriturismo il Molinello** rents four apartments, two built over a medieval mill. Hardworking Alessandro and Elisa share their organic produce and sometimes offer wine-tastings. With children, friendly dogs, toys, and a swimming pool, this is ideal for families (Qb-€70–100, apartment for up to 8-€130, 1-week stay required in summer, discounts and 2-night minimum off-season, mountain-bike rentals, near Asciano, 30 min southeast of Siena, tel. 0577-704-791, mobile 335-692-5720, fax 0577-705-605, www.molinello.com, info@molinello.com).

ROME

(Roma)

Rome is magnificent and brutal at the same time. Your ears will ring. If you're careless, you'll be run down or pickpocketed. You'll be frustrated by the kind of chaos that only an Italian can understand. You may even come to believe Mussolini was a necessary evil.

But Rome is required, and if your hotel provides a comfortable refuge; if you pace yourself; if you accept—and even partake in—the siesta plan; if you're well-organized for sightseeing; and if you protect yourself and your valuables with extra caution and discretion, you'll do fine. For me, Rome is in a three-way tie with Paris and London as Europe's greatest city.

Two thousand years ago, the word Rome meant civilization itself. Everything was either civilized (part of the Roman Empire, Latin- or Greek-speaking) or barbarian. Today, Rome is Italy's political capital, the capital of Catholicism, and the center of the ancient world, littered with evocative remains. As you peel through its fascinating and jumbled layers, you'll find Rome's buildings, cats, laundry, traffic, and 2.6 million people endlessly entertaining. And then, of course, there are its magnificent sights.

Tour St. Peter's, the greatest church on earth, and scale Michelangelo's 328-foot-tall dome, the world's largest. Learn something about eternity by touring the huge Vatican Museum. You'll find the story of creation—bright as the day it was painted—in the restored Sistine Chapel. Do the "Caesar Shuffle" through ancient Rome's Forum and Colosseum. Savor Europe's most sumptuous building, the Borghese Gallery, and take an early evening "Dolce Vita Stroll" down the Via del Corso with Rome's beautiful people. Enjoy an after-dark walk from Campo de' Fiori to the Spanish Steps, lacing together Rome's Baroque and bubbly nightspots.

Planning Your Time

For most travelers, Rome is best done quickly. It's great, but huge (pop. 2.6 million) and exhausting. Time is normally short, and Italy is more charming elsewhere. To "do" Rome in a day, consider it as a side-trip from Orvieto or Florence, and maybe before the night train to Venice. Crazy as that sounds, if all you have is a day, it's a great one.

Rome in a Day: Start with the Vatican City (2 hours in the Vatican Museum and Sistine Chapel, 1 hour in St. Peter's), taxi over the river to the Pantheon (picnic on its steps), then hike over Capitol Hill, through the Forum, and to the Colosseum. Have dinner on Campo de' Fiori and dessert on Piazza Navona.

Rome in Two to Three Days: On the first day, do the "Caesar Shuffle" from the Colosseum to the Forum, then over Capitol Hill to the Pantheon. After a siesta, join the locals strolling from Piazza del Popolo to the Spanish Steps (see my "Dolce Vita Stroll," page 533). On the second day, see the Vatican City (St. Peter's, climb the dome, tour the Vatican Museum). Have dinner on the atmospheric Campo de' Fiori, then walk to the Trevi Fountain and Spanish Steps (see my "Night Walk Across Rome," page 535). With a third day, add the Borghese Gallery (reservations required) and the National Museum of Rome.

ORIENTATION

Sprawling Rome actually feels manageable once you get to know it. The old core, with most of the tourist sights, sits in a diamond formed by the train station (in the east), the Vatican (west), the Borghese Gardens (north), and the Colosseum (south). The Tiber River runs through the diamond from north to south. It takes about an hour to walk from the train station to the Vatican.

Consider Rome in these layers:

The ancient city had a million people. The best of the classical sights stand in a line from the Colosseum to the Pantheon. (See map on page 543.)

Medieval Rome was little more than a hobo camp of 50,000—thieves, mean dogs, and the pope, whose legitimacy required a Roman address. A colorful tangle of lanes, the medieval city lies between the Pantheon and the river.

Window-shoppers' Rome twinkles with nightlife and ritzy shopping near Rome's main drag, Via del Corso—in the triangle formed by Piazza del Popolo, Piazza Venezia, and the Spanish Steps. (See "Dolce Vita Stroll" map, page 534.)

Vatican City, west of the Tiber, is a compact world of its own, with two great, huge sights: St. Peter's Basilica and the Vatican Museum. (See "Vatican City Overview" map, page 567.)

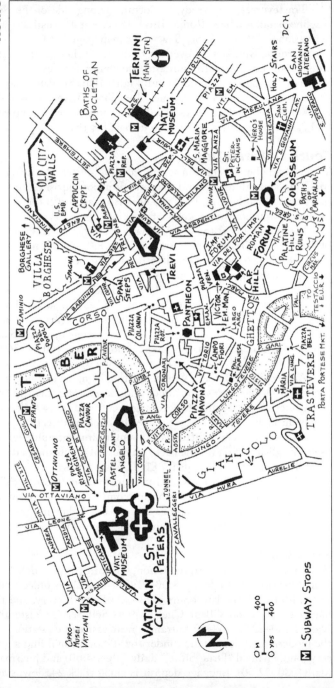

Rome

M - SUBWAY STOPS

Trastevere, the seedy, colorful, wrong-side-of-the-river neighborhood, is village Rome. This is the city at its crustiest—and perhaps most "Roman." (See Trastevere map, page 573.)

Baroque Rome is an overleaf that embellishes great squares throughout the town with fountains and church facades.

Since no one is allowed to build taller than St. Peter's dome, the city has no modern skyline. The Tiber River is basically ignored—after the last floods (1870), the banks were built up very high, and Rome turned its back on its naughty river.

Tourist Information

While Rome has several tourist information offices, the dozen or so TI kiosks scattered around the town at major tourist centers are handy and just as helpful. If all you need is a map, forget the TI and get one at your hotel or at a newsstand kiosk.

You'll find TIs at the airport (daily 8:00–19:00, tel. 06-6595-6074) and at the Termini train station (daily 8:00–21:00; near track 3, tel. 06-4890-6300, combined with travel agency). These TIs are especially helpful, if they're not too busy.

Smaller TIs (daily 9:00–18:00) include kiosks near the Forum (on Piazza del Tempio della Pace), at Via del Corso (on Largo Goldoni), in Trastevere (on Piazza Sonnino), on Via Nazionale (at Palazzo delle Esposizioni), at Castel Sant'Angelo, and at Santa Maria Maggiore Church. For more information, call 06-3600-4399 (answered daily 9:00–19:00; also see www.romaturismo.it).

At any TI, ask for a city map, a listing of sights and hours (in the free *Museums of Rome* booklet), and *Passepartout,* the free seasonal entertainment guide for evening events and fun. Don't book rooms through a TI; you'll save money by booking direct.

Roma c'è is a cheap little weekly entertainment guide with a useful English section (in the back) on musical events (new edition every Thu, sold at newsstands for €1.20, www.romace.it).

Web Sites: Check out www.romaturismo.com (music, exhibitions, and events), www.whatsoninrome.com (events and news), www.wantedinrome.com (job openings and real estate, but also festivals and exhibitions), and www.vatican.va (the pope's Web site).

Arrival in Rome

By Train: Rome's main train station, **Termini,** is a minefield of tourist services: a TI (daily 8:00–21:00), train info office (daily 7:00–21:00), ATMs, late-hours banks, 24-hour thievery, and the handy, cheery Food Village Chef Express Self-Service Ristorante (daily 11:00–22:30, WC at entrance, near east end of station). In the modern mall downstairs (under the station), you'll find a grocery (oddly named "Drug Store," daily 7:00–24:00) and pharmacy (daily 7:30–22:00). Luggage deposit is along track 24, downstairs

Greater Rome

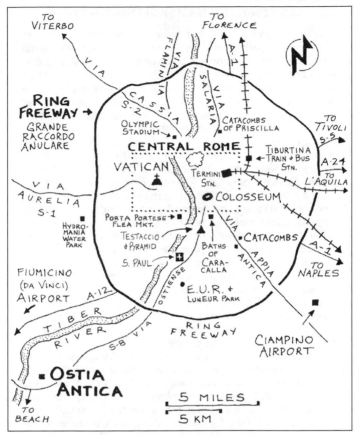

(€4 for up to 5 hrs, €0.60/hr thereafter, lines can be long). The train to Leonardo da Vinci/Fiumicino Airport runs from tracks 25 and 26 (see "Airports," page 609).

Termini is also a local transportation hub. The city's two Metro lines intersect at the Termini Metro station (downstairs). Buses (including the city orientation tour—see page 525) leave from the square directly in front of the main station hall. Taxis queue in front, along the right side of the square; avoid con men hawking "express taxi" services in unmarked cars (only use ones marked with the word *taxi* and a phone number). To avoid the long taxi line, simply hike out past the buses to the main street and hail one. The station has some sleazy sharks with official-looking business cards; avoid anybody selling anything at the station.

From the train station, most of my accommodation listings are easily accessible by foot (for hotels near the Termini train station) or

Soccer, the National Obsession

Winston Churchill said that Italians lose wars like soccer matches and soccer matches like wars. *Calcio* is the national obsession, regardless of age or social class. If you see an animated conversation, it's probably about soccer. Everyone's an expert, quick with opinions on a coach's lousy decision or a referee's unprofessional conduct. Fans routinely insult referees by yelling personal insults, such as *arbitro cornuto* (the referee is a cuckold—his wife sleeps around).

Rome has a special passion for soccer. It has two teams, Roma (representing the city) and Lazio (the region), and the rivalry is fanatic. When Romans are introduced, they ask each other, *"Laziale o romanista?"* The answer can actually compromise a relationship. Both Roma (jersey: yellow and red, symbol: she-wolf) and Lazio (jersey: light blue and white, symbol: imperial eagle) claim to be truly Roman. The Lazio team is older (founded in 1900), but Roma has more supporters. Lazio is supposed to be more upper class, Roma more popular, but the social division is blurred.

The most eagerly awaited sporting event of the year is the derby, when the two teams fight it out at the Olympic Stadium. All of Italy acknowledges that team spirit is most fervent in Rome. Fans prepare months in advance, and on the day of the match they fill the entire stadium with team colors, flags, banners, and smoke candles.

Witty slogans on banners work like dialogues. On one occasion, a Roma banner proclaimed, "Roma—only the sky is higher than you." The Lazio banner replied, "In fact, the sky is blue and white" (like its team colors). The exchange revealed that there had been a Lazio informer on the Roma side, traumatizing Roma fans for weeks. Many tourists go to these matches just for the folklore...to enjoy one of the most Roman of all experiences.

by Metro (for hotels in the Colosseum and Vatican neighborhoods).

By Bus: Long-distance buses (e.g., from Siena and Assisi) arrive at Rome's small **Tiburtina** station, which is on Metro line B, with easy connections to the Termini train station (a straight shot 4 stops away) and the entire Metro system.

By Plane: For information on Rome's airports and connections into the city, see "Airports" on page 609.

Dealing with (and Avoiding) Problems

Theft Alert: With sweet-talking con artists meeting you at the station, well-dressed pickpockets on buses, and thieving gangs of children at the ancient sites, Rome is a gauntlet of rip-offs.

There's no great physical risk, but green or sloppy tourists will be scammed. Thieves strike when you're distracted. Don't trust kind strangers. Keep nothing important in your pockets. Assume you're being stalked. (Then relax and have fun.) Be most on guard while boarding and leaving buses and subways. Thieves crowd the door, then stop and turn while others crowd and push from behind. The sneakiest thieves are well-dressed businessmen (generally with something in their hands); lately many are posing as tourists with fanny packs, cameras, and even Rick Steves guidebooks. Scams abound: Don't give your wallet to self-proclaimed "police" who stop you on the street, warn you about counterfeit (or drug) money, and ask to see your cash. If a bank machine eats your ATM card, see if there's a thin plastic insert with a tongue hanging out that thieves use to extract it.

If you know what to look out for, the gangs of children picking the pockets and handbags of naive tourists are no threat, but an interesting, albeit sad, spectacle. Gangs of city-stained children (just 8–10 years old—too young to be prosecuted, but old enough to rip you off) troll through the tourist crowds around the Colosseum, Forum, Piazza Repubblica, and train and Metro stations. Watch them target tourists who are overloaded with bags or distracted with a video camera. The kids look like beggars and hold up newspapers or cardboard signs to confuse their victims. They scram like stray cats if you're onto them. A fast-fingered mother with a baby is often nearby. The terrace above the bus stop near the Colosseum Metro stop is a fine place to watch the action...and maybe even pick up a few moves of your own.

Reporting Losses: To report lost or stolen passports and documents or to make an insurance claim, you must file a police report (at Termini train station, with Polizia at track 1 or with Carabinieri at track 20; offices are also at Piazza Venezia). To replace a passport, file the police report, then go to your embassy (see below). To report lost or stolen credit cards, see page 13.

Embassies: The U.S. Embassy is at Via Vittorio Veneto 119/A (Mon–Fri 8:30–13:00 & 14:00–17:30, closed Sat–Sun, 24-hour tel. 06-46741, www.usembassy.it), and the Canadian Embassy is at Via Zara 30 (tel. 06-445-981, www.canada.it).

Emergency Numbers: Police—tel. 113. Ambulance—tel. 118.

Pedestrian Safety: Walk with extreme caution. Scooters don't need to stop at red lights, and even cars exercise what drivers call the "logical option" of not stopping if they see no oncoming traffic. As noisy gasoline-powered scooters are replaced by electric ones, they'll be quieter (hooray) but more dangerous for pedestrians. Follow locals like a shadow when you cross a street (or spend a good part of your visit stranded on curbs). When you do cross alone, don't be a deer in the headlights. Find a gap in the traffic and walk with confidence while making eye contact with the approaching driver—they won't hit you if they can tell where you intend to go.

Staying/Getting Healthy: The siesta is a key to survival in summertime Rome. Lie down and contemplate the extraordinary power of gravity in the Eternal City. I drink lots of cold, refreshing water from Rome's many drinking fountains (the Forum has 3). There's a pharmacy (marked by a green cross) in every neighborhood, including a handy one in the Termini train station (daily 7:30–22:00, located downstairs, at west end), and a 24-hour pharmacy on Piazza dei Cinquecento 51 (next to Termini train station on Via Cavour, tel. 06-488-0019). Embassies can recommend English-speaking doctors. Consider MEDline, a 24-hour home medical service (tel. 06-808-0995, doctors speak English). Anyone is entitled to free emergency treatment at public hospitals. The hospital closest to the Termini train station is Policlinico Umberto 1 (entrance for emergency treatment on Via Lancisi, translators available, Metro: Policlinico). The American Hospital, a private hospital on the edge of town, is accustomed to helping Yankees (tel. 06-225-571).

Helpful Hints

Museum Prices: These can be upped when museums host special exhibits (no price break if you skip exhibit).

Internet Access: If your hotel doesn't offer free or cheap Internet access in their lobby, your hotelier can steer you to an Internet café nearby. Little cafés are scattered throughout Rome. The city's biggest Internet point is easyInternetcafé, centrally located on Piazza Barberini (cheap access, open 24/7, 250 terminals, www.easyinternetcafe.com). A smaller branch is in Trastevere, on Piazza in Piscinula.

Bookstores: Try Feltrinelli International (Via Vittorio Emanuele Orlando 84, daily 9:00–20:00, tel. 064-827-878), Almost Corner Bookshop in Trastevere (Via del Moro 45, tel. 06-583-6942), and the Anglo American Bookshop (Via della Vite 102, tel. 06-679-5222).

Laundry: Ask your hotelier for the nearest launderette (usually open daily 8:00–22:00, about €7 to wash and dry a 15-pound load). The Bolle Blu chain comes with Internet access (near train station at Via Palestro 59, and at Via Principe Amedeo 116, tel. 06-446-5804).

Travel Agencies: Get train tickets and railpass-related reservations and supplements at travel agencies, rather than dealing with the congested train station. The cost is often the same, though sometimes there's a minimal charge. Your hotel can direct you to the nearest travel agency. Quo Vadis, near the Vatican, is helpful (Via della Conciliazione, 22–24, tel. 06-6880-4941, fax 06-6880-3191, qv.viaggi@tiscalinet.it). Or purchase train tickets from the American Express office near the Spanish Steps (Mon–Fri 9:00–17:30, closed Sat–Sun, Piazza di Spagna 38, tel. 06-67641).

Getting Around Rome

Sightsee on foot, by city bus, by Metro, or by taxi. I've grouped your sightseeing into walkable neighborhoods. Make it a point to visit sights in a logical order. Needless backtracking wastes precious time.

Public transportation is efficient, cheap, and part of your Roman experience. It starts running at about 5:30 and stops at about 23:30, sometimes earlier. After midnight, there are a few very crowded night buses, and taxis become more expensive and hard to get. Don't try to hail one—go to a taxi stand.

You can use the same ticket on the bus or the Metro (€1, good for 75 min, valid for one Metro ride—including transfers—and unlimited buses); you can also buy an all-day bus/Metro pass (€4, good until midnight) or a one-week transit pass (€16—about the same as 2 taxi rides). You can buy tickets and passes at newsstands, tobacco shops (*tabacchi*, marked by a black-and-white *T* sign), and major Metro stations and bus stops, but not on board. Stamp your ticket before using it (machines are near subway turnstiles and on buses—watch others and imitate). If the validation machine won't work, you can write the date, time, and bus number on the ticket. For more information, visit www.atac.roma.it, or call 800-431-784.

It's smart to either buy an all-day pass or stock up on tickets early on. That way, you don't have to run around searching for an open *tabacchi* when you spot your bus approaching. Metro stations have no human ticket-sellers, and the machines are either broken or require exact change (it helps to put in smallest coin first).

Buses (especially the touristy #64) and the Metro are havens for thieves and pickpockets. Assume any commotion is a thief-created distraction. If one bus is packed, there's likely a second one on its tail with far fewer crowds and thieves. Once you know the bus system, it's easier than searching for a cab.

By Metro: The Roman subway system (Metropolitana) is simple, with two clean, cheap, fast lines that intersect at the Termini train station. Note that first and last compartments are generally the least crowded.

Rome's Metro

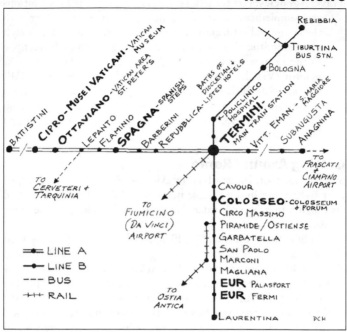

While much of Rome is not served by its skimpy subway, these stops are helpful:

Termini—train station, National Museum of Rome, and recommended hotels

Repubblica—Baths of Diocletian/Octagonal Hall, Via Naziona-le, and recommended hotels

Barberini—Cappuccin Crypt and Trevi Fountain

Spagna—Spanish Steps, Villa Borghese, and classy shopping area

Flaminio—Piazza del Popolo, start of recommended "Dolce Vita Stroll" down Via del Corso

Ottaviano—St. Peter's and Vatican City

Cipro-Musei Vaticani—Vatican Museum and recommended hotels

Colosseo—Colosseum, Roman Forum, and recommended hotels

E.U.R.—Mussolini's futuristic suburb

By Bus: Bus routes are clearly listed at the stops. Ask the TI for a bus map (bus info: tel. 06-4695-2027). Tickets have a bar code and must be stamped on the bus in the yellow box with the digital readout (be sure to retrieve your ticket). Punch your ticket as you board, or you are cheating. While relatively safe, riding without a stamped ticket on the bus is stressful. Inspectors fine even innocent-looking tourists €52.

Here are a few buses worth knowing about:

#64—Termini (train station), Piazza della Repubblica (sights), Via Nazionale (recommended hotels), Piazza Venezia (near Forum), Largo Argentina (near Pantheon), and St. Peter's Basilica (get off just past the tunnel). Ride it for a city overview and to watch pickpockets in action (can get horribly crowded).

#40—This express bus following the #64 route (get off at Piazza Pia—near Castel Sant'Angelo—for St. Peter's Basilica) is especially helpful—fewer stops, crowds, and pickpockets.

#8—This tram connects Largo Argentina with Trastevere (get off at Piazza Belli, just after crossing the Tiber River).

#62—Largo Argentina to St. Peter's Square.

#81—San Giovanni in Laterano, Colosseum, Largo Argentina, and Piazza Risorgimento (Vatican).

#H—Express connecting Termini train station and Trastevere, with a few stops on Via Nazionale (for Trastevere, get off at Piazza Belli, just after crossing the river).

#492—Stazione Tiburtina (bus station), Piazza Barberini, Piazza Venezia, Piazza Cavour (Castel Sant'Angelo), and Piazza Risorgimento (Vatican).

#271—Trastevere (from across Ponte Sisto Bridge) to the Vatican (Piazza Risorgimento).

#571—Express from Via Cavalleggeri (near St. Peter's Square) to the Colosseum.

#714—Termini (train station), Santa Maria Maggiore, San Giovanni in Laterano, and Terme di Caracalla (Baths of Caracalla).

#23—Links Vatican with Trastevere, stopping at Porta Portese (Sunday flea market), Trastevere (Piazza Belli), Castel Sant'Angelo, and Vatican Museum (nearest stop is Via Leone IV).

Rome has cute *elettrico* minibuses that wind through the narrow streets of old and interesting neighborhoods (daily, fewer on Sun). These are handy for sightseeing and fun for simply joyriding:

Elettrico **#116**—Through the medieval core of Rome: Ponte Vittorio Emanuele II (near Castel Sant'Angelo) to Campo de' Fiori, then to Piazza Barberini via the Pantheon, and finally through the scenic Villa Borghese park.

Elettrico **#117**—San Giovanni in Laterano, Colosseo, Via dei Serpenti, Trevi Fountain, Piazza di Spagna, and Piazza del Popolo.

By Taxi: I use taxis in Rome more often than in other cities. They're reasonable and useful for efficient sightseeing in this big, hot metropolis. Taxis start at about €2.50, then charge about €1 per kilometer (surcharges: €1 on Sun, €2.75 for nighttime hours of

Rome's Public Transportation

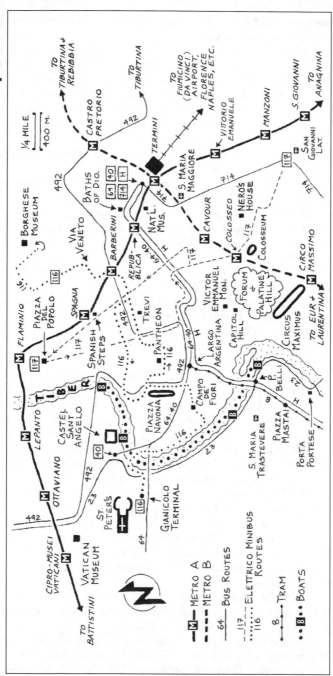

22:00–7:00, €1 for luggage, €7.25 extra for airport, tip by rounding up to the nearest euro). Sample fares: train station to Vatican-€9; train station to Colosseum-€6; Colosseum to Trastevere-€7. Three or four companions with more money than time should taxi almost everywhere. It's tough to wave down a taxi in Rome. Find the nearest taxi stand by asking a passerby or a clerk in a shop, "*Dov'è una fermata dei taxi?*" (doh-VEH OO-nah fehr-MAH-tah DEHee TAHK-see). Some taxi stands are listed on my maps. To save time and energy, have your hotel or restaurant call a taxi for you; the meter starts when the call is received (generally adding a euro or two to the bill). To call a cab on your own, dial 06-3570, 06-4994, or 06-88177. It's routine for Romans to ask the waiter in a restaurant to call a taxi when they ask for the bill. The waiter will tell you how many minutes you have to enjoy your coffee.

Beware of corrupt taxis. If hailing a cab on the street, be sure the meter is restarted when you get in (should be around €2.50; it may be higher if you called for the taxi). Many meters show both the fare and the time elapsed during the ride—and some tourists pay €8.30 for an eight-and-a-half-minute trip (more than the fair meter rate). When you arrive at the train station or airport, beware of hustlers conning naive visitors into unmarked rip-off "express taxis." Only use official taxis, with a *taxi* sign on top and a phone number marked on the door. By law, they must display a multilingual official price chart. If you have any problems with a taxi, point to the chart and ask the cabbie to explain it to you. Making a show of writing down the taxi number (to file a complaint) can motivate a driver to quickly settle the matter.

By Boat: Tourist-laden boats slowly float their way down the Tiber—trying to re-energize the city's neglected river (single ride-€1, day pass-€2.30, tour-€10, boats depart hourly, daily 8:00–19:30, maybe until 24:00 in summer, tel. 06-678-9361, www.battellidiroma.it). You can access the docks from the following bridges: Ponte Duca d'Aosta, Ponte Risorgimento, Ponte Cavour (Ara Pacis), Ponte Sant'Angelo (Vatican), Ponte Sisto (Trastevere), or Calata Anguillara (Isola Tiburtina).

By Car with Driver: You can hire your own private car with driver through Autoservizi Monti Concezio, run by gentle, capable, and English-speaking Ezio (car-€30/hr, minibus-€35/hr, 3-hr minimum, mobile 335-636-5907 or 349-674-5643, www.montitours.com, concemon@tin.it).

TOURS

Rome has many good, highly competitive tour companies. I've listed my favorites here, but without a lot of details on their offerings. Before your trip, spend some time on their Web sites to get

Daily Reminder

Sunday: These sights are closed: Vatican Museum (except for the last Sunday of the month, when it's free and crowded), Villa Farnesina, and the Catacombs of San Sebastian. In the morning, the Porta Portese flea market hops, and the old center is delightfully quiet.

Monday: Many sights are closed: National Museum of Rome, Borghese Gallery, Capitol Hill Museum, Catacombs of Priscilla, Octagonal Hall and Museum of the Bath (both at Baths of Diocletian), Castel Sant'Angelo, Montemartini Museum, E.U.R.'s Museum of Roman Civilization, Trajan's Market, Etruscan Museum, Protestant Cemetery in Testaccio, and Ostia Antica. All of the ancient sights (e.g., Colosseum and Forum) and the Vatican Museum, among others, are open. The Baths of Caracalla close early in the afternoon.

Tuesday: All sights are open in Rome, except for Nero's Golden House.

Wednesday: All sights are open, except for the Catacombs of San Callisto. St. Peter's Basilica may be closed in the morning for a papal audience.

Thursday: All sights are open, except for Galleria Doria Pamphilj and the Cappuccin Crypt.

Friday & Saturday: All sights are open in Rome.

to know your options, as each company has a particular teaching and guiding personality. Some are highbrow, while others are less scholarly. It's sometimes required, and always smart, to book a spot in advance (easy on the Web). While it may seem like a splurge to have a local or an American expat show you around, it's a treat that makes brutal Rome suddenly your friend.

Context Rome—Americans Paul Bennett and Lani Bevacqua offer walking tours for travelers with longer-than-average attention spans. Their orientation walks lace together lesser-known sights from antiquity to the present. Tours vary in length from two to four hours and range in price from €25 to €60. Try to book in advance, since their groups are limited to six and fill up fast (tel. 06-482-0911, U.S. tel. 888-467-1986, www.contextrome.com). They also offer orientation chats in your hotel—for many, well worth the price (€50/1 hr).

If you're interested in weeklong classes on Rome, look into the American Institute for Roman Culture—an innovative, educational organization run by Tom Rankin and his colleague, archaeologist Darius Arya (www.romanculture.org).

Through Eternity—This company offers several walking tours, all led by native English speakers who strive to bring the history to life. The tours, limited to groups of 20, include St. Peter's and the Vatican Museum (€40, museum entry not included, 5 hrs, almost daily); the Colosseum and Roman Forum (€25, 2.5 hrs, daily); and Rome at Twilight (€25, nightly). They also offer private tours of Rome, Tivoli, and Pompeii (tel. 06-700-9336, mobile 347-336-5298, 10 percent discount if booked online, www.througheternity.com, info@througheternity.com, Rob Allyn).

Rome Walks—These guides give tours in fluent English to small groups (generally fewer than 10 people). Sample tours include Colosseum/Forum/Palatine Walk (€50, includes admission to Colosseum, 3 hrs), Scandal Tour (€30, 2 hrs to dig up the dirt on Roman emperors, royalty, and popes), Vatican City Walk (€52, includes admission to Vatican Museum, 4 hrs), and a Twilight Rome Evening Walk (€25, all the famous squares that offer lively people scenes, 2 hrs). They also do private tours to more far-flung places such as Hadrian's Villa and Villa d'Este (mobile 347-795-5175, www.romewalks.com, info@romewalks.com, Annie).

Roman Odyssey —This expat tour company offers various two-to three-hour, €25 walks led by native English speakers who are also fully licensed local guides (15 percent discount for readers of this book in 2006, tel. 06-580-9902, mobile 328-912-3720, www.romanodyssey.com, Rahul).

Private Guides—Consider a personal tour. Any of the tour companies I list can provide a guide (around €50/hr). I work with Francesca Caruso, a licensed Italian guide who speaks excellent English, loves to teach and share her appreciation of her city, and has contributed generously to this book. She has a broad range of expertise and can tailor a walk to your interests (€100 for 2 hrs or more—she happily stretches the tour to half a day for eager students, individuals, and small groups, chris.fra@mclink.it).

Hop-on, Hop-off Bus Tour—The ATAC city bus #110 tour offers a quick, cheap orientation tour of Rome on big, red, double-decker buses with an open-air upper deck. In less than two hours, you'll have 80 sights pointed out to you (by a live guide in English and up to 3 other languages). While you can hop on and off, the service can be erratic (it can be mobbed midday and it's not ideal in bad weather). It's best to think of this as an efficient, two-hour quickie orientation with scant information and lots of images. The stops include Via Veneto, Via Tritone, Ara Pacis, Piazza Cavour, St. Peter's Square, Corso Vittorio Emanuele (for Piazza Navona), Piazza Venezia, Colosseum, and Via Nazionale. Bus #110 departs every 30 minutes—at the top and bottom of the hour—from in front of the Termini train station (runs daily March–Sept 9:00–20:00, Oct–Feb 10:00–18:00, tel. 06-4695-2252). Buy the €13 ticket at the info kiosk marked *i* near platform D.

Rome—Republic and Empire
(500 B.C.–A.D. 500)

Ancient Rome spanned about a thousand years, from 500 B.C. to A.D. 500. During that time, Rome expanded from a small tribe of barbarians to a vast empire, then dwindled slowly to city size again. For the first 500 years, when Rome's armies made her ruler of the Italian peninsula and beyond, Rome was a republic governed by elected senators. Over the next 500 years, a time of world conquest and eventual decline, Rome was an empire ruled by a military-backed dictator.

Julius Caesar bridged the gap between republic and empire. This ambitious general and politician, popular with the people because of his military victories and charisma, suspended the Roman constitution and assumed dictatorial powers about 50 B.C., then he was assassinated by a conspiracy of senators. His adopted son, Augustus, succeeded him, and soon "Caesar" was not just a name but a title.

Emperor Augustus ushered in the Pax Romana, or Roman peace (from A.D. 1–200), a time when Rome reached her peak and controlled an empire that stretched even beyond Eurail—from Scotland to Egypt, from Turkey to Morocco.

Archeobus—This hop-on, hop-off bus runs hourly from the Termini train station out to the Appian Way. This is a handy way to see the sights down this ancient Roman road, but it can be frustrating for various reasons (sometimes crowded, service can be sporadic, not ideal for hopping on and off). The trip, in an air-conditioned minibus, includes a basic, uninspired two-hour tour (longer if there's traffic) in Italian and English (€8; tickets sold at platform D in front of train station, hourly departures from station and Piazza Venezia 9:45–16:45, tel. 06-4695-4695).

SELF-GUIDED WALKS

Here are three walks that give you a moving picture of Rome, an ancient yet modern city. You'll walk through history ("Roman Forum Walk"), take a refreshing early-evening stroll ("The Dolce Vita Stroll"), and enjoy the thriving night scene ("Night Walk Across Rome").

Roman Forum Walk

The Roman Forum (Foro Romano) was the political, religious, and commercial center of the city. Rome's most important temples and halls of justice were here. This was the place for religious processions,

Roman Forum Walk

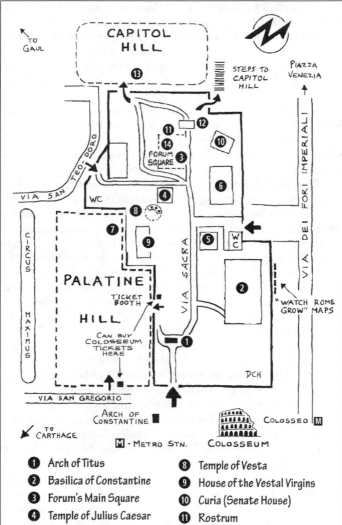

TO GAUL

CAPITOL HILL

STEPS TO CAPITOL HILL

PIAZZA VENEZIA

VIA SAN TEO. DORO

FORUM SQUARE

WC

CIRCUS MAXIMUS

PALATINE HILL

VIA SACRA

TICKET BOOTH

CAN BUY COLOSSEUM TICKETS HERE

WC

"WATCH ROME GROW" MAPS

VIA DEI FORI IMPERIALI

DCH

VIA SAN GREGORIO

ARCH OF CONSTANTINE

TO CARTHAGE

M - METRO STN.

COLOSSEO **M**

COLOSSEUM

① Arch of Titus
② Basilica of Constantine
③ Forum's Main Square
④ Temple of Julius Caesar
⑤ Temple of Antoninus and Faustina
⑥ Basilica Aemilia
⑦ Caligula's Palace
⑧ Temple of Vesta
⑨ House of the Vestal Virgins
⑩ Curia (Senate House)
⑪ Rostrum
⑫ Arch of Septimius Severus
⑬ Temple of Saturn
⑭ Column of Phocas

political demonstrations, elections, important speeches, and parades by conquering generals. As Rome's empire expanded, these few acres of land became the center of the civilized world.

Cost, Hours, Location: Free, daily 9:00–19:00 or until an hour before sunset, Metro: Colosseo, tel. 06-3996-7700. You can rent a dry but fact-filled €4 audioguide at the gift shop at the entrance on Via dei Fori Imperiali. Tours in English are offered almost hourly (€4); ask at the ticket booth at Palatine Hill (near Arch of Titus). Street vendors at several ancient sites sell small *Rome: Past and Present* books with plastic overlays that restore the ruins (marked €11, offer less).

• *Walk through the entrance nearest the Colosseum, hiking up the ramp marked* Via Sacra. *Stand next to the triumphal...*

❶ **Arch of Titus (Arco di Tito):** The arch commemorated the Roman victory over the province of Judea (Israel) in A.D. 70. The Romans had a reputation as benevolent conquerors who tolerated the local customs and rulers. All they required was allegiance to the empire, which could be shown by worshiping the emperor as a god. No problem for most conquered people, who already had half a dozen gods on their prayer lists anyway. But the Israelites believed in only one god and it wasn't the emperor. Israel revolted. After a short but bitter war, the Romans defeated the rebels, took Jerusalem, sacked their temple, and brought home 50,000 Jewish slaves...who were forced to build this arch.

• *Start down the Via Sacra into the Forum. After just a few yards, turn right and follow a path uphill to the three huge arches of the...*

❷ **Basilica of Constantine (a.k.a. Basilica Maxentius):** These gigantic arches represent only one third of the original Basilica of Constantine, a mammoth hall of justice. The arches were matched by a similar set along the Via Sacra side (only a few squat brick piers remain). Between them ran the central hall, which was spanned by a roof 130 feet high—about 55 feet higher than the side arches you see. (The stub of brick you see sticking up began an arch that once spanned the central hall.) The hall itself was as long as a football field, lavishly furnished with colorful inlaid marble, a gilded bronze ceiling, fountains, and statues, and filled with strolling Romans. At the far (west) end was an enormous marble statue of Emperor Constantine on a throne. (Pieces of this statue, including a hand the size of a man, are on display in Rome's Capitol Hill Museum.)

This basilica was begun by the emperor Maxentius, but after he was trounced in battle, the victor—Constantine—completed the massive building.

• *Now stroll deeper into the Forum, downhill along the Via Sacra, through the trees. Many of the large basalt stones under your feet were walked on by Caesar Augustus 2,000 years ago. Pass by the only original bronze door still swinging on its ancient hinges (green, on right) and continue between ruined buildings until the Via Sacra opens up to a flat, grassy area.*

❸ **The Forum's Main Square:** The original Forum, or main square, was this flat patch about the size of a football field, stretching to the foot of Capitol Hill. Surrounding it were temples, law courts, government buildings, and triumphal arches.

Rome was born right here. According to legend, twin brothers Romulus (Rome) and Remus were orphaned in infancy and raised by a she-wolf on top of Palatine Hill. Growing up, they found it hard to get dates. So they and their cohorts attacked the nearby Sabine tribe and kidnapped their women. After they made peace, this marshy valley became the meeting place and then the trading center for the scattered tribes on the surrounding hillsides.

• *At the near (east) end of the main square (the Colosseum is to the east) are the foundations of a temple now capped with a peaked wood-and-metal roof...*

❹ **The Temple of Julius Caesar (Tempio del Divo Giulio, or "Ara di Cesare"):** Julius Caesar's body was burned on this spot (under the metal roof) after his assassination. Peek behind the wall into the small apse area where a mound of dirt usually has fresh flowers—given to remember the man who, more than any other, personified the greatness of Rome.

Caesar (100–44 B.C.) changed Rome—and the Forum—dramatically. He cleared out many of the wooden market stalls and began to ring the square with even grander buildings. Caesar's house was located behind the temple, near that clump of trees. He walked right by here on the day he was assassinated ("Beware the Ides of March!" warned a street-corner Etruscan preacher).

Though popular with the masses, not everyone liked Caesar's urban design or his politics. When he assumed dictatorial powers, he was ambushed and stabbed to death by a conspiracy of senators, including his adopted son, Brutus *(Et tu, Brute?)*.

The funeral was held here, facing the main square. The citizens gathered and speeches were made. Mark Antony stood up to say (in Shakespeare's words), "Friends, Romans, countrymen, lend me your ears. I come to bury Caesar, not to praise him." When Caesar's body was burned, the citizens who still loved him threw anything at hand on the fire, requiring the fire department to come put it out. Later, Emperor Augustus dedicated this temple in his name, making Caesar the first Roman to become a god.

• *Behind and to the left of the Temple of Julius Caesar are the 10 tall columns of the...*

❺ **Temple of Antoninus and Faustina:** The respected Emperor Antoninus (A.D. 138–161) built this temple—originally called the Temple of Faustina—in honor of his late beloved wife. After the emperor's death, the temple became a monument to them both.

The 56-foot-tall Corinthian (leafy) columns must have been awe-inspiring to out-of-towners who grew up in thatched huts. Although the temple has been inhabited by a church, you can still see the basic layout—a staircase led to a shaded porch (the columns), which admitted you to the main building (now a church) where the statue of the god sat.

Picture the Forum covered with dirt as high as the green door—as it was until excavated in the 1800s.

• *There's a ramp next to the Temple of A. and F. Walk halfway up it and look to the left to view the...*

❻ **Basilica Aemilia:** A basilica was a Roman hall of justice. In a society that was as legal-minded as America is today, you needed a lot of lawyers—and a big place to put them. Citizens came here to work out matters such as inheritances and building permits, or to sue somebody.

Notice the layout. It was a long, rectangular building. The stubby columns all in a row form one long, central hall flanked by two side aisles. Medieval Christians required a larger meeting hall for their worship services than Roman temples provided, so they used the spacious Roman basilica (hall of justice) as the model for their churches. Cathedrals from France to Spain to England, from Romanesque to Gothic to Renaissance, all have the same basic floor plan as a Roman basilica.

• *Return again to the Temple of Julius Caesar. To the right of the temple are the three tall Corinthian columns of the Temple of Castor and Pollux. Beyond that is Palatine Hill—the corner of which may have been...*

❼ **Caligula's Palace (a.k.a. the Palace of Tiberius):** Emperor Caligula (ruled A.D. 37–41) had a huge palace on Palatine Hill overlooking the Forum. It actually sprawled down the hill into the Forum (some supporting arches remain in the hillside), with an entrance by the Temple of Castor and Pollux.

Caligula tortured enemies, stole senators' wives, and parked his chariot in handicap spaces. But Rome's luxury-loving emperors only added to the glory of the Forum, with each one trying to make his mark on history.

• *To the left of the Temple of Castor and Pollux, find the remains of a small, white, circular temple...*

❽ **The Temple of Vesta:** This was Rome's most sacred spot. Rome considered itself one big family, and this temple represented a circular hut, like the kind Rome's first families lived in. Inside, a fire burned, just as in a Roman home. And back in the days before lighters and matches, you never wanted your fire to go out. As long as the sacred flame burned, Rome would stand. The flame was tended by priestesses known as Vestal Virgins.

• *Around the back of the Temple of Vesta, you'll find two rectangular brick pools. These stood in the courtyard of...*

❾ The House of the Vestal Virgins: The Vestal Virgins lived in a two-story building surrounding a central courtyard with these two pools at one end. Rows of statues to the left and right marked the long sides of the building. This place was the model—both architecturally and sexually—for medieval convents and monasteries.

The six Vestal Virgins, chosen from noble families before they reached the age of 10, served a 30-year term. Honored and revered by the Romans, the Vestals even had their own box opposite the emperor in the Colosseum.

As the name implies, a Vestal took a vow of chastity. If she served her term faithfully—abstaining for 30 years—she was given a huge dowry, honored with a statue (like the ones at left), and allowed to marry (life begins at 40?). But if the Romans found any Virgin who wasn't, she was strapped to a funeral car, paraded through the streets of the Forum, taken to a crypt, given a loaf of bread and a lamp...and buried alive. Many women suffered the latter fate.

• *Head to the Forum's west end (opposite the Colosseum). You'll pass by a space that was left open by design—kind of a "proto-piazza." Consider how the piazza is still a standard part of any Italian town—reflecting and accommodating the gregarious and outgoing nature of the Italian people since Roman times. Stop at the big, well-preserved brick building (on right) with the triangular roof and look in.*

❿ The Curia: The Senate House (Curia) was the most important political building in the Forum. Though this current building is a 1930s reconstruction, this was the site of Rome's official center of government since the birth of the republic. Three hundred senators, elected by the citizens of Rome, met here to debate and create the laws of the land. Their wooden seats once circled the building in three tiers; the Senate president's podium sat at the far end. The marble floor is from ancient times. Listen to the echoes in this vast room—the acoustics are great. (Note: Although Julius Caesar was assassinated in "the Senate," it wasn't here—the Senate was temporarily meeting across town.)

• *Go back down the Senate steps to the metal guardrail and find a 10-foot-high wall at the base of Capitol Hill marked...*

⓫ Rostrum (Rostra): Nowhere was Roman freedom more apparent than at this "Speaker's Corner." The Rostrum was a raised platform, 10 feet high and 80 feet long, decorated with statues, columns, and the prows of ships.

Rome's orators, great and small, came here trying to draw a crowd and sway public opinion. Mark Antony rose to offer Caesar the laurel-leaf crown of kingship, which Caesar publicly (and hypocritically) refused while privately becoming a dictator. Men such as Cicero railed against the corruption and decadence that came with the city's newfound wealth. In later years, daring citizens even

Rome Falls

Again, Rome lasted 1,000 years—500 years of growth, 200 years of peak power, and 300 years of gradual decay. The fall had many causes, among them the barbarians who pecked away at Rome's borders. Christians blamed the fall on moral decay. Pagans blamed it on Christians. Socialists blamed it on a shallow economy based on the spoils of war. (George W. Bush blamed it on Democrats.) Whatever the reasons, the far-flung empire could no longer keep its grip on conquered lands, and it pulled back. Barbarian tribes from Germany and Asia attacked the Italian peninsula and even looted Rome itself in A.D. 410, leveling many of the buildings in the Forum. In 476, when the last emperor checked out and switched off the lights, Europe plunged into centuries of ignorance, poverty, and weak government—the Dark Ages.

But Rome lived on in the Catholic Church. Christianity was the state religion of Rome's last generations. Emperors became popes (both called themselves "Pontifex Maximus"), senators became bishops, orators became priests, and basilicas became churches. The glory of Rome remains eternal.

spoke out against the emperors, reminding them that Rome was once free.

• *The big arch to the right of the Rostrum is the...*

⓬ Arch of Septimius Severus: In imperial times, the Rostrum's voices of democracy would have been dwarfed by images of empire such as the huge, six-story-high Arch of Septimius Severus (A.D. 203). The reliefs commemorate the African-born emperor's battles in Mesopotamia. Near ground level, see curly-haired Severus marching captured barbarians back to Rome for the victory parade. Despite Severus' efficient rule, Rome's empire was crumbling under the weight of its own corruption, disease, decaying infrastructure, and the constant attacks by foreign "barbarians."

• *Pass underneath the Arch of Septimius Severus and turn left. On the slope of Capitol Hill are the eight remaining columns of the...*

⓭ Temple of Saturn: These columns framed the entrance to the Forum's oldest temple (497 B.C.). Inside was a humble, very old wooden statue of the god Saturn. But the statue's pedestal held the gold bars, coins, and jewels of Rome's state treasury, the booty collected by conquering generals.

• *Standing here, at one of the Forum's first buildings, look east at the lone, tall...*

⓮ Column of Phocas: This is the Forum's last great monument (A.D. 608), a gift from the powerful Byzantine Empire to a fallen empire—Rome. Given to commemorate the pagan Pantheon becoming a Christian church, it's like a symbolic last nail in ancient Rome's coffin. After Rome's 1,000-year reign, the city was looted by Vandals, the population of a million-plus shrank to 10,000, and the once-grand city center—the Forum—was abandoned, slowly covered up by centuries of silt and dirt. In the 1700s an English historian named Edward Gibbon stood here. Hearing Christian monks singing at these pagan ruins, he looked out at the few columns poking up from the ground, pondered the "Decline and Fall of the Roman Empire," and thought, "Hmm, that's a catchy title...."

The Dolce Vita Stroll

This is the city's chic stroll—from Piazza del Popolo (Metro: Flaminio) down a wonderfully traffic-free section of Via del Corso, and up Via Condotti to the Spanish Steps—each evening around 18:00 (Sat and Sun are best). Shoppers, people-watchers, and flirts on the prowl fill this neighborhood of Rome's most fashionable stores (open after siesta 16:30–19:30). Throughout Italy, early evening is the time to stroll.

Start on **Piazza del Popolo.** The delightfully car-free square is marked by an obelisk that was brought to Rome by Augustus after he conquered Egypt. (It used to stand in the Circus Maximus.) In medieval times, this area was just inside Rome's main entry.

The Baroque church of **Santa Maria del Popolo,** on the square, contains Raphael's Chigi Chapel (KEE-gee, third chapel on left) and two paintings by Caravaggio (the side paintings in chapel left of altar). The church is open daily (Mon–Sat 7:00–12:00 & 16:00–19:00, Sun 8:00–13:30 & 16:30–19:30, next to gate in the old wall, on far side of Piazza del Popolo, to the right as you face gate).

From Piazza del Popolo, shop your way down **Via del Corso.** If you need a rest or a viewpoint, join the locals sitting on the steps of various churches along the street.

At Via Pontefici, historians turn right and walk a block to see the massive, rotting, round-brick **Mausoleum of Augustus,** topped with overgrown cypress trees. Beyond it, next to the river, is Augustus' Ara Pacis, or Altar of Peace (likely open again in 2006 after renovation).

From the mausoleum, return to Via del Corso and the 21st century, continuing straight until **Via Condotti.** Shoppers, take a left on Via Condotti to join the parade to the **Spanish Steps.** The streets that parallel Via Condotti to the south (Borgognona and Frattini) are just as popular. You can catch a taxi home at the taxi stand a block south of the Spanish Steps (at Piazza Mignonelli, near American Express and McDonald's).

Historians: Ignore Via Condotti and forget the Spanish Steps. Stay on Via del Corso, which has been straight since Roman times,

The Dolce Vita Stroll

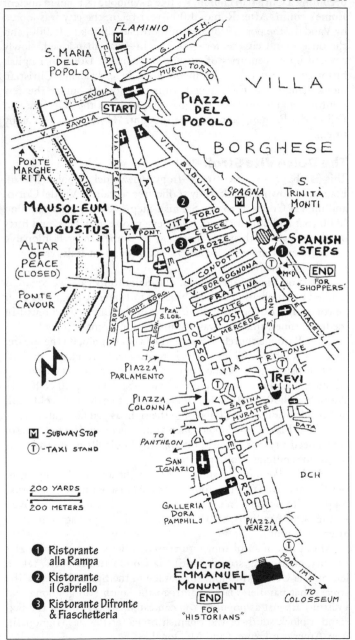

and walk a half mile down to the Victor Emmanuel Monument. Climb Michelangelo's stairway to his glorious (especially when floodlit) square atop Capitol Hill. From the balconies at either side of the mayor's palace, catch the lovely views of the Forum as the horizon reddens and cats prowl the unclaimed rubble of ancient Rome.

Night Walk Across Rome: Campo de' Fiori to the Spanish Steps

Rome can be grueling. But a fine way to enjoy this historian's rite of passage is an evening walk lacing together Rome's floodlit night spots and fine urban spaces with real-life theater vignettes.

Sitting so close to a Bernini fountain that traffic noises evaporate; jostling with local teenagers to see all the gelato flavors; enjoying lovers straddling more than the bench; jaywalking past flak-proof-vested *polizia;* and marveling at the ramshackle elegance that softens this brutal city for those who were born here and can imagine living nowhere else—these are the flavors of Rome best tasted after dark.

Start this mile-long walk at the **Campo de' Fiori** (Field of Flowers), my favorite outdoor dining room after dark (see page 598 for restaurant options). The statue of Giordano Bruno, an intellectual heretic who was burned on this spot in 1600, marks the center of this great and colorful square. Bruno overlooks a busy produce market in the morning and strollers after sundown. This neighborhood is still known for its free spirit and occasional demonstrations. When the statue of Bruno was erected in 1889, local riots overcame Vatican protests against honoring a heretic. Bruno faces his nemesis, the Vatican Chancellory (the big white building in the corner a bit to his right), while his pedestal reads: "And the flames rose up." Check out the reliefs on the pedestal for scenes from Bruno's trial and execution.

At the east end of the square (behind Bruno), the ramshackle apartments are built right into the old outer wall of ancient Rome's mammoth Theater of Pompey. This entertainment complex covered several city blocks, stretching from here to Largo Argentina. Julius Caesar was assassinated in the Theater of Pompey, where the Senate was renting space.

The square is lined with and surrounded by fun eateries. Bruno faces La Carbonara, the only real restaurant on the square. The Forno, next door to the left (7:30–20:00), is a popular place for hot and tasty take-out *pizza bianco* (plain pizza bread). Step in to at least observe the frenzy as pizza is sold hot out of the oven. Order an *etto* (100 grams) by pointing, then take your snack to the counter to pay.

Night Walk Across Rome

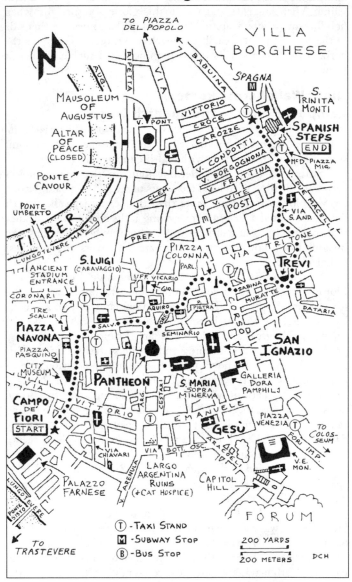

If Bruno did a hop, step, and jump forward, then turned right on Via dei Baullari and marched 200 yards, he'd cross the busy Corso Vittorio Emanuele and find **Piazza Navona.** Rome's most interesting night scene features street music, artists, fire-eaters, local Casanovas, ice cream, fountains by Bernini, and outdoor cafés (worthy of a splurge if you've got time to sit and enjoy Italy's human river).

This oblong square retains the shape of the original racetrack that was built by the emperor Domitian. (To see the ruins of the original entrance, exit the square at the far—or north—end, then take an immediate left, and look down to the left 25 feet below the current street level.) Since ancient times, the square has been a center of Roman life. In the 1800s, the city would flood the square to cool off the neighborhood.

The **Four Rivers fountain** in the center is the most famous fountain by the man who remade Rome in Baroque style, Gian Lorenzo Bernini. Four burly river gods (representing the four continents that were known in 1650) support an Egyptian obelisk that Bernini had moved here from the ancient Appian Way. The water of the world gushes everywhere. The Nile has his head covered, since the headwaters were unknown then. The Ganges holds an oar. The Danube turns to admire the obelisk. And the Rio de la Plata from Uruguay tumbles backward in shock, wondering how he ever made the top four. Bernini enlivens the fountain with horses plunging through the rocks and exotic flora and fauna from these newly discovered lands. Homesick Texans may want to find the armadillo. (It's the big, weird armor-plated creature behind the Plata river statue.)

The Plata river god is gazing upward at the church of St. Agnes, worked on by Bernini's former student turned rival, Francesco Borromini. Borromini's concave facade helps reveal the dome and epitomizes the curved symmetry of Baroque. Tour guides say that Bernini designed his river god to look horrified at Borromini's work. Or he may be shielding his eyes from St. Agnes' nakedness, as she was stripped before being martyred. However, the fountain was completed two years before Borromini even started work on the church.

At the **Tre Scalini** café (near the fountain), sample some *tartufo* "death by chocolate" ice cream, world-famous among connoisseurs of ice cream and chocolate alike (€4 to go, €8 at a table, open daily). Seriously admire a painting by a struggling artist. Request "Country Roads" from an Italian guitar player, and don't be surprised when he knows it. Listen to the white noise of gushing water and exuberant café-goers.

Leave Piazza Navona directly across from Tre Scalini café, go east past rose peddlers and palm readers, jog left around the guarded building, and follow the brown sign to the Pantheon. The

Rome at a Glance

▲▲▲Colosseum Huge stadium where gladiators fought. **Hours:** Daily 9:00–19:00 or until an hour before sunset.

▲▲▲Roman Forum Ancient Rome's main square, with ruins and grand arches. **Hours:** Daily 9:00–19:00 or until an hour before sunset.

▲▲▲Palatine Hill Ruins of emperors' palaces, Circus Maximus view, and museum. **Hours:** Daily 9:00–19:00 or until an hour before sunset.

▲▲▲Pantheon The defining domed temple. **Hours:** Mon–Sat 8:30–19:30, Sun 9:00–18:00, holidays 9:00–13:00.

▲▲▲National Museum of Rome Greatest collection of Roman sculpture anywhere. **Hours:** Tue–Sun 9:00–19:45, closed Mon.

▲▲▲Borghese Gallery Bernini sculptures and paintings by Caravaggio, Raphael, and Titian in a Baroque palazzo. Reservations mandatory. **Hours:** Tue–Sun 9:00–19:00, closed Mon.

▲▲▲Vatican Museum Four miles of the art of Western Civilization, culminating in the Sistine Chapel. **Hours:** March–Oct Mon–Fri 8:45–16:45 and Sat 8:45–13:45; Nov–Feb Mon–Sat 8:45–13:45; closed on numerous religious holidays and Sun, except last Sun of the month.

▲▲▲St. Peter's Basilica Most impressive church on earth, with Michelangelo's *Pietà* and dome. **Hours:** Church—daily April–Sept 7:00–19:00, Oct–March 7:00–18:00, often closed Wed mornings; dome—daily April–Sept 8:00–17:45, Oct–March 8:00–16:45.

▲▲Capitol Hill Hilltop square designed by Michelangelo with museum, grand stairway, and Forum overlooks. **Hours:** Always open.

▲▲Capitol Hill Museum Ancient statues, mosaics, and expansive view of Forum. **Hours:** Tue–Sun 9:00–20:00, closed Mon.

▲▲Churches near the Pantheon Four distinctive art-filled houses of worship (San Luigi dei Francesi, Santa Maria sopra Minerva, St. Ignazio, and Gesù) worth a visit for Pantheon sightseers. **Hours:** Roughly daily 7:00–12:30 & 16:00–19:00.

▲▲Catacombs Layers of tunnels with tombs, mainly Christian, outside the city. **Hours:** Open 8:30–12:00 & 14:30–17:30, until 17:00 in winter (San Callisto closed Wed and Feb, San Sebastian closed Sun and Nov, Priscilla closes at 17:00 year-round and all day Mon).

▲**St. Peter-in-Chains** Church with Michelangelo's *Moses*. **Hours:** Daily 7:00–12:30 & 15:30–18:00.

▲**Nero's Golden House** Sparse remains of Emperor Nero's sprawling home. This sight has been closed indefinitely—up to two years—because leaking water is ruining the frescoes and eroding the walls.

▲**Arch of Constantine** Honors the emperor who legalized Christianity. **Hours:** Always viewable.

▲**Mamertine Prison** Prison that held Saints Peter and Paul. **Hours:** Daily 9:00–19:00.

▲**Trajan's Column** Tall column with narrative relief, on Piazza Venezia. **Hours:** Always viewable.

▲**Galleria Doria Pamphilj** Fancy palace packed with art. **Hours:** Fri–Wed 10:00–17:00, closed Thu.

▲**Trevi Fountain** Baroque hotspot—bring coins to ensure a return trip to Rome. **Hours:** Always flowing.

▲**Baths of Diocletian** Once ancient Rome's immense public baths, now a Michelangelo church—Santa Maria degli Angeli—and the Octagonal Hall, a room with minor ancient Roman sculpture. **Hours:** Church—Mon–Sat 7:00–18:30, Sun 8:00–19:30. Octagonal Hall—Tue–Sat 9:00–14:00, Sun 9:00–13:00, closed Mon.

▲**Santa Maria della Vittoria** Church with Bernini's swooning *St. Teresa in Ecstasy*. **Hours:** Daily 7:00–12:00 & 15:30–19:00.

▲**Villa Borghese** Rome's "Central Park," with lake, Borghese Gallery, and Etruscan Museum. **Hours:** Always open.

▲**Cappuccin Crypt** Decorated with the bones of 4,000 monks. **Hours:** Fri–Wed 9:00–12:00 & 15:00–18:00, closed Thu.

▲**Castel Sant'Angelo** Hadrian's Tomb turned castle, prison, papal refuge, now museum. **Hours:** Tue–Sun 9:00–20:00, closed Mon.

Pantheon is straight down Via del Salvatore (cheap pizza place on left just before the Pantheon, WC at McDonald's).

Sit for a while under the floodlit and moonlit **Pantheon's** portico. The 40-foot single-piece granite columns of the Pantheon's entrance show the scale the ancient Romans built on. The columns support a triangular, Greek-style roof with an inscription that says "M. Agrippa" built it. In fact, it was built *(fecit)* by Emperor Hadrian (A.D. 120), who gave credit to the builder of an earlier structure. This impressive entranceway gives no clue that the greatest wonder of the building is inside—a domed room that inspired later domes, including Michelangelo's St. Peter's and Brunelleschi's Duomo (in Florence).

With your back to the Pantheon, veer to the right down Via Orfani. On the right, you'll see **Tazza d'Oro Casa del Caffè,** one of Rome's top coffee shops, dating back to the days when this area was licensed to roast coffee beans. Locals come here for its fine *granita di caffè con panna* (coffee slush with cream). Look back at the fine view of the Pantheon from here. Then take Via Orfani uphill to Piazza Capranica.

Piazza Capranica is home to the big, plain, Florentine Renaissance-style Palazzo Capranica. Big shots, like the Capranica family, built stubby towers on their palaces—not for any military use, but just to show off. Leave the piazza to the right of the palace, between the palace and the church. The street Via in Aquiro leads to a sixth-century B.C. **Egyptian obelisk** (taken as a trophy by Augustus after his victory in Egypt over Mark Antony and Cleopatra). The obelisk was set up as a sundial. Walk the zodiac markings to the front door of the guarded parliament building. To your right is Piazza Colonna, where we're heading next—unless you like gelato...

A short detour to the left (past Albergo National) brings you to Rome's most famous *gelateria*. **Giolitti's** is cheap for take-out or elegant and splurge-worthy for a sit among classy locals (open daily until very late, Via Uffici del Vicario 40); get your gelato in a cone *(cono)* or cup *(coppetta)*.

Piazza Colonna features a huge second-century column honoring Marcus Aurelius. The big, important-looking palace houses the headquarters for the deputies (or cabinet) of the prime minister. The **Via del Corso** is named for the Berber horse races—without riders—that took place here during Carnevale until the 1800s when a horse trampled a man to death in front of a horrified queen. Historically the street was filled with meat shops. When it became Rome's first gaslit street in the 1800s, these butcher shops were banned and replaced by classier boutiques, jewelers, and antique dealers. Nowadays most of Via del Corso is closed to traffic every evening and becomes a wonderful parade of Romans out for an evening stroll (see "Dolce Vita Stroll," page 533).

Cross Via del Corso, Rome's noisy main drag, continue through the Y-shaped shopping gallery from 1928, forking to the right, and head down Via dei Sabini to the roar of the water, light, and people of the Trevi Fountain.

The **Trevi Fountain** shows how Rome took full advantage of the abundance of water brought into the city by its great aqueducts. This watery Baroque avalanche was completed in 1762 by Nicola Salvi, hired by a pope who was celebrating the reopening of the ancient aqueduct that powers it. Salvi used the palace behind the fountain as a theatrical backdrop for the figure of "Ocean," who represents water in every form. The statue surfs through his wet kingdom—with water gushing from 24 spouts and tumbling over 30 different kinds of plants—while Triton blows his conch shell. (From here, the water goes underground, then bubbles up again at Bernini's Four Rivers Fountain in Piazza Navona.)

The magic of the square is enhanced by the fact that no streets directly approach it. You can hear the excitement as you approach, and then—bam—you're there. The scene is always lively, with lucky Romeos clutching dates while unlucky ones clutch beers. Romantics toss a coin over their shoulder, thinking it will give them a wish and assure their return to Rome. That may sound silly, but every year I go through this touristic ritual...and it actually seems to work.

Take some time to people-watch (whisper a few breathy *bellos* or *bellas*) before leaving. Face the fountain, then go past it on the right down Via delle Stamperia to Via del Triton. Cross the busy street and continue to the Spanish Steps (ask, "Dov'è Piazza di Spagna?"—Spagna rhymes with "lasagna"), a few blocks and thousands of dollars of shopping opportunities away.

The Piazza di Spagna, with the very popular **Spanish Steps**, is named for the Spanish Embassy to the Vatican, which has been here for 300 years. It's been the hangout of many Romantics over the years (Keats, Wagner, Openshaw, Goethe, and others). The British poet John Keats pondered his mortality, then died in the pink building on the right side of the steps. Fellow Romantic Lord Byron lived across the square at #66.

The Sinking Boat Fountain at the foot of the steps, built by Bernini or his father, Pietro, is powered by an aqueduct. All of Rome's fountains are powered by aqueducts; their spurts are determined by the varying water pressure. This one, for instance, is much weaker than Trevi's gush.

The piazza is a thriving night scene. Window-shop along Via Condotti, which stretches away from the steps. This is where Gucci and other big names cater to the trendsetting jet set. Facing the Spanish Steps, you can walk right about a block to tour one of the world's biggest and most lavish McDonald's (salad bar, WC).

Tips on Sightseeing in Rome

Museums: Plan ahead. The marvelous Borghese Gallery and Nero's Golden House (closed indefinitely due to water damage) both require reservations (smart to reserve well in advance; for specifics, see "Borghese Gallery" listing on page 557 and "Nero's Golden House" listing on page 544).

A special combo-ticket called the **Archeologia Card,** which costs €20, covers the National Museum of Rome, Colosseum, Palatine Hill, Baths of Caracalla, Crypt Balbi (medieval art), Museum of the Bath (Roman inscriptions), Palazzo Altemps (so-so sculpture collection), Tomb of Cecilia Metella (on Appian Way), and Villa of the Quintilli (barren Roman villa on the outskirts of Rome). The combo-ticket allows you to see nine sights for the price of three (purchase at participating sights, valid for 7 days). The big plus of this ticket is that you avoid the long lines at the Colosseum (assuming you purchase it somewhere other than the Colosseum).

Churches: Churches generally open early (around 7:00), close for lunch (roughly 12:00–15:00), and close late (around 19:00). Kamikaze tourists maximize their sightseeing hours by visiting churches before 9:00 and seeing the major sights that stay open during the siesta (St. Peter's, Colosseum, Forum, Capitol Hill Museum, and National Museum of Rome), while Romans are taking it cool and easy.

Many churches have "modest dress" requirements, which means no bare shoulders, miniskirts, or shorts—for men, women, or children. This dress code is only strictly enforced at St. Peter's and St. Paul's Outside the Walls.

There's a taxi stand in the courtyard outside McDonald's; or, if you'd prefer, the Spagna Metro stop (usually open until 23:30) is just to the left of the Spanish Steps, ready to zip you home.

SIGHTS

From the Colosseum Area to Capitol Hill

The core of the ancient city, where the grandest monuments were built, is between the Colosseum and Capitol Hill. The following sights are listed in roughly geographical order from the Colosseum area to Capitol Hill. Except for the small St. Peter-in-Chains Church and the Time Elevator Roma, the sights date from ancient Rome.

▲**St. Peter-in-Chains Church (San Pietro in Vincoli)**—Built in the fifth century to house the chains that held St. Peter, this church is most famous for its Michelangelo statue. Check out the much-venerated chains under the high altar, then focus on mighty Moses

Ancient Rome

(free, daily 7:00–12:30 & 15:30–18:00, modest dress required; the church is a 15-minute, uphill, zigzag walk from the Colosseum, or a shorter, simpler walk from the Cavour Metro stop—exiting the Metro stop, go up steep flight of steps, take a right at the top, and walk a block to church).

Pope Julius II commissioned Michelangelo to build a massive tomb, with 48 huge statues, crowned by a grand statue of this egomaniacal pope. The pope had planned to have his tomb placed in the center of St. Peter's Basilica. When Julius died, the work had barely been started, and no one had the money or necessary commitment to Julius to finish the project. Michelangelo finished one statue—Moses—and left a few unfinished statues: Leah and Rachel flanking Moses in this church, the *Prisoners* (now in Florence's Accademia), and the *Slaves* (now in Paris' Louvre).

This powerful statue of Moses—mature Michelangelo—is worth studying. The artist worked on it in fits and starts for 30 years. Moses has received the Ten Commandments. As he holds the stone tablets, his eyes show a man determined to stop his tribe from worshipping the golden calf and idols...a man determined to win salvation for the people of Israel. Why the horns? Centuries ago, the Hebrew word for "rays" was mistranslated as "horns."

▲**Nero's Golden House (Domus Aurea)**—The sparse remains of Emperor Nero's "Golden House" are closed indefinitely due to water damage. Nero (r. A.D. 54–68) was Rome's most notorious emperor. He killed his own mother, kicked his pregnant wife to death, and crucified St. Peter. When Rome burned in A.D. 64, Nero was accused of torching it to clear land for his domestic building needs. The Romans rebelled, the Senate declared him a public enemy, and Nero, with the help of a slave, killed himself.

While only hints of the splendid, colorful frescoes survive, the towering vaults and the sheer immensity of Nero's palace remain impressive. As you wander through rooms that are now underground, look up at the holes in the ceiling. Ponder how much of old Rome still hides underground...and why the subway is limited to two lines.

When the sight reopens, visits are allowed only with an escort (30 people, about every 30 min) and a mandatory reservation (€5 admission plus €1.50 reservation fee, Wed–Mon 9:00–19:45, last entry at 18:40, closed Tue). Schedule your visit online at www.pierreci.it or by calling 06-3996-7700 during office hours (reserve a few days in advance if you can). Guided tours in English are also offered twice daily for €10; request a tour when you book your reservation. Audioguides cost €2, but listen to the intro before entering or you'll be forever behind. If you show up without a reservation, you could luck out and be allowed in (chances are best on a late afternoon on a weekday). Nero's House is near the Colosseo Metro stop and 200 yards northeast of Colosseum; go through a park gate, up a hill, and it's on the left.

▲▲▲**Colosseum (Colosseo)**—This 2,000-year-old building is *the* great example of Roman engineering. Using concrete, brick, and their trademark round arches, Romans constructed much larger buildings than the Greeks. But in deference to the higher Greek culture, they finished their no-nonsense megastructure by pasting all three orders of Greek columns (Doric, Ionic, and Corinthian) as exterior decorations. The Flavian Amphitheater's popular name, "Colosseum," comes from the colossal statue of Nero that once stood in front of it.

Romans were into "big." By putting two theaters together, they created a circular amphitheater. They could fill and empty its 50,000 numbered seats as quickly and efficiently as we do our superstadiums. Teams of sailors hoisted canvas awnings over the stadium to give fans shade. This was where ancient Romans, whose taste for violence was the equal of modern America's, enjoyed their Dirty Harry and *Terminator*. Gladiators, criminals, and wild animals fought to the death in every conceivable scenario. The floor

Colosseum

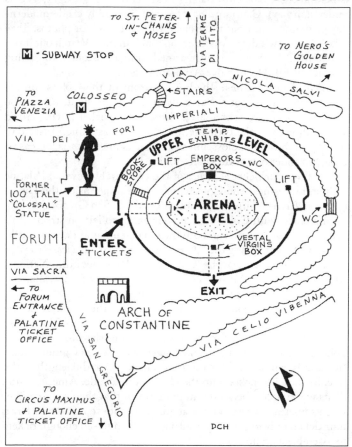

of the Colosseum is missing, exposing underground passages. Animals were kept in cages here and then lifted up in elevators; they'd pop out from behind blinds into the arena. The gladiator didn't know where, when, or by what he'd be attacked.

Cost, Hours, Location: €10 (includes Palatine Hill and special exhibits; also covered by €20 Archeologia Card). Audioguides are available at the ticket office (€4 for 2 hrs of use). Guided tours in English depart several times per day and last about one hour (€4). The Colosseum is open daily 9:00–19:00, or until an hour before sunset (tel. 06-3996-7700). Metro: Colosseo.

Like at the Forum, vendors outside the entrance of the Colosseum sell handy little *Rome: Past and Present* books with plastic overlays to un-ruin the ruins (marked €11, price soft). A crowded WC is inside the Colosseum, and a larger, cleaner WC is behind the Colosseum (facing ticket entrance, go right; WC is under stairway). Caution: For a fee, the incredibly crude modern-day gladiators snuff out their cigarettes and pose for photos. They take easy-to-swindle tourists for too much money. Watch out if you tangle with these guys (they're armed...and accustomed to getting as much as €100 from naive Asian tourists).

Avoid Long Lines: The lines in front of the Colosseum are for buying tickets, not for actually entering the sight. (Once you have your ticket, you can muscle through this ticket-buying crowd and go directly to the turnstile, which never has a line.) Instead of waiting in the long Colosseum ticket line (sometimes as long as an hour), consider one of these alternatives:

1. Buy your ticket at either of the two rarely crowded Palatine Hill entrances near the Colosseum—there's one inside the Forum (near the Arch of Titus) and another on Via di San Gregorio (facing Forum entry, with Colosseum at your back, go left on street). This €10 ticket includes entry to both the Colosseum and Palatine Hill.

2. Consider buying the €20 Archeologia Card at a less-crowded sight. The card covers the Colosseum, Palatine Hill, National Museum of Rome, Museum of the Bath, Baths of Caracalla, and more. Buy it at any of the included sights.

3. You can book a tour on the spot. These tours include Colosseum entry, allowing you to skip the line. This will cost you a few extra euros (€15 for the tour, including the €10 Colosseum ticket), but can save time and comes with a brief guided tour. Beware: It can be hard for you to instantly judge the length of the line, because it's tucked into the Colosseum arcade. American students working for the guides might tell you that there's a long line, when sometimes there is none at all. Also note that you may buy a tour ticket, only to get stuck waiting for them to sell enough tickets to assemble a group.

▲**Arch of Constantine**—The arch, next to the Colosseum, marks one of the great turning points in history—the military coup that made Christianity mainstream. In A.D. 312, Emperor Constantine defeated his rival Maxentius in one crucial battle. The night before, he had seen a vision of a cross in the sky. Constantine became sole emperor and legalized Christianity. With this one battle, a once obscure Jewish sect with a handful of followers was now the state religion of the entire Western world. In A.D. 300, you could be killed for being a Christian; later, you could be killed for not being one. Church enrollment boomed.

By the way, don't look too closely at the reliefs decorating this arch. By the fourth century, Rome was on its way down. Rather than struggle with original carvings, the makers of this arch plugged in bits and pieces scavenged from existing monuments. The arch is newly restored and looking great. But any meaning read into the stone will undoubtedly be very jumbled.

▲▲▲**Roman Forum (Foro Romano)**—This is ancient Rome's birthplace and civic center, and the common ground between Rome's famous seven hills (free, daily 9:00–19:00 or an hour before sunset, Metro: Colosseo, tel. 06-3996-7700). A €4 audioguide helps decipher the rubble (rent at gift shop at entrance on Via dei Fori Imperiali). Guided tours in English are offered nearly hourly (€4); ask for information at the ticket booth at the Palatine Hill (near Arch of Titus). See my self-guided walk on page 526.

▲▲▲**Palatine Hill (Monte Palatino)**—The hill above the Forum contains scant remains of the imperial palaces and the foundations of Rome, from Iron Age huts to the legendary house of Romulus (under corrugated tin roof in far corner). We get our word "palace" from this hill, where the emperors chose to live. The Palatine was once so filled with palaces that later emperors had to build out. (Looking up at it from the Forum, you see the substructure that supported these long-gone palaces.) The Palatine museum has sculptures and fresco fragments but is nothing special. From the pleasant garden, you'll get an overview of the Forum. On the far side, look down into an emperor's private stadium and then beyond at the dusty Circus Maximus, once a chariot course. Imagine the cheers, jeers, and furious betting.

While many tourists consider the Palatine Hill just extra credit after the Forum, it offers an insight into the greatness of Rome that's well worth the effort. (And, if you're visiting the Colosseum, you've got a ticket whether you like it or not.)

Cost, Hours, Location: €10 ticket also includes Colosseum, also covered by €20 Archeologia Card, daily 9:00–19:00 or until an hour before sunset, Metro: Colosseo. The main entrance and ticket office—which also sells Colosseum tickets, enabling smart sightseers to avoid that long line—is near the Arch of Titus and Colosseum. Another Palatine entrance is on Via di San Gregorio.

Audioguides cost €4. Guided tours in English are offered once daily (€3.50); ask for information at the ticket booth.

▲**Mamertine Prison**—This 2,500-year-old, cistern-like prison, which once held the bodies of Saints Peter and Paul, is worth a look (donation requested, daily 9:00–19:00, at the foot of Capitol Hill, near Forum's Arch of Septimius Severus). When you step into the room, you'll hit a modern floor. Ignore that and look up at the hole in the ceiling, from which prisoners were lowered. Then take the stairs down to the level of the actual prison floor. Downstairs, you'll see the column to which Peter was chained. It's said that a miraculous fountain sprang up in this room so that Peter could convert and baptize his jailers, who were also subsequently martyred. The upside-down cross commemorates Peter's upside-down crucifixion.

Imagine humans, amid fat rats and rotting corpses, awaiting slow deaths. On the walls near the entry are lists of notable prisoners (Christian and non-Christian) and the ways they were executed: *strangolati*, *decapitato*, *morto per fame* (died of hunger). The sign by the Christian names reads, "Here suffered, victorious for the triumph of Christ, these martyr saints."

▲**Trajan's Column, Market, and Forum (Colonna, Foro, e Mercati de Traiano)**—This offers the grandest column and best example of "continuous narration" from antiquity. Over 2,500 figures scroll around the 130-foot-high column, telling of Trajan's victorious Dacian campaign (circa A.D. 103, in present-day Romania), from the assembling of the army at the bottom to the victory sacrifice at the top. The ashes of Trajan and his wife were held in the mausoleum at the base while the sun once glinted off a polished bronze statue of Trajan at the top. Today, St. Peter is on top. Study the propaganda that winds up the column like a scroll, trumpeting Trajan's wonderful military exploits. You can see this close up for free (always open and viewable, just off Piazza Venezia, across the street from the Victor Emmanuel Monument). Viewing balconies once stood on either side, but it seems likely Trajan fans came away only with a feeling that the greatness of their emperor and empire was beyond comprehension (for a rolled-out version of the column's story, visit the Museum of Roman Civilization at E.U.R., page 584). This column marked **"Trajan's Forum,"** which was built to handle the shopping needs of a wealthy city of over a million. Commercial, political, religious, and social activities all mixed in the forum.

For a fee, you can go inside **Trajan's Market** (boring) and part of Trajan's Forum. The market was once filled with shops selling goods from all over the Roman Empire (€6.20, summer Tue–Sun 9:00–18:30, winter Tue–Sun 9:00–16:30, always closed Mon, entrance is uphill from the column on Via IV Novembre, tel. 06-679-0048). Trajan's Column is just a few steps off Piazza Venezia, on Via dei Fori Imperiali, across the street from the Victor Emmanuel Monument. Trajan's Forum stretches southeast of the column toward the Colosseum. The entrance to Trajan's Market is uphill from the column on Via IV Novembre.

Time Elevator Roma—The cheesy and overpriced visit is really just for kids (aged 5 and over). It starts with a stand-up, Italian-only, 15-minute intro, followed by a 30-minute, multi-screen show with seats jolting through the centuries. Equipped with headphones, you get nauseous in a comfortable, air-conditioned theater as the history of Rome unfolds before you—from the founding of the city, through its rise and fall, to its Renaissance rebound, and up to the present (€11, daily 11:00–19:30, shows every 30 min, no kids under 5, Via dei S.S. Apostoli 20, just off Via del Corso, 3-min walk from Piazza Venezia, tel. 06-9774-6243, www.time-elevator.it).

Capitol Hill Area

There are several ways to get to the top of Capitol Hill (also called "Capitoline Hill"). If you're coming from the north (from Piazza Venezia), take Michelangelo's impressive stairway to the right of the big, white Victor Emmanuel Monument. Coming from the south (the Forum), take either the steep staircase or the winding road, which converge near the top of the hill at a great Forum overlook, she-wolf statue, and refreshing water fountain. Block the spout with your fingers, and water spurts up for drinking. Romans, who call this *il nasone* (the big nose), joke that a cheap Roman boy takes his date out for a drink at *il nasone*. Near the *nasone* is a back-door entrance to the Victor Emmanuel Monument (described below).

▲▲**Capitol Hill (Campidoglio)**—This hill, once the religious and political center of ancient Rome, is still the home of the city's government. The mayoral palace and the twin buildings housing the Capitol Hill Museum (listed below) border Michelangelo's Renaissance square. The square's centerpiece is a copy of the famous equestrian statue of Marcus Aurelius (the original is behind glass in the adjacent museum—described below).

Michelangelo intended that people approach the square from his grand stairway off Piazza Venezia. From the top of the stairway, you see the new Renaissance face of Rome, with its back to the Forum. Michelangelo gave the buildings the "giant order"—huge pilasters make the existing two-story buildings feel one-storied and more harmonious with the new square. Notice how the statues atop these buildings welcome you and then draw you in. The terraces just downhill (past either side of the mayor's palace) offer grand views of the Forum.

▲▲**Capitol Hill Museum (Musei Capitolini)**—This museum encompasses two buildings (Palazzo dei Conservatori and Palazzo Nuovo) connected by an underground passage that leads to the vacant Tabularium and a panoramic overlook of the Forum (€8 ticket covers both buildings, €9.90 combo-ticket also includes Montemartini Museum—described on page 577, Tue–Sun 9:00–20:00, closed Mon, last entry 1 hr before closing, tel. 06-3996-7800, www.museicapitolini.org).

To identify the museum's two buildings, face the equestrian statue on Capitol Hill Square (with your back to the grand stairway leading up to the square). The Palazzo Nuovo is on your left; the Palazzo dei Conservatori (where you buy your ticket) is on your right (closer to the river). Ahead is the Palazzo Senatorio (mayoral palace, not open to public); below it—and out of sight—are the Tabularium and underground passage connecting the two museum buildings.

Buy your ticket (valid for 3 hrs) and consider renting the good €4 audioguide at Palazzo dei Conservatori.

Capitol Hill Area

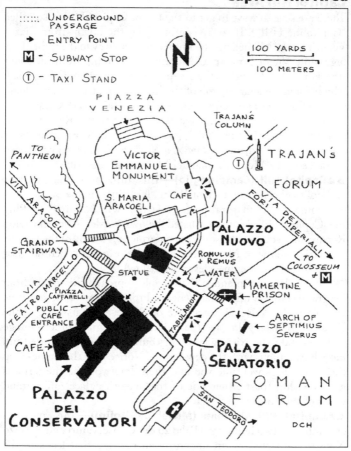

UNDERGROUND PASSAGE

→ ENTRY POINT

Ⓜ - SUBWAY STOP

Ⓣ - TAXI STAND

100 YARDS
100 METERS

PIAZZA VENEZIA

TRAJAN'S COLUMN

TRAJAN'S FORUM

TO PANTHEON

VICTOR EMMANUEL MONUMENT

VIA ARACOELI

S. MARIA ARACOELI

CAFÉ

PALAZZO NUOVO

VIA DEI FORI IMPERIALI

GRAND STAIRWAY

ROMULUS + REMUS

WATER

TO COLOSSEUM & Ⓜ

STATUE

MAMERTINE PRISON

VIA TEATRO MARCELLO

PIAZZA CAFFARELLI

PUBLIC CAFÉ ENTRANCE

TABULARIUM

ARCH OF SEPTIMIUS SEVERUS

CAFÉ →

PALAZZO SENATORIO

PALAZZO DEI CONSERVATORI

ROMAN FORUM

SAN TEODORO →

DCH

The **Palazzo dei Conservatori** is one of the world's oldest museums, at 500 years old. Inside the courtyard, have a look at giant chunks of a statue of Emperor Constantine; when intact, this imposing statue held court in the Basilica of Constantine in the Forum. The museum is worthwhile, with lavish rooms and several great statues. Tops is the original (500 B.C.) Etruscan *Capitoline Wolf* (the little statues of Romulus and Remus were added in the Renaissance). Don't miss the *Boy Extracting a Thorn* and the enchanting *Commodus as Hercules*. The second-floor painting gallery—except for two Caravaggios—is forgettable. The café upstairs, with a splendid patio with city views, is lovely at sunset.

Connect the two museums with the underground passage that leads to the **Tabularium**. Built in the first century B.C., this once held the archives of ancient Rome. The word *Tabularium* comes from "tablet," on which the Romans wrote their laws. You won't see any tablets, but you will see a superb head-on view of the Forum from the windows.

The **Palazzo Nuovo** houses mostly portrait busts of forgotten emperors. But it has three must-see statues: the *Dying Gaul*, the *Capitoline Venus* (both on the first floor up), and the original gilded bronze equestrian statue of Marcus Aurelius (behind glass in museum courtyard). This greatest surviving equestrian statue of antiquity was the original centerpiece of the square. While most such pagan statues were destroyed by Dark Age Christians, Marcus was mistaken for Constantine (the first Christian emperor) and therefore spared.

When you're ready to leave Capitol Hill, here are a couple of different options for reaching nearby sights:

Shortcut from Capitol Hill to Victor Emmanuel Monument: There's a clever little back-door access from the top of Capitol Hill directly to the top of the Victor Emmanuel Monument, saving you lots of uphill stair-climbing. Go up the wide steps in the left corner of the Capitol Hill square (if facing the Forum, the back-door entry is near the drinking fountain and she-wolf statue—follow signs to *terrazze*), pass through the iron gate at the top of the steps, and enter the small, unmarked door at #13 (on the right). You'll find yourself at the top of the monument with vast views, a café, and the entrance to the Museum of the Risorgimento (see "Victor Emmanuel Monument" listing, below). If you don't take this shortcut, you might decide to...

Descend from Capitol Hill to Piazza Venezia: Leaving Capitol Hill, head down the stairs leading to Piazza Venezia. At the bottom of the stairs, look left several blocks down the street to see a condominium actually built upon surviving ancient pillars and arches of Teatro Marcello.

Still at the bottom of the stairs, look up the long stairway to your right (which pilgrims climb on their knees) at the Santa Maria in Aracoeli church for a good example of the earliest style of Christian churches. While pilgrims find it worth the climb, sightseers can skip it. The contrast between this climb-on-your-knees ramp to God's house and Michelangelo's grand and elegant stairs leading to Capitol Hill (which you just came down) illustrates the changes Renaissance humanism brought civilization. As you walk toward Piazza Venezia, look down into the ditch on your right to see the ruins of an ancient apartment building from the first century A.D.; part of it was transformed into a tiny church (faded frescoes and bell tower). Rome was built in layers—almost everywhere you go, there's an earlier version beneath your feet.

Piazza Venezia —This vast square is the focal point of modern Rome. The Via del Corso, which starts here, is the city's axis, surrounded by Rome's classiest shopping district. In the 1930s, Benito Mussolini whipped up Italy's nationalistic fervor here from a balcony above the square (to your left with your back to Victor Emmanuel Monument). Fascist masses filled the square screaming, "Support the troops!"—or something like that. Mussolini lied to his people, mixing fear and patriotism to push his country to the right and embroil the Italians in expensive and regrettable wars. In 1945, they shot and hung Mussolini from a meat hook in Milan.

Victor Emmanuel Monument—This oversized monument to Italy's first king—built to celebrate the 50th anniversary of the country's unification in 1870—was part of Italy's push to overcome the new country's strong regionalism and to create a national identity. Open to the public, it offers a grand view of the Eternal City (free, 242 punishing steps to the top—unless you take the shortcut from Capitol Hill described above).

Romans think of the 200-foot-high, 500-foot-wide monument not as an altar of the fatherland, but as "the wedding cake," "the typewriter," or "the dentures." It wouldn't be so bad if it weren't sitting on a priceless acre of ancient Rome and if they had chosen better marble (this is too in-your-face white and picks up the pollution horribly). Soldiers guard Italy's Tomb of the Unknown Soldier as the eternal flame flickers. At the tomb, stand with your back to the flame and see how Via del Corso bisects Rome.

The Victor Emmanuel Monument houses a little-visited **Museum of the Risorgimento** explaining the movement and war that led to the unification of Italy in 1870 (free, daily 9:30–18:00, café).

Pantheon Area

To get to the Pantheon, you can walk (it's a 15-min walk from the Forum), take a taxi, or catch a bus. Bus #64 carries tourists and pickpockets daily and frequently between the train station and Vatican City, stopping at Largo Argentina, a few blocks south of the Pantheon. The *elettrico* minibus #116 runs between Campo de' Fiori and Piazza Barberini via the Pantheon (daily, fewer on Sun).

▲▲▲**Pantheon**—For the greatest look at the splendor of Rome, antiquity's best-preserved interior is a must (free, Mon–Sat 8:30–19:30, Sun 9:00–18:00, holidays 9:00–13:00, tel. 06-6830-0230). Because the Pantheon became a church dedicated to the martyrs just after the fall of Rome, the barbarians left it alone, and the locals didn't use it as a quarry. The portico is called "Rome's umbrella"—a fun local gathering in a rainstorm. Walk past its one-piece granite columns (biggest in Italy, shipped from Egypt) and through the original bronze doors. Sit inside under the glorious skylight and enjoy classical architecture at its best.

The dome, 142 feet high and wide, was Europe's biggest until

Pantheon Area

TO PIAZZA
DEL POPOLO

TO
SPANISH
STEPS

TO M
BARB.

PONTE
UMBERTO

T I B E R

LUNGOTEVERE MARZIO

PIAZZA
COLONNA

VIA TRITONE

S. LUIGI
(CARAVAGGIO)

ANCIENT
STADIUM
ENTRANCE

PARL.

TREVI

CORONARI

UFF. VICARIO

COPPELLE

SABINA

MURATTE

DATAR.

TRE
SCALINI

AQUIRO

P. PIETRA

SALV.

GIUST.

SEMINARIO

PIAZZA
NAVONA

PIAZZA
PASQUINO

SAN
IGNAZIO

CITY
MUSEUM

VIA

PANTHEON

S. MARIA
SOPRA
MINERVA

GALLERIA
DORA
PAMPHILJ

CAMPO
DE'
FIORI

VIA VITTORIO

ARG.

EST.

E MANUELE

PIAZZA
VENEZIA

B T

GESÙ

VIA BOTT. OSC.

ARACOELI

V.E.
MON.

FORI IMP.

TO
COLO-
SSEUM

PALAZZO
FARNESE

LARGO
ARGENTINA
RUINS
(& CAT HOSPICE)

CAPITOL
HILL

LUNGOTEVERE

PONTE
SISTO

F O R U M

TO
TRASTEVERE

T - TAXI STAND
M - SUBWAY STOP
B - BUS STOP

DCH

200 YARDS

200 METERS

the Renaissance. Michelangelo's dome at St. Peter's, while much higher, is about three feet narrower. The brilliance of this dome's construction astounded architects through the ages. During the Renaissance, Brunelleschi was given permission to cut into the dome (see the little square hole above and to the right of the entrance) to analyze the material. The concrete dome gets thinner and lighter with height—the highest part is volcanic pumice.

This wonderfully harmonious architecture greatly inspired Raphael and other artists of the Renaissance. Raphael, along with Italy's first two kings, chose to be buried here.

As you walk around the outside of the Pantheon, notice the "rise of Rome"—about 15 feet since it was built. The nearest WCs are at McDonald's and at bars on the square. You'll find perhaps Rome's most exuberant gelato at Gelateria della Palma, two blocks in front of the Pantheon (Via della Maddalena 20). For lunch or dinner ideas, see page 601.

▲▲**Churches near the Pantheon**—The **Church of San Luigi dei Francesi** has a magnificent chapel painted by Caravaggio (free, but bring coins to buy light, Fri–Wed 7:30–12:30 & 15:30–19:00, Thu 7:30–12:30, sightseers should avoid Mass at 7:30 and 19:00). The only Gothic church in Rome is **Santa Maria sopra Minerva,** with a little-known Michelangelo statue, *Christ Bearing the Cross* (free, daily 7:00–12:00 & 15:30–19:00, on a little square behind Pantheon, to the east). The **Church of St. Ignazio,** several blocks east of the Pantheon, is a riot of Baroque illusions with a false dome (free, daily 7:00–12:30 & 16:00–19:00). A few blocks away, back across Corso Vittorio Emanuele, is the rich and Baroque **Gesu Church,** headquarters of the Jesuits in Rome (free, daily 7:00–12:30 & 16:00–19:15). Modest dress is recommended at all churches.

▲**Galleria Doria Pamphilj**—This gallery, filling a palace on Piazza del Collegio Romano, offers a rare chance to wander through a noble family's lavish rooms with the prince who calls this downtown mansion home. Well, almost. Through an audioguide, the prince lovingly narrates his family's story, including how the Doria Pamphilj (pahm-FEEL-yee) family's cozy relationship with the pope inspired the word "nepotism." Highlights include paintings by Caravaggio, Titian, and Raphael, and portraits of Pope Innocent X by Diego Velázquez (on canvas) and Gian Lorenzo Bernini (in marble). The fancy rooms of the palace are interesting, with a mini-Versailles–like hall of mirrors and paintings lining the walls to the ceiling in the style typical of 18th-century galleries (€8, includes worthwhile audioguide, Fri–Wed 10:00–17:00, closed Thu, from Piazza Venezia walk 2 blocks up Via del Corso and take a left, Piazza del Collegio Romano 2, tel. 06-679-7323, www.doriapamphilj.it).

Piazza di Pietra (Piazza of Stone)—This square was actually a quarry set up to chew away at the abandoned Roman building. You can still see the holes that hungry medieval scavengers chipped into the columns to steal the metal pins that held the slabs together (2 blocks toward Via del Corso from Pantheon).

▲**Trevi Fountain**—This bubbly Baroque fountain, worth ▲ by day and ▲▲ by night, is a minor sight to art scholars...but a major nighttime gathering spot for teens on the make and tourists tossing coins. (For more information, see page 541.)

East Rome, near the Train Station

These sights are within a 10-minute walk of the train station. By Metro, use the Termini stop for the National Museum and the Piazza Repubblica stop for the rest.

▲▲▲**National Museum of Rome (Museo Nazionale Romano Palazzo Massimo alla Terme)**—This museum houses the greatest collection of ancient Roman art anywhere, and includes busts of emperors and a Roman copy of the *Greek Discus Thrower.* The

East Rome

ground floor is a historic yearbook of marble statues from the second century B.C. to the second century A.D., with rare Greek originals. The first floor is peopled by statues from the first through fourth centuries A.D. The second floor features a collection of frescoes and mosaics that once decorated Roman villas. Finally, descend into the basement to see fine gold jewelry, dice, an abacus, and vault doors leading into the best coin collection in Europe, with fancy magnifying glasses maneuvering you through cases of coins from ancient Rome to modern times.

Cost and Hours: €7, covered by €20 Archeologia Card, Tue–Sun 9:00–19:45, closed Mon, last entry 45 min before closing. An audioguide costs €4 (buy ticket first, then get audioguide at bookshop). The museum is about 100 yards from the Termini train station. As you leave the station, it's the sandstone-brick building on your left. Enter at the far end, at Largo di Villa Peretti (tel. 06-481-5576).

▲**Baths of Diocletian (Terme di Diocleziano)**—Around A.D. 300, Emperor Diocletian built the largest baths in Rome. This sprawling meeting place, with baths and schmoozing spaces to accommodate 3,000 bathers at a time, was a big deal in ancient Rome. The baths functioned until 537, when the barbarians cut Rome's aqueducts. While much of the complex is still closed, three sections are open: the Octagonal Hall, the Church of St. Mary of the Angels and Martyrs (both face Piazza della Repubblica—see below), and the skippable Museum of the Bath, which displays ancient Roman inscriptions on tons of tombs and tablets, but has nothing on the baths despite its name (museum entry-€5, covered by €20 Archeologia Card, audioguide-€4, Tue–Sun 9:00–19:45, closed Mon, last entry 45 min before closing, Viale E. de Nicola 79, entrance faces Termini train station, tel. 06-4782-6152).

Octagonal Hall: The Aula Ottagona, or Rotunda of Diocletian, was a private gymnasium in the Baths of Diocletian. The floor would have been 23 feet lower (look down the window in the center of the room). The graceful iron grid supported the canopy of a 1928 planetarium. Today, the hall's gallery, showing off fine bronze and marble statues—the kind that would have decorated the baths of imperial Rome. Most are Roman copies of Greek originals...gods, athletes, portrait busts. One merits a close look: the *Boxer at Rest* (1st century B.C.). Textbook Hellenistic, this bronze statue is realistic and full of emotion. Slumped over, losing, and exhausted, the boxer gasps for air (free, open sporadically, generally Tue–Sat 9:00–14:00, Sun 9:00–13:00, closed Mon, borrow the English-description booklet, handy WC hiding in the back corner through an unmarked door).

Church of St. Mary of the Angels and Martyrs (Santa Maria degli Angeli e dei Martiri): From Piazza della Repubblica, step through the Roman wall into what was the great central hall of the baths and is now a church (since the 16th century) that was designed by Michelangelo. When the church entrance was moved to Piazza Repubblica, the church was reoriented 90 degrees, turning the nave into long transepts and the transepts into a short nave. The 12 red-granite columns still stand in their ancient positions. The classical floor was 15 feet lower. Project the walls down and imagine the soaring shape of the Roman vaults (free, Mon–Sat 7:00–18:30, Sun 8:00–19:30, closed to sightseers during Mass).

▲**Santa Maria della Vittoria**—This church houses Bernini's statue of a swooning *St. Teresa in Ecstasy* (free, daily 7:00–12:00 & 15:30–19:00, about 5 blocks northwest of Termini train station on Largo Susanna, Metro: Repubblica).

Once inside the church, you'll find St. Teresa to the left of the altar. Teresa has just been stabbed with God's arrow of fire. Now, the angel pulls it out and watches her reaction. Teresa swoons, her eyes roll up, her hand goes limp, she parts her lips...and moans. The smiling, cherubic angel understands just how she feels. Teresa, a 16th-century Spanish nun, later talked of the "sweetness" of "this intense pain," describing her oneness with God in ecstatic, even erotic, terms.

Bernini, the master of multimedia, pulls out all the stops to make this mystical vision real. Actual sunlight pours through the alabaster windows; bronze sunbeams shine on a marble angel holding a golden arrow. Teresa leans back on a cloud and her robe ripples from within, charged with her spiritual arousal. Bernini has created a little stage-setting of heaven. And watching from the "theater boxes" on either side are members of the family that commissioned the work.

Santa Susanna Church—The home of the American Catholic Church in Rome, Santa Susanna holds Mass in English daily at 18:00 and on Sunday at 9:00 and 10:30. Their excellent Web site in English, www.santasusanna.org, contains tips for travelers and a long list of convents that rent out rooms. They arrange papal audiences (see page 566) and have an English library that includes my Venice, Florence, and Rome guidebooks (Mon–Fri 9:00–13:00 & 14:00–18:00, closed Sat–Sun, Via XX Settembre 15, near recommended Via Firenze hotels, Metro: Repubblica, tel. 06-4201-4554).

North Rome:
Villa Borghese and nearby Via Veneto

▲**Villa Borghese**—Rome's scruffy "Central Park" is great for people-watching (plenty of modern-day Romeos and Juliets). Take a rowboat out on the lake or visit the two museums listed below.

▲▲▲**Borghese Gallery (Galleria Borghese)**—This plush museum, filling a cardinal's mansion in the park, was recently restored and offers one of Europe's most sumptuous art experiences. You'll enjoy a collection of world-class Baroque sculpture, including Bernini's *David* and his excited statue of Apollo chasing Daphne, as well as paintings by Caravaggio, Raphael, Titian, and Rubens. The museum's slick mandatory reservation system keeps the crowds at a manageable size.

The essence of the collection is the connection of the Renaissance with the classical world. Notice the second-century Roman reliefs with Michelangelo-designed panels above either end of the portico

North Rome

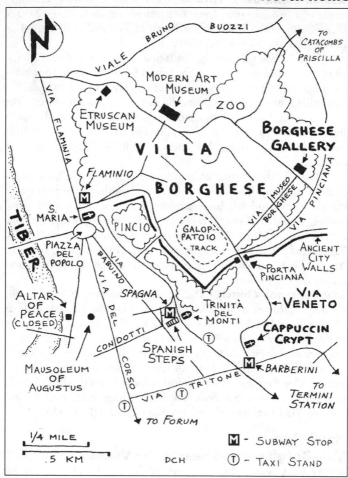

as you enter. The villa was built in the early 17th century by the great art collector Cardinal Borghese, who wanted to prove that the glories of ancient Rome were matched by the Renaissance.

In the main entry hall, opposite the door, notice the thrilling relief of the horse falling (1st century A.D., Greek). Pietro Bernini, father of the famous Bernini, completed the scene by adding the rider.

Each room seems to feature a Baroque masterpiece. The best of all is in Room III: Bernini's *Apollo and Daphne*. It's the perfect Baroque subject—capturing a thrilling, action-filled moment. In the mythological story, Apollo races after Daphne. Just as he's about to reach her, she turns into a tree. As her toes turn to roots

Borghese Gallery—Ground Floor

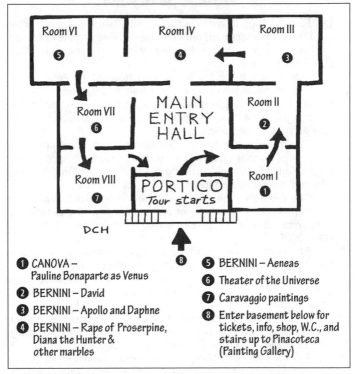

Room VI ⑤

Room IV ④

Room III ❸

Room VII ❻

MAIN ENTRY HALL

Room II ❷

Room VIII ❼

PORTICO
Tour starts

Room I ❶

DCH

❽

❶ CANOVA – Pauline Bonaparte as Venus

❷ BERNINI – David

❸ BERNINI – Apollo and Daphne

❹ BERNINI – Rape of Proserpine, Diana the Hunter & other marbles

⑤ BERNINI – Aeneas

❻ Theater of the Universe

❼ Caravaggio paintings

❽ Enter basement below for tickets, info, shop, W.C., and stairs up to Pinacoteca (Painting Gallery)

and branches spring from her fingers, Apollo is in for one rude surprise. Walk slowly around. It's more air than stone.

Cost and Hours: €8.50, includes €2 reservation fee, Tue–Sun 9:00–19:00, closed Mon. No photos are allowed.

Reservations: Reservations are mandatory and easy to get in English by booking online (www.ticketeria.it) or calling 06-328-101 (if you get an Italian recording, press 2 for English; office hours: Mon–Fri 9:00–18:00, Sat 9:00–13:00, office closed Sat in Aug and Sun year-round). Every two hours, 360 people are allowed to enter the museum. Entry times are 9:00, 11:00, 13:00, 15:00, and 17:00. Reserve a *minimum* of several days in advance for a weekday visit, at least a week ahead for weekends. Reservations are tightest at 11:00 and on weekends. When you reserve, request a day and time, and you'll get a claim number. While you'll be advised to come 30 minutes before your appointed time, I was told you can arrive 10 minutes beforehand. After that, you become a no-show, and your ticket is sold to stand-bys.

If you don't have a reservation, try calling to see if there are any openings, or just show up and hope for a cancellation. No-shows

From Pope to Pope

On March 30, 2005, 84-year-old Pope John Paul II appeared for the last time at his apartment window overlooking St. Peter's Square. Frail and unable to speak, he silently blessed the crowd. Three days later, he died.

John Paul's body lay in state in front of St. Peter's altar, beneath Michelangelo's dome and framed by Bernini's bronze canopy. Outside, hundreds of thousands of pilgrims lined up all the way down Via della Conciliazione, waiting up to 24 hours for one last look at their pope.

The morning of April 8, 300,000 mourners, dignitaries, and security personnel gathered in wind-blown St. Peter's Square for the funeral. As they carried out John Paul's coffin the crowd shouted *"Santo! Santo!"* insisting he be made a saint.

The next day, the coffin was carried from the altar down the steps into St. Peter's Crypt and buried near the tomb of St. Peter, marked by a simple stone slab reading: Joannes Paulus II (1920–2005).

Then came nine days of mourning as Cardinals representing the globe's 1.1 billion Catholics arrived to elect a new pope.

On April 18, 115 Cardinals dressed in crimson were stripped of their cell phones, given a vow of secrecy, and locked inside the Sistine Chapel for the "conclave" (from Latin *cum clave*, with key). Two votes failed to reach a two-thirds majority, and they burned the ballots in a temporary furnace, sending clouds of chemically-enhanced black smoke out over St. Peter's Square.

Finally, at 17:50 of April 19, an anxious crowd in St. Peter's Square saw a puff of white smoke from the Sistine Chapel's chimney. The bells in St. Peter's clock towers rang out gloriously (a new tradition) confirming that, indeed, a pope had been elected.

On the balcony of St. Peter's facade, a cardinal addressed the crowd below. "Brothers and sisters," he said in several languages, *"Habemus Papam."* We have a pope. As thousands chanted *"Viva il*

are released a few minutes after the top of the hour. Generally, out of 360 reservations, a few will fail to show (but more than a few may be waiting to grab them). You're most likely to land a stand-by ticket at 13:00. Visits are strictly limited to two hours. Concentrate on the ground floor, but leave yourself 30 minutes—any time during your visit—for the paintings of the Pinacoteca upstairs (highlights are marked by the audioguide icons). The fine bookshop and cafeteria are best visited outside your two-hour entry window.

Tours: Guided English tours are offered at 9:10 and 11:10 for €5; reserve with entry reservation (or consider the excellent audioguide tour for €4).

papa," 78-year-old Josef Ratzinger of Germany stepped up, raised his hands, and was presented as Pope Benedict XVI.

The 265th pope introduced himself as "a simple, humble worker in the vineyard of the Lord." But the man has a complex history, a reputation for intellectual brilliance, a flair for the piano, and a penchant for controversy for his unbending devotion to traditional Catholic doctrine.

Born in small-town Bavaria in 1927, he lived life under Nazi rule as many Germans did—outwardly obeying leaders while inwardly conflicted. Like many Germans, he joined the Hitler Youth, was drafted into the Army, sprayed flak from anti-aircraft guns, and saw Jews transported to death camps.

After the war, he became a rising voice of liberal Catholicism. But after the 1968 student revolts rocked Europe's Establishment, he became increasingly convinced that Church tradition was needed to offset the growing chaos of the world.

Ratzinger became Pope John Paul's closest advisor and good friend. Every Friday afternoon for two decades, they met for lunch, intellectual sparring, and friendly conversation.

Under John Paul, Ratzinger served as the Church's "enforcer" of doctrine, earning the nickname "God's Rottweiler." He spoke out against ordaining women, chastised Latin American priests for fomenting class warfare, reassigned bishops who were soft on homosexuality, reaffirmed opposition to birth control, and wrote thoughtful papers challenging the secular world's moral relativism.

The name of "Benedict" recalls both Pope Benedict XV (who healed World War I's divisions) and Europe's patron St. Benedict (c. 480–543), who symbolizes Europe's Christian roots. A true pan-European who speaks many languages, Benedict XVI is expected to continue John Paul's two priorities: defending Catholic doctrine in a changing world and building bridges with fellow Christians.

Getting There: The museum is in the Villa Borghese park. A taxi can get you within 100 yards of the museum (tell the cabbie your destination: gah-leh-REE-ah bor-GAY-zay). Getting to the museum by public transportation can be confusing, and requires a walk in the park. From the Spagna Metro stop, an escalator carries you up into the park, where you follow signs for 10 minutes. To avoid missing your appointment, allow yourself plenty of time to find the place.

Etruscan Museum (Villa Giulia Museo Nazionale Etrusco)—The Etruscan civilization thrived in this part of Italy around 600 B.C., when Rome was an Etruscan town. The Etruscan civilization is fascinating, but the Villa Giulia Museum is extremely low-tech and in a state of disarray. I don't like it, and fans of the Etruscans will prefer the Vatican Museum's section. Still, the Villa Giulia does have the famous "husband and wife sarcophagus" (a dead couple seeming to enjoy an everlasting banquet from atop their tomb—6th century B.C. from Cerveteri); the *Apollo from Veii* statue (of textbook fame); and an impressive room filled with gold sheets of Etruscan printing and temple statuary from the Sanctuary of Pyrgi (€4, Tue–Sun 8:30–19:30, closed Mon, closes earlier off-season, Piazzale di Villa Giulia 9, tel. 06-322-6571). For more on the Etruscans, see page 694.

▲**Cappuccin Crypt**—If you want to see artistically arranged bones, this is the place. The crypt is below the church of Santa Maria della Immacolata Concezione on Via Veneto, just up from Piazza Barberini. The bones of more than 4,000 monks who died between 1528 and 1870 are in the basement, all lined up for the delight—or disgust—of the always-wide-eyed visitor. The soil in the crypt was brought from Jerusalem 400 years ago, and the monastic message on the wall explains that this is more than just a macabre exercise: "We were what you are...you will become what we are now." *Buon giorno.* Pick up a few of Rome's most interesting postcards (donation, Fri–Wed 9:00–12:00 & 15:00–18:00, closed Thu, Metro: Barberini, tel. 06-487-1185). Just up the street, you'll find the American Embassy, Federal Express, Hard Rock Café, and fancy Via Veneto cafés filled with the poor and envious looking for the rich and famous.

Ara Pacis (Altar of Peace)—Now surrounded by a high fence, this may reopen in 2006 after restoration. In 9 B.C., after victories in Gaul and Spain, Emperor Augustus celebrated the beginning of the Pax Romana (the Roman Empire at peace) by building this altar of peace. Peace is almost worshipped here. The north and south walls show a procession with realistic portraits of the imperial family in Greek Hellenistic style. It's a memorable combination of Roman grandeur and Greek elegance. Even during restoration, the altar can sometimes be seen through the windows (a long block west of Via del Corso on Via di Ara Pacis, on east banks of river near Ponte Cavour, nearest Metro: Spagna).

Catacombs of Priscilla (Catacombe di Priscilla)—For the most intimate catacombs experience, many prefer this smaller, more obscure option to the crowded catacombs on Appian Way (San Callisto and San Sebastian). The Catacombs of Priscilla, which used to be situated under the house of a Roman noble family, were used for some of the most important burials during antiquity. Best of all, because they're on the opposite side of town from the most popular catacombs, you'll have them mostly to yourself. You'll actually be in the care of a nun with a flashlight as you walk through the evocative chambers claimed to show the first depiction of Mary with Jesus (€5, Tue–Sun 8:30–12:00 & 14:30–17:00, closed Mon, beyond Villa Borghese on Piazza Crati at Via Salaria 430, bus #63 from Largo Argentina, or €10 taxi ride, tel. 06-862-06272, www.catacombedipriscilla.com). For more on catacombs, see "Catacombs," page 582.

West Rome: Vatican City Area

▲▲▲**St. Peter's Basilica**—There is no doubt: This is the richest and most impressive church on earth. To call it vast is like calling God smart. Marks on the floor show where the next-largest churches would fit if they were put inside. The ornamental cherubs would dwarf a large man. Birds roost inside, and thousands of people wander about, heads craned heavenward, hardly noticing each other. Don't miss Michelangelo's *Pietà* (behind bulletproof glass) to the right of the entrance. Bernini's altar work and seven-story-tall bronze canopy *(baldacchino)* are brilliant.

For a quick walk through the basilica, follow these points (see map on page 564):

❶ The atrium is larger than most churches. Notice the historic doors (the Holy Door, on the right, won't be opened until the next Jubilee Year, in 2025—see page 565).

❷ The purple, circular porphyry stone marks the site of Charlemagne's coronation in A.D. 800 (in the first St. Peter's church that stood on this site). From here, get a sense of the immensity of the church, which can accommodate 95,000 worshippers standing on its six acres.

❸ Michelangelo planned a Greek-cross floor plan rather than the Latin-cross standard in medieval churches. A Greek cross, symbolizing the perfection of God, and by association the goodness of man, was important to the humanist Michelangelo. But accommodating large crowds was important to the Church in the fancy Baroque age, which followed Michelangelo, so the original nave length was doubled. Stand halfway up the nave and imagine the stubbier design Michelangelo had in mind.

❹ View the magnificent dome from the statue of St. Andrew. See the vision of heaven above the windows: Jesus, Mary, a ring of saints, rings of angels, and, on the very top, God the Father.

❺ The main altar sits directly over St. Peter's tomb and under Bernini's 70-foot-tall bronze canopy.

❻ The stairs lead down to the crypt to the foundation, chapels, and tombs of popes (including the simple tomb of John Paul II). Do this last, since it leads you out of the church.

❼ The statue of St. Peter, with an irresistibly kissable toe, is one of the few pieces of art that predate this church. It adorned the first St. Peter's church.

St. Peter's Basilica

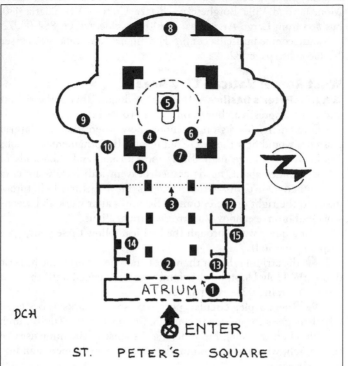

DCH

ENTER

ST.   PETER'S   SQUARE

1. Holy Door

2. Charlemagne's Coronation Site, A.D. 800

3. Extent of original "Greek Cross" Church Plan

4. St. Andrew Statue & View of Dome

5. Main Altar (Directly over Peter's Tomb)

6. Stairs Down to Crypt (Entrance May Move)

7. St. Peter Statue (With Kissable Toe)

8. BERNINI—Dove Window & "Throne of Peter"

9. St. Peter's Crucifixion Site

10. Museum Entrance

11. RAPHAEL—Transfiguration (Mosaic Copy)

12. Blessed Sacrament Chapel

13. MICHELANGELO—Pietà

14. Elevator to Roof and Dome-Climb (Possible Indoor Location)

15. Elevator to Roof and Dome-Climb (Possible Outdoor Location)

❽ St. Peter's throne and Bernini's starburst dove window is the site of a daily Mass (Mon–Sat at 17:00, Sun at 17:30).

❾ St. Peter was crucified here when this location was simply "the Vatican Hill." The obelisk now standing in the center of St. Peter's square marked the center of a Roman racecourse long before a church stood here.

❿ For most, the treasury (in the sacristy) is not worth the admission.

⓫ The church is filled with mosaics, not paintings. Notice the mosaic version of Raphael's *Transfiguration*.

⓬ Blessed Sacrament Chapel.

⓭ Michelangelo sculpted his *Pietà* when he was 24 years old. A pietà is a work showing Mary with the dead body of Christ taken down from the cross. Michelangelo's mastery of the body is obvious in this powerfully beautiful masterpiece. Jesus is believably dead, and Mary, the eternally youthful "handmaiden" of the Lord, still accepts God's will...even if it means giving up her son.

The Holy Door (just to the right of the *Pietà*) was bricked shut at the end of the Jubilee Year 2000 and won't be opened until 2025. Every 25 years, the Church celebrates an especially festive year derived from the Old Testament idea of the Jubilee Year (originally every 50 years), which encourages new beginnings and the forgiveness of sins and debts. In the Jubilee Year 2000, Pope John Paul II tirelessly—and with significant success—promoted debt relief for the world's poorest countries.

⓮ An elevator leads to the roof and the stairway up the dome (€6, allow an hour to go up and down). The dome, Michelangelo's last work, is (you guessed it) the biggest anywhere. Taller than a football field is long, it's well worth the sweaty climb for a great view of Rome, the Vatican grounds, and the inside of the basilica—particularly heavenly while there is singing. Look around—Rome has no modern skyline. No building is allowed to exceed the height of St. Peter's. The elevator takes you to the rooftop of the nave. From there, a few steps take you to a balcony at the base of the dome looking down into the church interior. After that, the one-way, 323-step climb (for some people claustrophobic) to the cupola begins. The rooftop level (below the dome) has a gift shop, WC, drinking fountain, and a commanding view.

Dress Code: The church strictly enforces its dress code: no shorts or bare shoulders (applies to men, women, and children); no miniskirts. You might be required to check any bags at a free cloakroom near the entry.

Hours of Church: Daily April–Sept 7:00–19:00, Oct–March 7:00–18:00. Mass is held daily (Mon–Sat at 8:30, 10:00, 11:00, 12:00, and 17:00; Sun and holidays at 9:00, 10:30, 11:30, 12:10, 13:00, 16:00, and 17:30; confirm schedule locally). The church often

Vatican City

This tiny independent country of just over 100 acres, contained entirely within Rome, has its own postal system, armed guards, helipad, mini-train station, and radio station (KPOP). Politically powerful, the Vatican is the religious capital of 800 million Roman Catholics. If you're not a Catholic, become one for your visit.

The pope is both the religious and secular leader of Vatican City. For centuries, locals referred to him as "King Pope." Italy and the Vatican didn't always have good relations. In fact, after unification (in 1870), when Rome's modern grid plan was built around the miniscule Vatican, it seemed as if the new buildings were designed to be just high enough so no one could see the dome of St. Peter's from street level. Modern Italy was created in 1870, but the Holy See didn't recognize it as a country until 1929, when the pope and Mussolini signed the Lateran Pact, giving sovereignty to the Vatican and a few nearby churches.

Like every European country, Vatican City has its own versions of the euro coin. You're unlikely to find one in your pocket, though, as they are snatched up by collectors before falling into actual circulation. With John Paul II's passing, the coins have been redesigned to feature a portrait of the new pope, Benedict XVI.

Small as it is, Vatican City has two huge sights: St. Peter's Basilica (with Michelangelo's *Pietà*) and the Vatican Museum (with the Sistine Chapel). A helpful **TI** is just to the left of St. Peter's Basilica (Mon–Sat 8:30–19:00, closed Sun, tel. 06-6988-1662; Vatican switchboard tel. 06-6982, www.vatican.va). The thief-infested bus #64 and the safer #40 express bus both stop near the basilica. The closest Metro stops are a 10-minute walk away from either sight: For St. Peter's, it's Ottaviano; for the Vatican Museum, it's Cipro-Musei Vaticani.

The Vatican **post office,** with offices on St. Peter's Square (next to TI) and in the Vatican Museum, is more reliable than Italy's mail service (Mon–Sat 8:30–19:00). The stamps are a collectible bonus. Vatican stamps are good throughout Rome, but to use the Vatican's mail service, you need to mail your cards from the Vatican; write your postcards ahead of time. (Note that the Vatican won't mail cards with Italian stamps.)

Seeing the Pope: Your best chances for a sighting are on Sunday and Wednesday. The pope usually gives a blessing at noon on Sunday from his apartment on St. Peter's Square (except summer, when he speaks at his summer residence at Castel Gandolfo, 25 miles from Rome; train leaves Rome's Termini station). St. Peter's is easiest (just show up) and, for most, enough of a "visit." Those interested in a more formal appearance (but not more intimate), can get a ticket for the Wednesday general audience (at 10:30) when the pope, arriving in his bulletproof Popemobile, greets and blesses the crowds at St. Peter's from a balcony or canopied

Vatican City Overview

CIPRO - MUSEI VATICANI

TO TERMINI

OTTAVIANO

VIA OTTAVIANO

VIA CANDIA

VIALE GIULIO CESARE

VIALE VATICANO

PIAZZA RISORGIMENTO

VATICAN MUSEUM →

SISTINE CHAPEL →

PAPAL APT.

TO CASTEL SANT'ANGELO + BUS #40 →

VIA CONCILIAZIONE

ST. PETER'S →

ST. PETER'S SQUARE + OBELISK

BUS #64

VATICAN BOUNDARY

DCH

Ⓣ - Taxi Stand
Ⓜ - Subway Stop
Ⓑ - Bus Stop

NOT TO SCALE: VATICAN MUSEUM ENTRY TO OBELISK IS A 15 MINUTE WALK

platform on the square (except in winter, when he speaks at 10:30 in the 7,000-seat Aula Paola VI Auditorium, next to St. Peter's Basilica). While anyone can observe from a distance, you need a ticket to actually get close to the papal action. Tickets are free and easy to get, but must be picked up the day before—on Tuesday for the Wednesday service. Your hotelier may be able to arrange a ticket for you; or you can contact Santa Susanna Church (they get the ticket and you pick it up on Tue at their church between 17:00 and 18:45, Via XX Settembre 15, near recommended Via Firenze hotels, Metro: Repubblica, tel. 06-4201-4554, www.santasusanna. org); or you can go to St. Peter's Basilica on Tuesday and wait in a long line for a ticket (Swiss Guards hand out tickets from their station at the Bronze Doors, just to the right of the basilica, after 12:00 on Tue). To find out the pope's schedule or to book a free spot for the Wednesday general audience (either for a seat on the square or in the auditorium), call 06-6988-4631. If you only want to see the Vatican—but not the pope—minimize crowd problems by avoiding these times.

Is the Pope Catholic?

Rome's tour guides, who introduce tourists to the city's great art and Christian history, field a lot of interesting questions and comments from their groups. Here are a few of their favorites:

- Was John Paul II the son of John Paul I?
- Who's the guy on the cross?
- Oh, to be here in Rome...where our Lord Jesus walked.
- Is this where Christ fought the lions?
- This guy who made so many nice things, Rene Sance, who is he? (Say it fast, and you'll get the gist.)
- What's the Sistine Chapel worth in U.S. dollars?
- How did Michelangelo get Moses to pose for him?
- What's Michelangelo doing now?

closes on Wednesday mornings during papal audiences. The best time to visit the church is early or late; I like to be here at 17:00, when the church is fairly empty, sunbeams can work their magic, and the late-afternoon Mass fills the place with spiritual music.

Tours: The Vatican TI conducts free 90-minute tours of St. Peter's (depart daily from TI at 14:15, many days also at 15:00, confirm schedule at TI, tel. 06-6988-1662). Audioguides can be rented near the checkroom.

Tours are the only way to see the Vatican Gardens; book at least a day in advance by calling 06-6988-4676 (€12, Tue, Thu, and Sat at 10:00, tours start at Vatican Museum tour desk and finish on St. Peter's Square).

To tour the Necropolis of St. Peter's and the saint's tomb, call the Excavations Office at 06-6988-5318 a minimum of a week before your visit (€1o, 2 hrs, office open Mon–Sat 9:00–17:00). The Crypt is open for free to the public, but this tour gets you closer to St. Peter's tomb.

Cost and Hours of Dome: The view from the dome is worth the climb (€6 elevator plus 323-step climb, allow an hour to go up and down, daily April–Sept 8:00–17:45, Oct–March 8:00–16:45).

▲▲▲**Vatican Museum (Musei Vaticani)**—The four miles of displays in this immense museum—from ancient statues to Christian frescoes to modern paintings—are topped by the Raphael Rooms and Michelangelo's glorious Sistine Chapel. (If you have binoculars, bring them.)

Even without the Sistine, this is one of Europe's top three or four houses of art. It can be exhausting, so plan your visit carefully, focusing on a few themes. Allow two hours for a quick visit, three or four for time to enjoy it. The museum has a nearly impossible-not-to-follow, one-way system. Tip: The Sistine Chapel has an exit (optional) that leads directly to St. Peter's Basilica, saving you the 10-minute walk back to the Vatican Museum exit; if you want to squirt out after seeing the Sistine, see the Pinacoteca painting gallery first (described below) and don't get an audioguide (which needs to be returned at the entry/exit).

Start, as civilization did, in **Egypt and Mesopotamia.** Next, the Pio Clementino collection features **Greek and Roman statues.** Decorating its courtyard are some of the best Greek and Roman statues in captivity, including the *Laocoön* group (1st century B.C., Hellenistic) and the *Apollo Belvedere* (a 2nd-century Roman copy of a Greek original). The centerpiece of the next hall is the *Belvedere Torso* (just a 2,000-year-old torso, but one that had a great impact on the art of Michelangelo). Finishing off the classical statuary are two fine fourth-century porphyry sarcophagi. These royal purple tombs were made (though not used) for the Roman emperor Constantine's mother and daughter. They were Christians—and therefore outlaws—until Constantine made Christianity legal (A.D. 312). The tombs, crafted in Egypt at a time when a declining Rome was unable to do such fine work, have details that are fun to study.

After long halls of tapestries, old maps, broken penises, and fig leaves, you'll come to what most people are looking for: The Raphael Rooms (or *stanza*) and Michelangelo's Sistine Chapel.

These outstanding works are frescoes. A fresco (meaning "fresh" in Italian) is technically not a painting. The color is mixed into wet plaster, and, when the plaster dries, the painting is actually part of the wall. This is a durable but difficult medium, requiring speed and accuracy, as the work is built one patch at a time.

After fancy rooms illustrating the "Immaculate Conception of Mary" (in the 19th century, the Vatican codified this hard-to-sell doctrine, making it a formal part of the Catholic faith) and the triumph of Constantine (with divine guidance, which led to his conversion to Christianity), you enter rooms frescoed by **Raphael** and his assistants. The highlight is the newly restored *School of Athens.* This is remarkable for its blatant pre-Christian classical orientation, especially since it originally wallpapered the apartments of Pope Julius II. Raphael honors the great pre-Christian thinkers—Aristotle, Plato, and company—who are portrayed as the leading artists of Raphael's day. The bearded figure of Plato is Leonardo da Vinci. Diogenes, history's first hippie, sprawls alone in bright blue on the stairs, while Michelangelo broods in the foreground—supposedly added later. Apparently, Raphael snuck a peek at the Sistine Chapel and decided that his arch-competitor was so good he had to put their personal differences aside and include him in this tribute to the artists of his generation. Today's St. Peter's was under construction as Raphael was working. In the *School of Athens*, he gives us a sneak preview of the unfinished church.

Next (unless you detour through the refreshingly modern Catholic art section) is the brilliantly restored **Sistine Chapel.** This is the pope's personal chapel and also the place where, upon the death of the ruling pope, a new pope is elected (as in April of 2005). The College of Cardinals meets here and votes four times a day until a two-thirds-plus-one majority is reached or a new pope is chosen.

The Sistine is famous for Michelangelo's pictorial culmination of the Renaissance, showing the story of creation, with a powerful God weaving in and out of each scene through that busy first week. This is an optimistic and positive expression of the High Renaissance and a stirring example of the artistic and theological maturity of the 33-year-old Michelangelo, who spent four years on this work.

Later, after the Reformation wars had begun and after the Catholic army of Spain had sacked the Vatican, the reeling Church began to fight back. As part of its Counter-Reformation, a much older Michelangelo was commissioned to paint the *Last Judgment* (behind the altar). Brilliantly restored, the message is as clear as the day Michelangelo finished it: Christ is returning, some will go to hell and some to heaven, and some will be saved by the power of the rosary.

In the recent and controversial restoration project, no paint was added. Centuries of dust, soot (from candles used for lighting and Mass), and glue (added to make the art shine) were removed, revealing the bright original colors of Michelangelo. Photos are allowed (without a flash) elsewhere in the museum, but as part of the deal with the company who did the restoration, no photos are allowed in the Sistine Chapel.

For a shortcut, a small door at the rear of the Sistine Chapel— likely labeled "Exit for private tour groups only"—allows groups and individuals (without an audioguide) to escape directly to St. Peter's Basilica. If you exit here, you're done with the museum. The Pinacoteca is the only important part left. Consider doing it at the start. Otherwise it's a 10-minute, heel-to-toe slalom through tourists from the Sistine Chapel to the entry/exit.

After this long march, you'll find the **Pinacoteca** (the Vatican's small but fine collection of paintings, with Raphael's *Transfiguration,* Leonardo's unfinished *St. Jerome,* and Caravaggio's *Deposition*), a cafeteria (long lines, uninspired food), and the underrated early-Christian art section, before you exit via the souvenir shop.

Cost and Hours: €12, March–Oct Mon–Fri 8:45–16:45, Sat 8:45–13:45; Nov–Feb Mon–Sat 8:45–13:45; closed Sun except last Sun of the month (when it's free, crowded, and open 8:45–13:45). Last entry is about 90 minutes before the closing time. The Sistine Chapel closes before the museum does.

The museum is closed on many holidays (mainly religious ones) including, for 2006: Jan 1 (New Year's), Jan 6 (Epiphany), Feb 11 (Vatican City established), March 19 (Saint Joseph), April 16–17 (Easter Sunday and Monday), May 1 (Labor Day), May 25 (Ascension Thursday), June 15 (Corpus Christi Day), June 29 (Saints Peter and Paul), Aug 15 plus either Aug 14 or 16 (Assumption of the Virgin), Nov 1 (All Saints' Day), Dec 8 (Immaculate Conception), and Dec 25–26 (Christmas). Other holidays may pop up—search for "closed dates" at www.vatican.va.

The museum is generally hot and crowded. The most crowded days are Saturday, the last Sunday of the month, Monday, rainy days, and any day before or after a holiday closure. Afternoons are best. On days the museum closes at 16:45, arriving by 13:00 works well. Most mornings, there's a line to get in that stretches around the block. (Stuck in the line? Figure about a 10-min wait for every 100 yards.)

Modest dress (no short shorts or bare shoulders) is appropriate and often required. Museum tel. 06-6988-4947.

Tours: Tours in English are offered daily at 10:30, 12:00, and 14:00 (€10 plus admission, 2 hrs, fax 06-6988-5100 to reserve up to 30 days before your visit; with a confirmed booking, you can skip the queue and enter through the exit—next to the entry—to reach the Guided Tours desk).

Or you can rent a €6 audioguide—but if you do, you lose the option of taking the shortcut from the Sistine Chapel to St. Peter's (because the audioguide must be returned at the Vatican Museum entrance).

▲**Castel Sant'Angelo**—Built as a tomb for the emperor; used through the Middle Ages as a castle, prison, and place of last refuge for popes under attack; and today, a museum, this giant pile of ancient bricks is packed with history (€5, Tue–Sun 9:00–20:00, closed Mon, audioguide-€4, near Vatican City, Metro: Lepanto or bus #64, tel. 06-3996-7600).

Ancient Rome allowed no tombs within its walls—not even the emperor's. So Emperor Hadrian grabbed the most commanding position just outside the walls and across the river and built a towering tomb (circa A.D. 139) well within view of the city. His mausoleum was a huge cylinder (210 by 70 feet) topped by a cypress grove and crowned by a huge statue of Hadrian himself riding a chariot. For nearly a hundred years, Roman emperors (from Hadrian to Caracalla, in A.D. 217) were buried here.

In the year 590, the Archangel Michael appeared above the mausoleum to Pope Gregory the Great. Sheathing his sword, the angel signaled the end of a plague. The fortress that was Hadrian's mausoleum eventually became a fortified palace, renamed for the "holy angel."

Castel Sant'Angelo spent centuries of the Dark Ages as a fortress and prison, but was eventually connected to the Vatican via an elevated corridor at the pope's request (1277). Since Rome was repeatedly plundered by invaders, Castel Sant'Angelo was a handy place of last refuge for threatened popes.

Touring the place is a stair-stepping workout. After you walk around the entire base of the castle, take the small staircase down to the original Roman floor (following the route of the Hadrian's funeral procession). In the atrium, study the model of the mausoleum as it was in Roman times. From here, a ramp leads to the right, spiraling 400 feet. At the end of the ramp, a bridge crosses over the room where the ashes of the emperors were kept. From here, the stairs continue out of the ancient section and into the medieval structure (built atop the mausoleum) that housed the papal apartments. Don't miss the Sala del Tesoro (Treasury), where the wealth of the Vatican was locked up in a huge chest. (*Do* miss the 58 rooms of the military museum.) From the pope's piggy bank, a narrow flight of stairs leads to the rooftop and perhaps the finest Rome view anywhere—pick out landmarks as you stroll around.

Ponte Sant'Angelo—The bridge leading to Castel Sant'Angelo was built by Hadrian for quick and regal access from downtown to his tomb. The three middle arches are actually Roman originals, and a fine example of the empire's engineering expertise. The statues of angels (each bearing a symbol of the passion of Christ—nail, sponge, shroud, and so on) are Bernini-designed and textbook Baroque. In the Middle Ages, this was the only bridge in the area that connected St. Peter's and the Vatican with downtown Rome. Nearly all pilgrims passed this bridge to and from the church. Its shoulder-high banisters recall a tragedy: During a Jubilee Year festival in 1450, the crowd got so huge that the mob pushed out the original banisters, causing nearly 200 to fall to their deaths.

Southwest Rome: Trastevere

Trastevere is the colorful neighborhood across *(tras)* the Tiber *(Tevere)* River. Trastevere (trahs-TAY-veh-ray) offers the best look at medieval-village Rome. The action unwinds to the chime of the church bells. Go there and wander. Wonder. Be a poet. This is Rome's Left Bank.

This proud neighborhood was long a working-class area. Now that it's becoming trendy, high rents are driving out the source of so much color. Still, it's a great people scene, especially at night. Stroll the back streets (for restaurant recommendations, see page 597).

Getting There: Trastevere is on the west side of the Tiber River, south of Vatican City and across the river from the Forum and Capitol Hill area. To get there by foot from Capitol Hill, cross the Tiber on Ponte Cestio (which goes over Tiber Island). You can

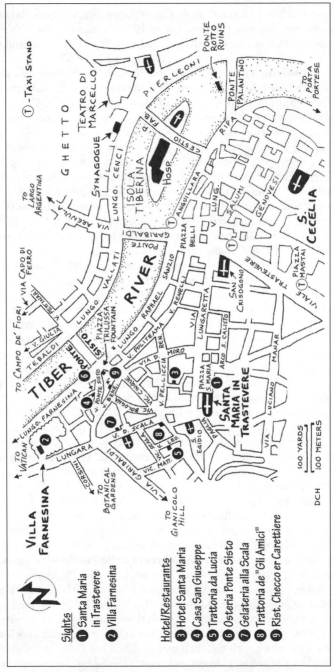

Trastevere

(T) - TAXI STAND

VILLA
FARNESINA

Sights
1 Santa Maria
in Trastevere
2 Villa Farnesina

Hotel/Restaurants
3 Hotel Santa Maria
4 Casa San Giuseppe
5 Trattoria da Lucia
6 Osteria Ponte Sisto
7 Gelateria alla Scala
8 Trattoria de "Gli Amici"
9 Rist. Checco er Carettiere

also reach it on tram #8 from Largo Argentina or express bus #H from the Termini train station and Via Nazionale; for either of these get off at Piazza Belli, just after crossing the Tiber. From the Vatican (Piazza Risorgimento), take bus #23 or #271.

Linking Trastevere with the "Night Walk Across Rome": You can walk from Trastevere to Campo de' Fiori to link up with the beginning of my "Night Walk Across Rome" (page 535): From Trastevere's church square (Piazza di Santa Maria), take Via del Moro to the river and cross at Ponte Sisto, a pedestrian bridge that has a good view of St. Peter's dome. Continue straight ahead for one block. Take the first left, which leads down Via di Capo di Ferro through the scary and narrow darkness to Piazza Farnese, with the imposing Palazzo Farnese. Michelangelo contributed to the facade of this palace, now the French Embassy. The fountains on the square feature huge, one-piece granite hot tubs from the ancient Roman Baths of Caracalla. One block from there (opposite the palace) is the atmospheric square of Campo de' Fiori.

▲**Santa Maria in Trastevere Church**—One of Rome's oldest churches, this was made a basilica in the fourth century, when Christianity was legalized (free, daily 9:00–17:30). It was the first church dedicated to the Virgin Mary. The portico (covered area just outside the door) is decorated with fascinating ancient fragments filled with early Christian symbolism. Most of what you see today dates from around the 12th century, but the granite columns come from an ancient Roman temple, and the ancient basilica floor plan (and ambience) survive. The 12th-century mosaics behind the altar are striking and notable for their portrayal of Mary—the first to show her at the throne with Jesus in Heaven. Look below the scenes from the life of Mary to see ahead-of-their-time mosaics (by Cavallini, from 1300), predating the Renaissance by 100 years.

The church is on Piazza di Santa Maria. While today's fountain is from the 17th century, there has been a fountain here since Roman times.

▲**Villa Farnesina**—This sumptuous 16th-century Renaissance villa, built for a wealthy Sienese banker, is decorated with paintings by Baldassare Peruzzi and a lovesick Raphael (€5, Tue–Fri 9:00–13:00, Mon and Sat 9:00–16:00, closed Sun, Via della Lungara).

Porta Portese Flea Market (Mercato delle Pulci)—For antiques and fleas, this is the granddaddy of markets. This Sunday-morning market is long and spindly, running between the actual Porta Portese (a gate in the old town wall) and the Trastevere train station. Starting at Porta Portese, walk through the long, tacky parade of stalls selling cheap bras and shoes. Along the way, check out the con artists with the shell games. Each has shills in the crowd "winning big money" to get suckers involved. Hang on to your wallet—literally, in your front pocket. This is a den of thieves. The heart of the market for real flea-market junk (hiding a few little antique treasures) is the area from Piazza Ippolito Nievo to the Trastevere station (6:30–13:00 Sun only, on Via Portuense and Via Ippolito Nievo; to get to the market, catch bus #75 from Termini station or tram #3 from Largo Argentina; get off the bus or tram on Viale Trastevere and walk toward the river—and the noise).

Near Trastevere: Jewish Quarter

From the 16th through the 19th centuries, Rome's Jewish population was forced to live in a cramped ghetto at an often-flooded bend of the Tiber River. While the medieval Jewish ghetto is long gone, this area—just across the river and towards Capitol Hill from Trastevere—is still home to Rome's synagogue and fragments of its Jewish heritage.

Synagogue (Sinagoga) and Jewish Museum (Museo Ebraico)— Rome's modern synagogue stands proudly on the spot where the medieval Jewish community lived in squalor for over 300 years. The site of a historic visit by Pope John Paul II, this synagogue features a fine interior and a simple museum filled with artifacts of Rome's Jewish community (€8 ticket includes synagogue and museum; May–Sept Mon–Thu 9:00–20:00, Fri 9:00–14:00, Sun 9:00–12:30, closed Sat; Oct–April Mon–Thu 9:00–17:00, Fri 9:00–14:00, Sun 9:00–12:30, closed Sat; on the riverbank road called Lungotevere dei Cenci near the bridge crossing Isola Tiberina, tel. 06-6840-0661).

South Rome

If you visit Ostia Antica (see page 585), you can maximize sightseeing efficiency by visiting any of the sights in south Rome on your return.

▲**St. Paul's Outside the Walls (Basilica San Paolo Fuori le Mura)**—This was the last major construction project of Imperial Rome (c. 380) and the largest church in Christendom until St. Peter's. After a tragic 19th-century fire, St. Paul's was rebuilt in the same general style and size as the original. Step inside and feel as close as you'll get in the 21st century to experiencing a monumental Roman basilica. Marvel at the ceiling, and imagine building it with those massive wood beams in A.D. 380.

It feels sterile, but in a good way—like you're already in heaven. Along with St. Peter's Basilica, San Giovanni in Laterano, and Santa Maria Maggiore, this church is part of the Vatican rather than Italy. The church was built upon the grave of the apostle Paul, whose body is buried under the altar (without his head, which San Giovanni in Laterano has). St. Paul was decapitated two miles from this spot.

Alabaster windows light the vast interior, and fifth-century

South Rome

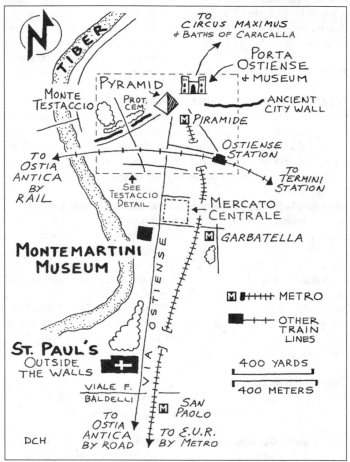

mosaics decorate the triumphal arch leading to the altar. Mosaic portraits of 264 popes, from St. Peter to the present, ring the place—with blank spots ready for future popes (pope #265—Benedict XVI—should show up here any day now). Find John Paul II (to right of the high altar: *Jo Paulus II*) and John Paul I (to his right, with a reign of 1 month and 3 days). Wander the ornate yet peaceful cloister—decorated with fragments from early Christian tombs and sarcophagi of people who wanted to be buried close to Paul (cloister closed 13:00–15:00).

The courtyard leading up to the church is typical of early Christian churches—even the first St. Peter's had this kind of welcoming zone (free, daily 7:00–18:00, modest dress code enforced, Via Ostiense 186, Metro: San Paolo).

▲Montemartini Museum (Musei Capitolini Centrale Monte-martini)—This museum houses a dreamy collection of 400 ancient statues, set evocatively in a classic 1932 electric power plant, among generators and *Metropolis*-type cast-iron machinery. While the art is not as famous as the collections you'll see downtown, the effect is fun and memorable—and you'll encounter absolutely no tourists (€4.20, €9.90 combo-ticket includes Capitol Hill Museum, Tue–Sun 9:30–19:00, closed Mon, Via Ostiense 106, a short walk from Metro: Garbatella, tel. 06-3996-7800, www.museicapitolini.org).

Baths of Caracalla (Terme di Caracalla)—Inaugurated by Emperor Caracalla in A.D. 216, this massive bath complex could accommodate 1,600 visitors at a time. Today it's just a shell—a huge shell—with all of its sculptures and most of its mosaics moved to museums. You'll see a two-story, roofless brick building surrounded by a garden, bordered by ruined walls. The two large rooms at either end of the building were used for exercise. In between the exercise rooms was a pool flanked by two small mosaic-floored dressing rooms. Niches in the walls once held statues.

In its day, this was a remarkable place to hang out. For ancient Romans, bathing was a social experience. The Baths of Caracalla functioned until Goths severed the aqueducts in the sixth century. In modern times, grand operas were performed here from 1938 to 1993. To keep the ruins from becoming more ruined, the performances were discontinued (€5, covered by €20 Archeologia Card, Mon 9:00–14:00, Tue–Sun 9:00–19:30, audioguide-€4, good €8 guidebook can be read in shaded garden while sitting on a chunk of column, Metro: Circus Maximus, plus a 5-min walk south along Via delle Terme di Caracalla, tel. 06-3996-7700). The baths' statues are displayed elsewhere: several are in Rome's Octagonal Hall, and the immense *Toro Farnese* (a marble sculpture of a bull surrounded by people) snorts in Naples' Archaeological Museum.

Testaccio—In the gritty Testaccio neighborhood, four fascinating but lesser sights cluster at the Piramide Metro stop between the Colosseum and E.U.R. (This is a quick and easy stop as you return from E.U.R. or when changing trains en route to Ostia Antica.)

Working-class since ancient times, the Testaccio neighborhood has recently gone trendy-bohemian. Visitors wander through an awkward mix of yuppie and proletarian worlds, not noticing—but perhaps feeling—the "Keep Testaccio for the Testaccians" graffiti. This has long been the neighborhood of slaughterhouses, and its restaurants are renowned for their ability to cook up the least palatable part of the animals...the fifth quarter. For a meal you won't forget, try **Trattoria "Da Oio" A Casa Mia** (closed Sun, Via Galvani 43, tel. 06-578-2680).

High-end shoe and clothing boutiques are moving into the neighborhood, and this is now one of the best areas in Rome to have

Testaccio

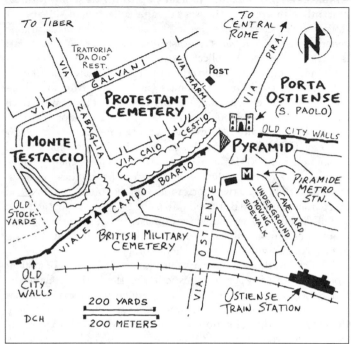

shoes custom-made. The Testaccio market (in the center) is hands-down the best, most authentic outdoor food market in Rome. This is where Romans shop while tourists flock to Campo de' Fiori.

Pyramid of Gaius Cestius: The Mark Antony/Cleopatra scandal (c. 30 B.C.) brought exotic Egyptian styles into vogue. A rich Roman magistrate, Gaius Cestius, had this pyramid built as his tomb. Made of brick covered in marble, it was completed in just 330 days (as stated in its Latin inscription) and fell far short of Egyptian pyramid standards. It was later incorporated into the Aurelian Wall, and it now stands as a marker to the entrance of Testaccio (next to the Piramide Metro stop).

Porta Ostiense: This formidable gate (also next to Piramide Metro stop) is from the Aurelian Wall, begun in the third century under Emperor Aurelius. The wall, which encircled the city, was 12 miles long and 26 feet high, with 14 main gates and 380 72-foot-tall towers. Most of what you'll see today is circa A.D. 400, but the barbarians reconstructed the gate later, in the sixth century. If you climb up (enter nearest the pyramid), you can enjoy a free ramble along the ramparts and exhibits and models of Ostia Antica (Rome's ancient port; see page 585) and the Ostian Way. (For more on the wall, visit the Museum of the Walls at Porta San Sebastian; see "Ancient Appian Way," below.)

Protestant Cemetery: The Cemetery for the Burial of Non-Catholic Foreigners (Cimitero Acattolico per gli Stranieri al Testaccio) is a tomb-filled park, running along the wall just beyond the pyramid. The cemetery is also the only English-style landscape (rolling hills, calculated vistas) in Rome, and a favorite spot for quiet picnics and strolls. From the Piramide Metro stop, walk between the pyramid and the Roman gate on Via Persichetti, then go left on Caio Cestio to the gate of the cemetery. Ring the bell to get inside (donation box, Tue–Sat 9:00–18:00, Sun 9:00–14:00, closed Mon; closes an hour earlier in winter).

Originally, none of the Protestant epitaphs were allowed to make any mention of heaven. Signs direct visitors to the graves of notable non-Catholics who died in Rome since 1738. Many of the buried were diplomats. And many, such as the poets Shelley and Keats, were from the Romantic Age. They came on the Grand Tour and—"captivated by the fatal charms of Rome," as Shelley wrote—never left. Head left toward the pyramid to find Keats' tomb, in the far corner. Keats died in his twenties, unrecognized. He wanted to be unnamed on a tomb that read, "Young English Poet, 1821. Here lies one whose name was writ in water." (To see Keats' tomb if the cemetery is closed, look through the tiny peephole on Via Caio Cestio, 10 yards off Via Marmarata.)

From inside the cemetery (nearest the pyramid), look down on Matilde Talli's cat hospice (flier at the gate). Volunteers use donations to care for these "Guardians of the Departed" who "provide loyal companionship to these dead."

Notice the beige travertine post office from 1932 (across the big street from cemetery). This is textbook Mussolini-era fascist architecture. The huge X design on the stairwells celebrates the 10th anniversary of the dictator's reign.

Monte Testaccio: Just behind the Protestant Cemetery (as you leave, turn left and continue 2 blocks down Caio Cestio) is a 115-foot-tall ancient trash mountain. It's made of broken *testae*—earthenware jars used to haul mostly oil 2,000 years ago, when this was a gritty port warehouse district. For 500 years, rancid oil vessels were discarded here. Slowly, Rome's lowly eighth hill was built. Because the caves dug into the hill stay cool, trendy bars, clubs, and restaurants compete with gritty car-repair places for a spot. The neighborhood was once known for a huge slaughterhouse and a Gypsy camp that squatted inside an old military base. Now it's home to the Testaccio Village, a site for concerts and techno-raves. The night scene at Monte Testaccio after 21:00 is youthful and lively with restaurants and clubs (Metro: Piramide).

Ancient Appian Way (Via Appia Antica)

Since the fourth century B.C., this has been Rome's gateway to the East. The wonder of its day, the Appian Way was the largest, widest, fastest road ever, called the "Queen of Roads." Eventually, this most important of Roman roads stretched 430 miles to the port of Brindisi—where boats sailed for Greece and Egypt. Twenty-nine such roads fanned out from Rome. Just as Hitler built the autobahn system in anticipation of empire maintenance, the emperors realized the military and political value of a good road system. A central strip accommodated animal-powered vehicles, and elevated sidewalks served pedestrians. The first section (near Rome) was perfectly straight, and lined with tombs and funerary monuments. Imagine a funeral procession passing under the pines and cypresses and past a long line of pyramids, private mini-temples, altars, and tombs.

Hollywood created the famous image of the Appian Way lined with the crucified bodies of Spartacus and his gang of slave rebels. This image is only partially accurate—Spartacus was killed in battle.

Today the road and the landscape around it are preserved as a cultural park, providing one of the best respites from the city for strolling or biking—especially on Sundays, when its active stretch closest to the city is closed to traffic.

Tourist's Appian Way: The road starts less than two miles south of the Colosseum at the massive San Sebastian Gate. The **Museum of the Walls,** located at the gate, offers an interesting look at Roman defense and a chance to scramble along a stretch of the ramparts (€2.60, Tue–Sat 9:00–19:00, Sun 9:00–14:00, closed Mon, tel. 06-7047-5284). A mile and a half down the road are the two most historic and popular catacombs, those of San Callisto and San Sebastian, described below. (More intimate, less crowded, and at the other end of town—north of the Villa Borghese—are the Catacombs of Priscilla; see page 562.)

Besides the two main catacombs described below, the Appian Way offers additional catacombs, ruins, and tombs. As you head north on the Appian Way (from its intersection with Via Cecilia Metella) toward the Catacombs of San Sebastian, you can't miss on the right the massive cylindrical **Tomb of Cecilia Metella**, one of the best preserved of the many tombs of prominent Romans that line the road. Just past the tomb on the right are the ruins of the **Villa and Circus of Maxentius** (the emperor defeated by Constantine in 312 A.D.). Farther along the Appian Way, past the Catacombs of San Sebastian and San Callisto, you'll see the **Church of Domine Quo Vadis,** built on the spot where Peter, while fleeing the city to escape Nero's persecution, saw a vision of Christ. Peter asked Jesus, "Lord, where are you going?" ("Domine quo vadis?" in Latin), to

Appian Way

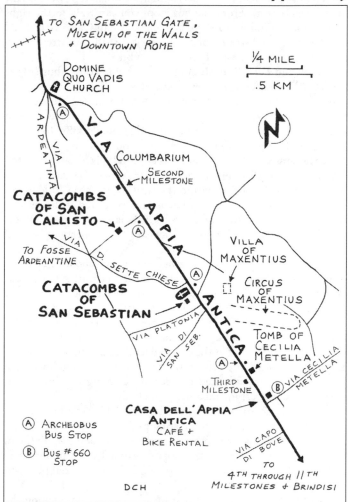

TO SAN SEBASTIAN GATE,
MUSEUM OF THE WALLS
& DOWNTOWN ROME

DOMINE
QUO VADIS
CHURCH

Ⓐ

¼ MILE

.5 KM

N

VIA ARDEATINA

VIA APPIA ANTICA

COLUMBARIUM

SECOND MILESTONE

CATACOMBS OF SAN CALLISTO

Ⓐ

VIA D. SETTE CHIESE

TO FOSSE ARDEANTINE

VILLA OF MAXENTIUS

Ⓐ

CIRCUS OF MAXENTIUS

CATACOMBS OF SAN SEBASTIAN

VIA PLATONIA

VIA DI SAN SEB.

TOMB OF CECILIA METELLA

VIA CECILIA METELLA

Ⓐ

THIRD MILESTONE

Ⓑ

Ⓐ ARCHEOBUS BUS STOP

Ⓑ BUS #660 STOP

CASA DELL' APPIA ANTICA
CAFÉ & BIKE RENTAL

VIA CAPO DI BOVE

TO 4TH THROUGH 11TH MILESTONES & BRINDISI

DCH

which Christ replied, "I am going to Rome to be crucified again." This miraculous sign gave Peter faith and courage and caused him to return to Rome. And just off the Appian Way on Via delle Sette Chiese is the evocative **Fosse Ardeantine,** a memorial tomb to 335 Italians gunned down by the Nazis as revenge for 32 German soldiers killed in a bomb attack in Rome during World War II.

Getting There: To reach the Appian Way, take the Archeobus from Rome's Termini train station (see "Archeobus," page 526) or take the Metro to the Colli Albani stop, then catch bus #660 to Via Appia Antica—its last stop and the start of an interesting stretch of the ancient road (the segment between the 3rd and 11th milestones is best). From the bus stop, you can walk to the right (north) for 15 minutes to the Catacombs of San Callisto, or head left (south) onto a stretch of the preserved road that stretches to the horizon. To get around faster, rent a bike.

Café and Bike Rental: At the Via Appia Antica bus stop is **Casa dell'Appia Antica,** where you can buy a light lunch or rent a bike (bike rental—€3/hr, Tue–Sun 10:00–18:00, closed Mon, at corner of Appian Way and Via Cecilia Metella, just beyond the Tomb of Cecilia Metella at Via Appia Antica 175, mobile 338-3465-440). Biking on the Appian Way is a treat (best on Sundays).

▲▲**Catacombs**—The catacombs are burial places for (mostly) Christians who died in ancient Roman times. By law, no one was allowed to be buried within the walls of Rome. While pagan Romans were into cremation, Christians preferred to be buried. But land was expensive, and most Christians were poor. A few wealthy, landowning Christians allowed their property to be used as burial places.

The 40 or so known catacombs circle Rome about three miles from its center. From the first through the fifth centuries, Christians dug an estimated 375 miles of tomb-lined tunnels, with networks of galleries as many as five layers deep. The tufa stone—soft and easy to cut, but which hardened when exposed to air—was perfect for the job. The Christians burrowed many layers deep for two reasons: to get more mileage out of the donated land, and to be near martyrs and saints already buried there. Bodies were wrapped in linen (like Christ's). Since they figured the Second Coming was imminent, there was no interest in embalming the body.

When Emperor Constantine legalized Christianity in A.D. 313, Christians had a new, interesting problem: There would be no more persecuted martyrs to bind them together and inspire them. Instead, the early martyrs and popes assumed more importance, and Christians began making pilgrimages to their burial places in the catacombs.

In the 800s, when barbarian invaders started ransacking the tombs, Christians moved the relics of saints and martyrs to the safety of churches in the city center. For a thousand years, the catacombs were forgotten. Around 1850, they were excavated and became part of the Romantic Age's Grand Tour of Europe.

When abandoned plates and utensils from ritual meals were found, 18th- and 19th-century Romantics guessed that persecuted Christians hid out in these candlelit galleries. This legend grew—even though it was untrue. By the second century, nearly two million people lived in Rome, and the 10,000 early Christians no longer had to camp out in the catacombs. They hid in plain view, melting into obscurity within the city itself.

The underground tunnels, while empty of bones, are rich in early Christian symbolism, which functioned as a secret language. The dove represented the soul. You'll see it quenching its thirst (worshipping), with an olive branch (at rest), or happily perched (in paradise). Peacocks, known for their "incorruptible flesh," embodied immortality. The shepherd with a lamb on his shoulders was the "good shepherd," the first portrayal of Christ as a kindly leader of his flock. The fish was used because the first letters of these words—"Jesus Christ, Son of God, Savior"—spelled "fish" in Greek. And the anchor is a cross in disguise. A second-century bishop had written on his tomb: "All who understand these things, pray for me." You'll see pictures of people praying with their hands raised up—the custom at the time.

Catacomb tours are essentially the same; which one you take is not important. The **Catacombs of San Callisto** (a.k.a. Callixtus), the official cemetery for the Christians of Rome and the burial place of third-century popes, is the most historic. Sixteen bishops (early popes) were buried here. Buy your €5 ticket and wait for your language to be called. They move lots of people quickly. If one group seems ridiculously large (more than 50 people), wait for the next tour in English (Thu–Tue 8:30–12:00 & 14:30–17:30, closed Wed and Feb, closes at 17:00 in winter, Via Appia Antica 110, tel. 06-5130-1580). Dig this: The catacombs have a Web site—www.catacombe.roma.it—that focuses mainly on San Callisto, featuring photos, site info, and a history.

The **Catacombs of San Sebastian** (Sebastiano) are 300 yards farther south down the road (€5, Mon–Sat 8:30–12:00 & 14:30–17:30, closed Sun and Nov, closes at 17:00 in winter, Via Appia Antica 136, tel. 06-785-0350).

E.U.R.

In the late 1930s, Italy's dictator, Benito Mussolini, planned an international exhibition to show off the wonders of his fascist society. But these wonders brought us World War II, and Il Duce's celebration never happened. The unfinished mega-project was completed in the 1950s, and today it houses government offices and big, obscure museums filled with important, rarely visited relics.

If Hitler and Mussolini won the war, our world might look like E.U.R. (AY-oor). Hike down E.U.R.'s wide, pedestrian-mean boulevards. Patriotic murals, aren't-you-proud-to-be-an-extreme-right-winger pillars, and stern squares decorate the soulless, planned grid and stark office blocks. Boulevards named for Astronomy, Electronics, Social Security, and Beethoven are more exhausting than inspirational. Today, E.U.R. is worth a trip for its Museum of Roman Civilization (described below). Because a few landmark buildings of Italian modernism are located here and there, E.U.R.

E.U.R.

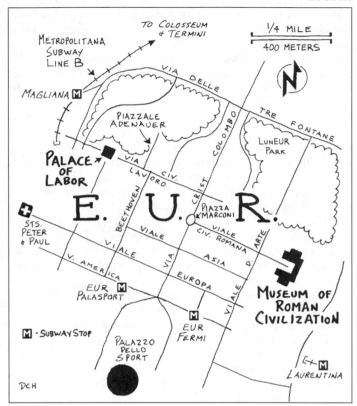

has become an important destination for architecture buffs.

The Metro skirts E.U.R. with three stops (10 min from the Colosseum). Use E.U.R. Magliana for the "Square Colosseum" and E.U.R. Fermi for the Museum of Roman Civilization (both described below). Consider walking 30 minutes from the palace to the museum through the center of E.U.R.

From the Magliana subway stop, stairs lead uphill to the **Palace of the Civilization of Labor** (Palazzo della Civiltà del Lavoro), the essence of fascist architecture. With its giant, no-questions-asked, patriotic statues and its black-and-white simplicity, this is E.U.R.'s tallest building and key landmark. It's understandably nicknamed the "Square Colosseum." Around the corner, Café Palombini is still decorated in a 1930s style and is quite popular with young Romans (daily 7:00–24:00, good gelato, pastries, and snacks, Piazzale Adenauer 12, tel. 06-591-1700).

▲Museum of Roman Civilization (Museo della Civiltà Romana)—With 59 rooms of plaster casts and models illustrating the greatness of classical Rome, this vast and heavy museum gives a strangely lifeless, close-up look at Rome. Each room has a theme, from military tricks to musical instruments. One long hall is filled with casts of the reliefs of Trajan's Column. The highlight is the 1:250-scale model of Constantine's Rome, circa A.D. 300 (€6.20, Tue–Sun 9:00–14:00, closed Mon, Piazza G. Agnelli; leave the E.U.R. Fermi Metro station on Via America, turn right, and walk past McDonald's, then at T-intersection turn left and go uphill 3 blocks to Via dell'Arte, you'll see its colonnade on the right; tel. 06-592-6041).

Near Rome

▲▲Ostia Antica—For an exciting day trip less than an hour from downtown Rome, pop down to the ancient Roman port of Ostia Antica. It's similar to Pompeii, but a lot closer and, in some ways, more interesting. Because Ostia was a working port town, it shows a more complete and gritty look at Roman life than does wealthy Pompeii. Wandering around today, you'll see the remains of the docks, warehouses, apartment flats, mansions, shopping arcades, and baths that served a once thriving port of 60,000 people. Later, Ostia became a ghost town, and is now excavated. Start at the 2,000-year-old theater, buy a map, explore the town, and finish with its fine little museum.

Getting There: From downtown Rome, you'll take a 45-minute combination Metro/train ride. It'll cost you just one Metro ticket each way (€2 total round-trip). From Rome, take the Metro (line B) to the Piramide stop (which really *is* next to a pyramid—see page 578). Exit and walk to the left, following overhead signs for the *Ferrovia Roma-Lido* train, which you'll ride to Ostia Antica (4/hr, keep your Metro ticket handy, get off at the stop before Lido Nord). At the train station at Ostia Antica, cross the road via the blue sky-bridge and walk straight down Via della Stazione di Ostia Antica, continuing straight until you reach the parking lot. The entrance is on the left.

Cost and Hours: €4, summer Tue–Sun 8:30–18:30 (you can linger on the grounds until 19:00), winter Tue–Sun 8:30–17:00, always closed Mon (tel. 06-5635-8099). The well-done audioguide (not always available) costs €5.

SLEEPING

The absolute cheapest beds in Rome are €20 in small, backpacker-filled hostels. A nicer hotel (around €130 with a bathroom and air-con) provides an oasis and refuge, making it easier to enjoy this intense and grinding city. If you're going door to door, prices are soft—so bargain. Built into a hotel's official price list is a kickback for a room-finding service or agency; if you're coming direct, they

Sleep Code

(€1 = about $1.20, country code: 39)
S = Single, **D** = Double/Twin, **T** = Triple, **Q** = Quad, **b** = bathroom, **s** = shower only. Breakfast is included in all but the cheapest places. Unless I note otherwise, the staff speaks English. You can assume a hotel takes credit cards unless you see "cash only" in the listing.

To help you sort easily through these listings, I've divided the rooms into three categories based on the price for a standard double room with bath:

$$$ **Higher Priced**—Most rooms €180 or more.
  $$ **Moderately Priced**—Most rooms between €120–180.
   $ **Lower Priced**—Most rooms €120 or less.

pay no kickback and may lower the price for you. Many hotels have high-season (mid-March–June, Sept–Oct) and low-season prices. If traveling outside of peak times, ask about a discount. Room rates are lowest in sweltering August. Easter, September, and Christmas are most crowded and expensive. On Easter (April 16 in 2006) and other major religious holidays (see list on page 711), the entire city can get booked up.

Traffic in Rome roars. My challenge: To find friendly places on quiet streets. With the recent arrival of double-paned windows and air-conditioning, night noise is not the problem it was. Even so, light sleepers should always ask for a *tranquillo* room. Many prices here are promised only to people who show this book and reserve directly, without using a room-finding service. And many places prefer hard cash.

Most hotels are eager to connect you with a shuttle service to the airport. It's reasonable and easy for departure, but upon arrival, I just catch a cab or the train into the city.

Almost no hotels have parking, but nearly all have a line on spots in a nearby garage (about €24/day).

Bed-and-breakfasts are booming in Rome, offering comfy doubles in the old center for €70–110. The Beehive is a good contact for booking B&Bs in Rome (www.cross-pollinate.com, page 590).

Rome has many **convents** that rent out rooms; the beds are twins and English is often in short supply, but the price is right. I list these nun-run places below: the expensive but divine Suore di Santa Elisabetta and the Istituto "Il Rosario" (both near Basilica Santa Maria Maggiore, see page 590), Casa San Giuseppe (secular but convent-run, in Trastevere, see page 594), and the most user-friendly of all, Casa per Ferie Santa Maria alle Fornaci dei Padri Trinitari (near the Vatican, see page 597). For more, see the Church of Santa Susanna's Web site (www.santasusanna.org, select "Coming To Rome," then "Convents").

Via Firenze

I generally stay on Via Firenze because it's safe, handy, central, and relatively quiet. It's a 10-minute walk from the Termini train station and the airport shuttle, and two blocks beyond Piazza della Repubblica and the TI. The Defense Ministry is nearby, so you've got heavily armed guards watching over you all night.

The neighborhood is well-connected by public transportation (with the Repubblica Metro stop nearby). Virtually all the city buses that rumble down Via Nazionale (#64, #70, #115, #640, and the #40 express) take you to Piazza Venezia (Forum) and Largo Argentina (Pantheon). From Largo Argentina, electric trolley #8 goes to Trastevere (get off at first stop after crossing the river) and the #64 bus (jammed with people and thieves) and the #40 express bus both continue to St. Peter's.

A 24-hour **pharmacy** near the recommended hotels is Farmacia Piram (Via Nazionale 228, tel. 06-488-4437).

$$ Hotel Oceania is a peaceful slice of air-conditioned heaven. This 15-room, manor house-type hotel is spacious and quiet, with spotless, tastefully decorated rooms, run by a pleasant father-and-son team. While Armando (the dad) serves world-famous coffee, Stefano (the son) works to give their hotel all the extra touches, including a plasma TV in the lounge for guests to watch classic movies set in Rome...and Italy episodes from my TV series (Sb-€118, Db-€148, Tb-€178, Qb-€198, prices good through 2006 with this book and cash, 25 percent less in Aug and winter, large roof terrace, family suite, Via Firenze 38, 3rd floor, tel. 06-482-4696, fax 06-488-5586, www.hoteloceania.it, info@hoteloceania.it; Anna, Radu, and Enrico round out the staff).

$$ Hotel Aberdeen, which perfectly combines high quality and friendliness, is warmly run by Annamaria, with support from cousins Sabrina and Cinzia and sister Laura. The 37 comfy, modern, air-conditioned, and smoke-free rooms are a terrific value. Enjoy the frescoed breakfast room (Sb-€87, Db-€135, Tb-€150, Qb-€165, these special prices promised through 2006 with this book, 30 percent less in Aug and winter, check Web site for deals, Via Firenze 48, tel. 06-482-3920, fax 06-482-1092, www.travel.it /roma/aberdeen, hotel.aberdeen@travel.it).

$$ Residenza Cellini is a gorgeous six-room place that feels like the guest wing of a neoclassical palace. It offers "ortho/anti-allergy beds" and four-star comforts and service (Db-€165, larger Db-€185, extra bed-€25, €30 less in Aug and mid-Nov–mid-March, prices good through 2006 with this book and cash, family apartment, air-con, elevator, Via Modena 5, tel. 06-4782-5204, fax 06-4788-1806, www.residenzacellini.it, residenzacellini@tin.it; Barbara, Gaetano, and Donato).

$ **Residence Adler** offers breakfast on a garden patio, wide halls, and eight quiet, simple, air-conditioned rooms in a good location. It's run the old-fashioned way by a charming family (Db-€120, Tb-€150, Qb-€180, Quint/b-€195, prices through 2006 with this book, additional 5 percent off if you pay with cash, 15 percent less in Aug and winter, elevator, Via Modena 5, 2nd floor, tel. 06-484-466, fax 06-488-0940, www.hoteladler-roma.com, info @hoteladler-roma.com, gracious Sr. Brando Massini doesn't speak English but tries).

$ **Hotel Nardizzi Americana** offers 33 simple, pleasant, air-conditioned rooms and a delightful rooftop terrace. Though loosely run, it's a fine value (Sb-€95, Db-€115, Tb-€145, Qb-€160, prices through 2006 with this book, 10 percent discounts for off-season and long stays, additional 10 percent off with cash, elevator, Via Firenze 38, 4th floor, tel. 06-488-0035, fax 06-488-0368, www .hotelnardizzi.it, info@hotelnardizzi.it).

Between Via Nazionale and Basilica Santa Maria Maggiore

$$ **Hotel Sonya** is small and family-run but impersonal, with 23 well-equipped rooms, a central location, and decent prices (Sb-€85, Db-€125, Tb-€140, Qb-€160, Quint/b-€180, prices through 2006 with this book, 5 percent less if you pay cash, big discounts off-season, air-con, elevator, free Internet in lobby, faces the opera at Via Viminale 58, Metro: Repubblica or Termini, tel. 06-481-9911, fax 06-488-5678, www.hotelsonya.it, hotelsonyaroma@katamail .com, Francesca).

$ **Hotel Pensione Italia,** in a busy, interesting, and handy locale, is placed safely on a quiet street next to the Ministry of the Interior. Thoughtfully run by Andrea, Nadine, and Gabriel, it has 31 comfortable, clean, bright, non-smoking rooms (Sb-€80, Db-€110, Tb-€145, Qb-€165, prices through 2006 with this book and cash, all rooms 30 percent off mid-July–Aug and Nov–mid-March, most rooms have fans, air-con-€8/day, elevator, Via Venezia 18, just off Via Nazionale, Metro: Repubblica or Termini, tel. 06-482-8355, fax 06-474-5550, www.hotelitaliaroma.com, info@hotelitaliaroma .com). They also have eight decent annex rooms across the street.

$ **Hotel Montreal,** run with care, is a bright, solid, business-class place on a big street a block southeast of Santa Maria Maggiore (rates are soft, but these prices are promised with this book in 2006: Db-€115, Tb-€140; in July–Aug and Nov–Feb rates drop to Db-€90, Tb-€120; air-con, elevator, good security, Via

Hotels in East Rome

1 Residenza Cellini &
 Residence Adler

2 Hotels Oceania & Nardizzi

3 Hotel Aberdeen

4 Hotel Sonya

5 Hotel Pensione Italia

6 Hotel Montreal

7 Istituto Il Rosario

8 Suore di Santa Elisabetta

9 To Gulliver's Place Rooms

10 Albergo Sileo &
 Fawlty Towers Hostel

11 Hotel Paba

12 Hotel Lancelot

13 The Beehive Hostel

14 Gulliver's House Hostel

15 Casa Olmata Hostel

Carlo Alberto 4, 1 block from Metro: Vittorio Emanuele, 3 blocks west of Termini train station, tel. 06-445-7797, fax 06-446-5522, www.hotelmontrealroma.com, info@hotelmontrealroma.com).

$ Suore di Santa Elisabetta is a heavenly Polish-run convent with a peaceful garden and tidy rooms. Often booked long in advance, it's a super value (S-€36, Sb-€45, D-€58, Db-€76, Tb-€96, Qb-€116, Quint/b-€125, 23:00 curfew, elevator, fine view roof terrace, a block southwest of Basilica Santa Maria Maggiore at Via dell'Omata 9, Metro: Termini or Vittorio Emanuele, tel. 06-488-8271, fax 06-488-4066, ist.it.s.elisabetta@libero.it).

$ Casa Olmata is a ramshackle, laid-back backpackers' place a block southwest of Basilica Santa Maria Maggiore, midway between the Termini train station and Colosseum (dorm beds-€20, S-€38, D-€57, laundry service, free Internet in lobby, video rentals, games, rooftop terrace with views and nearly free dinner parties, dinners twice weekly, communal kitchen, Via dell'Olmata 36, 3rd floor, Metro: Vittorio Emanuele, tel. 06-483-019, fax 06-486819, www .casaolmata.com, info@casaolmata.com, Mirella and Marco).

$ Gulliver's House Rome, run by helpful Simon and Sara, is a fun little hostel in a safe and handy location. Its 24 beds in cramped quarters work fine for backpackers. They host English-language movie evenings nightly in their lounge—you can start off the evening with my TV shows on Rome (€20 per bunk in 8-bed dorm, one D-€70, cash only, closed 12:00–16:00, 1:00 curfew, small kitchen, Via Palermo 36, tel. 06-481-7680, www.gullivershouse .com, stay@gullivershouse.com). They also offer five fun, funky double rooms at **Gulliver's Place,** in a large, secure building next to a university (D-€75, Db-€80, Tb-€100, air-con, elevator, east of the Termini train station at Viale Castro Pretorio 25, Metro: Castro Pretorio).

Sleeping Cheaply, Northeast of the Train Station

The cheapest beds in town are northeast of the Termini train station (Metro: Termini). Some travelers feel this area is weird and spooky after dark, but these hotels feel plenty safe. With your back to the train tracks, turn right and walk two blocks out of the station.

$ The Beehive gives vagabonds—old and young—a cheap, clean, and comfy home in Rome, thoughtfully and creatively run by a friendly young American couple, Steve and Linda. They offer seven great-value, artsy-mod double rooms (D-€70, this price promised through 2006 with this book) and an 8-bed dorm (€20 bunks; cash only, free Internet in lobby, private garden terrace, cheery café, 2 blocks north of Termini train station at Via Marghera 8, tel. 06-447-04553, www.the-beehive.com, info@the-beehive.com). Steve and Linda also run a B&B booking service (private rooms in the old center of Rome, Florence, and Venice; rates start at €30 per person, check out your options at www.cross-pollinate.com).

$ Albergo Sileo, with shiny chandeliers, has a contract to house train conductors who work the night shift—so its 10 simple, pleasant rooms are rented from 19:00–9:00 only. If you can handle this, it's a wonderful value. During the day, they store your luggage, and though you won't have access to a room, you're welcome to shower or hang out in the lobby or bar (D-€50, Db-€60, Tb-€65, Db for 24 hours-€62 when available, elevator, Via Magenta 39, 4th floor, tel. & fax 06-445-0246, www.hotelsileo.com, info@hotelsileo.com; friendly Alessandro and Maria Savioli don't speak English, but their daughter Anna does).

$ Fawlty Towers Hostel is well-run and ideal for backpackers arriving by train. It offers 50 beds and lots of fun, games, and extras (4-bed coed dorms-€22 per person, S-€47, D-€65, Db-€80, Q-€90, includes sheets, from station walk a block down Via Marghera and turn right to Via Magenta 39, tel. & fax 06-445-0374, www.fawltytowers .org, info@fawltytowers.org). Their nearby annex, Bubbles, offers similar beds and rates and shares the same reception desk.

Near the Colosseum

$$ Hotel Paba has six rooms, chocolate box-tidy and lovingly cared for by Alberta Castelli. Though it overlooks busy Via Cavour just two blocks from the Colosseum, it's quiet enough (Db-€135, extra bed-€35, 5 percent discount for cash, huge beds, breakfast served in room, air-con, elevator, Via Cavour 266, Metro: Cavour, tel. 06-4782-4902, fax 06-4788-1225, www.hotelpaba .com, info@hotelpaba.com).

$$ Hotel Lancelot, a favorite among United Nations workers, is a homey refuge. It's quiet, safe, and big (60 rooms), with a shady courtyard, bar, and restaurant. Well-run by Faris and Lubna Khan, it's popular with returning guests (Sb-€105, Db-€165, Tb-€190, Qb-€220, €15 extra for balcony, air-con, elevator, parking-€11/day, behind Colosseum near San Clemente Church at Via Capo d'Africa 47, tel. 06-7045-0615, fax 06-7045-0640, www.lancelothotel.com, info@lancelothotel.com, Lubna speaks the Queen's English).

Near Campo de' Fiori

You'll pay a premium (and endure a little extra night noise) to stay in the old center. But each of these places is romantically set deep in the tangled back streets near the idyllic Campo de' Fiori and, for many, worth the extra money.

$$ Casa di Santa Brigida overlooks the elegant Piazza Farnese. With soft-spoken sisters gliding down polished hallways, and pearly gates instead of doors, this lavish 23-room convent makes exhaust-stained Roman tourists feel like they've died and gone to heaven. If you don't need a double bed, this is worth the splurge (Sb-€100, twin Db-€170, 3 percent extra if you pay with credit card, air-con, tasty €20 dinners, roof garden, plush library, Monserrato 54, tel. 06-6889-2596, fax 06-6889-1573, brigida@mclink.it, many of the sisters are from India and speak English). If you get no response to your fax or e-mail within three days, consider that a "no."

$$ Hotel Smeraldo, with 50 rooms, is well run, clean, and a great deal (Sb-€95, Db-€125, Tb-€145, prices promised through 2006 with this book, 20 percent less off-season, buffet breakfast-€7 extra, centrally controlled air-con, elevator, flowery roof terrace, Vicolo dei Chiodaroli 9, midway between Campo de' Fiori and Largo Argentina, tel. 06-687-5929, fax 06-6880-5495, www.smeraldoroma .com, albergosmeraldoroma@tin.it, Massimo).

$$ Hotel in Parione, also run by Hotel Smeraldo, crams 16 modern, high-ceilinged rooms into a tiny, adjacent building. It offers similar amenities and a fabulous location (Sb-€90, Db-€115, prices promised through 2006 with this book, €25 less off-sea-son, breakfast-€7, air-con, elevator, roof terrace, Via dei Chiavari 32, tel. 06-6880-2560, fax 06-683-4094, www.inparione.com, info@inparione.com).

In the Jewish Quarter

$$ Hotel Arenula, with 50 decent rooms, is the only hotel in Rome's old Jewish quarter. While it has the ambience of a gym and attracts lots of students, it's a fine value in the thick of old Rome (Sb-€92, Db-€125, Tb-€146, claim a 5 percent discount with this book in 2006, 20 percent less in July–Aug and winter, air-con, just off Via Arenula at Via Santa Maria de' Calderari 47, tel. 06-687-9454, fax 06-689-6188, www.hotelarenula.com, hotel .arenula@flashnet.it, Rosanna).

Near the Pantheon

These places are buried in the pedestrian-friendly heart of ancient Rome, each within a four-minute walk of the Pantheon. You'll pay more here—but you'll save time and money by being exactly where you want to be for your early and late wandering.

$$$ Hotel Nazionale, a four-star landmark, is a 16th-century palace that shares a well-policed square with the Parliament build-ing. Its 92 rooms are served by lush public spaces, fancy bars, and a uniformed staff. It's a big, stuffy hotel with a revolving front door, but it's a worthy splurge if you want security, comfort, and ancient Rome at your doorstep (Sb-€210, Db-€325, giant deluxe Db-€450, 10 percent discount with this book in 2006, extra person-€65; less in Aug, winter, and when slow—check online for summer and weekend discounts; air-con, elevator, Piazza Montecitorio 131, tel. 06-695-001, fax 06-678-6677, www.nazionaleroma.it, hotel @nazionaleroma.it).

$$$ Albergo Santa Chiara is big, solid, and hotelesque, offering marbled elegance and all the hotel services in the old center. Its ample public lounges are dressy and professional, and its 100 rooms are quiet and spacious (Sb-€145, Db-€217, Tb-€250, ask for Rick Steves discount, check Web site for deals, elevator, behind Pantheon at Via di Santa Chiara 21, tel. 06-687-2979, fax 06-687-3144, www.albergosantachiara.com, info@albergosantachiara.com).

$$$ Hotel Due Torri, hiding out on a tiny, quiet street, is a little overpriced but beautifully located. It feels professional yet homey, with an accommodating staff, generous public spaces, and 26 comfortable-if-tight rooms (Sb-€118, Db-€190, family apartment-€250 for 3 and €275 for 4, air-con, Vicolo del Leonetto 23, a block off Via della Scrofa, tel. 06-6880-6956, fax 06-686-5442, www.hotelduetorriroma.com, hotelduetorri@interfree.it).

Near Piazza Venezia

$$ Hotel Giardino, thoughtfully run by Englishwoman Kate, offers 11 pleasant rooms in a central location three blocks northeast of Piazza Venezia (March–June and Sept–mid-Nov: Sb-€85, Db-€125; July–Aug and mid-Nov–Feb: Sb-€60, Db-€90; these prices promised through 2006 with this book and cash, check Web site for specials, air-con, double-paned windows, on a busy street off Piazza di Quirinale, Via XXIV Maggio 51, tel. 06-679-4584, fax 06-679-5155, www.hotel-giardino-roma.com, hotel_giardino@libero.it, Sergio also speaks English).

$ Istituto Il Rosario is a peaceful, well-run Dominican convent renting 40 rooms to both pilgrims and tourists in a good neighborhood (S-€38, Sb-€46, D-€72, Db-€80, Tb-€108, 23:00 curfew, roof terrace, midway between the Quirinale and Colosseum near bottom of Via Nazionale at Via Sant'Agata dei Goti 10, bus #40 or #64 from Termini, tel. 06-679-2346, fax 06-6994-1106, irodopre@tin.it).

Trastevere

Colorful and genuine in a gritty sort of way, Trastevere is a treat for travelers looking for a less touristy and more bohemian atmosphere. Choices are few here, but by trekking across the Tiber, you can have the experience of being comfortably immersed in old Rome. To locate the following two places, see the map on page 573.

$$ Hotel Santa Maria sits like a lazy hacienda in the midst of Trastevere. Surrounded by a medieval skyline, you'll feel as if you're on some romantic stage set. Its 19 small but well-equipped, air-conditioned rooms—former cells in a cloister—are all on the ground floor, circling a gravelly courtyard of orange trees and stay-awhile patio furniture (Db-€165, Tb-€210, Qb-€250; you must pay cash and stay at least 3 nights to get these 20–25 percent discounted

Hotels in the Heart of Rome

TO PIAZZA DEL POPOLO

TO SPANISH STEPS

TO Ⓜ BARB.

PONTE UMBERTO

TI BER

LUNGOTEVERE MARZIO

PIAZZA COLONNA

VIA TRITONE

ANCIENT STADIUM ENTRANCE

Ⓣ S. LUIGI (CARAVAGGIO)

UFF. VIC.

PARL.

Ⓣ

Ⓣ

TREVI

CORONARI

Ⓣ

AQUIRO

P. PIETRA

SABINA MURATTE

PIAZZA NAVONA

SALV. GIUST.

SEMINARIO

SAN IGNAZIO

PIAZZA PASQUINO

CITY MUSEUM

Ⓣ

Ⓣ

PANTHEON

S. MARIA SOPRA MINERVA

GALLERIA DORA PAMPHILJ

P. QUIR.

Ⓣ

CAMPO DE' FIORI

VITTORIO

ⒷⓉ EMANUELE

GESÙ

PIAZZA VENEZIA

Ⓣ

TO COLOS-SEUM

GIUBBO.

NARI

V. BOTT. OSC.

ARACELI

V.E. MON.

VIA IMPERIALT

PALAZZO FARNESE

LARGO ARGENTINA RUINS (+ CAT HOSPICE)

CAPITOL HILL

DCH

FORUM

TO TRASTEVERE

200 YARDS
200 METERS

N

Ⓣ - TAXI STAND
Ⓜ - SUBWAY STOP
Ⓑ - BUS STOP

❶ Casa di Santa Brigida
❷ Hotel Smeraldo
❸ Hotel in Parione
❹ Hotel Nazionale

❺ Albergo Santa Chiara
❻ Hotel Due Torri
❼ Hotel Giardino

rates, which are promised through 2006 with this book; you'll pay more for shorter stays and credit-card payment, smaller discounts off-season, suites available for 2–6 people, free loaner bikes and Internet access for guests, face church on Piazza Maria Trastevere and go right half a block to Vicolo del Piede 2, tel. 06-589-4626, fax 06-589-4815, www.htlsantamaria.com, hotelsantamaria@libero.it, Stefano).

$ Casa San Giuseppe is down a quiet, characteristic, laundry-strewn lane. While convent-run, it's a secular place renting 25 plain but peaceful, spacious, and spotless rooms (Sb-€75, Db-€105, Tb-€140, Qb-€160, air-con, elevator, just north of Piazza Trilussa, Vicolo Moroni 22, tel. 06-5833-3490, fax 06-5833-5754, casasangiuseppe@virgilio.it).

Near the Vatican Museum

Sleeping near the Vatican is expensive, but some enjoy calling this neighborhood home. Even though it's handy to the Vatican (when the rapture hits, you're right there), everything else is a long way away.

$$$ Hotel Sant'Anna is pricey, but located on a charming pedestrian street that fills up with restaurant tables at dinnertime. Its 20 comfy rooms, decorated with classical themes, are somewhere between tasteful and too much (Sb-€160, Db-€220; Db discounted to €150 in July–Aug, winter, and slow times; any time of year, ask for a Rick Steves discount; air-con, elevator, courtyard, Borgo Pio 133, near intersection with Mascherino, a couple blocks from entrance to St. Peter's, tel. 06-6880-1602, fax 06-6830-8717, www.hotelsantanna.com, santanna@travel.it, Viscardo).

$$$ Hotel Bramante sits like a grand medieval lodge in the shadow of the fortified escape wall that runs from the Vatican to Castel Sant'Angelo. The public spaces and 16 thoughtfully appointed rooms are generously sized, with rough wood beams and high ceilings (Sb-€140, Db-€195, Tb-€220, Qb-€230, these prices promised through 2006 with this book, air-con, no elevator, Vicolo delle Palline 24, tel. 06-6880-6426, fax 06-681-33339, www.hotelbramante.com, hotelbramante@libero.it, Maurizio and Loredana).

$$$ Hotel Alimandi Vaticano, facing the Vatican Museum, is beautifully designed. A new hotel run by the Alimandi family (see next listing), it features four stars, 24 spacious rooms, and all the modern comforts you can imagine (standard Db-€185, big Db with 2 double beds-€200, Tb-€210, Qb-€220, 5 percent discount with cash, air-con, elevator, Viale Vaticano 99, Metro: Cipro-Musei Vaticani, tel. 06-397-45562, fax 06-397-30132, www.alimandi.com, hotelali@hotelalimandie.191.it).

$$ Hotel Alimandi is a good value, run by the friendly and entrepreneurial Alimandi brothers—Paolo, Enrico, and Luigi—and the next generation, Marta, Irene, Barbara, and Germano. Their 35 rooms are air-conditioned, modern, and marbled in white (Sb-€90, Db-€160, Tb-€180, 5 percent discount for cash, closed Jan–mid-Feb, elevator, grand buffet breakfast served in great roof garden, small gym, pool table, piano lounge, down the stairs directly in front of Vatican Museum, Via Tunisi 8, Metro: Cipro-Musei Vaticani, reserve by phone, tel. 06-3972-6300, toll-free in Italy tel. 800-122-121, fax 06-3972-3943, www.alimandi.com, alimandi@tin.it). They offer free airport pick-up and drop-off for guests staying at either of their hotels, though you must reserve when you book your room and wait for a scheduled shuttle (every 2 hrs, see their Web site or lobby schedule).

$$ Hotel Spring House, part of the Best Western chain, has a hotelesque feel and 51 attractive rooms—some with balconies

Hotels and Restaurants in the Vatican Area

1. Hotel Sant'Anna
2. Hotel Bramante
3. Hotel Alimandi
4. Hotel Alimandi Vaticano
5. Hotel Spring House
6. To Hotel Gerber
7. To Casa per Ferie Rooms
8. Hostaria dei Bastioni Rest.
9. La Rustichella & Gelateria Millennium
10. To Tre Pupazzi Rest.
11. Perilli in Prati Rest.

or terraces (standard Db-€160, superior Db-€190, Tb-€195, Qb-€210, 15 percent discount July–Aug and Jan–Feb through 2006 with this book, air-con, elevator, free loaner bikes, Via Mocenigo 7, 2 blocks from Vatican Museum, Metro: Cipro-Musei Vaticani, tel. 06-3972-0948, fax 06-3972-1047, www.hotelspringhouse.com, info@hotelspringhouse.com, Stefania).

$$ Hotel Gerber, set in a quiet residential area, is modern and air-conditioned, with 27 well-polished, businesslike rooms (two S without air-con-€60, Sb-€105, Db-€140, Tb-€160, Qb-€180; discounts with this book through 2006: 10 percent discount beyond their best price in high season, 15 percent in low season; Via degli Scipioni 241, at intersection with Ezio, a block from Metro: Lepanto, tel. 06-321-6485, fax 06-321-7048, www.hotelgerber.it, info@hotelgerber.it, Peter and Simonetta speak English, but friendly dog Kira does not).

$ Casa per Ferie Santa Maria alle Fornaci dei Padri Trinitari houses pilgrims and secular tourists with simple class just a short walk south of the Vatican in 54 stark, identical, utilitarian, mostly twin-bed rooms. This is the most user-friendly convent-type place I found (Sb-€65, Db-€85, Tb-€120, groups welcome, air-con, elevator; bus #64 from train station to St. Peter's Station, then walk 100 yards to Piazza S. Maria alle Fornaci 27; tel. 06-393-67632, fax 06-393-66795, www.trinitaridematha.it, cffornaci@tin.it).

EATING

Romans spend their evenings eating rather than drinking, and the preferred activity is simply to enjoy a fine, slow meal, buried deep in the old city. Rome's a fun and cheap place to eat, with countless little eateries serving memorable €20 meals. In general, I'm impressed by how small the price difference is from a mediocre restaurant to a fine one. You can pay about 20 percent more for double the quality.

Although I've listed a number of restaurants, I recommend that you just head for a scenic area and explore. Piazza Navona, the Pantheon area, Campo de' Fiori, and Trastevere are neighborhoods packed with characteristic eateries. Sitting with tourists on a famous square, enjoying the scene works fine. (As my Roman friend explained: "When you're in a bad restaurant, the best way to survive is bread, olive oil, and salt.") But for more of a local flavor, consider my recommendations.

Trastevere

Colorful Trastevere is now pretty touristy. Still, Romans join the tourists to eat on the rustic side of the Tiber River. Start at the central square (Piazza Santa Maria). Then choose: Eat with tourists enjoying the ambience of the famous square, or wander the back streets in search of a mom-and-pop place with barely a menu. My recommendations are within a few minutes' walk of each other (between Piazza Santa Maria Trastevere and Ponte Sisto; see map on page 573).

Trattoria de "Gli Amici" serves good food on a super square (reservations smart—popular with dressy locals) or fine interior for a fair price while employing locals with disabilities. At this "Inn of the Friends," waiters do their work with a unique passion. Each has mental problems and is paired with a volunteer aide from the Community of Sant'Egidio. Pictures on the walls show what can be accomplished by mentally disabled people who are successfully integrated into the community like this (€7 pastas, €9 *secondi*, Mon–Sat from 19:30, closed Sun, 2 blocks off main square at Piazza Sant'Egidio 6, tel. 06-580-6033).

Trattoria da Lucia lets you enjoy simple, traditional food at a good price in a great scene. It offers the quintessential, rustic, 100 percent Roman Trastevere dining experience and has been family-run since World War II. You'll meet Renato, his uncle Ennio, and Ennio's mom—pictured on the menu in the 1950s (cheap, Tue–Sun 12:30–15:30 & 19:30–24:00, closed Mon, homey indoor or evocative outdoor seating, Vicolo del Mattonato 2, tel. 06-580-3601, no English spoken).

Osteria Ponte Sisto, a rough-and-tumble little place, special-izes in traditional Roman cuisine with a menu that changes often. Just outside the tourist zone, it caters mostly to Romans and offers a fine value (but be careful when ordering the unpriced fish dishes). It's also easy to find: Crossing Ponte Sisto (pedestrian bridge) toward Trastevere, continue across the little square (Piazza Trilussa) and you'll see it on the right (daily 12:30–15:00 & 19:30–24:00, Via Ponte Sisto 80, tel. 06-588-3411).

Ristorante Checco er Carettiere is a big, classic, family-run place that's been a Trastevere fixture for three generations. While it's a bit pricey, you'll eat well among lots of fun commotion (€13 pastas, €16 *secondi*, open daily, Via Benedetta 10/13, tel. 06-580-0985).

Gelateria alla Scala is a terrific little ice cream place that dishes up delightful cinnamon *(cannella)* and oh-wow pistachio (daily 12:00–24:00, Piazza della Scala 51, across from the church on Piazza della Scala). Seek this place out.

On and near Campo de' Fiori

While it is touristy, Campo de' Fiori offers a sublimely romantic setting. And, since it's so close to the collective heart of Rome, it remains popular with locals. For greater atmosphere than food value, circle the square, considering each place. Bars and pizzerias seem to overwhelm the square. The **Taverna** and **Vineria** (#16 and

#15) offer good perches from which to people-watch and nurse a glass of wine.

Ristorante la Carbonara has the ultimate Campo de' Fiori setting, with dressy waiters and superb on-the-square seating. While the service gets mixed reviews, the food and Italian ambience are wonderful (€10 pastas, €15 *secondi*, Wed–Mon, closed Tue, Campo de' Fiori 23, tel. 06-686-4783). Meals on small surrounding streets may be a better value, but they lack that Campo de' Fiori magic.

Ostaria da Giovanni ar Galletto is nearby, on the more elegant and peaceful Piazza Farnese. It has an upscale local crowd, pleasant outdoor seating, and reasonable prices. Say hi to Angelo, who's committed to serving fine food. Regrettably, service can be horrible and single diners aren't treated very well. Still, if you're in no hurry and ready to just savor my favorite *al fresco* setting in Rome, this is a good bet (Mon–Sat 12:15–15:00 & 19:30–23:00, closed Sun, tucked in corner of Piazza Farnese at #102, tel. 06-686-1714).

Osteria Enoteca al Bric is a mod bistro-type place run by a man who loves to cook and serve good wine. Wine-case lids decorate the wall like happy memories. With candlelit grace and no tourists, it's perfect for the wine snob in the mood for pasta and fine cheese. Aficionados choose their bottle from the huge selection that lines the walls near the entrance. Beginners order fine wine by the glass with help from the waiter when they order their meal (open from 19:30, closed Mon June–Sept, reserve after 20:30, 100 yards off Campo de' Fiori at Via del Pellegrino 51, tel. 06-687-9533). Al Bric offers my readers a special "Taste of Italy for Two" deal (fine plate of mixed cheese and meat with two glasses of full-bodied red wine and a pitcher of water) for €22 from 19:30, but you may need to finish by 20:30. This could be a light meal if you're kicking off an evening stroll, a substantial appetizer, or a way to check this place out for a serious meal later.

Filetti de Baccala, a tradition for many Romans, is basically a fish bar with paper tablecloths and cheap prices. Its grease-stained, hurried waiters serve old-time favorites—fried cod fillets, a strange bitter *puntarelle* salad, and their antipasto (delightful anchovies with butter)—to nostalgic locals (no credit cards, Mon–Sat 17:30–23:00, closed Sun, a block east of Campo de' Fiori tumbling onto long tables in a tiny and atmospheric square, Largo dei Librari 88, tel. 06-686-4018). Study what others are eating and order by pointing. Nothing is expensive (see the menu on wall). Urchins can get a cod stick to go and sit on the barnacle church doorsteps just outside. Say *ciao* to Marcello, who runs the place like a swim coach.

Trattoria der Pallaro, which has no menu, has a slogan: "Here, you'll eat what we want to feed you." Paola Fazi—with a towel wrapped around her head turban-style—and her family serve up a five-course meal of typically Roman food for €21, including

Restaurants in the Heart of Rome

1. Rest. la Carbonara, Taverna & Vineria
2. Ostaria da Giovanni ar Galletto
3. Osteria Enoteca al Bric
4. Filetti de Baccala
5. Trattoria der Pallaro
6. Rist. Grotte del Teatro di Pompeo
   & Hostaria Costanza
7. Cul de Sac Bar, L'Insalata Ricca Rest.
   & Ristorante Terra di Siena
8. Ristorante Pizzeria Sacro e Profano
9. Gelateria San Crispino
10. L'Antica Birreria Peroni

wine, coffee, and a tasty mandarin juice. Make like Oliver Twist asking for more soup and get seconds on the juice (Tue–Sun 12:00–15:00 & 19:00–24:00, closed Mon, indoor/outdoor seating on quiet square, a block south of Corso Vittorio Emanuele, down Largo del Chiavari to Largo del Pallaro 15, tel. 06-6880-1488).

Ristorante Grotte del Teatro di Pompeo, sitting atop an ancient theater, serves good food at great prices, perfect if you want to dine on a characteristic cobbled street, busy with strolling people and musicians. It's well-established, albeit a bit tired, but always popular (closed Mon and Aug, Via del Biscione 73, tel. 06-6880-3686). Their pasta radicchio (made with red endive) is good.

Hostaria Costanza has crisp-vested waiters, a local following, and lots of energy. You'll eat traditional Roman cuisine on a ramshackle patio or inside under arches from the ancient Pompeo Theater (closed Sun, Piazza Paradiso 63, tel. 06-686-1717).

Piazza Pasquino

Between Campo de' Fiori and Piazza Navona, these three bustling places have low prices and a happy clientele. As they are neighbors and each is completely different, check out all three before choosing:

Cul de Sac is packed with enthusiastic locals cobbling together fun meals from an Italian dim sum-type menu of traditional dishes (often crowded, daily 12:00–16:00 & 18:00–24:00, a block southwest of Piazza Navona on Piazza Pasquino). **L'Insalata Ricca,** next door, is a popular chain that specializes in hearty and healthy €7 salads and much less healthy pizzas (daily 12:00–15:45 & 18:45–24:00, Piazza Pasquino 72, tel. 06-6830-7881). **Ristorante Terra di Siena** is more traditional, with a Tuscan passion for meat (closed Sun, Piazza Pasquino 77, tel. 06-6830-7704).

Dining near the Pantheon

Ristorante da Fortunato is an Italian classic, with fresh flowers on the tables, and white-coated, black-tie waiters politely serving good meat and fish to local politicians, foreign dignitaries, and tourists with good taste. Don't leave without perusing the photos of their famous visitors—everyone from former Iraqi Foreign Minister Tariq Aziz to Bill Clinton has eaten here. The outdoor seating is fine for watching the river of Roman street life flow by. For a dressy night out, this is a reliable choice. When it comes to cuisine, Fortunato is a master of simple elegance (surprisingly reasonable, plan to spend €30, Mon–Sat 12:30–15:00 & 19:30–23:30, closed Sun, a block in front of the Pantheon at Via del Pantheon 55, tel. 06-679-2788).

Cheap and Colorful near the Pantheon

Eating on the square facing the Pantheon is a temptation (there's even a McDonald's that offers some of the best outdoor seating in town), and I'd consider it just to relax and enjoy the Roman scene. But if you walk a block or two away, you'll get less view and better food. Here are some suggestions:

Ristorante Enoteca Corsi is a wine shop that grew into a thriving lunch-only restaurant. The Paiella family serves straightforward, traditional cuisine at great prices to an appreciative crowd of office workers. Check the blackboard for daily specials (gnocchi on Thursday, fish on Friday, and so on). Friendly Ilaria and Manuela welcome diners to step into their wine shop and pick out a bottle. For the cheap take-away price, plus a euro or two, they'll uncork it at your table. With €5 pastas, €8.50 main dishes, and fine wine at a third the price you'd pay in normal restaurants, this is a superb value (Mon–Sat 12:00–15:00, closed Sun, a block toward the Pantheon from the Gesù church at Via del Gesù 87, tel. 06-679-0821).

Miscellanea is run by much-loved Mikki, who's on a mission to keep foreign students well-fed. You'll find cheap pasta, hearty and fresh €3 sandwiches, and a long list of €6 salads. Mikki often tosses in a fun little extra, including—if you have this book on the table—a free glass of Mikki's "sexy wine" (homemade from *fragolina*—strawberries). This place is popular with American students on foreign study programs (daily 11:00–24:00, indoor/outdoor seating, a block toward Via del Corso from the Pantheon at Via delle Paste 110).

Osteria da Mario, a homey little mom-and-pop joint with a no-stress menu, serves traditional favorites in a fun, homey little dining room or on tables spilling out onto a picturesque old Roman square (Mon–Sat 13:00–15:30 & 19:00–23:00, closed Sun, from the Pantheon walk 2 blocks up Via Pantheon, go left on Via delle Coppelle, take first right to Piazza delle Coppelle 51, tel. 06-6880-6349).

Restaurant Coco is a perfect place for a quick and atmospheric lunch with friendly service. They put out a wonderful €10 lunch buffet on weekdays. After grazing through the great selection of tempting dishes, you'll sit on the square among a produce market, watching local politicians stroll in and out of their dining hall across the way (classy indoor and rustic outdoor seating; €10 gets you a big main plate, bread, dessert, water and coffee; Mon–Fri 12:30–15:30, Piazza delle Coppelle 54, tel. 06-6813-6545).

Taverna le Coppelle is good—especially for pizza—with a checkered-tablecloth ambience (daily, Via delle Coppelle 39, tel. 06-6880-6557).

Restaurants near the Pantheon

100 YARDS

100 METERS

ⓉTAXI STAND
ⓂSUBWAY STOP
ⒷBUS STOP

❶ Ristorante da Fortunato
❷ Ristorante Enoteca Corsi
❸ Miscellanea Restaurant
❹ Osteria da Mario &
   Restaurant Coco
❺ Taverna le Coppelle

❻ Cafeteria Brek
❼ Antica Salumeria
❽ Crèmeria Monteforte
❾ Gelateria Giolitti
❿ Gelateria della Palma

Cafeteria Brek, on Largo Argentina just south of the Pantheon, is an appealing self-service restaurant with a modern, efficient atmosphere and cheap prices (daily 12:00–15:30 & 19:00–22:15, skip the sandwiches and pizza slices downstairs and go to the cafeteria upstairs, northwest corner of square, Largo Argentina 1, tel. 06-6821-0353).

Picnic on the Pantheon Porch: **Antica Salumeria** is an old-time *alimentari* (grocery store, daily 8:00–21:00) on the Pantheon square. Eduardo speaks English and will help you assemble your picnic: artichokes, mixed olives, bread, cheese, meat, and wine (with plastic glasses). While you can create your own (sold by the weight, more fun, and cheaper), they also sell quality ready-made sandwiches. Now take your peasant's feast over for a temple-porch picnic. Enjoy the shade at the base of a column and munch your meal. For dessert…

Gelato

Three fine *gelaterie* are within a two-minute walk of the Pantheon. Rome's most famous and venerable ice-cream joint is **Gelateria Caffè Pasticceria Giolitti** (with cheap take-away prices and elegant Old World seating, just off Piazza Colonna and Piazza Monte Citorio at Via Uffici del Vicario 40, tel. 06-699-1243). Another good option is **Gelateria della Palma** (2 blocks directly in front of the Pantheon at Via della Maddalena 20). Bright with neon and filled with every type of candy imaginable, kids of all ages will enjoy their huge selection of colorful, tasty *gelati*. However, taste purists look down on bright colors. For mellower hues and more traditional quality, try **Crèmeria Monteforte,** facing the right side of the Pantheon (Tue–Sun 11:00–24:00, closed Mon, Via della Rotonda 22).

Near the Spanish Steps

To locate these restaurants, see the "Dolce Vita Stroll" map on page 534.

Ristorante il Gabriello is inviting and small—modern under medieval arches—and offers a peaceful and local-feeling respite from all the top-end fashion shops in the area. Claudio serves with charisma, while his brother cooks creative Roman cuisine using fresh, organic products from his wife's farm. Simply close your eyes and point to anything on the menu (pastas-€9, *secondi*-€12; dinner only, Mon–Sat 19:00–24:00, closed Sun, air-con, dress respectfully—no shorts please, reservations smart, Via Vittoria 51, 3 blocks from Spanish Steps, tel. 06-6994-0810). Italians normally just trust the waiter and say "Bring it on." Tourists are understandably more cautious, but you can be trusting here. Invest €40 (not including wine) in "Claudio's Extravaganza," and he'll shower you with edible kindness.

These two neighboring places are nothing special, just lively and simple, offering €8 plates with good indoor and outdoor seating near the Spanish Steps. **Ristorante Difronte,** with a fresh, stylish ambience, serves big, fun €8 salads and pizzas (Tue–Sun 12:00–15:30 & 17:30–24:00, closed Mon, Via della Croce 38, tel. 06-678-0355). Stepping next door takes you back about 100 years to the bustling **Fiaschetteria,** serving traditional Italian cuisine (closed Sun, Via della Croce 39).

Ristorante alla Rampa, just around the corner from the touristy crush of the Spanish Steps, offers Roman cooking, appealing indoor/outdoor ambience at a moderate price, and impersonal service. They take no reservations, so arrive by 19:30, or be prepared to wait. If the antipasto bar is open, try the €9 *piatto misto all'ortolana*—a self-service trip to an antipasto spread of meat, fish, and veggies. Even though you get just one trip to the buffet, this can be a simple meal in itself (closed Sun, 100 yards east of Spanish Steps at Piazza Mignanelli 18, tel. 06-678-2621).

Near the Trevi Fountain

L'Antica Birreria Peroni is Rome's answer to a German beer hall. Serving hearty mugs of the local Peroni beer and lots of just plain fun, beer-hall food, the place is a hit with locals for a cheap night out (Mon–Sat 12:00–24:00, closed Sun, midway between Trevi Fountain and Capitol Hill, a block off Via del Corso at Via di San Marcello 19, tel. 06-679-5310).

Ristorante Pizzeria Sacro e Profano fills an old church with spicy south Italian (Calabrian) cuisine and some pricey, exotic dishes. Run with enthusiasm and passion by Pasquale and friends, this is just far enough away from the Trevi mobs. Their hearty €13 *antipasti* plate offers a delightful montage of Calabrian taste treats—plenty of food for a light, memorable meal (Mon–Sat 12:00–15:00 & 18:00–22:00, closed Sun, a block off Via del Tritone at Via dei Maroniti 29, tel. 06-679-1836). For dessert...

Around the corner, **Gelateria San Crispino,** well-respected by locals, serves particularly tasty, gourmet gelato using creative ingredients such as balsamic vinegar, pear, and cinnamon (Wed–Mon 12:00–24:00, closed Tue, Via della Panetteria 42, tel. 06-679-3924).

Eating Cheaply between the Colosseum and St. Peter-in-Chains Church

You'll find good views but poor value in the restaurants directly behind the Colosseum. To get your money's worth, eat at least a block away. Here are two handy eateries at the top of Terme di Tito (a block uphill from Colosseum, near St. Peter-in-Chains church—of Michelangelo's *Moses* fame; se page 542).

Caffè dello Studente is a lively spot popular with local engineering students attending the nearby U. of Rome. Pina, Mauro, and their perky daughter Simona (speaks English, but you can teach her some more) give my readers a royal welcome and serve typical *bar gastronomia* fare: toasted sandwiches and simple pastas and pizzas. You can get your food to go *(da portar via)*; stand up and eat at the crowded bar; sit at an outdoor table and wait for a menu; or—if it's not busy—show this book when you order at the bar and sit without paying extra at a table (Mon–Sat 7:30–21:00, Sun 9:00–18:00, tel. 06-488-3240).

Ostaria da Nerone, next door, is more of a restaurant: less friendly and more aggressive. Their €7.50 *antipasti* plate is the best value; add €2 and you get meat and shellfish (Mon–Sat 12:00–15:00 & 19:00–23:00, closed Sun, indoor/outdoor seating, Via delle Terme di Tito 96, tel. 06-481-7952, run by Teo).

Munching near Via Firenze

You have plenty of eating options near my recommended hotels on Via Firenze.

Ristorante del Giglio is a circa-1900 place with a long family tradition of serving traditional Roman dishes. You'll eat in a big elegant hall of about 20 tables with dressy locals and tourists following the recommendation of the many nearby hotels (€8 pastas, €15 *secondi*, Mon–Sat 12:00–15:00 & 19:00–23:00, closed Sun, Via Torino 137, tel. 06-488-1606).

Ristorante da Giovanni is a reasonable, budget option that has fed locals and hungry travelers now for 50 years (tired but filling €14 *menu*, Mon–Sat 12:00–15:00 & 19:00–22:30, closed Sun and in Aug, just off Via XX Settembre at Via Antonio Salandra 1, tel. 06-485-950).

Cafeteria Nazionale, with woody elegance, offers light lunches—including salads—at fair prices. It's noisy with local office workers being served by frantic red-vested wait staff (Mon–Sat 7:00–20:00, closed Sun, Via Nazionale 26–27, at intersection with Via Agostino de Pretis, tel. 06-4899-1716). Their lunch buffet is a delight but gets picked over early (small dish €7.50, Mon–Sat 12:00–15:00).

Restaurant Target is a modern, handy place serving decent pizza and pasta near recommended hotels (Mon–Sat 12:00–15:30 & 19:00–24:00, Sun 19:00–24:00, indoor/outdoor seating, don't expect great service, Via Torino 33, tel. 06-474-0066).

The **McDonald's** restaurants on Piazza della Repubblica (free piazza seating outside), Piazza Barberini, and Via Firenze offer air-conditioned interiors and salad bars.

Flann O'Brien Irish Pub is an entertaining place for a light meal (of pasta or something *other* than pasta, such as grilled beef, served early and late, when other places are closed), fine Irish beer, live sporting events on TV, and perhaps the most Italian crowd of all. Walk way back before choosing a table (daily 7:30–24:00, Via Nazionale 17, at intersection with Via Napoli, tel. 06-488-0418).

Snack Bar Gastronomia is a local joint with one table and a booming take-out business—especially popular for its Greek-style yogurt with fruit and honey (€3–5, confirm price before ordering as there are several versions; fresh meat or veggie sandwiches,

Restaurants in East Rome

1 Ost. da Nerone & Caffè dello Studente

2 Ristorante del Giglio

3 Ristorante da Giovanni

4 Cafeteria Nazionale

5 Restaurant Target

6 Flann O'Brien Irish Pub

7 Snack Bar Gastronomia

salads, freshly squeezed juices, daily 7:00–24:00, Via Firenze 34). An old-fashioned *alimentari* (grocery), with everything you'd need for a picnic, is across the street (7:00–19:30), just uphill from the McDonald's.

Near the Vatican Museum and St. Peter's

Avoid the restaurant pushers handing out fliers near the Vatican: bad food and expensive menu tricks. Try any of these instead (see map on page 596).

Perilli in Prati is bright, modern, and just far enough away from the tourist hordes. While friendly Lucia and Massimo specialize in pizza and grilled meats, the highlight is their excellent lunch buffet on weekdays (€5.50 small plate or €7.50 for large, Mon–Fri 12:00–15:00, also open Mon–Sat for dinner, 1 block from Ottaviano Metro stop, Via Otranto 9, tel. 06-370-0156).

Hostaria dei Bastioni, run by Antonio and his family, has tasty food and friendly service. It's conveniently located midway on your hike from St. Peters' to the Vatican Museum, with noisy street-side seating and a quiet interior. The house fettuccine and the risotto with seafood are good (pastas-€6, *secondi*-€8–12, no cover charge, Mon–Sat 12:00–15:00 & 19:00–23:30, closed Sun, at corner of Vatican wall, Via Leone IV 29, tel. 06-3972-3034).

La Rustichella serves a sprawling *antipasti* buffet (€7 for a single meal-sized plate). Arrive when they open at 19:30 to avoid a line and have the pristine buffet to yourself (Tue–Sun 12:30–15:00 & 19:30–23:00, closed Mon, near Metro: Cipro-Musei Vaticani, opposite church at end of Via Candia, Via Angelo Emo 1, tel. 06-3972-0649). Consider the fun and fruity **Gelateria Millennium** next door.

Viale Giulio Cesare is lined with cheap **Pizza Rustica** shops, self-serve places, and inviting eateries. Restaurants such as **Tre Pupazzi** (closed Sun, tel. 06-686-8371), which line the pedestrian-only Borgo Pio—a block from Piazza San Pietro—are worth a look.

Turn your nose loose in the wonderful **Via Andrea Doria open-air market,** three blocks north of the Vatican Museum (Mon–Sat roughly 7:00–13:30, until 16:30 Tue and Fri except summer, corner of Via Tunisi and Via Andrea Doria). If the market is closed, try the nearby **IN's supermarket** (Mon–Sat 8:30–13:30 & 16:00–20:00, closed Thu eve and Sun, a half block straight out from Via Tunisi entrance of open-air market, Via Francesco Caracciolo 18).

Testaccio

For restaurant location, see the map on page 578.

Trattoria "Da Oio" A Casa Mia serves quality, inexpensive, traditional cuisine to a local crowd. It's a upbeat little eatery where you understand the Testaccio passion for the "fifth quarter." (Testaccio, dominated for centuries by its slaughterhouses, is noted for restaurants expert at preparing undesirable meat parts.) The menu is big on soft meats (closed Sun, Via Galvani 43, tel. 06-578-2680).

TRANSPORTATION CONNECTIONS

Termini is the central station (see "Arrival in Rome" on page 514; Metro: Termini). Tiburtina is the bus station (4 Metro stops away from train station; Metro: Tiburtina).

From Rome by Train to: Venice (6/day, 5–8 hrs, overnight possible), **Florence** (12/day, 2 hrs, most stop at Orvieto en route), **Assisi** (every 2 hrs, 2.5 hrs, many direct), **Pisa** (8/day, 3–4 hrs), **Genoa** (7/day, 6 hrs, overnight option), **Milan** (12/day, 5 hrs, overnight possible), **Naples** (6/day, 2 hrs), **Brindisi** (2/day, 9 hrs, overnight available), **Amsterdam** (2/day, 20 hrs, overnight unavoidable), **Bern** (5/day, 10 hrs, overnight possible), **Frankfurt** (4/day, 14 hrs, overnight available), **Munich** (5/day, 12 hrs, overnight option), **Nice** (2/day, 10 hrs, overnight possible), **Paris** (5/day, 16 hrs, overnight available), **Vienna** (3/day, 13–15 hrs, overnight option).

By Bus to: Assisi (3/day, 3 hrs), **Siena** (7/day, 3 hrs), **Sorrento** (1–2/day, 4 hrs; this is the quickest and easiest way to go straight to Sorrento).

Airports

Rome's two airports—Fiumicino (a.k.a. Leonardo da Vinci) and the small Ciampino—share the same Web site (www.adr.it).

Fiumicino Airport

Rome's major airport has a TI (daily 8:00–19:00, tel. 06-6595-6074), ATMs, banks, luggage storage, shops, and bars.

A slick, direct **train** connects the airport and Rome's central Termini train station in 30 minutes. Trains run twice hourly in both directions from roughly 6:00 to 23:00. From the airport, trains depart at :07 and :37 past the hour. From the airport's arrival gate, follow signs to *Stazione/Railway Station*. Buy your ticket from a machine or the Biglietteria office (€9.50). Make sure the train you board is going to the central "Roma Termini" station, not "Roma Orte" or others.

Going from the Termini train station to the airport, trains depart at :20 and :50 past the hour, usually from track 25 or 26; to reach these tracks, take a long 10-minute walk along track 24 to the end of the station (near the corner of Giovanni Giolitti and Via Lamarmora, moving walkways are inside the building to the right on the lower level). Check the departure boards for "Fiumicino

Aeroporto"—the local name for the airport—and confirm with an official or a local on the platform that the train is indeed going to the airport (€9.50, buy ticket from computerized yellow ticket machines, any *tabacchi* shop in station, or at the desk near entrance to track 26). Read your ticket: If it requires validation, stamp it in the yellow machine near the platform before boarding. Know whether your plane departs from terminal A, B, or C.

Shuttle van services run to and from the airport. Consider Rome Airport Shuttle (€23/person, 30 percent more late night or early morning, tel. 06-4201-4507 or 06-420-13469, www .airportshuttle.it).

Your hotel can arrange a **taxi** to the airport at any hour for about €40. To get from the airport into town cheaply by taxi, try teaming up with any tourist also just arriving (most are heading for hotels near yours in the center). Be sure to wait at the taxi stand. Avoid unmarked, unmetered taxis; these guys will try to tempt you away from the taxi stand line-up by offering an immediate (rip-off) ride.

For **airport information,** call 06-65951. To inquire about flights, call 06-6595-3640 (Alitalia: tel. 06-2222, British Airways and SAS: tel. 06-6501-0771, Delta: toll-free tel. 800-477-999, KLM/Northwest: tel. 06-6501-1441, Lufthansa: tel. 06-6568-4004, Swiss International: tel. 848-868-120, United: tel. 848-800-692, Air Europa: tel. 06-6595-5695).

Ciampino Airport

Rome's smaller airport (tel. 06-794-941) handles budget airlines, such as easyJet or Ryanair, and charter flights. To get to downtown Rome from the airport, you can take the LILA/Cotral bus (2/hr, 40 min) to the Anagnina Metro stop, where you can connect by Metro to the stop nearest your hotel. Rome Airport Shuttle (listed above) also offers service to and from Ciampino.

Driving in Rome

The Grande Raccordo Anulare circles greater Rome. This ring road has spokes that lead you into the center. Entering from the north, leave the autostrada at the Settebagni exit. Following the ancient Via Salaria (and the black-and-white *Centro* signs), work your way doggedly into the Roman thick of things. This will take you along the Villa Borghese park and dump you right on Via Veneto in central Rome. Avoid rush hour and drive defensively: Roman cars stay in their lanes like rocks in an avalanche. Parking in Rome is dangerous. Park near a police station or get advice at your hotel. The Villa Borghese underground garage is handy (Metro: Spagna). Garages charge about €24 per day.

Consider this: Your car is a worthless headache in Rome. Avoid a pile of stress and save money by parking at the huge, easy, and relatively safe lot behind the train station in the hill town of Orvieto (follow *P* signs from autostrada) and catching the train to Rome (every 2 hrs, 75 min).

NAPLES

(Napoli)

If you like Italy as far south as Rome, go further south. It gets better. If Italy is getting on your nerves by the time you get to Rome, think twice about going further. Naples is Italy in the extreme—its best (birthplace of pizza and Sophia Loren) and its worst (home of the Camorra, Naples' "family" of organized crime). Just beyond Naples are three of the best ancient Rome sights anywhere: the impressive ruins of Pompeii and Herculaneum...and the brooding volcano that did them both in, Mount Vesuvius.

Naples—Italy's third-largest city (with 1 million people in the city proper, sprawling to 2 million in greater Naples)—has almost no open spaces or parks, which makes its position as Europe's most densely populated city plenty evident. Watching the police try to enforce traffic sanity is almost comical in Italy's grittiest, most polluted, and most crime-ridden city.

But Naples surprises the observant traveler with its good humor, decency, and impressive knack for living, eating, and raising children in the streets. Overcome your fear of being run down or ripped off long enough to talk with people. Enjoy a few smiles and jokes with the man running the neighborhood tripe shop or the woman taking her day-care class on a walk through the traffic. Ask a local about the New Year's Eve tradition of tossing chipped dinner plates off of balconies into the streets.

Twenty-five hundred years ago, Neapolis ("new city") was a thriving Greek commercial center. Two centuries ago, it was the capital of its own kingdom—the "Paris of the south." Then, locals lament, after it joined the newly united Italy, its riches were swallowed up by the new country. As Naples' wealth was used to fund the industrial expansion in the north, it lost its status and glamour.

Planning Your Time in the Region

On a quick trip, give the entire area—Naples, Sorrento, and the Amalfi Coast (covered within 3 chapters)—a minimum of three days. With Sorrento as your sunny springboard (see next chapter), spend a day in Naples, a day exploring the Amalfi Coast, and a day split between Pompeii and the town of Sorrento. While Paestum (Greek temples), Mount Vesuvius, Herculaneum (an ancient Roman site like Pompeii), and the island of Capri are decent options, they are worthwhile only if you give the area more time. All sights mentioned are covered in this book. For more information on transportation, see page 632.

Regional Pass: If you're planning serious time in the area, consider getting the Campania ArteCard. This €25, three-day pass offers free entry to two sights of your choice in this area (Pompeii and Herculaneum are the most expensive, so choose those as your freebies) and 50 percent off on all other sights covered by the card, including Naples' Archaeological Museum and Royal Palace, Paestum, and many more. The card also covers Naples' Metro, buses, and funiculars, as well as the regional Circumvesuviana trains (7-day version costs €28 and covers all sights but no transportation). For details, visit www .campaniartecard.it. ArteCards are sold at participating sights, Naples' Metro and train stations, travel agencies, and Naples' airport.

Naples, the Amalfi Coast, and Paestum

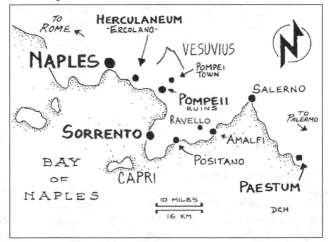

Naples

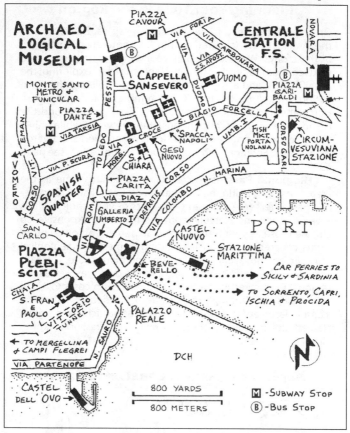

Nevertheless, it remains southern Italy's leading city, offering a fascinating collection of museums, churches, and eclectic architecture. The pulse of Italy throbs in Naples. This tangled mess—the closest thing to "reality travel" you'll find in western Europe—still somehow manages to breathe, laugh, and sing...with a captivating Italian accent.

Planning Your Time

Naples makes an ideal day trip either from Rome or the comfortable home base of Sorrento an hour south (see next chapter), though I've listed a few accommodations for those who want to overnight here.

On a quick visit, start with the Archaeological Museum (see page 625), do "The Slice-of-Neapolitan-Life Walk" (see page 618), and celebrate your survival with pizza. Of course, Naples is huge.

But even with limited time, if you stick to the described route and grab a cab when you're lost or tired, it's fun. Treat yourself well in Naples; the city is cheap by Italian standards.

For a blitz tour from Rome, you could have breakfast on the early Rome–Naples express train (about 7:00–9:00), do Naples and Pompeii in a day, and be back in Rome in time for *Letterman*. That's exhausting but more memorable than a fourth day in Rome.

Remember that in the afternoon, Naples' street life slows and many sights close as the temperature soars. The city comes back to life in the early evening.

ORIENTATION

Tourist Information
The TI is in the Napoli Centrale train station (Mon–Sat 8:30–20:00, maybe also Sun 9:00–13:00; with your back to the tracks, TI is in the lobby to your left, look for *Ente Provinciale Turismo* sign; for info call 081-402-394). Pick up a map and—even though the odds are against you—ask for the *Qui Napoli* booklet; when they say they're "finished," ask for an old one. If you want to visit Vesuvius, confirm the bus is running (see page 642).

Local Guide: Pina Esposito specializes in art and archaeology and does fine tours of Naples, Pompeii, Herculaneum, PaestumHer, and Capri (€100/2 hrs, €150/half-day, mobile 338-763-4224, annamariaesposito1@virgilio.it). She can often be found outside the Archaeological Museum; you could ask for her there.

Arrival in Naples
By Train: There are several Naples stations. You want Napoli Centrale (facing Piazza Garibaldi), which has a TI, baggage check,

Naples Transportation

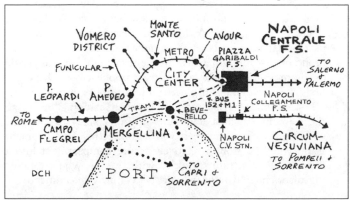

and the Circumvesuviana stop for commuter trains to Sorrento and Pompeii. Centrale is a dead-end station, and through trains often stop first at Piazza Garibaldi (it's fine to get off here, it's essentially the same place—a subway station just downstairs from Centrale), Campi Flegrei, or Napoli Mergellina across town before they arrive at Centrale. While on the train to Naples, ask the conductor which Naples stations your train stops at. Get off at Mergellina or Campi Flegrei only if your train does not stop at Centrale or Garibaldi. The stations of Campi Flegrei and Mergellina are connected to Centrale by a direct subway route: the Metropolitana Linea 2 (a railpass or train ticket to Napoli Centrale covers the ride, subway trains depart about every 12 min). You can store baggage at the Centrale train station (€11/12 hrs, daily 7:00–23:00, *deposito bagagli* near track #24, follow the corridor around to the left).

By Boat: If arriving at Port Beverello, you can take a taxi, bus, or tram to the Napoli Centrale train station. With your back to the water, walk to the right end of the port to find the taxi stand (about €10 to train station or Archaeological Museum, more for luggage, 10-min ride). To go by bus or tram, buy a €1 ticket in the *tabacchi* behind the taxi stand, then walk towards the gigantic Castel Nuovo to the main street. Take a right, so that you are crossing the piazza heading away from the castle; cross the street to the first median, and walk up it to the bus signs. Buses #152 and #M1—and tram #1—all head to Piazza Garibaldi, where the train station is located (6/hr, 15 min, validate ticket in yellow box when you board).

Helpful Hints

Theft Alert: Lately, Naples—which is governed by an activist mayor—has been occupied by an army of police, and feels much safer. Still, err on the side of caution. Don't venture into neighborhoods that make you uncomfortable. Walk with confidence, as if you know where you're going and what you're doing. Assume able-bodied beggars are thieves. Keep your money belt completely hidden. Stick to busy streets and beware of gangs of hoodlums. A third of the city is unemployed, and past local governments set an example that the Mafia would be proud of. Assume con artists are cleverer than you. Any jostle or commotion is probably a thief-team smokescreen. Dishonest taxis claim museums are closed and push tours instead.

Your biggest risk of theft is when catching or riding the Circumvesuviana commuter train (Naples to Pompeii to Sorrento). Remember, if you're connecting from a major train, you'll go from a relatively secure compartment into a crowded Naples train sprinkled with thieves, who are hunting disoriented American tourists. While I recommend the

Circumvesuviana and ride it comfortably and safely, each year I hear of many who get ripped off on this ride. You won't be mugged—just conned or pickpocketed. Con artists may say you need to "transfer" by taxi to catch the Circumvesuviana; you don't. There are no porters at the Centrale station or in the basement where the Circumvesuviana station is located; assume anyone offering to help you with your bags is a thief. Any displayed credentials are bogus.

Traffic: In Naples, red lights are discretionary, and pedestrians need to be wary, particularly of the motor scooters. Some tourists jaywalk in the shadow of bold and confident locals for sport.

Getting Around Naples

Naples' subway, the Servizio Metropolitana, runs from the Centrale station through the center of town (direction: Pozzuoli), stopping at Piazza Cavour (a 5-min walk from Archaeological Museum) and Montesanto (top of Spanish Quarter and Spaccanapoli street). Tickets cost €1 and are good for 90 minutes. All-day tickets cost €3. If you can afford a taxi, don't mess with the buses. A short taxi ride costs around €5 (insist on the meter; €2 supplement after 22:00, €1.50 supplement charged on Sun).

   Getting to the Archaeological Museum and "Slice-of-Neapolitan-Life Walk": From the Centrale train station, follow signs to *Metropolitana* downstairs. Buy tickets from the yellow kiosk opposite the Circumvesuviana ticket windows. Ask which track *("Binario?")* to Piazza Cavour; it's usually track 4 *("quattro,"* direction Pozzuoli).

   The only option is Linea 2—go through a *solo metropolitana* turnstile and ride the subway one stop (runs about every 12 minutes). As you leave the Metro at the Piazza Cavour station, follow signs to Linea 1 through the underpass. It's a maze to get out, but just follow the signs to *Museo*, even if they seem to be pointing in strange directions. Take the elevator or escalators up, and once you pass through the skylighted Metro entrance, take a right, go up the stairs, and continue to the museum down the corridor (to your left, at 11 o'clock, then up the stairs).

   For less walking, take the bus from Piazza Garibaldi at the Centrale train station. Grab a ticket from a *tabacchi* store (also good for the Metro) and spot the orange buses (marked "anm") on the northwest end of Piazza Garibaldi. Take bus #201 or #CS (5/hr, 15 min, usually one is waiting there) and tell your driver *"Museo."* Take a left when you hop off the bus, and it's a 20-yard walk to the museum entrance.

SELF-GUIDED WALK

The Slice-of-Neapolitan-Life Walk

For a ▲▲▲ experience, walk from the Archaeological Museum (see page 625) through the heart of town and back to the Napoli Centrale station (allow at least 2 hours, plus lunch and sightseeing stops). Sights are listed in the order you'll see them on this walk.

Naples, a living medieval city, is its own best sight. Couples artfully make love on Vespas, surrounded by more fights and smiles per cobble here than anywhere else in Italy. Rather than seeing Naples as a list of sights, see the one great museum and then capture its essence by taking this walk through the core of the city. Should you become overwhelmed or lost, step into a store and ask for directions to get you back to the train station: *"Dov'è la stazione centrale?"* (DOH-vay lah staht-zee-OH-nay chen-TRAH-lay?), or ask, *"Dov'è?"* and point to the next sight in this book.

Part 1: Via Toledo and the Spanish Quarter

The first part of this walk is a straight one-mile ramble down this boulevard to Galleria Umberto I, near the Royal Palace.

Ideally, begin by touring the Archaeological Museum (see page 625; at the top of Piazza Cavour, near Metro: Cavour). When you leave the museum, cross the street, immediately turn left, then take a right to walk under the grand, arched, former shopping mall of Galleria Principe. Exit and turn right to Via Pessina. (This walk ends near great pizzerias, but if you can't wait, try La Tana dell'Arte, just past the Galleria; see "Eating," page 630.)

Busy Via Pessina leads downhill to **Piazza Dante**, marked by a statue of Dante, the medieval poet. Here you can feel Italy… but many locals feel the repression of the central state. When Napoleon was defeated, Naples became its own independent kingdom. But with Italian unification in 1861, Naples went from being a thriving cultural and political capital to a provincial town, its money used to help establish the industrial strength of the north. Originally, a statue of a Spanish Bourbon king stood here. The grand red-and-gray building is typical of Bourbon buildings from that period. With the unification of Italy, the king, symbolic of Italy's colonial subjugation, was replaced by Dante—considered the father of the Italian language and a strong symbol of Italian nationalism.

Poor old Dante looks out over the urban chaos with a hopeless gesture. The Alba Gate, part of Naples' old wall and the entrance to a small street often lined with book vendors, is to Dante's right. Via Pessina, the long, straight road that we're walking, originated as a military road built by Spain in the 16th century. It skirted the old town wall to connect the Spanish military headquarters

The Slice-of-Neapolitan-Life Walk

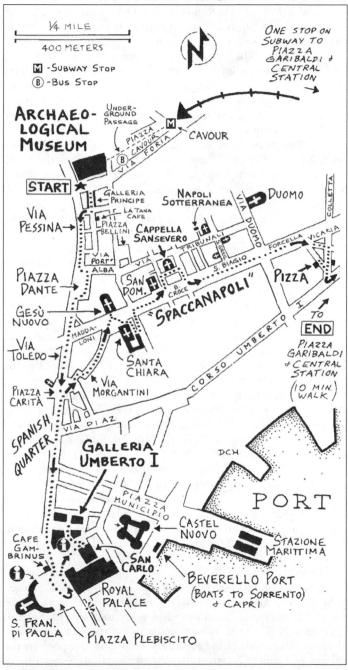

(now the museum) with the Royal Palace (down by the bay). A new subway station has recently been built here on Piazza Dante. Construction was slowed by the city's rich underground history: 13 feet down—Roman ruins; 23 feet down—Greek ruins.

Continue walking downhill, remembering that here in Naples, red lights are considered "decorations." When crossing a street, try to cross with a local. The people here are survivors; a long history of corrupt and greedy colonial overlords has taught Neapolitans to deal with authority creatively. Many credit this aspect of Naples' past for the advent of organized crime here.

Via Pessina becomes Via Toledo (another reminder of Spanish rule), Naples' principal shopping street. In 1860, from the white marble balcony (on the neoclassical building) overlooking Piazza Sette Settembre, the famous revolutionary Giuseppe Garibaldi declared Italy united and Victor Emmanuel its first king. Not until 1870, when Rome fell, was the dream of Italian unity actually realized.

Continue straight on Via Toledo (even though the arterial jogs left). At the next left (Via Maddaloni), about three blocks below Piazza Dante, you'll come to the long, straight street nicknamed **Spaccanapoli** (literally, "split Naples").

Before crossing it, look left. Look right. Since ancient times, this thin street (which changes names several times: Maddaloni, Via B. Croce, Via S. Biagio dei Librai, Forecella, and Vicaria) has bisected the city. (We'll return to this intersection later. If you want to abbreviate this walk, turn left here and skip ahead to the Spaccanapoli section, below.)

Via Toledo runs through Piazza Carità, surrounded by fascist architecture from 1938, with stern, straight, obedient lines. Wander south down Via Toledo a few blocks, past more fascist architecture—the two banks on the left. Try robbing the second one (Banco di Napoli, Via Toledo 178). Step across the street and notice the Banco di Napoli's architecture: typical fascist arches and reliefs, built to celebrate the bank's 400th anniversary (est. 1539—how old is your bank?). On the next corner, another bank (Banca Commerciale Italiana) fills an older palace and has a Caravaggio painting on its second floor (you're welcome to drop in and ask, "*Posso vedere il Caravaggio?*" and hope that it's back from its world tour).

From the Banco di Napoli, side-trip uphill three blocks into the **Spanish Quarter**—a classic world of *basso* (low) living. In such tight quarters, families generally do it in the road. This is *the* cliché of life in Naples, as shown in so many movies. The Spanish Quarter is Naples at its rawest, poorest, and most characteristic. The only things predictable about this Neapolitan tide pool are the ancient grid plan of its streets (which survives from Greek times), the friendliness of its shopkeepers, and the boldness of its mopeds. Concerned locals will tug on their lower eyelids, warning you to be wary. Pop into a grocery shop and ask the man to make you his best ham and mozzarella sandwich. The price should be around €3.

Return to Via Toledo (clogged with more people than cars) and work your way down to the immense **Piazza Plebiscito,** which celebrates the 1861 vote (*plebiscito*—plebiscite) when Naples chose to join Italy. Walk to the middle of the square. From here, you'll see the Church of San Francesco di Paola, with its Pantheon-inspired dome and broad, arcing colonnades. Opposite is the **Royal Palace,** which has housed Spanish, French, and even Italian royalty. Each of the eight kings in the niches is from a different dynasty (left to right: Norman, German, French, Spanish, Spanish, Spanish, French—the brother-in-law of Napoleon—and, finally, Italian: Victor Emmanuel II, King of Savoy). The statues were done at the request of V.E. II's son, so his dad is the most dashing of the group.

The huge and lavish Royal Palace welcomes the public (€4, Thu–Tue 9:00–19:00, closed Wed, shorter hours off-season, audio-guide–€4 or €5/2 people). The grand neoclassical staircase leads up to 30 plush rooms on one floor. You'll follow a one-way route (with some English descriptions) featuring paintings by "the Caravaggio Imitators," Neapolitan tapestries, fine inlaid stone tabletops, and more. Don't miss the huge Hercules room and the chapel with a fantastic nativity scene (a commotion of ceramic figurines from the 18th century).

If you continue 50 yards past the Royal Palace, you'll enjoy a fine **harbor view** with Mount Vesuvius smoldering ominously in the distance. Look back to see the vast "Bourbon red" palace—its color inspired by Pompeii. Above the Piazza Plebiscito on the hilltop is Naples' Carthusian Monastery and Castle of St. Elmo. This street continues to Naples' romantic harborfront—the "Santa Lucia Promenade" (from where the famous song, *Santa Lucia,* was first sung).

The **Gran Caffè Gambrinus,** facing Piazza Plebiscito, takes you back to the elegance of 1860. It's a classic place to sample a unique Neapolitan pastry called *sfogliatella* (crispy, scallop shell-shaped pastry filled with sweet ricotta cheese). Or you might prefer the mushroom-shaped, rum-soaked bread-like cakes called *babà,* which come in a huge variety. Stand at the bar, pay double to sit, or just wander around and try to imagine the café buzzing with the ritzy intellectuals, journalists, and artsy bohemian types who would have munched on *babà* during Naples' 19th-century heyday (Mon–Sun 7:00–1:30 in the morning, Piazza Plebiscito 1, tel. 081-417-582).

Now walk away from the Piazza to go behind the palace, where you can peek inside the neoclassical **Teatro San Carlo,** Europe's oldest and Italy's second-most-respected opera house, after Milan's

La Scala (guided visits-€5, tours in English about every 20 min, Mon–Sat 9:00–18:00, closed Sun, tel. 081-664-545). The huge castle on the harborfront just beyond the palace houses government bureaucrats and the Civic Museum, featuring 14th–16th-century art (€5, Mon–Sat 9:00–19:00, closed Sun, tel. 081-420-1241).

Next, go through the tall, yellow arch at the end of Via Toledo or across from the opera house and into the Victorian iron and glass of the 100-year-old shopping mall, **Galleria Umberto I.** Gawk up.

For Part 2 of this walk, double back up Via Toledo to Piazza Carità, veering right on Via Morgantini to Via Maddaloni (or avoid the backtrack and uphill walk by catching a €6 taxi to the church of Gesu Nuovo; JAY-zoo noo-OH-voh).

Part 2: Spaccanapoli back to the Centrale Train Station
You're back at the straight-as-a-Greek-arrow Spaccanapoli, formerly the main thoroughfare of the Greek city of Neapolis.

Stop at Piazza Gesu Nuovo to visit the two bulky old churches (both churches free, Mon–Sat 6:30–13:30 & 16:00–18:30, Sun 6:30–16:00). The square is marked by a towering, 18th-century Baroque monument to the Counter-Reformation. The Jesuit order was powerful in Naples due to its Spanish heritage. But locals never attacked Protestants here with the full fury of the Spanish Inquisition.

Check out the austere, fortress-like, 17th-century church of **Gesu Nuovo**. The unique, pyramid-grill facade survives from a fortified 15th-century noble palace. Step inside for a brilliant Neapolitan Baroque interior. The second chapel on the right features a much-kissed statue of Giuseppe Moscati, a Christian doctor famous for helping the poor. Moscati was fast-tracked to sainthood in 1987 (only 6 years after he died). Continue on to the third chapel and enter the Sale Moscati for a huge room filled with Ex Votos—tiny red-and-silver plaques of thanksgiving for miracles attributed to Saint Moscati. Each has a symbol of the ailment cured. Naples' practice of "Ex Votos," while incorporated into its Catholic rituals, goes back to its pagan Greek roots. Rooms from Moscati's nearby apartment are on display, and a glass case shows possessions and photos of the great doctor. As you leave the Sale Moscati, notice the big bomb casing hanging in the corner. It fell through the church's dome in 1943, but never exploded...yet another miracle.

Across the street, the simpler church of **Santa Chiara** dates from the 14th century, during a period of French royal rule under the Angevin dynasty. Consider the stark contrast between this church (Gothic) and the Gesu Nuovo (Baroque). Notice the huge inlaid marble Angevin coat of arms on the floor. The faded Trinity (c. 1414, left of entry) is an example of the fine frescoes that once covered the walls. Most were stuccoed over during Baroque times or destroyed in 1943 by WWII bombs. The altar is adorned with four finely carved Gothic tombs of Angevin kings. A chapel stacked with Bourbon royalty is just to the right.

Exiting out of the church, take a right and head to the back of the church. Continue through the archway straight ahead, and pass all the parked cars to reach the farthest door on the right. Here is the bright and ornate majolica-tiled cloistered courtyard of Santa Chiara (€4, Mon–Fri 9:30–18:30, Sun 9:30–14:30). Note the sprawling nativity scene immediately on your right as you enter—a cartoonish, 3-D snapshot of Old World Napoli.

Now continue straight down traffic-free Via B. Croce. Since this is a university district, you'll see lots of students and bookstores. This neighborhood is also extremely superstitious. Look for incense-burning women with carts of good-luck charms for sale. At Via Santa Chiara, a detour to the left leads to shops of antique musical instruments.

Further down Spaccanapoli, you'll see the next square, Piazza S. Domenico Maggiore, marked by an ornate 17th-century plague monument (built to thank God for ending the plague). The well-loved **Scaturchio Pasticceria** is another good place to try *sfogliatella* (€1.30 to go, costs double at a table in the square, daily 7:20–20:40, tel. 081-551-6944).

From this square, detour left along the right side of the castle-like church, then follow yellow signs and take the first right for one block to **Cappella Sansevero** (€5, Mon and Wed–Sat 10:00–18:00, Sun 10:00–13:30, closed Tue, Via de Sanctis 19). No photos are allowed in the chapel (postcards for sale in gift shop).

This small chapel is a Baroque explosion mourning the body of Christ, who lies on a soft pillow under an incredibly realistic veil. It's also the personal chapel of Raimondo de Sangro, an eccentric Freemason. The monuments to his relatives have a second purpose: to share the Freemason philosophy of freedom through enlightenment. For example, the statue of *Despair* (by Francesco Queirolo, 1759) struggling with a marble rope net (carved out of a single piece of marble) shows how knowledge—in the guise of an angel—frees the human mind. Nearby *Modesty* poses coyly under her full-length marble veil (by Antonio Corradini, 1752).

Study the incredible *Veiled Christ* in the center. Carved out of marble, it's like no other statue I've seen (by Giuseppe "how-deedoodat" Sammartino, 1753). The Christian message (Jesus died for our salvation) is accompanied by a Freemason message (the veil represents how the body and ego are an obstacle to real spiritual freedom.) As you walk from Christ's feet to his head, notice how the expression of Jesus' face goes from suffering to peace. Standing directly behind him, the veil over the face and knees disappears.

To the right of *Despair* and the net, an inlaid Escher-esque maze on the floor leads to de Sangro's tomb. The maze is another Freemason reminder of how the quest for knowledge gets you out of the maze of life. Your Sansevero finale is downstairs: two mysterious...skeletons. Perhaps another of the mad inventor's fancies: Inject a corpse with a fluid to fossilize the veins so they'll survive the body's decomposition. While that's the legend, it was most likely constructed to illustrate how the circulation system works.

Return to Via B. Croce (a.k.a. Spaccanapoli), turn left, and continue your cultural scavenger hunt. At the intersection of Via Nilo, find the statue of the Nile (on left)—a reminder of the multiethnic make-up of Greek Neapolis (this was the Egyptian quarter). Locals like to call this statue *The Body of Naples*, with the overflowing cornucopia symbolizing the abundance of their fine city. (I asked a Neapolitan man to describe the local women, who are famous for their beauty, in one word. He replied simply, "Abundant.") This intersection is considered the center of old Naples.

Five yards farther down (on the right) is the tiny **"Chapel of Maradona"**— a niche on the wall dedicated to Diego Maradona, a soccer star who played for Naples in the 1980s. Locals consider soccer almost a religion (see page 706)...and this guy was practically a diety. You can even see a "hair of Diego" and a teardrop from the city when he went to another team for more money. Unfortunately his reputation has been sullied with organized crime, drugs, and police problems.

A few blocks further, at the tiny square, Via San Gregorio Armeno leads left into a colorful district (and also to the underground Napoli Sotterranea archaeological site—see "Sights," page 628). The kitschy Baroque church on the left has a Vesuvius lava shrine in its portico. You'll see many shops that sell tiny components of fantastic manger scenes.

As Via B. Croce becomes Via S. Biagio dei Librai, notice the gold and silver shops. Some say stolen jewelry ends up here, is melted down immediately, and appears in a saleable form as soon as it cools. The inimitable Sr. Grassi runs the Ospedale delle Bambole (doll hospital) at #81.

Cross busy Via Duomo. The street and side-street scenes along Via Vicaria intensify. This is known as a center of the Camorra (organized crime).

Paint a picture with these thoughts: Naples has the most intact street plan of any ancient Roman city. Imagine this city then (retain these images as you visit Pompeii), with street-side shop fronts that close up after dark to form private homes. Today it's just one more page in a 2,000-year-old story of a city: all kinds of meetings, beatings, and cheatings; kisses, near misses, and little-boy pisses.

You name it, it occurs right on the streets today, as it has since ancient times. People ooze from crusty corners. Black-and-white death announcements add to the clutter on the walls. Widows sell cigarettes from buckets. For a peek behind the scenes in the shade of wet laundry, venture down a few side streets. Buy two carrots as a gift for the woman on the fifth floor if she'll lower her bucket to pick them up. The neighborhood action seems best around 18:00.

At the tiny fenced-in triangle of greenery, veer right onto Via Forcella, which leads to busy Via Pietro Colletta. A tiny round traffic island protects a chunk of the ancient Greek wall of Neapolis (4th century B.C.). Turning right on Via Pietro Colletta, walk 50 yards and step into the North Pole. Reward yourself for surviving this safari with a stop at the oldest *gelateria* in Naples, **Polo Nord Gelateria** (with 4 generations of family working here since 1931). Sample their *bacio* or "kiss" flavor before ordering (Mon–Sat 10:00–24:00, Sun 10:00–14:00 & 17:00–24:00, Via Pietro Colletta 41). Via Pietro Colletta leads past Napoli's two most competitive **pizzerias** (see "Eating," page 630) to Corso Umberto.

Turn left on the grand-boulevard-like Corso Umberto. It's a 10-minute walk from here to the Centrale train station (if you're tired, hop on a bus; they all go to the station). To finish the walk, continue on Corso Umberto—past a gauntlet of purse/CD/sunglasses salesmen and shady characters hawking stolen camcorders—to the vast, ugly Piazza Garibaldi. On the far side is the Centrale station.

SIGHTS

Archaeological Museum (Museo Archeologico)

For lovers of antiquity, this museum rates ▲▲▲ and by itself makes Naples a worthwhile stop. It offers the best possible peek into the artistic jewelry boxes of Pompeii and Herculaneum. When Pompeii was excavated (early 1800s), Naples' Bourbon king bellowed, "Bring me the best of what you find!" The actual excavation sights are impressive but barren; the finest art and artifacts ended up here.

Cost, Hours, Information: €6.50, extra for special exhibits, Wed–Mon 8:30–19:00, closed Tue, tel. 848-800-288). **Audioguides** cost €4 (at ticket desk, rentable for 3 hrs). For a guided **tour**, try to find Pina—look for her licensed guide nametag. She pulls together small groups for €10 tours (1.5 hrs).

To visit the **Secret Room**, which contains lascivious art from Pompeii, you have to make an appointment at the counter immediately on your left as you enter (depends on crowds, ask when you buy your ticket).

Photos are allowed without a flash. The shop sells a worthwhile green guidebook, *National Archeological Museum of Naples*, for

€7.50. Baggage check is obligatory and free. For a pleasant lunch, two pizzerias are two blocks downhill.

Orientation: The museum's entire collection is being rearranged. When you visit, the art may be in a different location than I've described below. Ask for a floor plan at the ticket counter.

The huge first floor (top of the grand staircase) contains frescoes from Pompeii, vases from Paestum, and bronze statues from Herculaneum (a nearby town destroyed in the same eruption that devastated Pompeii). The Pompeii mosaics and the Secret Room (Gabinetto Segreto) are on the small mezzanine level (up the grand staircase and to the left). The Farnese Collection of marble statues is on the ground floor (turn right past the staircase). Stairs behind the grand staircase lead to the basement WCs. If you can't find a particular work, ask a museum custodian, *"Dov'è?"* (Where?), followed by the item's name.

Statues, Frescoes, and Artifacts (top floor): Climb the stairs to the top floor. Before you enter the great hall (left), head to the right to visit the collection of bronze statues. These 50 statues (79 B.C. copies of 4th-century B.C. originals) decorated the holiday home (Villa dei Papyri in Herculaneum) of Julius Caesar's father-in-law. Look into the lifelike blue eyes of the two intense *atleta* (athletes) bent on doing their best. *Resting Hermes* (with his tired little heel wings) is taking a break. The *Drunken Faun* (singing and snapping his fingers to the beat, with a wineskin at his side) is clearly living for today—true to the *carpe diem* preaching of the Epicurean philosophy. Julius Caesar's father-in-law was an Epicurean philosopher, and his library—with 2,000 papyrus scrolls—supported his outlook.

Next, step into the huge hall. This was the great hall of the university (17th and 18th centuries) until the building became the royal museum in 1777. The sundial (from 1791) still works. At noon, a sunray strikes the spot indicating today's date...if you know your zodiac. With your back to the entrance, the rooms on your left feature the Pompeii frescoes, paintings, and artifacts (including interesting ancient glass). Just beyond the glass objects, a model shows the Pompeii archaeological site circa 1879 *(plastico di Pompeii)*. The wall model shows the site in 2004, after more excavations. Still with your back to the entrance, the rooms on your right feature ancient Greek art: a model of Paestum and ancient vases discovered on-site. Paestum, a temple complex south of Naples, was part of a once-thriving region known as Greater Greece; for more about Paestum, see page 684 in the Amalfi Coast chapter. If you contrast all of this ancient art with the darkness of medieval Europe, it's easy to see how the classical era inspired and enlightened the Renaissance greats.

House of the Faun Mosaics: On the mezzanine floor below (directly under the bronze statues from Herculaneum), you'll find a small, exquisite collection of Pompeian mosaics. Most of these mosaics were taken from Pompeii's House of the Faun. The house's delightful centerpiece was a 20-inch-high statue of the *Dancing Faun*. This rare surviving Greek bronze statue (from the 4th century B.C.) is surrounded by some of the best mosaics from the age. A highlight is the grand *Battle of Alexander,* a second-century B.C. copy of a third-century B.C. Greek original. It decorated a floor in the House of the Faun. It was found intact; the damage you see occurred as this treasure was moved from Pompeii to the king's collection here. The painting (on left, made before it was moved) shows how it once looked. Notice the dynamism, shading, perspective—everything the Renaissance artists later worked so hard to accomplish.

The **Secret Room** (Gabinetto Segreto), on the other side of the partition from the *Battle of Alexander* mosaic, contains a sizable assortment of erotic frescoes, well-spun pottery, and perky statues that once decorated bedrooms, meeting rooms, brothels, and even shops at Pompeii and Herculaneum. You'll have to make an appointment to view the room (see "Cost, Hours, Information," above). You might be escorted by a local guide (offering a 20-minute tour primarily in Italian but, if you ask nicely, likely in English). Even without a guide, the art speaks for itself (and comes with good printed descriptions in English).

These bawdy statues and frescos—often found in Pompeii's grandest houses—were entertainment for guests. (By the time they made it to this museum, in 1819, the frescoes could only be viewed with permission from the king.) The Roman nobles commissioned the wildest scenes imaginable. Think of them as ancient dirty jokes: a faun playfully pulling the sheet off a beautiful woman, only to be grossed out by the plumbing of a hermaphrodite. (Perhaps the original "*Mamma mia!*") Find the homosexual pygmies from Africa in action. Venus, the patron goddess of Pompeii, was a favorite pin-up girl. In a particularly high-quality statue, a goat and satyr illustrate the act of sodomy.

The room full of phallic talismans make the point that a massive penis was not necessarily a sexual symbol, but a magical amulet used against the evil eye. The phallus symbolized fertility, happiness, good luck, riches, straight A's, and general well-being. Across from the talismans, a room is furnished and decorated as an ancient brothel might have been (c. A.D. 79).

So, now that your travel buddy is finally showing a little interest in art...the best stuff awaits downstairs.

Farnese Collection (ground floor): The museum's ground floor alone has enough Greek and Roman art to put any museum on the map. Its highlight is the Farnese Collection, a grand hall of huge, bright, and wonderfully restored statues excavated from

Rome's Baths of Caracalla. The *Toro Farnese*—a tangled group with a woman being tied to a bull—is the largest intact statue from antiquity and (at 13 feet) the tallest ancient marble group ever found. Actually a third-century A.D. copy of a lost bronze Hellenistic original, it was carved out of one piece of marble. It was "restored" by Michelangelo and others at the Pope's request—meaning that they integrated surviving bits into a new work. Panels on the wall show which pieces are actually by Michelangelo (in blue on the chart: the head of the boy in front, the upper part of the aunt, and the dog).

Here's the story: Once upon an ancient Greek time, King Lykos was bewitched by Dirce and abandoned his pregnant wife (standing regally in the background). The single mom gave birth to twin boys (shown here), who grew up to kill their deadbeat dad and tie Dirce to the horns of a bull to be bashed against a mountain. You can almost hear the bull snorting.

At the far end of the hall (opposite the *Toro*, behind Hercules), a small room contains the sumptuous Farnese Cup, a large ancient cameo made of agates (2nd century B.C., from Egypt). Its decorations are both Egyptian (the Nile toting a lush cornucopia) and Greek (Medusa's head).

Don't leave without visiting *Il Doriforo.* (Ask a guard, *"Dov'è Il Doriforo?"*) This seven-foot-tall "spear-thrower" (the literal translation of "Doriforo") is a marble copy of a fifth-century B.C. bronze original by Polycletus. Found in a Pompeii gym, it inspired athletes with the ideal proportions of Greek beauty. This much-copied Greek statue—so full of motion, and so realistic in its *contrapposto* pose (weight on one foot)—inspired Donatello and Michelangelo.

More Sights

Napoli Sotterranea—This archaeological site, an underground man-made maze of passageways and ruins from Greek and Roman times, is tourable only with a guide. Visits in English are at set times (€9.30, includes tour, Mon–Sun 12:00, 14:00, and 16:00; also 10:00 and 18:00 Sat–Sun, last visit of the day may be cancelled, tel. 081-296-944). Descend 121 steps under the modern city to explore; bring a light sweater. First stop is the old Greek quarry, used to build the city of Neopolis, and later converted into an immense aqueduct by the Romans. Next is an excavated portion of the Greco-Roman theater; rumor has it that Emperor Nero sang here for his Naples debut, and didn't even stop for the earthquake.

To get to the site from the Piazza Cavour Metro stop, exit the Metro station, and go left on the main street, heading east, away from the Archaeological Museum. Take a right on Via Duomo (the first main street), and then a right at the third street (not counting alleyways)—Via Tribunali—to Piazza Gaetano 68.

Markets—Naples' **fish market** is fun for photos, with sawed-off swordfish, wriggly eels in pans, and mussels taking a shower. It's at Piazza Nolana, a few blocks southwest of the train station (at the piazza, follow your nose and go through the old gate, down the small street, Vico Sopramuro). A bigger **general market** starts at the far corner of Piazza Capuana (several blocks northwest of the train station), filling the street Via Sant'Antonio Abate with a mix of clothes, olives, bags of gnocchi, hanging hams, shoes, produce, umbrellas, and shoppers on foot or on Vespas. These colorful markets are both open daily (Mon–Sat 7:00–18:00, Sun 8:00–13:00).

SLEEPING

With Sorrento just an hour away (see next chapter), I can't imagine why you'd sleep in Naples. But, if needed, here are several places. Except for Hotel Siri, each is within a couple of blocks of the train station. The area can feel unnerving, especially after dark.

$$ Hotel Siri is a peaceful oasis a 10-minute walk from the station, with 16 spacious, bare-bones rooms (Sb-€40, Db-€70, Tb-€100, includes meager breakfast, air-con, Via Mignogna 15, tel. 081-554-3122, fax 081-554-3098, www.hotelsiri.it, info@hotelsiri .it, no English spoken). Leaving the train station, walk along Piazza Garibaldi on its left side, turn left on Corso Umberto, and take the second left onto Via Mignogna; the hotel is ahead on the left.

$$ Grand Hotel Europa, a gem in the seedy neighborhood around the train station, has modern rooms decorated with not-quite-right reproductions of famous paintings (Sb-€73, Db-€83, Tb-€93, prices guaranteed through 2006, air-con, cheery breakfast room, elegant restaurant, turn right out of station onto Corso Novara

---

Sleep Code

(€1 = about $1.20, country code: 39)
S = Single, **D** = Double/Twin, **T** = Triple, **Q** = Quad, **b** = bathroom, **s** = shower only. Unless otherwise noted, credit cards are accepted, English is spoken, and breakfast is included.

To help you sort easily through these listings, I've divided the rooms into three categories based on the price for a standard double room with bath:

$$$ **Higher Priced**—Most rooms €110 or more.
$$ **Moderately Priced**—Most rooms between €75–110.
$ **Lower Priced**—Most rooms €75 or less.

and take the first right—on Corso Meridionale—to #14, tel. 081-267-511, www.grandhoteleuropa.com, info@grandhoteleuropa.com).

$$ Hotel Guiren is a comfortable, safe place to call home, with 37 polished, quiet rooms two blocks from the station (Sb-€65, Db-€85, Tb-€110, includes breakfast, air-con, Via Bologna 114, tel. 081-286-530, fax 081-200-893, www.hotelguiren.it, info@hotelguiren .it). Exit the station by the McDonald's, go along the right side of the square two blocks, and turn right onto Via Bologna.

$ Hotel Ginevra, which rents 21 rooms, has a touch of the crustiness characteristic of the neighborhood (D-€55, Db-€65, superior Db-€80, T-€75, Tb-€85, superior Tb-€100, Q-€80, Qb-€110, miserly €5 breakfast in room—don't bother, cash only, 10 percent discount through 2006 with this book if you ask, noisy, air-con, lots of stairs; turn right out of station onto Corso Novara and walk 2 blocks, turn right on Via Genova to #116, 2nd floor; tel. & fax 081-283-210, www.hotelginevra.it, info@hotelginevra.it).

EATING

Drop by one of the two most traditional pizzerias (both at the end of the walking tour, described above). Naples, baking just the right combination of fresh dough, mozzarella, and tomatoes in traditional wood-burning ovens, is the birthplace of pizza. For something other than pizza, consider the last two listings.

Antica Pizzeria da Michele, a few blocks from the train station, is for pizza purists. Filled with locals, it serves two kinds of pizza: *margherita* (tomato sauce and mozzarella) or *marinara* (tomato sauce, oregano, and garlic, no cheese). A pizza with beer costs €5 (Mon–Sat 10:00–24:00, closed Sun; from the station, head left off Piazza Garibaldi, turn left onto Corso Umberto—juts off Piazza Garibaldi at 11 o'clock with the station to your back—then turn right on Via Pietro Colletta, look for the vertical red *Antica Pizzeria* sign, at intersection of Via Pietro Colletta and Via Cesare Sersale, tel. 081-553-9204).

Pizzeria Trianon, across the street, has been Da Michele's archrival since 1923. It offers more choices, slightly higher prices (€3.80–7.50), air-conditioning, and a cozier atmosphere. Waiting for your meal, you can survey the evolution of a humble wad of dough into a smoldering, bubbly feast in their entryway pizza kitchen (daily 10:00–15:30 & 18:30–23:00, Via Pietro Colletta 42, tel. 081-553-9426).

La Tana dell'Arte, a handy pizzeria with outdoor seating on a quiet pedestrian square, is located just past Galleria Principe, near the Archaeological Museum. The fresh homemade pastas are a unique find among the menu of flash-fired Neopolitan pizzas (daily 12:00–17:00 & 19:00–24:00, Via Bellini 29, tel. 081-549-1844).

La Cantina dei Mille, a block in front of the train station, is a traditional family-style place serving good, basic food to good, basic people (Tue–Sun 9:00–16:00 & 17:00–24:00, closed Mon, with your back to the station it's about halfway up the left side of Piazza Garibaldi to #126, tel. 081-283-448).

Next door, **Iris'** cadre of bow-tied waiters sling good, reasonably-priced seafood, pastas, and pizzas in a comfortable *ristorante* with an outdoor patio (Sun–Fri 12:00–16:00 & 17:00–24:00, closed Sat, Piazza Garibaldi 121-125, tel. 081-269-988).

TRANSPORTATION CONNECTIONS

From Naples by Boat to: Sorrento (7/day, 40 min, €7.50), **Capri** (2/hr, 40 min, €12), **Amalfi** (mid-May–mid-Oct only, 4/day, 90 min, €10). For a map showing boat connections, see page 633.

By Train to: Rome (2/hr, 2–3 hrs), **Florence** (12/day, 3.5–5 hrs, more with change in Rome), **Brindisi** (8/day, 5–8 hrs, overnight possible; from Brindisi, ferries sail to Greece), **Milan** (hrly, 6.5–9 hrs, overnight possible, more with a change in Rome), **Venice** (3 direct/day or about hourly with change in Rome or Bologna, 8–10 hrs), **Palermo** (5/day, 10 hrs), **Nice** (2/day, 12 hrs with change in Genoa), **Paris** (3/day, 14–18 hrs with change in Rome or Milan).

Naples Airport: Naples International Airport (Capodichino) is located four miles northeast of the city center (tel. 081-789-6111 or 081-789-6259, www.gesac.it). Orange buses marked "anm" and Alibus shuttle buses run between the airport and Napoli Centrale train station (daily 6:30–23:30). You can also catch a bus from the airport direct to Sorrento (€6, pay driver, 6/day in each direction, 75 min, www.gesac.it).

Pompeii, Herculaneum, and Vesuvius

Stopped in their tracks by the eruption of Mount Vesuvius in A.D. 79, Pompeii and Herculaneum offer the best look anywhere at what life in Rome must have been like 2,000 years ago. Of the two sites, Pompeii is grander. An entire city of well-preserved ruins are yours to explore. Herculaneum is smaller and more intimate. Vesuvius, as ominous as a viper, rises up on the horizon. Once a killer, the volcano is tamer now. Today you can climb it—by bus.

Getting Around the Region

To connect Naples, Sorrento, and the Amalfi Coast, you can travel on land by train, bus, and taxi. When possible, consider taking a boat—it's faster, scenic, cooler, and you can take photos of the coastline that you can't get from the bus or train. For specific travel times and costs, check the Transportation Connections sections of the Naples, Sorrento, and Amalfi Coast chapters.

By Circumvesuviana Train: This useful commuter train—popular with commuters, tourists, and pickpockets—links Naples, Herculaneum, Pompeii, and Sorrento. At the Napoli Centrale station, signs direct you downstairs to the Circumvesuviana. In the long corridor in the basement, the ticket windows—marked *Circumvesuviana*—are on your left. Schedules are posted on the wall just to the right of window 4. When you buy your ticket, ask which track your train will depart from (*"Che binario?"*; kay bee-NAH-ree-oh). Don't go through the turnstiles opposite the ticket windows. Instead, follow Circumvesuviana signs down the corridor and jog right when it does, down another long corridor that has turnstiles at the end (insert your ticket). The platforms are just beyond.

The Circumvesuviana also has its own terminal (one Metro stop or a 10-minute walk beyond the Centrale station), but there's no reason to use it unless you are headed in that direction. Two trains per hour, marked *Sorrento*, take you to Herculaneum (Ercolano) in 25 minutes, Pompeii in 40 minutes, and Sorrento, the end of the line, in 70 minutes—see list of stops in sidebar, page 613 (€3.20 one-way, not covered by railpass). Not all of the trains go as far as Sorrento; look at the schedule carefully or confirm with a local before boarding to make sure the train is going where you want to. Express trains marked *DD* (12/day) get you to Sorrento 20 minutes quicker. When returning to the Napoli Centrale station on the Circumvesuviana, get off at the second-to-the-last station, the Collegamento FS or Garibaldi stop (Centrale station is just up the escalator). Note: When returning from Sorrento, your Circumvesuviana ticket includes a ride anywhere on the Naples Metro system. After you validate your ticket, it's good for up to three hours in one direction, even if you make a stopover somewhere; if you're feeling spontaneous, jump out for free at any town before hopping back on the train to your final destination, as long as it's within the three-hour window.

While I have not had a problem, many readers report being ripped off on this train (see "Theft Alert," page 616).

By Bus: SITA buses (often blue or green-and-white) connect the towns. Buses that travel along the highly touristed Amalfi Coast can be crowded—for tips, see "From Sorrento to the Amalfi Coast by Bus" on page 668.

By Taxi: Some people prefer paying the price for door-to-

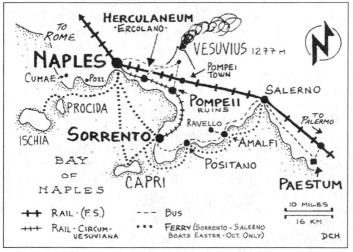

TO ROME · NAPLES · CUMAE · Pozz. · PROCIDA · ISCHIA · SORRENTO · HERCULANEUM -ERCOLANO- · VESUVIUS 1277 M · POMPEI TOWN · POMPEII RUINS · RAVELLO · AMALFI · POSITANO · SALERNO · TO PALERMO · PAESTUM · BAY OF NAPLES · CAPRI · RAIL · (F.S.) · RAIL · CIRCUM-VESUVIANA · BUS · FERRY (SORRENTO - SALERNO BOATS EASTER - OCT. ONLY) · 10 MILES · 16 KM · DCH

door transport. For €80–100, you can ride a taxi from Naples 30 miles directly to your Sorrento hotel; agree on a set price without the meter and pay upon arrival. You can hire a cab on Capri for about €50/hr. Taxis in the Amalfi Coast are generally expensive, and more than willing to overcharge you, but they can be a good convenience, especially with a larger group. See " Amalfi Coast Tours by Taxi" on page 670.

By Boat: Four primary ferry companies service the Naples, Sorrento, and Amalfi Coast areas: Caremar, SNAV, Metro del Mare, and one company that goes by three names—LMS, LMP, or Alilauro. Each company has different destinations and prices, some competing for the same trips. The quicker the trip, the higher the price. Caremar tends to have longer travel times on *traghetti veloci* (fast ferries) or *navi* (ships), rather than the super-quick *aliscafi* (hydrofoils). A hydrofoil skims between Naples and Sorrento—it's faster, safer from pickpockets, and more scenic than the Circumvesuviana (7/day, departing every 2 hours, 40 min, €7.50). Taking a taxi from the Napoli Centrale train station to the port costs about €10 (supplement for bags, Sundays, eves after 22:00, and holidays).

Check schedules at the boat dock (near Piazza Plebescito), or easier, at any TI. The number of boats that run per day depends on the season; expect at least two more boats daily in July and August. Trips are canceled in bad weather.

If you plan to arrive and leave a destination by boat, make note upon your arrival of return times, since the last boat usually leaves before 19:00.

Pompeii

A thriving commercial port of 20,000, Pompeii grew from Greek and Etruscan roots to become an important Roman city. Then, it was buried under 30 feet of hot mud and volcanic ash in the A.D. 79 eruption. Pompeii was rediscovered in the 1600s and excavations began in 1748. For archaeologists, Pompeii is a shake-and-bake windfall, teaching them almost all they know about daily Roman life. For travelers, it's a ▲▲▲ sight.

Cost, Hours, Information: €10, €18 combo-ticket includes Herculaneum and three lesser sites (valid 3 days), can be free or 50 percent off with Campania ArteCard (see "Planning Your Time in the Region" on page 613). Open daily April–Oct 8:30–19:30, Nov–March 8:30–17:00, tel. 081-857-5347. The ticket office stops selling tickets 1.5 hours before closing time. A good map is included with admission (pick up at TI window to left of WCs; for more information, check www.pompeiisites.org). A free baggage check is near the site entrance turnstiles (retrieve bags by 19:20).

Stop by the bookshop. A guidebook on Pompeii makes this site more meaningful. (Books are also on sale in Sorrento.) The small Pompeii and Herculaneum "past and present" book has a helpful text and allows you to re-create the ruins with plastic overlays—with the "present" actually being 1964 (available for €11 in bookstore unless they're "finished"; if you buy from a street vendor, pay no more than €11). Good audioguides are available at the ticket booth for €6.50 (€10 for 2, ID required).

Live guides cluster near the ticket booth. If you gather 10 people, the price is reasonable when split (around €10 apiece, total cost about €115, 2 hrs). For a local guide, consider Gaetano Manfredi (tel. 081-863-9816, mobile 338-725-5620). Gaetano reports that imposters are stealing his business; confirm it's him by asking for his mobile number.

If you want to visit Mt. Vesuvius, you can catch a bus from Pompeii's Piazza Esedra and Piazza Anfiteatro (runs daily 8:00–15:30, 60 min up with stop at bar, 40 min down, Vesuviana Mobilità).

Getting to Pompeii

Pompeii is halfway between Naples and Sorrento, roughly 30 minutes from either by direct Circumvesuviana train (runs at least hourly, see page 632). Get off at the Pompei Scavi/Villa dei Misteri stop on the Naples–Sorrento train line. A different Circumvesuviana line, which does *not* go to Sorrento, has a Pompeii stop that leaves you far from the excavation site entrance. Check your bag at the Pompei Scavi train station (at the bar, €1.50, pick up by 19:00 in summer,

Circumvesuviana Stops between Naples and Sorrento

I list these so that you can look at the scenery instead of your watch.

Napoli
Napoli Collegamento FS (a.k.a. Piazza Garibaldi; below Centrale station)
Gianturco
S. Giovanni
Barra
S. Maria d. Pozzo
S. Giorgio
Cavalli di Bronzo
Bellavista
V. Liberta
Ercolano Scavi (Herculaneum)
Ercolano Miglio d'Oro
Torre del Greco
V.S. Antonio
V. del Monte
V. Monaci

Villa della Ginestra
Leopardi
V. Viuli
Trecase
Torre Annunziata
Pompei Scavi (Pompeii site)
Moregine
Ponte Persica
Pioppaino
V. Nocera
C. Mare Stabia
C. Mare Terme
Pozzano
Scraio
Vico Equense
Seiano
Meta
Piano di Sorrento
S. Agnello
Sorrento

18:00 Oct–Feb) or, better yet, at the Pompeii ruins for free. From the train station, turn right and walk down the road about a block to the entrance (first left turn). The TI is further down the street, but not a necessary stop for your visit.

SELF-GUIDED TOUR

Welcome to Pompeii

Allow at least three hours to tour the site. Consider the following route, starting at the Porta Marina (town gate) after the ticket booth. Before Vesuvius blew, the sea came nearly to this gate. As you approach the Porta Marina, notice the two openings—big for chariots, small for pedestrians.

From the Porta Marina, Via Marina leads straight to Pompeii's main square, the forum.

The **forum** *(foro)*, Pompeii's commercial, religious, and political center, stands at the intersection of the city's two main streets. While the most ruined part of Pompeii, it's grand nonetheless—with temples, lots of pedestals that once sported statues (now in the

Pompeii

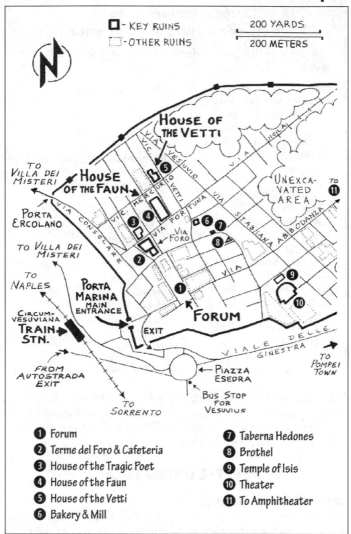

- ◼ – KEY RUINS
- ⬚ – OTHER RUINS

200 YARDS
200 METERS

House of the Vetti

House of the Faun

TO VILLA DEI MISTERI

PORTA ERCOLANO

TO VILLA DEI MISTERI

TO NAPLES

VIA CONSOLARE

VIC. MERCURIO

VIA VESUVIO

VIC. O VETTI

VIA FORTUNA

VIA FORO

VIA STABIANA

VIA ABBONDANZA

VIA NOLA

UNEXCAVATED AREA

TO

CIRCUM-VESUVIANA **TRAIN STN.**

FROM AUTOSTRADA EXIT

PORTA MARINA MAIN ENTRANCE

EXIT

FORUM

VIALE DELLE GINESTRA

TO POMPEI TOWN

PIAZZA ESEDRA

BUS STOP FOR VESUVIUS

TO SORRENTO

1 Forum
2 Terme del Foro & Cafeteria
3 House of the Tragic Poet
4 House of the Faun
5 House of the Vetti
6 Bakery & Mill

7 Taberna Hedones
8 Brothel
9 Temple of Isis
10 Theater
11 To Amphitheater

museum in Naples), and the basilica (Pompeii's largest building, the ancient equivalent of law courts and stock market—on the right as you enter). The Curia (home of the government) stands at the end of the forum. It's built of brick and mortar, a Roman invention. While brick now, it was once faced with marble. Note that while Pompeii was destroyed by the eruption of A.D. 79, it was also devastated by an earthquake in A.D. 62. It's safe to assume any brick you see dates from between A.D. 62 and A.D. 79—

Pompeii—Before the Eruption

Pompeii was a booming Roman trading city. Most streets would have been lined with stalls and jammed with customers from sunup to sundown. Chariots vied with shoppers for street space, and many streets were off-limits to chariots during shopping hours (see street signs with pictures of men carrying vases—this meant pedestrians only).

Fountains overflowed into the streets, flushing the gutters into the sea (thereby cleaning the streets). The stones you see at intersections allowed pedestrians to cross the constantly gushing streets. A single stone designated a one-way street (just enough room for one chariot, the stone straddled by its two oxen), and more stones meant a two-way chariot street. There were no posh neighborhoods. Rich and poor mixed it up, as elegant homes existed side by side with simple homes throughout Pompeii. While nearby Herculaneum would have been a classier place to live (traffic-free streets, more elegant homes, far better drainage), Pompeii was *the* place for action and shopping. It served its estimated 20,000 residents with more than 40 bakeries, 30 brothels, and 130 bars, restaurants, and hotels. Rome controlled the entire Mediterranean 2,000 years ago—making it a kind of free-trade zone—and Pompeii was a central and booming port town. With most buildings covered by brilliant, white ground-marble stucco, Pompeii in A.D.. 79 was an impressive town. Remember, Pompeii's best art is in the Naples Archaeological Museum (see page 625).

restoration work done by Pompeians after the quake.

Walk (away from the Curia) along the fenced, roofed area that runs alongside the forum. Behind the iron fence are piles of pottery and, at the end, some eerie casts of volcano victims. With the unification of Italy in the 1860s, national spirit fueled efforts to excavate Pompeii. During this period, archaeologists made these molds (during excavations, when they detected hollows underfoot—left by decomposed bodies—they'd pour liquid plaster into the cavities, let it dry, and dig up the casts).

Such a busy square needed a public toilet. Just past the warehouse, turn left into an ancient public WC. Notice the ditch that led to the sewer (marked by an arch in the corner). The stone supports once held wooden benches with the appropriate holes. Even back then, this area had pay toilets.

Continue on, leaving the forum through the gate at the end. Take an immediate right, then a left. You're on Via del Foro, passing a convenient 21st-century cafeteria (decent value, gelato, books, WCs upstairs; a fancier restaurant in a more elegant ancient gymnasium setting is adjacent).

Head down Via del Foro and enter the impressive baths, **Terme del Foro** (on the left, past the cafeteria). You'll enter through the gymnasium. After working out, clients would find four rooms: a waiting room, warm bath *(tepidarium)*, hot bath *(caldarium)*, and cold-plunge bath *(frigidarium)*.

The *tepidarium* is ringed by mini-statues or *telamones* (male caryatids, figures used as supporting pillars), which divided clients' lockers. They'd undress and warm up here, perhaps stretching out on one of the benches near the bronze heater for a massage. Notice the ceiling: half crushed by the eruption and half surviving, with its fine blue-and-white stucco work.

Next, in the *caldarium*, you'd get hot. Notice the engineering. The double floor was heated from below—so nice with bare feet (look into the grate to see the brick support towers). The double walls with brown terra-cotta tiles held the heat. Romans soaked in the big tub, which was filled with hot water. To keep condensation from dripping annoyingly from the ceiling, the fluting (ribbing) was added to carry the drips down the walls.

Next came the cold plunge in the *frigidarium*—a circular marble basin with the spout spewing frigid water, opposite the entry.

Exit the baths. Notice the oxcart wheel grooves and stepping-stones in the street. During ancient rainstorms, streets would turn into filthy rivers. Do as the ancient Romans did. Keep your feet dry by using the stepping-stones to cross the street. Directly in front of you is an ancient fast-food stand (notice the holes in the counters for pots). To your left, a few doors down, is the **House of the Tragic Poet** (Casa del Poeta Tragico), with its famous "Beware of Dog" (Cave Canum) mosaic in the entryway. On either side, grooves in the doorway indicate a shop with sliding doors.

Face the House of the Tragic Poet, then walk to your right two blocks to the House of the Faun (Casa del Fauno). Notice the holes drilled into the curbs—to hitch your animal or perhaps to support an awning from your storefront.

Pompeii's largest home (with 40 rooms), the **House of the Faun,** provided Naples' Archaeological Museum with many of its top treasures, including the original dancing faun (you'll see a copy here) and the famous mosaic of the Battle of Alexander. Wander past the welcome mosaic (*HAVE,* or "hail to you") and through its courtyards. The back courtyard leads to the exit. It's lined by pillars rebuilt after the A.D. 62 earthquake. Take a close look at the brick, mortar, and fake marble-stucco veneer.

Back on the street, turn right and look for the exposed 2,000-year-old lead pipes in the wire cage (ahead and down on the ground to your right). The lead was imported from Roman Britannia. A huge water tank—fed by an aqueduct—stood at the high end of

The Eruption of Vesuvius

At noon on August 24, A.D. 79, Mount Vesuvius blew, sending a mushroom cloud of ash, dust, cinders, and rocks 12 miles into the air. It spewed for 18 hours straight, with southerly winds blowing the cloud southward. The white-grey ash settled like snow on Pompeii, collapsing roofs and floors, but leaving the walls intact. Two thousand of the town's 20,000 residents were entombed under eight feet of fine powder.

The next morning, Vesuvius' column of ejected material collapsed, picking up speed as it fell to earth, creating a cloud of ash, pumice, and gas. The red-hot avalanche (a "pyroclastic flow") sped down the side of the mountain at nearly 100 mph. Four minutes later, it engulfed the city of Herculaneum four miles away, burying it in nearly 60 feet of hot mud. The mud cooled into stone, freezing the moment in time.

town. Three independent pipe systems supplied water to the city from here: one each for baths, private homes, and public water fountains. In case of a water shortage, supply could be limited. Democratic priorities prevailed: first the baths were cut, then the private homes. The last water to be cut was that which fed the public fountains (where people got their water for drinking and cooking).

Take your first left on Vicolo dei Vetti. Enter Pompeii's best-preserved home, the House of the Vetti (Casa dei Vetti).

The **House of the Vetti** (may still be under restoration in 2006), which has retained its mosaics and frescoes, was the bachelor pad of two wealthy merchant brothers. In the entryway, see if you can spot the erection. This is not pornography. There's a meaning here: The penis and the sack of money balance each other on the goldsmith's scale above a fine bowl of fruit. The meaning: Only with a balance of fertility and money can you have abundance.

Step into the atrium, its ceiling open to the sky to collect light and rainwater. The pool, while decorative, was a functional water-supply tank. It's flanked by large money boxes anchored to the floor. The brothers were certainly successful merchants, and possibly moneylenders, too.

Exit on the right, passing the tight servant quarters, and go into the kitchen, with its bronze cooking pots (and a touchable lead pipe on the back wall). The passage dead-ends in the little Venus Room, with its erotic frescoes behind glass.

Return to the atrium and pass into the big colonnaded garden. It was planted according to the plan indicated by traces of roots excavated in the volcanic ash. This courtyard is ringed by richly frescoed entertainment rooms. Circle counterclockwise. The dining room is finely decorated in "Pompeian red" (from iron rust) and black. Study the detail. Notice the lead humidity seal between the wall and the floor designed to keep the moisture-sensitive frescoes dry. (Had Leonardo taken this clever step, his *Last Supper* in Milan might be in better shape today.) Continuing around, notice the square white stones inlaid in the floor. Imagine them reflecting like cat eyes as the brothers and their friends wandered around by oil lamp late at night. Frescoes in the Yellow Room (near the exit) show off the ancient mastery of perspective, which was not matched elsewhere in Europe for nearly 1,500 years.

Leaving the House of the Vetti, go left past the pipes again. Then turn right, following Vicolo dei Vetti to Via della Fortuna. Intersections like this, with public fountains, were busy neighborhood centers, where rent was high and people gathered.

Turn left on Via della Fortuna and take a quick right on Vicolo Storto, which leads down a curving street to the **bakery and mill** *(forno e mulini)*. The ovens look like a modern-day pizza oven. The stubby stone towers are flour grinders: After grain was poured into the top, donkeys pushed wooden bars that turned the stones, and eventually powdered grain dropped out the bottom as flour—flavored with tiny bits of rock. Perhaps this is why sifters were invented.

Take the first left after the bakery onto Via degli Augustali, and check out the mosaics on the left at the **Taberna Hedones**. This must be the tavern of hedonism; see the cute welcome mosaic—like the one we saw earlier at the House of the Faun—reading *HAVE* ("hail to you"), with the bear licking his wounds.

Next turn right, over the street dam, and follow the signs to the **brothel** *(lupanare)*, at #18. Prostitutes were nicknamed *lupe* (she-wolves). Wander into the brothel, a simple place with stone beds and pillows. The ancient graffiti includes stroke tallies and exotic names of the women, indicating they came from all corners of the Mediterranean. The faded frescoes above the cells may have served as a kind of menu for services offered. Note the idealized portrayal of women (white, considered beautiful) and man (dark, considered horny). Outside at #17 is a laundry—likely to boil the sheets (thought to guard against venereal disease).

Leaving the brothel, go down the hill to Pompeii's main drag, Via Abbondanza. The forum (and exit) is to the right. (The huge amphitheater—which you can skip—is 10 min to your left.) Go straight down Via dei Teatri, then left before the columns, downhill to the **Temple of Isis** (on the right). This Egyptian temple served Pompeii's Egyptian community. The little shrine with the plastic roof housed holy water from the Nile. Pompeii must have had a synagogue, but it has yet to be excavated.

Exit the temple where you entered and take an immediate right down an alleyway to our last stop, the **theater**. Originally a Greek theater (Greeks built theirs with the help of a hillside), this marks the spot of the birthplace, in 470 B.C., of the Greek port here. During Roman times, the theater sat 5,000 in three price ranges: the five marble terraces up close (filled with romantic wooden seats for two), the main section, and the cheap nosebleed section (surviving only on the right). The square stones above the cheap seats used to support a canvas rooftop. Notice the high-profile boxes, flanking the stage, for guests of honor. From this perch, you can see the gladiator barracks—the colonnaded courtyard beyond the theater. They lived in tiny rooms, trained in the courtyard, and fought in the nearby amphitheater.

There's much more to see; 75 percent of Pompeii's 164 acres has been excavated. But this tour's over. When you're ready to leave, the exit is to the left of the steep hill at the entrance to the Foro. When it forks, head right to get back to the site entrance to pick up bags or revisit the bookshop. *HAVE!*

Herculaneum
(Ercolano)

Smaller, less ruined, and less crowded than its famous big sister, Herculaneum—a ▲▲ sight—offers a closer peek into ancient Roman life but lacks the grandeur of Pompeii (there's barely a colonnade).

Cost, Hours, Information: €10, €18 combo-ticket includes Pompeii and three lesser sites (valid 3 days), can be free or 50 percent off with Campania ArteCard (see "Planning Your Time in the Region" on page 613). Open daily April–Oct 8:30–19:30, Nov–March 8:30–17:00, ticket office closes 60 min earlier. The informative, interesting **audioguide** sheds light on the ruins and life in Herculaneum in the first century A.D. (€6.50, €10 for 2, ID required, turn in 30 min before closing). WCs are to the left of the audioguide kiosk. Tel. 081-739-0963, www.pompeiisites.org.

Getting to Herculaneum: Herculaneum is 15 minutes from Naples and 45 minutes from Sorrento on the same Circumvesuviana train that goes to Pompeii (see page 632 for information). To get to the ruins, leave the Ercolano station and turn right, then left, following yellow signs; go eight blocks straight downhill from the station to the end of the road. The site entrance is 200 yards beyond and on your left as you curve around its perimeter.

➋ **Self-Guided Tour:** Caked and baked by the same A.D. 79 eruption that pummeled Pompeii, Herculaneum is a small community of intact buildings with plenty of surviving detail. Unlike Pompeii, which was buried in ash and pumice, Herculaneum was buried under nearly 60 feet of boiling mud, which hardened into baked tufa, perfectly preserving the city until excavations began in 1738.

As you enter the site from the tunnel and make your way to the arches, you are walking across what was formerly Herculaneum's beach. The **arches** you see were boat storage areas. During excavations in 1981, hundreds of bodies were found here, between the wall of volcanic stone behind you and the city in front of you. Herculaneum's 4,000 citizens had a little more time than the people of Pompeii to flee the eruption. They tried to escape to the sea but were forced back to shore by a violent tidal wave.

The **baths** nearest the entrance illustrate the city's devastation. After you descend into the baths, look back at the steps. You'll see the original wood charred in the disaster, protected by the wooden planks you just walked on. At the bottom of the stairs, in the waiting room to the right, notice where the floor collapsed under the sheer weight of the volcanic mud. (The sunken pavement reveals the baths' heating system; hot air generated by wood-burning furnaces circulated between different levels of the floor.) A doorway in the room in front of the stairs is still filled with rock-hard mud. Despite the damage, elements of refinement remain intact, such as the delicate stuccoes in the *caldarium* (hot bath).

Stroll the city and find the **House of Deer** (Casa dei Cervi), named for the statues of deer being attacked by dogs in the garden courtyard (these are copies; originals are in Archaeological Museum in Naples). The **Seat of the Augustali** (Sede degli Augustali), decorated with frescoes of Hercules (for whom this city was named), was a forum for freed slaves climbing their way up the ladder of Roman society. The **Bottega ad Cucumas** wine shop still has its drink list frescoed on the wall. Don't miss the **gymnasium** complex with its Hydra of Lerna, a sculpted bronze fountain featuring the seven-headed monster defeated by Hercules as one of his 12 labors.

Vesuvius

The 4,000-foot-high Vesuvius, mainland Europe's only active volcano, has been sleeping restlessly since 1944.

Getting to Vesuvius: The summit is accessible year-round by car, taxi (€80 round-trip), or by the usually white or gray Vesuviana Mobilità bus. The bus runs from **Herculaneum** (daily at 8:00 and 12:45, €7.60 round-trip), **Pompeii** (10/day from Piazza Esedra and Piazza Anfiteatro, daily 8:00–15:30, 1 hr, €8.60 round-trip), and **Naples** (buses leave at 9:25 and 10:40 from Hotel Terminus in Piazza Garibaldi—the square in front of the train station, and return 12:30 and 14:00, runs mid-May–late Aug, €13.10 round-trip, 1 hr, confirm times at tel. 081-963-4420). Pay your fare when you board. Be prepared for a long wait for the return trip. Beware of expensive pit stops: The bus may make a bathroom stop at a tourist shack along the way—if you use the WC, you may be expected to purchase a candy bar or some other item at premium prices.

At Vesuvius: Site entry with a mandatory guide is €6.50. From the bus stop and parking lot, it's a steep 30-minute hike to the top for a sweeping view of the Bay of Naples (often cold and windy, bring a sweater or coat, especially Oct–April). Up here, it's desolate and lunar-like. The rocks are hot. Walk the entire crater lip for the most interesting views; the far end overlooks Pompeii. Be still and alone to hear the wind and tumbling rocks in the crater. Any steam? Closed when erupting.

SORRENTO AND CAPRI

Without a hint of big-city Naples and just an hour to the south, serene Sorrento makes an ideal home base for exploring all the fascinating sights in the region, from Naples to the Amalfi Coast to Paestum. And just a short cruise from Sorrento is the jet-setting island of Capri, offering more charm and fun (outside of the crowded months of July and August) than its glitzy reputation would lead you to believe.

Sorrento

Wedged on a ledge under the mountains and over the Mediterranean, spritzed by lemon and olive groves, Sorrento is an attractive resort of 20,000 residents and—in the summer—as many tourists. It's as well-located for regional sightseeing as it is a fine place to stay and stroll. The Sorrentines have gone out of their way to create a completely safe and relaxed place for tourists to come and spend money. Everyone seems to speak fluent English and works for the Chamber of Commerce. This gateway to the Amalfi Coast (see next chapter) has an unspoiled old quarter, a lively main shopping street, and a spectacular cliffside setting. Locals are proud of the many world-class romantics who've vacationed here. In 1921, the famed tenor Enrico Caruso chose Sorrento as the place to spend his last weeks.

Planning Your Time

With Sorrento as your home base, spend a minimum of three days and nights in the region. On your way to or from Sorrento, visit

Naples as a day-trip. After settling in Sorrento, spend a day touring the Amalfi Coast by bus, and another day split between Sorrento and Pompeii (accessible by Circumvesuviana train—see page 632). With more time, catch a quick boat ride to the nearby island of Capri or linger on the Amalfi Coast (see next chapter), getting as far south as Paestum's Greek temples.

ORIENTATION

Sorrento is long and narrow. The main drag, Corso Italia (50 yards in front of the Circumvesuviana train station), runs parallel to the sea from the station through the town center and out to the cape, where it's renamed Via Capo. The town's center is the square called Piazza Tasso. Everything mentioned here (except the hotels on Via Capo) is within a 10-minute walk of the station. Sorrento hibernates in January and February, when many places close down.

Tourist Information

The TI, located inside the Foreigners' Club, hands out a free monthly *Surrentum* magazine with a great city map and schedules of boats, buses, concerts, and festivals (Mon–Sat 8:45–18:15, closed Sun, shorter hours off-season, tel. 081-807-4033, www.sorrentotourism .com, info@sorrentotourism.com). To reach the TI (Soggiorno e Turismo) from the train station, go left on Corso Italia and walk five minutes to Piazza Tasso; turn right at the end of the square, then head down Via L. de Maio through Piazza Sant'Antonino to the Foreigners' Club mansion at #35. You'll pass fake "tourist offices" (travel agencies selling bus and boat tours) along the way. If you arrive after the TI closes, look for key TI handouts in the lobby of the Foreigners' Club (open until midnight).

If you need just quick advice, the fake tourist office—located in a green caboose right when you come out of the station—can be of help. While they hope you'll purchase one of their overpriced excursions, they're willing to give basic information on directions, buses, and ferries.

Arrival in Sorrento

By Train: Those arriving by train (the last stop of the Circumvesuviana) find taxis waiting to overcharge them (no meters, generally €12 for any ride) and an Amalfi bus stop. It's a five-minute walk to the city center, Piazza Tasso (walk a block in front of the station and turn left on Corso Italia), and a 10-minute walk to most of my recommended hotels (but catch a bus for hotels on Via Capo).

By Boat: You'll dock at Marina Piccola, Sorrento's little harbor. To get to Piazza Tasso, it's a 10-minute uphill hike or a short bus ride. A line of usually orange and orange-and-blue city buses

Sorrento

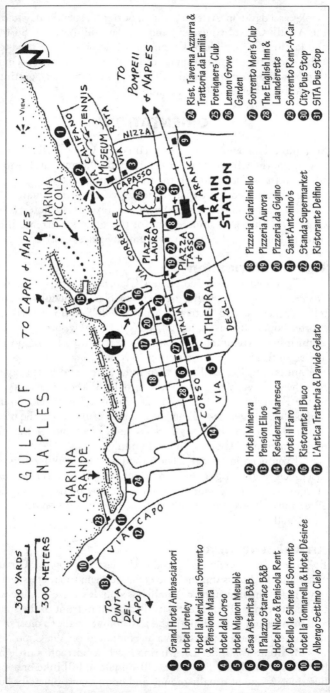

1 Grand Hotel Ambasciatori
2 Hotel Loreley
3 Hotel la Meridiana Sorrento & Pensione Mara
4 Hotel del Corso
5 Hotel Mignon Meublè
6 Casa Astarita B&B
7 Il Palazzo Starace B&B
8 Hotel Nice & Penisola Rent
9 Ostello le Sirene di Sorrento
10 Hotel la Tonnarella & Hotel Désirée
11 Albergo Settimo Cielo
12 Hotel Minerva
13 Pension Elios
14 Residenza Maresca
15 Hotel il Faro
16 Ristorante il Buco
17 L'Antica Trattoria & Davide Gelato
18 Pizzeria Giardiniello
19 Pizzeria Aurora
20 Pizzeria da Gigino
21 Sant'Antonino's
22 Standa Supermarket
23 Ristorante Delfino
24 Rist. Taverna Azzurra & Trattoria da Emilia
25 Foreigners' Club
26 Lemon Grove Garden
27 Sorrento Men's Club
28 The English Inn & Launderette
29 Sorrento Rent-A-Car
30 City Bus Stop
31 SITA Bus Stop

wait at the harbor; buy your €1 bus ticket at the souvenir shop and exchange booth just to the left of the buses. All buses stop at Piazza Tasso.

Helpful Hints

Laundry: A handy laundry is at Corso Italia 30; enter through the alley (daily 8:00–21:00, bring coins, €8/load, includes soap, full-service—11 pounds for €12, tel. 081-078-1185).

Where It's At: The **Foreigners' Club** provides reasonably-priced snacks and drinks, music, dancing, views, and a handy place for visitors to meet locals (open April-Oct, behind TI, public WC, tel. 081-877-3263); see "Nightlife" and "Eating" below. Drop in for the view overlooking the harbor and the Bay of Naples.

Getting Around Sorrento

By Bus: Orange and orange-and-blue city buses all stop in the main square (Piazza Tasso). Bus #A runs to Meta beach and the hotels on Via Capo, Bus #B and #C to the port (Marina Piccola), and Bus #D to the fishing village (Marina Grande). Tickets cost €1 within the city limits (buy at *tabacchi* shops and newsstands, purchase before boarding, and stamp upon entering).

By Rental Wheels: Sorrento Rent-A-Car rents mopeds and Vespas (about €40/day, daily 9:00–13:00 & 16:00–21:00, Corso Italia 210, tel. 081-878-1386, europcar@sorrento.it). Penisola Rent, across the street, has comparable prices and tiny "smart cars" (daily 8:30–21:00, located in Hotel Nice, tel. 081-877-4664, info@penisolarent .com). In summer, forget renting a car unless you enjoy traffic jams.

By Taxi: Taxis are expensive, charging at least €12 for the short ride from the station to hotels. Because of heavy traffic and the complex one-way system, you can often walk faster.

SELF-GUIDED WALK

Welcome to Sorrento

Get to know Sorrento with this lazy self-guided town stroll. Begin on the main square, Piazza Tasso. Stand under the flags with your back to the sea.

1. Piazza Tasso: As in any southern Italian town, this "piazza" is Sorrento's living room. It may be noisy and congested, but locals want to be where the action is...part of the scene. The most expensive apartments and top cafés are on or near this square. Buses stop here on their way to Marina Piccola (where boats depart for Naples and Capri, at the harbor, a 10-minute hike below you), to the train station (left), and to Via Capo (right).

This square spans a gorge that divided the town until the 19th century. The old town (on your right) still has some surviving ancient Greek streets. The new town (to your left) was farm country just two centuries ago. If you walk a block inland and look down, you'll see steps from the fifth century B.C.

Sorrento's name came from the Greek word for "siren," the legendary half-bird, half-woman who sang an intoxicating lullaby. No one had ever sailed by the sirens without succumbing to their incredible musical charms...and dying. But Ulysses was determined to hear the song. He put wax in his oarsmen's ears and had himself lashed to the mast of his ship. Oh, it was nice. The sirens, thinking they had lost their powers, threw themselves into the sea, and the place became safe to inhabit. Ulysses' odyssey was all about the westward expansion of Greek culture, and to the ancient Greeks, places like Sorrento were the wild, wild west.

With your back still to the sea, head to the far right corner of the square, behind the statue of Signor Tasso, the square's name-sake (he was a 16th-century Renaissance poet who was born here). Pop into the flower shop (#18, big courtyard on left) for the feeling of an 18th-century aristocratic palace's courtyard, lined with characteristic tiles. Then find the narrow...

2. Via Santa Maria della Pietà: Here, just a few yards off the noisy main drag, is a street that goes back centuries before Christ. About 100 yards down the lane at #24, find a 13th-century palace (no balconies back then...for security reasons). Continuing on for 10 yards, you'll find a tiny shrine across the street. It's typical of southern Italy, where the faithful pray to their saint, who contacts Mary, who contacts Jesus, who contacts God. This shrine is a bit more direct—starting right with Mary.

Continue down the lane. It ends at the cathedral (which, although the seat of the local bishop, is nothing special besides the *intarcio* (inlaid wood) doors. Turn right to get to busy Corso Italia. Cross the street, and go straight (on Via Padre R. Giuliani), following the old, Greek street plan (east–west for the most sunlight, north–south for the prevailing and cooling breeze). While the gust is welcome in the summer, even in ancient times, documents report of locals complaining about the cold winter wind making them sick. One block ahead is a fine old covered portico, the...

3. Sorrento Men's Club: This has been a retreat for retired working-class men for generations. Strictly no women—and no phones.

Italian men venerate their mothers. (Italians joke that that Jesus must have been a southern Italian, because his mother believed her son was God, he believed his mom was a virgin, and he lived at home with her until he was 30.) But Italian men have also built into their culture ways to be on their own. Here, men play cards and gossip under 15th-century Renaissance frescos (redone in the 18th century).

At the Men's Club, turn right. Via San Cesareo, a touristy shopping street, leads back to Piazza Tasso. Notice the huge ancient doorways with their tiny doors—to carefully let in people during a dangerous age. At the noisy street on the edge of Piazza Tasso, turn left and fight the traffic downhill to the next square, dedicated to St. Antonino, Sorrento's patron saint. His statue humbly looms among the palms, facing the basilica where his reliquary lies.

Quit the walk now, or continue along a long, downhill road that dead-ends at the waterfront (you can catch a bus to get back if it's before 20:00).

4. Hike Down to Marina Grande: Gradually wind your way with the traffic downhill. After a block or so, on the right is a fine cliffside public square overlooking the harbor. From here, an elevator takes people down to Marina Piccola, where lounge chairs and vacationers working on tans line the sundeck. Enjoy the view of the little harbor and the Bay of Naples. The Franciscan church fronting this square comes with a great little cloister (pop in to see Sicilian Gothic—a 13th-century mix of Norman, Gothic, and Arabic styles).

Continuing downhill, the road turns into stairs that zig-zag down to the Marina Grande—Sorrento's big harbor. Just before reaching the harbor, you pass under an ancient Greek gate, a reminder that Marina Grande is a separate town with its own proud residents. It's said that even their cats look different. Sorrentines—who believe that Marina Grande dwellers come from Saracen (Turkish pirate) stock—still scare their children by saying, "Behave—or the Turks will take you away."

Marina Grande's economy is still based on its fishing fleet. People respect old traditions. Women wear black when a relative dies (one year for an uncle, three for a husband). Men get off easy, just wearing a black button if their wife dies. There are several recommended restaurants on the harbor; two are gritty family-run joints right on the beach (see "Eating," page 656). On the far side, Ristorante Delfino comes with a sundeck for a lazy drink before or after your lunch.

From here, buses return to the center hourly (usually at :25 past the hour, note schedule, buy €1 ticket from driver).

SIGHTS AND ACTIVITIES

▲**Strolling**—Take time to explore the surprisingly pleasant old city between Corso Italia and the sea. Views from the public park next to Imperial Hotel Tramontano are worth the detour. Duck into the Church of England. The evening *passeggiata* (along Corso Italia and Via San Cesareo) peaks around 22:00.

Lemons

Around here, *limoni* are ubiquitous: screaming yellow painted on ceramics, dainty bottles of *limoncello*, and lemons at the fruit stand the size of a softball. The area of the Amalfi Coast and Sorrento produces several different kinds of lemons. T h e gigantic, bumpy lemons are actually citrons, called *cedri*, and are more for show—they're pulpier, rather than juicier, and make a good marmalade. The juicy *sfusato sorrentino*, grown only in Sorrento, is shaped like an American football, while the *sfusato amalfitano*, with knobby points on both ends, is less juicy but equally aromatic. These two kinds of luscious lemons are used in sweets such as *granita* (shaved ice doused in lemonade), *limoncello* (a candy-like liquor with a big kick, called *limoncino* on the Cinque Terre), *delizia* (a dome of fluffy cake filled and slathered with a thick, whipped lemon cream), *spremuta di limone* (fresh squeezed lemon juice), and of course, gelato or *sorbetto alla limone*.

▲**Lemon Grove Garden (L'Agruminato)**—This small park consists of an inviting lemon and orange grove lined with paths. The owners of the grove are seasoned green thumbs, working the orchard through many generations. They've even grafted orange tree branches onto a lemon tree, so that both fruits now grow on the same tree. The garden is dotted with benches, tables, and an inviting little tasting (and buying) stand. They offer free samples of chilled *limoncello* (a local specialty made of lemons, sugar, and pure alcohol) and various other homemade liquors made from basil, mandarins, or fennel (free, daily April–Sept 9:30–21:00, Oct–March 10:00–16:00). The shop selling all their organic, homemade products is outside the Corso Italia entrance. Enter the garden on Corso Italia (100 yards to the north of the train station on Corso Italia #165, where tiles mark "*L'Agruminato, il giardino della città*"), or at intersection of Via Capasso and Via Rota (next to Hotel La Meridiana Sorrento).

▲**Swimming near Sorrento**—If you require immediate tanning, you can rent a chair on the pier by the port. There are no great beaches in Sorrento—the gravely, jam-packed private beaches of Marina Piccola are more for partying than pampering. There's just a tiny spot for public use. The best sandy, family-friendly beach is two miles away at Meta. While the Meta Circumvesuviana stop is a very long walk from the beach (or a €25 cab ride), the orange bus #A goes directly from Piazza Tasso to the beach (last stop, schedule posted for hourly returns). At Meta, you'll find pizzerias, snack bars, and a little free section of beach—but it's mostly dominated by several sprawling private beach complexes. If you go, pay for a spot in one of these. Lido Metamare seems best, and the manager, Aldo, offers readers of this book 30 percent off on everything, including the entry fee, through 2006 (€2.50 entry; also available—and discounted—are lockable changing cabins, lounge chairs, etc.). It's a very Italian scene, with light lunches, a playground, manicured beach, loud pop music...and no international tourists.

Tarzan might take Jane to the wild and stony beach at **Punta del Capo,** a 15-minute bus ride from Piazza Tasso (2/hr, get off at last stop—in front of American Bar—then walk 10 min past ruined Roman Villa di Pollio). Otherwise, from the American Bar bus stop, you can walk to **Marina di Poulo,** a tiny fishing town popular in the summer for its sandy beach, surfside restaurants, and beachfront disco (15-min walk, follow signs).

Tennis—The Sorrento Sport Snack Bar has fine courts open to the public (daily 9:30–23:00, until 20:00 in winter, €15/hr including rackets and balls for 2 people, call for reservation, across from recommended Ambasciatori Hotel at Via Califano 5, tel. 081-807-1616).

Scuba Diving—To go where there are no shops, dive deep into the Mediterranean. First, boat out for one hour to the protected marine zone that lies between Sorrento and Capri. There, you can try the beginners' dive (€90, includes instruction and complete supervision, 14:00 daily year-round), or the dives for experienced, certified divers (1 dive-€55, 2 dives-€90, April–Oct 9:00 and 14:00). The whole experience takes about three hours, and the prices include all equipment, transportation, and the dive itself, which lasts about 40 minutes for both novices and experts (20 yards east of port at Via Marina Piccola 63, tel. 081-877-4812, www.sorrentodivingcenter .it, info@sorrentodivingcenter.it).

NIGHTLIFE

English vacationers come here in droves. Many have holidayed here annually for decades. The town is filled with pubs that try to help British guests feel right at home. **The English Inn** offers a rough-feeling pub or a more refined-feeling garden out back (daily, 24 hrs, closed Dec; serves baked beans on toast, fish and chips, draft beer; fun music, Internet access, Corso Italia 53, tel. 081-807-4357). **Matilda's,** a big late-night dance club with several floors of loud and youthful action, is more popular with Italians (as central as can be, just below Piazza Tasso). The **Foreigners' Club** offers live Neapolitan songs, Sinatra-style classics, and jazzy elevator-type music nightly at 21:00 throughout the summer. It's just right for old-timers feeling frisky (in the center, see "Tourist Information," page 645).

SLEEPING

Sorrento offers the whole range of rooms. Hotels often charge the same for a room whether it has a view, balcony, or neither. At hotels that offer sea views, ask for a room *"con balcone, con vista sul mare"* (with a balcony, with a sea view). *"Tranquillo"* is taken as a request for a room off the street. Hotels listed are either near the station and city center or along the way to Punta del Capo, a 20-minute walk (or short bus ride) from the station. While many hotels close for the winter, you should have no trouble finding a room any time outside of August, when the place is jammed and many hotel prices go way up. Outside of summer, prices can be soft—it doesn't hurt to ask for a discount. Splurge for a hotel with air-conditioning if you wilt in the heat, but be aware it often costs extra. Note: The spindly, more exotic, and more tranquil Amalfi Coast town of Positano (see next chapter) is also a good place to spend the night.

East of the Center

To reach these hotels, head a block in front of the train station, turn right onto Corso Italia, then left down Via Capasso, which winds right and becomes Via Califano.

$$$ **Grand Hotel Ambasciatori** is a sumptuous four-star hotel with 100 rooms, a cliffside setting, a sprawling garden, and a pool. This is Humphrey Bogart-land, with plush public spaces, a relaxing stay-a-while ambience, and a free elevator to its "private beach." The beach is actually a sundeck built out over the water, shared with Hotel Loreley (Db-€250, Db-€310 with seaview, 10 percent off with cash and this 2006 book, those who reserve in advance pay higher rates than walk-ins, closed Jan–March, air-con, some balconies, parking, Via Califano 18, tel. 081-878-2025, fax 081-807-1021,

---

Sleep Code

(€1 = about $1.20, country code: 39)
S = Single, **D** = Double/Twin, **T** = Triple, **Q** = Quad, **b** = bathroom, **s** = shower only. Unless otherwise noted, credit cards are accepted, English is spoken, and breakfast is included.

To help you sort easily through these listings, I've divided the rooms into three categories based on the price for a standard double room with bath:

$$$ **Higher Priced**—Most rooms €150 or more.
  $$ **Moderately Priced**—Most rooms between €100–150.
    $ **Lower Priced**—Most rooms €100 or less.

www.manniellohotels.it, ambasciatori@manniellohotels.it).

$$ Hotel la Meridiana Sorrento, a fine three-star place with everything but character, offers business-class public spaces and 45 modern rooms (Db-€117, Tb-€165, required Aug half-pension at Db-€185 and Tb-€264, prices soft when slow, extra for air-con, big rooftop terrace with grand views, next door to public Lemon Grove Garden, Via Rota 1, tel. 081-807-3535, fax 081-807-3484, www.lameridianasorrento.com, info@lameridianasorrento.com).

$ Hotel Loreley, a rambling, spacious, colorful, old Sorrentine villa, feels like a sanatorium. Of its 27 rooms, 19 have seaview balconies, but the unpredictable management cannot guarantee you'll get a view room. The noisy streetside rooms lack views but are air-conditioned, which helps drown out the traffic noise. A €3 elevator takes you to the hotel's beach, a sundeck built out over the water and shared with Hotel Ambasciatori (non-view Db-€90, seaview Db-€95, in August half-pension at Db-€125 is required but the dinner's decent, prices good through 2006 with this book, some free parking, Via Califano 2, tel. 081-807-3187, fax 081-532-9001, e-mail to info@sorrentohotelmignon.com but make it clear you're booking for Loreley). The attached restaurant (see "Eating," page 656) has a terrace with a panoramic view of the sea.

$ Pensione Mara is a dirty-ashtray kind of place, with five simple ground-floor rooms in a dull building with a good location (Db-€45, Tb-€65, Qb-€85, these prices promised through 2006 with this book, cash only, no breakfast, from Via Capasso, turn right at Hotel La Meridiana to Via Rota 5; tel. & fax 081-878-3665, Adelle speaks a little English).

In the Town Center

$$ Hotel del Corso, a funky, Old World, three-star hotel, is central, family-run, and comfortable, with 26 spacious rooms. The staff can be curt (Db-€110, Tb-€150, Qb-€170, ask for €10/day Rick Steves discount, bottom-floor rooms like new, ask for room off busy street, air-con, rooftop sun terrace, Corso Italia 134, near Piazza Tasso, tel. 081-807-1016, tel. & fax 081-807-3157, www.hoteldelcorso.com, info@hoteldelcorso.com).

$ Casa Astarita B&B is a shining gem in the middle of town, with a crazy-quilt tiled entryway; six bright, tranquil, air-conditioned rooms (3 with little balconies); and a fully-stocked communal fridge and sideboard for help-yourself breakfasts (Db-€95, Tb-€110, prices promised with this book through 2006, double-paned windows, elevator, Internet in lobby, just past Ristorante Parrucchiano as you're coming from the station on Corso Italia at #67, tel. 081-877-4906, fax 081-807-1146, www.casastarita.com, info@casastarita.com, Annamaria and Rita).

$ Il Palazzo Starace B&B offers seven peaceful, tidy, and rather dark rooms in a little alley off Corso Italia (opposite Hotel del Corso), one block from Piazza Tasso (Db-€90, includes small breakfast at a bar around the corner, no elevator but a luggage dumbwaiter; ring bell at Via S.M. della Pietà #9, then climb 3 floors; tel. 081-878-4031, fax 081-532-9344, www.palazzostarace .com, palazzostarace@tiscali.it).

$ Hotel Mignon Meublè rents 24 basic rooms in a central location a block off Corso Italia (Sb-€85, Db-€100, Tb-€130, air-con, double-paned windows on first floor, some balconies but no views; from station, turn left on Corso Italia, 10-min walk to Via Sersale 9; tel. 081-807-3824, fax 081-877-4348, www.sorrentohotelmignon .com, info@sorrentohotelmignon.com, friendly and warm Anna).

$ Hotel Nice rents 28 simple, cramped rooms with high ceilings 100 yards in front of the train station on the noisy main drag. Ask for a room off the street, facing a little garden of lemon and orange trees (Db-€85, Tb-€100, Qb-€120, 10 percent discount with cash and this 2006 book, air-con, elevator, rooftop terrace, Corso Italia 257, tel. 081-878-1650, fax 081-878-3086, hotelnice@tiscali.it).

$ Residenza Maresca is a humble two-building, 12-room sideline for the recommended Pizzeria Giardiniello, which serves as the reception (see directions under "Eating," page 656). Eight of the 12 modern, large rooms are at the end of Corso Italia (at #5). Witty owner Franco may struggle with his English and be tardy when he meets you for check-in, but the price can't be beat (Db-€60, cash only, air-con, mini-fridge, Via Accademia 7-9, tel. 081-878-4616, casamarescaresidence@libero.it).

$ Ostello le Sirene di Sorrento, a tiny hostel four blocks from the train station, offers 50 of the cheapest beds in town (€18 for a bunk in 8- to 10-bed dorms with bath, includes breakfast, cash only, membership not required, Internet in lobby, Via degli Aranci 160, tel. & fax 081-877-1371, www.hostel.it, info@hostel.it).

With a View on Via Capo

These hotels are outside of town, near the cape (straight out Corso Italia, which turns into Via Capo; from the city center, it's a 15-min walk, a €15 taxi ride, or a cheap bus ride). The bus situation is goofy because there are two competing companies. To get from the train station to Via Capo, you can catch a SITA bus (usually blue or green, any except those heading for Positano/Amalfi) or an orange or orange-and-blue Circumvesuviana bus (Bus #A). Tickets for both (€1) are sold at the station newsstand and tobacco shops, but not on the buses. The orange buses run more frequently (3/hr). The first two hotels are my favorite Sorrento splurges, and the last two hotels are clearly the best budget bets. If you're in Sorrento to stay put and luxuriate, these accommodations are perfect (although I'd rather luxuriate in Positano—see next chapter).

$$ Albergo Settimo Cielo, the aptly named "Seventh Heaven," offers all the views and lazy resort trappings you could want, run by a family that really hustles to give a fine value. At this dressy cliffhanger, the reception is just off the road, and the elevator takes you down through four floors with 50 rooms—all with grand views, two-thirds with balconies (Sb-€115, Db-€135, Tb-€175, Qb-€205, 5 percent discount if you mention this book when reserving and show this book at reception desk, air-con June–Sept, free parking, inviting pool and sun terrace, Internet in lobby, Via Capo 27, tel. 081-878-1012, fax 081-807-3290, www.hotelsettimocielo.com, info@hotelsettimocielo.com). It's 300 steps above Marina Grande.

$$ Hotel Minerva is like a sun worshipper's temple. Catch the elevator at Via Capo 32. Getting off at the fifth floor, you'll step into a spectacular terrace with outrageous Mediterranean views and a small, cliff-hanging swimming pool and a cold-water Jacuzzi *con vista* complementing 60 large, tiled *limoncello* rooms (Db-€140, Tb-€155, Qb-€170, plus €10 for a balcony, these prices—discounted about €30—are promised with this book through 2006 only if claimed at time of inquiry, watch out for the occasional moldy room, no summer half-pension requirement, air-con, Internet in lobby, parking-€10/day, Via Capo 30-32, tel. 081-878-1011, fax 081-878-1949, www.minervasorrento.com, minerva@acampora.it).

$$ Hotel la Tonnarella is a freshly renovated Sorrentine villa with several terraces, stylish tiles, a dreamy chandeliered dining room, and disinterested owners. Eighteen of its 24 rooms have views of the sea (non-view Db-€150, seaview Db-€155, Db with view balcony-€160, Db with view terrace-€165, view suite-€200, €22/person half-pension available in Aug, rooms near kitchen come with clanging pots and pans, air-con, small beach with free elevator access, Via Capo 31, tel. 081-878-1153, fax 081-878-2169, www.latonnarella.it, info@latonnarella.it).

$ Hotel Désirée, run by friendly Corinna, is a simpler affair, with humbler vistas but no traffic noise. Half of the 22 slightly scruffy rooms have high, cliff-facing views, balconies, or both (all same price). Most rooms have fans, and there's a fine roof sunning terrace, lovable cats, and no half-pension requirements (maximum prices: Sb-€61, small Db-€78, Db-€90, Tb-€108, Qb-€126, cash only, laundry-€8, rooms on bottom floor in better condition, shares driveway and free beach access with La Tonnarella, Via Capo 31, tel. & fax 081-878-1563). Corinna, who speaks English, is hugely helpful with tips on exploring the peninsula.

$ The humble Pension Elios, run by Maria and daughter Gianna, offers 14 simple but spacious rooms—most with balconies and views—and a panoramic sun terrace (Db-€65, Tb-€80, family rooms, cheaper off-season but closed Dec, cash only, free parking, Via Capo 33, tel. 081-878-1812, a little English spoken).

Near the Port
$$ Hotel il Faro, located near Marina Piccola, is handy to visitors traveling by hydrofoil to Naples or Capri, and to buses into the center. Its rooftop terrace, crammed with sunning lounge chairs, overlooks the ocean. Some of its neat and modern 50 rooms have balconies, many with views (Sb-€90, non-view Db-€120, seaview Db-€130, non-view Tb-€150, seaview Tb-€170, July–Aug add €10/person, 15 percent discount promised with this book through 2006, air-con, tel. 081-878-1390, fax 081-807-3144, www.hotelilfaro .com, info@hotelilfaro.com). They also run the attached Ristorante Pizzeria Vela Bianca, offering a 10 percent discount to hotel guests.

EATING

Downtown Splurges
In a town proud to have no McDonald's, consider eating well for a few extra bucks. Both of these places are worthwhile splurges in the old center.

Ristorante il Buco, once the cellar of an old monastery, is now a small, dressy restaurant serving delightfully presented, top-quality food. They showcase good wine (especially from Campania) and offer snappy service. The owner, Peppe, designs his menu around whatever's fresh, and travels in the winter to assemble a wine list sure to offer connoisseurs something new and memorable (€14 pastas, €20 *secondi*, always a good vegetarian selection, dinners run about €45–50 plus wine, several tasting *menus* available or order à la carte, Thu–Tue 12:00–15:00 & 19:00–23:00, closed Wed and Jan, just off Piazza Sant'Antonino; facing the basilica, go under the grand arch on the left and immediately enter the restaurant, Il Rampa Marina Piccola 5, tel. 081-878-2354). Reservations are generally necessary to sit inside under their elegant vault. For outside dining, I'd go elsewhere.

L'Antica Trattoria serves more traditional cuisine from an inviting menu in a *romantico* candlelit ambience. Aldo and sons will take good care of you in a place busy with contagiously fun waiters and enthusiastic eaters (*menus* for €29, €35, and €40; always vegetarian options). Its wine list is more predictable, featuring well-known wines from the region. Walk around the labyrinthine place before you select a place to sit (daily 12:00–15:00 & 19:00–23:30, closed Mon Nov–Feb, air-con, shaded and verdant terrace, non-smoking sections, reservations smart, Via P.R. Giulani 33, tel. 081-807-1082).

Eating Well and Cheaply Downtown
Pizzeria Giardiniello is a family show, offering good food, friendly smiles, and a peaceful, tropical garden setting (€5 pizzas and pastas, daily 12:00–24:00, Via Accademia 7, tel. 081-878-4616). Like an

old sailor checking the lines, Franco makes sure you're well-fed. Franco's son, Luigi, runs a wine-and-tapas bar downstairs (nightly 18:00 until past midnight).

Pizzeria Aurora, located on Piazza Tasso, makes 50 different kinds of prizewinning pizzas and calzones (€6–10). Sit inside to watch the *pizzaiolo* create your dinner, or outside for optimum people-watching (daily 12:00–16:00 & 18:30–24:00, Piazza Tasso 10/11, east of taxi stand, tel. 081-878-1248).

Pizzeria da Gigino, lively and small, makes huge, tasty, Naples-style pizzas in their wood-burning oven (Wed–Mon 12:00–15:00 & 18:30–24:00, closed Tue but daily July–Aug; just off Piazza Sant'Antonino, take first road to the left of Sant'Antonino as you face him, pass under archway and take first left; tel. 081-878-1927).

Sant'Antonino's nearby offers friendly service, red-checkered tablecloths, an outdoor patio spotted with lemon trees, an open kitchen, decent prices, and edible food (daily 12:00–16:00 & 19:00–24:00, closed Wed Dec–March, just off Piazza Sant'Antonino on Santa Maria delle Grazie 6, tel. 081-877-1200).

If you fancy a picnic dinner on your balcony, on the hotel terrace, or in the public garden, you'll find many markets and take-out pizzerias in the old town. The **Standa supermarket** at Corso Italia 223 has it all (Mon–Sat 8:30–13:20 & 16:30–20:25, Sun 9:30–13:00 & 17:00–22:30).

Gelato: A few doors downhill from L'Antica Trattoria, **Davide Gelato** has many repeat customers—so many flavors, so little time. Walk the most enticing chorus line in Italy before ordering. Sample Profumi di Sorrento (an explosive sorbet of mixed local fruits) and lemon mousse (mid-June–mid-Sept daily 9:30–24:00, otherwise closed Mon; Via P.R. Giuliani 39, 2 blocks off Corso Italia).

Dinners with Sea Views

For a decent dinner *con vista*, the following places come with great view terraces.

Ristorante Delfino gets their seafood right off the fishermen's boats at Marina Grande, and serves it up in big portions to hungry locals in a quiet and bright pier restaurant. It's lovingly run by effervescent Luisa, her brothers Andrea and Roberto, and her husband Antonio. They take good care of their guests, play Dean Martin, and give travelers who carry this book a little glass of *limoncello* to cap the experience (daily 11:30–15:30 & 18:30–23:00, closed Nov–Easter; Marina Grande, facing the water, go all the way to the left and follow signs; tel. 081-878-2038). If you're here for lunch, Delfino comes with great sundeck and lounge chairs.

Ristorante Taverna Azzurra and **Trattoria da Emilia,** both on the tranquil Marina Grande waterfront, are good for straightforward, typical Sorrentine home-cooking, including *maccheroni,* *gnocchi di mamma,* and fresh fish (Azzurra—daily 12:00–midnight, tel. 081-877-2510; Emilia—daily 19:30–22:30, closed Tue Oct–March, tel. 081-807-2720).

The **Foreigners' Club Restaurant** is a place where the English Patient could recuperate. It has the best sea views in town (under breezy palms), live music nightly in summer at 21:00, and passable meals. It's a good spot for dessert or an after-dinner *limoncello* (March–Oct daily, bar opens at 9:30, snacks served 11:30–15:00, dinner 19:00–23:00, closed in winter, Via L. De Maio 35, tel. 081-877-3263).

Hotel Loreley's restaurant serves reasonably priced, so-so meals with a spectacular sea view. Unfortunately, nighttime romance is drowned out by the fluorescent lights but it's fine for a daytime visit (daily 12:00–14:30 & 19:00–21:30, 10-min walk east of town center, Via Califano 2; see "Sleeping," page 652).

TRANSPORTATION CONNECTIONS

It's impressively fast to zip by boat from Sorrento to most coastal towns and islands during the summer, when there are many more departures. In fact, locals routinely get around quicker by fast boat than by car or train (see "Boats," below, and the map on page 633).

From Sorrento to Naples, Pompeii, and Herculaneum by Circumvesuviana Train: This commuter train runs about every 30 minutes between Naples and Sorrento. From Sorrento, it's 30 minutes to Pompeii, 45 minutes to Herculaneum (€1.80 one-way for either trip), and 70 minutes to Naples (€3.20 one-way). The schedule is printed in the free *Surrentum* magazine (available at TI). See Naples' "Transportation Connections," page 631, for more information on the Circumvesuviana and theft precautions. Note: The risk of theft is limited mostly to suburban Naples. Going between Sorrento and Pompeii or Herculaneum is much safer.

From Sorrento to the Naples Airport: Six buses run daily to and from the airport; confirm the schedule at the TI (€6, pay driver, 75 min, depart Piazza Tasso, wait at bus stop under flags where the stairs lead down to Marina Piccola, look for bus with *Curreri* written high on windshield, www.gesac.it).

To the Amalfi Coast: See next chapter.

To Rome: Most people ride the Circumvesuviana for an hour to Naples, then catch the express train to Rome. But the direct Sorrento–Rome bus can actually be more convenient. Marozzi buses leave Sorrento's Piazza Tasso daily for Rome's Tibertina station (€16, 4 hrs, leaves Mon–Sun at 6:00 and 17:00, different colored buses but look for *Marozzi*, buy tickets on board or at any travel agency, tel. 0805-790-111, www.marozzivt.it).

Boats

The number of boats that run per day varies according to the season. The frequency indicated here is for May through September, with two to four more boats per day in July and August. All schedules should be checked with the TI.

By Boat to: Capri (at least hourly: fast ferry, 25 min, €5.80; and the fastest and priciest, jet boat, 20 min, €10.50; depart by 9:30 at the latest—these early boats can be jammed but it's worth it to avoid crowds on Capri), **Naples** (7/day, 40 min, €7.50: for more info see page 631), **Positano** (3/day daily mid-May–mid-Oct only, otherwise only weekends, 50 min for €10; 90 min for €7.50), **Amalfi** (6/day daily mid-May–mid-Oct only, may be some off season, 50 min, €7). For a slightly less touristy alternative to Capri, consider the nearby island of **Ischia** (1/day, Easter–Nov only, departure usually around 9:30, otherwise from Naples, 55 min, €14).

Getting to Sorrento's Port: To get from Sorrento's Piazza Tasso to the port, walk down the stairs near the statue's left side or take orange shuttle bus #B or #C (3/hr). Boat tickets are sold only at the port. Various lines go to different destinations, but for Sorrento-Capri two lines compete—LMP and Caremar, with ferries and hydrofoil, ranging in prices and trip duration (check schedules, best deal is the less-frequent 25-minute fast ferry with Caremar for €5.80). See "Planning Your Time," for Capri, below, for advice on buying one-way vs. round-trip tickets.

Capri

Capri was made famous as the vacation hideaway of Roman emperors Augustus and Tiberius. In the 19th century, it was the haunt of Romantic Age aristocrats on their Grand Tour of Europe. But these days, the island is a world-class tourist trap, packed with gawky, name-tag-wearing visitors searching for the rich and famous, and finding only their prices.

The "Island of Dreams" is a zoo in July and August—overrun with tacky, low-grade group tourism at its worst. Other times of year, hosever, it provides a relaxing and scenic break from the cultural gauntlet of Italy.

Planning Your Time

This is the best day-trip plan from Sorrento: Take an early jet boat to Capri (buy ticket at 8:00, boat leaves at 8:25 and arrives at 9:00—smart). Go directly to the Blue Grotto, then catch a bus from the Grotto to Anacapri and ride the chairlift to Monte Solare. From the summit, hike down (or return by chairlift). Stroll out from the base of the chairlift to Villa San Michele for the view, then catch a bus to Capri for the rest of your stay. At the end of the day, ride the funicular down to Marina Grande to catch the boat back to Sorrento. For an efficient way to connect destinations, many travelers coming from Sorrento check their bag at the harbor, see Capri, and sail from here directly to Naples.

If you buy a one-way ticket to Capri (there's no round-trip discount), you'll have maximum schedule flexibility and can take either company's boat back. (Check times for the last return crossing upon arrival; at Capri get a schedule from the TI or check at boat-ticket kiosk.) During July and August, however, it's wise to get a round-trip boat ticket with a late return (improving your odds of getting a spot on a boat when they're most crowded; available from LMP line)—and you can use the ticket to return earlier if you like. Be 20 minutes early or you can be bumped.

Day-trippers come down from Rome, creating a daily rush hour in each direction. The trip to the Blue Grotto is just a 20-minute boat ride away from the arrival dock, but the commotion there can amount to a two-hour delay (see page 664). If you're heading to Capri specifically to see the Blue Grotto, be sure to check that the tide isn't too high or the water too rough—ask the TI or your hotelier before heading over.

ORIENTATION

First thing—pronounce it right: KAH-pree, not kah-PREE like the song or the pants. The island is small—just four miles by two miles—and is separated from the Sorrento Peninsula by a narrow strait. There are only two towns to speak of (Capri and Anacapri). The island also has some scant Roman ruins and a few interesting churches and villas. But its chief attraction is its famous Blue Grotto, and its best activity is a chairlift up the island's Monte Solaro followed by a scenic hike down.

Local Guide: Roberta Mazzarella is good (about €180/day, depending on itinerary, mobile 339-135-7619, robertamazzarella @yahoo.it).

Arrival in Capri

Get oriented on the boat before you dock. As you near the harbor, Capri spreads out before you: The dock is **Marina Grande** (TI, boats to **Blue Grotto,** buses to anywhere, funicular to the town of Capri). **Capri town** fills the ridge high above the harbor. Emperor Tiberius' palace ruins, **Villa Jovis,** cap the peak on the left. The dramatic *"Mamma mia!"* road arcs around the highest mountain on the island (**Monte Solare**) on the right leading up to **Anacapri** (the island's second town, just out of sight). Notice the zigzag steps that date from ancient times below that road. The white house on the

Capri

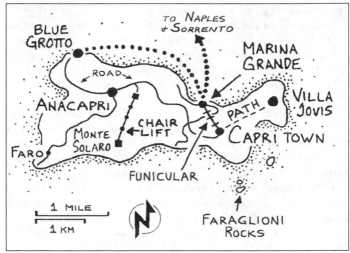

ridge above the zigzags is **Villa San Michele** (where you'll go later for a grand view of boats like the one you're on now).

Upon arrival, get your bearings. Boats dock in two places: On the long pier or directly by the main street. If your boat arrived on the main street, take a right to get to the long pier. Stand with your back to the pier: The **funicular** is across the street. The fourth little shop to the right of the funicular (no sign, sells clothes and souvenirs) provides **baggage storage** in the back of the store (€2.50/day per bag, March–Sept daily 8:30–18:00). The kiosk that sells **bus and funicular tickets** is around the end of the pier to your right. Kiosks that sell return **boat tickets** (2 competing companies) are behind that; across the street from all this are the **public WCs**.

The **TI** is behind you on the dock (April–Oct daily 8:30–20:45; Nov–March Mon–Sat 9:00–13:00 & 15:30–18:30, closed Sun; pick up €0.80 map only if you'll be venturing to the outskirts of Capri town or Anacapri, tel. 081-837-0634). Bar Augusto, a few doors down to the left of the funicular, has **Internet access** (daily 6:00–20:00).

From the port, you have three transit options: boat to the Blue Grotto (best early—ideally upon arrival), bus to Anacapri, or ride the funicular up to Capri town (5 min, 4/hr; if funicular isn't running, use bus—departs from station 50 yards uphill to right).

Getting Around Capri

The buses and funicular are covered by the same ticket options: €1.30 per ride, €2.10 for 60 minutes of unlimited use (best option if going straight to Blue Grotto by public bus), or €6.70 for an all-day pass. Schedules are clearly posted at all bus stations. You can hire a taxi for about €50 per hour—negotiate.

Buses from the Port at Marina Grande: Buses pick up just beyond where you bought your ticket. Get in line under the appropriate sign: either under S. Costanzo for going up to the town of **Capri** (4/hr), where you could then transfer to Anacapri (7 min, 4/hr, there's routinely a long queue for this Capri-to-Anacapri bus); or direct to **Anacapri** (2/hr).

Buses from Anacapri: Buses go to **Capri town** (at least 4/hr, can be packed; guarantee a seat by catching the bus before the Anacapri stop, at the end-of-the-line stop called "Caprile"—a 10-min walk away, ask for directions). Buses also run to the **Blue Grotto** (from a different end-of-the-line stop called "Piazza del Cimitero," which is a 5-min walk on the main road from Anacapri's main square). If you're coming from the town of Capri and want to transfer to the Blue Grotto buses, don't get off when the driver announces "Anacapri." Instead, ride one more stop, then transfer to the well-signed *Grotta Azzurra* (Blue Grotto) buses.

Capri Town

This is a cute but touristy shopping town. The *funiculare* drops you just around the corner from Piazza Umberto, the town's main square. The **TI** fills a closet under the bell tower on Piazza Umberto (less crowded than its sister on the port—and with same hours, tel. 081-837-0686, WC downstairs behind TI). From the city hall (Municipio, lowest corner), a lane leads into the medieval part of town, which has plenty of eateries. The lane past the many-domed church (past Bar Tiberio, on left) has been dubbed by locals "Rodeo Drive" because it's the fashion shopping strip. Walk down Rodeo Drive to Quisisana Hotel, the island's top old-time hotel, or go to the left, down a lane lined with elegant villas for the "Beverly Hills walk." For great views, take the street on the right that heads downhill. At the "T" in the road, you can go left to the 14th-century Certosa Monastery (free, Tue–Sat 9:00–14:00, Sun 9:00–13:00, closed Mon), or right to the public garden, Giardini Augusto (free, daily 9:00–18:00).

Emperor Tiberius' now-ruined villa, **Villa Jovis,** is a scenic 45-minute hike from Capri town. Tiberius ruled Rome from here for a decade (c. A.D. 30). There are no statues and no mosaics. You go for evocative stones and a lovely view (€2, €1 English flier, daily from 9:00 until an hour before sunset).

SLEEPING

(€1 = about $1.20, country code: 39)

$$ Casa per Ferie Villa Helios is a church-run former convent renting rooms to raise money for the adjacent seniors' home. Located away from the tourist intensity, at the top of Capri town with a view terrace and a charming dignity, its 24 rooms are spacious, simple, and pleasant (Db-€110, €30 more mid-May–mid-Sept, extra bed-€30, includes breakfast, family rooms, some with air-con, Via Croce 4, tel. & fax 081-837-0240, www.villahelios.it, info@villahelios.it).

Anacapri

Capri's second town has no sea views but some fun and interesting activities. From the busy square where the bus drops you, head down the pedestrian street with the curvy pavement to reach the **TI** (Mon–Sat 9:00–15:00, closed Sun, often closed Nov–Easter, tel. 081-837-1524).

Straight ahead from the chairlift exit (Piazza Vittoria), a pedestrian path leads across the square and past the deluxe Capri Palace Hotel (venture in if you can get past the treacherous swimming pool windows), under the Villa San Michele, and to a sweeping island view. (The view is even better from the villa—see below.)

SIGHTS AND ACTIVITIES

Villa San Michele—The 19th-century mansion of Capri's grand personality, Avel Munthe, offers an insight into the scene here when this was the only comfortable refuge for Europe's artsy gay community. Oscar Wilde, D. H. Lawrence, and company hung out here back when being gay could land you in jail...or worse. Munthe, a Swedish doctor who lived here until 1949, left this impressive mansion littered with Roman statues, the Olivetum (museum of local birds and bugs), and a delightful garden. From the sphinx, you'll enjoy one of Capri's best views (€5, daily 9:00–18:00).

▲St. Michael's Church—This church has a remarkable majolica floor showing paradise on earth in a classic 18th-century Neapolitan style. The entire floor is ornately tiled, featuring an angel (with flaming sword) driving Adam and Eve from paradise. The devil is wrapped around the trunk of a beautiful tree. The animals—happily ignoring this momentous event—all have human expressions (€1, daily 9:45–16:30, in town center, 100 yards after the TI take a right to the church).

Capri in Miniatura—A 22' x 11' miniature replica of Capri, crafted with stone, ceramic, and real vegetation—including sculpted bonsai trees—sprawls across the center of a sunny courtyard. Small aquarium-like dioramas on the periphery of the courtyard depict Old World islanders' daily life. Avoid stopping in between 14:00–15:00, when cruise ships crowds shuffle through (€3, Mon–Sun 9:00–19:30, closed Nov–March, Via G. Orlandi 105, tel. 081-837-1169).

Faro—The lighthouse is a favorite place to enjoy the sunset with a private beach, pool, small restaurants, and a few fishermen. Reach it by bus from Anacapri (cemetery stop, Piazza del Cimitero).

▲▲**Chairlift up to Monte Solaro**—From Anacapri, ride the chairlift to the 1,900-foot summit of Monte Solaro for a commanding view of the Bay of Naples. Work on your tan as you float over hazelnut, walnut, chestnut, apricot, peach, kiwi, and fig trees and past a montage of tourists (mostly cruise-ship types; when the Grotto is closed—as it often is—they bring passengers here instead). As you ascend, consider how real estate has been priced out of reach of locals. The ride takes 15 minutes each way, and you'll want at least half an hour on top.

At the summit, you'll enjoy the best panorama possible: lush cliffs busy with seagulls enjoying the ideal nesting spot. The Faraglioni Rocks are an icon of the island—with tour boats squeezing through every few minutes. The pink building nearest the rocks was an American R&R base during World War II. Eisenhower and Churchill met here. On the peak closest to Cape Sorrento, you can see the distant ruins of the emperor's palace, Villa Jovis. Pipes from the Sorrento Peninsula bring water to Capri, which long ago exceeded the supply of its three natural springs. The Galli Islands mark the Amalfi Coast in the distance. Cross the bar terrace for views of Mount Vesuvius and Naples (€6 round-trip, €4.50 one-way, daily in summer 9:30–17:00, last run down at 17:30, Nov–March last run 15:30).

A highlight for many visitors is the pleasant 40-minute downhill hike from the top of Monte Solaro, through lush vegetation and ever-changing views, past the 14th-century Chapel of Santa Maria Cetrella, and back into Anacapri.

Blue Grotto (Grotto Azzurra)

Three thousand tourists a day pay about €20 and spend a couple of hours visiting Capri's Blue Grotto (rated ▲▲). I did—early, without the frustration of crowds, and with choppy waves nearly making entrance impossible...and it was great.

The actual cave experience isn't much: a five-minute dinghy ride through a three-foot-high entry hole to reach a 60-yard-long cave, where the sun reflects brilliantly blue on its limestone bottom. But the experience—getting there, getting in, and getting back—is a scenic hoot. You get a fast ride on a 30-foot boat partway around the gorgeous island, seeing bird life and dramatic limestone cliffs with a scant narration. You'll understand why Roman emperors appreciated the invulnerability of the island—it's surrounded by cliffs, with only one access point, and therefore easy to defend. Then, at the grotto's "distribution center," you pile with mostly Japanese tourists into awaiting eight-foot dinghies, where ruffian rowers elbow their way to the tiny hole and pull fast and hard on the cable at the low point of the swells to squeeze you into the grotto. Then your man rows you around, spouting off a few descriptive lines and singing *O Sole Mio*. Depending upon the strength of the sunshine that day, the blue light inside is brilliant. Typically, they extort an extra tip (about €2) out of you before taking you back outside to your big boat.

Cost and Logistics: The round-trip boat from Marina Grande costs €8.50 (daily 9:00 until an hour before sunset, boats don't run in stormy weather or during high tides—check this out *before* you purchase boat ticket). Once you reach the grotto, you pay €4.50 for a rowboat to take you in for the five-minute row around the inside of the grotto (after your rower jockeys for position for at least 20 minutes), plus €4 to cover the admission to the grotto (total €18, but your rower will expect a tip at the end—€2 is enough, though don't tip if rower did poorly. Anyone can dive in for free after 18:00, when the boats stop running—a magical experience and a favorite among locals.

If the waves or high tide make entering dangerous, they don't go in—the grotto can close with no notice, sending tourists (flush with anticipation) home without a chance to squeeze through the little hole.

You can take the boat back, or be dropped off on a small dock next to the grotto by request and return by bus to Anacapri (no discount on round-trip boat ticket, stairs lead to bus stop, schedule posted at the stop, generally 3/hr, buy ticket from driver). By taking the bus from Anacapri directly to the grotto, you save around €5, and see a beautiful, calmer side of the island (every 20 min from Piazza del Cimitero, a 5-min walk on the main road beyond Piazza Vittoria in Anacapri; your 60-min ticket is enough time to visit the grotto and take the bus back to town).

If you're coming from Capri's port, allow one to three hours for the entire visit, depending on the chaos at the caves (early trips often come with the boatmen in their dinghies hitching a ride behind your boat and less chaos at the entry point).

TRANSPORTATION CONNECTIONS

From Capri by Boat to: Positano (mid-May–Sept only; 2/day fast boat—40 min, €15; 1/day slow boat—50 min, €12.50), **Amalfi** (mid-May–Sept only; 2/day by slow boat—75 min, €11.50; 2/day by hydrofoil—1 hr, €14), **Sorrento** (at least hourly; fast ferry—25 min, €5.80; fastest and priciest jet boat—20 min, €10.50), **Naples** (2/hr, 40 min, €12). Confirm the schedule carefully—last boats usually leave between 18:00–20:10.

AMALFI COAST
AND PAESTUM

The Amalfi Coast (Costa Amalfitana) is chaotic, scenic, in-love-with-life Italy at its best.
With its stunning scenery, hill- and harbor-
hugging towns, and historic ruins, Amalfi is
Italy's coast with the most.

The bus trip from Sorrento to Salerno
along the breathtaking Amalfi Coast is one
of the world's great bus rides. It will leave your mouth open and
your film exposed. You'll gain respect for the Italian engineers
who built the roads in the 1800s—and even more respect for the
bus drivers who drive it. Cantilevered garages, hotels, and villas
cling to the vertical terrain, and beautiful sandy coves tease from
far below and out of reach. As you hyperventilate, notice how the
Mediterranean, a sheer 500-foot drop below, really twinkles. And
if you know where to look, you'll see the villas of Sophia Loren,
Franco Zefferelli, and Gore Vidal.

Planning Your Time

On a quick trip, use Sorrento as your home base and do the Amalfi
Coast as a day trip. But for a small-town vacation from your vaca-
tion, spend a few more days on the coast, perhaps sleeping in
Positano or Amalfi town.

Trying to decide between staying in Sorrento, Positano, or
Amalfi? Sorrento is the largest and most touristy of the three, with
the best transportation connections. Positano is the most chic and
picturesque, with a decent beach. The town of Amalfi has the most
actual sights and the best hiking opportunities.

Getting Around the Amalfi Coast

Amalfi Coast towns are pretty but are generally touristy, congested, overpriced, and a long hike above tiny, pebbly beaches. Most beaches are private, and access to those is generally expensive. Check and understand your bills in this greedy region. The real thrill here is the scenic Amalfi drive. This is pretty treacherous stuff—even if you have a car, you may want to take the bus or hire a taxi. Some enjoy doing the coast by scooter or motorbike (rent in Sorrento, be sure to get a helmet). The most logical springboard for this trip is Sorrento (see previous chapter), but Positano and Amalfi work, too.

For most travelers, the best strategy is to take the bus along the Amalfi Coast one way and return by boat. Instead of busing from Sorrento to Salerno (end of the line) and back, take the bus to Salerno, then catch the ferry back to Amalfi or Positano, and from either town, hop a ferry to Sorrento.

Perhaps the simplest option is to take the bus to Positano and boat from there back to Sorrento (or vice-versa). Note that ferry service for this trip decreases to weekends only off-season (mid Oct–early June), and that boats don't run in stormy weather.

Looking for exercise? Consider an Amalfi Coast hike (see "Hikes," page 681). Numerous trails connect the main towns along the coast with villages on the hills. Get a good map and/or book before you venture out.

The Amalfi Coast by Bus

From Sorrento: Blue or green-and-white SITA buses depart from Sorrento's train station nearly hourly (in peak season, 20/day) and stop at all Amalfi Coast towns (Positano in 40 min, €1.30; Amalfi in another 50 min, €2.40, tickets valid for 2 hrs), ending up in Salerno at the far end of the coast in just under three hours (one easy transfer in Amalfi; return trips might also transfer in Positano). Buses start running as early as 6:30 and run as late as 20:00 (22:00 in summer). Buy tickets at the tobacco shop nearest any bus stop before boarding. (There's a *tabacchi*/newsstand at street level in the Sorrento station.) Line up under the "Riservato SITA" sign (where a schedule is posted on the wall) in front of the station (10 steps down). Carefully note the lettered codes (explained in English at the bottom) that differentiate daily buses from weekend-only buses. Leaving Sorrento, grab a seat on the right for the best views. Returning, it's fun to sit directly behind the driver for a box seat over the twisting hairpin action.

Avoiding Crowds on the Bus: Buses are routinely unable to handle the demand during summer months and holidays. Occasionally, an extra bus is added to handle the overflow. Generally, if you don't get on, you're well-positioned to catch the

Getting Around the Amalfi Coast

NOT TO SCALE

NAPLES
VESUVIUS
PROCIDA
HERCULANEUM
POMPEII
RAVELLO
AMALFI
SALERNO
ISCHIA
SORRENTO
6·35m·€4
PAESTUM
8·30m·€9
POSITANO
3.50m·€10.50
CAPRI
3·40m·€15
4·60m·€14

7·40m·€7.5
20·40m·€12
15·20m·€10.50

N

‡‡‡ RAIL
--- BUSES
••• BOATS
···· SEASONAL BOATS (GENERALLY MAY THROUGH SEPT.)
BOAT CODE:
    1ST NUMBER – DEPARTURES PER DAY
    2ND NUMBER – LENGTH OF TRIP IN MINUTES
    3RD NUMBER – COST (ONE-WAY) IN EUROS
NOTE: SLIGHTLY SLOWER/CHEAPER BOATS EXIST
    IN SOME CASES. ASK & CONFIRM LOCALLY.

DCH

next bus (bring a book). In the morning, arrive early (buses start running as early as 6:30 and depart about every 30 min, crowds make departures from 9:00–11:00 very frustrating). Count the line: buses pull in empty and seat 48 (plus 25 standing).

Returning to Sorrento: The congestion can be so bad in the summer, during July and August in particular, that return buses don't even stop in Positano (they were filled in Amalfi). Those trying to get back to Sorrento are stuck with taking an extortionist taxi (except for Carmello Monetti—the local cabbie recommended below) or, if in Positano, hopping a boat if they're running. If touring the coast by bus, do Positano first and come home from Amalfi to avoid the problem of packed buses.

The Amalfi Coast by Boat

There are several competing companies who often claim to know nothing about their rivals' services. It's wise any time of year to check posted schedules, pick up ferry schedules from the TI, and confirm times to figure out the best plan. The boats servicing

Sorrento, Positano, and Amalfi start operating on weekends after Easter, then run daily from mid-June through mid-October (4/day in peak season, 45 min, €6, buy ticket on dock, pick up schedule at TI, www.metrodelmare.com). No boats run off-season.

From Salerno, ferries run from June through September from Piazza Concordia to Amalfi (6/day, 35 min, €4) and Positano (6/day, 70 min, €6, tickets and info at TravelMar, Piazza Concordia, tel. 089-872-950). Salerno's dock is conveniently located at the Amalfi Coast bus stop.

The Amalfi Coast by Taxi

Given the hairy driving, impossible parking, congested buses, and potential fun, you might consider splurging to hire your own car and driver for the Amalfi day. (Don't bother for Pompeii, as the Circumvesuviana serves it so conveniently and only licensed guides can take you into the site.)

Fun-loving **Carmello Monetti** (a jolly, singing, in-love-with-life, grandfatherly type who speaks "inventive English"), his son Raffaele (much better English, fewer smiles, more information) and cousin Tony (similar to Raffaele) have long taken excellent care of my readers' transportation needs from Sorrento.

Sample trips and rates for their taxi: Amalfi Coast Day (Positano-Amalfi-lunch in Ravello), seven hours, €180; Amalfi Coast and Paestum, 10 hours, €250; transfer to Naples airport or train station, one hour, €90. To get these special prices, promised for up to four people through 2006, mention this book.

The Monettis can take six passengers—at a higher rate schedule—in their air-conditioned minivan. Payment is cash only (Raffaele's mobile 335-602-9158, Carmello's mobile 338-946-2860, "office" run by Raffaele's English-speaking wife, Susanna: fax 081-878-4795, www.monettitaxi17.it, monettitaxi17@libero.it). Their reservation system is simple, easygoing, and reliable.

Be careful: Many cabbies claim to be the Monettis. The Monettis drive Mercedes station wagon taxi #17, usually found at Sorrento's Piazza Tasso. Couples wanting to reduce their costs can tell Susanna they're open to sharing (but be sure to agree on your itinerary with the other party first), allowing her to try to fill the minivan or put two couples in the car. Carmello's specialty is helping Italo-Americans find their families in southern Italy. E-mail him in advance if you want to find your long-lost relatives, and he can put together a meeting and transportation package. If in any kind of a jam, call Raffaele's mobile phone for information.

Umberto and Giovanni Benvenuto offer transport and narrated excursions throughout the Amalfi Coast as well as to Rome, Naples, Pompeii, and more. They are more up-market and formal, with rates explained on their Web site (Via Roma 54, tel.

334-307-8342, mobile 330-353-294, www.benvenutolimos.com, info @benvenutolimos.com).

Rides Only: If you're hiring a cabbie off the street for a ride and not a tour, here are sample fares from Sorrento to Positano: up to four people one-way for around €55 in a car, or up to six people for €75 in a minibus. Figure on paying 50 percent more to Amalfi. While taxis must use a meter within a city, a fixed rate is OK otherwise. Negotiate—ask about a round-trip.

SELF-GUIDED TOUR

Hugging the Amalfi Coast

The trip from Sorrento to Salerno is one of the all-time great white-knuckle rides. Gasp from the right side of the bus as you go out and from the left as you return to Sorrento. (Those on the wrong side really miss out.) Traffic is so heavy that private tour buses are only allowed to go in one direction (eastbound from Sorrento)—summer traffic is infuriating. Policemen are actually posted at tough bends at peak hours to help fold in side-view mirrors.

Here's a loosely guided tour of what you're seeing, from west to east:

Leaving Sorrento, the road winds up into the hills past lemon groves and hidden houses. Traveling the coast, you'll see several Saracen (Turkish pirate) watchtowers. The gray-green trees are olives. Dark, green-leafed trees planted in dense groves are lemon—many destined to become *limoncello.*

Atop the ridge outside of Sorrento, look to your right: the two small islands after Sorrento are the **Galli Islands;** the bigger one (on the left) is Ulysses Island (see page 648 for the ancient connection). These islands, once owned by the famed ballet dancer Rudolf Nureyev, mark the boundary between the Bay of Naples and the Bay of Salerno. Technically, the Amalfi Coast drive begins here.

The limestone cliffs, plunging into the sea, were traversed by an ancient trail that became a modern road in the mid-19th century. Fruit stands sell produce from farms and orchards just over the hill. Limestone absorbs the heat, making this south-facing coastline a suntrap, with temperatures as much as 10 degrees higher than in nearby Sorrento. Bougainvillea and geraniums grow like weeds in the summer.

Just south of Positano, **St. Peter's Hotel** (camouflaged below the tiny St. Peter's church) is about the most posh stop on the coast. Notice the elevator to the beach and dock. Bring your credit card.

Praiano has sparse accommodations (try Hotel Holiday, Db-€70–85, Via Umberto I 105, tel. 089-874-041 or 089-874-169, www.holidayamalficoast.it). It's notable for its cathedral, with the characteristic majolica-tiled roof and dome—a reminder of this region's

Amalfi Coast

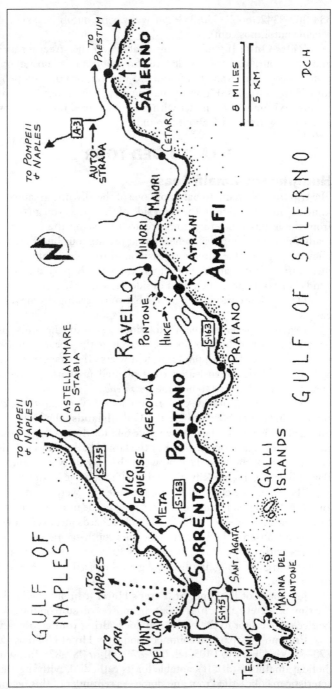

respected ceramics industry. Just past the tunnel stands a Saracen watchtower.

Marina di Praiano is a tiny and unique fishing hamlet wedged into a tight ravine with a couple of good restaurants, and a small hotel.

The next Saracen tower guarded the harbor of the Amalfi navy until it was destroyed by a tidal wave in 1343.

The most dramatic dance of man and nature here ends at **Amalfi** and **Atrani** (both described below). As you leave Amalfi, look up to the left. The white house that clings to a cliff (Villa Rondinaia) was home for many years to the writer Gore Vidal. Atop the cliff is the town of **Ravello** (see below). From here, the western half of the Amalfi Coast is mostly wild and unpopulated until you hit Salerno.

Positano

According to legend, the Greek god Poseidon created Positano for Pasitea, a nymph he lusted after. History says the town was founded when ancient Greeks at Paestum decided to move out of the swamp (and escape malaria). Specializing in scenery and sand, Positano hangs halfway between Sorrento and Amalfi town on the most spectacular stretch of the coast.

The village, a ▲▲▲ sight from a distance, is a pleasant gathering of cafés and expensive women's clothing stores, with a good but pebbly beach. Positano is famous for its fashions—90 percent of its shops are fashion boutiques.

Squished into a ravine, with narrow alleys that cascade down to the harbor, Positano requires you to stroll whether you're going up or heading down. The center of town has no main square (unless you count the beach). There's little to do here but eat, window-shop, and enjoy the beach and views (hence the town's popularity).

Consider seeing Positano as a day trip from Sorrento: take the bus out and the afternoon ferry home, but be sure to check the boat schedules when you arrive—the last ferry often leaves before 18:00.

The "skyline" looks like it did a century ago. Notice the town's characteristic Saracen-inspired rooftop domes. Filled with sand, these provide insulation—cool in summer and hot in winter. It's been practically impossible to get a building permit in Positano for 25 years now, and those making renovations can make no external changes. The steep stairs are a way of life for the 4,000 hardy locals. Only one street in Positano allows motorized traffic—the rest are steep pedestrian lanes. Because hotels don't take large groups (bus access is too difficult), the town—unlike Sorrento—has been

Positano

P – PARKING
— ROADS FOR CARS
-- PEDESTRIAN
   STREETS

1. Hotel Marincanto
2. Albergo California
3. Residence la Tavolozza
4. Hotel Savoia
5. Villa Maria Antonietta
6. Hotel Bougainville
7. Brikette Hostel
8. Bar Mulino Verde

spared the ravages of big-bus tourism.

Spend the night to enjoy the magic of Positano. The town has a local flavor at night, when the grown-ups stroll and the kids play soccer on the church porch.

ORIENTATION

Tourist Information

The TI is a half-block from the beach, in a small building at the bottom of the church steps (April–Sept Mon–Sat 8:00–20:00, Sun 8:00–13:00, shorter hours Oct–March, tel. 089-875-067).

Arrival in Positano

The main coast highway winds above the town. Regional SITA buses (blue or green-and-white) stop at two scheduled bus stops located at either end of town: Chiesa (at Bar Internazionale, nearer Sorrento) and Sponda (nearer Amalfi town). From either stop, roads lead downhill through the town to the beach. To minimize your descent, use the Sponda stop (the second Positano stop, if you're coming from Sorrento). It's a 20-minute stroll/shop/munch from here to the beach (and TI).

If you're catching the SITA bus back to Sorrento, remember that it may leave from the Sponda stop five minutes before the printed departure. There's no room for the bus to wait, so in case the driver is early, you should be, too (€1.30, departures about hourly, daily 7:00–20:00, buy tickets from Bar Mulino Verde or Positour Agency—both are on Via Colombo, about 300 yards below the stop). If the walk up to the stop is too tough, take the dizzy little local orange bus (marked *Interno Positano*), which constantly loops through Positano, connecting the lower town with the highway's two bus stops (€1, 2/hr, buy tickets on board, convenient stop at the corner of Via Colombo and Via dei Mulini heads up to Sponda). Bar Mulino Verde (as close as cars, taxis, and the shuttle bus can get to the beach) is located just across from the stop for the little orange bus, with a fine, breezy terrace you can enjoy if you're waiting.

Drivers must go with the one-way flow, entering the town only at the Chiesa bus stop (closest to Sorrento) and exiting at Sponda. Driving is a headache here.

ACTIVITIES

Beach—Positano's pebbly and sandy primary beach (Spiaggia Grande), colorful with umbrellas and stretching wide around the cove, is mostly private (€10–15/person, April–Oct, cost includes use of sun beds and umbrellas, free section on the west end, near where the boats take off). The nearest WC is behind the waterfront Bucca di Bacco bar.

Boat Trips—At the west side of the beach (as you face the sea), you'll see a series of booths selling boat tickets. Some little boats make the three-minute journey to Fornillo Beach—a quieter beach just around the bend. The ride is free if you agree to eat at a certain restaurant, or rent a beach lounge and umbrella (usually cheaper than at Spiaggia Grande); otherwise, they'll rip you off, charging €5 for the boat ride. Fornillo, which is smaller and less wild, is an easy 10-min walk from Spiaggia Grande (take trail near ticket booths).

Consider renting a rowboat or taking various boat tours to a nearby cave (La Grotta dello Smeraldo—Emerald Cave), fishing village (Nerano), or small islands. Of course, there are also trips to the bigger Amalfi Coast destinations—see "Transportation Connections," below.

SLEEPING

These hotels (but not the hostel) are all on Via Colombo, which leads from the Sponda SITA bus stop down into the village. Prices given are for the highest season (June-Sept)—at other times, they should be at least €10 less per day.

$$$ Hotel Marincanto is a newly restored four-star hotel with a bright terrace practically teetering on a cliff (Db-€200, superior seaview Db-€230, suites with seaview balconies-€270–375, private stairs to beach, large sundeck, 50 yards below the Sponda bus stop at Via Colombo 50, tel. 089-875-130, fax 089-875-595, www.marincanto.it, info@marincanto.it).

$$ Hotel Savoia is family run and rents 39 sizeable, breezy, bright, air-conditioned rooms (viewless Db-€130, Db with view-€190, deluxe Db-€210, at least €10/day off with this 2006 book, Via Colombo 73, tel. 089-875-003, fax 089-811-844, www.savoiapositano.it, info@savoiapositano.it).

$$ Albergo California has lofty views, spacious rooms (15 of 20 with sea views), and a grand terrace draped with vines (Db-€130, windowless Db-€100, prices promised with this book through 2006, air-con, free parking, Via Colombo 141, tel. 089-875-382, fax 089-812-154, www.hotelcaliforniapositano.it, info@hotelcaliforniapositano.it, Maria and Antonio).

$$ Hotel Bougainville rents 14 basic rooms (viewless Db-€95, Db with sea view-€130, breakfast included only with this book through 2006, air-con, some traffic noise and fumes, Via Colombo 25, tel. & fax 089-875-047, www.bougainville.it, hotel@bougainville.it, Carlo, Luisa, and sons).

$ Residence la Tavolozza is an attractive eight-room hotel, warmly run by Celeste (cheh-LEHS-tay), her sisters, and daughter. Flawlessly restored, each room comes with a view, a balcony, fine

Sleep Code

(€1 = about $1.20, country code: 39)
S = Single, **D** = Double/Twin, **T** = Triple, **Q** = Quad, **b** = bathroom, **s** = shower only. Unless otherwise noted, credit cards are accepted, English is spoken, and breakfast is included.

To help you sort easily through these listings, I've divided the rooms into three categories based on the price for a standard double room with bath:

$$$ **Higher Priced**—Most rooms €150 or more.
$$ **Moderately Priced**—Most rooms between €100–150.
$ **Lower Priced**—Most rooms €100 or less.

tile, and silence (Db-€85 promised through 2006 with this book, families can ask for "Royal Apartment," cash only, holds room until 16:00 with phone call—don't be a no-show, lavish breakfast extra, air-con, Via Colombo 10, tel. & fax 089-875-040, celeste .dileva@tiscali.it, a little English spoken).

$ **Villa Maria Antonietta** is a humble family place with seven decent rooms, all with a view of the back alley and the ocean beyond. Head down a grungy lane off the elegant main drag and then up a few big flights of stairs (Db-€80, cash only; follow signs from Via Colombo 41, it's behind Albergo Savoia; tel. 089-875-071, Maria).

$ **Brikette Hostel** offers your best cheap, dorm-bed option in this otherwise ritzy town. Renting 65 beds and offering a great sun and breakfast terrace, it's bright and clean with the normal hostel rules: 11:00–14:30 lockout, cushy midnight curfew, and checkout by 10:00 (dorm bed-€22, Db-€75, includes breakfast, closed Nov-March, Via G. Marconi 358, leave bus at Chiesa/Bar Internazionale stop and backtrack uphill 500 feet, tel. & fax 089-875-857, www .brikette.com, info@brikette.com, Cristiana is full of energy). She also rents four hotel-style rooms on top (D-€65, one big suite Db-€90, family deals).

EATING

The pizzerias and restaurants facing the beach, while overpriced, are pleasant and convenient. At the waterfront, I like **Cambuso,** but the neighboring places also leave people fat and happy.

If a picnic dinner on your balcony or the beach sounds good, sunny Emilia at **Delikatessen** can supply the ingredients (*antipasto misto* to go at €1.60/100 grams, sandwiches made and sold by weight; March–Oct Mon–Sat 7:00–22:00, Sun 7:00–20:00; Nov–Feb daily 7:00–20:00, just below car park at Via del Mulini 5, tel. 089-875-489). **Vini e Panini,** another small grocery, is a block from the beach a few steps above the TI (Mon–Sat 8:00–14:00 & 16:30–21:30, Sun 8:00–14:00, tel. 089-875-175, just off church steps).

TRANSPORTATION CONNECTIONS

Always check boat schedules, since the last boats often leave Positano before 18:00. The schedule varies drastically according to time of year—be sure to check it with the TI.

From Positano by Boat to: **Amalfi** (8/day, 30 min, March–Oct only, €9), **Capri** (3/day total, 40 min on fast boat, €15; 50 min by slow boat, €12.50, mid-May-Sept only), **Sorrento** (3/day daily mid-May–mid-Oct only, otherwise only weekends, 50 min for €10; 90 min for €7.50). Direct boats to **Naples** are unlikely, but check with the TI; you can also change boats in Sorrento.

Amalfi Town

The Amalfi Coast is named for this town. It was founded (according to legend) when the girlfriend of Hercules was buried here. After Rome fell, Amalfi was one of the first cities to trade goods—coffee, carpets, and paper—between Europe and points East. Its heyday was the 10th and 11th centuries, when it was a powerful maritime republic—a trading power with a fleet that controlled this region and rivaled Genoa and Venice. The Republic of Amalfi founded a hospital in Jerusalem and claims to have founded the Knights of Malta order—even giving them the Amalfi cross, which became the famous Maltese cross. Amalfi minted its own coins and established "rules of the sea"—the basics of which survive today. Paper has been a vital industry here since the glory days in the Middle Ages. They'd pound rags into pulp in a big vat, pull it up using a screen, and air-dry it to create paper (the same technique used to make paper still sold in Amalfi shops). For a demonstration of this ancient technique, check out the Paper Museum (see below).

In 1343, this little powerhouse was destroyed by a freak tidal wave caused by an undersea earthquake. That disaster, compounded by devastating plagues, left Amalfi a humble backwater. Today, its 7,000 residents live off tourism (and paper).

ORIENTATION

The waterfront of this most famous of the Amalfi Coast villages is dominated by a bus station, a parking lot, two gas stations, a statue of local boy Flavio Gioia—the inventor of the compass (see sidebar)—and a TI.

Amalfi, the most big-bus accessible of the towns along the coast, is a classic tourist trap. It's packed during the day with big bus tours (whose drivers pay €50 an hour to park while their groups shop for *limoncello* and ceramics).

Before you enter the town, notice the colorful tile above the Porta della Marina gateway, showing off the domain of the maritime Republic of Amalfi. Just to the left, along the busy road, are a series of arches that indicate the long, narrow, vaulted halls of its arsenal—where ships were built in the 11th century.

Venture into the town, and you find its once rich and formidable medieval shell is filled with trendy shops, a main square sporting a springwater-spewing statue of St. Andrew, and a cathedral—the town's most important sight.

The further you get away from the water, the more local Amalfi gets. The Paper Museum is 10-minute walk up Via Lorenzo d'Amalfi, the main drag. From here, the road narrows and you can

---

Flavio Gioia

You'll see a statue of Flavio Gioia towering above the chaos of cars and buses on the seaside piazza. Amalfi residents credit this hometown boy with the invention of the magnetic compass back in 1302, but historians can't verify he actually existed. While an improvement to the compass did occur in Amalfi during that time period, the Chinese and Arabs had been using rudimentary compasses for years. In Gioia's time, seamen used a needle bobbing around in water as a kind of medieval GPS. If Gioia existed at all, he probably just figured out how to secure that needle inside a little box.

Locals, however, have no doubts that Flavio Gioia is an inventor extraordinaire.

---

turn off onto a path leading to the shaded Valle dei Mulini; it's full of paper-mill ruins that recall this once proud and prosperous industry. The ruined castle clinging to the rocky ridge above Amalfi is Torre dello Ziro, a good lookout point for intrepid hikers (see below). Amalfi is not as picturesque as Positano or as well-connected as Sorrento, but take some time to explore the town. Amalfi's charms will reveal themselves, especially early and late in the day when tourist crowds dissipate.

Tourist Information

The TI is on Corso della Repubbliche Marinare 27 (Mon–Fri 8:30–13:30 & 15:00–17:00, maybe until 20:00 June–Aug, Sat 8:30–13:00, closed Sun, tel. 089-871-107, www.azienturismoamalfi.com). It's a five-minute walk from the waterfront, and a two-minute walk from the main square. Facing the church on the main square, take a right. Head towards the water, take the first left, and look to the left for a courtyard; you'll see the post office and the TI.

Helpful Hints

Internet Access: L'Altra Costiera, on the main drag, looks more like a travel agency but has Internet service (daily 9:00–21:00, Via Lorenzo d'Amalfi 34, tel. 089-873-6082). Or try Lo Scrigno Internet Point Full System, just off Piazza dei Dogi (tel. 089-873-6339).

Laundry: The full-service laundry offers same-day service (Mon–Sat 8:00–13:00 & 15:30–20:30, closed Sun, drop off before 10:00 and pick up same day after 19:00). It's a one-minute walk west from main square. Across from the cathedral steps, walk through the set-back archway with a sign for *Piazza dei Dogi*. In this little piazza, the laundry is in the far left corner.

Hiking Guidebook: The best book on hiking is *Sorrento Amalfi Capri Car Tours and Walks*, on sale at many local bookstores. It has useful, color-coded maps and info on public transportation to the trailheads.

SIGHTS

Cathedral—This church is "Amalfi Romanesque" (a mix of Moorish and Byzantine flavor, built c. 1000–1300) with a fanciful neo-Byzantine facade from the 19th century. The 1,000-year-old bronze door was given to Amalfi by a wealthy local merchant who had it made in Constantinople. Climb the imposing stairway—which functions as a handy outdoor theater for town events—and go inside (€2.50, daily in summer 9:00–19:00, winter 10:00–17:00, closed Jan–Feb, pick up English flier, tel. 089-871-324).

Visitors are directed on a one-way circuit through the cathedral complex with these four stops:

"Cloister of Paradise": This courtyard of 120 graceful columns was the cemetery of the nobles (note their stone sarcophagi). Don't miss the fine view of the bell tower and its majolica tiles.

Basilica of the Crucifix: The original ninth-century church is now a museum filled with the art treasures of the cathedral. The Angevin Mitre, with a "pavement of tiny pearls" setting off its gold and gems, has been worn by bishops since the 14th century. On the far wall is a plank from a Saracen pirate ship that wrecked just outside of town in 1544 during another freak storm. This storm was caused by a saint, rather than an earthquake—and saved the town, rather than destroyed it. The plank still reminds locals how St. Andrew (see below) rescued the town from certain Turkish pillage and plunder.

Crypt of St. Andrew: Like Venice needed Mark to get on the pilgrimage map, Amalfi got St. Andrew—one of the apostles who left his nets to become the original "fishers of men." What are believed to be his remains (under the huge bronze statue) were brought here from Constantinople in 1206 during the Crusades—an indication of the wealth and importance of Amalfi back then.

Cathedral: The interior is notable for its fine 13th-century wooden crucifix. The painting behind it shows St. Andrew martyred on an X-shaped cross flanked by two Egyptian granite columns supporting a triumphal arch. Before leaving, check out the delicate mother-of-pearl crucifix (right of door in back).

▲**Paper Museum**—At this cavernous, cool 13th-century paper mill-turned-museum, a multilingual guide collects groups at the entrance (no particular times) for a 45-minute tour recounting the history and process of paper making, a long-time industry for the town of Amalfi (€3.50, March–Oct daily 10:00–18:30, sporadic hours Nov–Feb, a 10-min walk up the main street from the cathedral, tel. 089-830-4561, www.museodellacarta.it).

ACTIVITIES

Hikes—Amalfi is the starting point for several fine hikes (see hiking guidebook listed under "Helpful Hints," above). Here are two:
Hike #1: This loop trail leads up the valley past paper-mill ruins, ending in the small town of **Pontone**; you can get lunch there, and head back down to the town of Amalfi (allow 3 hours total). Bring a good map, since it's easy to veer off the main route. Start your hike by following the main road (Via Lorenzo d'Amalfi) away from the sea.

After the Paper Museum, jog right, then left to join the trail, leading through the shaded woods along a babbling stream. Heed the signs to stay away from the ruins of paper mills (no matter how tempting), since many are ready to collapse on unwary hikers. Continue up to the tiny town of Pontone, where Trattoria l'Antico Borgo offers wonderful cuisine and a great view (Via Noce 4, tel. 089-871-469). After lunch, return to Amalfi via a steep stairway.

If you're feeling ambitious, before you head back to Amalfi, add a one-hour detour (30 min each way) to visit the ridge-hugging **Torre dello Ziro** (ask a local how to find the trail to this tower). You'll be rewarded with a spectacular view.

Hike #2: For an easier hike—more of a stroll—head to the nearby town of **Atrani**. This village, just a 15-minute stroll beyond Amalfi town, is a world apart; its 1,500 residents consider themselves definitely *not* from Amalfi. Leave Amalfi via the main road, and stay on the water side until the sidewalk ends. Cross the street and head up the stairs; the paved route takes you over the hill, and drops you into Atrani in about 15 minutes. Piazza Umberto is the core of town, with cafés and a little grocery store (that makes sandwiches). Amazingly, Atrani has none of the trendy resort feel of Amalfi, with relatively few tourists, a delightful town square, and a free, sandy beach.

From Atrani, you can continue up to **Ravello** (see below). But be warned, unless you're part mountain goat, you'll probably prefer catching the bus to Ravello from the town of Amalfi instead.

SLEEPING

(€1 = about $1.20, country code: 39)
Sleeps are better in Positano, but if you're marooned in Amalfi, here are some options. High season on the Amalfi Coast (July–Aug) demands the highest prices; prices listed here are peak-season rates.

$$ Hotel Amalfi, with 40 rooms and a garden, is a fine choice (Db-€75–135, extra for air-con, roof-terrace breakfast, no sea views, 50 yards from cathedral, head up the pedestrian street and take staircase to the left before underpass, Via dei Pastai 3, tel. 089-872-440, fax 089-872-250, www.hamalfi.it, hamalfi@starnet.it).

$$ Residenze del Duca is a little five-room boutique B&B taking advantage of its wonderful location in the heart of this touristy enclave (Db-€100–160, free Internet in lobby, air-con, glimpses of ocean through the rooftops; up a lot of stairs just 25 yards uphill from Piazza Duomo, take a left at Via Mastalo II Duca 3; tel. 089-873-6365, www.residencedelduca.it, info@residencedelduca.it).

$$ Hotel Bussola, a five-minute walk north along the harbor, rises above the ocean with its 60 swanky, sunny rooms, most boasting terraces with a breezy ocean view (Db-€124, extra for air-con, Lungomare dei Cavalieri, 16, 089-871-533, www.labussolahotel.it, info@labussolahotel.it).

In Atrani: **$ A'Scalinatella** is an informal backpackers' hostel, with a honeycomb of cramped two- to six-bed dorms, way-over-priced private rooms, and communal kitchen. It's a small-town Amalfi hideaway, without the glitz and hill-climbing of Positano. The English-speaking owners, Filippo and Gabriele, rent the only beds in town (€21 per bed in 4- to 6- bed rooms, D-€60, Db-€90, prices very soft, includes breakfast, cash only, no membership required, 100 yards up from main square at Scalinatella Piazza Umberto I #5, tel. 089-871-492, www.hostelscalinatella .com, scalinatella@amalficoast.it).

Ravello

Ravello sits atop a lofty perch 1,000 feet above the sea, and offers an interesting church, two villas, and a chance to catch a glimpse of celebrities such as American author Gore Vidal. He is one of a sizable group of rich and famous artists—including Richard Wagner, D. H. Lawrence, William Longfellow, and Greta Garbo—who have succumbed to Ravello's charms.

To see the sights listed below, start at the bus stop and walk through the tunnel to the main square, where you'll find the church on the right, Villa Rufolo on the left, and the **TI** (pick up the color-coded trail map called *Passeggiata/Walks,* tel 089-857-096). A 10-minute walk through the town (follow the signs) leads to Villa Cimbrone.

SIGHTS AND ACTIVITIES

Duomo—You can't miss Ravello's cathedral, located right on the main square. The two main features of this church are the bronze doors, with 54 scenes of the life of Christ, and the carved marble pulpit supported by six lions. The geometric designs show Arabic influence.

Villa Rufolo—The villa, built in the 13th century, has pleasant Arabic/Norman gardens. During the concert season (March-Oct), locals build a bandstand to perch on the edge of the cliff, giving concert attendees the combination of wonderful music and a dizzying view. Wagner visited here and was impressed enough to set the second act of his opera *Parsifal* in the villa's magical gardens. A concert on the cliff is a sublime experience (villa entry-€4, daily June–Sept 9:00–20:00, Oct–May 9:00–18:00, tel. 089-858-149, www .ravelloarts.org).

Villa Cimbrone—This villa, located at the other end of Ravello, was built in the 20th century by Englishman William Bechett. It offers extensive gardens and a killer film-devouring view from the "Terrace of Infinity." Consider buying a picnic in town and munching it here discreetly with magnificent Italian panoramas at your feet. A wander through the gardens will reveal reproductions of famous sculptures and lots of great views (€4, daily 9:00–sunset).

Hike to Amalfi Town from Villa Cimbrone—To walk downhill from Ravello's Villa Cimbrone to the town of Amalfi (a path for hardy hikers only), retrace your steps back toward town. Take the first left that turns into a stepped path winding its way below the cliff. Pause here to look back up at the rock with a big white mansion—Villa La Rondinaia, where Gore Vidal lived for many years. Continue down the fairly steep path about 40 minutes to the town of Atrani, where several bars on the main square offer well-deserved refreshment. From here, it's about 15 minutes to walk back to Amalfi (see the hike section on Atrani, above, under "Hikes").

TRANSPORTATION CONNECTIONS

Ravello and the town of Amalfi are connected by a winding road and a bus. Coming from Amalfi town, buy your ticket at the bar on the waterfront, and ask where the bus stop is; buses usually stop to the left as you face the water, near the statue of Flavio Gioia on the waterfront Piazza Flavio Gioia. Line up early, since the buses are often crowded.

Paestum

Paestum (PASTE-oom) has one of the best collections of Greek temples anywhere—and certainly the most accessible to Western Europe. Serenely situated, it's surrounded by fields and wildflowers, and has only a modest commercial strip.

This town was founded as Poseidonia by Greeks in the sixth century B.C. and became a key stop on an important trade route. In the fifth century B.C., the Lucans, a barbarous inland tribe, conquered Poseidonia, changed its name to Paistom, and tried to adopt the cultured ways of the Greeks. The Romans, who took over in the third century B.C., gave Paestum the name it bears today. The final conquerors of Paestum, malaria-carrying mosquitoes, kept the site wonderfully deserted for nearly a thousand years. Rediscovered in the 18th century, Paestum today offers the only well-preserved Greek ruins north of Sicily.

ORIENTATION

Tourist Information: At the TI, next to Paestum's museum, pick up a free map and info booklet of the site (July–Aug Mon–Sat 9:00–19:00, Sun 9:00–13:00, hours may vary, tel. 082-881-1016, info@infopaestum.it). If you ask politely, you might be able to store luggage at the TI, site, or museum.

Arrival at Paestum: Buses from Salerno (see "Transportation Connections," below) stop near a corner of the ruins (at a little bar/café). Arriving by train, exit the station and walk through the old city gate; the ruins are an eight-minute walk straight ahead.

Cost, Hours, Information: €4 for the museum, €4 for the site, €6.50 for a combo-ticket. The site is free (or 50 percent off) with the Campania ArteCard (see page 613).

Both the museum and site open daily at 9:00 (except the 1st and 3rd Mon of each month, when museum is closed though the site is open). Year-round, the museum closes at 19:00 (last ticket sold at 18:30). The site closes one hour before sunset (as late as 19:30 June–Aug, as early as 15:45 in Dec, last ticket sold 1 hr before closing). Several mediocre guidebooks are offered at the museum's bookshop, including a €13 past-and-present guide. Dull €4 audioguides are available to rent at the museum entrance and sometimes at the site entrance and cover both (ID required). The site and museum have separate entrances. The museum, just outside the ruins, is in a cluster with the TI and a small paleo-Christian basilica.

Planning Your Time: Allow two hours, including the museum. Depending on your interest and the heat of the day, start with either the museum or the site.

Paestum

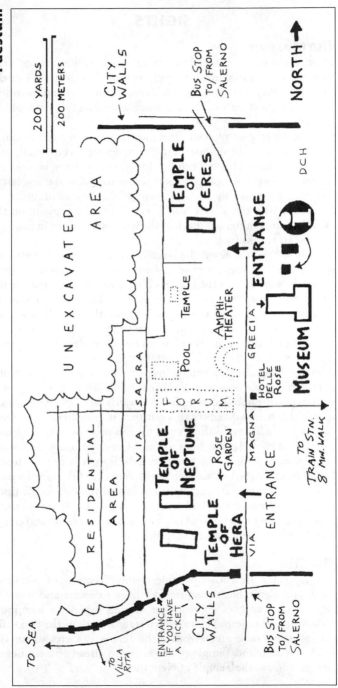

SIGHTS

The Museum

Paestum's museum offers you the rare opportunity to see artifacts—dating from prehistoric to Greek to Roman times—at the site where they were discovered. These beautifully crafted works help bring Paestum to life. There are good English descriptions throughout.

The large ground floor (the most impressive part) contains Greek artifacts. The upstairs, after remodeling is completed, may still contain the prehistory exhibits (displays of pottery, blades, and arrowheads) as well as the Roman Room (contains statues, busts, and inscriptions dating from the time of the Roman occupation). No matter where you start, you'll feel like you've come in on the middle of something, but much of the work is described in English, and the art speaks for itself.

On the ground floor, the large carvings overhead—wrapping around the first room you see as you enter the museum—once adorned a sanctuary of the goddess Hera (wife of Zeus) outside the city. Some of the carvings show scenes from the life of Hercules. In the various ground-floor rooms, you'll see startlingly well-preserved Greek vases, crumbling armor, and paintings.

The highlight of the museum is a rare example of Greek painting, known as the *Diver's Tomb* (480 B.C.). These slabs—showing a diver and four scenes of banqueting—originally were the sides of a tomb. The simple painting of a diver arcing down into a pool was the top of the tomb (painting faced inward). Though the deceased might have been a diver, it's thought the art more likely represents our dive from life to death. It's rare to see a real Greek statue (most are Roman copies), even rarer to see a Greek painting. The many other painted slabs in the museum date from a later time under Lucan rule. The barbarous people who conquered the Greeks tried to appropriate their art and style, but lacked the Greeks' distinct, light touch. Regardless, the Lucan paintings, as well as the crisply drawn pictures on dozens of Greek vases, are instructive and enjoyable. Consider them ancient snapshots.

The Site

The key ruins are the impossible-to-miss Temples of Neptune, Hera, and Ceres, but the scattered village ruins are also interesting. Lonely Ceres, in an evocative setting, is about a 10-minute walk from Neptune and Hera, which stand together. The two main entrances to the site are in front of the Temple of Ceres and on the south side near the Temple of Hera. If you already have a ticket, you can enter at the Temple of Neptune.

The Temple of Neptune is simply overwhelming. Constructed in 450 B.C., it's a textbook example of the Doric style. Archaeologists are not sure which deity the misnamed temple was dedicated to, but Apollo, Zeus, and Hera are the top contenders. Better preserved than the Parthenon in Athens, this huge structure is a tribute to Greek engineering and aesthetics. Contemplate the word "renaissance"—the rebirth of this grand Greek style of architecture. Notice how the columns angle out and the base bows up (scan the short ends of the temple). This was a trick ancient architects used to create the illusion of a perfectly straight building. All important Greek buildings were built using this technique. Now imagine it richly and colorfully decorated with marble and statues.

Adjacent to the Temple of Neptune is the almost-delicate Temple of Hera, dedicated to the Greek goddess of marriage in 550 B.C.

SLEEPING

(€1 = about $1.20, country code: 39)
Paestum at night, with views of the floodlit ruins, is magic.

$ Hotel delle Rose, with 10 small, fine rooms and a respectable restaurant, is near the Neptune entrance, on the street bordering the ruins (Db-€60, includes breakfast, Via Magna Grecia 193, tel. 082-881-1070, www.hotelristorantedellerose.com, info @hotelristorantedellerose.com, no English spoken).

$ Agriturismo Seliano offers spacious, spotless rooms on a farm, a pool, and great cooking using produce from the garden (Db-€80 with breakfast, €125 July–Aug, run by an English-speaking baroness, serves a fine €15 lunch or dinner, air-con, near beach, 2 miles from ruins, best for drivers, tel. 082-872-4544, fax 082-872-3634, www.agriturismoseliano.it, seliano@agriturismoseliano.it).

$ Hotel Villa Rita is a tidy, quiet, country hotel set on two acres within walking distance of the beach and the temples, with 15 clean, air-conditioned rooms, a swimming pool, and free parking (Db-€75, 5-min walk west of Hera entrance, Via Principe di Piemonte—a.k.a. Via Nettuno—9; tel. 0828-811-081, fax 0828-722-555, www.hotelvillarita.it, info@hotelvillarita.it).

TRANSPORTATION CONNECTIONS

Salerno and Paestum
Salerno, the big city just north of Paestum, is the nearest transportation hub. From Naples or Sorrento, you'll change buses or trains in Salerno to get to Paestum. Salerno's **TI** has bus, ferry, and train schedules (Mon–Sat 9:00–14:00 & 15:30–20:00, closed Sun, shorter hours off-season, on Piazza Veneto, just outside train station, tel. 089-231-432, toll-free 800-213-289).

Salerno Connections

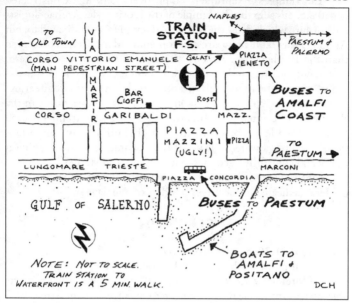

Salerno to Paestum by Bus: Four companies (CSTP, SCAT, Giuliano, and Lettieri) offer a Salerno–Paestum bus service, all conveniently leaving from the same stop at Piazza della Concordia on the waterfront (2–3/hr, 70 min, schedules extremely sparse on Sun). Buy the €3 round-trip ticket on the bus, except on CSTP buses (CSTP prefers you buy a ticket at their office, next to TI at Piazza Veneto/train station, but driver will grumpily sell you a ticket on bus if necessary). No clear schedule is posted at the Salerno stop. Simply ask a local or a bus rep at the stop for the next bus to Paestum; otherwise, get a schedule at the TI (more impartial, since they don't represent a particular company and their schedule shows all companies and times). Note that orange city buses use the same stop; ignore these.

When leaving Paestum, catch a northbound bus from either of the intersections that flank the ruins (see map on page 685). Flag down any bus, ask "Salerno?", and buy the ticket on board (except for CSTP buses—try to buy ticket at bar closest to stop).

Salerno to Paestum by Train: The train from Salerno to Paestum (hrly, 40 min, direction: Paola or Sapri) runs far less frequently than the buses, though it's a quicker ride because it's immune from traffic jams; check schedules at Salerno's TI or train station. Paestum's train station is an eight-minute walk from the ruins (from station, go through old city wall, ruins are straight ahead). If you plan to leave Paestum by train, buy your train ticket at the bar/café near the TI because the station is not staffed (train schedules at TI). Leaving Paestum, trains bound for Salerno (direction: Battipaglia) usually continue to Naples.

Naples to Salerno by Train: 3/hr, 60–90-min trip (don't board the extra-slow Diretto train; note that some trains stop at Pompeii).

Sorrento to Salerno by Bus: The scenic three-hour Amalfi Coast drive (blue SITA bus, 12/day, 3 hrs, easy transfer in Amalfi) drops you at the Salerno train station, where the TI is located, or you can get off earlier at the seaside Piazza della Concordia, if you want to catch the bus to Paestum.

If you plan to take a bus from Salerno to Sorrento (or points in between), the bus stop is directly in front of Salerno's train station exit, on the median strip under the *Fermata SITA* sign. Buy your bus ticket at the newsstand inside the train station and tell the vendor your destination (prices vary). If it's closed, try the ticket windows in the train station or walk two blocks to Bar Cioffi (CHOH-fee), across the square from Piazza della Concordia (see map on page 688). Ticket vendors change periodically; if Bar Cioffi no longer sells tickets, ask anyone or a clerk at a *tabacchi* shop, "Who sells bus tickets to _____?" by saying, "*Chi vende i biglietti dell'autobus per _____?*" (kee VEHN-dee ee beel-YET-tee del-OW-toh-boos pehr _____).

Sorrento to Salerno by Train: Ride the Circumvesuviana to Naples' Centrale station (2/hr, 70 min) and catch the Salerno train (2/hr, 45 min). Or ask about the tricky shortcut to Pompeii; specify you want to go to "Pompei Scavi" (or you may end up in the modern city of Pompeii).

Salerno to Amalfi Towns by Ferry to: Amalfi (6/day, 35 min, €4), **Positano** (6/day, 70 min, €6). Most ferries depart from Salerno's Piazza della Concordia, see map page 688 (tickets and info at TravelMar, Piazza della Concordia, tel. 089-872-950).

Drivers: While the Amalfi Coast is a thrill to drive off-season, summer traffic is miserable. From Sorrento, Paestum is 60 miles and three hours via the coast and a much smoother two hours by autostrada. To reach Paestum from Sorrento via the autostrada, drive toward Naples, catch the autostrada (direction: Salerno), skirt Salerno (direction: Reggio), exit at Battipaglia, and drive straight through the roundabout. During your ride, you'll see many signs for "*mozzarella di bufala,*" the cheese made from the milk of water buffalo that graze here. Try it here—it can't be any fresher.

ITALIAN HISTORY

Italy has a lot of history, so let's get started.

Origins

A she-wolf breastfed two human babies, Romulus and Remus, who grew to build the city of Rome in 753 B.C.—you buy that? Closer to fact, farmers and shepherds of the Latin tribe settled near the mouth of the Tiber River, a convenient trading location. The crude settlement was sandwiched between two sophisticated civilizations—Greek colonists to the south ("Magna Grecia," or greater Greece), and the Etruscans of Tuscany, whose origins and language are still a mystery to historians. Baby Rome was both dominated and nourished by these societies.

When an Etruscan king raped a Roman (509 B.C.), her husband led a revolt, driving out the Etruscan kings and replacing them with elected Roman senators and (eventually) a code of law ("Laws of the Twelve Tables," 450 B.C.). The Roman Republic was born.

The Roman Republic Expands (c. 500 B.C.–A.D. 1)

Located in the center of the peninsula, Rome was perfectly situated for trading salt and wine. Roman businessmen, backed by a disciplined army, expanded through the Italian peninsula, establishing a Roman infrastructure as they went. Rome soon swallowed up its northern Etruscan neighbors, conquering them by force and absorbing their culture.

Next came "Magna Grecia," with Rome's legions defeating the Greek general Pyrrhus after several costly, "Pyrrhic" victories (c. 275 B.C.). Rome now ruled a united federation stretching from Tuscany to the toe, with a standard currency, a system of roads (including the Via Appia), and a standing army of a half million soldiers ready for the next challenge—Carthage.

Carthage (modern-day Tunisia) and Rome fought the three bitter Punic Wars for control of the Mediterranean (264–201 B.C. and 146 B.C.). The balance of power hung precariously in the Second Punic War (218–201 B.C.), when Hannibal of Carthage crossed the sea to Spain with a huge army of men and elephants. He marched 1,200 miles overland, crossed the Alps, and forcefully penetrated Italy from the rear. Almost at the gates of the city of Rome, he was finally turned back. Rome prevailed and, in the mismatched Third Punic War, burned the city of Carthage to the ground (146 B.C.).

The well-tuned Roman legions easily subdued sophisticated Greece in three Macedonian Wars (215–146 B.C.). Though Rome conquered Greece, Greek culture dominated the Romans. From hairstyles to statues to temples to the evening's entertainment, Rome was forever "Hellenized," becoming the curators of Greek culture, passing it down to future generations.

By the first century B.C., Rome was master of the Mediterranean. Booty, cheap grain, and thousands of captured slaves poured in, turning the economy from small-farmers to unemployed city dwellers living off tribute from conquered lands. The Republic had changed.

Civil Wars and the Transition to Empire (1st Century B.C.)

With easy money streaming in and traditional roles obsolete, Romans bickered among themselves over their slice of the pie. Wealthy landowners (patricians, the ruling Senate) wrangled with the middle- and working classes (plebeians) and with the growing population of slaves, who demanded greater say-so in government. In 73 B.C., Spartacus—a Greek-born soldier-turned-Roman-slave who'd been forced to fight as a gladiator—escaped to the slopes of Mount Vesuvius, where he amassed an army of 70,000 angry slaves. After two years of fierce fighting across Italy, the Roman legions crushed the revolt and crucified 6,000 rebels along the Via Appia as a warning.

Amid the chaos of class war and civil war, charismatic generals who could provide wealth and security became dictators—men such as Sulla, Crassus, Pompey...and Caesar. Julius Caesar (100–44 B.C.) was a cunning politician, riveting speaker, conqueror of Gaul, author of *The Gallic Wars*, and lover of Cleopatra, Queen of Egypt. In his four-year reign, he reformed and centralized the government around himself. Disgruntled Republicans feared he would become a king. At his peak of power, they surrounded Caesar in the Senate on the "Ides of March" (March 15, 44 B.C.) and stabbed him to death.

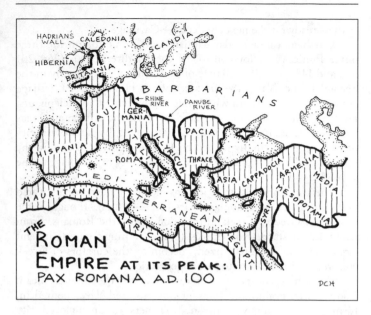

THE ROMAN EMPIRE AT ITS PEAK: PAX ROMANA A.D. 100

Julius Caesar died, but the concept of one-man rule lived on in his adopted son. Octavian defeated rival Mark Antony (another lover of Cleopatra, 31 B.C.) and was proclaimed Emperor Augustus (27 B.C.). Augustus outwardly followed the traditions of the Republic while in practice acting as a dictator with the backing of Rome's legions and the rubber-stamp approval of the Senate. He established his family to succeed him (making the family name "Caesar" a title), and set the pattern of rule by emperors for the next 500 years.

The Roman Empire (c. A.D. 1–500)

In his 40-year reign, Augustus ended Rome's civil wars and ushered in 200 years of prosperity and relative peace called the Pax Romana. Rome ruled an empire of 54 million people, stretching from Scotland to Africa, from Spain to the Cradle of Civilization (modern-day Iraq). Conquered peoples were welcomed into the fold of prosperity, linked by roads, common laws, common gods, education, and the Latin language. The city of Rome, with over a million inhabitants, was decorated with Greek-style statues and monumental structures faced with marble. It was the marvel of the known world.

The empire prospered on a (false) economy of booty, slaves, and cheap imports. On the Italian peninsula, traditional small farms were swallowed up by large farming and herding estates. In this "global economy," the Italian peninsula became just one province of many in a worldwide, Latin-speaking empire, ruled by an emperor who was likely born elsewhere. The empire even survived the often turbulent and naughty behavior of emperors like Caligula (37–41) and Nero (54–68).

Decline and Fall

Rome peaked in the second century under the capable emperors Trajan (98–117), Hadrian (117–138), and Marcus Aurelius (161–180). For the next three centuries, the Roman Empire declined, shrinking in size and wealth, a victim of corruption, disease, an overextended army, its false economy, and the constant pressure of "barbarian" tribes pecking away at the borders. By the third century, the army had become the real power, hand-picking figurehead emperors to do its bidding—in a 40-year span, 15 emperors were saluted then assassinated by fickle generals.

Trying to stall the disintegration, Emperor Diocletian (284–305) split the empire into two administrative halves under two equal emperors. Constantine (306–337) solidified the divide by moving the capital of the empire from decaying Rome to the new city of Constantinople (330, present-day Istanbul). Almost instantly, the once-great city of Rome became a minor player in imperial affairs. (The eastern "Byzantine" half of the empire would thrive and live on for another thousand years.) Constantine also legalized Christianity (313), and the once-persecuted cult soon became virtually the state religion, the backbone of Rome's fading hierarchy.

By 410, "Rome" had shrunk to the city itself, surrounded by a protective wall. Barbarian tribes from the north and east poured in to loot and plunder. The city was sacked by Visigoths (410), vandalized by Vandals (455), and the pope had to plead with Attila the Hun for mercy (451). The peninsula's population fell to six million, trade and agriculture were disrupted, schools closed, and the infrastructure collapsed. Peasants huddled near powerful lords for protection from bandits, planting the seeds of medieval feudalism.

In 476, the last emperor sold his title for a comfy pension, and Rome fell like a huge column, kicking up dust that would plunge Europe into a thousand years of darkness. For the next 13 centuries, there would be no "Italy," just a patchwork of rural dukedoms and towns, victimized by foreign powers. Italy lay helpless.

Invasions (A.D. 500–1000)

In 500 years, Italy suffered through a full paragraph of invasions: Lombards (568) and Byzantines (under Justinian, 536) occupied the north. In the south, Muslim Saracens (827) and Normans (1061) established thriving kingdoms. Charlemagne, King of the Franks (a Germanic tribe), defeated the Lombards and, on Christmas Day, A.D. 800, he knelt before the pope in St. Peter's in Rome to be crowned "Holy Roman Emperor." For the next thousand

Under the Etruscan Sun
(c. 900 BC–A.D. 1)

Around 550 B.C.—just before the Golden Age of Greece—the Etruscan people of central Italy had their own Golden Age. Though their origins are mysterious, their mix of Greek-style art with Roman-style customs helped lay a civilized foundation for the rise of Rome. As you travel through Italy—particularly in Tuscany (from "Etruscan"), Umbria, and North Latium—you'll find traces of the long-lost Etruscans.

The Etruscans first appeared in the ninth century, when a number of cities sprouted up in sparsely-populated Tuscany and Umbria, including today's hill towns of Cortona, Chiuisi, and Volterra. Perhaps they were immigrants from Western Turkey, but more likely they were just the local farmers who moved to the city, became traders and craftsmen, and welcomed new ideas from Greece.

More technologically advanced than their neighbors, they mined metal, exporting it around the Mediterranean, both as crude ingots and as some of the finest-crafted jewelry in the known world. The Etruscans drained and irrigated large tracts of land, creating the fertile farm land of central Italy's breadbasket. With their disciplined army, warships, merchant vessels, and (from the Greek perspective) pirate galleys they ruled central Italy and the major ports along the Tyrrhenian Sea. For nearly two centuries (c. 700-500 B.C.), much of Italy lived a golden age of peace and prosperity under the Etruscan sun.

Judging from the many luxury items that have survived, the Etruscans enjoyed the good life. Frescoes show men and women looking remarkably like how the Greeks and Romans described them: healthy, vibrant, and well-dressed, playing flutes, dancing with birds, or playing party games. Etruscan artists celebrated individual people, showing their wrinkles, crooked noses, silly smiles, and funny haircuts.

Thousands upon thousands of surviving ceramic plates, cups, and vases attest to the importance of food. Hosting a banquet was a symbol that you'd arrived. Men and women ate together, propped on their elbows on dining couches, surrounded by colorful frescoes and terracotta tiles. According to contemporary accounts, the Etruscans were Europe's best-dressed people, even their slaves. They ate off dinnerware either imported from Greece or made in the Greek style—red and black ceramics, decorated with warriors, nymphs, sphinxes, and gods. The banqueters were entertained with music and dancing and served by elegant and well-treated slaves.

Scholars today have deciphered the Etruscans' Greek-style alphabet and some individual words, but they've yet to fully master the grammar or crack the code. Virtually no long Etruscan documents survive.

Much of what we know of the Etruscans comes from their tombs, often clustered in a necropolis. The tomb was your home in the hereafter, fully furnished for the afterlife, complete with all the deceased's belongings. The sarcophagus might have a statue on the lid of the deceased at a banquet—lying across a dining couch, spooning with his wife, smiles on their faces, living the good life for all eternity.

Seven decades of wars with Greeks (545–474 B.C.) disrupted the trade routes and drained the League, just as a new Mediterranean power was emerging...Rome. In 509 B.C., the Romans overthrew their Etruscan king, and Rome expanded, capturing Etruscan cities one by one (the last in 264 B.C.). Etruscan resisters were killed, the survivors intermarried with Romans, their kids grew up speaking Latin, and the culture became Romanized. By Julius Caesar's time, the only remnants of Etruscan culture were Etruscan priests, who became Rome's professional soothsayers. The shape a flock of birds made, the bend in a lightning flash, or a scar on a goat's liver could tell a priest how a client's business might fare next year. Interestingly, the Etruscan prophets had foreseen their own demise, having predicted that Etruscan civilization would last 10 centuries.

But Etruscan culture lived on in Roman religion (pantheon of gods, household gods, and divination rituals), art (realism), lifestyle (the banquet), and in a taste for Greek styles—the mix that became our "Western civilization."

Etruscan Sights in Italy

Here are some of the more important and more touristically-accessible Etruscan sights (all are mentioned in this book):

Rome: Traces of original Etruscan engineering projects (e.g., Circus Maximus), Vatican Museum artifacts, and Villa Giulia Museum, with the famous "husband and wife sarcophagus."

Orvieto: Archaeological Museum (coins, dinnerware, and a sarcophagus), necropolis, and underground tunnels and caves.

Volterra: Etruscan gate (Porta dell'Arco, from 4th century B.C.) and Etruscan Museum (funerary urns).

Chiusi: Museum, tombs, and tunnels.

Cortona: Museum and dome-shaped tombs.

years, Italians would pledge nominal allegiance to weak, distant German kings as their "Holy Roman Emperor," an empty title meant to resurrect the glory of ancient Rome united with medieval Christianity.

Through all of the invasions and chaos, the glory of ancient Rome was preserved in the pomp, knowledge, hierarchy, and wealth of the Christian Church. Strong popes (Leo I, 440–461; and Gregory the Great, 590–604) ruled like small-time emperors, governing territories in central Italy called the Papal States.

A.D. 1000–1300

Italy survived Y1K, and the economy picked up. Sea-trading cities like Venice, Genoa, Pisa, Naples, and Amalfi grew wealthy as middlemen between Europe and the Orient. During the Crusades (e.g. First Crusade 1097–1130), Italian ships ferried Europe's Christian soldiers eastward, then returned laden with spices and high-mark-up luxury goods from the Orient. Trade spawned banking, and Italians became capitalists, loaning money at interest to Europe's royalty. Italy pioneered a new phenomenon in Europe— cities *(comuni)* that were self-governing commercial centers. The medieval prosperity of the cities laid the foundation of the future Renaissance.

Politically, the Italian peninsula was dominated by two rulers—the pope in Rome and the German "Holy Roman Emperor" (with holdings in the north). It split Italy into two warring political parties—supporters of the popes (called Guelfs, centered in urban areas) and those of the emperors (Ghibellines, popular with the rural nobility).

The Unlucky 1300s

In 1309, the pope—enticed by Europe's fast-rising power, France— moved from Rome to Avignon, France. At one point, two rival popes reigned, one in Avignon and the other in Rome, and excommunicated each other. The papacy eventually returned to Rome (1377), but the schism had created a breakdown in central authority that was exacerbated by an outbreak of bubonic plague (Black Death, 1347–1348) that killed a third of Italians.

In the power vacuum, new powers emerged in the independent cities. Venice, Florence, Milan, and Naples were under the protection and leadership of local noble families *(signoria)* such as the Medici in Florence. Florence thrived in the wool and dyeing trade, which led to international banking, with branches in all Europe's capitals. A positive side-effect of the terrible Black Death was that the smaller population got a bigger share of the land, jobs, and infrastructure. By century's end, Italy was poised to enter its most glorious era since antiquity.

The Renaissance (1400s)

The Renaissance (Rinascimento)—the "rebirth" of ancient Greek and Roman art styles, knowledge, and humanism—began in Italy (c. 1400), and spread through Europe over the next two centuries. Many of Europe's most famous painters, sculptors, and thinkers—Michelangelo, Leonardo, Raphael, etc.—were Italian.

It was a cultural boom that changed people's thinking about every aspect of life. In politics, it meant democracy. In religion, it meant a move away from Church dominance and toward the assertion of man (humanism) and a more personal faith. Science and secular learning were revived after centuries of superstition and ignorance. In architecture, it was a return to the balanced columns and domes of Greece and Rome. In painting, the Renaissance meant 3-D realism.

Italians dotted their cities with public-financed art—Greek gods, Roman-style domed buildings. They preached Greek-style democracy, and explored the natural world. The cultural boom was financed by booming trade and lucrative banking. In the Renaissance, the peninsula once again became the trend-setting cultural center of Europe.

End of the Renaissance, France and Spain Invade (1500s)

In May, 1498, Vasco da Gama of Portugal landed in India, having found a sea route around Africa. Italy's monopoly on trade with the East was broken. Portugal, France, Spain, England, and Holland—nation-states under strong central rule—began to overtake decentralized Italy. Italy's once-great maritime cities now traded in an economic backwater, just as Italy's bankers (such as the Medici in Florence) were going bankrupt. While the Italian Renaissance was all the rage throughout Europe, it declined in its birthplace. Italy—culturally sophisticated but weak and decentralized—was ripe for the picking by Europe's rising powers.

France and Spain invaded (1494 and 1495)—initially invited by Italian lords to attack their rivals—and began divvying up territory for their noble families. Italy also became a battleground in religious conflicts between Catholics and the new Protestant movement. In the chaos, the city of Rome was brutally sacked by foreign mercenary warriors (1527).

Foreign Rule (1600–1800)

For the next two centuries, most of Italy's states were ruled by foreign nobles, serving as prizes for the winners of Europe's dynastic wars. Italy ceased to be a major player in Europe, politically or economically. Italian intellectual life was often cropped short by a conservative Catholic Church trying to fight Protestantism. Galileo,

Top 10 Italians

Romulus: Breastfed on wolf milk, this legendary orphan grew to found the city of Rome (traditionally in 753 B.C.). Over the next seven centuries, his descendants dominated the Italian peninsula, ruling from Rome as a Republic.

Julius Caesar (100–44 B.C.): After conquering Gaul (France), subduing Egypt, and winning Cleopatra's heart, Caesar ruled Rome with king-like powers. Senators stabbed him to death trying to preserve the Republic, but the concept of one-man rule lived on.

Augustus (born Octavian, 63 B.C.–A.D. 14): Julius's adopted son became the first of the Caesars that ruled Rome during its 500 years as a Europe-wide power. He set the tone for emperors both good (Trajan, Hadrian, Marcus Aurelius) and bad (Caligula, Nero, and dozens of others).

Constantine (c. 280–337 A.D.): Raised in a Christian home, this emperor legalized Christianity, almost instantly turning a persecuted sect into a Europe-wide religion. With the Fall of Rome, the Church, directed by strong popes, guided Italians through the next 1000 years of invasions, plagues, political decentralization, and darkness.

Lorenzo the Magnificent (1449–1492): Soldier, poet, lover, and ruler of Florence in the 1400s, this Renaissance Man embodied the "rebirth" of ancient enlightenment. Lorenzo's wealthy Medici family funded Florentine artists who pioneered a realistic 3-D style.

Michelangelo Buonarroti (1475–1564): His statue of *David*—slaying an ignorant brute—stands as a monumental symbol of Italian enlightenment. Along with fellow geniuses Leonardo da Vinci and Raphael, Michelangelo spread the Italian Renaissance (painting, sculpture, architecture, literature, and Ideas) to a world-wide audience.

Gianlorenzo Bernini (1598–1680): The "Michelangelo of Baroque" kept Italy a major exporter of sophisticated trends. Bernini's

for example, was forced by the Inquisition to renounce his belief that the earth orbited the sun (1633). But Italy did export Baroque art (Gian Lorenzo Bernini) and the budding new medium of opera.

The War of the Spanish Succession (1713)—a war in which Italy did not participate—gave much of northern Italy to Austria's ruling family, the Hapsburgs (who now wore the crown of "Holy Roman Emperor"). In the south, Spain's Bourbon family ruled the Kingdom of Naples (known after 1816 as the Kingdom of the Two Sicilies), making it a culturally sophisticated but economically backward area, preserving a medieval, feudal caste system.

ornate statues and architecture decorated palaces of the rising power France even as Italy was reverting to an economically stagnant patchwork of foreign-ruled states.

Victor Emmanuel II (1820–1878): As the only Italian-born ruler on the peninsula, this King of Sardinia became the rallying point for Italian unification. Aided by the general Garibaldi, writer Mazzini, and politician Cavour (with soundtrack by Verdi), he became the first ruler of a united, democratic Italy in September 1870. (The preceding proper nouns have since come to adorn streets and piazzas throughout Italy.)

Benito Mussolini (1883–1945): A kinder, gentler Hitler, he derailed Italy's fledgling democracy, becoming dictator of a fascist state, leading the country into defeat in World War II. No public places honor Mussolini, but many streets and piazzas throughout Italy bear the name of Giacomo Matteotti (1885–1924), a politician whose outspoken opposition to Mussolini got him killed by Fascists.

Federico Fellini (1920–1993): Fellini's films chronicle Italy's postwar years in gritty black and white—the poverty, destruction, and disillusionment of the war followed by the optimism, decadence, and materialism of the economic boom. He captured the surreal chaos of Italy's abrupt social change from traditional Catholic to a secular, urban world presided over by Mafia bosses and weak government.

Top Italian Number 11 (_____–_____): Has Italy produced another recent Italian who's dominant enough to make his or her mark on the world? Could it be politician Silvio Berlusconi, Italy's longest-reigning head of state since World War II? Opera singer Luciano Pavarotti? Former president of the European Union, Romano Prodi? Or big-pec-ed model "Fabio" Lanzoni, named "Sexiest Man on Earth" by Cosmopolitan magazine? The world awaits.

In 1720, a minor war (the War of Austrian Succession) created a new state at the foot of the Alps, called the Kingdom of Sardinia (a.k.a. the Kingdom of Piedmont or Savoy). Ruled by the Savoy family, this was the only major state on the peninsula actually ruled by Italians. It proved to be a toehold to the future.

Italy Unites—The Risorgimento (1800s)

In 1796, Napoleon Bonaparte swept through Italy and changed everything. He ousted Austrian and Spanish dukes, confiscated Church lands, united scattered states, and crowned himself "King

Italian Unification

Note: Dates indicate the year of annexation to the Kingdom of Sardinia (after 1861, the Kingdom of Italy).

of Italy" (1805). After his defeat (1815), Italy's old ruling order (namely, Austria and Spain) was restored. But Napoleon had planted a seed: What if Italians could unite and rule themselves like Europe's other modern nations?

For the next 50 years, a movement to unite Italy slowly grew. Called the Risorgimento—a word that means "rising again"—the movement promised a revival of Italy's glory. It started as a revolutionary, liberal movement punishable by death. Members of a secret society called the Carbonari (led by a professional revolutionary named Giuseppe Mazzini) exchanged secret handshakes, printed flyers, planted bombs, and assassinated conservative rulers. Their small revolutions (1820–1821, 1831, 1848) were easily and brutally slapped down, but the cause wouldn't die.

Gradually, Italians of all stripes warmed to the idea of unification. Whether it was a united dictatorship, a united papal state, a united kingdom, or a united democracy, most Italians could agree that it was time for Spain, Austria, and France to leave.

The March on Rome

In October 1922, Benito Mussolini, head of the newly-formed Fascist Party, boldly proposed a coup d'etat, saying: "Either the government will be given to us, or we will take it by marching on Rome." Throughout Italy, black-shirted Fascists occupied government buildings in their hometowns. Others grabbed guns, farming hoes, and kitchen knives and set off to converge on the outskirts of Rome. (Estimates of the size of the Fascist band range from 300 to the 300,000 of Fascist legend.) Mussolini sent the government an ultimatum to surrender. Though the Fascists were easily outmanned and outgunned by government forces, the show of force intimidated the king into avoiding a nasty confrontation. He invited Mussolini to Rome. Mussolini arrived the next day (by first-class train), was made prime minister, then marched his black-shirted troops triumphantly through the streets of Rome.

The movement coalesced around the Italian-ruled Kingdom of Sardinia and its king, Victor Emmanuel II. In 1859, Sardinia's prime minister, Camillo Cavour, cleverly persuaded France to drive Austria out of north Italy, leaving the north in Italian hands. A plebiscite (vote) was held, and several central Italian states (including some of the pope's) rejected their feudal lords and chose to join the growing Kingdom of Sardinia.

After victory in the north, Italy's most renowned Carbonari general, Giuseppe Garibaldi (1807–1882), steamed south with a thousand of his best soldiers *(I Mille)* and marched on the Spanish-ruled city of Naples (1860). The old order simply collapsed. In two short months, Garibaldi had achieved a seemingly impossible victory against a far superior army. Garibaldi sent a one-word telegram to the king of Sardinia: *"Obbedisco"* (I obey). The following year, an assembly of deputies from throughout Italy met in Turin and crowned Victor Emmanuel II "King of Italy." Only the pope in Rome held out, protected by French troops. When the city finally fell easily to the unification forces on September 20, 1870, the Risorgimento was complete. Italy went ape.

The Risorgimento was largely the work of four men: Garibaldi (the sword), Mazzini (the spark), Cavour (the diplomat), and Victor Emmanuel II (the rallying point). Today, street signs throughout Italy honor them and the dates of their great victories.

Mussolini and War (1900–1950)

Italy—now an actual nation-state, not just a linguistic region—entered the 20th century with a progressive government (a constitutional monarchy), a collection of colonies, and a flourishing

Silvio Berlusconi
(1936–   )

Italy's richest man ($12 billion) is also its most powerful. As the owner of most of Italy's major TV stations—as well as magazines, books, the AC Milan soccer team, and large construction companies—his decisions influence many aspects of Italians' everyday lives. Did I mention he's also prime minister, having been re-elected in May of 2005? Silvio Berlusconi is now Italy's longest-reigning head of state since World War II.

Berlusconi first came to power in 1994 after single-handedly creating his own political party, called *Forza Italia* ("Go, Italy!"—a soccer chant used to root on the national squad). Politically, the party follows a moderate course while also courting northern Italian extremists who want to break from the south, as well as southern neo-fascists and xenophobes.

A self-made man, Berlusconi sees himself as the champion of individual freedom against a stagnant bureaucracy. This makes him skeptical of expanding the European Union and of imposing economic restrictions like the Kyoto Protocol on global warming. Berlusconi supported George W. Bush's invasion of Iraq despite overwhelming public opposition.

Berlusconi's fans think he's exactly the right man for the job—a forceful captain of industry who can run government more efficiently than left-wing bureaucrats. He's dynamic, enthusiastic, comfortable on TV, and very image-conscious (including airbrushed photos, a face-lift, and hair plugs). Newspapers call him *Il Cavaliere* ("the horseman"), reinforcing

---

northern half of the country. In the economically backward south (the Mezzogiorno), millions of poor peasants emigrated to the Americas. World War I (1915–1918) left 650,000 Italians dead, but being on the winning Allied side, survivors were granted possession of the alpine regions. In the postwar cynicism and anarchy, many radical political parties rose up—Communist, Socialist, Popular, and Fascist.

Benito Mussolini (1883–1945), a popular writer for socialist and labor-union newspapers, led the Fascists. ("Fascism" comes from Latin *fasci*, the bundles of rods that symbolized unity in ancient Rome.) Though only a minority (6 percent of the parliament in 1921), they intimidated the disorganized majority with organized violence by black-shirted Fascist gangs. In 1922, Mussolini seized the government (see sidebar) and began his rule as dictator for the next two decades.

Mussolini solidified his reign among Catholics by striking an agreement with the pope (Concordato, 1929), giving Vatican City

his image as a bold, even "cavalier" adventurer.

Critics, on the other hand, dislike many things about Berlusconi—most notably, they're convinced he's a crook. During the 1990s, when Italians finally broke the back of the Mafia, many of Berlusconi's business associates were convicted of corruption. Berlusconi himself was tried and convicted in 1997 and 1998 of tax evasion and bribery. After being re-elected in 2001, he promptly passed laws giving himself immunity. The case is on appeal.

Aside from actual crimes, people wonder how Berlusconi can possibly avoid conflicts of interests as head of so many powerful institutions, both private and public. If the government, the media, and much of the economy are controlled by one man, what does that say about democracy? Italy's economy is currently stagnant, which is especially hard on the middle class. Nobody seems to be getting ahead...except Berlusconi and his associates. But so far, Berlusconi's coalition of centrist and right-wing parties has given him just enough political capital to keep the many critics at bay.

The Prime Minister is elected to a five-year term, but a lack of confidence in the government may force earlier elections—in which case, Berlusconi would likely face a center-left coalition (called *Ulivo,* or "Olive Tree") headed by former Prime Minister Romano Prodi. Whether Italy heads center-left or center-right, there now appears to be one thing that's been missing from Italian politics for 50 years—a center.

to the pope while Mussolini ruled Italy, with the implied blessing of the Catholic Church. Italy responded to the great worldwide Depression (1930s) with big public works projects (including Rome's subway), government investment in industry, and an expanded army.

Mussolini allied his country with Hitler's Nazi regime, drawing an unprepared Italy into World War II (1940). Italy's lame army was never a factor in the war, and when Allied forces landed in Sicily (1943), Italians welcomed them as liberators. The Italians toppled Mussolini's government and surrendered to the Allies, but Nazi Germany sent troops to rescue Mussolini. The war raged on as Allied troops inched their way north against German resistance. Italians were reduced to dire poverty. In the last days of the war (April 1945), Mussolini was captured by the Italian resistance. They shot him and his girlfriend and hung their bodies upside down in a public square in Milan.

Postwar Italy

At War's end, Italy was physically ruined and extremely poor. The nation rebuilt in the '50s and '60s (the "economic miracle") with Marshall Plan aid from America. Many Italian men moved to northern Europe to find work; many others left the farm and flocked to cities. Italy regained its standing among nations, joining the United Nations, NATO, and, eventually, the European Union.

However, the government remained weak, changing on average once a year, shifting from right to left to centrist coalitions (60 governments since World War II). All Italians acknowledged that the real power lay in the hands of backroom politicians and organized crime—a phenomenon called *Tangentopoli*, or "Bribe City." The country remained strongly divided between the rich, industrial north and the poor, rural south.

Italian society changed greatly in the 1960s and '70s, spurred by liberal interpretations of the Catholic Church's Council of Vatican II (1962–1965). The once-conservative Catholic country legalized divorce and contraception, and the birth rate plummeted. In the 1970s, the economy slowed thanks to inflation, strikes, and the worldwide energy crisis. Italy suffered a wave of violence from left- and right-wing domestic terrorists and organized crime, punctuated with the assassination of the prime minister Aldo Moro (1978). A series of coalition governments in the 1980s brought some stability to the economy.

In the early 1990s, the judiciary launched a campaign to rid politics of corruption and Mafia ties. Though still ongoing, the investigation sent a message that Italy would no longer tolerate evils that were considered necessary just a generation earlier. In 2001, billionaire Silvio Berlusconi, the owner of many of Italy's media outlets and Italy's richest person, financed his own political party (*Forza Italia*, or "Go, Italy!"), won 30 percent of the popular vote, and became prime minister, heading a center-right coalition (see sidebar). In 2003, Berlusconi backed the U.S. invasion of Iraq, a policy that polarized Italy.

As you travel through Italy today, you'll encounter a thriving country with a rich history and a per capita income rivaling its neighbors to the north. Italy is enthusiastically part of Europe...yet it's as wonderfully Italian as ever.

APPENDIX

Italian Sports

Flip on the hotel TV or thumb through a local newspaper, and you'll see that sports are big in Italy—but not American sports. There's little interest in baseball, American football, or hockey. Instead, Italian sports idols are soccer players (Francesco Totti), skiers (Alberto Tomba), cyclists (Paolo Savodelli), and motorcycle riders (Valentino Rossi). The world's top-paid athlete through most of the 1990s was not Michael Jordan, Tiger Woods, John Elway, or Derek Jeter—but a German race-car driver for Ferrari, Michael Schumacher.

Italy's undisputed number-one sport is soccer (called *il calcio*; see the sidebar on page 706). All other sports are a distant second, and on the night of a big match, expect to see sports bars jammed with loud fans, followed by a horn-blowing parade of cars after a victory (see page 516 of Rome chapter).

In the home country of Ferrari, Alfa Romeo, and Maserati, another popular spectator sport is motor racing—not stock cars like American NASCAR, but Formula One/Grand Prix. And since many Italians grow up zipping through narrow streets on small Vespas, it's little wonder that motorcycle racing *(moto)* is a major sport here. Sports that are only somewhat popular in America—tennis, golf, winter sports, and Olympic events (track and field)—are even more popular in Italy, especially if it involves homegrown talent.

Then there are the truly European sports—particularly cycling. During the 25-day Giro d'Italia (won in May of 2005 by an Italian, Paolo Savodelli), the entire route takes on a festive atmosphere. And Italians, who routinely play *bocce* in their parks and piazzas, also watch the pros do it on TV.

Europe is catching on to new sports trends emerging from

Italian Football (Soccer) Leagues

It seems that on almost any given night of the year, there's yet another "absolutely crucial" football match in Italy. That's because the only way to feed fans' insatiable appetite for the game is to run the sport year-round, with different leagues playing their seasons concurrently, staggering playoffs and finals throughout the year.

Italy's top domestic league is known as Serie A. It's comprised of **professional football clubs** (the for-profit teams like those in America's NFL, NBA, or Major League Baseball). Italy's **national team** is called *La Squadra Azzura* ("The Blue Team," named for the uniforms). It plays against other countries' national teams in international, Olympic-style competitions. The best Italian players play both for their professional club, and for the national team.

Serie A football clubs are usually based in a major city (e.g., AS Roma, AC Milan, or Juventus of Turin), and employ the best players money can buy. For example, AS Roma fields well-known players not just from Italy, but also from Brazil, France, Nigeria, and many other countries. The Serie A season normally runs from September to May, as clubs from around Italy play each other—usually on Sundays—for the league title (known as the *scudetto*, and won by Juventus in 2005). While the Serie A season is going on, the top four Italian teams are also playing in the Champions League, which pits the best teams from a host of other domestic European leagues (England, France, Spain) hoping to emerge as Europe's top club (Liverpool of England did it in 2005).

Besides the Serie A football clubs, smaller Italian cities have their own clubs, which compete in Serie B, C, and so on. Each year, a handful of the best "B" clubs get promoted to the "A" league (cue celebrations in the streets)...while the worst of the "A" clubs

America, like extreme sports (motocross, snowboarding, skateboarding) or beach volleyball. And America's "big three" are growing, if slowly. The NFL has a European "farm league" for trying out new talent, with teams in many European cities—but none in Italy. Basketball, however, is fast becoming a major Italian sport. Fans carry on with soccer-style rowdiness, and the Italian teams groom players and coaches who go on to careers in the NBA.

Let's Talk Telephones

This is a primer on telephoning in Europe. For specifics on Italy, see "Telephones" in the Introduction.

Making Calls within a European Country: What you dial depends on the phone system of the country you're in. About half of all European countries have phone systems that use area codes; the other half uses a direct-dial system without area codes.

get demoted to the "B" league (cue weeping and gnashing of teeth). Promotion to Serie A is a big deal in small-town Italy, but in reality, the upper echelon of Italian soccer is dominated by a handful of elite teams—Roma, Milan, Juventus—based in big-market, big-money cities.

In addition to its professional football clubs, Italy also fields a national team that takes on other countries. Only Italians can play on it, so whenever they play, national pride is on the line. The team competes in two huge international tournaments: the World Cup (the most important, held every 4 years—hosted by Germany in 2006) and the European Championships (a.k.a. the "Euro Cup," or simply the "Euro," held every 4 years, hosted by Portugal in 2004, and by Austria and Switzerland jointly in 2008). Both of these tournaments involve two years of matches (usually on weeknights) just to qualify for, and culminate in a final game watched by millions and millions of fans.

With so many different leagues and tournaments (World Cup, Champions League, European Championships, Serie A)—each requiring months of qualifying rounds—scheduling can be a nightmare. Consider Italy's most famous player, Francesco Totti. On Sunday, he plays for Roma against AC Milan in an "absolutely crucial" Italian league match. On Wednesday, he switches jerseys and joins Italy's national squad for a World Cup-qualifying match, against France (and one of his Roma teammates). A few days later, he returns to his club team in Rome to face Real Madrid in a Champions League match watched by all of Italy and Spain. Then it's suiting up for *La Squadra Azzura* again for a "friendly" (an exhibition match), against a visiting squad from Brazil—and another of his AS Roma teammates. Whew!

If you're calling within a country that uses a direct-dial system (Italy, Belgium, the Czech Republic, Denmark, France, Norway, Portugal, Spain, and Switzerland), you dial the same number whether you're calling across the street or across the country.

In countries that use area codes (such as Austria, Britain, Croatia, Finland, Germany, Hungary, Ireland, the Netherlands, Poland, Slovakia, Slovenia, and Sweden), you dial the local number when calling within a city, and you add the area code if calling long-distance within the country. Example: The phone number of a hotel in Munich is 089-264-349. To call it in Munich, dial 264-349; to call it from Frankfurt, dial 089-264-349.

Making International Calls: You always start with the international access code (011 if you're calling from the U.S. or Canada, 00 from Europe), then dial the country code of the country you're calling (see list of country codes, below).

European Calling Chart

Just smile and dial, using this key:
AC = Area Code, LN = Local Number.

European Country	Calling long distance within ...	Calling from the U.S.A./ Canada to ...	Calling from a European country to ...
Austria	AC + LN	011 + 43 + AC (without the initial zero) + LN	00 + 43 + AC (without the initial zero) + LN
Belgium	LN	011 + 32 + LN (without initial zero)	00 + 32 + LN (without initial zero)
Britain	AC + LN	011 + 44 + AC (without initial zero) + LN	00 + 44 + AC (without initial zero) + LN
Croatia	AC + LN	011 + 385 + AC (without initial zero) + LN	00 + 385 + AC (without initial zero) + LN
Czech Republic	LN	011 + 420 + LN	00 + 420 + LN
Denmark	LN	011 + 45 + LN	00 + 45 + LN
Finland	AC + LN	011 + 358 + AC (without initial zero) + LN	00 + 358 + AC (without initial zero) + LN
France	LN	011 + 33 + LN (without initial zero)	00 + 33 + LN (without initial zero)
Germany	AC + LN	011 + 49 + AC (without initial zero) + LN	00 + 49 + AC (without initial zero) + LN
Greece	LN	011 + 30 + LN	00 + 30 + LN
Hungary	06 + AC + LN	011 + 36 + AC + LN	00 + 36 + AC + LN
Ireland	AC + LN	011 + 353 + AC (without initial zero) + LN	00 + 353 + AC (without initial zero) + LN
Italy	LN	011 + 39 + LN	00 + 39 + LN

European Country	Calling long distance within ...	Calling from the U.S.A./ Canada to ...	Calling from a European country to ...
Netherlands	AC + LN	011 + 31 + AC (without initial zero) + LN	00 + 31 + AC (without initial zero) + LN
Norway	LN	011 + 47 + LN	00 + 47 + LN
Poland	AC + LN	011 + 48 + AC (without initial zero) + LN	00 + 48 + AC (without initial zero) + LN
Portugal	LN	011 + 351 + LN	00 + 351 + LN
Slovakia	AC + LN	011 + 421 + AC (without initial zero) + LN	00 + 421 + AC (without initial zero) + LN
Slovenia	AC + LN	011 + 386 + AC (without initial zero) + LN	00 + 386 + AC (without initial zero) + LN
Spain	LN	011 + 34 + LN	00 + 34 + LN
Sweden	AC + LN	011 + 46 + AC (without initial zero) + LN	00 + 46 + AC (without initial zero) + LN
Switzerland	LN	011 + 41 + LN (without initial zero)	00 + 41 + LN (without initial zero)
Turkey	AC (if no initial zero is included, add one) + LN	011 + 90 + AC (without initial zero) + LN	00 + 90 + AC (without initial zero) + LN

- The instructions above apply whether you're calling a fixed phone or mobile phone.
- The international access codes (the first numbers you dial when making an international call) are 011 if you're calling from the U.S.A./Canada, or 00 if you're calling from anywhere in Europe.
- To call the U.S.A. or Canada from Europe, dial 00, then 1 (the country code for the U.S.A. and Canada), then the area code and number. In short, 00 + 1 + AC + LN = Hi, Mom!

What you dial next depends on the particular phone system of the country you're calling. If the country uses area codes, you drop the initial zero of the area code, then dial the rest of the area code and the local number. Example: To call the Munich hotel (mentioned above) from Spain, dial 00, 49 (Germany's country code), then 89-264-349.

Countries that use direct-dial systems (no area codes) differ in how they're accessed internationally by phone. For instance, if you're making an international call to Italy, the Czech Republic, Denmark, Norway, Portugal, or Spain, you simply dial the international access code, country code, and the phone number in full. But if you're calling Belgium, France, or Switzerland, you drop the initial zero of the phone number. Example: The phone number of a Paris hotel is 01 47 05 49 15. To call it from Rome, dial 00, 33 (France's country code), then 1 47 05 49 15 (the phone number without the initial zero).

Calling America or Canada from Europe: Dial the international access code (00 for Europe), then dial 1, the area code, and local phone number. Example: My number here at Europe Through the Back Door (in Edmonds, WA) is 425/771-8303. To call me from Europe, dial 00-1-425-771-8303.

Country Codes

After you've dialed the international access code (00 if calling from Europe, 011 if calling from the U.S. or Canada), dial the code of the country you're calling.

Austria—43	Italy—39
Belgium—32	Morocco—212
Britain—44	Netherlands—31
Canada—1	Norway—47
Croatia—385	Poland—48
Czech Rep.—420	Portugal—351
Denmark—45	Slovakia—421
Estonia—372	Slovenia—386
Finland—358	Spain—34
France—33	Sweden—46
Germany—49	Switzerland—41
Gibraltar—350	Turkey—90
Greece—30	U.S.A.—1
Ireland—353	

Useful Italian Phone Numbers
Emergency (English-speaking police help): 113
Emergency (military police): 112
Road Service: 116

Directory Assistance (for €0.50, an Italian-speaking robot gives the number twice, very clearly): 12
Telephone help (in English; free directory assistance): 170

U.S. Embassies
In Rome: American Embassy at Via Vittorio Veneto 119/A (Mon–Fri 8:30–13:00 & 14:00–17:30, closed Sat–Sun, tel. 06-46741, www.usembassy.it); Canadian Embassy at Via Zara 30 (tel. 06-445-981, www.canada.it).
In Milan: U.S. Consulate at Via Principe Amedeo 2/10, tel. 02-290-351.
In Florence: U.S. Consulate at Lungarno Vespucci 38, 055-266-951.
In Naples: U.S. Consulate at Piazza della Repubblica, 081-5838-111.

Public Holidays and Festivals
Italy (including most major sights) closes down on national holidays. Each town has a local festival honoring its patron saint. For more information on festivals, check out www.italiantourism.com, www.discoveritalia.com, www.hostetler.net, and www.whatsonwhen.com.

Note that this isn't a complete list; holidays strike without warning. Dates listed are for 2006.

Jan 1:	New Year's Day
Jan 6:	Epiphany Fair (religious festival), Rome
Feb 17–Feb 28:	Carnevale (Mardi Gras, www.carnivalofvenice.com), Venice
April 6–10:	Vinitaly (wine festival), Verona
April 16:	Easter Sunday (and *Scoppio del Carro* fireworks in Florence)
April 17:	Easter Monday
April 25:	Liberation Day
June:	Florence Music Festival, Florence (all month)
May 1:	Labor Day
May 25:	Ascension Day
June 2:	Anniversary of the Republic
June 16–17:	Festival of St. Ranieri, Pisa
June 24:	St. John Day, Calcio Fiorentino (costumed soccer game, fireworks), Florence
June 29:	Sts. Peter and Paul Day, most fervently celebrated in Rome
July–Aug:	Opera season, Verona
July 2:	Palio horse race, Siena
July 15–16:	Feast of the Redeemer (parade, fireworks), Venice

2006

JANUARY						
S	**M**	**T**	**W**	**T**	**F**	**S**
1	2	3	4	5	6	7
8	9	10	11	12	13	14
15	16	17	18	19	20	21
22	23	24	25	26	27	28
29	30	31				

FEBRUARY						
S	**M**	**T**	**W**	**T**	**F**	**S**
			1	2	3	4
5	6	7	8	9	10	11
12	13	14	15	16	17	18
19	20	21	22	23	24	25
26	27	28				

MARCH						
S	**M**	**T**	**W**	**T**	**F**	**S**
			1	2	3	4
5	6	7	8	9	10	11
12	13	14	15	16	17	18
19	20	21	22	23	24	25
26	27	28	29	30	31	

APRIL						
S	**M**	**T**	**W**	**T**	**F**	**S**
						1
2	3	4	5	6	7	8
9	10	11	12	13	14	15
16	17	18	19	20	21	22
23/30	24	25	26	27	28	29

MAY						
S	**M**	**T**	**W**	**T**	**F**	**S**
	1	2	3	4	5	6
7	8	9	10	11	12	13
14	15	16	17	18	19	20
21	22	23	24	25	26	27
28	29	30	31			

JUNE						
S	**M**	**T**	**W**	**T**	**F**	**S**
				1	2	3
4	5	6	7	8	9	10
11	12	13	14	15	16	17
18	19	20	21	22	23	24
25	26	27	28	29	30	

JULY						
S	**M**	**T**	**W**	**T**	**F**	**S**
						1
2	3	4	5	6	7	8
9	10	11	12	13	14	15
16	17	18	19	20	21	22
23/30	24/31	25	26	27	28	29

AUGUST						
S	**M**	**T**	**W**	**T**	**F**	**S**
		1	2	3	4	5
6	7	8	9	10	11	12
13	14	15	16	17	18	19
20	21	22	23	24	25	26
27	28	29	30	31		

SEPTEMBER						
S	**M**	**T**	**W**	**T**	**F**	**S**
					1	2
3	4	5	6	7	8	9
10	11	12	13	14	15	16
17	18	19	20	21	22	23
24	25	26	27	28	29	30

OCTOBER						
S	**M**	**T**	**W**	**T**	**F**	**S**
1	2	3	4	5	6	7
8	9	10	11	12	13	14
15	16	17	18	19	20	21
22	23	24	25	26	27	28
29	30	31				

NOVEMBER						
S	**M**	**T**	**W**	**T**	**F**	**S**
			1	2	3	4
5	6	7	8	9	10	11
12	13	14	15	16	17	18
19	20	21	22	23	24	25
26	27	28	29	30		

DECEMBER						
S	**M**	**T**	**W**	**T**	**F**	**S**
					1	2
3	4	5	6	7	8	9
10	11	12	13	14	15	16
17	18	19	20	21	22	23
24/31	25	26	27	28	29	30

Aug 15:	Assumption of Mary
Aug 16:	Palio horse race, Siena
Sept 3:	Historical Regatta (boat parade), Venice
Sept:	Chestnut Festivals (festivals, chestnut roasts), most towns, mainly north of Rome
Sept 13–14:	Volto Santo, Lucca
Sept 19:	Festival of San Gennaro (religious festival), Naples
Nov 1:	All Saints' Day
Dec 8:	Immaculate Conception of Mary
Dec:	Christmas Market, Rome, Piazza Navona, and crêches in churches throughout Italy
Dec 25:	Christmas
Dec 26:	St. Stephen's Day

Numbers and Stumblers

- Europeans write a few of their numbers differently than we do. 1 = 1 , 4 = 4 , 7 = 7 . Learn the difference or miss your train.
- In Europe, dates appear as day/month/year, so Christmas is 25/12/06.
- Commas are decimal points and decimals commas. A dollar and a half is 1,50, and there are 5.280 feet in a mile.
- When pointing, use your whole hand, palm down.
- When counting with fingers, start with your thumb. If you hold up your first finger to request one item, you'll probably get two.
- What Americans call the second floor of a building is the first floor in Europe.
- Europeans keep the left "lane" open for passing on escalators and moving sidewalks. Keep to the right.

Metric Conversion (approximate)

1 inch = 25 millimeters	32 degrees F = 0 degrees C
1 foot = 0.3 meter	82 degrees F = about 28 degrees C
1 yard = 0.9 meter	1 ounce = 28 grams
1 mile = 1.6 kilometers	1 kilogram = 2.2 pounds
1 centimeter = 0.4 inch	1 quart = 0.95 liter
1 meter = 39.4 inches	1 square yard = 0.8 square meter
1 kilometer = 0.62 mile	1 acre = 0.4 hectare

Climate Chart

First line, average daily low; second line, average daily high; third line, days of no rain.

	J	F	M	A	M	J	J	A	S	O	N	D
Rome												
	40°	42°	45°	50°	56°	63°	67°	67°	62°	55°	49°	44°
	52°	55°	59°	66°	74°	82°	87°	86°	79°	71°	61°	55°
	13	19	23	24	26	26	30	29	25	23	19	21
Milan												
	32°	35°	43°	49°	57°	63°	67°	66°	61°	52°	43°	35°
	40°	46°	56°	65°	74°	80°	84°	82°	75°	63°	51°	43°
	25	21	24	22	23	21	25	24	25	23	20	24

Converting Temperatures: Fahrenheit and Celsius

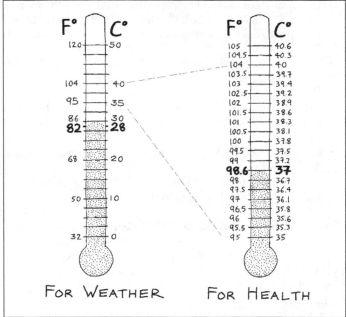

Europe takes its temperature using the Celsius scale, while we opt for Fahrenheit. For weather, just remember that 28°C is 82°F—perfect. For health, 37°C is just right.

Roman Numerals

In the U.S., you'll see Roman numerals—which originated in ancient Rome—used for copyright dates, clocks, and the Super Bowl. In Italy, you're likely to observe these numbers chiseled on statues and buildings. If you want to do some numeric detective work, here's how. In Roman numerals, as in ours, the highest numbers (thousands, hundreds) come first, followed by smaller numbers. Many numbers are made by combining numerals into sets: V = 5, so VIII = 8 (5 plus 3). Roman numerals follow a subtraction principle for multiples of fours (4, 40, 400, etc.) and nines (9, 90, 900, etc.); the number four, for example, is written as IV (1 subtracted from 5), rather than IIII. The number nine is IX (1 subtracted from 10).

Rick Steves' Italy 2006—written in Roman numerals—would translate as *Rick Steves' Italy MMVI*. Big numbers such as dates can look daunting at first. The easiest way to handle them is to read the numbers in discrete chunks. For example, Michelangelo was born in MCDLXXV. Break it down: M (1,000) + CD (100 subtracted from 500, or 400) + LXX (50 + 10 + 10, or 70) + V (5) = 1475. It was a very good year.

M = 1000	XL = 40
CM = 900	X = 10
D = 500	IX = 9
CD = 400	V = 5
C = 100	IV = 4
XC = 90	I = duh
L = 50	

Making Your Hotel Reservation

Most hotel managers know basic "hotel English." Faxing or e-mailing are the preferred methods for reserving a room. They're more accurate than telephoning and much faster than writing a letter. Use this handy form for your fax or find it online at www.ricksteves.com/reservation. Photocopy and fax away.

One-Page Fax

To: _____ @ _____
       hotel   *fax*

From: _____@ _____
         name   *fax*

Today's date: _____ / _____ / _____
                    day   *month*   *year*

Dear Hotel _____ ,
Please make this reservation for me:

Name: _____

Total # of people: _____ # of rooms: _____ # of nights: _____

Arriving: _____ /_____ /_____   My time of arrival (24-hr clock): _____
              day   *month*   *year*   (I will telephone if I will be late)

Departing: _____ /_____ /_____
                day   *month*   *year*

Room(s): Single _____ Double _____ Twin _____ Triple _____ Quad _____

With: Toilet _____ Shower _____ Bath _____ Sink only _____

Special needs: View ____ Quiet ____ Cheapest ____ Ground Floor ____

Please fax, mail, or e-mail confirmation of my reservation, along with the type of room reserved and the price. Please also inform me of your cancellation policy. After I hear from you, I will quickly send my credit-card information as a deposit to hold the room. Thank you.

_____
Signature

_____
Name

_____
Address

_____
City   *State*   *Zip Code*   *Country*

_____
E-mail Address

Italian Survival Phrases

Good day.	**Buon giorno.**	bwohn JOR-noh
Do you speak English?	**Parla inglese?**	PAR-lah een-GLAY-zay
Yes. / No.	**Sì. / No.**	see / noh
I (don't) understand.	**(Non) capisco.**	(nohn) kah-PEES-koh
Please.	**Per favore.**	pehr fah-VOH-ray
Thank you.	**Grazie.**	GRAHT-seeay
I'm sorry.	**Mi dispiace.**	mee dee-speeAH-chay
Excuse me.	**Mi scusi.**	mee SKOO-zee
(No) problem.	**(Non) c'è un problema.**	(nohn) cheh oon proh-BLAY-mah
Good.	**Va bene.**	vah BEHN-ay
Goodbye.	**Arrivederci.**	ah-ree-vay-DEHR-chee
one / two	**uno / due**	OO-noh / DOO-ay
three / four	**tre / quattro**	tray / KWAH-troh
five / six	**cinque / sei**	CHEENG-kway / SEHee
seven / eight	**sette / otto**	SEHT-tay / OT-toh
nine / ten	**nove / dieci**	NOV-ay / deeAY-chee
How much is it?	**Quanto costa?**	KWAHN-toh KOS-tah
Write it?	**Me lo scrive?**	may loh SKREE-vay
Is it free?	**È gratis?**	eh GRAH-tees
Is it included?	**È incluso?**	eh een-KLOO-zoh
Where can I buy / find...?	**Dove posso comprare / trovare...?**	DOH-vay POS-soh kohm-PRAH-ray / troh-VAH-ray
I'd like / We'd like...	**Vorrei / Vorremmo...**	vor-REHee / vor-RAY-moh
...a room.	**...una camera.**	OO-nah KAH-meh-rah
...a ticket to ___.	**...un biglietto per ___.**	oon beel-YEHT-toh pehr
Is it possible?	**È possibile?**	eh poh-SEE-bee-lay
Where is...?	**Dov'è...?**	DOH-veh
...the train station	**...la stazione**	lah staht-seeOH-nay
...the bus station	**...la stazione degli autobus**	lah staht-seeOH-nay DAYL-yee OW-toh-boos
...tourist information	**...informazioni per turisti**	een-for-maht-seeOH-nee pehr too-REE-stee
...the toilet	**...la toilette**	lah twah-LEHT-tay
men	**uomini, signori**	WOH-mee-nee, seen-YOH-ree
women	**donne, signore**	DON-nay, seen-YOH-ray
left / right	**sinistra / destra**	see-NEE-strah / DEHS-trah
straight	**sempre diritto**	SEHM-pray dee-REE-toh
When do you open / close?	**A che ora aprite / chiudete?**	ah kay OH-rah ah-PREE-tay / keeoo-DAY-tay
At what time?	**A che ora?**	ah kay OH-rah
Just a moment.	**Un momento.**	oon moh-MAYN-toh
now / soon / later	**adesso / presto / tardi**	ah-DEHS-soh / PREHS-toh / TAR-dee
today / tomorrow	**oggi / domani**	OH-jee / doh-MAH-nee

In the Restaurant

I'd like...	**Vorrei...**	vor-REHee
We'd like...	**Vorremmo...**	vor-RAY-moh
...to reserve...	**...prenotare...**	pray-noh-TAH-ray
...a table for one / two.	**...un tavolo per uno / due.**	oon TAH-voh-loh pehr OO-noh / DOO-ay
Non-smoking.	**Non fumare.**	nohn foo-MAH-ray
Is this seat free?	**È libero questo posto?**	eh LEE-bay-roh KWEHS-toh POH-stoh
The menu (in English), please.	**Il menù (in inglese), per favore.**	eel may-NOO (een een-GLAY-zay) pehr fah-VOH-ray
service (not) included	**servizio (non) incluso**	sehr-VEET-seeoh (nohn) een-KLOO-zoh
cover charge	**pane e coperto**	PAH-nay ay koh-PEHR-toh
to go	**da portar via**	dah POR-tar VEE-ah
with / without	**con / senza**	kohn / SEHN-sah
and / or	**e / o**	ay / oh
menu (of the day)	**menù (del giorno)**	may-NOO (dayl JOR-noh)
specialty of the house	**specialità della casa**	spay-chah-lee-TAH DEHL-lah KAH-zah
first course (pasta, soup)	**primo piatto**	PREE-moh peeAH-toh
main course (meat, fish)	**secondo piatto**	say-KOHN-doh peeAH-toh
side dishes	**contorni**	kohn-TOR-nee
bread	**pane**	PAH-nay
cheese	**formaggio**	for-MAH-joh
sandwich	**panino**	pah-NEE-noh
soup	**minestra, zuppa**	mee-NEHS-trah, TSOO-pah
salad	**insalata**	een-sah-LAH-tah
meat	**carne**	KAR-nay
chicken	**pollo**	POH-loh
fish	**pesce**	PEH-shay
seafood	**frutti di mare**	FROO-tee dee MAH-ray
fruit / vegetables	**frutta / legumi**	FROO-tah / lay-GOO-mee
dessert	**dolci**	DOHL-chee
tap water	**acqua del rubinetto**	AH-kwah dayl roo-bee-NAY-toh
mineral water	**acqua minerale**	AH-kwah mee-nay-RAH-lay
milk	**latte**	LAH-tay
(orange) juice	**succo (d'arancia)**	SOO-koh (dah-RAHN-chah)
coffee / tea	**caffè / tè**	kah-FEH / teh
wine	**vino**	VEE-noh
red / white	**rosso / bianco**	ROH-soh / beeAHN-koh
glass / bottle	**bicchiere / bottiglia**	bee-keeAY-ray / boh-TEEL-yah
beer	**birra**	BEE-rah
Cheers!	**Cin cin!**	cheen cheen
More. / Another.	**Ancora un po.' / Un altro.**	ahn-KOH-rah oon poh / oon AHL-troh
The same.	**Lo stesso.**	loh STEHS-soh
The bill, please.	**Il conto, per favore.**	eel KOHN-toh pehr fah-VOH-ray
tip	**mancia**	MAHN-chah
Delicious!	**Delizioso!**	day-leet-seeOH-zoh

For hundreds more pages of survival phrases for your trip to Italy, check out *Rick Steves' Italian Phrase Book & Dictionary* or *Rick Steves' French, Italian, and German Phrase Book*.

INDEX

CREDITS

Researchers

To annually update his four books on Italy, Rick relies on the help of these *fantastica* researchers:

Heidi Sewell
Heidi Sewell lived in Italy for two years, learning to speak Italian and roll her own pasta. When she's not leading tours and scouring the Italian Peninsula for Back Doors worthy of Rick Steves' guidebooks, she resides in Seattle with her husband Ragen.

Amanda Scotese
Amanda Scotese freelances as a journalist and editor in San Francisco. Her travels in Italy include a stint selling leather jackets in Florence's San Lorenzo Market, basking in the Sicilian sun, and of course, helping out with Rick Steves' guidebooks and tours.

Images

Front color matter: St. Peter's, Rome	Rick Steves
Front color matter: Cinque Terre	Rick Steves
Front color matter: Trevi Fountain, Rome	Richard T. Nowitz
Venice: Church of San Giorgio Maggiore	Dave Hoerlein
Towns Near Venice: Verona—Roman Arena	Dave Hoerlein
The Dolomites: Alpe di Siusi	Julie Coen
The Lakes: Bellagio	Rick Steves
Milan: Cathedral (Duomo)	Dave Hoerlein
The Cinque Terre: Corniglia	Rick Steves
Riviera Towns near the Cinque Terre: Portofino	Dave Hoerlein
Florence: View from Piazzale Michelangelo	Rick Steves
Pisa and Lucca: Field of Miracles	Rick Steves
Siena: Il Campo	Dave Hoerlein
Assisi: Basilica of St. Francis	Rick Steves
Hill Towns of Central Italy: Civita di Bagnoregio	Dave Hoerlein
Rome: Piazza Navona	Rick Steves
Naples: Mt. Vesuvius	Dave Hoerlein
Sorrento and Capri: Capri	Dave Hoerlein
Amalfi Coast and Paestum: Positano	Dave Hoerlein

Start your trip at
www.ricksteves.com

Rick Steves' website is packed with over 3,000 pages of timely travel information. It's also your gateway to getting FREE monthly travel news from Rick—and more!

Free Monthly European Travel News

Fresh articles on Europe's most interesting destinations and happenings. Rick will even send you an e-mail every month (often direct from Europe) with his latest discoveries!

Timely Travel Tips

Rick Steves' best money-and-stress-saving tips on trip planning, packing, transportation, hotels, health, safety, finances, hurdling the language barrier...and more.

Travelers' Graffiti Wall

Candid advice and opinions from thousands of travelers on everything listed above, plus whatever topics are hot at the moment (discount flights, packing tips, scams...you name it).

Rick's Annual Guide to European Railpasses

The clearest, most comprehensive guide to the confusing array of rail-pass options out there, and how to choo-choose the railpass that best fits your itinerary and budget. Then you can order your railpass (and get a bunch of great freebies) online from us!

Great Gear at the Rick Steves Travel Store

Enjoy bargains on Rick's guidebooks, planning maps and TV series DVDs—and on his custom-designed carry-on bags, wheeled bags, day bags and light-packing accessories.

Rick Steves Tours

Every year more than 6,000 lucky travelers explore Europe on a Rick Steves tour. Learn more about our 30 different one-to-three-week itineraries, read uncensored feedback from our tour alums, and sign up for your dream trip online!

Rick on Radio and TV

Read the scripts and run clips from public television's "Rick Steves' Europe" and public radio's "Travel with Rick Steves."

Respect for Your Privacy

Ordering online from us is secure. When you buy something from us, join a tour, or subscribe to Rick's free monthly travel news e-mails, we promise to never share your name, information, or e-mail address with anyone else. You won't be spammed!

Have fun raising your Travel I.Q. at
www.ricksteves.com

Travel smart...carry on!

The latest generation of Rick Steves' carry-on travel bags is easily the best—benefiting from two decades of on-the-road attention to what really matters: maximum quality and strength; practical, flexible features; and no unnecessary frills. You won't find a better value anywhere!

Convertible, expandable, and carry-on-size:

Rick Steves' Back Door Bag $99

This is the same bag that Rick Steves lives out of for three months every summer. It's made of rugged water-resistant 1000 denier Cordura nylon, and best of all, it converts easily from a smart-looking suitcase to a handy backpack with comfortably-curved shoulder straps and a padded waistbelt.

This roomy, versatile 9" x 21" x 14" bag has a large 2600 cubic-inch main compartment, plus three outside pockets (small, medium and huge) that are perfect for often-used items. And the cinch-tight compression straps will keep your load compact and close to your back—not sagging like a sack of potatoes.

Wishing you had even more room to bring home souvenirs? Pull open the full-perimeter expando-zipper and its capacity jumps from 2600 to 3000 cubic inches. When you want to use it as a suitcase or check it as luggage (required when "expanded"), the straps and belt hide away in a zippered compartment in the back.

Attention travelers under 5'4" tall: This bag also comes in an inch-shorter version, for a compact-friendlier fit between the waistbelt and shoulder straps.

Convenient, expandable, and carry-on-size:

Rick Steves' Wheeled Bag $129

At 9" x 21" x 14" our sturdy Rick Steves' Wheeled Bag is rucksack-soft in front, but the rest is lined with a hard ABS-lexan shell to give maximum protection to your belongings. We've spared no expense on moving parts, splurging on an extra-long button-release handle and big, tough inline skate wheels for easy rolling on rough surfaces.

Wishing you had even more room to bring home souvenirs? Pull open the full-perimeter expando-zipper and its capacity jumps from 2600 to 3000 cubic inches.

Rick Steves' Wheeled Bag has exactly the same three-outside-pocket configuration as our Back Door Bag, plus a handy "add-a-bag" strap and full lining.

Our Back Door Bags and Wheeled Bags come in black, navy, blue spruce, evergreen and merlot.

For great deals on a wide selection of travel goodies, begin your next trip at the Rick Steves Travel Store!

Visit the Rick Steves Travel Store at
www.ricksteves.com

FREE-SPIRITED TOURS FROM
Rick Steves

Small Groups
Great Guides
No Grumps

Best of Europe ■ **Eastern Europe**
Italy ■ **Village Italy** ■ **South Italy**
France ■ **Britain** ■ **Ireland**
Heart of France ■ **South of France**
Turkey ■ **Spain/Portugal**
Germany/Austria/Switzerland
Scandinavia ■ **London** ■ **Paris** ■ **Rome**
Venice ■ **Florence…and much more!**

Looking for a one, two, or three-week tour that's run in the Rick Steves style? Check out Rick Steves' educational, experiential tours of Europe.

Rick's tours are an excellent value compared to "mainstream" tours. Here's a taste of what you'll get…

- **Small groups:** With just 24-28 travelers, you'll go where typical groups of 40-50 can only dream.

- **Big buses:** You'll travel in a full-size 40-50 seat bus, with plenty of empty seats for you to spread out and be comfortable.

- **Great guides:** Our guides are hand-picked by Rick Steves for their wealth of knowledge and giddy enthusiasm for Europe.

- **No tips or kickbacks:** To keep your guide and driver 100% focused on giving you the best travel experience, we pay them well—and prohibit them from accepting tips and merchant kickbacks.

- **All sightseeing:** Your tour price includes all group sightseeing, with no hidden extra charges.

- **Central hotels:** You'll stay in Rick's favorite small, characteristic, locally-run hotels in the center of each city, within walking distance of the sights you came to see.

- **Visit www.ricksteves.com:** You'll find all our latest itineraries, dates and prices, be able to reserve online, and request a free copy of our "Rick Steves Tour Experience" DVD!

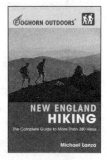
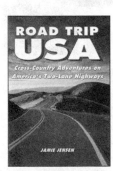

Rick Steves

More *Savvy*. More *Surprising*. More *Fun*.

COUNTRY GUIDES 2006

England
France
Germany & Austria
Great Britain
Ireland
Italy
Portugal
Scandinavia
Spain
Switzerland

CITY GUIDES 2006

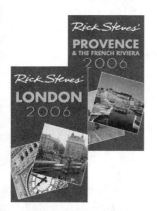

Amsterdam, Bruges & Brussels
Florence & Tuscany
London
Paris
Prague & The Czech Republic
Provence & The French Riviera
Rome
Venice

BEST OF GUIDES

Best of Eastern Europe
Best of Europe

As the #1 authority on European travel, Rick gives you inside information on what to visit, where to stay, and how to get there—economically and hassle-free.

www.ricksteves.com

PHRASE BOOKS & DICTIONARIES

French
French, Italian & German
German
Italian
Portuguese
Spanish

MORE EUROPE FROM RICK STEVES

Easy Access Europe
Europe 101
Europe Through the Back Door
Postcards from Europe

RICK STEVES' EUROPE DVDs

All 43 Shows 2000-2005
Britain
Eastern Europe
France & Benelux
Germany, The Swiss Alps & Travel Skills
Ireland
Italy
Spain & Portugal

PLANNING MAPS

Britain & Ireland
Europe
France
Germany, Austria & Switzerland
Italy
Spain & Portugal

For a complete list of Rick Steves' guidebooks, see page 8.

Thanks to Gene Openshaw for his contributions on art and history.

Avalon Travel Publishing
1400 65th Street, Suite 250
Emeryville, CA 94608

AVALON
publishing group incorporated

Avalon Travel Publishing
An Imprint of Avalon Publishing Group, Inc.

Printed in the U.S.A. by Worzalla. Third Printing February 2005.
Distributed by Publishers Group West, Berkeley, California

ISBN (10) 1-56691-727-1
ISBN (13) 978-1-56691-727-8
ISSN 1084-4422

For the latest on Rick's lectures, guidebooks, tours, and public television series, contact
Europe Through the Back Door, Box 2009, Edmonds, WA 98020, tel. 425/771-8303, fax
425/771-0833, www.ricksteves.com, rick@ricksteves.com.

Europe Through the Back Door Managing Editor: Risa Laib
ETBD Editors: Cameron Hewitt, Jennifer Hauseman, Kevin Yip, Lauren Mills
Avalon Travel Publishing Series Manager: Patrick Collins
Avalon Travel Publishing Project Editor: Madhu Prasher
Copy Editor: Chris Hayhurst
Research Assistance: Heidi Sewell, Amanda Scotese, David C. Ho
Production and Typesetting: Patrick David Barber, Holly McGuire
Cover Design: Kari Gim, Laura Mazer
Interior Design: Jane Musser, Laura Mazer, Amber Pirker
Maps & Graphics: David C. Hoerlein, Laura VanDeventer, Lauren Mills, Mike
    Morgenfeld
Front Cover Photos: front image, Vernazza harbor © Russell Mountford/Lonely Planet
    Images; back image, Michelangelo's David, Florence, Italy © Rick Steves
Front Matter Color Photos: p. i, view of St. Peter's Dome, Rome © Rick Steves; p. viii,
    Cinque Terre © Rick Steves; p. xii, Trevi Fountain, Rome © Richard T. Nowitz